European
Photography
Guide 7

Edited by
Peter Badge and
Vladimír Birgus

European Photography

© 1982, 2000 European Photography,
Andreas Müller-Pohle. All rights reserved
in all countries. No part of this directory
may be reproduced in any form or by any
electronic or mechanical means, including
information storage and retrieval systems,
without written permission from the
publisher.

Die Deutsche Bibliothek –
CIP-Einheitsaufnahme
Ein Titeldatensatz für diese Publikation
ist bei der Deutschen Bibliothek erhältlich.

Seventh edition 2000
Sixth edition 1997
Fifth edition 1994
Fourth edition 1991
Third edition 1987
Second edition 1984
First edition 1982

Available in the U.S. through D.A.P.
Distributed Art Publishers, 155 Sixth Ave.
2nd Floor, New York, NY 10013-1507,
Tel (212) 627-1999, Fax (212) 627-9484

ISBN 3-923283-54-7
Copy editor: Bernd Neubauer
Printed and bound in Germany

European Photography, P.O. Box 3043,
D-37020 Göttingen, Germany
europhoto@equivalence.com
www.equivalence.com

Contents

Preface / Vorwort

Austria 9

Belarus 17

Belgium 20

Bulgaria 33

Croatia 36

Czech Republic 38

Denmark 53

Estonia 58

Finland 60

France 65

Germany 89

Great Britain 136

Greece 157

Hungary 161

Ireland 165

Italy 166

Latvia 186

Lithuania 189

Luxembourg 191

Netherlands 192

Norway 204

Poland 206

Portugal 216

Romania 220

Russia 222

Slovakia 232

Slovenia 238

Spain 242

Sweden 252

Switzerland 259

Ukraine 268

Yugoslavia 270

Index Section 275

Preface

You have in your hands the seventh completely revised and extended edition of the *European Photography Guide*, the most comprehensive reference work on the photography-and-art scene in Europe. With more than 2,600 entries from 32 countries, this *Guide* is more complete and exhaustive than its predecessors, while at the same time an attempt has been made to condense the volume of information. Under each country listed you will find the tried and tested categories Galleries and Museums, Festivals and Fairs, Magazines, Book Publishers, Critics and Journalists, Schools and Workshops, Associations, Grants and Awards. The category Video Art has been replaced by New Media and now also embraces activities and institutions in the field of digital imagery. Due to repeated requests, the new categories Auctions and Bookshops have been introduced.

Research for this edition was done with the help of a questionnaire – a procedure we will replace from now on by e-mail and online updates. For further details, please visit our website www.equivalence.com. There you will also find selected country files that can be downloaded free of charge; an online offer for purchasing the complete *European Photography Guide* is being prepared.

More than forty country correspondents and advisors have collaborated on this edition of the *European Photography Guide*. They, and all those who supported us with their suggestions and criticism, will continue to be an indispensable constituent of the editorial concept behind this publication. As ever, our heartfelt thanks to them.

Vorwort

Vor Ihnen liegt die siebte, vollständig aktualisierte und erweiterte Ausgabe des *European Photography Guide*, des umfassendsten Referenzwerkes zur Foto- und Kunstszene Europas. Mit über 2600 Einträgen aus 32 Ländern ist dieser *Guide* kompletter und verläßlicher als seine Vorgänger, zugleich haben wir uns um eine Straffung des Informationsangebots bemüht. Innerhalb der Länderordnung folgt die Gliederung den bewährten Rubriken Galerien und Museen, Festivals und Messen, Zeitschriften, Buchverlage, Kritiker und Journalisten, Schulen und Workshops, Vereinigungen sowie Preise und Stipendien. Die Rubrik Video Art wurde ersetzt durch Neue Medien und umfaßt nun auch Aktivitäten und Institutionen im Bereich des digitalen Bildes. Auf vielfache Anregung neu hinzugekommen sind die Rubriken Auktionen und Fotobuchläden.

Die vorliegende Ausgabe wurde wiederum mittels Fragebogen recherchiert – ein Verfahren, das wir von nun an durch E-Mail- und Online-Aktualisierungen ersetzen werden. Bitte besuchen Sie hierzu unsere Website www.equivalence.com. Dort finden Sie auch ausgewählte Länderdateien zum kostenlosen Download; ein kostenpflichtiges Online-Angebot des kompletten *European Photography Guide* ist in Vorbereitung.

Über vierzig Länderkorrespondenten und Berater haben an dieser Ausgabe des *European Photography Guide* mitgewirkt. Sie und alle, die uns mit Anregungen und Kritik unterstützen, werden auch in Zukunft ein unverzichtbares Element des editorischen Konzepts dieser Publikation sein. Wie immer, ihnen einen herzlichen Dank.

Advisors

Carl Aigner, Krems, editor of *Eikon* magazine, university lecturer, artistic director of the Kunsthalle Krems, Krems (Austria)

Vilnis Auzinš, Riga, director of the Latvian Museum of Photography, photographer, critic and curator (Latvia)

Helen Back, Birmingham, information manager of Seeing the Light (Great Britain)

Ruxandra Balaci, Bucharest, curator and critic, National Museum of Art, Bucharest (Romania)

Gabriel Bauret, Paris, freelance curator and editor (France)

Lucia Benická, Poprad, curator and critic, director of the House of Photography in Poprad (Slovakia)

Yevgeni Berezner, Moscow, critic and curator, deputy director at ROSIZO State Center in Moscow (Russia)

Jure Breceljnik, Ljubljana, photographer and curator (Slovenia)

Andrey Chezhin, Saint Petersburg, photographer, curator (Russia)

Peter Dabac, Zagreb, photographer, custodian of the Tošo Dabac Photographic Archive (Croatia)

Birgit Filzmaier, Zollikon, art historian, critic, curator, consultant (Switzerland)

Dr. Andrzej Florkowski, Poznan, photographer, lecturer at the Academy of Fine Arts in Poznan (Poland)

Joan Fontcuberta, La Roca (Barcelona), visual artist – photography, editor of *PhotoVision* (Spain)

Marek Grygiel, Warsaw, director of Mala Galeria, curator at the Center of Contemporary Art, editor of *Tapeta*, picture editor of Gazeta *Wyborcza* (Poland)

Lajos Györi, Budapest, critic, curator, collector (Hungary)

Károly Kincses, Kécskemét, curator and critic, director of the Hungarian Museum of Photography in Kecskemét (Hungary)

Hans-Michael Koetzle, Munich, editor of *Leica World*, art critic, curator (Germany)

Árpád Kiss-Kuntler, Budapest, critic, editor-in-chief of *Foto* (Hungary)

Dr. Zelimir Koscevic, Zagreb, curator, art critic, Museum of Contemporary Art in Zagreb (Croatia)

Barbara Kosinska-Filocha, Warsaw, editor, critic (Poland)

Nikolay Laoutliev, Plovdiv, director of Laoutliev Gallery, photographer and curator (Bulgaria)

Tomaš Lauko, Ljubljana, photographer (Slovenia)

Peeter Linnap, Tallinn, photographer, critic, lecturer, curator (Estonia)

Jan-Erik Lundström, Umeå, director of BildMuseet, critic (Sweden, Norway, Finland)

Dr. Václav Macek, Bratislava, curator, critic, head of the Department of Film Studies at the Academy of Performing Arts, director of FOTOFO, editor of *Imago* magazine (Slovakia)

Goran Malic, Belgrade, photographer, photo historian, television editor (Yugoslavia)

Juli R. Masterova, Kharkov, critic (Ukraine)

Stavros Moressopoulos, Athens, president of Hellenic Centre of Photography, editor of *Fotografia*, critic (Greece)

Tatiana Pavlova, Kharkov, art critic, curator (Ukraine)

Attila Pöcze, Budapest, curator, collector, owner of Vintage Galéria (Hungary)

Iglena Rousseva, Sofia, photographer, critic, associate professor at the National Academy of Theatre and Cinema, editor of *Fotooko* (Bulgaria)

Dr. Helmutas Šabasevicius, Vilnius, art critic, lecturer at the Vilnius Academy of Arts, editor of *Krantai* (Lithuania)

Igor Savchenko, Minsk, photographer and curator (Belarus)

Lars Schwander, Copenhagen, curator at Fotografisk Center, Copenhagen, and Louisiana Museum of Modern Art, Humlebæk (Denmark)

Laima Skeiviené, Vilnius, art critic and art researcher (Lithuania)

Adam Sobota, Wroclaw, curator of photography at the National Museum, Wroclaw (Poland)

Dr. Valery Stigneev, Moscow, photographer, critic, curator, art historian at the State Institute of History and Theory of Art (Russia)

Kateryna Stukalova, Kiev, critic, documentation assistent at the Center of Contemporary Art in Kiev (Ukraine)

Dr. Johan Swinnen, Antwerp, critic, professor of the History and Theory of Photography, Free University of Brussels and University of Ghent (Belgium, Netherlands)

Irina Tschmyreva, Moscow, art critic, historian of photography, chief scientific officer at ROSIZO State Center in Moscow (Russia)

Roberta Valtorta, Milan, critic, professor of Photographic Language at Centro Bauer, Milan, and of the History of Photography at the University of Udine (Italy)

Dmitry Vilensky, Saint Petersburg, photographer, curator, critic (Russia)

Rhonda Wilson, Birmingham, director of Seeing the Light, writer, image maker (Great Britain)

Prof. Stefan Wojnecki, Poznan, photographer, critic, head of photography at the Poznan Academy of Fine Arts (Poland)

equivalence

The site for photography and new media from
European Photography and Andreas Müller-Pohle

Austria

Population: 8.0 million
Capital: Vienna, 1.6 million
Currency: Schilling (S)
International code: ++43
Tourist information: Öster-reich-Werbung, Margareten-str. 1, A-1040 Wien
Tel (01) 587 20 00,
Fax (01) 588 66 20

Galleries & Museums

Galerie Lisi Hämmerle, Im Rathaus-bezirk, Anton Schneider Str. 4a/I, A-6900 Bregenz. Tel (05574) 47319, Fax (05574) 47319. E-mail office@ galerie-lisihaemmerle.at. Website www.galerie-lisihaemmerle.at

Kunsthaus Bregenz, Karl Tizian Platz, A-6900 Bregenz. Tel (05574) 485940, Fax (05574) 485948. E-mail kub@ kunsthaus-bregenz.at. Website www. kunsthaus-bregenz.at. Open: Tue–Sun 10–18 (Wed –21). Director: Prof. Edelbert Köb. Curator: Dr. Rudolf Sagmeister. Founded 1997. 4 rooms, 2,000 m². 1 photo exhibition/year

Koralm-Fotogalerie, Frauentalerstr. 48, A-8530 Deutschlandsberg. Fax (03462) 8002480. Open: Mon–Fri 9–19, Sat–Sun 9.30–11. Director/ curator: Erich Nauschnig. Founded 1982. 5 rooms, 350 m². 10 photo exhibitions/year

Fotogalerie Camera Austria, Sparkas-senplatz 2, A-8010 Graz. Tel (0316) 8155500, Fax (0316) 8155509. E-mail camera.austria@styria.com. Website www.camera-austria.at. Open: Mon–Fri 14–18, Sat–Sun 11–15. Director: Manfred Willmann. Founded 1975. 2 rooms, 210 m². 6–8 photo exhibitions/year. Artists: Nobuyoshi Araki, Sabine Bitter, Boris Mikhailov, Nan Goldin, Thomas Florschuetz, Gosbert Adler, Seiichi Furuya, David Gold-blatt, Michael Schmidt, Nick Wap-lington

Neue Galerie am Landesmuseum Joanneum, Sackstr. 16, A-8010 Graz. Tel (0316) 8291-55/86, Fax (0316) 815401. E-mail neue-galerie-graz @sime.com. Website www. neuegalerie.at. Open: Tue–Fri 10–18, Sat–Sun 10–13. Director/ curator: Dr. Werner Fenz. Founded 1941. 16 rooms, 880 m². 2–3 photo exhibitions/year

Fotoforum West, Adolf-Pichler-Platz 8, A-6020 Innsbruck. Tel (0512) 572236, Fax (0512) 5722364. Open: Tue–Fri 15–19, Sat 10–13. Director/ curator: Rupert Larl. Founded 1991. 2 rooms, 350 m². 12 photo exhibi-tions/year

Galerie Dieter Tausch, Adolf-Pichler-Platz 12, A-6020 Innsbruck. Tel (0512) 562769, Fax (0512) 582132. Open: Tue–Fri 15–18. Director: Dieter Tausch. Founded 1980. 3 rooms, 160 m². 4 photo exhibitions/year. Artists: Rupert Larl, Clemens Bruch, Helene Schnitzer

Galerie Stadtpark, Wichnerstr., A-3500 Krems/Stein. Tel (02732) 84705, Fax (02732) 81276. E-mail acisatak@ eunet.at. Open: Wed–Sat 11–19. Director: Christina Lackner. Founded 1919. 2 rooms, 160 m². 1–2 photo exhibitions/year. Artists: Thomas Joshua Cooper, Thomas Freiler, Norbert Fleischmann, Hans Schar-nagl, Ecke Bonk, Isa Genzken, Viktor

Rogy, Maria Hahnenkamp, Hamish Fulton, Heimo Zobernig

Kunsthalle Krems, Steiner Landstr. 8, A-3504 Krems/Stein. Tel (02732) 8266919, Fax (02732) 8266916. E-mail office@krems.kunsthalle.at. Website www.krems.kunsthalle.at. Open: Tue–Sun 10–18. Director/curator: Carl Aigner. Founded 1991. 5 rooms, 1,200 m². 1–3 photo exhibitions/year. Artists: Leo Kandl, Heinz Cibulka, Walter Ebenhofer, Robert F. Hammerstiel, John Hilliard

Neue Galerie der Stadt Linz, Wolfgang-Gurlitt-Museum, Blütenstr. 15, A-4020 Linz. Tel (0732) 7070360-0/1, Fax (0732) 736190. E-mail neue. galerie@mag.linz.at. Website www. neuegalerie.linz.at. Open: daily 10–18 (Thu –22) (Jan–Jun + Sept–Dec); Mon + Wed–Fri 10–18 (Thu –22), Sat 10–13 (Jul–Aug). Director: Prof. Peter Baum. Curator: Dr. Nowak-Thaller. Founded 1947. 3 rooms, 3,050 m². 3 photo exhibitions/year. Artists: Gustav Klimt, Egon Schiele, Lovis Corinth, Max Pechstein, Otto Mueller, Oskar Kokoschka, Arnulf Rainer, Andy Warhol, Christian Ludwig Attersee, Karel Appel

Euregio Galerie, Prager Fotoschule, P. O. Box 17, A-4212 Neumarkt i. M. Tel (07941) 8651, Fax (07941) 86514. E-mail pfs@magnet.at. Website www.prager-fotoschule.at. Open: Wed 16–19, Sat–Sun 10–12, 13–18. Director: Sepp Puchner. Founded 1998. 4 rooms, 140 m². 8 photo exhibitions/year. Artists: Roman Sejkot, Kurt Hörbst, Wilhelm Petri, Peter Bauer, Christian Hafstadler, Daniela Ruzicka

Galerie 5020, IG bildender KünstlerInnen Salzburgs, Sigmund-Haffner-Gasse 12/1, A-5020 Salzburg. Tel (0662) 848817, Fax (0662) 848817.

E-mail galerie5020@salzburg.co.at. Open: Tue–Fri 14–18, Sat 10–13

Galerie Fotohof, Erhardplatz 3, A-5020 Salzburg. Tel (0662) 849296, Fax (0662) 8492964. E-mail fotohof @salzburg.co.at. Website www. fotohof.or.at/. Open: Mon–Fri 15–19, Sat 10–13. Founded 1981. 2 rooms, 140 m². 12 photo exhibitions/year. Artists: Cora Pongracz, Peter Dressler, Valie Export, Dieter Huber, Rolf Koppel, Paul Albert Leitner, Inge Morath, Michaela Moscouw, Otmar Thormann, Manfred Willmann

Österreichische Fotogalerie im Rupertinum, Wiener Philharmoniker Gasse 9, A-5010 Salzburg. Tel (0662) 80422568, Fax (0662) 80422542. E-mail rupertinum@land-sbg.gr.at. Website www.sbg.gr.at. Open: Tue–Sun 10–17 (Wed –21). Director: Prof. Peter Weiermair. Curator: Dr. Margit Zuckriegl. Founded 1983. 7 rooms, 700 m². 3–4 photo exhibitions/year. Artists: Ernst Haas, Inge Morath, Otmar Thormann, Heinz Cibulka, Franz Hubmann, Peter Dressler, Herwig Kempinger, Ilse Haider, Robert F. Hammerstiel, Anton Josef Trcka, Weegee

Fotogalerie Wien, Währinger Str. 59, A-1090 Wien. Tel (01) 4085462, Fax (01) 4030478. E-mail office.f.w@ xpoint.at. Website www.fotogalerie-wien.at. Open: Tue–Fri 14–19. Sat 10–14. Directors: Susanne Gamauf, Klaus Pamminger. Founded 1980. 2 rooms, 140 m². 10 photo exhibitions/year

Fotosammlung in der Albertina, Augustinerstr. 1, A-1010 Wien. Tel (01) 5348371, Fax (01) 5337697. E-mail info @albertina.at. Website www. albertina.at

Galerie Faber, Fine Arts Photography, Brahmsplatz 7, A-1040 Wien. Tel (01)

5057518, Fax (01) 5057518. E-mail office@jmcfaber.at. Website www. jmcfaber.at. Open: Tue–Fri 14–18, Sat 11–17 and by appointment. Director: Johannes Faber. Founded 1982. 3 rooms, 150 m². 10 photo exhibitions/ year. Artists: Paul Albert Leitner, Jan Saudek, Ladislav E. Berka, Trude Fleischmann, Emil Mayer, František Drtikol, Josef Sudek, Otmar Thormann, Heinrich Kühn, Rudolf Koppitz

Kunsthalle Exnergasse, WUK, Währinger Str. 59, A-1090 Wien. Tel (01) 40121-41/42, Fax (01) 4012167. E-mail kunsthalle.exnergasse@wuk.at. Website www.wuk.at/kunsthalle. Open: Tue–Fri 14–19, Sat 10–13. Director: Franziska Kasper. Founded 1989. 1 room, 400 m². 1 photo exhibition/ year

Kunsthalle Wien am Karlsplatz, Treitlstr. 2, A-1040 Wien. Tel (01) 5218914, Fax (01) 5218920. E-mail kunsthallewien@to.or.at. Website www.to.or.at/kunsthallewien. Open: Wed–Mon 10–18 (Thu –20). Director: Dr. Gerald Matt. Founded 1992. 3 rooms, 1,700 m²

Kunsthalle Wien im Museumsquartier, Museumplatz 1/6/1, A-1040 Wien. Tel (01) 5218914, Fax (01) 5218960. E-mail kunsthallewien@to.or.at. Website www.to.or.at/kunsthallewien. Open: Wed–Mon 10–18 (Thu –20)

Museum Moderner Kunst Stiftung Ludwig, Museum des 20. Jahrhunderts, Arsenalstr. 1, A-1030 Wien. Tel (01) 7996900, Fax (01) 7996901. E-mail museum@mmkslw.or.at. Website www.mmkslw.or.at/mmkslw. Open: Tue–Sun 10–18. Director: Dr. Lóránd Hegyi. Curators: Monika Faber, Dr. Rainer Fuchs. Founded 1962. 1 room, 1,500 m². 1 photo exhibition/year.

Artists: Anton Josef Trcka, Manasse, Rudolf Koppitz, Vilem Reichmann

Museum Moderner Kunst Stiftung Ludwig, Palais Liechtenstein, Fürstengasse 1, A-1090 Wien. Tel (01) 3176900, Fax (01) 3176901. E-mail museum@mmkslw.or.at. Website www.mmkslw.or.at/mmkslw. Open: Tue–Sun 10–18. Director: Dr. Lóránd Hegyi. Curators: Monika Faber, Dr. Rainer Fuchs. Founded 1979. 21 rooms, 2,000 m². 1 photo exhibition/year

Österreichisches Museum für Angewandte Kunst, MAK, Stubenring 5, A-1010 Wien. Tel (01) 711360, Fax (01) 7131026. E-mail office@mak.at. Open: Tue–Sun 10–18 (Thu –21)

Wiener Secession, Vereinigung Bildender Künstler, Friedrichstr. 12, A-1010 Wien. Tel (01) 58753070, Fax (01) 587530734. E-mail secession.pr@to.or.at. Website www.secession.at. Open: Tue–Sun 10–18 (Thu –20). Director: Matthias Herrmann. Founded 1897. 3 rooms, 851 m². 4 photo exhibitions/year

FLUSS – Niederösterreichische Fotoinitiative, Schloßplatz 2, A-2120 Wolkersdorf. Tel (02245) 5455, Fax (02245) 6155. E-mail fluss@aon.at. Open: Sat–Sun 14–18. Directors: Heinz Cibulka, Charlotte Gohs. Founded 1989. 8 rooms, 200 m². 10 photo exhibitions/year

Festivals & Fairs

Ars Electronica, ORF Landesstudio Oberösterreich, Europaplatz 3, A-4010 Linz. Tel (0732) 69000, Fax (0732) 6900250. E-mail prixars@aec.at. Website www.aec.at

Österreichische Triennale zur Fotografie, Jakoministr. 16/2, A-8010

Graz. Tel (0316) 811831, Fax (0316) 811885. E-mail fototriennale@mur.at. Website www.fototriennale.mur.at

Magazines

Camera Austria, Sparkassenplatz 2, A-8010 Graz. Tel (0361) 8155500, Fax (0361) 8155509. E-mail camera.austria@thing.or.at. Website www.thing.or.at/thing/camera.austria. Editors: Christine Frisinghelli, Manfred Willmann. German/English. Founded 1980. Copy price: S 160.00. Annual subscription: S 600.00, 4 issues/year

Der Photograph, Verlag für photographische Literatur, Opernring 6, A-1010 Wien. Tel (01) 5128712, Fax (01) 5137833. E-mail vphl@fayer.co.at. Website www.photobook.at. Editor: Andreas Barylli. German. Copy price: S 37.00. Annual subscription: S 370.00, 11 issues/year

Eikon, Internationale Zeitschrift für Photographie und Medienkunst, Gumpendorfer Str. 118a/19, A-1060 Wien. Tel (01) 5977088, Fax (01) 5977087. E-mail office@eikon.or.at. Website www.eikon.or.at. Editor: Carl Aigner. German (with original contributions in foreign languages). Founded 1991. Copy price: S 190.00. Annual subscription: S 490.00, 4 issues/year

Fotogeschichte, Beiträge zur Geschichte und Ästhetik der Fotografie, Buchfeldgasse 12/4, A-1080 Wien. Tel (01) 4067733, Fax (01) 4067733. E-mail fotohistor@aol.com. Website www.fotoinfo.de/fotogeschichte

Frame, Frameworks Verlagsgesmbh, Gumpendorfer Str. 89, A-1060 Wien. Tel (01) 59727810, Fax (01) 597278115.

E-mail frameworks@frame.co.at. Website www.frame.co.at

Springerin, Hefte für Gegenwartskunst, Folio-Verlag Wien/Bozen, Museumsplatz 1/Fürstenhof, A-1070 Wien. Tel (01) 5229124, Fax (01) 5229125. E-mail springerin@springerin.at

Book Publishers

Ariadne Verlag, Geibelgasse 14, A-1150 Wien. Tel (01) 89532555, Fax (01) 895324420. E-mail music@ariadne.vienna.at

Christian Brandstätter, Verlag & Edition, Wickenburggasse 26, A-1080 Wien. Tel (01) 40838-14/15, Fax (01) 4087200. E-mail books@cbv.co.at

Edition Camera Austria, Sparkassenplatz 2, A-8010 Graz. Tel (0361) 8155500, Fax (0361) 8155509. E-mail camera.austria@thing.or.at. Website www.thing.or.at/thing/camera.austria

Fotohof Edition, Erhardplatz 3, A-5020 Salzburg. Tel (0662) 849296, Fax (0662) 8492964. E-mail fotohof@salzburg.co.at. Website www.fotohof.or.at/

Löcker Verlag, Annagasse 3a, A-1015 Wien. Tel (01) 5120282, Fax (01) 512028222. E-mail lverlag@loecker.at. Website www.loecker.at

Otto Müller Verlag, Ernest-Thun-Str. 11, A-5020 Salzburg. Tel (0662) 8819740, Fax (0662) 872387. E-mail otto.muellerverlag@salzburg.co.at

Residenz Verlag GmbH, Gaisbergstr. 6, A-5020 Salzburg. Tel (0662) 641986, Fax (0662) 643548. E-mail residenz@oebr.co.at. Website www.residenzverlag.at

«Eine passende Hose kann glücklicher machen als alles andere» Thomas Bernhard

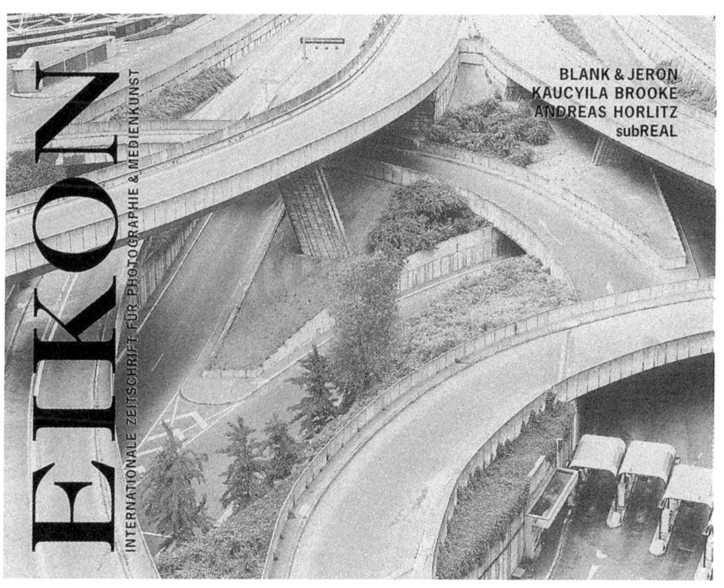

EIKON –
Internationale Zeitschrift für Photographie & Medienkunst
Heft 31 • März–Mai 2000

EIKON 31 enthält – neben Institutionspräsentationen,
Ausstellungsbesprechungen, Rezensionen, Veranstaltungs-
und Ausschreibungshinweisen sowie einem Ausstellungskalender
– eigens für EIKON gestaltete Beiträge von folgenden Künstlern:
Blank & Jeron, Kaucyila Brooke, Andreas Horlitz und subREAL.

Detaillierte Information: *http://www.eikon.or.at/zeitschrift/*

öS 190,– /DM 28,– (zzgl. öS 30,–/DM 5,– Porto/Versandkosten)
Abonnement für 4 Nummern: öS 490,–/DM 70,– (zzgl. öS 120,–/
DM 20,– Porto/Versandkosten)
Tel.: (+43-1) 597 70 88, Fax: (+43-1) 597 70 87
E-Mail: office@eikon.or.at

13 Austria

Schroll-Verlag, Spengergasse 39, A-1051 Wien. Tel (01) 5445641, Fax (01) 544564166. E-mail prepress@ agens-werk.at

Triton Verlag, Wilhelminerstr. 73, A-1160 Wien. Tel (01) 93610515/ 4699103

Verlag Niederösterreichisches Pressehaus, Gutenbergstr. 12, A-3100 St. Pöllen. Tel (02742) 8021415, Fax (02742) 8022464. E-mail r.wonka@ np-buch.at

Verlag Turia & Kant, Linke Wienzeile 100, A-1060 Wien. Tel (01) 5862677, Fax (01) 5862677

Bookshops

Buchhandlung Lia Wolf, Bäckerstr. 2, A-1010 Wien. Tel (01) 5124094, Fax (01) 512409419. E-mail lia.wolf@ lia.wolf.at. Website www.lia.wolf.at

Auctions

Dorotheum, Dorotheergasse 17, A-1010 Wien. Tel (01) 51560378

Critics & Journalists

Carl Aigner, Ledergasse 13/9, A-3500 Krems. Tel (02732) 8266919, Fax (02732) 8266916. Editor of *Eikon*, Wien; *EXTRA – Wiener Zeitung*, Wien; *European Photography*, Göttingen

Anna Auer, Fleischmarkt 16/2/2/31, A-1011 Wien. Tel (01) 5137196

Reinhard Braun, Bauernfeldstr. 26/6, A-8020 Graz. Tel (0316) 584632, Fax (0316) 584632. E-mail reinhard.braun @thing.at. Website www.thing.at/ braun. *Springerin, Eikon,* Wien; *Camera Austria,* Graz

Dr. Werner Fenz, Neue Galerie am Landesmuseum Joanneum, Sackstr. 16, A-8010 Graz. Tel (0316) 829155, Fax (0316) 815401. E-mail neue-galerie-graz@sime.com. Director of Neue Galerie am Landesmuseum Joanneum, Graz

Christine Frisinghelli, Camera Austria, Sparkassenplatz 2, A-8010 Graz. Tel (0316) 8155500, Fax (0316) 8155509. E-mail camera.austria@ styria.com. Website www.camera-austria.at. Editor of *Camera Austria,* Graz

Johanna Hofleitner, Ybbsstr. 18/15, A-1020 Wien. Tel (01) 7266140, Fax (01) 7266140. E-mail jhofleitner@to.or. at. *Artforum*, New York; *European Photography*, Göttingen; *Flash Art*, Milan; *Blocnotes*, Paris; *Eikon, Die Presse,* Wien; *Neue Zürcher Zeitung*, Zürich

Dr. Kurt Kaindl, Sparkassenstr. 5, A-5020 Salzburg. Tel (0662) 420124, Fax (0662) 42012420. E-mail k.kaindl@ salzburg.co.at. Editor of "Edition Fotohof im Otto Müller Verlag", Salzburg

Michael Mauracher, Stauffenstr. 17, A-5020 Salzburg. Tel (0662) 849296, Fax (0662) 8492964

Franz Niegelhell, Plüddemanngasse 93, A-8010 Graz. Tel (0316) 465211

Timm Starl, c/o Fotogeschichte, Buchfeldgasse 12/4, A-1080 Wien. Tel (01) 4067733, Fax (01) 4067733. E-mail fotohistor@aol.com. Website www.fotoinfo.de/fotogeschichte

Barbara Steiner, Untere Donaustr. 33/ 2/23, A-1020 Wien

Prof. Peter Weiermair, Rupertinum, P. O. Box 527, A-5010 Salzburg. Tel (0662) 80422541, Fax (0662) 80422542. E-mail peter.weiermair@land-sbg. gr.at

Jana Wisniewski, Widerhofergasse 3/23, A-1090 Wien. Tel (01) 3196771, Fax (01) 3195138. E-mail artspace@ ins.at. *Salzburger Nachrichten*, Salzburg; *Eikon*, Wien

Dr. Margit Zuckriegl, Österreichische Fotogalerie im Rupertinum, Wiener Philharmoniker Gasse 9, A-5010 Salzburg. Tel (0662) 80422568, Fax (0662) 80422542. E-mail rupertinum @land-sbg.gr.at. Director of Österreichische Fotogalerie im Rupertinum, Salzburg

Schools & Workshops

Akademie der Bildenden Künste, Schillerplatz 3, A-1010 Wien. Tel (01) 58816, Fax (01) 5877977. Website www.akbild.ac.at

FLUSS – Niederösterreichische Fotoinitiative, Schloßplatz 2, A-2120 Wolkersdorf. Tel (02245) 5455, Fax (02245) 6155. E-mail fluss@aon.at

Hochschule für Angewandte Kunst, Oskar Kokoschka Platz 2, A-1010 Wien. Tel (01) 711330, Fax (01) 71133222. E-mail christian.schneider @merkur.hsak.ac.at

Höhere Bundeslehranstalt für Kunst und Design, Abt. Audiovisuelle Mediengestaltung, Ortweingasse 4, A-8013 Graz. Tel (0316) 6084310, Fax (0316) 6084257. E-mail la@ htlortwein-graz.ac.at. Website www.htlortwein-graz.ac.at

Höhere Graphische Bundeslehr- und Versuchsanstalt, Leyserstr. 6, A-1140 Wien. Tel (01) 9823914, Fax (01) 9823914-111. E-mail direktion@ graphische.at. Website www. graphische.at

Internationale Sommerakademie für Bildende Kunst, Kapitelgasse 5, A-5010 Salzburg. Tel (0662) 842113/ 843727, Fax (0662) 849638. E-mail soak.salzburg@magnet.at. Website www.land-sbg.gv.at/ sommerakademie

Prager Fotoschule, P. O. Box 17, A-4212 Neumarkt i. M. Tel (07941) 8651, Fax (07941) 86514. E-mail pfs@ magnet.at. Website www.prager-fotoschule.at

Salzburg College, Leopoldskronstr. 56, A-5020 Salzburg. Tel (0662) 829082, Fax (0662) 820236

Schule für Künstlerische Photographie, Gartenstr. 5/2, A-1050 Wien. Tel (01) 5448649, Fax (01) 5444100

Universität für künstlerische und industrielle Gestaltung, Hauptplatz 8, A-4010 Linz. Tel (0732) 28980, Fax (0732) 783508. Website www.ufg.uc.at

Associations

Berufsvereinigung Bildender Künstler Österreichs, Schloß Schönbrunn, Ovalstiege, A-1130 Wien. Tel (01) 8135269, Fax (01) 8174739

Bundesinnung der Photographen Österreichs, Wiedner Hauptstr. 63, A-1045 Wien. Tel (01) 501053283, Fax (01) 7153920. E-mail bigb@ wk.or.at

Lomographische Gesellschaft, Stiftgasse 15–17/8, A-1070 Wien. Tel (01) 5248488, Fax (01) 5248488. E-mail lomo@lomo.com. Website www.lomo.com

Österreichisches Institut für Photographie und Medienkunst, Gumpendorfer Str. 118a/19, A-1060 Wien. Tel (01) 5977088, Fax (01) 5977087. E-mail office@eikon.or.at

Verband Österreichischer Galerien moderner Kunst, Museumsquartier, Stiege 5/Messeplatz 1, A-1070 Wien. Tel (01) 5229126, Fax (01) 5229127. E-mail verband.oegmk@eunet.at. Website www.kunstnet.or.at/kunst

Vereinigung Bildender Künstlerinnen Österreichs, Maysedergasse 2, A-1010 Wien. Tel (01) 5136473

Verwertungsgesellschaft Bildender Künstler (VBK), Tivoligasse 67, A-1120 Wien. Tel (01) 8152691, Fax (01) 8137835. E-mail vbk@magnet.at

Grants & Awards

Camera Austria Preis für zeitgenössische Fotografie der Stadt Graz, to recognize an outstanding work published in *Camera Austria*, no age limit, S 100,000, every two years. Contact: Camera Austria, Sparkassenplatz 2, A-8010 Graz. Tel (0316) 8155500, Fax (0316) 8155509. E-mail camera. austria@styria.com. Website www. camera-austria.at

Förderungspreis für Fotografie, for young Austrian artists, no age limit, S 75,000, every year. Contact: BKA / Abt. II/3, MR, Johannes Hörhan, Schottengasse 1, A-1014 Wien. Tel (01) 53120-2315/7530, Fax (01) 531207538. E-mail johannes.hoerhan@ bmwf.gv.at. Website www.fotonet.at

Großer Österreichischer Staatspreis für Fotografie, to recognize a lifetime achievement, for Austrian artists, S 300,000, occasional. Contact: BKA / Abt. II/3, MR, Johannes Hörhan, Schottengasse 1, A-1014 Wien. Tel (01) 53120-2315/7530, Fax (01) 531207538. E-mail johannes.hoerhan@ bmwf.gv.at. Website www.fotonet.at

Landesförderungspreis für Fotografie in der Steiermark, for artists born or living for five years in the Styria, total amount S 80,000, every year. Contact: Neue Galerie am Landesmuseum Joanneum, Sackstr. 16, A-8010 Graz. Tel (0316) 829155, Fax (0316) 815401. E-mail neue-galerie-graz@sime.com

Römerquelle-Fotopreis, to recognize new talent and outstanding work, Austrian artists, total amount S 200,000, every two years. Contact: Römerquelle-Fotopreis, Dr. Hansjörg Wachta, Oldenburggasse 49, A-1232 Wien. Tel (01) 6673284, Fax (01) 6673582

Rupertinum-Fotopreis, for Austrian artists, no age limit, S 70,000, every two years. Contact: Österreichische Fotogalerie im Rupertinum, Wiener Philharmoniker Gasse 9, A-5010 Salzburg. Tel (0662) 80422568, Fax (0662) 80422542

Würdigungspreis für Fotografie, for Austrian artists, no age limit, S 150,000, every year. Contact: BKA / Abt. II/3, MR, Johannes Hörhan, Schottengasse 1, A-1014 Wien. Tel (01) 53120-2315/7530, Fax (01) 531207538. E-mail johannes.hoerhan@ bmwf.gv.at. Website www.fotonet.at

New Media

Ars Electronica, Festival for art, technology and society, Hauptstr. 2, A-4040 Linz. Tel (0732) 72720, Fax (0732) 72777. E-mail info@aec.at

Medienwerkstatt Wien, Neubaugasse 40a, A-1070 Wien. Tel (01) 5263667, Fax (01) 5267168. E-mail medienwerkstatt@to.or.at. Website www.to.or.at/~medienwerkstatt

Belarus

Population: 10.3 million
Capital: Minsk, 1.7 million
Currency: Belarusian Rubel
(BuR)
International code: ++375
Ministry of Sport and Tourism,
8, Kirova St., BY-220600 Minsk
Tel (0172) 277237, 260147,
Fax (0172) 252175

Galleries & Museums

Belorussky gosudarstvenny muzei istorii Velikoi otechestvennoi voiny, Belarusian State Museum of History of the Great Patriotic War, prosp. F. Skoriny 25 a, BY-220030 Minsk. Tel (017) 2275665, Fax (017) 2271166. Open: Tue–Sun 10–18. Contact: Irina Voronkova. Founded 1967. 3 rooms, 320 m². 3–4 photo exhibitions/year

Galereya Evropeiskogo gumanitarnogo universiteta, European Humanities University Gallery, prosp. F. Skoriny 24, BY-220030 Minsk. Tel (017) 2768159, Fax (017) 2768159 E-mail art@ehu.unibel.by. Open: Mon–Sat 9–18. Contact: Tatiana Bembel. Founded 1999. 2 rooms 86 + 96 m². 4 photo exhibitions/year

Galereya Natsional'noj biblioteki Belarusi, Gallery of the National Library of Belarus, ul. Krasnoarmeiskaya 9, BY-220030 Minsk. Tel (017) 2261840, Fax (017) 2292494. E-mail sol@nacbibl.minsk.by. Website www.natlib.org.by. Open: Tue–Sun 10–19. Director: Irina Domanskaya. Founded 1998. 1 room, 106 m². 3–4 photo exhibitions/year

Galereya Nova, Gallery Nova, Yanka Kupala Central Public Library, ul. Very Khoruzhey 16, BY-220123 Minsk. Tel (017) 2344621, Fax (017) 2342235. E-mail novagallery@mail.ru. Open: by appointment. Contact: Uladzimir Parfianok. 1 room. 8–10 photo exhibitions/year

Galereya Vilnius, Vilnius Gallery, ul. Kalinovskogo 55, BY-220030 Minsk. Tel (017) 2517110, Fax (017) 2342235. E-mail innreut@netscape.net. Open: Sat–Thu 12–20. Contact: Inna Reut. Founded 1997. 1 room, 55 m². 2 photo exhibitions/year

Gosudarstvenny muzei istorii teatral'noi i muzikal'noi kultury Belarusi, State Museum of History of Theatre and Musical Culture of Belarus, ul. Starovilenskaya 14, BY-220029 Minsk. Tel (017) 2686403. Open: Mon–Fri 9–17.30. Curator: Galina Bordusova. Founded 1995. 2 rooms, 200 m². 2–3 photo exhibitions/year

Khudozhestvennaya galereya Belart, Belart Fine Arts Gallery, ul. K. Marx 8/21, BY-220050 Minsk. Tel (017) 2276124, Fax (017) 2277101. Open: Mon–Fri 10–18. Director: Irina Metlinskaya. Founded 1997. 3 rooms 18, 13 + 54 m². 2–3 photo exhibitions/year

Muzei Belorusskoi akademii iskusstv, Belarusian Arts Academy Museum, prosp. F. Skoriny 81a, BY-220012 Minsk. Tel (017) 2328151, Fax (017) 2322041. Open: Mon–Fri 10–13, 14–18. Director: Irina Persikova. 1 room, 220 m². 3–4 photo exhibitions/year

Muzei sovremennogo izobrazitelnogo iskusstva, Contemporary Fine Art Museum, prosp. F. Skoriny 47, BY-220005 Minsk. Tel (017) 2134468, Fax

(017) 2848621. Open: Tue–Sat 10–18.
Curator: Larisa Dobrovolskaya.
Founded 1998. 2 rooms 55 + 216 m².
3–4 photo exhibitions/year

Natsional'ny khudozhesvenny muzei,
National Museum of Fine Arts, ul.
Lenina 20, BY-220600 Minsk. Tel
(017) 227-7163/4562/3258, Fax (017)
2275672. Open: Wed–Mon 11–19.
Director: Olga Kovalenko. Founded
1939. 2 rooms, 250 + 80 m². 1–2 photo
exhibitions/year

**Natsional'ny muzei istorii i kul'tury
Belarusi,** National Museum of History and Culture of Belarus, ul. K.
Marx 12, BY-220050 Minsk. Tel (017)
2261504, Fax (017) 2273665. Website
www.natlib.org.by/web/hist-cult-
museum/home.htm. Open: Thu–Tue
11–19. Director: Tatiana Voronova.
Curator: Nadezhda Savchenko.
Founded 1957. 3 rooms, 60, 100 +
210 m². 3–4 photo exhibitions/year

Art-centr imeni Marka Shagala, Marc
Chagall Art Center, ul. Putna 2, BY-
210026 Vitebsk. Tel (0212) 360387,
Fax (0212) 372629. 1–2 photo exhibi-
tions/year

Centr sovremennogo iskusstva, Contemporary Art Center, ul. Pravdy 5,
BY-210064 Vitebsk. Tel (0212) 360293.
Director: Valentina Kirillova. Founded 1998

Magazines

Mastatstva, Art Magazine, ul.
Chicherina 1, 220029 Minsk. Tel (017)
2893467. Editor: Alexey Dudarev.
Belarusian (English summaries).
Founded 1983, 12 issues/year

Monolog, ul. Belomorskaya 7-21,
BY-220013 Minsk. Tel (017) 2324392.
E-mail agandreev@hotmail.com.

Editor: Alexey Andreev. Russian.
Founded 1995

Book Publishers

Belarus, prosp. Masherova 11, BY-
220600 Minsk. Tel (017) 2238742

Izdatel'stvo Vinograd, P. O. Box 377,
BY-220050 Minsk 50. Tel (017)
2277121, Fax (017) 2277121

Critics & Journalists

Mikhail Barazna, prosp. Rokossovs-
kogo 109-76, BY-220085 Minsk.
Tel (017) 2328151/2476982

Irina Bigday, ul. Knorina 6-15, BY-
220049 Minsk. Tel (017) 2660878/
2368790, Fax (017) 2651712. E-mail
bt@belarustoday.com, belarustoday@
irex.minsk.by

Alexander Davydchik, ul. Shugayeva
19-2-217, BY-220141 Minsk. Tel (017)
2605181. E-mail alexica@mail.ru

Dmitry Korol, ul. Vostochnaya 56-23,
BY-220113 Minsk. Tel (017) 2625382.
E-mail 5623@mail.ru

Nadezhda Korotkina, ul. Kalinovskogo 99-41, BY-220103 Minsk. Tel
(017) 2631661. *Mastatstva,* Minsk

Valery Lobko, ul. Shugayeva 3-2-200,
BY-220041 Minsk. Tel (017) 2603279,
Fax (017) 2603279. E-mail valeryl@
nsys.by

Arsen Melikian, ul. Molodyozhnaya
21-106, BY-220007 Machulishchi,
Minsk region. Tel (017) 5047114.
E-mail melikian@ehu.unibel.by

Uladzimir Parfianok, ul. Bakinskaya
16-76, BY-220007 Minsk. Tel (017)
2248017. E-mail novagallery@mail.ru,
vp@belkoda.nsys.by

Inna Reut, ul. Odovskogo 103-7,
BY-220015 Minsk. Tel (017) 2517110.
E-mail innareut@netscape.net,
semyonova@ehu.unibel.by

Igor Savchenko, Kharkovskaya 78-3-
57, 220074 Minsk. Tel (017) 2519256

Schools & Workshops

Belarusskaya akademiya iskusstv,
Belarusian Academy of Arts, prosp.
F. Skoriny 81, BY-220012 Minsk. Tel
(017) 2328151, Fax (017) 2322041

**Belorussky gosudarstvenny univer-
sitet – fakul'tet zhurnalistiki,** Belarusian State University – Faculty of
Journalism, ul. Moskovskaya 15, BY-
220001 Minsk. Tel (017) 2265951

Tekhnikum tekhnologicheskij, Technological Technical School, ul. Krasnaya 19b, BY-220005 Minsk. Tel (017)
2847815

Associations

**Assotsiatsiya "Sovremennoe iskusst-
vo",** "Contemporary Art" Association, ul. Cherviakova 18-63, BY-
220068 Minsk. Tel (017) 2379284

Fotoklub "Minsk", Photoclub
"Minsk", P. O. Box 179, BY-220039
Minsk 39. Tel (017) 2242585/2068955

Fotoklub "Raduga", Photoclub
"Raduga", P. O. Box 62, BY-212030
Mogilev – 2GOS

Belgium

Population: 10.2 million
Capital: Brussels, 950,000
Currency: Franc (BF)
International code: ++32
Tourist information:
Toerisme Vlaanderen, Gras-
markt 61, B-1000 Bruxelles
Tel (02) 50 40-300/390,
Fax (02) 50 40 270, 513 88 03.
Office du promotion du touris-
me de Wallonie-Bruxelles, 61
rue Marché aux herbes,
B-1000 Bruxelles
Tel (02) 50 40 200,
Fax (02) 513 69 50

Galleries & Museums

Instituut voor Fotografie en Nieuwe Media – Vlaanderen, Institute for Photography and New Media – Flanders, B-Antwerpen. Tel (03) 2564034, Fax (03) 2564034. E-mail info@ifon.be. Website www.ifon.be

Galerie DB-S, Vlaamse Kaai 76, B-2000 Antwerpen. Tel (03) 2378305, Fax (03) 2385319. Open: Wed–Sat 14–18. Director: Inge de Bisschop. Curator: Marc Steculorum. Founded 1985. 1 room, 120 m². 4 photo exhibitions/year. Artists: Henze Boekhout, Frank Schramm, Jitka Hanzlova, Jean-Paul Brohez, Hans Aarsman, Knut Maron, David Williams, Manel Esclusa

Museum van Hedendaagse Kunst Antwerpen, Leuvenstraat 32, B-2000 Antwerpen. Tel (03) 2385960, Fax (03) 2162486. E-mail muhka@skynet.be. Website www.muhka.be. Open: Tue–Sun 10–17. Director: Florent Bex. Founded: 1987. 3 rooms, 1,500 m² . Artists: Thierry Decordier, Luc Tuymans, Richard Deacon, Dan Flavin, Richard Artschwager

Museum voor Fotografie, 47 Waalse Kaai, B-2000 Antwerpen. Tel (03) 2429321, Fax (03) 2429310. E-mail info@fotografie.provant.be. Website www.provant.be. Open: Tue–Sun 10–17. Director: Eugène van Hoye. Curator: Pool Andries. Founded 1965. 5 rooms, 1,200 m². 18 photo exhibitions/year

Ruimte Morguen, 21–22 Waalse Kaai, B-2000 Antwerpen. Tel (03) 2480845. Open: Thu–Sat 14–18. Directors: Leen Derks, Marc Schepers. Founded 1982. 2 rooms, 70 m². 3 photo exhibitions/year. Artists: Pierre Antoine, François Elie, Frederick Bell, Marc Schepers, Renate Paulsen, Chris Baaten, Charl van Ark, Marco Jacobs

Argos, Werfstraat 13 rue du Chantier, B-1000 Bruxelles. Tel (02) 2290003, Fax (02) 2237331. E-mail info@argosarts.org. Director: Frie Depraetere. Founded 1989

Art Kiosk – Art Gallery, av. J. Volderslaan 9, B-1060 Bruxelles. Tel (02) 5346611, Fax (02) 5343688. E-mail art.kiosk@glo.be. Open: Thu–Sat 10–18.30. Director/curator: Agnes Rammant. Founded 1995. 5 rooms, 110 m². 3 photo exhibitions/year. Artists: Olga Tobreluts, Bella Matveeva, Andrej Barov, Timur Noviko, Oleg Mazlov, Viktor Kuznetsov, Orlan, Edward Lucie-Smith, Eric Rondepierre

Centre d'Art Contemporain, 63 avenue des Nerviens, B-1040 Bruxelles.

Instituut voor
Fotografie en Nieuwe Media
Vlaanderen

Institute for
Photography and New Media
Flanders

www.ifon.be

Tel/Fax +32 3 2564034
E-mail: info@ifon.be

Tel (02) 7350531/7356649, Fax (02) 7355190. Open: Mon–Fri 9–13, 14–17, Sat 13–18. Director: Fabienne Dumont. Founded 1983. 3 rooms, 150 m². 1 photo exhibition/year

Dorothée de Pauw Gallery, 70 rue de Hennin, B-1050 Bruxelles. Tel (02) 6494380, Fax (02) 6496519. E-mail de.pauw.gallery@skynet.be, info@depauwgallery.com. Website www.depauwgallery.com. Artists: Carla Arocha, Heno op de Beeck, Jock Sturges, Hein Hage, Nick Waplington, Richard Caldicott, Seydou Keïta

Espace Photographique Contretype, 1 avenue de la Jonction, B-1060 Bruxelles. Tel (02) 5384220, Fax (02) 5389919. E-mail contrety@hebel.net. Website www.magic.be/contretype. Open: Tue–Sun 13–18. Director: Jean-Louis Godefroid. Founded 1979. 4 rooms, 39 running meters. 6 photo

exhibitions/year. Artists: Anne Denis, Daniel Brunemer, André Jasinski, Dirk Braeckman, Julien Coulommier, Gast Bouschet, Chantal Maes, Lucia Radochonska, Jean-Louis Vanesch

Galerie Rodolphe Janssen, 35 rue de Livourne, B-1050 Bruxelles. Tel (02) 5380818, Fax (02) 5385660. E-mail rodolphe.janssen@skynet.be. Open: Tue–Sat 14–19. Director: Rodolphe Janssen. Founded 1989. 1 room, 250 m². 2 photo exhibitions/year. Artists: Balthasar Burkhard, Lynne Cohen, Hiroshi Sugimoto, Karl Blossfeldt, John Davies, Eadweard Muybridge, Sam Samore, Philip-Lorca DiCorcia, Michel François, Lawrence Beck

Galerie Willy D'Huysser, 35 pl. du Grand Sablon, B-1000 Bruxelles. Tel (02) 5113704, Fax (02) 5144245. Open: Mon–Sat 11–18, Sun 10–14. Director:

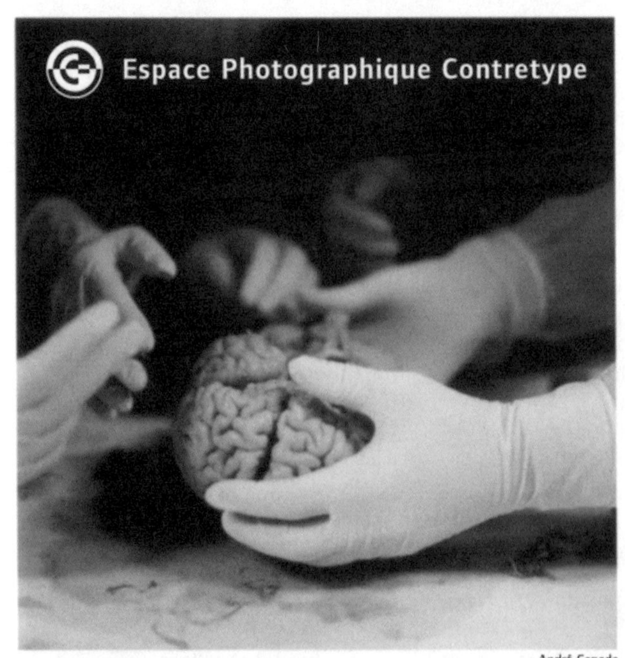

André Cepeda

Willy D'Huysser. Founded 1970.
1 room, 400 m². 2 photo exhibitions/
year. Artists: Carlos Da Ponte, Jean Le
Gac, Christian Carez, Calum Colvin,
Jean-Pierre Raynaud, Greta Buysse,
Geoffroy De Volder, Bruno Jacqmain,
Ronny Delrue, Danny Leriche

**Institut de Radioélectricité et de
Cinématographie,** 75 avenue Victor
Rousseau, B-1190 Bruxelles. Tel (02)
3401100, Fax (02) 3401116

Le Botanique, Centre Culturel de la
Communauté Française, 236 rue
Royale, B-1210 Bruxelles. Tel (02)
2261211, Fax (02) 2196660. E-mail
expo@botanique.be. Website www.
ais.be/botanique. Open: Tue–Sun
11–18. Director: Catherine De Braeke-
leer. Founded 1984. 3 rooms, 1,160
m². 2 photo exhibitions/year

Velge & Noirhomme, rue de la Ré-
gence 17 Regentschapsstraat, B-1000
Bruxelles. Tel (02) 5125010, Fax (02)
5121115. E-mail lotus@skynet.be.
Open: Tue–Sat 11–18.30. Director:
Alain Noirhomme. Founded 1995.
3 rooms, 150 m². 1 photo exhibition/
year. Artists: Stephen Sack, Philippe
de Gobert, Hervé Charles, Robert
Silvers

Xavier Hufkens Gallery, 6–8 rue Saint
Georges, B-1050 Bruxelles. Tel (02)
6466330, Fax (02) 6469342. E-mail
info@xavierhufkens.com. Website
www.artnet.com/xhufkens.html.
Open: Tue–Sat 12–18. Director: Xavier
Hufkens. Founded 1987. 6 rooms,
400 m². 3 photo exhibitions/year.
Artists: Jan Vercruysse, Bruce Weber,
Robert Mapplethorpe, James Welling,
Michelangelo Pistoletto, Adam Fuss,
Jean-Marc Bustament

Musée de la Photographie, 11 avenue
Paul Pastur, B-6032 Charleroi (Mont-
sur-Marchienne). Tel (071) 435810,

Fax (071) 364645. E-mail museephoto
@infonie.be. Website www.musee.
photo.infonie.be. Open: Tue–Sun 10–
18. Director: Xavier Canonne. Curator: Marc Vausort. Founded 1987. 35
rooms, 2,000 m². 15 photo exhibi-
tions/year

Palais des Beaux-Arts, pl. du Manège,
B-6000 Charleroi. Tel (071) 314420,
Fax (071) 334297. Open: Tue–Sun 10–
18. Director: Laurent Busine. Founded 1957. 2 rooms, 1,500 m²

Fotogalerij Cultureel Centrum Hasselt,
5 Kunstlaan, B-3500 Hasselt. Tel (011)
229931, Fax (011) 243207. Open: 10–
19. Directors: J. P. Grootaers, V. Du-
mon. Founded 1976. 1 room, 530 m².
6 photo exhibitions/year. Artists:
Roland Castro, Dominique Van Huf-
fel, Philippe Sohiez, Gilbert De
Keyser

Provinciaal Museum Hasselt, 33 Zui-
velmarkt, B-3500 Hasselt. Tel (011)
295960, Fax (011) 295961. E-mail
pcbk@limburg.be. Website www.
limburg.be/begijnhof. Open: Tue–
Sat 10–17, Sun 14–17. Director:
Danny Pauly. Founded 1958. 9
rooms, 857 m². 1 photo exhibition/
year

Cultureel Centrum, 40 Dekenstraat,
B-3550 Heusden-Zolder. Tel (021)
533315, Fax (021) 533124. Director:
R. Geladé. Founded 1974. 2 rooms,
85 m². 10 photo exhibitions/year

Galerie Périscope, 20 rue du Mouton
Blanc, B-4000 Liège. Tel (04) 2247050,
Fax (04) 2247051. E-mail jlderu@
yahoo.com. Open: daily 13–24.
Director: Jean–Luc Deru. Founded
1993. 1 room, 25 m². 5 photo exhibi-
tions/year

Cultureel Centrum Gildhof, 9 Sint-
Michielstraat, B-8700 Tielt. Tel (051)
402935, Fax (051) 408329. Open: 9–12,

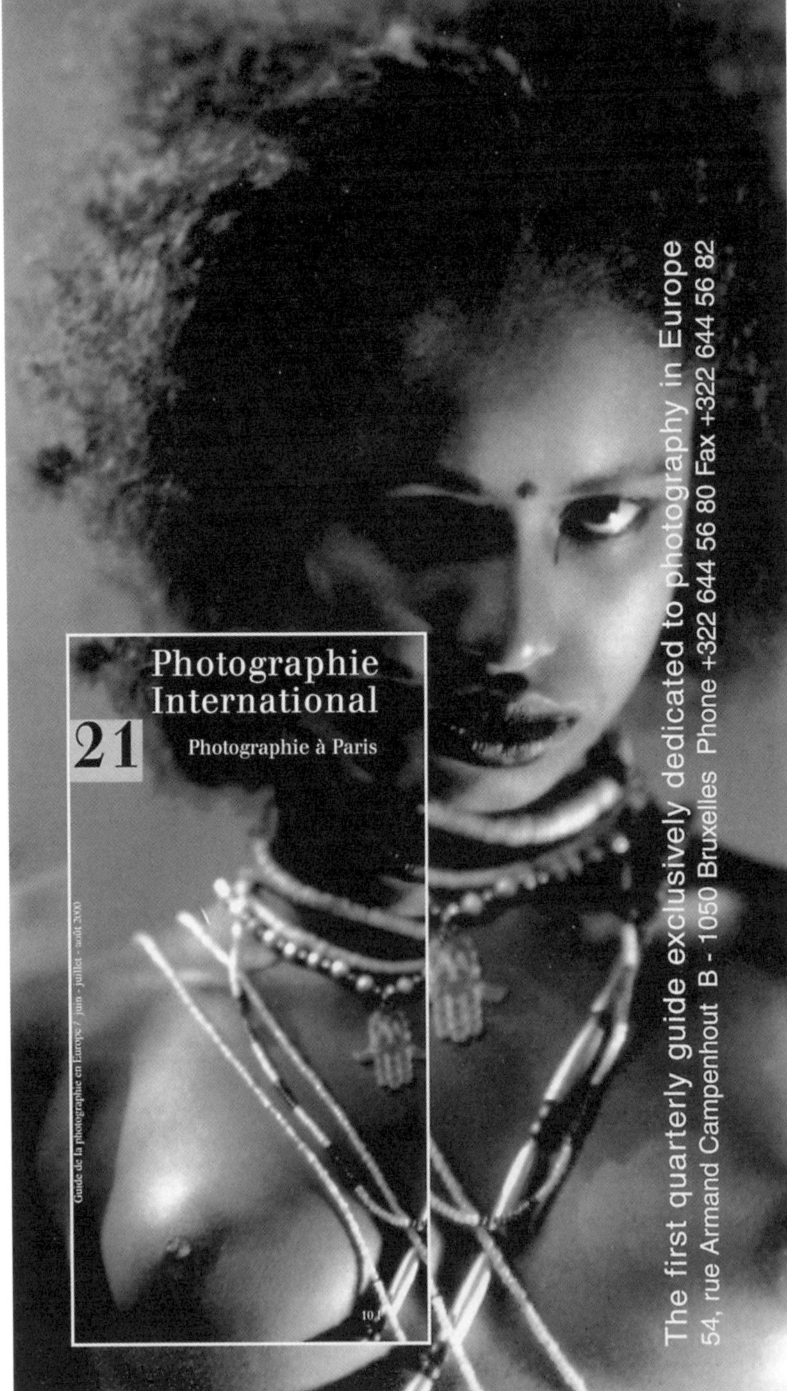
Photographie
International
Photographie à Paris
21
Guide de la photographie en Europe / juin - juillet - août 2000
10 F
The first quarterly guide exclusively dedicated to photography in Europe
54, rue Armand Campenhout B - 1050 Bruxelles Phone +322 644 56 80 Fax +322 644 56 82

14–17 (closed 15 Jul – 15 Aug). Director/curator: Erik Demoen. Founded 1980. 3 rooms, 250 m². 10 photo exhibitions/year

De Warande, 42 Warandestraat, B-2300 Turnhout. Tel (014) 419494, Fax (014) 420821. E-mail tento@ warande.be. Website www. warande.be. Open: Tue–Sat 14–18, Sun 10–12, 14–18. Director: Jan Cools. Founded 1972. 3 rooms, 900 m². 12 photo exhibitions/year

Festivals & Fairs

Fotografiecircuit – Vlaanderen, Jan Van Broeckhoven, Braderijstraat 8, B-2000 Antwerpen. Tel (0496) 262618. E-mail jan.van. broeckhoven@atv.be

Internationaal Fotofestival Knokke-Heist, Cultureel Centrum "Scharpoord", Meerlaan 32, B-8300 Knokke-Heist. Tel (050) 630-430/380

Internationaal Fotofestival Turnhout, fofetu, Veldstraat 27, B-2300 Turnhout. Website www.fofetu.org

Laboratorium, Antwerpen Open, Wapper 2, B-2000 Antwerpen. Tel (03) 2248534, Fax (03) 2248501. E-mail laboratorium@ antwerpenopen.be. Website laboratorium.antwerpenopen.be

Seneffe Arts & Culture, Gaëtan de Laever, rue Lucien Plasman 4, B-7180 Seneffe. Tel (064) 521754, Fax (064) 521752. E-mail g.delaever @seneffe.be

View-finder asbl, 17a rue du Bourgmestre, B-1050 Bruxelles. Tel (02) 6404290, Fax (02) 6404290. E-mail viewfinder@village.uunet.be. Website www.bitume.citeweb.net

Zomer van de Fotografie, Jan Van Broeckhoven, Braderijstraat 8, B-2000 Antwerpen. Tel (0496) 262618. E-mail jan.van.broeckhoven@atv.be

Magazines

Contretype, 1 avenue de la Jonction, B-1060 Bruxelles. Tel (02) 5384220, Fax (02) 5389919. E-mail contrety@ hebel.net. Website www.magic.be/ contretype/. Editor: Jean-Louis Godefroid. French. Founded 1985. Annual subscription: BF 600.00, 5 issues/year

Forum International, Cederreef 9/1, B-9230 Wetteren. Tel (09) 3663108, Fax (09) 3663167

Obscuur, c/o Uitgeverij Ludion, Muinkkaai 42, B-9000 Gent. Tel (09) 2334816, Fax (09) 2334862. Editor: Erik Eelbode. Copy price: BF 295. Annual subscription: BF 995, 3 issues/year

Photographie Ouverte, Revue du Musée de la Photographie, 11 avenue Paul Pastur, B-6032 Charleroi (Mont-sur-Marchienne). Tel (071) 435810, Fax (071) 364645. E-mail museephoto@infonie.be. Website www.musee.photo.infonie.be. Editor: Georges Vercheval. French. Founded 1979. Copy price: BF 100.00. Annual subscription: BF 1,000, 6 issues/year

Photoscoop, Foto-Video, Golden Hopestraat 1, B-1620 Drogenbos. Tel (02) 3782127, Fax (02) 3783729. Editor: Raymond Naumann. Dutch/French. Founded 1994. Copy price: BF 100.00. Annual subscription: BF 400.00, 4 issues/year

Book Publishers

ARP Editions, Editions photographiques, rue François Bossaerts 131, B-1030 Bruxelles. Tel (02) 2159401, Fax (02) 2453120. E-mail sign@ skynet.be

Uitgeverij Ludion, Muinkkaai 42, B-9000 Gent. Tel (09) 2334816, Fax (09) 2334862

Bookshops

Blow Up Photography Bookshop, Kloosterstr. 160, B-2000 Antwerpen. Tel (03) 2572020, Fax (03) 2572020. E-mail blowup@pandora.be. Website www.blowup.be

Copyright Art & Architecture Bookshop, Haarstraat 22, B-2000 Antwerpen. Tel (03) 2329416, Fax (09) 2333173. E-mail copyright@ village.uunet.be

Copyright Art & Architecture Bookshop, Jakobijnenstraat 8, B-9000 Gent. Tel (09) 2235794, Fax (09) 2333173. E-mail copyright@ village.uunet.be

Foto Art, Nieuwe Gentweg 148–150, B-8000 Brugge. Tel (050) 330532, Fax (050) 346153. E-mail fotoart@pi.be. Website www.fotoart.be

Librairie Objectifs, rue de I'Homme Chrétien 1a, B-1000 Bruxelles

Posada Art Books, rue de la Madeleine 29, B-1020 Bruxelles

Auctions

Michel Grommen, 33 rue du Pont, B-4000 Liège

Critics & Journalists

Pascal Baetens, W. Coosemansstraat 122, B-3010 Kessel-Lo. Tel (016) 258411, Fax (016) 258470. E-mail pascal.baetens@advalvas.be. *Photographie*, Düsseldorf; *De Fotograaf*, Amsterdam; *Infotravel*, Bruxelles

Jean-Marc Bodson, rue du Prévot 112, B-1050 Bruxelles. Tel (02) 3445404. La Libre Belgique, Bruxelles

Alain D'Hooghe, 105 avenue Emile de Beco, B-1050 Bruxelles. Tel (02) 6405522, Fax (02) 6401850

Johan De Vos, Grote Peperstraat 11, B-9100 Sint-Niklaas. Tel (03) 7762098, Fax (03) 7663562. *Knack Magazine*, *Kunst & Cultuur*, Bruxelles; *Focus*, Amsterdam; Radio I Brt, Bruxelles

Erik Eelbode, Steenhouwersstraat 1, B-9050 Ledeberg. Tel (09) 2318781. Editor of *Obscuur*

Guy Gilsoul, rue de Pologne 25, B-1060 Bruxelles. Tel (02) 5376069. Musée de la Photographie, Charleroi

Pascal Goffaux, RTBF 52 boulevard Reyers, B-1044 Bruxelles. Tel (02) 73729-19/20, Fax (02) 7374692. E-mail pgx@rtbf.be

Marc van Gysegem, 21 Hertecantlaan, B-9290 Berlare. Tel (052) 423237, Fax (052) 426111

Bernard Marcelis, 37 rue des Eperonniers, B-1000 Bruxelles. Tel (02) 5119643, Fax (02) 5119643. *Art Press*, Paris

Josiane Roisselle, rue des Canadiens 41, B-7180 Seneffe. Tel (075) 200506. E-mail jr@epacar.be

Dr. Johan Swinnen, Boudewijnsstraat 59, B-2018 Antwerpen. Tel (03) 2900365, Fax (03) 2900367. E-mail

FOTOGRAFIE *in* DIALOOG

Filosofie van de fotografie
van Walter Benjamin tot Roland Barthes

Fotografie in België: *inleiding en interviews.*
Willem Elias en Johan Swinnen / *Uitgeverij Groeninghe, 1999*

Het uitgangspunt van Fotografie in dialoog was het verzamelen van interviews met Belgische en in België werkende fotografen-kunstenaars en fotohistorici geboren voor 1930.
24 bezielde mensen komen door middel van deze boekuitgave in een hernieuwde belangstelling. De foto's en teksten van deze generatie 'vaders en moeders van de Belgische fotografie' horen bij ons cultureel erfgoed en reflecteren een inzicht op onze eigen traditie.
De fotografie van gisteren bepaalt immers het beeld van vandaag. Het is een signalement over de sfeer van deze pioniersjaren waarin de variëteit van het materiaal en de vele artistieke en creatieve invalshoeken kenmerkend zijn. Daarnaast biedt Fotografie in dialoog een begrijpelijk overzicht van filosofen die over fotografie hebben gepubliceerd. Fotografische praktijk en filosofie geven parallelle antwoorden op het tijdsbeeld en drukken dikwijls dezelfde wereldvisies uit. Of we het ons realiseren of niet, de camera verandert de werkelijkheid en herinterpreteert de wereld rondom ons. De camera laat ons de wereld letterlijk anders zien.
En de filosofie van fotografie toont aan dat fotografie in ieder geval geen neutraal medium is.
Het verband tussen fotografie en filosofie is dat van beeld en woord. De filosofische teksten verschenen tijdens de actiefste periode van de betreffende fotografen, nl. Tussen het eerste filosofische essay (1931, Benjamin) en het eerste filosofische boek over fotografie (1980, Barthes).

Prijs: **28** EURO (gesigneerd door de auteurs)
verzending inbegrepen in Europese Unie

HOE BESTELLEN?   Voor België: via Gemeentekrediet
E-mail: johan@swinnen.com   068-2176061-87
Tel + 32 3 29 003 65   Voor Nederland: via ING Bank
Fax +32 3 29 003 67   659974029

johan@swinnen.com. *European Photography*, Göttingen; Free University Brussels, Bruxelles; De Vries Foundation, Zeist

Karel R. L. Van Deuren, 19/1 Troyentenhoflaan, B-2600 Antwerpen-Berchem. Tel (03) 32184109. *Foto*, Leusden; *Fotohistorisch Tijdschrift*, Den Haag; *Vlaanderen*, Tielt

Jean-Pierre Van Tieghem, 64 avenue Emile Duray, B-1050 Bruxelles. Tel (02) 6485926

Jean-Marie Wynants, Le Soir (rédaction), 120 rue Royale, B-1000 Bruxelles. Tel (02) 2255432, Fax (02) 22559-14/10. E-mail jean.marie.wynants@lesoir.be. Website www.lesoir.com/. Musée de la Photographie, Charleroi; *Le Soir*, Bruxelles

Schools & Workshops

Académie des Beaux-Arts Alphonse Darville, 26 rue Dourlet, B-6000 Charleroi. Tel (071) 417511

Académie Royale des Beaux-Arts de Bruxelles, 144 rue du Midi, B-1000 Bruxelles

Arrêt sur l'Image, rue V. Rauter 201, B-1070 Bruxelles. Tel (02) 5238849, Fax (02) 5204228

Centrum voor Volwassenenonderwij Technicum Noord-Antwerpen, 43 Londenstraat, B-2000 Antwerpen. Tel (03) 2024530, Fax (03) 2311171. E-mail technicum@glo.be

Coloma Instituut, Tervuursesteenweg 2, B-2800 Mechelen. Tel (015) 422703, Fax (015) 420422. E-mail coloma@colomainstituut.be

CVO Elishout avondschool COOVI, 1 E. Gryonlaan, B-1070 Bruxelles. Tel (02) 5267740, Fax (02) 5267713. E-mail elishout.avondschool.coovi@skynet.be

École de Photographie de la Ville de Bruxelles, 57 rue Claessens, B-1020 Bruxelles. Tel (02) 4220360, Fax (02) 4220368. E-mail jp.baron@brunette.brucity.be. Website www.brunette.brucity.be/claessens/photo/index.htm

Gemeentelijke Academie voor Beeldende Kunsten, 1 Molderdijk, B-2400 Mol

Gemeentelijke Tekenacademie, 23 Schoolstraat, B-9230 Wetteren. Tel (09) 3660054, Fax (09) 3660054. E-mail academie.wetteren@skynet.be. Website www.wetteren.be/academie.htm

Hoger Instituut voor Schone Kunsten, Higher Institute for Fine Arts, Lange Leemstraat 338, B-2018 Antwerpen. Tel (03) 2867840, Fax (03) 2815026. E-mail hisk@hisk.edu. Website www.hisk.edu

Hoger Onderwijs Imelda Instituut, 132 Ninoofsesteenweg, B-1080 Bruxelles

Hoger Onderwijs Imelda Instituut HONIM, Birminghamstraat 41, B-1080 Bruxelles. Tel (02) 4104631, Fax (02) 4104134. Website www.honim.wenk.be

Hogeschool Sint-Lucas Brussel, 70 Paleizenstraat, B-1030 Bruxelles. Tel (02) 2501110, Fax (02) 2501111. E-mail info.lukas@sintlukasbrussel.be

Inraci, 75 avenue Victor Rousseau, B-1180 Bruxelles. Tel (02) 3401100, Fax (02) 3401116. E-mail helb@inraci.be. Website www.inraci.be

Instituut Saint-Luc, 26 rue St. Marie, B-4000 Liège. Tel (04) 2223982, Fax (04) 2233908

Katholieke Hogeschool Limburg, Dep. Audiovisuele & Beeldende Kunsten,

In its quality of post-graduate educational programme, the Higher Institute for the Visual Arts is a leading institution in the field of the visual plastic arts. The HISK is an independent institution and is directed towards young artists in general. HISK offers individual studios to some thirty five young visual artists, thus enabling them to develop their own individual oeuvre and style, independently of fixed curricula or programmes, yet within a professional climate, stimulated, guided and supported by experts.

HISK
Studios for visual artists

Hoger Instituut *voor* Schone Kunsten

Higher Institute *for* Fine Arts

Lange Leemstraat 338 . B-2018 Antwerpen . Belgium

tel +32 3 2867840 . **fax** +32 3 2815026

e-mail hisk@hisk.edu . **internet-site** www.hisk.edu

REIND M. DE VRIES FOUNDATION
EUROPEAN PHOTOGRAPHY PRIZE

The prize of 25.000 EURO is to be awarded

in appreciation of an artistic, theoretical,

scientific, technological or agogical achievement

of contribution that has proved to be essential

or substantially significant to the progress

and promotion of photography

in the real sense of the word.

THE FINAL DATE FOR ENTRIES IS 1 SEPTEMBER 2000.

www.devriesfoundation.org

Stichting Reind M. de Vries Prijs
c/o Museum voor Fotografie
Waalse Kaai 47
B-2000 Antwerpen, Belgium

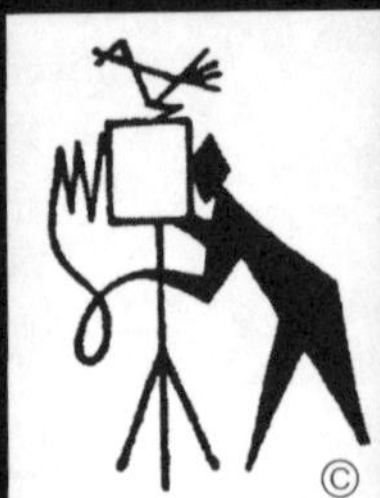

CORRESPONDENCE:
Johan Swinnen:
e-mail: info @ devriesfoundation.org
tel. + 32 3 257 19 92
fax + 32 3 238 43 35

30 Belgium

Weg Naar As 50, B-3600 Genk. Tel
(089) 300850, Fax (089) 300859. E-mail
khlim@skynet.be

**Koninklijke Academie voor Audio-
visuele en Beeldende Kunst,** Optie
fotografie, Hogeschool Gent, Jozef
Kluyskensstraat 2, B-9000 Gent. Tel
(09) 2660800, Fax (09) 2660801. E-mail
wim_sas@skynet.be. Website www.
acad.hogent.be/fotografie

Koninklijk Technisch Atheneum 2,
101 Ledebaan, B-9300 Aalst. Tel (053)
769250, Fax (053) 784505. E-mail
kta2.aalst@gemeenschepsonderwijs.be.
Website www.schoolweb.argo.be/
kta/aalst/ledebaan

La Cambre Ensav, 21 Abbaye de la
Cambre, B-1000 Bruxelles. Tel (02)
6489619, Fax (02) 6409693. E-mail
ensav.lacambre@sup.cfwb.be.
Website www.lacambre.be

Le "75", 10 avenue J. F. Debecker,
B-1200 Bruxelles. Tel (02) 7612702,
Fax (02) 7612713. E-mail ecok.75@
chello.be

Périscope, Assoc. sans but lucratif
pour la promotion des arts visuels,
355 rue Ste. Marguerite, B-4000 Liège.
Tel (04) 2247050, Fax (04) 2247051

Rijkscentrum Hoger Kunstonderwijs,
2 E. de Thibaultlaan, B-1040 Bruxelles. Tel (02) 7334551, Fax (02) 7358809.
E-mail sbk.etterbeek@argo.be

**Stedelijk Instituut voor Sierkunsten
en Ambachten,** 2 Cadixstraat, B-2000
Antwerpen. Tel (03) 2060060, Fax (03)
2060085. E-mail sisa@village.uunet.
be. Website www.gallery.uunet.be/
sisa

**Stedelijke Academie voor Schone
Kunsten,** 86 Katelijnestraat, B-8000
Brugge

**Stedelijke Academie voor Schone
Kunsten,** 12 Kunstlaan, B-3500
Hasselt. Tel (011) 227832, Fax (011)
261495

**Stedelijke Academie voor Schone
Kunsten,** 30 L. Vanderkelenstraat,
B-3000 Leuven

**Stedelijke Academie voor Schone
Kunsten,** Boonhemstraat 1, B-9100
Sint-Niklaas. Tel (03) 7763300, Fax
(03) 7763453

**Vrij Instituut voor secundair Onder-
wijs,** 228 Industrieweg, B-9030 Maria-
kerke. Tel (09) 2163636, Fax (09)
2163637. E-mail viso-mariakerke@
ping.be. Website www.hiprocampus.
com

Vrij Instituut voor Kunstambachten,
35 Bredastraat, B-2008 Antwerpen

Vrije Universiteit Brussel, 2 Pleinlaan,
B-1050 Bruxelles. Tel (032) 26292325,
Fax (032) 26292337. E-mail rhebbeli@
vub.ac.be. Website www.vub.ac.be

Associations

Europhot, House of International
Associations, 40 rue Washington,
B-1050 Bruxelles

Grants & Awards

Stichting Reind M. de Vries Prijs,
c/o Museum voor Fotografie, Johan
Swinnen, Waalse Kaai 47, B-2000
Antwerpen. Tel (03) 2571992, Fax
(03) 2383435. E-mail info@
devriesfoundation.org. Website
www.devriesfoundation.org

New Media

Argos, International Video & Film,
Frie Depraetere, Werfstraat 13 rue du
Chantier, B-1000 Bruxelles. Tel (02)
2290003, Fax (02) 2237331. E-mail
info@argosarts.org

**Festival International du Film Indé-
pendant (Mondial de la Vidéo),** Robert Malengreau, 12 rue Paul Emile
Janson, B-1000 Bruxelles. Tel (02)
6493340, Fax (02) 6493340. E-mail
centre.multimedia@euronet.be

**International Internet FilmVideoFesti-
val "King Nobel",** VTB-VAB Smal-
film- & Videoclub "Spotlight", c/o
Bernard Benoot Baljuwweg 1, B-9080
Lochristi. Tel (09) 3557114, Fax (09)
3557114. E-mail Bernard.Benoot@
ping.be. Website www.ping.be/film

Festival Video Liège International,
ASBL Film et Culture, rue Alex
Bouvy 34, B-4020 Liège. Tel (04)
3441512, Fax (04) 344 1514

Bulgaria

Population: 9 million
Capital: Sofia, 1.3 million
Currency: Leva (Lv)
International code: ++359
Tourist information: Bulgarian
Association of Tourism and
Recreation, ul. Knjaz Alexander
Batemberg 12, BG-1000 Sofia
Tel (02) 84131

Galleries & Museums

Laoutlieff Gallery, Zlatarska 11a,
BG-4000 Plovdiv. Tel (032) 264589/
229544, Fax (032) 229544. Open:
10–20. Contact: Nikolay Laoutliev.
Founded 1980. 1 room, 60 m². 8–10
photo exhibitions/year

State Fine Arts Gallery, ul. Kniaz
Aleksander I. 15, BG-4000 Plovdiv.
Tel (032) 224220. 420 m². 2 photo
exhibitions/year

Art Center MONO, ul. Christo
Belchev 8, BG-1000 Sofia. Tel (02)
9803078, Fax (02) 9803078. Contact:
Ilia Zaykov. 2 rooms, 100 m². 3–4
photo exhibitions/year

ATA Galeria, Center for Contemporary Art, ul. Christo Belchev 25, BG-
1000 Sofia. Tel (02) 9819617, Fax (02)
9808025. E-mail ray@mail.bol.bg.
100 m². Artist: Iglena Rousseva

Galeria K.E.V.A., Bulgarian Photographic Association, ul. G. S. Rakovski 114, BG-1000 Sofia. Tel (02)
870417, Fax (02) 870417. E-mail bpa@
comedy.art.acad.bg. Website

www.photone.ch. Artist: Stanka
Conkova

Galeria Sredec, Sredec Gallery, Euro-
Bulgarian Cultural Center, Al. Stam-
bolijski 17, BG-1000 Sofia. Tel (02)
9880084. E-mail cip@culture-link.
nat.bg. Website www.culture-link.
nat.bg. 60 m². Artists: Dimitr Vil-
kov, Students of New Bulgarian
University

**Gallery of Fine Arts of the Associa-
tion of Bulgarian Fine Artists,** ul.
Shipka 6, BG-1000 Sofia. Tel (02)
43351, Fax (02) 463129. Several rooms
from 100 m² to 400 m². 2–3 photo
exhibitions/year

National Gallery of Fine Art, ul.
Kniaz Aleksander Batemberg 6,
BG-1000 Sofia. Tel (02) 883559.
Open: Tue–Sun 10–18

National Palace of Culture, Bul-
garia Square 1, BG-1000 Sofia.
Tel (02) 91662841. Several rooms.
Artist: Garo Keshishan

Rossen Kolarov Gallery, jk. Liulin 10
bl. 155, BG-1000 Sofia. E-mail rossen-
kolarov@hotmail.com. 1 room, 45 m².
3–4 photo exhibitions/year

Sofijska gradska galeria, Sofia Municipal Art Gallery, ul. General Gurko
1, BG-1000 Sofia. Tel (02) 872181.
Open: Wed–Sun 10.30–18.30. 2 rooms,
1,000 m². 2–3 photo exhibitions/year
Artist: Javor Popov

Festivals & Fairs

**International Meetings of Photog-
raphy,** P. O. Box 910, BG-4000
Plovdiv

**International Photo Salon "Art –
Document – Photo",** FODAR Foundation, 4, "Loukovit" str., BG-5800

Pleven. Tel (02) 6436168, Fax (02) 6436168. E-mail style33@ mbox.digsys.bg

Photovacation festival, Photographic Society, P. O. Box 56, BG-1680 Sofia. E-mail photovacation@fotof.com

Magazines

Fotooko, P. O. Box 162, BG-1606 Sofia. Tel (02) 9885727. E-mail photoeye@bgnet.bg. Website www.photoeye.dir.bg. Editors: Iglena Rousseva, Boyko Yordanov. Bulgarian. Copy price: DM 9.00, 6 issues/year

Critics & Journalists

Adriana Bancheva, ul. Chan Krum 37, BG-1000 Sofia

Jara Boubnova, Institute for Contemporary Art, 3, Frityof Nanssen str. BG-1000 Sofia. E-mail iaraica@ mbox.cit.bg

Prof. Roumen Georgiev, National Academy of Theatre and Cinema Kr. Serafov, ul. G. S. Rakovski 108a, BG-1000 Sofia. Tel (02) 9879862, Fax (02) 897389

Nikolay Laoutliev, Laoutlieff Gallery Zlatarska 11a, BG-4000 Plovdiv. Tel (032) 264589, 229544, Fax (032) 229544. E-mail lilia-mor@yahoo.com

Krassimir Linkov, ul. Komsomolska 27b, BG-4000 Plovdiv

Georgi Lozanov, "Kultura" newspaper, 4, "Knjaz Alexander Battenberg" str. BG-1040 Sofia. Tel (02) 9800495/ 440951

Boris Missirkov, Tsar Osloboditel blvd. 25, BG-1000 Sofia. Tel (02)

443362, (0288) 224232. E-mail badeff@usa.net, bpa@comedy.art. acad.bg. Bulgarian Photographic Association, Sofia

Georgi Papakochev, ul. Bacho Kiro 2, BG-1000 Sofia

Ralica Peikova, ul. Gurguliat 16, BG-1000 Sofia. Tel (02) 9865495

Iglena Rousseva, ul. Nezabravka 33a, BG-1113 Sofia. Tel (02) 658857. E-mail rousseva@bol.bg. Associate Professor of NATFIZ, chief editor of *Fotooko*, Sofia

Maria Vassileva, Institute for Contemporary Art, 3, Frityof Nanssen str. BG-1000 Sofia. Tel (02) 803791. E-mail mariaart@mail.bol.bg

Boyko Yordanov, Photo Information Center, ul. Vitosha 45, P. O. Box 162, BG-1606 Sofia. Tel (02) 562200. E-mail pic-bg@hotmail.com

Schools & Workshops

National Academy of Theatre and Cinema Kr. Sarafov, Department of Film, Television and Still Photography, ul. G. S. Rakovski 108A, BG-1000 Sofia. Tel (02) 9879862, Fax (02) 897389. E-mail natfiz@bgcict.acad.bg

New Bulgarian University, Department of Photography (Soros Foundation). Tel (02) 768965

School of Polygraphy and Photography, ul. Zlatishi Prokhod 5, BG-1408 Sofia

Sofia University, Faculty of Journalism, ul. Moskovska 49, BG-1000 Sofia

Associations

Art Center MONO, ul. Christo Belchev 8, BG-1000 Sofia. Tel (02) 9803078, Fax (02) 9803078. E-mail artemono@mail.orbitel.bg

Association of Advertising Photographers, ul. G. S. Rakovski 146, BG-1000 Sofia. Tel (02) 9810572, Fax (02) 9809753. E-mail association@com.bg

Bulgarian Photo-Club, ul. Moskovska 49, BG-1000 Sofia. E-mail bulphotoclub@mail.orbitel.bg

Bulgarian Photographic Association, ul. G. S. Rakovski 114, BG-1000 Sofia. Tel (02) 870417, Fax (02) 870417. E-mail bpa@comedy.art.acad.bg

Photographic Academy, ul. Vitosha 45, BG-1000 Sofia. Tel (02) 9885727

Photo Information Center, ul. Vitosha 45, P. O. Box 162, BG-1606 Sofia. Tel (02) 562200. E-mail pic-bg@hotmail.com. Contact: Boyko Yordanov

Grants & Awards

Bulgarian Photographic Association, ul. G. S. Rakovski 114, BG-1000 Sofia. Tel (02) 870417, Fax (02) 870417. E-mail bpa@comedy.art.acad.bg

Plovdiv Photographic Foundation, Nikolay Laoutliev, 61 Ruski Str. 61, P. O. Box 910, BG-4000 Plovdiv

New Media

Computer Space, International Forum for Computer Arts, SCAS/Student Computer Art Society, 10 Narodno sabranie sqr., BG-1000 Sofia. Tel (02) 870293, Fax (02) 870293. E-mail forum@scas.acad.bg, info@scas.acad.bg. Website www.scas.acad.bg

Interspace Media Arts Center, Vassil Levski blvd. 8, BG-1000 Sofia. Tel (02) 664352. E-mail home@i-space.org

Croatia

Population: 4.8 million
Capital: Zagreb, 930,000
Currency: Kuna (Hkn)
International code: ++385
Tourist information: Turisticki
Informativni Centar, Trg Bana
Jelacica 11, CRO-10000 Zagreb
Tel (01) 48 140-51/52,
Fax (01) 48 140 56

Galleries & Museums

Muzej grada Rijeke, City Museum of
Rijeka, Muzejski trg 1/1, CRO-51000
Rijeka. Tel (051) 336711, Fax (051)
336521. E-mail muzej-grada-rijeke@
ri.tel.hr. Director: Ervin Dubrovic.
Founded 1994. 2 photo exhibitions/
year. Artists: Viktor Hreljanovic, Igor
Emili, Šime Radovcic

Galerija fotografija, Fotoklub Split,
Marmontova 5, CRO-21000 Split. Tel
(021) 347597. Contact: Mario Javor-
cic, Ante Verzotti. 2 rooms, 70 m².
20 photo exhibitions/year

Arhiv Tošo Dabac, Archive Tošo
Dabac, Ilica 17, CRO-10000 Zagreb.
Tel (01) 4833677, Fax (01) 4833453.
Open: by appointment only. Contact:
Petar Dabac. Founded 1970. 1 room,
19 m². Artists: Petar Dabac, Tošo
Dabac

Fotogalerija Spot, Fotoklub Zagreb,
Ilica 29, CRO-10000 Zagreb. Tel (01)
4833359, Fax (01) 4833359. Open:
Mon–Fri 11–15, Tue 18–21. Director:
Vinko Šebrek. Founded 1957. 3
rooms, 120 m². 8–10 photo exhibi-
tions/year. Artists: Luka Mjeda,
Marija Braut, Bolto Ranilovic,
Zvonimir Atletic, Ivan Medar, Zvoni-
mir Dumancic, Erika Šmider, Bozidar
Grigic, Velizar Vesovic,Vladimir
Vucinovic, Oto Hohnjec

Muzej suvremene umjetnost Zagreb,
Museum of Contemporary Art
Zagreb – Department of Photogra-
phy, Habdeliceva 2, CRO-10000
Zagreb, P. O. Box 537. Tel (01)
4851930, Fax (01) 4851931. E-mail
msu@msu.tel.hr. Website www.
mdc.hr/msu. Open: Thu–Sat 11–19,
Sun 10–13. Curators: Dr. Zelimir
Koščevic, Tihomir Milovac. Founded
1954. 7 rooms, 300 m². Artists: Man
Ray, Boris Cvjetanovic, Josef Sudek,
Tošo Dabac, Ana Opalic, Josip Kla-
rica, August Sander, Dennis Adams

Muzej za umjetnost i obrt, Museum
of Art and Crafts, Trg M. Tita 10,
CRO-10000 Zagreb. Tel (01) 4826922/
4828086, Fax (01) 4828088. E-mail
muo@muo.hr. Website www.muo.hr.
Director: Vladimir Malekovic.
Curators: Marija Tonkovic, Biserka
Osrecki. Founded 1880. 12 rooms,
1,600 m². 2–3 photo exhibitions/year.
Artists: Zeljko Koprolcec, Stephan
Lupino, Damir Fabijanic

Critics & Journalists

Iva Brezovecki Bidjin, Sollarova 1,
CRO-10000 Zagreb. E-mail iva-bb@
yahoo.com

Vesna Delic-Gozze, Dubrovacki
Muzej, Knezev Dvor, CRO-20000
Dubrovnik. Tel (020) 426469

Ervin Dubrovic, A. Dubrovica 2, CRO-
51211 Matulji. Tel (051) 276281,
336711, Fax (051) 336521. E-mail
muzej-grada-rijeke@ri.tel.hr

Vladimir Gudac, Atelier Uncanska 2,
CRO-10250 Lucko

Branka Hlevnjak, Gajeva 36, CRO-
10000 Zagreb. Tel (01) 4577804, Fax
(01) 4577804. E-mail b-hlevnjak18@
yahoo.com

Dina Ivan, Vecernji list, Slavonska
Avenija 4, CRO-10000 Zagreb. Tel
(01) 6300444, Fax (01) 6300675.
Vecernji list, Zagreb

Dr. Radovan Ivancevic, Bosanska 7,
CRO-10000 Zagreb. Tel (01) 3760001,
Fax (01) 3760001. E-mail rivancev@
zg.tel.hr

Dr. Zelimir Koščevic, Museum of
Contemporary Art, Zagreb, Habde-
liceva 2, P. O. Box 537, CRO-10000
Zagreb. Tel (01) 4851930, Fax (01)
4851931. E-mail msu@msu.tel.hr.
Home: Langova 15, CRO-10430
Samobor. Tel (01) 3362884. E-mail
zelimirk@zamir.net

Branka Slijepcevic, Draškoviceva 10,
CRO-10000 Zagreb. Tel (01) 253198/
6112346. E-mail Branka.Slijepcevic@
pomet.adu.hr

Marija Tonkovic, Vocarska cesta 28b,
CRO-10000 Zagreb. Tel (01) 4635472

Antun Travirka, Ante Starcevica 11e,
CRO-23000 Zadar. Tel 435844/200542

Schools & Workshops

Akademija dramske umjetnosti,
Academy of Performing Arts, Trg M.
Tita 5, CRO-10000 Zagreb. Tel (01)
4828506, Fax (01) 4828508. E-mail
dekanat@ pomet.adu.hr. Website
www.adu.hr

**Škola primijenjenih umjetnosti i
dizajna,** School of Applied Arts and
Design, Trg M. Tita 11. CRO-10000

Zagreb. Tel (01) 4828099, Fax (01)
4828099

Associations

Hrvatski fotosavez, Croatian Photographic Union, Dalmatinska 12, CRO-
10000 Zagreb. Tel (01) 4848793, Fax
(01) 4848793

New Media

**International Festival of Film, Video &
New Media,** Split Festival of New
Film, P. O. Box 244 (Kralja Tomislava
15), CRO-21000 Split. Tel (021) 348001,
Fax (021) 348002. E-mail split.filmfest
@st.tel.hr. Website www.st.carnet.hr/
split-filmfest/

Czech Republic

Population: 10.5 million
Capital: Prague, 1.2 million
Currency: Ceska koruna (Kc)
International code: ++420
Tourist information:
Ceská centrála cestovního
ruchu, Czech Tourist Authori-
ty, Vinohradská 46, P. O. Box
32, CZ-120 41 Praha 2
Tel (02) 21 58 01 11,
Fax (02) 24 24 75 16

Galleries & Museums

Muzeum výtvarného umení, Museum of Fine Art, Malé námestí 1/74, CZ-256 01 Benešov u Prahy. Tel (0301) 24601, Fax (0301) 726177. E-mail desmuz@czn.cz. Website www.desmuz.leknet.cz. Open: Tue–Sat 10–13, 14–16. Director: Tomáš Fassati. Founded 1990. 8 rooms, 300 m². 2–3 photo exhibitions/year. Artists: Rudolf Bruner-Dvorák, Jan Pohribný, František Provazník, Olga Bleyová, Dana Bleyová

Dum umení mesta Brna, Brno House of Art, Malinovského námestí 2, CZ-601 07 Brno. Tel (05) 42211808, Fax (05) 42211662. Open: Tue–Sun 10–18. Director: Dr. Pavel Liška. Curator: Dr. Jana Vránová. Photo exhibitions since 1958. 2 rooms, 160 m + 165 m². 5–6 photo exhibitions/year. Artists: Anton Corbijn, Václav Zykmund, Jaromír Funke, Paul den Hollander, Peter Neusser, Pavel Dias, Vladimír

Birgus, Jindrich Štreit, Karel Cudlín, Markéta Luskacová, Viktor Kolár

Galerie AB, Kounicova 15, CZ-602 00 Brno. Tel (05) 750814. Open: Mon–Fri 9–18. Curator: Miroslav Myška. 45 m². Artists: Vilém Reichmann, Irena Armutidisová, Vojtech Bartek, Vít Mádr, Jarmila Šimánová, Vlastimil Trešnák, Igor Šefr

Galerie Ambrosiana, Jezuitská 11, CZ-602 00 Brno. Tel (05) 42214439, Fax (05) 44214439. Open: Mon–Fri 10–12, 13.30–17.45. Contact: Vladimír Ambroz. Founded 1990. 1 room, 55 m². 2–4 photo exhibitions/year. Artists: Jan Saudek, František Drtikol, Vladimír Zidlický, Rudo Prekop, Peter Zupník, Václav Jirásek

Galerie Foma, Bratislavská 7, CZ-602 00 Brno. Tel (05) 45221926. Director: Dr. Jan Vrba. Curator: Evzen Sobek. 40 m². 10 photo exhibitions/year. Artists: Miro Myška, Jindrich Štreit, Evzen Sobek, Andrea Velnerová

Moravská galerie v Brne, Moravian Gallery in Brno, Husova 18, CZ-662 26 Brno. Tel (05) 42217630-33, Fax (05) 42216651. Open: Wed–Sun 9.30–18. Director: Dr. Kaliopi Chamonikola. Curator: Dr. Antonín Dufek. Photographic department founded 1962. Several exhibition rooms, 75–250 m². 10–12 photo exhibitions/year. Artists: Josef Sudek, Jaromír Funke, František Drtikol, Karel Kašparík, Josef Koudelka, Jindrich Štreit, Jan Svoboda, Martin Parr, Frank Horvat, Pavel Mára, Markéta Luskacová

Moravské zemské muzeum – Etnografický ústav, Moravian Museum, Dept. of Ethnography, Koblizná 2, CZ-602 00 Brno. Tel (05) 42211161, Fax (05) 42212792. E-mail etno@anet.mzm.cz. Director: Dr. Helena Dvoráková. Curator: Dr. Helena Beránková. 3 rooms, 150, 56, 20 m². 2–3 photo exhibitions/year. Artists: Guido Boggiani, K. O. Hrubý, Jan Beran, Aurellio Amendola, Josef Braun

Galerie Škola, Základní škola, Pastviny 70, CZ-624 00 Brno. Tel (05) 41223028. E-mail kohout@telecom.cz. Open: Mon–Fri 8–20 (Sep–Jun). Contact: Igor Slavík. Founded 1996. 1 room. 6–8 photo exhibitions/year. Artists: David Boukal, Jan Tabery, Evzen Sobek, Igor Slavík, Katarina Hanová, Igor Šefr, David Kurc, Armin Bardel, Piotr Szymon

Galerie Pod kamennou zábou, Piaristické námestí 2, CZ-370 01 Ceské Budejovice. Tel (038) 6359687. Open: Mon–Fri 10–12, 13–17.30, Sat– Sun 13–17.30. Contact: Jaroslav Kutis. Founded 1995. 2 rooms, 80 m² (additional 3 rooms, 250 m², available on request). 3 photo exhibitions/ year. Artists: Zdenek Stolbelko, Aleš Kuneš, David Boukal, Jindrich Štreit, Michaela Brachtlová

Galerie 4, Kamenná 2, CZ-350 22 Cheb. Tel (0166) 422838, Fax (0166) 422838. E-mail G4@seznam.cz. Website www. egeria.cz/G4. Open: Tue– Sat 10–18. Contact: Zbynek Illek. Founded 1985. 4 rooms, 170 m². 12 photo exhibitions/year. Artists: Markéta Luskacová, Jan Saudek, Jindrich Štreit, Weegee, Václav Podestát, Jeffrey Silverthorne, Vladimír Birgus, Vladimír Kozlík, Roman Sejkot

Galerie výtvarného umení, Gallery of Fine Art, Uprkova 2, CZ-695 01 Hodonín. Tel (0628) 21051, Fax (0628) 21701. E-mail gvuhodonin@ hod.czn.cz. Website www.ccsystem. cz/gvuhodonin. Open: Tue–Fri 9–17, Sat–Sun 13–17. 2–4 photo exhibitions/year. Artists: Josef Sudek,

Vladimír Zidlický, Jan Šplíchal, Jaroslav Pulicar, Jana Smahelová, Jirí Horák

Foma Bohemia, Gocárova trída, CZ-500 03 Hradec Králové. Open: Mon–Fri 9–17. Contact: Jana Neugebauerová. 1 room, 30 m². 10–12 photo exhibitions/year. Artists: Ján Šmok, Dana Kyndrová, Milan Michl

Muzeum východnich Cech, Museum of East Bohemia, Eliščino nábrezí 465, CZ-500 01 Hradec Králové. Tel (049) 55146246, Fax (049) 5512899. E-mail mvc@mvc.anet.cz. Open: Tue–Sun 9–12, 13–17. Director: Dr. Zdenek Zahradník. Curator: Jirí Zikmund. Several rooms, 3,000 m². 1–3 photo exhibitions/year. Artists: Milan Michl, Bohdan Holomícek, Jirí Havel, Alexandr Skalický

Galerie Jána Šmoka, Ján Šmok Gallery, Dvorákova 12, CZ-586 01 Jihlava. Tel (066) 7311938. E-mail susg@jitel.cz. Website www.susg.cz. Part of Soukromá strední umelecká škola grafická, High Art Graphic School, Jihlava. Open: Mon–Fri 9–12, 13–16. Contact: Milan Dušák, Dr. Ivan Zluva. Founded 1999. 8 rooms, 300 m². Artists: Ján Šmok, FAMU students

Malá galerie Ceské sporitelny, Little Gallery of the Czech Saving Bank, námestí Svobody 1960, CZ-272 00 Kladno. Tel (0312) 627690. Open: Mon–Fri 8–17. Contact: Jirí Hanke. Founded 1977. 1 room, 60 m². 12 photo exhibitions/year. Artists: Zdenek Tmej, Ivan Pinkava, Pavel Mára, Jacqueline Salmon, Jaroslav Rajzík, Karel Kuklík, Pavel Dias, Zdenek Lhoták, Viktor Kolár, Jan Pohribný, Annette Fournet, Bill Davis, Jaroslav Kucera, Miroslav Vojtechovský

Galerie U Bílého jednorozce, Gallery by the White Unicorn, námestí Míru 149, CZ-339 01 Klatovy. Tel (0186) 22049. Part of the Galerie Klatovy – Klenová, Klenová 1, CZ-340 21 Janovice nad Uhlavou. Tel (0186) 692208, Fax (0186) 692208. E-mail info@galerie-klatovy.cz, klatovy@galerie-klatovy.cz. Website www.galerie-klatovy.cz. Open: daily 9–12, 13–17. Director: Dr. Marcela Flašarová. Founded 1990. Several rooms. 5 photo exhibitions/year. Artists: Jan Pohribný, Josef Sudek, Josef Moucha, Jaroslav Pulicar, Jan Svoboda, Iren Stehli, Jindrich Štreit, Peter Fryer, Pavel Odvody, Bohdan Holomícek

Fotogalerie Kralupy, Seifertovo námestí 698, CZ-278 01 Kralupy nad Vltavou. Tel (0205) 712086, Fax (0205) 23885. E-mail rosikl@kaucuk.cz. Open: Mon–Fri 8–19. Contact: Ladislav Rosík. Founded 1971. 1 room, 35 m². 10 photo exhibitions/year. Artists: Milan Borovicka, Dana Kyndrová, Miloslav Stibor, Ladislav Rosík, Jirí Hanke, Jindrich Štreit

Malá výstavní sín – Fotogalerie, Small Exhibition Hall – Photogallery, Jablonecká 5, CZ-460 01 Liberec. Tel (048) 5108332, Fax (048) 5203015. E-mail sks.lbc@volny.cz. Open: Mon–Fri 10–17, Sat 10–11.30, 13–17. Contact: Jaromír Typlt. 3 rooms, 71 m². 10–13 photo exhibitions/year. Artists: Jan Reich, Taras Kuščynskyj, Bohdan Holomícek, Jaroslav Bárta, Miroslav Hák, Vladimír Birgus, Tomáš Pospech

Severoceské muzeum, North Bohemian Museum, Masarykova 11, CZ-460 01 Liberec. Tel (048) 5108319/5108283, Fax (048) 5108319. Open: Tue 12–17, Wed–Sun 9–17. Curator: Katerina Neváková. Founded 1873. 3 rooms, 450 m². 1–2 photo exhibitions/year. Artists: Guido Boggiani, Taras Kuščynskyj, Vilém Bohác, Catherine Steinmann

Galerie umelecké fotografie, Gallery of Art Photography, Brnenská 32, CZ-571 01 Moravská Trebová. Tel (0462) 315103. Website www.mtrebova-city.cz/galerie. Open: Wed 14–17, Sat 14–17, Sun 14–16. Contact: Rudolf Zukal. Founded 1995. Permanent exposition, 6 photo exhibitions/year. Artists: Jan Beran, Vilém Reichmann, Taras Kuščynskyj, K. O. Hrubý, Antonín Hinšt, Miroslav Myška, Ludvík Baran, Jirí Bartoš

Fotogalerie Zelená sedma, námestí Karla IV. 241, CZ-362 21 Nejdek. Tel (017) 3925216, Fax (017) 3925708. Open: Mon–Fri 9–17. Contact: Zdenek Pánek. Founded 1998. 1 room, 30 m². 10 photo exhibitions/year. Artists: Heinz K. Henisch, Stanislav Wieser, Dalibor Stach, Jan Šibík

Foto Art, T. G. Masaryka 391, CZ-549 01 Nové Mesto nad Metují. Tel (0441) 72461, Fax (0441) 72461. E-mail fotoart@fotoart.cz. Website www.fotoart.cz. Contact: Roman Unger. 1 room. 10 photo exhibitions/year. Artists: Ludvík Baran, Miloslav Stibor, Miloš Vojír, Roman Unger, Pavel Rejtar

Divadlo hudby, Theatre of Music, Denisova 10, CZ-772 00 Olomouc. Tel (068) 5223565. Open: during performances. Contact: Dr. Libuše Šlezarová. 1 room, 24 m². 3–4 photo exhibitions/year

Galerie Caesar, Radnice, Horní námestí, CZ-771 00 Olomouc. Open: Tue–Sun 10–17. Contact: Miroslav Šnajdr. Founded 1990. 1 room, 50 m². 2–3 photo exhibitions/year. Artists: Michal Macku, Jindrich Štreit, Eva Fuková, Vladimír Birgus, Milena Valusková

Muzeum umení Olomouc, Museum of
Art Olomouc, Denisova 47, CZ-771 11
Olomouc. Tel (068) 5228470/5225005,
Fax (068) 5223166. E-mail info@
almuart.cz. Website www.almuart.cz.
Open: Tue–Sun 10–18. Contact: Dr.
Pavel Zatloukal. Founded 1952.
Several rooms. 1–3 photo exhibi-
tions/year. Artists: Jan Saudek,
Karel Kašparik, Group DOFO

Dum umení, House of Art, Pekarská,
CZ-746 01 Opava. Tel (0653) 212231.
E-mail klimes@opv.czn.cz. Open:
Tue–Sun 10–17. Director: Martin
Klimeš. Founded 1975. Several
rooms, 600 m². 2–4 photo exhibitions/
year. Artists: Dušan Šimánek, Jan
Pohribný, Jindrich Štreit, Guido Bog-
giani, Jirí Štencek, Martin Popelár,
Teachers of the Institute of Creative
Photography, Vilém Reichmann

Galerie Institutu tvurcí fotografie,
Gallery of the Institute of Creative
Photography, Slezská univerzita,
Bezrucovo námestí 13, CZ-746 01
Opava. Tel (0653) 684383, Fax (0653)
684383. E-mail itf@fpf.slu.cz. Open:
Mon–Fri 8–18. Contact: Vojtech
Bartek. Founded 1991. 2 rooms,
100 m². 5–6 photo exhibitions/year.
Artists: Jan Šibík, Jaroslav Krejcí,
Jindrich Štreit

Slezské zemské muzeum, Silesian
Provincial Museum, Ostrozná 42,
CZ-746 01 Opava. Tel (0653) 211742.
Open: Tue–Fri 9–12, 13–17, Sat–Sun
9–12. Curator: Ludek Wünsch.
Founded 1814. Several rooms. 2–3
photo exhibitions/year. Artists: Pavel
Dias, Václav Podestát, Aleš Kuneš,
René Burri, Michal Macku, Viktor
Kolár, Rudolf Bruner-Dvorák, Frank
Horvat, Martin Parr, Pavel Mára

Galerie Fiducia, Nádrazní 30, CZ-
701 00 Ostrava. Tel (069) 6114360.
Open: Mon–Fri 10–22, Sat 18–22.

Contact: Roman Polášek. 1 room,
50 m². 3–4 photo exhibitions/year.
Artists. Martin Smékal, Jaroslav
Malík

Galerie Opera, Národní divadlo
moravskoslezské – Divadlo Jirího
Myrona, Cs. legií 14, CZ-701 04
Ostrava. Tel (069) 6115460/(0653)
684383, Fax (069) 6112881/(0653)
684383. Open: daily 17–21. Curator:
Dr. Vladimír Birgus. 2 rooms, 300 m².
10 photo exhibitions/year. Artists:
Martin Parr, Frank Horvat, Josef
Koudelka, René Burri, Paul den
Hollander, Viktor Kolár, Jindrich
Štreit, Jan Pohribný, Pavel Mára,
Robo Kocan, Vilém Reichmann,
Zdenek Tmej, Karel Ludwig, Jan
Šibík, Michal Macku, Andrej Bán

Minigalerie Waldemar, A. Macka
4, CZ-701 00 Ostrava 1. E-mail
fotogalerie@atlas.cz. Open: Mon–Fri
9–22. Curator: Michal Kubícek. 1
room, 30 m². 8–10 photo exhibitions/
year. Artists: Jirí Kudelka, Miroslav
Glogar, Václav Vlach, Zuzana Ole-
járová

**Výtvarné centrum Chagall – Galerie
Na schodišti,** Art Center Chagall,
Repinova 16, CZ-702 00 Ostrava.
Tel (069) 6112019, Fax (069) 6124344.
Open: Mon–Sat 9–22, Sun 13–22.
Director: Dr. Petr Pavlinák. Founded
1990. 1 room, 80 m². 6 photo exhibi-
tions/year. Artists: František Krasl,
Václav Marcol, Jan Byrtus, Emanuel
Krenek, Jaroslav Malík, Jakub Chle-
boun, Ladislav Kamarád

Galerie Maecenas, námestí Republiky 40, CZ-301 16 Plzen. Tel (019)
7032710. Open: Mon 13–17, Tue–Fri
10–12, 13–17, Sat 10–14. Part of X
Centrum, Dominikánská 12, CZ-
301 12 Plzen. 3 rooms, 124 m². 2–3
photo exhibitions/year. Artists:

Yves Leresche, Cecil Beaton, Jindrich Štreit

Galerie ve sklepe, námestí Republiky 40, CZ-301 16 Plzen. Tel (019) 7032730. Open: Mon 13–17, Tue–Fri 10–12, 13–17, Sat 10–14. Part of X Centrum, Dominikánská 12, CZ-301 12 Plzen. 4 rooms, 165 m². 2–3 photo exhibitions/year. Artists: Guido Boggiani, Cecil Beaton

Stop Gallery, Dominikánská 2, CZ-301 16 Plzen. Tel (019) 7032720. Open: Mon 13–17, Tue–Fri 10–12, 13–17, Sat 10–14. Part of X Centrum, Dominikánská 12, CZ-301 12 Plzen. 1 room, 75 m². 2–4 photo exhibitions/ year. Artists: Jan Šibík, Michal Bartoš, Jaroslav Beneš, Václav Podestát

Ceské centrum fotografie, Czech Center of Photography, Náplavní 1, CZ-120 00 Praha 2. Tel (02) 296587. E-mail jas.gal@telecom.cz. Open: Mon–Sun 11–19. Director: Dr. Jirí Jaskmanický. 1 room. 12 photo exhibitions/year. Artists: Jan Lukas, Josef Sudek, Ivo Loos, Miroslav Hák, Drahomír Josef Ruzicka, Jaroslav Rössler, Alexandr Hackenschmied, Edward S. Curtis

Dobra Galerie, Slavíkova 20, CZ-130 00 Praha 3. Open: Mon–Fri 10–12, 13–18. Contact: Rifo Dobra. 1 room, 30 m². Artists: Josef Vetrovský, Josef Sudek, Gabina Fárová, Oldrich Karásek, Jaromír Funke

Galerie FAMU, Smetanovo nábrezí 2, CZ-116 65 Praha 1. Tel (02) 24233337, Fax (02) 24230285. E-mail vojtechovsky@f.amu.cz. Open: Mon–Fri 10–17. Contact: Prof. Miroslav Vojtechovský, Renáta Vávrová. Founded 1984. Several rooms. 10–15 photo exhibitions/year. Artists: Tibor Honty, Karel Plicka, Zdenek Stolbenko, Jirí Lehovec, Michaela Brachtlová, students of FAMU

Galerie Fronta, Spálená 53, CZ-110 00 Praha 1. Tel (02) 296508. Open Tue–Sun 10–12.30, 14–17.30. Contact: Bohuslav Holý. 2 rooms, 100 m². 3–4 photo exhibitions/year. Artists: Iren Stehli, Milota Havránková, Jaroslav Fišer, Jirí Pekárek, Libuše Jarcovjáková, Ivana Fixlová, Helena Márová, Miroslav Hucek

Galerie hlavního mesta Prahy, Prague City Gallery, Staromestská radnice, Old Town Townhall, Staromestské námestí, CZ-110 00 Praha 1 & Dum U Kamenného zvonu, House by the Stone Bell, Staromestské námestí 13, Municipal Library, Mariánské nám 1, CZ-110 00 Praha 1. Tel (02) 24482088/ 24810036. Open: Tue–Sun 9–17 (Staromestská radnice)/Tue–Sun 10–18 (Dum u kamenného zvonu). Curator: Dr. Karel Srp. Several rooms in three buildings. 2–3 photo exhibitions/ year. Artists: Dagmar Hochová, Markéta Luskacová, Jan Reich, Vladimír Špacek, Markéta Othová, Veronika Bromová, Lukáš Jasanský and Martin Polák, Jaromir Funke

Galerie Josefa Sudka, Josef Sudek's Gallery (part of the Museum of Decorative Arts), Úvoz 24, CZ-110 00 Praha 1. Open: Tue–Sun 10–12, 13–18. Curator: Jan Mlcoch. Founded 1995. 2 rooms, 42 m². 5 photo exhibitions/year. Artist: Josef Sudek, Alois Zych, Jaroslav Krupka, Jindrich Vanek, Karel Novák, Jirí Toman

Galerie Lichtenštejnský palác, Gallery Liechtenstein Palace, Malostranské námestí 13, CZ-118 11 Praha 1. Contact: Prof. Ivan Štraus. Founded 1993. Several rooms, 400 m². 1–2 photo exhibitions/year. Artists: Patrick Lichfield, Karel Plicka, Students of FAMU

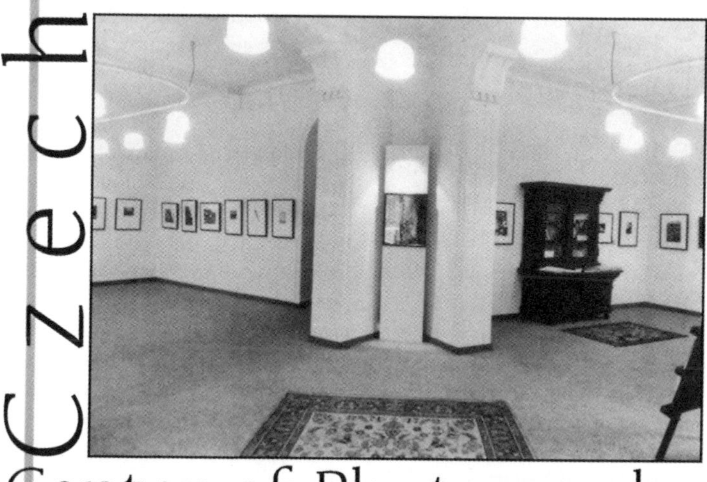

Center of Photography

is a photographics gallery in Prague established in 1997. The center provides room for the exhibitions of both, classical and experimental photography by known and unknown authors of local and foreign origin. Among others the Gallery has also organized exhibition of the founder of Russian pictorials Sergey Lobovikov, American photographers Sally Mann and E. S. Curtis, American photographer of czech origin Jan Lukas and avant–garde group of photographers Aventinum trio or a legend of Czech photography Josef Sudek. Gallery is currently developing publishing as another field of its activities. We prepare publishing of Alexander Hackenschmied monography and Jaroslav Rössler monography.

MARCH: DRAHOMÍR JOSEF RŮŽIČKA
APRIL - JUNE: ALEXANDER HACKENSCHMIED
JULY: FRANTIŠEK DRTIKOL
AUGUST: VÁCLAV ZYKMUND
SEPTEMBER: VIKTOR KOPASZ
OCTOBER: VÁCLAV JIRÁSEK
NOVEMBER: JAN SVOBODA
DECEMBER: JAROSLAV RÖSSLER

Commercial activities are an integral part of our work. In our center you can find the representative collections of works of more than fourty czech photographers as the most significant Czech artists like J. Sudek, J. Rössler, M. Hák and many others. Our gallery exclusively represents authors as Alexander Hackenschmied, Tibor Honty, Petr Helbich, Ladislav Postupa and others.

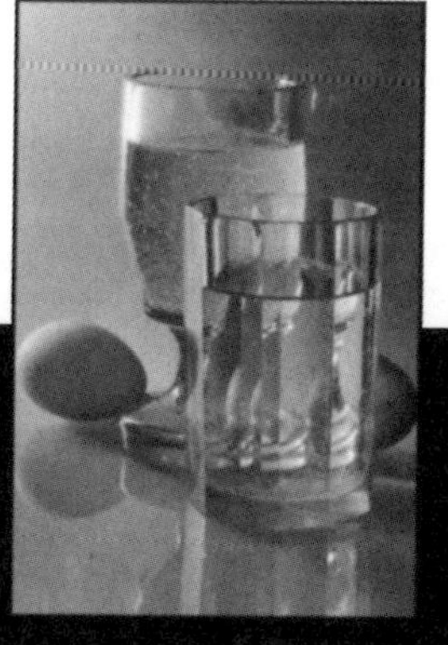

CZECH CENTER OF PHOTOGRAPHY

NÁPLAVNÍ 1, 120 00 PRAGUE 2, CZECH REPUBLIC
TEL./FAX: +4202 29 65 87
E-MAIL: jas.gal@telecom.cz

Galerie Pecka, Vratislavova 24, CZ-120 00 Praha 2. Tel (02) 294926, Fax (02) 294926. Open: Mon–Sun 10–18. Contact: Jaroslav Pecka. Founded 1991. 2 rooms, 100 m². 3–4 photo exhibitions/year. Artists: Vasil Stanko, Václav Jirásek, William Ropp, Antonín Kratochvíl, Veronika Zapletalová

Galerie Rudolfinum, Alšovo nábrezí 12, CZ-110 00 Praha 1. Tel (02) 24893295, Fax (02) 2319293. Open: Tue–Sun 10–18. Director: Dr. Petr Nedoma. Several rooms, 200–2,000 m². 2–3 photo exhibitions/year. Artists: Cindy Sherman, Nan Goldin, Jürgen Klauke, Jan Langhans, František Drtikol, Milon Novotný, Václav Stratil, Jirí David

Galerie Štepánská 35, Francouzský institut, French Institute, Štepánská 35, P. O. Box 850, CZ-111 21 Praha 1. Tel. (02) 2223-1783/2997/0577, Fax (02) 22230579. E-mail ifp@telecom.cz. Website www.ifp.cz. Open: Tue–Fri 10–18. Contact: Jean-Pierre Attal. Founded 1993. 2 rooms, 210 m². 3–5 photo exhibitions/year. Artists: Henri Cartier-Bresson, Jacques-Henri Lartigue, André Villers, Jeanloup Sieff, Helmut Newton, Jan Reich, Frank Horvat, Luc Choquer, Marc Riboud

Galerie Václava Špály, Národní 30, CZ-110 00 Praha 1. Tel (02) 24946738, Fax (02) 24046738. Director: Jaroslav Krbušek. 3 rooms. 1–2 photo exhibitions/year. Artists: Josef Sudek, Josef Šnobl, Paul Pouvre, Andreas Müller-Pohle, Veronika Bromová, Václav Chochola, Zdenek Tmej, Karel Ludwig, Karel Hájek

Galerie Velryba, Opatovická 24, CZ-110 00 Praha 1. Tel (02) 208088/24233337. Open: Mon–Fri 13–21, Sat–Sun 17–22. Curators: Prof. Dr. Vladimír Birgus, Renáta Vávrová. 1 room, 30 m². 11 photo exhibitions/year.

Artists: Robo Kocan, Stephanie Kiwitt, Petr Zinke, Krzyszof Zielinski, Roman Dietrich, Hynek Alt, Marian Beneš, Viktor Stoilov, Dorota Bylica, Vuk Latinovic

Komorní galerie Domu fotografie Josefa Sudka, The Chamber Gallery of Josef Sudek House of Photography, U radnice 5, CZ-110 00 Praha 1. Tel (02) 24819098/2322254. Open: Tue–Sun 10–19. Contact: Daniela Mrázková, Vera Mateju. Founded 1997. 2 rooms, 75 m². Artists: Karel Cudlín, Milan Borovicka, Zdenek Virt, Miloslav Stibor, Norbert Záliš, Ben Fernandez, Jan Ságl, Rostislav & Zlatuše

Mánes, Masarykovo nábrezí 250, CZ-110 00 Praha 1. Tel (02) 291808, Fax (02) 291808. Open: Tue–Sun 10–18. Contact: Dr. Vlasta Ciháková-Noshiro. 2 rooms, 1,000 m². 1–2 photo exhibitions/year. Artists: Don McCullin, Stanislav Tuma, Jan Lukas, Leoš Nebor, Jindrich Štreit

Mánes – fotografická galerie, Mánes – Photogallery, Masarykovo nábrezí 250, CZ-110 00 Praha 1. Open: Mon–Sun 10–16. Contact: Jaroslav Šimon. 1 room, 50 m². 12 photo exhibitions/year. Artists: Dana Kyndrová, Piotr Szymon, Grzegorz Klatka, Jirí Hanke

Muzeum hlavního mesta Prahy, Museum of the City of Prague, Na porící 52, CZ-180 00 Praha 8 (expositions), Kozná 1, CZ-110 00 Praha 1 (administration). Tel (02) 24223696-8, Fax (02) 24214306. Open: Tue–Sun 10–18. Contact: Dr. Zdenek Míka, Dr. Katerina Becková, Dr. Jan Jungmann. Founded 1883. 2–3 rooms, 430 m². 1–2 photo exhibitions/year. Artists: Jindrich Eckert, Ladislav Sitenský

Národní galerie – Sbírka moderního a soucasného umeni, National Gallery – Collection of Modern and Contemporary Art, Veletrzní palác, Dukelských hrdinu 47, CZ-170 00 Praha 7. Tel (02) 24301111, Fax (02) 24301167. E-mail smsu@ngprague.cz. Open: Tue–Sun 10–18 (Thu –21). Director: Dr. Katarína Rusnáková. Several rooms. 1–3 photo exhibitions/year. Artists: Annie Leibovitz, Zofia Kulik, Antonín Kratochvíl, Markéta Othová, Students of FAMU

Národní technické muzeum, National Technical Museum, Kostelní 42, CZ-170 00 Praha 7. Tel (02) 20399111, Fax (02) 33371801. E-mail info@ ntm.cz. Open: Tue–Sun 9–17. Director: Ivo Janoušek. Founded 1908. Several rooms, circa 1,100 m². 5–7 photo exhibitions/year. Artists: Karol Kállay, David Bailey, Karel Otto Hrubý, Cedo Butina, Rudolf Jung, Rudolf Bruner-Dvorák, Tono Stano

Obecní dum, Municipal House, námestí Republiky 5, CZ-110 00 Praha 1. Open: Mon–Sun 10–18. Contact: Dušan Seidl. Several rooms. 1–2 photo exhibitions/year. Artists: Jan Saudek, Jindrich Štreit

Obecní galerie Beseda, Malostranské námestí 21, CZ-118 00 Praha 1. Tel (02) 538383, Fax (02) 538383. Open: Tue–Sun 13–18. Contact: Jirina Borkovcová, Stanislav Tuma. Founded 1996. 3 rooms, 80 m². 2–3 photo exhibitions/year. Artists: Zdenko Feyfar, Dagmar Hochová, Václav Chochola, Taras Kuščynskyj, Jan Pohribný, Petr Velkoborský, Jan Reich, Stanislav Tuma, Antonín Malý, Emila Medková, Chad Evans Wyatt

Prazský dum fotografie, Prague House of Photography, Haštalská 1, CZ-110 00 Praha 1. Tel (02) 24810779/

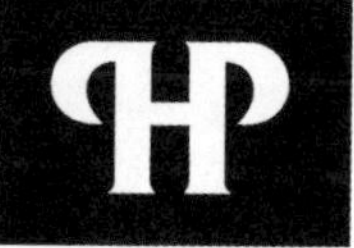

Prague House of Photography

Haštalská 1, CZ - 110 00 Praha 1 • e-mail: php@ecn.cz
Tel.: +420 2 24810779, Tel./fax: +420 2 24810781

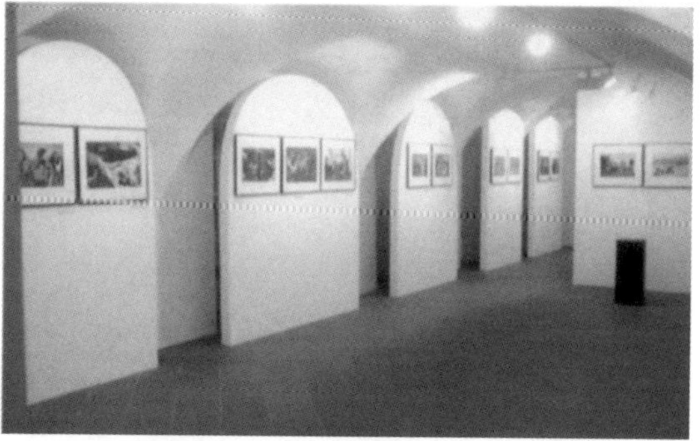

Prague House of Photography, estabilished in the spring of 1989 is the only non-profit center of photography in the Czech capital. PHP presents a continuous international program of historical and contemporary exhibitions, lectures, publications, summer workshops, fine photography print sales and artist services.

Open daily 11 a.m.- 6 a.m.

PUBLISHING HOUSE KANT

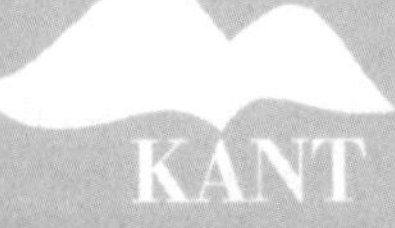

KANT

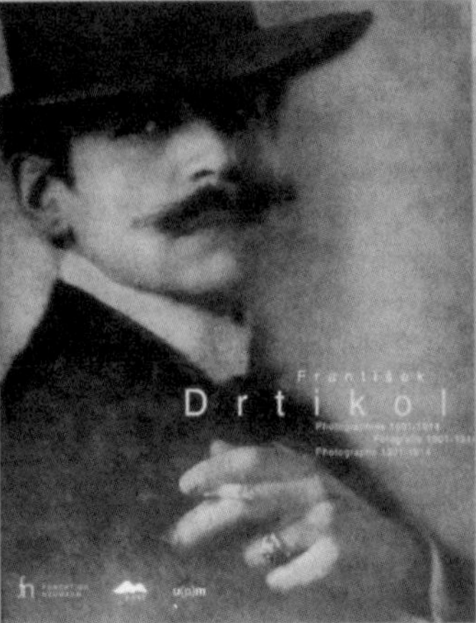

FRANTIŠEK DRTIKOL
Photographs 1901–1914

72 pgs., 38 color and 13 duotones
ISBN: 80-86217-08-6

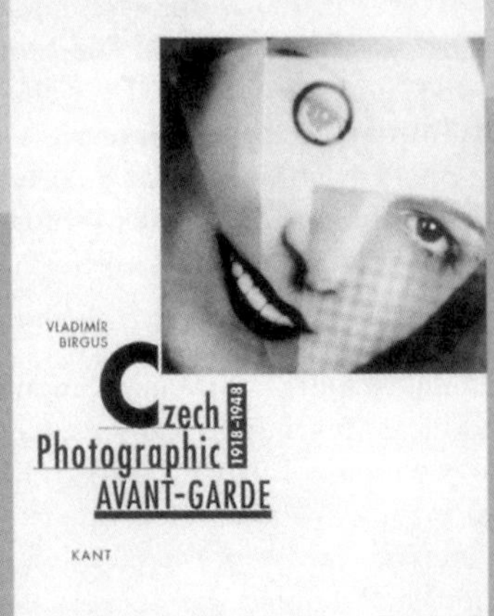

Czech Photographic
AVANT–GARDE 1918–1948

304 pgs., 16 color and 280 duotones
ISBN:80-96217-09-4

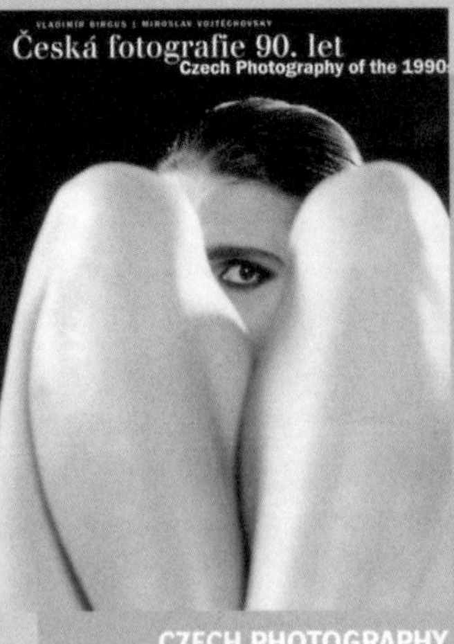

CZECH PHOTOGRAPHY
of the 1990s

208 pgs., 10 color and 98 duotones
ISBN: 80-86217-00-0

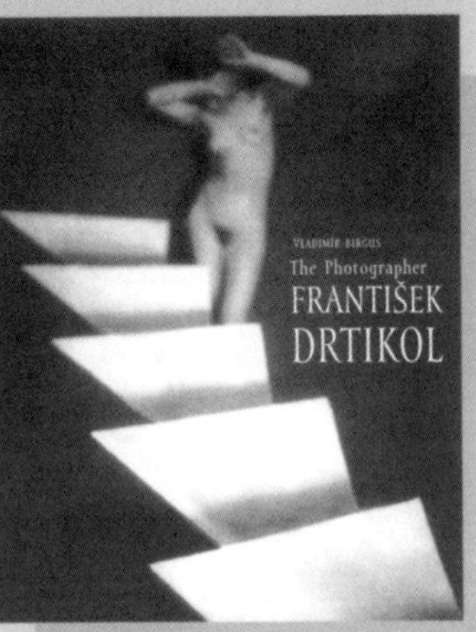

The Photographer
FRANTIŠEK DRTIKOL

208 pgs., 8 color and 128 duotones
ISBN:80-86217-20-5

KANT, Kladenská 29, 160 00 Praha 6, Czech Republic
tel.:/fax: 0042(2) 366 817, e-mail: kant@znet.cz

24810781, Fax (02) 24810781. Open: daily 11–18. Contact: Eva Králová. Founded 1991. 2 rooms, 150 m². 9 photo exhibitions/year. Artists: Markéta Luskacová, Elinor Carucci, František Drtikol, Jaromír Funke, Tibor Honty, Karel Ludwig, André Kertész, August Sander, René Burri, Raul Hausmann, Ernestine Ruben, Ján Šmok, Zdenek Lhoták

Prazský hrad, Prague Castle, Správa Prazského hradu, programová divize – výstavní oddelení, CZ-119 08 Praha-Hrad. Tel (02) 24371111/24373616, Fax (02) 24372255/24310896. Website www.hrad.cz. Open: Tue–Sun 10–18. Contact: Dr. Ladislav Kesner. Founded 1993. Several rooms from 400 m² to 580 m². 4–5 photo exhibitions/year. Artists: Inge Morath, William Klein, Josef Koudelka, Roman Vishniac, Josef Sudek, Erich Lessing, Magnum, Cecil Beaton, Antonín Kratochvíl, Pavel Banka

Umeleckoprumyslové muzeum, Museum of Decorative Arts, 17. listopadu 2, CZ-110 00 Praha 1. Tel (02) 24811241, Fax (02) 24811666. Open: Tue–Sun 10–18. Contact: Dr. Helena Koenigsmarková, Jan Mlcoch. 1 room, 240 m². Founded in 1902. 1–2 photo exhibitions/year. Artists: František Drtikol, Josef Sudek, Josef Koudelka, Magnum, Jan Svoboda

Galerie Mestské knihovny, Gallery of the Municipal Library, Bezrucova 519, CZ-756 61 Roznov pod Rad-hoštem. Tel (0651) 563349, Fax (0651) 563349. Open: Tue–Sun 10–17. Curator: Aleš Zanta. Founded 1994. 1 room, 64 m². 4–5 photo exhibitions/year. Artists: Miroslav Bílek, Jakub Sobotka, Tomáš Pospech, Jindrich Štreit, Jaroslav Malík, Michal Bartoš

Galerie Šternberk, Radnicní 3, CZ-785 01 Šternberk. Tel (0643) 3488.

Contact: Pavel Brunclík. Photographic part of the gallery founded 1996. 24 m². 2–3 photo exhibitions/year. Artists: Josef Sudek, Daniel Šperl, Jindrich Štreit, Martin Popelár, Petr Zatloukal, Zdenek Stolbenko, Jolana Havelková, Miroslav Schubert

Galerie Zlutá ponorka, Gallery Yellow Submarine, Havlíckova 7, CZ-669 01 Znojmo. Tel (0624) 224034/261271, Fax (0624) 224034. E-mail info@ illusion.cz. Open: Mon–Sun 16–2. Contact: Josef Plotzer. Founded 1993. 1 room, 65 m². 11 photo exhibitions/year. Artists: Veronika Bromová, David Kraus, Andrej Bán, Robert Vano, Boris Filemon, Jan Šibík, Martin Vybíral

Festivals & Fairs

Funkeho Kolín, Jolana Havelková, Na hradbách 132, CZ-280 00 Kolín

Interkamera, M.I. P. Praha, Legerova 3, CZ-120 00 Praha 2. Tel (02) 242622-37/39, Fax (02) 24262238

Magazines

Advanced – Foto Video, Velvarská 45, CZ-160 00 Praha 6. Tel. (02) 33326215, Fax (02) 3124908. E-mail advanced@atemi.cz. Website www. fotoavideo.cz. Czech. Copy price: Kc 49.00, 12 issues/year

Ateliér, Masarykovo nábrezí 250, CZ-110 00 Praha 1. Tel (02) 291884, Fax (02) 291884. Editor: Dr. Blanka Jirácková. Czech (English summaries). Copy price: Kc 27.00, 26 issues/year

Bulletin Moravské galerie v Brne, Moravská galerie, Husova 16, CZ-662 26 Brno. Tel (05) 42216104, Fax

(05) 42213721. Editor: Dr. Bronislava Gabrielová. Czech (English summaries)

Fotografie Magazín, Dobrovského 25, CZ-170 55 Praha 7. Tel (02) 33072022. E-mail fotografie.magazin@ economia.cz. Editor: Daniela Mrázková. Czech (English, German and Russian summaries). Founded 1945. Copy price: Kc 48.00, 12 issues/year

Geographic Camera, magazine for travel photography, Holubická 2, CZ-161 00 Praha 6. Tel (02) 35301205, Fax (02) 35300870. E-mail photolife@ volny.cz. Editor: Petra Soukupová. Czech. Copy price: Kc 50.00. Annual subscription: Kc 330.00, 6 issues/year

Labyrint, magazine for literature, fine art, music and cinema, P. O. Box 52, Jablonecká 715, CZ-190 00 Praha 9. Tel (02) 2321934, Fax (02) 2321934. Editor Joachim Dvorák. Czech. Founded 1990. Annual subscription: DM 42.00, 2 issues/year

Listy o fotografii, Acta photographica Univesitas Silesianae Opaviensis, Institut tvurcí fotografie Slezské univerzity, Bezrucovo nám. 13, CZ-746 01 Opava. Tel (0653) 684383, Fax (0653) 216948. E-mail ITF@fpf.slu.cz. Editors: Vladimír Birgus, Tomáš Pospech. Czech. Founded 1994

Photo Life, Holubická 2, CZ-161 00 Praha 6. Tel (02) 35301205, Fax (02) 35300870. E-mail photolife@volny.cz. Editor: Petra Soukupová. Czech. Copy price: Kc 50.00. Annual subscription: Kc 350.00, 6 issues/year

Revolver Revue & Kritická príloha, Jindrišská 5, CZ-110 00 Praha 1. Editor: Terezie Pokorná. Czech. Copy price: Kc 125.00 (Revolver Revue), Kc 68.00 (Kritická príloha)

Umelec, magazine for contemporary art and culture, Borivojova 49, CZ-130 00 Praha 3. Tel (02) 22719229, Fax (02) 22721240. E-mail umelec@ mail.divus.cz. Website www. divus.cz/umelec. Editor: Lenka Lindaurová. Czech/English. Copy price: Kc 70.00. Annual subscription: Euro 26.00, 12 issues/year

Book Publishers

Foto Mida, U trí lvu 11, CZ-370 01 Ceské Budejovice. Tel (038) 6353315, Fax (038) 6353315. E-mail fotomida@ iol.cz

Grada Publishing, U pruhonu 22, CZ-170 00 Praha 7. Tel (02) 20386439, Fax (02) 20386400. E-mail matulik@ grada-publishing.cz

Kant, Kladenská 29, CZ-160 00 Praha 6. Tel (02) 366817, Fax (02) 366817. E-mail kant@znet.cz

Kuklik, Slovinská 13, CZ-101 00 Praha 1. Tel (02) 737253

Studio JB, Jeronýmova 136, CZ-512 51 Lomnice nad Popelkou. Tel (0431) 92260

Torst, Opatovická 24, CZ-110 00 Praha 1. Tel (02) 24916082

Bookshops

Ceské centrum fotografie, Czech Center of Photography, Náplavní 1, CZ-120 00 Praha 2. Tel (02) 296587

Dum knihy – Jan Kanzelsberger, House of Book – Jan Kanzelsberger, Václavské námestí 4, CZ-110 00 Praha 1. Tel (02) 24219214

Prazský dum fotografie, Prague House of Photography, Haštalská 1,

CZ-110 00 Praha 1. Tel (02) 248107-
79/81, Fax (02) 24810781

Auctions

Aukcní agentura a Antikvariát Prošek,
Sinkulova 24, CZ-147 00 Praha 4

Ceské centrum fotografie, Czech
Center of Photography, Náplavní 1,
CZ-120 00 Praha 2. Tel (02) 296587

Dorotheum Praha, Ovocný trh 2, CZ-
110 00 Praha 1. Tel (02) 24222001, Fax
(02) 24222011

Critics & Journalists

Prof. Dr. Ludvík Baran, Koulova 8,
CZ-160 00 Praha 6. Tel (02) 3119027.
Fotografie Magazín, Ateliér, Praha

Prof. Dr. Vladimír Birgus, Na poríc-
ním právu 4, CZ-128 00 Praha 2. Tel
(02) 24920867/(603) 892886/(02)
24233337 (FAMU), Fax (02) 24920867.
E-mail birgus@cesnet.cz. FAMU and
Institute of Creative Photography of
Silesian University, Opava; *European
Photography,* Göttingen; *Ateliér, Advanced, Mladá fronta Dnes,* Praha;
Imago, Bratislava; *Photonews,* Hamburg; Kant, Torst, Praha

Blanka Chocholová, Vodnická 318,
CZ 149 00 Praha 4. Tel (02) 67911693.
Institute of Creative Photography of
Silesian University, Opava; *Ateliér,*
Kant, Praha

Josef Chuchma, Petrzílkova 2260/26,
CZ-155 00 Praha 5. Tel (02) 5618087/
22062440. E-mail kultura@mafra.cz.
*Mladá fronta Dnes, Respekt, Literární
noviny,* Praha

Dr. Antonín Dufek, Moravská galerie,
Husova 18, CZ-662 26 Brno. Tel (05)

42217630-33, Fax (05) 42216651.
Bulletin Moravské galerie, Brno; *Ateliér,*
Praha; *Imago,* Bratislava; Academia,
Praha; Foto Mida, Ceské Budejovice

Tomáš Dvorák, Rackova 1049, CZ-
165 00 Praha 6. Tel (02) 20922196.
Ateliér, Lidové noviny, Praha

Dr. Anna Fárová, Španelská 12, CZ-
120 00 Praha 2. *Ateliér, Revolver Revue,*
Praha; Torst, Praha; *Aperture,* New
York; *Photo Poche,* Paris

Tomáš Fassati, Bezrucova 6, CZ-
256 01 Benešov u Prahy. Tel (0301)
24601, Fax (0301)726177. E-mail
desmuz@czn.cz. Director of Museum
of Fine Art, Benešov; *Ateliér,* Praha

Jolana Havelková, Na hradbách 132,
CZ-280 00 Kolín. *Hospodárské noviny,
Ateliér,* Praha

Michal Janata, Švýcarská 2428, CZ-
272 02 Kladno. *Ateliér, Týden,* Praha

Prof. Dr. Zdenek Kirschner, FAMU,
Smetanovo nábrezí 2, CZ-116 65
Praha 1. Tel (02) 24233337. E-mail
kirschner@f.amu.cz. *Fotografie
Magazín, Ateliér,* Praha

Dr. Josef Kroutvor, Umeleckopru-
myslové muzeum, 17. listopadu 2,
CZ-110 00 Praha 1. Tel (02) 51093111.
*Ateliér, Revolver Revue, Literární
noviny, Umení a remesla,* Praha;
Museum of Decorative Arts, Volvox
Globator, Praha

Aleš Kuneš, Štefánikova 44, CZ-
150 00 Praha 5. Tel (02) 8557112.
Institute of Creative Photography of
Silesian University, Opava; *Lidové
noviny, Ateliér, Listy o fotografii,
Analogon, Divus,* Praha

Dr. Pavel Liska, Dum umení mesta
Brna, Malinovského namestí 2, CZ-
601 07 Brno. *Ateliér,* Praha

50 Czech Republic

Dr. Vera Mateju, Hastalská 4, CZ-110 00 Praha 1. Tel (02) 24814966. *Fotografie Magazín, Hospodárské noviny,* Praha

Jan Mlcoch, Umeleckoprumyslové muzeum – Museum od Decorative Arts, 17. listopadu 2, CZ-110 00 Praha 1. Tel (02) 51093254. *Ateliér, Lidove noviny,* Praha; *Kant,* Praha

Josef Moucha, Lukešova 1607, CZ-142 00 Praha 4. Tel (02) 4714625. *Ateliér, Mladá fronta Dnes, Respekt, Revolver Revue, Iluminace,* Praha; *Imago,* Bratislava

Daniela Mrázková, Dykova 16, CZ-101 00 Praha 10. Tel (02) 51641434/33072022, Fax (02) 51641434. Editor of *Fotografie Magazín,* Praha; *Foundation, Czech Photo, Reflex, Hospodárské noviny,* Praha

Karel Oujezdský, Ceský rozhlas, Vinohradská 12, CZ-120 00 Praha 2. Tel (02) 24094204/24094212. Czech Radio, Praha; *Ateliér,* Praha

Martina Pachmannová, Záverka 11, CZ-169 00 Praha 6. Tel (02) 29511805. *Ateliér, Umelec,* Praha

Suzanne Pastor, Hyacintová 426, CZ-252 43 Pruhonice. Prague House of Photography, Praha

Václav Podestát, Na palcátech 547, CZ-331 41 Kralovice. Tel (0182) 397451. Institute of Creative Photography, Silesian University, Opava; *Plzenský deník,* Plzen; *Ateliér, Fotografie Magazín,* Praha

Tomáš Pospech, Sklený kopec 1711, CZ-753 01 Hranice. Tel (0642) 204074. Institute of Creative Photography, Silesian University, Opava; *Listy o fotografii,* Opava; *Mladá fronta Dnes,* Ostrava; *Ateliér,* Praha; *Hranický týden,* Hranice

Dr. Zdenek Primus, Premyslova 9, CZ-120 00 Praha 2. *Ateliér,* Praha

Vladimír Remeš, Dykova 16, CZ-101 00 Praha 10. Tel (02) 51641434, Fax (02) 51641434. *Fotografie Magazín,* Praha

Pavel Scheufler, Druhanická 479, CZ-190 16 Praha 9 – Ujezd nad Lesy. Tel (02) 81970539. FAMU, Czech Radio, Grada, Praha; *Advanced, Ateliér, Photo Life,* Praha; Foto Mida, Ceské Budejovice; Grada, Praha

Robert Silverio, Prátelství 876, CZ-104 00 Praha 10. Tel (02) 67711836. Katedra fotografie FAMU, Praha; *Ateliér, Lidové noviny, Kritická príloha Revolver Revue, Labyrint,* Praha

Dr. Karel Srp, Vostrovská 42, CZ-160 00 Praha 6. Tel (02) 3112858. Prague City Gallery, Mariánské námestí 1, CZ-110 00 Praha 1. *Umení, Ateliér,* Praha; Torst, Praha

Jan H. Vitvar, Jaselská 14, CZ-160 00 Praha 6. Tel (02) 24323212. *Mladá fronta Dnes,* Praha

Prof. Miroslav Vojtechovský, Ke Strašnicím 2402, CZ-100 00 Praha 10. Tel (02) 7816224/24233337. E-mail vojtechovsky@f.amu.cz. FAMU, Kant, Praha; *Fotografie Magazín, Photo Life, Ateliér,* Praha; Votobia, Olomouc

Dr. Jana Vránová, Dum umení mesta Brna, Malinovského nám. 2, CZ-601 07 Brno. Tel (05) 42211808, Fax (05) 42211662. *Brnenský vecerník, Bulletin Moravské galerie,* Brno; *Ateliér,* Praha

Schools & Workshops

Fakulta sociálních ved Karlovy univerzity, Smetanovo nábrezi 6, CZ-116 65 Praha 1

FAMU – Filmová a televizní fakulta Akademie múzických umení, Film and Television Faculty of the Academy of Performing Arts, Departmenmt of Photography, Smetanovo nábrezí 2, CZ-116 65 Praha 1. Tel (02) 24233337. Fax (02) 24230285. E-mail vokacova@ f.amu.cz

Hradecká fotografická konzervator, Okruzní 1130, CZ-500 03 Hradec Králové

Institut marketingu a reklamní tvorby, Institute of Marketing and Advertising, Fakulta technologická Vysokého ucení technického, Štefánikova 36, CZ-760 01 Zlín. Tel (067) 30621

Institut tvurcí fotografie Slezské univerzity, Institute of Creative Photography of Silesian University, Bezrucovo námestí 13, CZ-746 01 Opava. Tel (0653) 684383/684111, Fax (0653) 684383/216948. E-mail itf@fpf.slu.cz

Lidová konzervator Ostrava, Wattova 5, CZ-701 00 Ostrava. Tel (069) 6136805, Fax (069) 215762

Prazská fotografická škola, Prague School of Photography, Námestí Jirího z Lobkovic 22, CZ-130 00 Praha 3. Tel (02) 72738290, Fax (02) 72738290

Soukromá strední umelecká škola grafická, Krízová 18, CZ 586 01 Jihlava. Tel (066) 7310355. E-mail atelier@jitel.cz

Soukromá škola uzitého umení a podnikání Michael, Machkova 1646, CZ-149 00 Praha 4

Strední odborné ucilište, Charbulova 106, CZ-618 00 Brno

Strední odborné ucilište, Ruská 147, CZ-405 01 Decín

Strední odborné ucilište, Sládeckova 38, CZ-715 00 Ostrava-Michálkovice

Strední odborné ucilište sluzeb, Zejdlicova 681, CZ-588 13 Polná. Tel (066) 7212523-4, Fax (066) 7212482. E-mail soupolna@mbox.vol.cz

Strední odborné ucilište, Hloubetínská 26/78, CZ-194 00 Praha 9

Strední integrovaná škola obchodu, sluzeb a podnikání, Prícná 1108, CZ-708 00 Ostrava-Poruba. Tel (069) 6732232

Strední umeleckoprumyslová škola, Karla Pokorného 1742, CZ-708 00 Ostrava-Poruba. Tel (069) 6915307

Strední umeleckoprumyslová škola, Všehrdova 267, CZ-686 53 Uherské Hradište. Tel (0632) 551500, Fax (0632) 552354. E-mail supsuh@ pvtnet.cz

Strední škola umeleckých remesel, Husova 10, CZ-602 00 Brno. Tel (05) 43235477/43235012, Fax (05) 43235950. E-mail ssur.husova.brno@ telecom.cz

Univerzita J. E. Purkyne, J. E. Purkyne University, Ateliér fotografie Institutu výtvarné kultury, Velká Hradební 13, CZ-400 01 Ústí nad Labem. Tel (047) 5210876, Fax (047) 5210876. E-mail matousek@ rek.ujep.cz

Vysoká škola umeleckoprumyslová, Academy of Applied Arts, ateliér fotografie, Námestí Jana Palacha, CZ-110 00 Praha 1. Tel (02) 24811172

Vyšší odborná škola grafická a Strední prumyslová škola grafická, Hellichova 22, CZ-118 00 Praha 1. Tel (02) 533117/539514, Fax (02) 533118. E-mail spsghellich@mbox.vol.cz. Website www.volweb.cz/spsghellich

Associations

Aktiv volné fotografie, Prague House of Photography, Haštalská 1, CZ-110 00 Praha 1. Tel (02) 24810779/24810781, Fax (02) 24810781

Asociace fotografu, Voršilská 3, CZ-110 00 Praha 1

Ceské foto – sdruzení na podporu fotografie, P. O. Box 5, CZ-111 21 Praha 1. Tel (0431) 671260

Czech Photo, Mánesova 13, CZ-120 00 Praha 2. Tel (02) 24819098

Komora fotografu, Chamber of Photographers, Novotného lávka 5, CZ-110 00 Praha 1

Spolecenost pratel fotografie, Association of Friends of Photography, Mánesova 13, CZ-120 00 Praha 2. Tel (02) 33072022

Svaz ceských fotografu, Union of Czech Photographers, Seifertova 43, CZ-130 00 Praha 3. Tel (02) 22716425

Syndikát novináru Ceské republiky, Union of Journalists of the Czech Republic, Parízská 9, CZ-116 30 Praha 1. Tel (02) 2325109/2320686

Volné sdruzení výchoceských fotografu, Open Union of East Bohemian Photographers, Okruzní 1130, CZ-500 03 Hradec Králové. Tel (049) 42769, Fax (049) 46560

Grants & Awards

Award of City of Prague, Czech Press Photo. Contact: Fotografie Magazín, Daniela Mrázková, Dobrovského 25, CZ-170 55 Praha 7. Tel (02) 51641434/33072022, Fax (02) 51641434. E-mail fotografie.magazin@economia.cz

Photographic Book of the Year, prizes for the best Czech and Slovak photographic books, catalogues and calendars, every year. Contact: Fotografie Magazín, Dobrovského 25, CZ-170 55 Praha 7. Tel (02) 51641434/33072022, Fax (02) 51641434. E-mail fotografie.magazin@economia.cz

Prizes of Interkamera, for achievment in photography, technology and ecology, every second year during the fair Interkamera. Contact: Interkamera, M.I.P. Praha, Legerova 3, CZ-120 00 Praha 2. Tel (02) 24262237, Fax (02) 24262238

Prizes of the Chamber of Photographers, for outstanding Czech contributions in photography and photographic technology, every year. Contact: Komora fotografu, Novotného lávka 5, CZ-116 68 Praha 1. Tel (02) 21082335, Fax (02) 21082289

Denmark

Population: 5.3 million
Capital: Copenhagen, 1.4 million
Currency: Krone (DKr)
International code: ++45
Tourist information: Danmarks Turistraad, Vesterbrogade 6d, DK-1620 København V
Tel 33111415,
Fax 33931416

Galleries & Museums

Galleri Image, Toldbodgade 8, DK-8000 Århus C. Tel 86202429, Fax 86202429. E-mail beate@post.tele.dk. Open: Tue–Sun 13–17. Directors: Beate Cegielska, Saul Shapiro. Curator: Beate Cegielska. Founded 1977. 2 rooms, 120 m². 10 photo exhibitions/year. Artists: Luis Paredes, Lisbet Nielsen, Anthony Haughey, Helga Bu, Luis González Palma, Ewa Andrzejewska, Joakim Eskildsen, Johnny Jensen, Charlotte C. Haslund-Christensen, Martine Mougin

Danmarks Fotomuseum, Museumsgade 28, DK-7400 Herning. Tel 97225322. Website www.fotomuseum.dk. Open: Tue–Sun 12–16.30. Director: Bjarne Meldgaard. Founded 1984. 8 rooms, 535 m². 8 photo exhibitions/year

Det Nationalhistoriske Museum paa Frederiksborg, Moderne Samling, Frederiksborg Slot, DK-3400 Hillerød. Tel 42260439, Fax 48240966. E-mail frederiksborgmuseet@ frederiksborgmuseet.dk. Website www.frederiksborgmuseet.dk. Open: 10–17. Director: Jesper S. Knudsen. Curators: Tove H. Thage, Martin Brandt. Founded 1993. 14 rooms, 700 m². 1–2 photo exhibitions/year. Artists: Joyce Tenneson, Henrik Saxgren, Piotr Topperzer, Jesper Westley, Rigmor Mydtskov, Thierry Geoffroy-Colonel, Ole Haupt, Marianne Grøndahl, Morten Krogvold, Per Morten Abrahamsen

Louisiana Museum of Modern Art, Gl. Strandvej 13, DK-3050 Humlebæk. Tel 49190719, Fax 49193505. E-mail curatorial@louisiana.dk. Website www.louisiana.dk. Open: 10–17 (Wed –22). Director: Poul Erik Tojner. Curator: Lars Schwander. Founded 1958. 28 rooms, 10,000 m². 2 photo exhibitions/year. Artists: Pablo Picasso, Alberto Giacometti, Henry Moore, Jean Dubuffet, Yves Klein, Mark Rothko, Andy Warhol, Cindy Sherman, Anselm Kiefer, Robert Frank

Arken, Museum for Moderne Kunst, Skovvej 100, DK-2635 Ishøj. Tel 43540222, Fax 43540522. E-mail reception@arken.dk. Website www.arken.dk. Open: Tue–Sun 10–17 (Wed –21). Director: Christian Gether. Founded 1996. 7 rooms, 3,000 m². 2–3 photo exhibitions/year

Det Kongelige Bibliotek, The National Museum of Photography, Christians Brygge 8, DK-1219 København K. Tel 33474747, Fax 33329846. E-mail ifj@kb.dk. Website www.kb.dk/fotomuseum. Open: Mon–Sat 10–19. Director: Ingrid Fischer Jonge. Founded 1996. 1 room, 400 m². 4 photo exhibitions/year. Artists: Francis Bedford, Desire Charnay, Maxime Ducamp, William Henry Fox Talbot, Francis Frith, Nan Goldin, Thomas Ruff

Fotografisk Center, Gammel Strand 48, DK-1202 København K. Tel 33930996, Fax 33930997. E-mail fc@photography.dk. Website www.photography.dk. Open: Tue–Sun 11–17. Director/curator: Lars Schwander. Founded 1996. 4 rooms, 200 m². 8–10 photo exhibitions/year. Artists: Duane Michals, Yoko Ono, Nathalie Amand, Hamadou Bocoum, Torben Eskerod, Tove Kurtzweil, Viggo Rivad, Man Ray

Kunstakademiets Bibliothek, Collection of Architectural Photography, Kongens Nytorv 1, DK-1050 København K. Tel 33744800, Fax 33744888. E-mail kab@kb.dk. Website www.kulturnet.dk/homes/kab. Open: by appointment only. Director: Hakon Lund. Curator: Marie-Louise Berner. Founded 1854. 1 room. 0–1 photo exhibition/year. Artists: Frédéric Flacheron, August Lorent, Edouard Baldus, James Robertson and Felice A. Beato, Maurizio Lotze, Bisson Frères

Museet for Fotokunst, Brandts Klædefabrik, Brandts Passage 37 & 43, DK-5000 Odense C. Tel 66137816, Fax 66137310. E-mail mff@brandts.dk. Website www.brandts.dk. Open: Tue–Sun 10–17. Director: Finn Thrane. Curators: Finn Thrane, Lis Steincke. Founded 1987. 5 rooms, 600 m². 10–12 photo exhibitions/year. Artists: Josef Koudelka, Frantisek Drtikol

Festivals & Fairs

Odense Foto Triennale, Museet for Fotokunst, Brandts Passage 37 & 43, DK-5000 Odense. Tel (066) 137816, Fax (066) 137310. Website www.brandts.dk

Magazines

Dansk Fotografisk Tidsskrift, Dansk Fotografisk Forening, Bornholmsgade 1, 1.tv, DK-1266 København K. Tel 33120090, Fax 33932601. Editor: Keld Nielsen. Danish. Founded 1879. Copy price: DKr 40.00. Annual subscription: DKr 150.00, 4 issues/year

Katalog, Journal of Photography and Video, Brandts Passage 37 & 43, DK-5000 Odense C. Tel 49251122, Fax 66137310. E-mail mff@brandts.dk. Website www.brandts.dk/katalog. Editor: Henning Wettendorff. English/Danish. Founded 1988. Copy price: DKr 95.00. Annual subscription: DKr 275.00, 3 issues/year

Øjeblikket, Forlaget Basilisk, Nansensgade 77, DK-1366 København K

Book Publishers

Borgens Forlag, Valbygaardsvej 33, DK-2500 Valby. Tel 31462100, Fax 36441488

Forlaget Politisk Revy, Nansensgade 70, st., DK-1366 København K. Tel 33914141, Fax 33915115. E-mail politiskrevy@forlagene.dk. Website www.forlagene.dk/politiskrevy

Fotografisk Center, Gammel Strand 48, DK-1202 København K. Tel 33930996, Fax 33930997. E-mail fc@photography.dk. Website www.photography.dk

Gyldendal, Klareboderne 3, DK-1001 København K. Tel 33110775, Fax 33110323

Rhodos Internationalt Forlag, Strandgade 36, DK-1401 København K. Tel 32543020, Fax 32954742. E-mail rhodos@rhodos.dk. Website www.rhodos.dk

JOURNAL OF PHOTOGRAPHY & VIDEO

55   Denmark

Bookshops

Fotografisk Center, Gammel Strand 48, DK-1202 København K. Tel 33930996, Fax 33930997. E-mail fc@photography.dk. Website www.photography.dk

Louisiana Museum of Modern Art, Bookshop, Gl. Strandvej 13, DK-3050 Humlebæk. Tel 49190719, Fax 49161125. E-mail museumshop@louisiana.dk. Website www.louisiana.dk

Critics & Journalists

Lars Kiel Bertelsen, Nordkapvej 13, DK-8200 Århus N. Tel 86108141/89421865, Fax 89421855. E-mail kultlkb@hum.au.dk. Website www.hum.au.dk/kunsthis/kultlkb/home.htm. *Katalog,* Odense; ARK, Århus

Carsten Brandt, Jelsbuen 27, DK-2620 Albertslund. Tel 43626778. E-mail cbrandt@csc.dk

Mogens Damgaard, Fyens Stiftstidende, Blangstedgårdsvej 2–6, DK-5220 Odense SØ

Ingrid Fischer Jonge, Fiskedamsgade 10, 5. tv, DK-2100 København Ø. Tel 31387176

Rune Gade, Absalonsgade 16, DK-1658 København V. Tel 31312415. E-mail rune_gade@online.pol.dk. *Dagbladet information, Tidsskriftet Øjeblikket,* København

Anthony Georgieff, Vinkelager 50, st tv, DK-2720 København. Tel 38794968, Fax 38794968. E-mail anthony1@image.dk. *Katalog,* Odense; *European Photography,* Göttingen

Birna Marianne Kleivan, Fælledvej 16, DK-2200 København K. Tel 35374545, Fax 35374544. E-mail birnakleivan@hotmail.com

Mette Kia Krabbe Meyer, Gothersgade 161.3, DK-1123 København K. Tel 33141192. E-mail krabbemeyer@get2net.dk

Lotte Tauber Larsen, Lipkesgade 26, I, DK-2100 København Ø. Tel 35430315, Fax 35430315

Tage Poulsen, Katholmvej 1B, DK-2720 Vanløse. Tel 38749818. *Katalog,* Odense

Mette Sandbye, Københavns Universitet, Institut für litteraturvidenskab, Njalsgade 80, DK-2300 København S. Tel 35329263. E-mail sandbye@hum.ku.dk. Website www.hum.au.dk/nordisk/realisme. *Katalog,* Odense; *Weekendavisen,* København

Lars Schwander, Andreas Bjørns Gade 19, DK-1428 København K. Tel 33930996, Fax 33930997. E-mail schwander@forum.dk. Website www.artonline.dk. Curator at Fotografisk Center, København, and Louisiana Museum of Modern Art, Humlebæk

Martin Sne, Vendersgade 3, DK-1363 København K. Tel 33142465

Erik Steffensen, Sølvgade 6 A, DK-1307 København K. Tel 33919107

Tove Thage, Frederiksborg Slot 7, DK-3400 Hillerød. Tel 42268702, Fax 48240966

Finn Thrane, Hverringevej 177, DK-5300 Kerteminde. Tel 65321828, Fax 65321828. Director of Museet for Fotokunst, Odense

Henning S. Wettendorff, Mimersvej 16, DK-3000 Helsingør. Tel 49251122, Fax 49251122. E-mail henning@wettendorff.dk. Editor of *Katalog,* Odense

Schools & Workshops

Danmarks Designskole, Strandboule-
varden 47, DK-2100 København Ø.
Tel 35277500, Fax 35277600. E-mail
reception@dk-designskole.dk.
Website www.dk-designskole.dk

Fatamorgana, Teglgaardsstræde 5,
1. sal, DK-1452 København K. Tel
33156866, Fax 33156866. E-mail
fatamorgana@fata.dk. Website
www.fata.dk

K.U.B.A., Øster Farimagsgade 16 F,
DK-2100 København Ø. Tel 31381183

Kunstakademiets Konservatorskole,
Esplanaden 34, 4.th, DK-1263
København K

Roskilde University, Communication
Studies, DK-4000 Roskilde

Royal Academy of Fine Arts, Kongens
Nytorv 1, DK-1021 København K. Tel
33744500, Fax 33744666. Website
www.kunstakademiet.dk

Samsø Folkehøjskole, Skolebakken
10, DK-8308 Samsø. Tel 86590411,
Fax 86591132. E-mail samsing@
pip.dknet.dk

The Danish School of Journalism,
The Department of Photojournalism,
Olof Palmes Alle 11, DK-8200 Århus
N. Tel 89440440, Fax 86168910. E-mail
photo@djh.dk. Website www.djh.dk

Vestbirk Højskole, Grunveld Niel-
sensvey 1–5, DK-8752 Østbirk. Tel
75781171, Fax 75780090

Vrå Folkehøjskole, Høgskolevey 1,
DK-9760 Vrå. Tel 98981010, Fax
98982031

Associations

BKF (Danish Artists' Association),
Bremerholm 28, DK-1069
København K

Dansk Fotografisk Forening, Bornholmsgade 1, DK-1266 København K.
Tel 33120090, Fax 33932601

Dansk Fotohistorisk Selskab, Tegl-
gårdsvej 308, DK-3050 Humlebæk

**Støttekredsen (Members' Associa-
tion),** Museet for Fotokunst, Brandts
Passage 37, DK-5000 Odense C. Tel
66137816, Fax 66137360. E-mail
lis.steinke@brandts.dk. Website
www.brandts.dk

New Media

**Copenhagen Film und Video Work-
shop Festival,** Danish Film Institute
Workshop and Filmhouse Denmark,
Vognmagergade 10, DK-1120
København K. Tel 33931914, Fax
33931912

Danish Film Institute Workshop,
Laurids Skausgade 12, DK-6100
Haderslev. Tel 74528695, Fax
74532461. E-mail hansvb@dfi.dk.
Website www.dfi.dk

The Danish Video Art Data Bank,
Themstrupvej 36, DK-4690 Haslev.
Tel 56312121, Fax 56312121. E-mail
soeborg@inet.uni2.dk. Website
www.videoart.suite.dk

Estonia

Population: 1.46 million
Capital: Tallinn 420,000
Currency: Kroon (EEK)
International code: ++372
Tourist information: Estonian
Tourist Board, Mündi 2,
EE-10146 Tallin
Tel 699 04 20,
Fax 699 04 32

Galleries & Museums

Gallery of Estonian Academy of Art, Tartu mnt. 1, EE-10145 Tallin. Contact: Ketle Tiitsaar

Kiek in de Kök, Komandandi Tee 2, EE-10130 Tallin. Tel 6446686. Open: Tue–Fri 10.30–17.30, Sat–Sun 10.30–16.30. Contact: Maruta Varrak. Founded 1972. 2 rooms, 80 running meters. 18–20 photo exhibitions/year

Linnagalerii, Harju 13, EE-10130 Tallin. Tel 6441913, Fax 6442818. Open: Tue–Sat 11–18. Contact: Anu Livak. Founded 1991. 2 rooms, 124 m². 2–4 photo exhibitions/year. Artists: Arne Maasik, Herkki Merila, Mati Karmin, Peeter Laurits

Photocellar "LEE", Photomuseum, Raekoja 4/6, EE-10146 Tallin. Tel 6448767. Open: daily except Tuesday 11–17. Founded 1992. 1 room, 35 m². 13 photo exhibitions/year. Artists: Ann Tenno, Peep Puks, Peeter Langovits, Kristel Lukats, Jaan Roomus, Aravo Iho, Heido Tooming, Peeter Tooming, Vidar Lindqvist, Margus Hendrikson, Toomas Kaasik, Juliana Volor, Raimo Virtanen, Jaak Veiderma, Hans Duggen, Eric Renner, Sergey Osmachkin

Photomuseum, Town Hall Prison, Raekoja 4/6, EE-10146 Tallin. Tel 6448767. Open: daily except Tuesday 10.30–17.30. Contact: Mall Parmas. Founded 1980. 6 rooms, 200 m². 4 photo exhibitions/year

Illegaard, Ulikooli 5, EE-51014 Tartu. Tel (027) 454424. Open: daily 12–18. Contact: Ave Vaino, Sirje Ginter. Founded 1990. 1 room, 70 m². 5–6 photo exhibitions/year. Artists: Einar Tiits, Riita Jarnela, Raimo Korhonen, Jo Selsing, Martin Parr

Festivals & Fairs

Photofestivals Narvas Spring & Narvas Automn, Valeri Boltusin, Puskini 8, EE-20308 Narva

Magazines

Estonian Art, Estonian Institute, P. O. Box 3469, EE-10506 Tallin. Tel 6314355, Fax 6314356. E-mail einst@einst.ee. Website www.einst.ee/Ea

Kunst.ee., Heie Treier, Vabudase väljak 6, EE-10141 Tallin

Teater-Muusika-Kino, Narva Mnt. 5, EE-10117 Tallin. Tel 6601882, Fax 6616162. Editor: Jüri Aarma. Estonian (English summaries). Founded 1981, 12 issues/year

Vikerkaar, Literature & Art, Pikk 2, EE-10123 Tallin. Tel 6464059. Editor: Märt Väljataga. Estonian, 12 issues/year

Critics & Journalists

Anders Härm, Rahe 18, EE-10618 Tallin. Tel 6562512

Mari Laanemets, Oismäe tee 121-60, EE-13515 Tallin. Tel 6569724

Peeter Linnap, Paasiku 4-128, EE-13916 Tallin. Tel 6337556, Fax 6327347. Center for Contemporary Photography, Tallinn Fine Art University, Tallin; *European Photography*, Göttingen

Piret Räni, Arbu 8-54, EE-13617 Tallin. Tel 6327347, Fax 6327347

Heie Treier, Hobusepea 2, EE-10133 Tallin

Reet Varblane, Sirp, Pärnu mnt. 8, EE-10148 Tallin. Tel 6448868

Associations

Center for Contemporary Photography, Paasiku 4, EE-10100 Tallin

EFÜ – Estonian Society for Photographic Art, P. O. Box 3163, EE-10100 Tallin

New Media

dig_in_time: International Offline@ online Media Art Festival, Videos, short films, net.art, CD-ROMs, lectures, artist presentations, Raivo Kelomees, E-Media Center, Estonia Academy of Arts, Tartu Str. 1, EE-10145 Tallin. Tel 6267336, Fax 56235191. E-mail offline@online.ee. Website www.artun.ee/digintime/

Interstanding 4, Soros Centre for Contemporary Arts, EE-Tallin. Tel 6314050, Fax 6314049. E-mail post@skkke.ee / Estonian Academy of Arts, Tel 6267300, Fax 6267350. E-mail ando@artun.ee. Website www.artun.ee/center/i2, www.interstanding2.ee

Finland

Population: 5.1 million
Capital: Helsinki, 546,000
Currency: Mark (Fmk)
International code: ++358
Tourism information: Finnish
Tourist Board, P. O. Box 249,
FIN-00131 Helsinki
Tel (09) 41 76-92 11/93 00,
Fax (09) 41 76 93 01

Galleries & Museums

Galleria Diana, Korkeavuorenkatu 2
bF72, FIN-00140 Helsinki. Tel (09)
662433, Fax (09) 662422. Open: Tue–
Fri 10–18, Sat–Sun 10–16. Director:
Ulla Koski. Founded 1988. 375 m²

Laterna Magica, Photographic Gallery, Rauhankatu 7, FIN-00170 Helsinki. Tel (09) 1357559/5250559, Fax
(09) 8043949. E-mail mikko.pekari@
laterna.net. Website www.laterna.net.
Open: Mon–Fri 10–18, Sat 10–14.
Director: Mikko Pekari. Founded
1989. 2 rooms, 100 m². 20 photo ex-
hibitions/year. Artists: Caj Bremer,
Tuija Lindström, Christer Strömholm,
Stefan Bremer, Pentti Sammallahti,
Simo Rista, Hannele Rantala

Nykytaiteen Museo, Contemporary
Museum of Art, Kaivokatu 2, FIN-
Helsinki. Tel (09) 173361, Fax (09)
17336237. Website www.fng.fi/.
Open: Tue–Fri 9–18 (Wed–Thu –20),
Sat–Sun 11–17. Director: Tuula Ar-
leio. Founded 1990. 5 rooms, 500 m².
1–2 photo exhibitions/year. Artists:
Francis Bacon, Joseph Beuys, Marcel
Broodthaers, Richard Long, Robert
Motherwell, Jan Fabre, Gary Hill,
Donald Judd, Yves Klein, Jiri Kolar

The Finnish Museum of Photography,
Cable Factory, Tallberginkatu 1 G,
FIN-00180 Helsinki. Tel (09) 6866360,
Fax (09) 68663630. E-mail fmp@
fmp.fi. Website www.fmp.fi. Open:
Tue–Sun 12–19. Director: Asko
Mäkelä. Curator: Pirkko Siitari.
Founded 1969. 3 rooms, 900 m².
8–10 photo exhibitions/year

Valokuvagalleria Hippolyte, Photo-
graphic Gallery Hippolyte, Kalevan-
katu 18 b, FIN-00100 Helsinki. Tel
(09) 6123344, Fax (09) 6123343. E-mail
photo@artists.fi. Open: Tue–Fri 12–17,
Sat–Sun 12–16. Director: Marjatta
Tikkanen. Curator: Jan Kaila. Found-
ed 1977. 3 rooms, 68 m². 12 photo ex-
hibitions/year. Artists: Ulla Jokisalo,
Timo Kelaranta, Tuija Lindström,
Boris Mikhailov, Esko Mannikkö,
Jorma Puranen, Heli Rekula, Igor
Savchenko, Jan Svenungsson, Paul
Graham

Galleria Fotokram, The Center of
Creative Photography, Kramsunkatu
1, FIN-40600 Jyväskylä. Tel (014)
615730, Fax (014) 615730. Open: Thu–
Sun 12–18. Director: Martti Kapanen.
Founded 1986. 2 rooms, 84 m². 10
photo exhibitions/year

**Fotocentrum Raseborg Valokuva-
keskus,** Galleri Zebra, Keskuskatu 90,
FIN-10300 Karjaa. Tel (019) 36499, Fax
(019) 2411147. Open: Mon–Fri 13–19,
Sat 10–14. Director: Vidar Lindquist.
Founded 1992. 3 rooms, 200 m². 11
photo exhibitions/year. Artists: Ben
Kaila, Martti Anttila, Paul Brück,
Vidar Lindquist, Matti Saanio, Kaj
Pettersson

Konserttitalon valokuvagalleria,
Keskuskatu 33, FIN-48100 Kotka. Tel

(05) 234702, Fax (05) 234274. Open:
Mon–Fri 8–16. Director: Marianna
Siltala. Founded 1986. 1 room, 76 m².
12 photo exhibitions/year

**Victor Barsokevitsch Photographic
Center,** Kuninkaankatu 14–16, FIN-
70100 Kuopio. Tel (017) 2615599,
Fax (017) 2615844. E-mail
vb.valokuvakeskus@co.inet.fi.
Website www.vb.kuopio.fi. Open:
Mon–Fri 10–19, Sat–Sun 12–16 (Jun–
Aug), Mon–Fri 11–17, Sat–Sun 12–16
(Sep–May). Director: Laura Luosta-
rinen. Founded 1987. 5 rooms,
140 m². 8–10 photo exhibitions/year

Oulu Taidemuseo, Oulu Art Muse-
um, Kasarmintie 7, FIN-90100 Oulu.
Tel (08) 55847450, Fax (08) 55847499.
E-mail keskus.taidemuseo@ouka.fi.
Website www.ouka.fi/taidemuseo.
Open: Tue–Sun 11–18 (Wed –20).
Director: Ulla Maria Pallasmaa.
Founded 1963. 7 rooms, 1,330 m².
1 photo exhibition/year. Artists: Rax
Rinnekangas, Esko Mannikkö, Pekka
Turunen, Veli Granö, Elina Brotheus,
Stefan Bremer

Pohjoinen valokuvakeskus, Northern
Photographic Center, Hallituskatu
5 & 7, FIN-90100 Oulu. Tel (08)
3110611, Fax (08) 3116705. E-mail
alla.raisanen@pvk.inet.ti. Website
www.ouka.ti/pvk. Open: Mon–Fri
10–20, Sat 10–14, Sun 12–18. Director:
Arja-Liisa Räisänen. Founded 1987.
4 rooms, 77 m². 10 photo exhibitions/
year. Artists: Tiina Itkonen, Marja
Vuorelainen, Matti Saanio, Jorma Pur

Rantagalleria, Center of Culture, Hallituskatu 7, FIN-90100 Oulu. Tel (08)
3116005, Fax (08) 3116705. E-mail
rantag@na.netppl.fi. Website www.
netppl.fi/'rantag. Open: Mon–Sun
10–20. Director: Pirjo Lempeä.
Founded 1981. 4 rooms, 77 m².
12 photo exhibitions/year

Porin Taidemuseo, Pori Art Museum,
Eteläranta, FIN-28100 Pori. Tel (02)
6211082, Fax (02) 331789. Open: Tue–
Sun 11–18 (Wed –20). Director: Mar-
ketta Seppälä. Founded 1981. 4 rooms,
1,000 m². 1 photo exhibition/year.
Artists: Rauni Liukko, Jussi Kivi,
Geoffrey Hendricks, Arno Rafael
Minkkinen

Rovaniemi Art Museum, Lapinkä-
vijäntie 4, FIN-96100 Rovaniemi.
Tel (016) 3222820, Fax (016) 3223052.
E-mail leena.lohiniva@rovaniemi.fi.
Open: Tue–Sun 10–17. Curator: Leena
Lohiniva. Founded 1986. 5 rooms,
700 m². 2–5 photo exhibitions/year.
Artists: Arto Liiti, Marja Helander,
Johanna Vuoksenmaa, Kapa, Mikko
Hietaharju

Valokuvakeskus Nykyaika, Photographic Center Nykyaika, Kehrä-
saari B, FIN-33200 Tampere. Tel (03)
2146677, Fax (03) 2148080. E-mail
backlight@backlight.fi. Website
www.backlight.fi. Open: Tue–Fri
12–18, Sat–Sun 12–16. Director: Antti
Haapio. Curator: Ulrich Haas-Pursia-
inen. Founded 1982. 4 rooms, 100 m².
10 photo exhibitions/year. Artists:
Sally Mann, Jaschi Klein, Heinz Cibulka, Chipex, Wim Wenders, Esko
Mannikko, Thomas Ruff

Aineen Taidemuseo, The Aine Art
Museum, Torikatu 2, FIN-95400 Tor-
nio. Tel (016) 432438, Fax (016) 432586.
Open: Mon–Fri 11–19, Sat–Sun 11–17
(summer); Tue–Fri 11–19, Sat–Sun 11–
17 (winter). Director: Yrjö Nurkkala.
Founded 1986. 5 rooms, 623 m².
1 photo exhibition/year

Valokuvakeskus Peri, Peri Center of
Photography, Uudenmaankatu 1,
FIN-20500 Turku. Tel (02) 2514364,
Fax (02) 2514843. E-mail galleria.peri
@dlc.fi. Open: Tue–Sun 12–19. Cura-
tor: Ville Kettunen. Founded 1987.

4 rooms, 150 m². 18 photo exhibitions/year

Festivals & Fairs

Pohjoinen Valokuva, Northern Photography Triennal, Hallituskatu 5, FIN-90100 Oulu. Tel (08) 3110611, Fax (08) 3116705. E-mail alla.raisanen@pvk.inet.ti. Website www.ouka.ti/pvk

Valokuvataide-Arkitaide, Helsinki Photography Festival, Kalevankatu 18b, FIN-00100 Helsinki. Tel (09) 6123344, Fax (09) 6123343. E-mail photo@artist.fi

Magazines

Form Function Finland, Erottajankatu 15–17a, FIN-00130 Helsinki. Tel (09) 62208114, Fax (09) 629489. E-mail form.function@designforum.fi. Website www.finnishdesign.fi. Editor: Anne Stenros. English. Founded 1980. Copy price: Fmk 45.00. Annual subscription: Fmk 235.00 (Europe), 4 issues/year

Kameralehti, Photography Magazine, Malminrinne 1B, FIN-00180 Helsinki. Tel (09) 6940134, Fax (09) 6940166. E-mail kamera@kamera-lethi.fi. Website www.kamera-lehti.fi. Editor: Pekka Punkari. Finnish. Founded 1950. Copy price: Fmk 39.00. Annual subscription: Fmk 351.00, 10 issues/year

Musta Taide, Photo magazine, Lemuntie 7 A, FIN-00510 Helsinki. Tel (09) 7016477, Fax (09) 7535537. Editor: Tuomo-Juhani Vuorenmaa. Finnish. Founded 1990. Copy price: Fmk 40.00–150.00. Annual subscription: Fmk 300.00

Taide, Kasarminkatu 23a, FIN-00130 Helsinki. Tel (09) 626467, Fax (09) 626482

Valokuva, Korkeavuorenkatu 2 b F 72, FIN-00140 Helsinki. Tel (09) 663433, Fax (09) 662422. E-mail valokuva@valokuv.pp.fi. Editor: Kati Lintonen. Finnish (English summaries). Founded 1921. Copy price: Fmk 40.00. Annual subscription: Fmk 350.00, 6 issues/year

Book Publishers

Musta Taide, Lemuntie 7 A, FIN-00510 Helsinki. Tel (09) 7016477, Fax (09) 7535537

Bookshops

Laterna Magica, Antique Books, Rauhankatu 7, FIN-00170 Helsinki. Tel (09) 1357559/5350559, Fax (09) 8043949. E-mail mikko.pekari@laterna.net. Website www.laterna.net

Critics & Journalists

Philip Dean, Uomarinne 1 E 72, FIN-01600 Vantaa. Tel (09) 5668861, Fax (09) 662433. University of Art & Design, Helsinki; *Valokuva*, Helsinki

Jukka Järvinen, Mustankivenaukio 3 B 29, FIN-00980 Helsinki. Tel (09) 3257264, Fax (08) 3116705. E-mail jukkajarvinen@artic.net. Website www.xoom.com/moottori/index.html. *Kaltio-Magazine*, Oulu

Kari Kemppainen, Kalevankatu 38 c 45, FIN-00180 Helsinki. Tel (040) 7383041. E-mail kari.kemppainen@kaapeli.fi

Kati Lintonen, Korkeavuorenkatu 2 b
F 72, FIN-00140 Helsinki. Tel (09)
663433, Fax (09) 662433

Martti Lintunen, Liesipolku 7 C, FIN-
00630 Helsinki. Tel (09) 7542130, Fax
(09) 7543525

Mikko Pekari, Rauhankatu 7, FIN-
00170 Helsinki. Tel (09) 1357559, Fax
(09) 8043949. YLE/TV2, Tampere;
Laterna Magica/Photo Gallery,
Helsinki; *Musta Taide*, Helsinki

Mika Ripatti, Pispankatu 21 as. 4,
FIN-33240 Tampere

Leena-Maija Rossi, Sepankatu 15 c 50,
FIN-00150 Helsinki. Tel (09) 628839,
Fax (09) 628839. E-mail lmrossi@
helsinki.fi. Helsingin Sanomat,
University of Helsinki, Helsinki

Merja Salo, Haapalahdenkatu 15 B,
FIN-00300 Helsinki. Tel (09) 4362390

Leena Saraste, Agricolakatu 13 B 21,
FIN-00530 Helsinki

Sakari Sunila, Mäyrätie 14 as. 32,
FIN-00800 Helsinki

Anu Uimonen, Mechelininkatu 26 A
II, FIN-00100 Helsinki. Tel (09)
447906, Fax (09) 1222609. E-mail
anu.uimonen@sanoma.fi. Helsingin
Sanomat, Helsinki

Timo Valjakka, Suomenlinna B 37,
FIN-00190 Helsinki. Tel (09) 668143,
Fax (09) 668594

Hannu Vanhanen, Amattikoulunkatu
15 A 3, FIN-33230 Tampere

Leo Vossi, Pajukatu 3 as 21, FIN-
04260 Kerava

Schools & Workshops

**Keski-Suomen käsi- ja taideteol-
lisuusoppilaitos,** Valokuvakauksen
linja, Miilutie 2, FIN-41900 Petä-
jävesi

**Lahden taide- ja käsiteollisuusoppi-
laitos,** Kannaksenkatu 22, FIN-15140
Lahti

Svenska Konstskola, Juthasvagen 6 a,
FIN-66900 Karleby NY

Taideteollinen Korkeakoulu, University of Art and Design Helsinki,
Dept. of Photography, Hämeentie
135 C, FIN-00560 Helsinki. Tel (09)
75631/75630593, Fax (09) 75630223.
E-mail studies@uiah.fi. Website
www.uiah.fi

Turun taiteen ja viestinnän oppilaitos,
Valokuvakausen linja, Ratapihankatu
53, FIN-20100 Turku

Associations

Finnfoto ry, Mannerheimintie 76 B,
FIN-00250 Helsinki. Tel (09)
4543742, Fax (09) 4543743. E-mail
tuula.kojonen@finnfotory.fi. Website www.finnfotory.fi

Pohjoinen valokuvakeskus, Northern
Photographic Center, Hallituskatus,
FIN-90100 Oulo. Tel (08) 3110611,
Fax (08) 3116705. E-mail alla.
raisanen@pvk.inet.fi. Website
www.ouka.fi/pvk

Suomen Luonnonvalokuvaajat ry,
The Finnish Association of Nature
Photographers, Nervanderinkatu
11, FIN-00100 Helsinki. Tel (09)
4002949, Fax (09) 4002949. E-mail
luonnonvalokuvaajat@co.jyu.fi.
Website www.co.jyu.fi/
luonnonvalokuvaajat

Suomen Mainosvalokuvaajat ry, The
Finnish Advertising Photographers,
c/o Studio 8x10 Ltd, Itälahdenkatu 9

A, FIN-00210 Helsinki. Tel (09) 6925811, Fax (09) 6923781

Suomen Valokuvaajain Liitto ry, The Finnish Photographers' Association, Perustamisvuosi 1919, Jäsenmäärä 305, Mannerheimintie 76 B, FIN-00250 Helsinki. Tel (09) 75102300, Fax (09) 75102222. E-mail lea.hertuua@photoas.pp.fi

Vakka-Suomen Taideyhdistys ry, Uivelopolku 3, FIN-23500 Uusikaupunki. E-mail vstaideyhdistys@uusikaupunki.fi

Valokuvataiteilijoiden Liitto ry, Union of Artist Photographers, Kalevankatu 18 b, FIN-00100 Helsinki. Tel (09) 6123344, Fax (09) 6123343. E-mail photo@artist.fi

Grants & Awards

Fotofinlandia, for Finnish photographers, total amount Fmk 87,000, every year. Contact: Finnfoto, Mannerheimintie 76 B, FIN-00250 Helsinki. Tel (09) 4543742, Fax (09) 4543743

Kopiosto Grant, for Finnish photographers, total amount Fmk 100,000–140,000, every year. Contact: Finnfoto, Mannerheimintie 76 B, FIN-00250 Helsinki. Tel (09) 4543742, Fax (09) 4543743

New Media

Kiasma Mediatheque & screenings, Kiasma, Museum of Contemporary Art, Mannerheiminaukio 2, FIN-00100 Helsinki. Tel (09) 17336538, Fax (09) 17336575. E-mail info.kiasma@fng.fi. Website www.kiasma.fng.fi

MuuMedia Festival – Annual Nordic Media Arts Festival, Av-ARK, Tallberginkatu 1 E 76, FIN-00180 Helsinki. Tel (09) 6854404, Fax (09) 6854187. E-mail mmf@av-arkki.fi. Website www.av-arkki.fi/mmf/

France

Population: 58.6 million
Capital: Paris, 9.3 million
Currency: Franc (F)
International code: ++33
Tourist information: Maison de la France, 20 avenue de l'Opéra, F-75001 Paris Tel (01) 42961023

Galleries & Museums

Galerie Arena, 16 rue des Arènes, F-13200 Arles. Tel (04) 90993333, Fax (04) 90993359. E-mail comm.enp@ provnet.fr. Website www.provnet.fr/ users/enp. Director: Alain Leloup. Founded 1979. 1 room, 100 m². 2–3 photo exhibitions/year

Musée Réattu, 10 rue du Grand-Prieuré, F-13200 Arles. Tel (04) 90493768, Fax (04) 90493697. Open: 9–12.30, 14–19 (summer); 10–12.30, 14–17.30 (winter). Director: Michéle Moutashar. Founded 1868. 1 room, 200 m². 4 photo exhibitions/year. Artists: Ansel Adams, Brassaï, Henri Cartier-Bresson, Lucien Clergue, Robert Doisneau, Izis, Yousuf Karsh, William Klein, Man Ray, Edward Weston

Centre Méditerranéen de la Photographie, P. O. Box 323, F-20297 Bastia Cedex. Tel (04) 95315608, Fax (04) 95315275. E-mail cmo.fortini@ wanadoo.fr. Curator: Marcel Fortini. Founded 1990. 3 rooms, 350 m². 10 photo exhibitions/year. Artists: Dolores Marat, Nadia Benchallol, Alain Fleischer, Laurent van der Stockt, André Merian, Antonio Biasiucci, Mimmo Jodice, Albano Silva Pereira, Paulo Nozolino

Espace Image, Scène nationale de Bayonne et du Sud-Aquitaine, place de la Liberté, F-64100 Bayonne. Tel (05) 59558505, Fax (05) 59552170. E-mail snbayonne@wanadoo.fr. Open: Tue–Sat 13–19. Director: Dominique Burucoa. Founded 1991. 1 room, 50 m². 6 photo exhibitions/ year. Artists: Henri Cartier-Bresson, Ferdinando Scianna, Alex Webb, Bruno Lasnier, William Klein, Patrice Zamora, Jacques-André Pavlovsky

Espace Images, Espace François Mitterrand, rue du 27 Juin, F-60000 Beauvais. Tel (03) 44063600, Fax (03) 44063605. Open: Tue+Thu+Fri 13–17, Wed+Sat 9–17. Director: Patrice Laplace. Curator: Nathalie Girandeau. Founded 1994. 1 room, 70 m². 5–6 photo exhibitions/year

Galerie Zero, l'infini chemin des trois Croix, Espace Valentin, F-25048 Besançon Cedex. Tel (03) 81507543, Fax (03) 81531359

Musée Français de la Photographie, 78 rue de Paris, F-91570 Bièvres. Tel (01) 69351650, Fax (01) 60192111. Open: 10–12, 14–18. Director: Eric Bourgougnon. Curator: Elisabeth Guimard. Founded 1960. 3 rooms, 350 m². 3 photo exhibitions/year

A.R.P.A., 17 rue de Candale, F-33000 Bordeaux. Tel (05) 56918812. Open: 14–19. Director: Jean-Marc Lacabe. Founded 1979. 1 room, 60 m². 5 photo exhibitions/year

Arrêt sur l'Image Galerie, 13 rue Buffon, F-33000 Bordeaux. Tel (05) 56485636, Fax (05) 56485639. Open: Mon–Sat 14.30–19. Director: Nathalie Lamire-Fabre. Curator: Sylvie Bouny.

Founded 1993. 1 room, 25 m². 6 photo exhibitions/year. Artists: Pierre Boulat, Alice Springs, Beat Presser, Jean-Bernard Fabre

Musée Albert Kahn, Jardins et Collections, 14 rue du Port, F-92100 Boulogne-Billancourt. Tel (01) 46045280, Fax (01) 46038659. Open: 11–18 (Oct–Apr), 11–19 (May–Sep). Director: Jeanne Beausoleil. Founded 1909. 1 room, 750 m². 2–3 photo exhibitions/year. Artists: Stéphane Passet, Auguste Léon, Georges Chevalier, Roger Dumas, Frédéric Gadmer, Fernand Cuville, Léon Busy

Centre Atlantique de la Photographie, P. O. Box 7339, F-29273 Brest Cedex. Tel (02) 98463580, Fax (02) 98339501. Open: Tue–Sat 13–19, Sun 14–18. Director: François Nicolas Hardy. Founded 1996. 2 rooms, 250 m². 5 photo exhibitions/year. Artists: Mark Power, Serge Picard, Michael Ackerman, Massimo Vitali, Silvana Reggiardo

Musée de la Mer, Ile Sainte-Marguerite, F-06400 Cannes. Tel (04) 93385526, Fax (04) 93388150. Open: Wed–Mon 10.30–12, 14–16.30 (Oct–Mar), 10.30–12, 14–17.30 (Apr–Jun), 10.30–12, 14–18.30 (Jul–Sep). Curator: Marie Wallet. Founded 1987. 3 rooms. 4 photo exhibitions/year

L'Abattoir, Centre Régional de Créations Européennes, 5 place de l'Obélisque, F-71100 Chalon-sur-Saône. Tel (03) 85480522, Fax (03) 85936862. Director: Florence Dell' Accio

Musée Nicéphore Niépce, 28 quai des Messageries, F-71100 Chalon-sur-Saône. Tel (03) 85484198, Fax (03) 85486320. Director: François Cheval. Founded 1972. 10 rooms, 1,300 m². 5 photo exhibitions/year. Artists: Nicéphore Niépce, Louis-Jacques-Mandé Daguerre, William Henry Fox Talbot, Antoine Henri Becquerel, Ducos du Hauron, Alphonse Louis Poitevin, Charles Nègre

Espace Malraux, Carré Curial, 67 place François Mitterrand, F-73001 Chambéry Cedex. Tel (04) 79855543, Fax (04) 79852629. Open: Tue–Fri 13–19, Sat 10–18. Director: Dominique Gambon. Curator: Philippe Quotunel. Founded 1990. 3 rooms, 400 m². 8–10 photo exhibitions/year. Artists: Don McCullin, Raymond Depardon, Gilles Caron, Robert Doisneau, André Kertesz, Alexander Rodchenko, Willy Ronis, Claude Batho, Duane Michals

L'Hippodrome, Scène nationale, place du Barlet, F-59502 Doubai Cedex. Tel (03) 27870778, Fax (03) 27872959. E-mail hippo@etnet.fr. Website www.etnet.fr/hippo. Open: 14–19. Director: Jean Escher. Founded 1986. 2 rooms, 50 running meters. 6 photo exhibitions/year

Centre Régional de la Photographie, Nord Pas-de-Calais, place des Nations, F-59282 Douchy-les-mines. Tel (03) 27435650, Fax (03) 27313193. Open: Mon–Fri 14–18, Sat–Sun 15–18. Director: Pierre Devin. Founded 1986. 2 rooms, 120 m². 6 photo exhibitions/year. Artists: Bernard Plossu, Marc Trivier, Dominique Auerbacher, Bruce Gilden, Michael Schaffer, Mimmo Jodice, Yves Guillot, Arno Fischer

MJC de Rosendaël, Château Coquelle, rue de Belfort, F-59240 Dunkerque. Tel (03) 28639991. Open: Tue–Sat 14–19. Director: René Cambier. 150 m². 8 photo exhibitions/year

Galerie du Théâtre de l'Agora, place de l'Agora, P. O. Box 46, F-91002 Évry Cedex. Tel (01) 60916560, Fax (01)

60916575. Open: Tue–Sat 14–19. Curator: Patrick Drouaud. Founded 1986. 2 rooms. 5–10 photo exhibitions/year. Artists: Stephane Couturier, Emmanuel Sougez, Jean-Yves Cousseau, Françoise Huguier, Noel Jagbour, Larry Fink, Jeanloup Sieff, Dolorés Marat

Galerie du Théâtre, 137 boulevard Georges Pompidou, F-05000 Gap. Tel (04) 92525252, Fax (04) 92525242

Maison Robert Doisneau, 1 rue de la Division du Général Leclerc, F-94250 Gentilly. Tel (01) 47408833, Fax (01) 45479783

Artothèque, 5 Grand Place, F-38100 Grenoble. Tel (04) 76229134, Fax (04) 76094054. E-mail micheledollmann@bm-grenoble.fr. Website www.bm-grenoble.fr. Open: Tue–Sat. Director: Michèle Dollmann. Founded 1976. 1 room, 160 m². 4–5 photo exhibitions/year. Artists: Edouard Boubat, Toni Catany, Arnaud Claass, Robert Doisneau, Patrick Faigenbaum, Bernard Faucon, William Klein, Knut Wolfgang Maron, Bernard Plossu, Denis Roche

Centre d'Art d'Ivry, 93 avenue Georges Gosnat, F-94200 Ivry-sur-Seine. Tel (01) 49602506, Fax (01) 49602507. E-mail credac@worldnet.fr. Open: Mon–Sat 14–19, Sun 11–18. Directors: Thierry Sigg, Madeleine van Doren. Founded 1986. 5 rooms, 700 m². 1–2 photo exhibitions/year. Artists: Georges Rousse, Sinje Dillenkofer, Deidi von Schaewen, Gerhard Vormwald, Alain Fleischer

L'Imagerie, 19 rue Jean Savidan, F-22300 Lannion. Tel (02) 96465725, Fax (02) 96465725. E-mail l-imagerie@wanadoo.fr. Website www.perso.wanadoo.fr/imagerie.22. Open: Mon+Wed–Sat 15–18.30 (winter),

Mon–Sat 10–12, 15–19 (summer). Director: Jean-François Rospape. Founded 1984. 2 rooms, 400 m². 6 photo exhibitions/year

Arrêt sur Images, Centre de Diffusion de la Photographie, 5 rue Sainte-Claire, F-32700 Lectoure. Tel (05) 62688372, Fax (05) 62688303. Open: Tue–Fri 9–12, 14–18, Tue–Fri 15–19 (summer). Director/curator: François Saint-Pierre. Founded 1987. 6 rooms, 180 m². 4 photo exhibitions/year

Galerie L'Œil Écoute, 7 rue du Pont Saint-Martial, F-87000 Limoges. Tel (05) 55323078. Open: Wed–Sat 14–18. Directors: Philippe Leduc, Yves Lapeyre. Founded 1992. 1 room, 20 m². 6 photo exhibitions/year. Artists: Yves Lapeyre, Alain Desvergnes, François Puyplat

Galerie Le Lieu, Maison de la Mer, quai de Rohan, F-56100 Lorient. Tel (02) 97211802, Fax (02) 97840378. E-mail galerie.lelieu@a3imail.com. Open: Tue–Sat 11–18, Sun 15–18. Director: Patrick Bernier. Founded 1989. 1 room, 300 m². 8 photo exhibitions/year. Artists: Edouard Boubat, Martin Parr, Karen Knorr, Toto Frima, Josef Sudek, Mazao Gozu, Anthony Haughey, Frederic Gallier, Jun Shiraoka

Le Réverbère 2, 38 rue Burdeau, F-69001 Lyon. Tel (04) 72000672, Fax (04) 72000672. Open: Wed–Sat 14–19 and by appointment. Director: Catherine Derioz. Founded 1981. 3 rooms, 300 m². 4–5 photo exhibitions/year. Artists: Arièle Bonzon, Dirk Braeckman, Jacques Damez, Bernard Descamps, William Klein, Lionel Fourneaux, Denis Roche, Beatrix von Conta, Jean-Claude Palisse, Yves Rozet

Vrais Rêves, 6 rue Dumenge, F-69004 Lyon. Tel (04) 78306542, Fax (04) 78294439. E-mail vraisrev@worldnet. fr. Website www.worldnet.net/ ~vraisrev. Open: Thu–Sat 15–19 and by appointment. Director: Raymond Viallon. Founded 1980. 2 rooms, 150 m². 7 photo exhibitions/year. Artists: Michel Brunier, Toni Catany, Luc Ewen, Mario Giacomelli, Yannig Hedel, Irina Ionesco, Marc Le Mené, Michel Medinger, Marc Peverelli, Unglee, Vladimír Zidlicky

Galerie sel d'Argent, 31 rue Ph. Laguiche, F-71000 Mâcon. Tel (03) 85393106. Open: Wed–Fri 17–19.15, Sat 10–12, 16–19. Director: Susanne Neubauer. Founded 1993. 1 room, 60 m². 5–6 photo exhibitions/year. Artists: Gil Cépède, Xavier Benony, Jean-Marc Biry, Marco Signorini, Anna Pisula-Mandziey

Centre de la Vieille Charité, 2 rue de la Charité, F-13000 Marseille. Tel (04) 91562838, Fax (04) 91906307. Open: Tue–Sun 11–18 (summer), Tue–Sun 10–17 (winter). Director: C. Diserens. Curator: Macha Toufany. 1 room, 600 m². 1 photo exhibition/year

Les Ateliers Nadar, 3 rue Lafon, F-13006 Marseille. Tel (04) 91334121, Fax (04) 91337322. Open: Wed–Sat 14–18.30. Directors/curators: Monique Deregibus, Olivier Menanteau. Founded 1990. 3 rooms, 70 m². 3 photo exhibitions/year. Artists: Monique Deregibus, Olivier Menanteau

Musée d'Art Contemporain, 69 avenue d'Haïfa, F-13008 Marseille. Tel (04) 91250107, Fax (04) 91721727. Open: Tue–Sun 11–18 (summer), Tue–Sun 10–17 (winter). Directors: Nathalie Abou-Isaac, Philippe Vergne. Founded 1994. 3,500 m². 3 photo exhibitions/year

Centre Photographique Nicéphore, 16 rue Dom-Vaissette, F-34000 Montpellier. Tel (04) 67583834, Fax (04) 67929242. Open: Tue–Sat 14–19. Director/curator: Laurent Bertran de Balanda. 2 rooms, 100 m². 6 photo exhibitions/year. Artists: Olivier Proust, Christopher Taylor, Lusia Simons

La Galerie Photo, Salle Dominique Bagouet, esplanade Charles-de-Gaulle, F-34000 Montpellier. Tel (04) 67604311, Fax (04) 67604358

La Filature – La Galerie, 20 allée Nathan Katz, F-68090 Mulhouse Cedex. Tel (03) 89362828, Fax (03) 89362800. E-mail webmaster@ lafilature.org. Website www. lafilature.org. Open: Tue–Sat 11– 18.30, Sun 14–18. Director: Christopher Crines. Curator: Paul Cottin. Founded 1993. 1 room, 350 m². 4–6 photo exhibitions/year. Artists: Isabel Muñoz, André Kertész, Bohdan Holomicek, Paulo Nozolino, Gilles Peress, Libuse Rudinska, Werner Bischof

Musée des Beaux-Arts de Nantes, 10 rue Georges Clemenceau, F-44000 Nantes. Tel (02) 51250640, Fax (02) 51250649. Director: Jean Aubert. 3 rooms, 2,000 m². 1 photo exhibition/ year. Artists: Martin Barré, Sarkis, Soulages, Guiseppe Penone, Joan Mitchell, Tony Grand, Giulio Paolini

Galerie Municipale du Château, Espace graphique, 14 rue Droite, F-06300 Nice. Tel (04) 93859436, Fax (04) 93859436. Open: Tue–Sat 10.30– 13, 14–18. Director: Nadine Babani. Founded 1990. 1 room, 35 m². 6–7 photo exhibitions/year

Musée d'Art Moderne et d'Art Contemporain, promenade des Arts, F-06300 Nice. Tel (04) 93626162, Fax

(04) 93130901. Open: Fri 11–22, Sat–Wed 11–18. Director: Pierre Chaigneau. Curator: Muriel Amssens. Founded 1990. 10 rooms, 40,000 m². Artists: Bernard Descamps, Gilbert & George, Robert Doisneau, Bernard Faucon, Serge Gal, Michel Guillemin, Bernard Guillot, Vera Isler, Robert Mapplethorpe

Theatre de la Photographie et de l'Image, 27 bd Dubouchage, F-06000 Nice. Tel (04) 93801100, Fax (04) 93801155. E-mail theatre.photo@ wanadoo.fr. Open: Tue–Sat 10–12, 14–18. Contact: Jean-Pierre Giusto, Nadine Babani. 600 m². 3–4 photo exhibitions/year. Artists: Gabriele Basilico, Eric Bourret, Claude-Raymond Dityvon, Jacques Godard, Daniel Guillaume, Michael Kenna, Bogdan Konopka, Vladimir Nitkitin, Dorka Raynor, Alexei Titarenko

Musée d'Art Contemporain, Carré d'Art, place de la Maison Carrée, F-30000 Nîmes. Tel (04) 66763570, Fax (04) 66763585. Open: Tue–Sun 10–18. Director: Guy Tosatto

A l'Enseigne des Oudin, 58 rue Quincampoix, F-75004 Paris. Tel (01) 42718365, Fax (01) 42711538. E-mail oudin@club-internet.fr. Website www.pariserve.tm.fr. Open: Tue–Sat 11–13, 15–19. Director: Alain Oudin. Founded 1978. 1 room, 50 m². 3 photo exhibitions/year. Artists: Thierry Cauwet, Henri Maccheroni, Man Ray, Jean Vérame, Pierre Molinier, Irina Ionesco, Marie Chamant, Dominique Digeon, Christian Paraschiv, Philippe Duval

A l'Image du Grenier sur l'Eau, 45 rue des Francs Bourgeois, F-75004 Paris. Tel (01) 42710231, Fax (01) 42786677. E-mail image.di-maria@wanadoo.fr. Open: Mon–Sat 10–19, Sun 14–19. Directors: Sylvain & Yves di Maria.

Founded 1977. 1 room, 50 m². 2 photo exhibitions/year. Artists: Étienne Carjat, Albert Monier, Edouard Denis Baldus, François Kollar, Lehnert & Landrock, Baron Wilhelm von Gloeden, Remy Duval, Robert Doisneau

Art Rencontres Internationales, 5 bis Cité Aubry, F-75020 Paris. Tel (01) 43704815, Fax (01) 43716089. E-mail atett.ponant@wanadoo.fr. Open: 10–13, 14–19. Director: Pierre Ponant. Founded 1985. 1 room, 100 m². 3 photo exhibitions/year. Artists: Philippe Gerbaud, Gabor Bachman, Michel Mallard, Yorgo Tloupas

Bibliothèque Nationale de France, Département des Estampes et de la Photographie, 58 rue de Richelieu, F-75002 Paris. Tel (01) 47038392, Fax (01) 47038307. E-mail anne.sanciaud@ bnf.fr. Open: 12–18.30. Curators: Anne Sanciaud-Azanza, Philippe Arbaizar. Founded 1971. 2 rooms, 60 m². 2–4 photo exhibitions/year

Bièvres – Foire à la Photographie, Photo Club du Val de Bièvres, 28 ter rue Gassendi, F-75014 Paris. Open: 9.30–12, 14–19. Director/curator: André Fage. Founded 1949. 2 rooms, 100 m². 11 photo exhibitions/year

Camera Obscura, 12 rue Ernest Cresson, F-75014 Paris. Tel (01) 45456708, Fax (01) 45456790. Open: Tue–Sat 14–19. Director: Didier Brousse. Founded 1993. 2 rooms, 60 m². 5 photo exhibitions/year. Artists: Didier Ben Loulou, Tomio Seike, Yasuhiro Ishimoto, Paolo Roversi, Koichiro Kurita, Willy Ronis, Julie Ganzin, Lucien Hervé, Franco Zecchin, Philippe Pache

Centre International d'Art Contemporain Château Beychevelle, 76 rue de Prony, F-75017 Paris. Tel (01) 47541271, Fax (01) 47643904. Open:

10–18 (Jul–Oct). Director: Brigitte Huard. Founded 1990. 7 rooms, 560 m². 1 photo exhibition/year. Artists: Shigeo Anzai, Keiichi Tahara, Luis Gonzales-Palma, Ernest Pignon Ernest, Marcel Odenbach, Maria Lugossy, Giuseppe Bergomi, José Hernandez, Erik Samakh, Joris Heetman & Anne Liberati

Centre National de la Photographie, Fondation Salomon Rothschild, 11 rue Berryer, F-75008 Paris. Tel (01) 53761232, Fax (01) 53761233. E-mail regisdurand1@wanadoo.fr. Website www.photographie.com. Open: Wed–Mon 12–19. Director/curator: Régis Durand. Founded 1982. 7 rooms, 600 m². 10 photo exhibitions/year. Artists: Vik Muniz, Irving Penn

Espace d'Art Yvonamor Palix, 13 rue Keller, F-75011 Paris. Tel (01) 48063670, Fax (01) 47000121. Open: Tue–Sat 14–19. Director: Yvonamor Palix. Founded 1991. 3 rooms, 85 m². 3 photo exhibitions/year. Artists: Sandy Skoglund, Paloma Navares, Aziz & Cucher, Keith Cottingham, Daniel Canogar, Olivier Richon, Diller & Scofidio, Dumb Type

Fondation Cartier pour l'art contemporain, 261 boulevard Raspail, F-75014 Paris. Tel (01) 42185650, Fax (01) 42185652. Website www. fondation.cartier.fr. Open: Tue–Sun 12–20

Galerie 1900–2000, 8 rue Bonaparte, F-75006 Paris. Tel (01) 43258420, Fax (01) 46347452. E-mail gal1900@club-internet.fr. Website www.galerie 1900-2000.com. Open: Mon 14–19, Tue–Sat 10–12.30, 14–19. Directors: Marcel Fleiss, David Fleiss. Founded 1981. 1 room, 50 m². 3 photo exhibitions/year. Artists: Dora Maar, Man Ray, James Abbe, Jean Kallina, Ingrid Dinter, Robert Doisneau, Henri Cartier-Bresson, Paul Wolff, Lionel Beyol-Themines, Germaine Krull

Galerie 213, 213 boulevard Raspail, F-75014 Paris. Tel (01) 43228323, Fax (01) 43220331. E-mail galerie213@ wanadoo.fr. Open: Tue–Sat 11–19. Artists: Mario Sorrenti, Elaine Constantine, Elser Esser, Marcy Robinson, Steve Hiett, Peter Fraser

Galerie Agathe Gaillard, 3 rue du Pont-Louis-Philippe, F-75004 Paris. Tel (01) 42773824, Fax (01) 42777836. Open: Tue–Sat 13–19. Director: Agathe Gaillard. Founded 1975. 2 rooms, 120 m². 6–7 photo exhibitions/ year. Artists: Manuel Alvarez Bravo, Edouard Boubat, Henri Cartier-Bresson, Jean-Philippe Charbonnier, Mario Giacomelli, Ralph Gibson,

Hervé Guibert, Marc Riboud, Krysztof Pruszkowski, Pierre Reimer

Galerie Alain Gutharc, 47 rue de Lappe, F-75011 Paris. Tel (01) 47003210, Fax (01) 40217274

Galerie Anne Barrault, 22 rue Saint Claude, F-75003 Paris. Tel (01) 44789167, Fax (01) 44789167. E-mail annebarrault@free.fr. Website www.annebarrault.free.fr. Open: Tue–Sat 14–19. Artists: Philippe Bazin, Anne Deguelle, Bill Jacobson, Eric Nehr

Galerie Baudoin Lebon, 38 rue Sainte Croix de la Bretonnerie, F-75004 Paris. Tel (01) 42720910, Fax (01) 42720220. E-mail baudoin.lebon@ wanadoo.fr. Open: Tue–Sat 11–13, 14.30–19. Directors: Baudoin Lebon. Founded 1976. 4 rooms, 250 m². 5 photo exhibitions/year. Artists: Dieter Appelt, Walker Evans, Robert

WE BUY VINTAGE
EASTERN EUROPEAN
PHOTOGRAPHS

20TH CENTURY PHOTOGRAPHY

CSABA MOROCZ

11, RUE DE PROVENCE   75009 PARIS
TEL 33 1 42 46 75 05   FAX 33 1 48 00 93 24
e-mail : csaba@freesurf.fr   www.cmorocz-photo.com
SUR RENDEZ-VOUS

Mapplethorpe, Joel-Peter Witkin, Patrick Burban, Aram Dervent, Keiichi Tahara, Ernestine Ruben

Galerie Carré Noir, 2 impasse Lebouis, F-75014 Paris. Tel (01) 40470439, Fax (01) 40470439. Open: Tue–Sat 14.30–19

Galerie Condé, Goethe-Institut, 31 rue de Condé, F-75006 Paris. Tel (01) 40466960, Fax (01) 40466961. E-mail sobieraj@paris.goethe.org. Website www.goethe.de/fr/par. Open: Mon–Fri 12–20, Sat 12–20. Director: Dr. Dieter Strauss. Curator: Anke Sobieraj. Founded 1973. 1 room, 40 m². 5 photo exhibitions/year. Artists: Sinje Dillenkofer, Klaus Elle, Andreas Müller-Pohle, Helga Paris, Corinna Rosteck, Thomas Ruff, Jörg Sasse, Joachim Schmid, Ursula Kraft, Matthias Hoch

Galerie des Archives, 4 impasse Beaubourg, F-75003 Paris. Tel (01) 42780577, Fax (01) 42781940. Open: 11–13, 14–19. Directors: Fabienne Leclerc, Christophe Durand-Ruel. Founded 1989. 2 rooms, 150 m². Artists: Pep Agut, David Boeno, Patrick Corillon, Mark Dion, Gary Hill, Florence Paradeis

Galerie du Jour Agnès B., 44 rue Quincampoix, F-75004 Paris. Tel (01) 44545590, Fax (01) 44545599. E-mail jour@agnesb.fr. Website www.agnesb.fr. Open: Tue–Sat 10–19. Director: Pierre Chevalier. Founded 1984. 3 rooms, 120 m². 3 photo exhibitions/year. Artists: Aurèle, Thomas Florschuetz, Joel Hubaut, Louis Jammes, Thierry Le Fébure, Mike Lash, Claude Leveque, Made In Eric, Jonas Mekas, Martin Parr

Galerie Esther Woerdehoff, 36 rue Falguière, F-75015 Paris. Tel (01) 43214483, Fax (01) 43214503. E-mail galerie@falguiere36.org. Website www.falguiere36.org. Open: 13–16.30 and by appointment. Director/curator: Esther Woerdehoff. Founded 1996. 1 room, 160 m². 4 photo exhibitions/year. Artists: Eugene Bavcar, Connie Imboden, Leonard Freed, Jérôme Galland, Olivier Mériel, Inge Morath, Andreas Müller-Pohle, Mario Cravo Neto, Arthur Tress, Michael von Graffenried

Galerie Fait et Cause, 58 rue Quincampoix, F-75004 Paris. Tel (01) 42742636, Fax (01) 42742288. Artist: Robert Doisneau

Galerie Farideh Cadot, 77 rue des Archives, F-75003 Paris. Tel (01) 42780836, Fax (01) 42786361. Open: 14–19. Director: Farideh Cadot. Founded 1976. 3 rooms, 300 m². 2 photo exhibitions/year. Artists: Meret Oppenheim, Georges Rousse, Eve Sonneman, Jorge Molder, Markus Raetz, Mac Adams, Pierre Molinier, Luciano Castelli, Gwen Akin, Allan Ludwig

Galerie Françoise et Alain Paviot, 57 rue Sainte-Anne, F-75002 Paris. Tel (01) 42601001, Fax (01) 42604477. E-mail paviotfoto@wanadoo.fr. Open: Tue–Sat 14.30–19 and by appointment. Director: François Paviot. Founded 1994. 1 room, 90 m². 4–5 photo exhibitions/year. Artists: Eugène Atget, Henri Cartier-Bresson, Robert Doisneau, Anna & Bernhard Blume, Dieter Appelt, Rudolf Bonvie, Brassaï, Man Ray, Charles Nègre

Galerie J & J Donguy, 57 rue de la Roquette, F-75011 Paris. Tel (01) 47001094, Fax (01) 40218384. Open: 13–19. Director: Jacques Donguy. Founded 1981. 2 rooms, 250 m². 4 photo exhibitions/year. Artists: Joe Gantz, Gérard Malanga, Pierre Molinier, Jean Daive, Denis Roche, Bela Kolárová

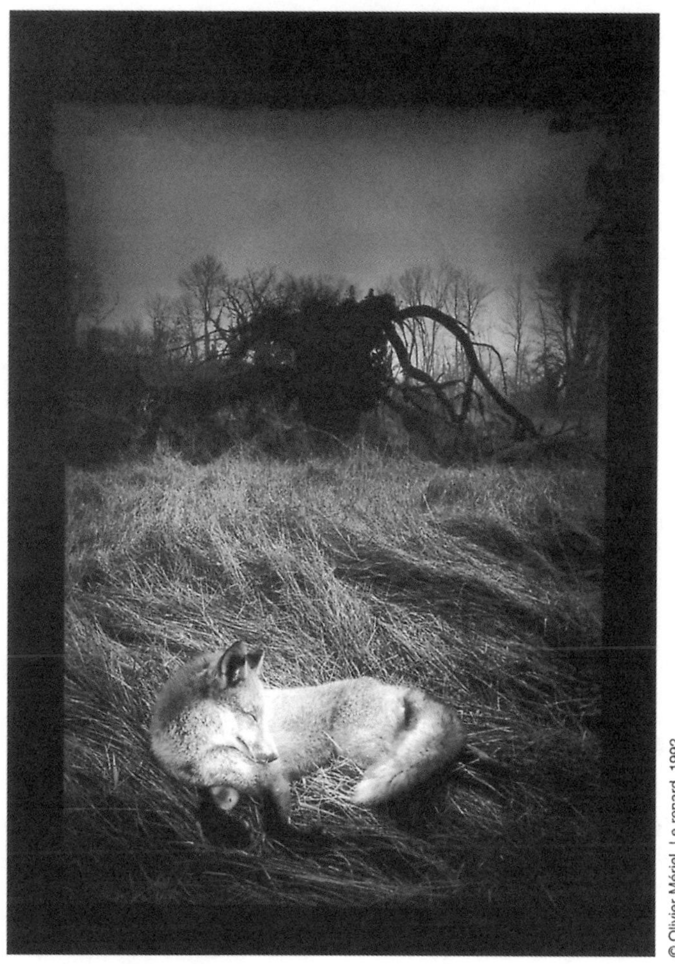

Falguière 36

Galerie Esther Woerdehoff

36, rue Falguière
75015 Paris
Tél. 01 43 21 44 83
Fax 01 43 21 45 03
http://www.falguiere36.org
e-mail : galerie@falguiere36.org

Evgen Bavčar
Kurt Blum
Zabo Chabiland
Claire de Virieu
Philipp Giegel
Frank Horvat
Connie Imboden
Elliott Erwitt
Leonard Freed

Jérôme Galland
Monique Jacot
Yves Leresche
Olivier Mériel
Inge Morath
Andreas Müller-Pohle
Mario Cravo Neto
Arthur Tress
Michael von Graffenried

Galerie Karsten Greve, 5 rue Debelleyme, F-7500 Paris. Open: Tue–Sat 11–19. Director: Karsten Greve. Artists: Josef Albers, John Chamberlain, Yves Charbonnier, Adam Fuss, Loic Le Groumellec, Detleff Orlopp

Galerie Laage-Salomon, 57 rue du Temple, F-75004 Paris. Tel (01) 42781171, Fax (01) 42713449. E-mail laagesalomon@compuserve.com. Open: Tue–Sat 14–19. Director: Gabrielle Salomon. Curator: Delphine Perru. Founded 1977. 2 rooms, 150 m². 4 photo exhibitions/year. Artists: Roger Ackling, Monique Frydman, John Baldessari, Hamish Fulton, Fariba Hajamadi, Hannah Collins, Tracey Moffatt, Axel Hütte, Candida Höfer, Karen Knorr

Galerie Laurent Herschtritt, 5 rue Jacques Callot, F-75006 Paris. Tel (01) 56243474, Fax (01) 56243474. Open: Tue–Sat 14–19. Director: Laurent Herschtritt. Founded 1999. 2 rooms, 35 m². 5–6 photo exhibitions/year

Galerie les Filles du Calvaire, 17 rue des Filles du Calvaire, F-75003 Paris. Tel (01) 42744705, Fax (01) 42744706. Open: Tue–Sat 13–19. Artists: François Daireaux, Elizabeth Lennard, Catherine Poncin, Philippe Le Goff, Ariele Bonzon, Paul Pouvreau, Mireille Loup, Florence Chevallier

Galerie Maeght, 42 rue du BAC, F-75007 Paris. Tel (01) 45484515, Fax (01) 42222283. Website www. imaginet.fr/~jules/. Open: Tue–Sat 10–13, 14–19. Director: Yoyo Maeght. Founded 1957. 2 rooms, 100 m². 1 photo exhibition/year

Galerie Marion Meyer, 15 rue Guénégaud, F-75006 Paris. Tel (01) 46330438, Fax (01) 40469141. E-mail m-meyer@club-internet.fr. Open: Tue–Sat 11–13, 14.30–19. Artists:

Louis Stettner, Man Ray, Brassaï, Rob Wynne

Galerie Michèle Chomette, 24 rue Beaubourg, F-75003 Paris. Tel (01) 42780562, Fax (01) 42726205. Open: Tue–Sat 14–19 and by appointment. Director: Michèle Chomette. Founded 1985. 5 rooms, 100 m². 6 photo exhibitions/year. Artists: Lewis Baltz, Patrick Bailly-Maître-Grand, Arnaud Claass, Alain Fleischer, François Méchain, Bernard Plossu, Eric Rondepierre, Riwan Tromeur, Holger Trülzsch, Nancy Burson

Galerie Nationale du Jeu de Paume, place de la Concorde, F-75008 Paris. Tel (01) 47031250, Fax (01) 47031251. Director: Daniel Abadie. Founded 1991. 2–3 photo exhibitions/year

Galerie Pierre Brullé, 23 rue de Tournon, F-75006 Paris. Tel (01) 43251873, Fax (01) 44070055. Artist: Bruno Roy

Galerie Polaris, 8 rue Saint Claude, F-75003 Paris. Tel (01) 42722127, Fax (01) 42760629. E-mail polaris@ easynet.fr. Open: Tue–Sat 13–19.30. Director: Bernard Utudjian. Founded 1985. 2 rooms, 105 m². 6 photo exhibitions/year. Artists: Eric Emo, Stéphane Couturier, Anthony Hernandez, Bert Sissingh, Eric Larrayadieu, Martine Locatelli, Brigitte Bauer, Nigel Rolfe

Galerie Régine Lussan, 7 rue de l'Odéon, F-75006 Paris. Tel (01) 46333750. Open: afternoons daily, Sun closed. Director: Régine Lussan. Founded 1974. 2 rooms, 50 m². 2 photo exhibitions/year. Artists: Claus Semmler, Akira Fukaesaku, Pierre Loti

Galerie Renn, 14–16 rue de Verneuil, F-75007 Paris. Tel (01) 42612571, Fax

(01) 42612571. Open: Tue–Sat 12–19.
Artist: Thomas Flechtner

Galerie Samia Saouma, 16 rue des
Coutures Saint-Gervais, F-75003
Paris. Tel (01) 42784044, Fax (01)
42786400. Open: Tue–Sat 11–13, 14–
19. Director: Samia Saouma. 1 room,
85 m². 2–3 photo exhibitions/year.
Artists: Pierre & Gilles, Jeanne
Dunning, Gregory Crewdson

Galerie Suzel Berna, 18 rue des
Tournelles, F-75004 Paris. Tel (01)
48873033, Fax (01) 48873023. Open:
Wed–Sun 14–19.30. Curator: Nathalie Emprin

Galerie Thaddaeus Ropac, 7 rue
Debelleyme, F-75003 Paris. Tel (01)
42729900, Fax (01) 42726166. Open:
Tue–Sat 10–19. Director: Caroline
Smulders. Founded 1990. 3 rooms,
350 m². 2 photo exhibitions/year.
Artists: Dennis Hopper, Marie-Jo
Lafontaine, Anne & Patrick Poirier,
Martine Aballea

Galerie Thierry Marlat, 2 rue de
Jarente, F-75004 Paris. Tel (01)
44617979, Fax (01) 44617989. Open:
Tue–Sat 14–19. Director: Thierry
Marlat. Artists: Eugene Atget, Horst
P. Horst, Richard Avedon, Erwin
Blumenfeld, Brassaï, Man Ray, Jock
Sturges, Helmut Newton, Irving
Penn, Javier Vallhonrat

Galerie Vu, 2 rue Jules Cousin, F-
75004 Paris. Tel (01) 53018585, Fax
(01) 53018580. E-mail vu@abvent.fr.
Open: Wed–Sat 14–19. Artists: Michel
Vanden Eeckhoudt, Chema Madoz,
Jane Evelyn Atwood, Isabel Muñoz,
Bernard Faucon, Graciela Iturbide,
Antoine d'Agata, Gotthard Schuh

Galerie Xippas, 108 rue Vieille-du-
Temple, F-75003 Paris. Tel (01)
40270555, Fax (01) 40270716. E-mail

xippas@club-internet.fr. Open: Tue–
Fri 10–13, 14–19, Sat 10–19

Galerie Yvon Lambert, 108 rue Vieille
du Temple, F-75003 Paris. Tel (01)
42710933, Fax (01) 42718747. Open:
Tue–Fri 10–13, 14.30–19, Sat 10–19.
Director/curator: Yvon Lambert.
Founded 1967. 4 rooms, 400 m².
Artists: David Armstrong, Bernard
Faucon, Nan Goldin, Douglas Gor-
don, Anselm Kiefer, Jeong-a Koo,
Joey Kötting, Louise Lawler, Sharon
Lockhart, Fiorenza Menini

Gilbert Brownstone et Cie, 26 rue
Saint Gilles, F-75003 Paris. Tel (01)
42784321, Fax (01) 42740400. Open:
11–13, 14–19. Director/curator:
Gilbert Brownstone. Founded 1985.
2 rooms, 200 m². 1–2 photo exhibi-
tions/year. Artists: Seton Smith,
Bettina Rheims, Javier Vallhonrat

Goethe-Institut, Centre Culturel
Allemand, 17 avenue d'Iéna, F-
75116 Paris. Tel (01) 44439230, Fax
(01) 44439240. E-mail amthor-croft@
paris.goethe.org. Website www.
goethe.de. Open: Mon–Fri 9–21.
Curator: Claudia Amthor-Croft.
Founded 1962. 2 rooms, 150 m².
3 photo exhibitions/year. Artists:
Tina Bara, Kurt Buchwald, Michael
Scheffer, Gundula Schulze, Maria
Sewcz, Thomas Florschuetz, Maix
Mayer, Andreas Rost, Ludwig
Rauch

La Laverie, 9 rue Keller, F-75011 Paris.
Tel (01) 47001138, Fax (01) 47001138.
Open: Tue–Sat 14–19. Director/
curator: Suko Lam. Founded 1994.
1 room, 30 m². 10 photo exhibitions/
year. Artists: Jean-Claude Bélegou,
Liu Hsin-Yu, So Hing-Keung, Olga
Gaupmann, Hou Tsung-Hui, Wu
Chung-Wei, Chen Shun-Chu,
Ng Sai Kit

Lagerfeld Gallery, Caroline Lebar, 40 rue de Seine, F-75006 Paris. Tel (01) 55427550, Fax (01) 40460595. E-mail pressing@club-internet.fr

Le bar Floréal. photographie, 43 rue des Couronnes, F-75020 Paris. Tel (01) 43495522, Fax (01) 43496934. Open: Mon–Fri 10–19. Director: Alex Jordan. Founded 1985. 2 rooms, 70 m². 3 photo exhibitions/year. Artists: Bernard Baudin, Sabine Delcour, Alex Jordan, Jean-Pierre Vallorani, André Lejarre, Olivier Pasquiers, Kristof Guez, Jean-Luc Cormier

Maison de la Villette, angle de l'avenue Corentin Cariou et du quai de la Charente, F-75019 Paris. Tel (01) 40037559, Fax (01) 40037511. Open: Tue–Sun 13–18. Director: Jean-Michel Gourden. Founded 1956. 3 rooms, 700 m². 3 photo exhibitions/year. Artists: Robert Doisneau, Willy Ronis, Michel Maiofiss, Jean Mougin, Patrice Molinard

Maison Européenne de la Photographie, 82 rue François Miron, F-75004 Paris. Tel (01) 44787500, Fax (01) 44787515. Website www.pictime.fr/maison-europeenne/. Open: Wed–Sun 11–20. Director: Jean-Luc Monterosso. Founded 1996. 6 rooms, 1,500 m². 10–12 photo exhibitions/year. Artists: Irving Penn, Robert Frank, William Klein, Weegee, Pierre & Gilles, Bettina Rheims, Henri Cartier-Bresson

Musée Carnavalet, 23 rue de Sévigné, F-75003 Paris. Tel (01) 42722113, Fax (01) 40278559. Open: Tue–Sun 10–17.40. Director: Jean-Marc Leri. Curator: Françoise Reynaud. Founded 1880. 300 m². 2 photo exhibitions/year. Artists: Charles Marville, Eugène Atget, Brassaï, Ilse Bing, Henri Cartier-Bresson, William Klein, Edouard Boubat, Frank Horvat, Keiichi Tahara

Musée d'Art Moderne de la Ville de Paris, 11 avenue du Président Wilson, F-75116 Paris. Tel (01) 53674000. Open: Tue–Fri 12–19, Sat–Sun 10–19

Musée de l'Holographie, Forum des Halles 15–21, Grand Balcon niveau-1, F-75001 Paris. Tel (01) 42969683, Fax (01) 42743357. Open: Mon–Sat 10–19, Sun 13–19. Founded 1980. 2 rooms, 400 m². 2 photo exhibitions/year. Artists: Margaret Benyon, Dieter Jung, John Kaufman, Dan Schweizer

Musée National d'Art Moderne, Centre Georges Pompidou, 19 rue Beaubourg, F-75191 Paris Cedex 04. Tel (01) 44781233, Fax (01) 44781208. Open: Mon+Wed–Fri 12–22, Sat–Sun 10–22. Curator: Alain Sayag. Artists: Man Ray, Brassaï, André Kertész

NCE, La Galerie Itinérante, 391 rue des Pyrénées, F-75020 Paris. Tel (01) 46363205, Fax (01) 46363640. E-mail info@nce-photo.fr. Website www.nce-photo.fr. Open: by appointment only. Director/curator: Nathalie Casabo Emprin. Founded 1995. 5–6 photo exhibitions/year. Artists: Edouard Boubat, Stefan Bremer, Barbara Crane, Frances Dalchele, Jean Dieuzaide, Harri Larjosto, Arno Rafael Minkkinen, Jorma Puranen, Shanta Rao, Michel Semeniako

Passage de Retz, 9 rue Charlot, F-75003 Paris. Tel (01) 48043799, Fax (01) 48043860. E-mail jfk.retz@wanadoo.fr. Director: Jacqueline Kyohuan. Founded 1994. 4 rooms, 700 m². 2 photo exhibitions/year. Artists: Boris Carmi, Lin Fei, Anna Sahar, Marc Garanger, Pessi Geresh

Patrimoine de la photographique – Hotel Sully, 62 rue Saint-Antoine, F-75004 Paris. Tel (01) 42744775.

Open: Tue–Sun 10–18.30. Curator:
Pierre Bonhomme. 4 rooms, 500 m².
5 photo exhibitions/year. Artists:
René-Jacques, François Kollar, Denise
Colomb, Jacques-Henri Lartigue,
Roger Corbeau, Raymond Voinquel,
André Kertész

Picto Bastille, 53 bis rue de la Ro-
quette, F-75011 Paris. Tel (01)
53362121, Fax (01) 53362100. Open:
Mon–Fri 8.30–19. Director: Monique
Plon. Founded 1988. 1 room, 100 m².
50–55 photo exhibitions/year. Artists:
Roger Pic, Edouard Boubat, Gaston
Bergeret, Alexandre Trauner, Frank
Horvat, Marc Garanger, Jean-Marc
Charles, Fernand Michaud, Jacque-
line Salmon

Serge Aboukrat, 7 place Furstemberg,
F-75006 Paris. Tel (01) 44070298, Fax
(01) 44070298

Sylviane de Decker Heftler, 4 rue
Perronet, F-75007 Paris. Tel (01)
45444028, Fax (01) 45491750. Open:
by appointment only. Director:
Sylviane de Decker Heftler. Founded
1987. Artists: Robert Adams, John
Coplans, Patrick Feigenbaum, Jan
Groover, Marc Pataut, Rhona Bitner

Viviane Esders, 40 rue Pascal, F-75013
Paris. Tel (01) 43311010, Fax (01)
47076613. E-mail esders@club-
internet.fr. Open: by appointment
only. Director: Viviane Esders.
Founded 1979

**Centre Photographique d'Île de
France,** Hôtel de ville, F-77340 Pontault-Combault. Tel (01) 64434710,
Fax (01) 64434716. E-mail cpif@club-
internet.fr. Open: Tue–Sun 13–18.30.
Director: Sylvain Lizon. Founded
1989. 2 rooms, 350 m². 8 photo exhi-
bitions/year

Centre Culturel du Triangle, boulevard de Yougoslavie, F-35200 Rennes.

Tel (02) 99222727, Fax (02) 99222733.
Open: Tue–Sun 13.30–20. Director:
Christian Druart. Curator: Yvette Le
Gall. Founded 1985. 2 rooms, 300 m².
6 photo exhibitions/year. Artists:
Antonio Biasiucci, Didier Ben Loulou,
Lehnert & Landrock, Hélène Hour-
mat, Fabrice Picard, Jill Culliner,
Oliver Umhauer, Yvan Le Bosec,
Didier Petit

**Centre International d'Art Contem-
porain Château Beychevelle,** F-33250
Saint-Julien-Beychevelle. Tel (05)
56592346, Fax (05) 56590304. Open:
10–18 (Jul–Oct). Director: Brigitte
Huard. Founded 1990. 7 rooms,
560 m². 1 photo exhibition/year.
Artists: Shigeo Anzai, Keiichi Tahara,
Luis Gonzales-Palma, Marcel Odenbach, Maria Lugossy, Giuseppe Bergomi, José Hernandez, Erik Samakh,
Joris Heetman

Galerie du Forum, 18 rue de la Ré-
publique, F-31300 Toulouse. Tel (05)
61426347, Fax (05) 61307469. Open:
Mon–Sat 14–19. Director: Bernard
Verdier. Founded 1995. 1 room,
40 m². 7 photo exhibitions/year.
Artists: Jean Dieuzaide, V. Lorenzo,
C. Santoro, Jean-Paul Morro, Sylvie
Fontayne, Dominique Roux, Patrick
Le Bescont

Galerie Municipale du Château d'Eau,
1 place Laganne, F-31300 Toulouse.
Tel (05) 61770940, Fax (05) 61420270.
Open: Wed–Mon 13–19. Director:
Michel Dieuzaide. Curator: Laurence
Horiot. Founded 1974. 3 rooms,
250 m². 10 photo exhibitions/year.
Artists: Edouard Boubat, André
Kertész, William Klein, Brassaï, Ralph
Gibson, Jan Saudek, Josef Koudelka,
Lucien Clergue, Gisèle Freund

Galerie-Atelier de Photographie,
Espace Saint-Cyprien, 56 allées
Charles de Fitte, F-31300 Toulouse.

Tel (05) 61427575/61222777, Fax (05) 61223589. Open: 9–18. Director: Martine Michard. Founded 1987. 2 rooms, 120 m². 4 photo exhibitions/year. Artists: Lenni van Dinther, René Sultra, Maria Barthelemy, Gerd Bonfert, Eugene Bavcar, Vladimír Zidlicky, Arièle Bonzon, Biet & Vyain, Anne Montaut, François Saint-Pierre

Galerie Nadar, Médiathèque André Malraux, 26 rue Famelart/P. O. Box 599, F-59208 Tourcoing Cedex. Tel (03) 20250377, Fax (03) 20013951/20255159. Open: Tue+Fri 13–18.30, Wed+Thu 10–18.30, Sat 10–17.30. Director: Jean-Pierre Zanetti. Curator: Jean-Pierre Salomon. Founded 1988. 1 room, 150 m². 8 photo exhibitions/year

Gallery L'Aquarium, 8 rue Ferrand, F-59300 Valenciennes. Tel (03) 27225763, Fax (03) 27225760. Open: Tue–Sat 15–19. Director/curator: Antonio Guzman. Founded 1993. 1 room, 88 m². 2–3 photo exhibitions/year. Artists: Jeff Wall, Philippe Oudard, Olivier Richon, Lewis Baltz, Jean-Marc Bustamante, Candida Höfer, Ken Lum, Hannah Collins, Karen Knorr, Andreas Gursky

Galerie Robert Doisneau, Centre Culturel André Malraux, 1 place de l'Hôtel de Ville, F-54504 Vandœuvre-les-Nancy Cedex. Tel (03) 83561500, Fax (03) 83532185. Open: Mon–Sat 14–19. Director: Denis Cussenot. Founded 1986. 3 rooms, 350 m². 8 photo exhibitions/year. Artists: Arnaud Stines, Jean-Yves Camus, William Ropp, Eric Didym, Patrick Jacques, Claude Philippot, Florence Mouraux

Festivals & Fairs

Biarritz Terre d'Images, 79 bis, rue d'Espagne, F-64200 Biarritz. Tel (05) 59230882, Fax (05) 59235986

Biennale d'Art Contemporain, Maison de Lyon, place Bellecour, F-69002 Lyon. Tel (04) 72402626, Fax (04) 78382892

Biennale Internationale de l'Image, 20 rue Raymond Poincaré, F-54000 Nancy. Tel (03) 83271150, Fax (03) 83279348

Biennale Photographique, Centre Méditerranéen de la Photographie, P. O. Box 323, F-20279 Bastia Cedex. Tel (04) 95315608, Fax (04) 95315275

Bièvres-Foire à la Photographie, Photo Club du Val de Bièvres, 28 ter rue Gassendi, F-75014 Paris. Tel (01) 43221172

Cholet-Quinzaine de la Photographie, Groupe d'animation photographique de Cholet, 8 rue de Terves, F-49340 Nuaillé. Tel (02) 41464111

Découvertes, Parc des Expositions de Paris, Porte de Versailles, 62 rue de Miromesnil, F-75008 Paris. Tel (01) 49532700, Fax (01) 49532788

Festival de l'Image, 1 rue du Docteur Gallouédec, F-72000 Le Mans. Tel (02) 43241435

FIAC, Reed-OIP, 11 rue du Colonel Pierre Avia, F-75726 Paris Cedex 15. Tel (01) 41904747, Fax (01) 41904789

Image/Imatge, Rencontres audiovisuelles des régions sud, 7 avenue François Jammes, F-64300 Orthez. Tel (05) 59694112, Fax (05) 59694112

Images et Pages, salon du livre de photographies, Association Hélio,

123 rue d'Anvers, F-59200 Tourcoing.
Tel (03) 20263087

Journées de l'Image Professionnelle,
Mas du Soleil, Grand Draille, F-13990
Fontvieille

Journées Photographiques à Grignan,
Centre Vivant d'Art Contemporain,
Vieux Village, Grande rue, F-26230
Grignan. Tel (04) 75465555, Fax (04)
75469484

Le Printemps de la Photo, 125 rue
Fondu Haute, F-46000 Cahors. Tel
(05) 65353005, Fax (05) 65220732

L'Été Photographique de Lectoure,
Centre Photographique de Lectoure,
5 rue Claire, F-32700 Lectoure. Tel
(05) 62688372, Fax (05) 62688303

Mai Photographies, Association
l'œil quimperois, P. O. Box 219,
F-29101 Quimper Cedex. Tel (02)
98535347

Mois de la Photo à Paris, Maison
Européenne de la Photographie, 82
rue François Miron, F-75004 Paris.
Tel (01) 44787500, Fax (01) 44787515.
Website www.mep-fr.org

Mois de la Photographie, M. le Maire,
Hôtel de Ville, P. O. Box 68, F-21240
Talant. Tel (03) 80446024, Fax (03)
80446020

Montpellier Photovisions, Hôtel de
Varennes, 2 place Pétrarque, F-34000
Montpellier. Tel (04) 67604311, Fax
(04) 67604358

**Normandie-Rencontres Photographi-
ques,** 38 rue de Fontenelle, F-76000
Rouen. Tel (02) 35712436

**Rencontres Internationales de la
Photographie,** 10 Rond-Point des
Arènes, F-13632 Arles Cedex. Tel
(04) 90967606, Fax (04) 90499439

**Rencontres Photographiques en
Bretagne,** 11 bis, place Anatole-Le-
Braz, F-56100 Lorient

Rencontres Photographiques, Groupe
de Recherche et d'Animation Photographique, 86 rue de Verdun, F-11000
Carcassonne. Tel (04) 68252474

Rencontres Photographiques, Association L'Œil Écoute, 7 rue du Pont
Saint-Martial, F-87000 Limoges. Tel
(05) 55323078

Septembre de la Photo, 27 bd
Dubouchage, F-06300 Nice. Tel (04)
92049970, Fax (04) 92049980. E-mail
jean-pierre.giusto@ville-nice

**Théâtre de la Photographie et de
l'Image,** 27 bd Dubouchage, F-06300
Nice. Tel (04) 92049970, Fax (04)
92049980. E-mail jean-pierre.giusto@
ville-nice

Visa pour l'Image, Hôtel Pams, 18 rue
Emile Zola, F-66000 Perpignan. Tel
(05) 68359710, Fax (05) 68359709

Magazines

Art Press, 2 rue François Villon,
F-75015 Paris. Tel (01) 53686565,
Fax (01) 53686565. E-mail contact@
artpress.com. Website www.
artpress.com. Editor: Catherine
Millet. French/English. Founded
1972. Copy price: F 40.00. Annual
subscription: F 495.00 (France),
F 780.00 (Europe), 12 issues/year

Beaux-Arts, Publications Nuit et Jour,
33 avenue du Maine, F-75015 Paris.
Tel (01) 56541234, Fax (01) 45383001.
E-mail bamag@infonie.fr

Colors, 70 rue des Archives, F-75003
Paris. Tel (01) 44787900, Fax (01)
44787920. Editor: Carlos Mustienes

Connaissance des arts, 23 rue des Jeûners, F-75002 Paris. Tel (01) 44885500, Fax (01) 44885188. E-mail cda@cdesarts.com. Website www.utopix.ch/cda/. Editor: Philip Jodidio. French. Founded 1952. Copy price: F 50.00. Annual subscription: F 520.00, 11 issues/year

Études photographiques, Sociéte française de photographie, 71 rue de Richelieu, F-75002 Paris. Tel (01) 42600457, Fax (01) 42600457. E-mail etudes@photographie.com. Copy price: F 118.00. Annual subscription: F 216.00 (France), F 262.00 (Europe), 2 issues/year

Galeries Magazine, 88 rue Saint Martin, F-75004 Paris. Tel (01) 48878700, Fax (01) 48875303. Editors: Yves J. Hayat, Florette Camard. French/English. Founded 1985. Copy price: F 37.00. Annual subscription: F 250.00 (Europe), 6 issues/year

Journal des Arts, Publications Artistiques Françaises, 55–57 avenue d'Italie, F-75013 Paris. Tel (01) 56619500, Fax (01) 53940715. E-mail pub@artindex.tm.fr

Le Journal, Centre National de la Photographie, Hôtel Salomon de Rothschild, 11 rue Berryer, F-75008 Paris. Tel (01) 53761232, Fax (01) 53761233. E-mail centre.national.de.la.photographie@wanadoo.fr. Editor: Claire Jacquet. French. Founded 1997. Copy price: F 10.00. Annual subscription: F 40.00, 4 issues/year

L'Oeil, Publications Artistiques Françaises, 55–57 avenue d'Italie, F-75013 Paris. Tel (01) 56619500, Fax (01) 53940715. E-mail pub@artindex.tm.fr

Le Photographe, Le magazine des professionnels photo, vidéo numérique, 150 rue Galliéni, F-92100 Boulogne-Billancourt. Tel (01) 41861600, Fax (01) 41861690. Editor: Bernard Perrine. French. Founded 1910. Copy price: F 45.00. Annual subscription: F 530.00, 10 issues/year

Phot'Argus, Edition V. M., 116 boulevard Malesherbes, F-75017 Paris. Tel (01) 42272544, Fax (01) 47665714. Editor: Gérard Bouhot. French. Founded 1965. Annual subscription: F 320.00, 8 issues/year

Photo work, 126 rue des Trois-Epis, F-68230 Turckeim. Tel (03) 89272648, Fax (03) 89273727. Editor: Yannick Ansel. French. Founded 1978. Copy price: F 50.00. Annual subscription: F 200.00, 4 issues/year

Photo, 63 Champs-Elysées, F-75008 Paris. Tel (01) 41347327, Fax (01) 41347152. Editor: Eric Neveu. French. Founded 1967. Copy price: F 25.00. Annual subscription: F 200.00, 8 issues/year

Plages, 1762 rue du Vieux Pont de Sèvres, F-92100 Boulogne. Tel (01) 46083556, Fax (01) 46083556

Profession Photographe, Créer-Déclencher-Diffuser, 36 boulevard de la Bastille, F-75012 Paris. Tel (01) 43430737, Fax (01) 43078543. Website www.profession-photographe.com. Editor: Dominique Le Fur. French/English. Founded 1984. Copy price: F 25.00. Annual subscription: F 220.00, 3 issues/year

Revue Noire, 8 rue Cels, F-75014 Paris. Tel (01) 43209200, Fax (01) 43229260. E-mail renoir@club-internet.fr

Book Publishers

A. van Ginneken, St. Sulpice, P. O. Box 1, F-31410 Noe. Tel (05) 61872400, Fax (05) 61870630

Actes Sud, Le Méjan, 47 rue du Docteur Fanton, F-13200 Arles. Tel (04) 90498691, Fax (04) 90969525

Anatolia, 21 rue du Palais des Guilhems, F-34000 Montpellier. Tel (04) 67606040, Fax (04) 43547643

Booking International, 16 rue des Grands-Augustins, F-75006 Paris. Tel (01) 43542750, Fax (01) 43256492

Créaphis, Ecole des Filles, Le Village, F-26400 Grane. Tel (04) 75627489

Éditions Alain Sebe Images, 128 avenue Président Wilson, P. O. Box 37, F-83550 Vidauban. Tel (04) 94731280, Fax (04) 94735887

Éditions Assouline, 26 rue Danielle Casanova, F-75002 Paris. Tel (01) 42603384, Fax (01) 42603385. E-mail assouline@assouline.com. Website www.assouline.com

Éditions de la Martiniere, 27 rue Saint André des Arts, F-75006 Paris. Tel (01) 46330423, Fax (01) 46340027

Éditions Denoël, 9 rue du Cherche-Midi, F-75006 Paris. Tel (01) 43362728, Fax (01) 43366396

Éditions du Collectionneur, 53 rue Claude Bernard, F-75005 Paris

Éditions du Regard, 1 rue du Delta, F-75009 Paris. Tel (01) 53218680, Fax (01) 53218690

Éditions du Seuil, 27 rue Jacob, P. O. Box 80, F-75261 Paris Cedex 06. Tel (01) 40465050, Fax (01) 43290829

Éditions Hazan, 35–37 rue de Seine, F-75006 Paris. Tel (01) 44411700, Fax (01) 44411709

Editions Images en Manœuvres, Domaine de l'Observance, 2 place Francis-Chirat, F-13002 Marseille. Tel (04) 91917406, Fax (04) 91903085

Éditions Nathan, 9 rue Méchain, F-75676 Paris Cedex 14. Tel (01) 45875000, Fax (01) 43312169. E-mail brivero@nathan.fr

Éditions Pierre Belfond, 216 boulevard Saint-Germain, F-75007 Paris. Tel (01) 45443823, Fax (01) 45449804

Éditions V. M., 116 boulevard Malesherbes, F-75017 Paris

Fanlac, 12 rue Pr.-Peyrot, P. O. Box 2043, F-24002 Périgueux. Tel (05) 53534190, Fax (05) 53080585

Filigranes, Lec'h Geffroy, F-22140 Trézélan. Tel (02) 96453202, Fax (02) 96453691

FotoFolio, 36 rue Falguière, F-75015 Paris. Tel (01) 43214483, Fax (01) 43214503

Librairie Artheme Fayard, 75 rue des Saints Pères, F-75006 Paris. Tel (01) 45443845, Fax (01) 42224017

Lionel Hoebeke, 12 rue du Dragon, F-75006 Paris. Tel (01) 42228381, Fax (01) 45440496

Maeght, 12 rue Carvès , F-92100 Montrouge. Tel (01) 47468610, Fax (01) 47460532

Marval, 7 place St. Sulpice, F-75006 Paris. Tel (01) 43253333, Fax (01) 43258888. Website www.marval.com

Philippe Sers, 53 rue La Fayette, F-75009 Paris

Plume, 28 rue de Sévigné, F-75004 Paris. Tel (01) 40299609, Fax (01) 40299611

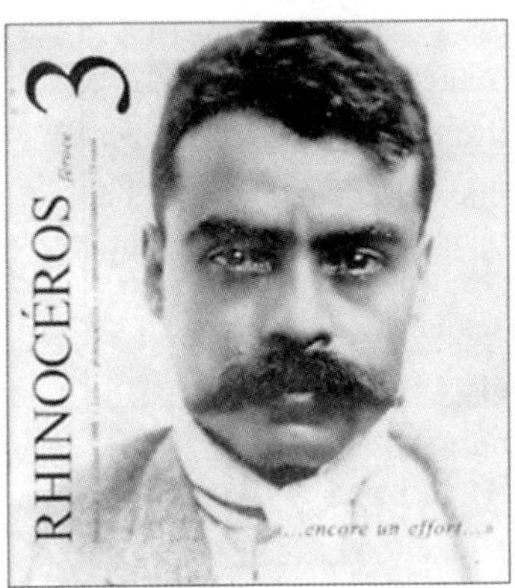

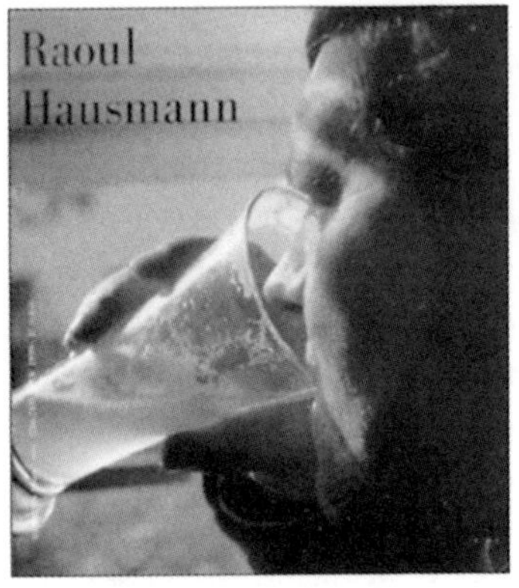

rhinocéros féroce
catalogue périodique de photographies et de livres rares (75 euros/an)

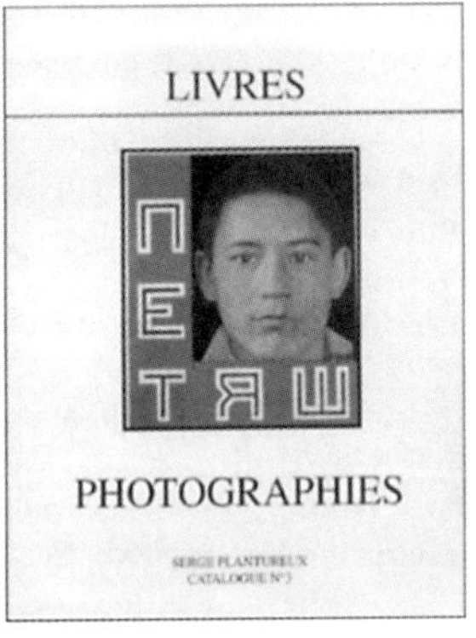

petites histoires de photographies
catalogue de 550 livres d'enfants illustrés de photographies (30 euros)

w w w . p a t r i m o i n e p h o t o g r a p h i q u e . f r

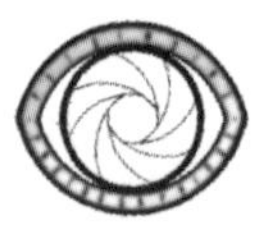

SERGE PLANTUREUX
61, rue du faubourg poissonnière 75009 Paris
tel (33).1.44.79.07.13   fax (33).1.44.79.08.19

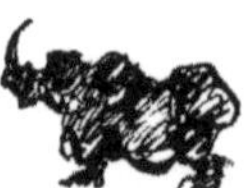

82 France

Bookshops

A l'Enseigne des Oudin, 58 rue Quincampoix, F-75004 Paris. Tel (01) 42718365, Fax (01) 42711538. E-mail oudin@club-internet.fr. Website www.pariserve.tm.fr

Comptoir de l'Image, 44 rue de Sévigne, F-75004 Paris

Fnac Etoile, 26, 30 avenue des Ternes, F-75017 Paris

Fnac Montparnasse, 136 rue de Rennes, F-76006 Paris

Gibert Joseph, 26 bd. St. Michel, F-75006 Paris

La Chambre Claire, 14 rue Saint-Sulpice, F-75006 Paris

La Hune, 170 bd. St. Germain, F-75006 Paris

Librairie Contacts, 24 rue du Colisée, F-75008 Paris

Librairie de la Maison Européenne de la Photographie, 5/7 rue de Fourcy, F-75004 Paris

Librairie du Centre Georges Pompidou, Plateau Beauborg, F-75191 Paris

Librairie Maupetit, 142 la Canebiere, F-13002 Marseille

Librairie Mollat, 15 rue Vital Carles, F-33000 Bordeaux

Photo Librairie, 49 avenue de Villiers, F-75017 Paris

Serge Plantureux – Livres anciens, 61 rue du faubourg Poissonnière, F-75009 Paris. Tel (01) 44790713, Fax (01) 44790819

Temps de Pose, 19 rue de la Rochefoucault, F-75009 Paris

Auctions

Etude Binoche, 5 rue la Boétie, F-75008 Paris. Tel (01) 47427801, Fax (01) 47428755

Etude Pescheteau-Badin, Godeau, Leroy, 16 rue de la Grange Bateliére, F-75009 Paris. Tel (01) 47708838, Fax (01) 48010445

Etude Tajan, 37 rue des Mathurins, F-75008 Paris. Tel (01) 53303030, Fax (01) 53303031

Galerie de Chartres, 1 bis, place du Géneral de Gaulle, F-28000 Chartres. Tel (02) 37840433, Fax (02) 37363471

Millon et Associe's, 19 rue de la Grange-Bataliére, F-75009 Paris. Tel (01) 48009944, Fax (01) 48009858

Olivier Coutau-Bégarie, 60 avenue de la Bourdonnais, F-75007 Paris. Tel (01) 45561220, Fax (01) 45557045

Viviane Esders/Esders Concept, 40 rue Pascal, F-75013 Paris. Tel (01) 43311010, Fax (01) 47076613. E-mail esders@club-internet.fr

Critics & Journalists

Jean Arrouye, 650 avenue de Mazenod, F-13100 Aix-en-Provence. Tel (04) 42210142, Fax (04) 42203359

Gabriel Bauret, 1 rue du Clos de Rame, Fontenay-Mauvoisin, F-78200 Mantes-la-Jolie. Tel (01) 34765286, Fax (01) 34765565

Pierre Borhan, 63 rue de Bretagne, F-75003 Paris. Tel (01) 42743060, Fax (01) 42743080

Christian Bouqueret, 21 rue Beaurepaire, F-75010 Paris. Tel (01) 40030273, Fax (01) 40030273

Alexandre Castant, 134 bis, avenue de Saint-Ouen, F-75018 Paris. Tel (01) 42263007, Fax (01) 44857619

Christian Caujolle, Agence Vu, 17 boulevard Henri IV, F-75004 Paris. Tel (01) 53018585, Fax (01) 53018580

Jean-François Chevrier, 28 rue des Gravilliers, F-75003 Paris. Tel (01) 42771954

Alain Dister, 9 rue Aristide Bruant, F-75018 Paris. Tel (01) 42237226, Fax (01) 42233763. E-mail disterphot@aol.com. *L'oel*, Paris; France Culture, Paris

Régis Durand, 27 ter boulevard Diderot, F-75012 Paris. Tel (01) 43403113. Director of Centre National de la Photographie, Paris; *Art Press*, Paris

Viviane Esders, 40 rue Pascal, F-75013 Paris. Tel (01) 43311010, Fax (01) 47076613. E-mail esders@club-internet.fr. *Architectural Digest*, Paris

Alain Fleig, 5 rue Berthollet, F-75005 Paris. Tel (01) 47075919

Michel Frizot, 53 rue de la Roquette, F-75011 Paris. Tel (01) 40213079

Christian Gattinoni, 9 rue de Laghouat, F-75018 Paris. Tel (01) 42593275, Fax (01) 53410885. E-mail chgattinoni@minitel.net. *Arts Croises*, Aix-en-Provence; *Exporevue.com*, France Culture, Paris

Jean-Claude Gautrand, 45 rue d'Avon, F-75020 Paris. Tel (01) 43721036

Michel Guerrin, 21 bis rue Claude-Bernard, F-75242 Paris Cedex 05. Tel (01) 42172000

Marion Kalter, 4 passage Sainte Avoye, F-75003 Paris. Tel (01) 48874374, Fax (01) 48876848. *European Photography*, Göttingen

Bernard Lamarche-Vadel, Château de la Rougère, F-53380 La Croixille. Tel (02) 43685713, Fax (02) 43685662

Hervé Le Goff, 127 rue Saint Denis, F-75001 Paris. Tel (01) 45080372

Jean-Claude Lemagny, 150 rue de Charonne, F-75011 Paris

Guy Mandéry, 16 rue des Orteaux, F-75020 Paris. Tel (01) 43567947

Dr. Günter Metken, 14 rue du Cardinal Lemoine, F-75005 Paris

Bernard Millet, Mission Departementale d'Action Culturelle, 15 rue Goyrand, F-13100 Aix-en-Provence. Tel (04) 42930367

Jean-Luc Monterosso, Maison Européenne de la Photographie, 82 rue François Miron, F-75004 Paris. Tel (01) 44787508. Director of Maison Européene de la Photographie, Paris

Gilles Mora, Lasclèdes, Brax, F-47310 La Plume. Tel (05) 53967828, Fax (05) 53982189

Claude Nori, 59 rue Froidevaux, F-75014 Paris. Tel (01) 43227057. *Contrejour*, Paris

Michel Nuridsany, 19 rue des Grands Augustins, F-75006 Paris. Tel (01) 43290439

Brigitte Ollier, Libération, 11 rue Béranger, F-75003 Paris. Tel (01) 42761752, Fax (01) 42721072

Robert Pujade, 24 avenue Sylvain Giraud, F-13510 Eguilles. Tel (04) 42926364

Patrick Remy, 22 place Charles Fillion, F-75017 Paris. Tel (01) 42632167, Fax (01) 53310482. E-mail patremy@club-internet.fr

Denis Roche, 87 rue de Reuilly, F-75012 Paris

Patrick Roegiers, 10 avenue Littré, F-94100 St. Maur. Tel (01) 48891740, Fax (01) 48894769

André Rouillé, 19 rue Levert, F-75020 Paris. Tel (01) 47971187, Fax (01) 43661707. E-mail rouille@map-prod. net. Website www.map-prod.net

Alain Sayag, Musée National d'Art Moderne, Centre Georges Pompidou, 19 rue Beaubourg, F-75191 Paris Cedex 04. Tel (01) 44781233, Fax (01) 44781208. Curator of Photography, Centre Georges Pompidou, Paris

Schools & Workshops

Atelier de Photographie, Espace Saint-Cyprien, 56 allées Charles de Fitte, F-31300 Toulouse. Tel (05) 61427575, Fax (05) 61223589

Centre de Formation des Techniques de Communications Visuelles, 5 rue René-Robin, F-94200 Ivry

Centre de Formation Technologique de la Chambre de Commerce et d'Industrie de Paris "Les Gobelins", 73 boulevard Saint-Marcel, F-75013 Paris. Tel (01) 47077482

Centre d'étude et de Recherche de l'Image et du Son, 82 rue François Rolland, F-94310 Nogent-sur-Marne

Cours Professionels de la Chambre des Métiers, 42 rue Bassano, F-75008 Paris. Tel (01) 47208520

École de Photographie de Paris, Icart-Photo, 10 rue Baudin, F-92300 Levallois-Perret. Tel (01) 47480010, Fax (01) 47581331

École des Arts de Valenciennes, 8 rue Ferrand, F-59300 Valenciennes. Tel (03) 27225759, Fax (03) 27225760

École Française d'Enseignement Technique, 110 rue de Picpus, F-75012 Paris. Tel (01) 43468696, Fax (01) 43410393

École Louis Lumière, 8 rue Rollin, F-75005 Paris

École Municipale des Beaux-Arts de Metz, 1 rue de la Citadelle, F-57000 Metz. Tel (03) 87755778, Fax (03) 87750616

École Municipale des Beaux-Arts d'Orléans, 2 rue de la Bibliothèque, F-45000 Orléans

École Municipale des Beaux-Arts, F-13009 Lumigny-Marseille

École Nationale de la Photographie, 16 rue des Arènes, P. O. Box 149, F-13200 Arles. Tel (04) 90993333, Fax (04) 90993359. E-mail comm. enp@provnet.fr. Website www. provnet.fr/users/enp

École Nationale des Arts Décoratifs de Nice, 20 rue Stéphane Liegard, F-06000 Nice

École Nationale Supérieure des Arts Décoratifs, 31 rue d'Ulm, F-75005 Paris

École Nationale Supérieure Estienne, 18 boulevard Auguste-Blanqui, F-75013 Paris

École Nationale Supérieure Louis Lumière, 7 allée du Promontoire, P. O. Box 22, F-93161 Noisy-le-Grand Cedex. Tel (01) 48154010, Fax (01) 43056344. E-mail llumiere@ imaginet.fr

École Supérieure d'Arts Graphiques, 31 rue du Dragon, F-75006 Paris

École Technique Privée de la Photographie et de l'Audiovisuel, 7 rue Eugène Labiche, F-31200 Toulouse. Tel (05) 34401200, Fax (05) 34401201.

E-mail ecole@etpa-toulouse.com.
Website www.etpa-toulouse.com

Image Ouverte, 4 chemin des Carteyrades, F-30870 Clarensac. Tel (04) 66814585, Fax (04) 66815920

Speos, Paris Photographic Institut, 8 rue Jules Vallés, F-75011 Paris. Tel (01) 40091858, Fax (01) 40098497. E-mail pymahe@speos.fr. Website www.speos.fr

Université Paris VIII, Département Image photographique, 2 rue de la Liberté, F-93526 Saint-Denis Cedex. Tel (01) 49406615, Fax (01) 49406532. E-mail photo-mmedia@univ-paris8.fr

Associations

A.R.P.A., 17 rue de Candale, F-33000 Bordeaux. Tel (05) 56918812

Art & Recherche, Association 1901, 8 rue Ferrand, F-59300 Valenciennes. Tel (03) 27225763, Fax (03) 27225760

Association Photographique Contemporaine en Bretagne, Centre Culturel du Triangle, boulevard de Yougoslavie, P. O. Box 22036, F-35022 Rennes Cedex. Tel (02) 99530192, Fax (02) 99508085

Association Regionale de Diffusion de l'Image, Photographie en Région Basse-Normandie, 4 place F. Mitterrand, F-14200 Herouville, Saint Clair. Tel (02) 31951740, Fax (02) 31951740. E-mail ardiphot@cybercable.fr. Website www.herouville.net/ardi

Centre d'Action Culturelle Théâtre de la Ville, P. O. Box 509, F-15005 Aurillac Cedex. Tel (04) 71483014

Centre Photographique d'Ile de France, Ferme Briarde, Hôtel de Ville, 107 avenue de la République, F-77340

Pontault-Combault. Tel (01) 64434741, Fax (01) 64434716

Foire Internationale d'Art Contemporain, 62 rue de Miromesnil, F-75008 Paris. Tel (01) 49532700, Fax (01) 49532786

Fondation Cartier pour l'art contemporain, 261 boulevard Raspail, F-75014 Paris. Tel (01) 42185650, Fax (01) 42185652. Website www. fondation.cartier.fr

Forum de l'Image, 6 avenue Albert-Durand, F-31706 Blagnac Cedex. Tel (05) 61307298, Fax (05) 61307469

Gens d'Images, Association des Gens d'Images, Secrétariat Général , P. O. Box 37, F-75014 Paris

Groupe d'Animation Photographique de Cholet, 8 rue de Terves Nuaillé, F-49340 Trementines. Tel (02) 41620061

Hélio, 123 rue d'Anvers, F-59200 Tourcoing. Tel (03) 20263087

Image/Imatge, 7 avenue F. Jammes, F-64300 Orthez. Tel (05) 59694112, Fax (05) 59694112

L'Oeil Écoute, 7 rue du Pont Saint-Martial, F-87000 Limoges. Tel (05) 55323078

L'Oeil Quimpérois, 21 rue Pen Ar Steir, P. O. Box 1103, F-29101 Quimper Cedex. Tel (02) 98953397, Fax (02) 98535347

Metz pour la Photographie, 9 rue des Trinitaires, F-57000 Metz. Tel (03) 87754540

Montpellier Photovisions, Hôtel de Varennes, 2 place Pétrarque, F-34000 Montpellier. Tel (04) 67604311, Fax (04) 67604358

Patrimoine Photographique, 19 rue Réaumur, F-75003 Paris. Tel (01)

42743060, Fax (01) 42743080. E-mail patrimoine-photo@patrimoine-photo.org. Website www.patrimoine-photo.org

Photo Club 30 x 40, Centre International de Séjour, 6 avenue Maurice Ravel, F-75012 Paris

Photographies and Co, Ancien Presbytère, Le Village, Sausseuzemare en Caux, F-76110 Le Havre-Goderville. Tel (02) 35271778, Fax (02) 35271778

Priorité Ouverture, 9 rue Thiers, F-51100 Reims. Tel (03) 26402223, Fax (03) 26400825

Sellit 150, 11 bis, place Anatole la Braz, F-56100 Lorient. Tel (02) 97211802

SIRP, Palais de Congrés, P. O. Box 102, F-17206 Royan. Tel (05) 46385201, Fax (05) 46239591

Société de la Propriété Artistique et des Dessins, et Modèles (SPADEM), 12 rue Henner, F-75009 Paris

Société Française de Photographie, Bibliothèque Nationale de France, 4 rue Vivienne, F-75002 Paris. Tel (01) 42600598, Fax (01) 42600457. E-mail sfp@wanadoo.fr. Website www.sfp.photographie.com, www.etudes-photographie.com

UMMAF, 27 rue de l'Université, F-75007 Paris

Vienne la Photographie, Galerie 74, 16 rue Teste du Bailler, F-38200 Vienne. Tel (04) 74315568

Grants & Awards

Académie de France à Rome/Villa Médicis, Centre National des Arts Plastiques, Délégation aux Arts Plastiques, 27 avenue de l'Opéra,

F-75001 Paris. Tel (01) 40157300, Fax (01) 40157414

Fondation CCF pour la Photographie, 103 avenue des Champs Elysées, F-75419 Paris Cedex 08. Tel (01) 40702713, Fax (01) 40707353

Grand Prix Scam du Portfolio Photographique, F 20,000, every year. Contact: Scam Hôtel de Massa, 38 faubourg Saint-Jacques, F-75014 Paris. Tel (01) 40513330, Fax (01) 44072997. E-mail sjoseph@scam.fr

Kodak Prize of the Photographic Critique, to recognize young professional photographers of French nationality or residency, recommendation necessary, every year. Contact: Kodak Pathé, 26 rue Villiot, F-75594 Paris Cedex 12. Tel (01) 40013000, Fax (01) 40013323

Prix Henri Vincenot de la Photographie, photographs taken in or dealing with the Bourgogne, F 15,000, exhibition and catalog. Contact: Mairie de Talant, P. O. Box 68, F-21240 Talant. Tel (03) 80446024, Fax (03) 80446020

Prix Niépce, for photographers in mid-career, age 45 and over, F 70,000, every year. Contact: Prix Niépce, Gens d'images, Nathalie Bocher-Lenoir, 21 rue du Montparnasse, F-75283 Paris Cedex 06. Tel (01) 44394346, Fax (01) 44394448

Villa Médicis Hors les Murs, Ministère des Affaires Etrangères, AFAA, 1 bis avenue de Villars, F-75007 Paris. Tel (01) 53698300, Fax (01) 53693300

New Media

A Bao A Qou, 13 Villa Eugène Leblanc, F-75019 Paris. Tel (01) 40334992, Fax (01) 40334992.

APA Art Video Danse, Geneviève Charras, 6 rue Sédillot, F-67000 Strasbourg. Tel (03) 88370703, Fax (03) 88777375

Arcanal, Reine Prat, 92 avenue Kleber, F-75116 Paris. Tel (01) 47273060, Fax (01) 47048651

Centre Audiovisuel Simone de Beauvoir, Claudine Delvaux, 2 rue de la Manutention, F-75116 Paris. Tel (01) 47236748, Fax (01) 47236749

Centre de Recherche Pierre Schaeffer, Pierre Bongiovanni, P. O. Box 5, F-25310 Hérimoncourt. Tel (03) 81309030, Fax (03) 81309525. E-mail eric@cicv.fr. Website www.cicv.fr

Centre Georges Pompidou/Musée National d'Art Moderne, Christine van Assche, F-75197 Paris Cedex 04. Tel (01) 44781233

Festival Cinema/Video de Lyon, Musée d'Art Contemporain de Lyon, 81 Cité internationale, quai Charles de Gaulle, F-69463 Lyon cedex 06. Tel (04) 72691717, Fax (04) 72691700. E-mail info@moca-lyon.org

Heure Exquise!, Le Fort, cour sud, avenue de Normandie, P. O. Box 113, F-59370 Mons-en-Barcoeul. Tel (03) 20432432, Fax (03) 20432433. E-mail exquise@nordnet.fr. Website www.altern.org/heureexquise

Institut National de l'Audiovisuel, Philippe Queau, 4 avenue de l' Europe, F-94360 Bry sur Marne. Tel (01) 49822000, Fax (01) 49832582

Les dérives magnétiques, Rendez-vous annuel autor des nouvelles technologies et de l'image en mouvement, Le Mas Babas, F-30190 Sainte-Anastasie. Tel (04) 66810276/ 67605982, Fax (04) 66631664. E-mail rezo@mnet.fr. Website www.mnet.fr/lemas

Rencontres Arts Electroniques, Festival for Experimental Underground Film and Video Art, Station Arts electroniques, Université Rennes 2, 6 avenue Gaston Berger, F-35043 Rennes cedex. E-mail station@uhb.fr. Website www.uhb.fr/culture/station/Welcome.html

Rencontres Internationales Art Cinema/Art Video, Triennial international event of symposia, projections, 71 rue Leblanc, F-75015 Paris. Tel (01) 44260873, Fax (01) 40600716

Rencontres Vidéos Arts Plastiques, Centre d'art contemporain de Basse-Normandie, 7 passage de la Poste, P. O. Box 59, F-14203 Hérouville Saint-Clair cedex. Tel (02) 31955087, Fax (02) 31953760. E-mail wharf@cybercable.tm.fr

Vidéoformes, Festival International d'art vidéo et multimedia & expositions, P. O. Box 71, F-63003 Clermont-Ferrand Cedex 1. Tel (04) 73170217, Fax (04) 73930545. E-mail videoformes@nat.fr. Website www.nat.fr/videoformes

Germany

Population: 82 million
Capital: Berlin, 3.4 million
Currency: Mark (DM)
International code: ++49
Tourist information:
Deutscher Tourismusverband
e. V., Bertha-von-Suttner-
Platz 13, D-53111 Bonn
Tel (0228) 98 52 20,
Fax (0228) 69 87 22

Galleries & Museums

Ludwig Forum für internationale Kunst, Jülicher Str. 97–109, D-52058 Aachen. Tel (0241) 1807104, Fax (0241) 1807101. Open: Tue+Thu 10–17, Wed+Fri 10–20, Sat–Sun 11–17. Director: Wolfgang Becker. Founded 1991. 13 rooms, 6,000 m². 3 photo exhibitions/year

Suermondt-Ludwig-Museum, Studio, Wilhelmstr. 18, D-52070 Aachen. Tel (0241) 479800, Fax (0241) 37075. Open: Tue–Fri 11–19 (Wed –21), Sat–Sun 11–17. Director: Dr. Ulrich Schneider. Curator: Sylvia Böhmer. Founded 1877/1994. 2 rooms (for photography), 77 m². 5–6 photo exhibitions/year. Artists: Albert Renger-Patzsch, Florence Henri, Ilse Bing, Erich Lessing, Louis Stettner, Lotte Jacobi, Dorothea Lange, Grete Stern, Chargesheimer

Kunsthaus Apolda Avantgarde, Bahnhofstr. 42, D-99510 Apolda. Tel (03644) 562480, Fax (03644) 562480.

Open: Tue–Sun 10–18 (also on bank holidays)

Photo-Galerie Altstadt, Hunoldsgraben 36, D-86150 Augsburg. Tel (0821) 515763. Open: Mon–Fri 16.30–18.30, Sat 11–13. Director: Ilona Pitschel. Founded 1990. 1 room, 20 m². 3 photo exhibitions/year

Staatliche Kunsthalle Baden-Baden, Lichtentaler Allee 8a, D-76530 Baden-Baden. Tel (07221) 300763, Fax (07221) 38590. E-mail kunsthalle.baden-baden@t-online.de. Open: Tue–Sun 11–18 (Wed –20). Director: Matthias Winzen. Founded 1909. 11 rooms, 650 m². 3 photo exhibitions/year. Artists: Thomas Ruff, Mette Tronvoll, Robert Lebeck

Bauhaus-Archiv, Museum für Gestaltung, Klingelhöferstr. 14, D-10785 Berlin. Tel (030) 2540020, Fax (030) 25400210. E-mail bauhaus@bauhaus.de. Website www.bauhaus.de. Open: Wed–Mon 10–17. Director: Dr. Peter Hahn. Curator: Sabine Hartmann. Founded 1960. 2 rooms, 1,000 m². 2 photo exhibitions/year. Artists: Lucia Moholy, Umbo

Berlinische Galerie, Museum für moderne Kunst, Photographie und Architektur, Stresemannstr. 110, Martin-Gropius-Bau, D-10963 Berlin. Tel (030) 43095342, Fax (030) 43095319. E-mail berlinischegalerie@t-online.de. Website www.berlinischegalerie.de. Director: Prof. Jörn Merkert. Curators: Janos Frecot, Ulrich Domröse. Founded 1979. 1,800 m²

Busche Galerie, Bundesallee 32, D-10717 Berlin. Tel (030) 88424676, Fax (030) 88424677. Open: Tue–Fri 13–18.30, Sat 11–14. Director/curator: Dr. Ernst A. Busche. Founded 1989. 1–2 photo exhibitions/year. Artists:

Dieter Hacker, Boris Becker, Beat Streuli

Cafe Aroma Photogalerie, Hochkirchstr. 8, D-10829 Berlin. Tel (030) 7825821, Fax (030) 6927458. Open: 16–2. Director: Gino Puddu. Founded 1987. 3 rooms, 100 m². 4 photo exhibitions/year. Artists: Fran Wolffram, Frank David, Paolo Primiero, Roland Albrecht

Das Verborgene Museum, Schlüterstr. 70, D-10625 Berlin. Tel (030) 3133656. Open: Thu–Fri 15–19, Sat–Sun 12–16. Director: Marion Beckers. Founded 1986. 2 rooms, 50 m². 1 photo exhibition/year. Artists: Marianne Breslauer, Lotte Jacobi, Eva Besnyö, Else Thalemann, Gertrud Arndt, Gerda Leo, Gerta Taro, Ré Soupault, Ursula Arnold, Yva (Else Simon)

Fotogalerie, Kommunale Galerie Friedrichshain, Helsingforser Platz 1, D-10243 Berlin. Tel (030) 2961684. Open: Tue–Sat 13–18, Thu 10–18. Director: Renate Haenel. Founded 1985. 4 rooms, 135 m². 7–8 photo exhibitions/year. Artist: Jan Reich

Galerie argus fotokunst, Marienstr. 9, D-10117 Berlin. Tel (030) 2835901, Fax (030) 2833049. E-mail argusberlin@ gmx.de. Open: Wed–Sun 14–18. Director/curator: Norbert Bunge. Founded 1996. 3 rooms, 80 m². 6 photo exhibitions/year. Artists: Ursula Arnold, René Burri, Christian Borchert, Uwe Steinberg, Clemens Kalischer, Arno Fischer, Max Jacoby, Will McBride, Eva Kemlein, Antanas Sutkus

Galerie Barbara Thumm, Dircksenstr. 41, D-10178 Berlin. Tel (030) 28390347, Fax (030) 28390457. E-mail b.thumm@ berlin.snafu.de. Website www. bthumm.de. Open: Tue–Fri 13–19, Sat 13–18. Director: Barbara Thumm.

Founded 1998. 1 room, 140 m². 2 photo exhibitions/year. Artists: Fiona Banner, Daniela Brahm, Twin Gabriel, Teresa Hubbard & Alexander Birchler, Sabine Honig, Mariele Neudecker, Heidi Specker, Bridget Smith

Galerie Berinson, Auguststr. 22, D-10117 Berlin. Tel (030) 28387990, Fax (030) 28387999. Open: Tue–Sat 15–19. 1 room. Artists: Hans Bellmer, Weegee

Galerie Camera Work, Atelierhaus, Kantstr. 149, D-10623 Berlin. Tel (030) 31504783, Fax (030) 31504784. E-mail info@camerawork.de. Website www. camerawork.de. Open: Tue–Fri 10–19, Sat 10–14. Directors: Christian Diener, Gerd Elfering. Artists: Irving Penn, Richard Avedon, Peter Beard, Helmut Newton, Horst P. Horst, André Kertész

Galerie Eigen+Art, Auguststr. 26, D-10117 Berlin. Tel (030) 2806605, Fax (030) 2806616. E-mail eigen.art@ berlin.snafu.de. Website www.eigen-art.de. Open: Tue–Sat 11–18. Director: Gerd Harry Lybke. Founded 1983. 2 rooms, 100 m². 2 photo exhibitions/year. Artists: Christiane Borland, Birgit Brenner, Nina Fischer/Maroan El Sani, Christine Hill, Jörg Herold, Rémy Markowitsch, Maix Mayer, Yana Milev, Olaf Nicolai, Annelies Štrba

Galerie Eva Poll, Lützowplatz 7, D-10785 Berlin. Tel (030) 2617091, Fax (030) 2617092. E-mail galerie@poll-berlin.de. Website www. germangalleries.com/poll. Open: Mon 10–13, Tue–Fri 11–18.30, Sat 11–15. Director: Eva Poll. Founded 1968. 6 rooms, 350 m². 1 photo exhibition/year. Artists: Gundula Schulze el Dowy, Michael Ruetz, Maxim Kantor, Harald Duwe, G. L. Gabriel, Volker Stelzmann, Christine

Jackob-Marks, Ulrich Baehr, Hans
Scheib

Galerie Françoise Knabe, Thomas-
Dehler-Str. 3, D-10787 Berlin. Tel
(030) 2624812, Fax (030) 2624812.
E-mail galerie.knabe@t-online.de.
Open: Tue–Fri 10–19, Sat 10–15.
Director: Françoise Knabe. Founded
1989. 4 rooms, 80 m². 4 photo exhi-
bitions/year. Artists: Peter Badge,
John Duncan, David Farrell, Gudrun
Kemsa, Natacha Lesueur, Julien
Maire, Laura Padgett, Frank van
der Salm, Olivier Richon, Paul
Seawright

Galerie Lichtbilder, Kulturamt Mitte,
Weinmeisterstr. 8, D-10178 Berlin.
Tel (030) 2817332, Fax (030) 2817332.
E-mail scheune@macht.de. Web-
site www.galerie.de/am-
scheunenviertel. Open: Tue–Fri 15–
19, Sat 15–18. Director/curator:
Tanja Hofmann. Founded 1987. 3
rooms, 116 m². 12 photo exhibitions/
year. Artists: Florian von Ploetz,
Oliver Möst, Jan Mende, Christian
Stöger, Andreas Neumann, Jörg
Janzer, Gudrun Brückel, Beate
Honsell-Weiss, Helmut-Ulrich Weiss

Galerie Rudolf Kicken, Linienstr. 155,
D-10115 Berlin. Tel (030) 28877882,
Fax (030) 28877883. E-mail kicken@
kicken-gallery.com. Website www.
kicken-gallery.com. Open: Tue–Sun
11–18. Directors: Rudolf Kicken,
Anette Kicken. Founded 1972.
Artists: Dieter Appelt, Helmut
Newton, László Moholy-Nagy,
Man Ray, Albert Renger-Patzsch,
Alexander Rodtschenko, August
Sander, Anna & Bernhard Blume,
Klaus Rinke, Albert Watson

Galerie Tammen & Busch, Fidicin-
str. 40, D-10965 Berlin. Tel (030)
69401227, Fax (030) 88835601. E-mail
bbusch@berlin.schafu.de. Website

www.tammen-busch.de. Open:
Tue–Fri 13–18, Sat 11–14, Sun 15–18.
Directors: Bernd Busch, Werner
Tammen. Curator: Jacqueline Rugo.
Founded 1991. 2 rooms, 300 m².
2 photo exhibitions/year. Artists:
Bernd Borcherdt, Kain Karawahn

Galerie Wohnmaschine, Tucholskystr.
36, D-10117 Berlin. Tel (030) 30872015,
Fax (030) 30872016. E-mail info@
wohnmasche.de. Website www.
wohnmaschine.de. Open: Tue–Fri
14–19, Sat 11–17. Director: Friedrich
Loock. Founded 1988. 2–5 photo
exhibitions/year. Artists: Thorsten
Goldberg, Anton Henning, York der
Knöfel, Peter Moors, Robert Lippok,
Florian Merkel, Andreas Rost, Joerg
Waehner, Gunda Förster, Maya Roos

Georg-Kolbe-Museum, Sensburger
Allee 25, D-14055 Berlin. Tel (030)
3042144, Fax (030) 3047041. E-mail
kolbe.museum@t-online.de. Website
www.georg-kolbe-museum.de.
Open: Tue–Sun 10–17. Director: Dr.
Ursel Berger. Founded 1950. 1 photo
exhibition/year

Giedre Bartelt Galerie, Wielandstr.
31, D-10629 Berlin. Tel (030) 8852086,
Fax (030) 8852086. E-mail giedre.
bartelt@t-online.de. Website www.
home.t-online.de/home/giedre.
bartelt. Open: Tue–Fri 14–18.30, Sat
11–14 and by appointment. Director/
curator: Giedre Bartelt. Founded
1996. 2 rooms, 55 m². 1–4 photo
exhibitions/year. Artists: Violeta
Bubelyte, Alvydas Lukys, Torsten
Warmuth, Maggy Drolshagen

Golem Photo Art, International
Gallery, Nehringstr. 29, D-14059
Berlin. Tel (030) 32102552, Fax (030)
3224969. E-mail jovester@t-online.de.
Open: Mon–Fri 17–20 and by
appointment. Contact: Johannes
Vester. Founded 2000. 1 room, 55 m².

3–4 photo exhibitions/year. Artists: Vjatscheslaw Livanow, Honorata, Johannes Vester

Haus am Waldsee, Argentinische Allee 30, D-14163 Berlin. Tel (030) 8018935, Fax (030) 8022028. Website www.hausamwaldsee-berlin.de. Open: Tue–Sun 12–20. Director: Barbara Straka. Founded 1946. 12 rooms, 400 m². 1–2 photo exhibitions/year

Haus der Kulturen der Welt, John-Foster-Dulles-Allee 10, D-10557 Berlin. Tel (030) 397870, Fax (030) 3948679. Open: 10–20. Director: Hans-Georg Knopp. Curator: Alfons Hug. Founded 1989. 2 rooms, 1,000 m². 4 photo exhibitions/year. Artists: Frank Darius, Michael Friedel, Obie Oberholzer, Manuel Alvarez Bravo, Bouna Medoune Seye, Santu Mofokeng, Rogelio Lopez Cuenca, Touhami Ennadre

IfA-Galerie, Neustädtische Kirchstrasse 15, D-10117 Berlin. Tel (030) 226796-16/17, Fax (030) 22679618. E-mail barsch@ifa.de. Website www.ifa.de. Open: Tue–Sun, 14–19

KMZA – Kunst- und Medienzentrum Adlershof, Dörpfelderstr. 56, D-12489 Berlin. Tel (030) 67776811, Fax (030) 67776812. E-mail longest@longest.de. Website www.kmza.de. Open: Mon, Thu–Fri 11–19, Tue 11–17, Sun 14–19. Director/curator: Longest F. Stein. Founded 1998. 7 rooms, 400 m². 4–5 photo exhibitions/year. Artists: Bernd Borchardt, Tina Bara, Kurt Buchwald, Miron Zownir, Maria Sewcz, Martin Zeller, Matthias Hoch, Bertram Kober

Künstlerhaus Bethanien, Mariannenplatz 2, D-10997 Berlin. Tel (030) 6169030, Fax (030) 61690330. E-mail kb@bethanien.de. Website www.bethanien.de. Open: Wed–Sun 14–19. Director: Christoph Tannert. Founded 1974. 3 rooms, 900 m². Artists: Christina Glidden, Maria Hedlund, Won Ju Lim, Ine Lawers, Wouter van Riessen, Sarah Morris, Louise Paramor, Peter Robinson, Noé Sendas, Mette Tronvoll

Kunstraum im BDI, Bundesverband der Deutschen Industrie e. V., Haus der Deutschen Wirtschaft, Breite Str. 29/2. OG., D-10178 Berlin. Tel (030) 20281406, Fax (030) 20282406. E-mail kulturkreis@bdi-online.de

Neue Gesellschaft für Bildende Kunst e. V., Oranienstr. 25, D-10999 Berlin. Tel (030) 6153031, Fax (030) 6152290. E-mail ngbk@snafu.de. Website www.snafu.de/~ngbk. Open: 12–18.30. Director: Leonie Baumann. Founded 1969. 1 room, 300 m². 3 photo exhibitions/year

Neue Nationalgalerie, Potsdamer Str. 50, D-10785 Berlin. Tel (030) 2660, Fax (030) 2624715. Open: Tue–Fri 9–17, Sat–Sun 10–17. Director: Dr. Britta Schmitz. Founded 1968. 14 rooms, 6,092 m². 1 photo exhibition/year. Artists: Thomas Ruff, Dieter Appelt, Bernhard & Anna Blume, Klaus Rinke

Neuer Berliner Kunstverein, Chausseestr. 128–129, D-10115 Berlin. Tel (030) 2807020, Fax (030) 2807019. E-mail nbk@nbk.org. Website www.nbk.org. Open: Tue–Fri 12–18, Sat–Sun 12–16. Director/curator: Dr. Alexander Tolnay. Founded 1969. 2 rooms, 300 m². 1–2 photo exhibitions/year

Photography Now, Invalidenstr. 115, D-10115 Berlin. Tel (0170) 2819702. E-mail photography.now@t-online.de. Director: Claudia Stein. Founded 1998

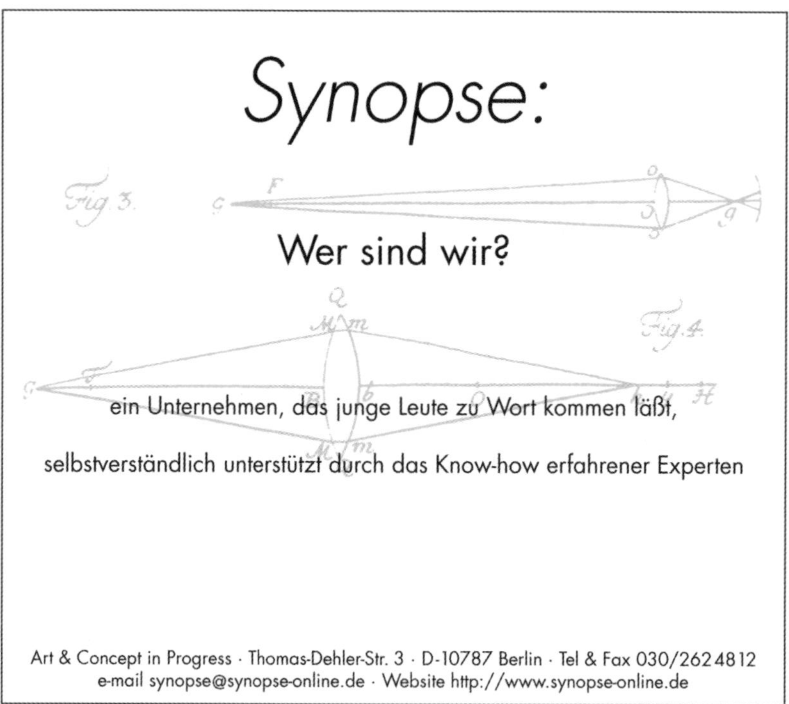

Picture Perfect, Auguststr. 19, D-10117 Berlin. Tel (030) 28387883, Fax (030) 28387885. Open: Wed–Fri 13–18, Sat 12–18. 3 rooms, 150 m². Director: Elke Niemann. Founded 2000. Artists: Hugo Erfurth, Trude Fleischmann, Wilhelm von Gloeden, Lehnert & Landrock, Max Krajewsky, Germaine Krull, Gerhard Riebicke, Sasha Stone, Herbert Tobias, Yva (Else Simon)

Raab Galerie, Potsdamer Str. 58, D-10785 Berlin. Tel (030) 26192-17/18, Fax (030) 2629217. E-mail raab-galerie@bln.de. Website www.germangalleries.com/raab. Open: Mon–Fri 10–19, Sat 10–16. Director: Ingrid Raab. Founded 1978. 2 rooms, 1,300 m². 2–3 photo exhibitions/year. Artists: Rainer Fetting, Luciano Castelli, K.-H. Hödicke, Pierre & Gilles, Timur Novikov, Karl Lager-feld, Dead Chickens, Albrecht Kunkel, Peter Chevaillier, Elvira Bach

Schwules Museum, Mehringdamm 61, Gartenhaus Parterre, D-10961 Berlin. Tel (030) 6931172, Fax (030) 6934037. Open: Wed–Sun 14–18 (Thu –21). Directors/curators: Andreas Sternweiler, Wolfgang Theis. Founded 1985. 2 rooms, 180 m². 2 photo exhibitions/year. Artist: Ingo Taubhorn

Staatliche Museen zu Berlin, Hamburger Bahnhof, Invalidenstr. 50–51, D-10557 Berlin. Tel (030) 3978340, Fax (030) 39783413. E-mail aussenamt@smb.spk-berlin.de. Website www.smb.spk-berlin.de/d/. Open: Tue–Fri 10–18, Sat–Sun 11–18. Director: Prof. Dr. Peter Klaus Schuster. Founded 1996. 23 rooms, 9,000 m²

Staatliche Museen zu Berlin, Kunst-bibliothek, Matthäikirchplatz 6, D-10785 Berlin. Tel (030) 2662028, Fax (030) 2662958. E-mail aussenamt@ smb.spk-berlin.de. Website www. smb.spk-berlin.de/d/. Open: Tue–Fri 10–18, Sat–Sun 11–18. Director: Prof. Peter Klaus Schuster. Curator: Christine Kühn. Founded 1867. 1 room, 285 m². 1–2 photo exhibitions/year. Artists: Ernst Juhl, Fritz Matthies-Masuren, László Moholy-Nagy, Albert Renger-Patzsch, Helmar Lerski, Thomas Florschuetz, Dieter Appelt, Max Burchartz

Synopse, Art Consulting, Thomas-Dehler-Str. 3, D-10787 Berlin. Tel (030) 2624812, Fax (030) 2624812. E-mail info@synopse-onlinde.de. Website www.synopse-online.de. Open: by appointment only. Directors: Françoise Knabe, Peter Badge. Founded 2000. 1 room, 80 m²

Tschechisches Zentrum, Leipziger Str. 60, D-10117 Berlin. Tel (030) 2082592, Fax (030) 2044415. E-mail mehnert@ berlin.czech.cz. Website www.czech. cz. Open: Mon–Fri 13–18. Director: Jan Bondy. Curator: Simona Mehnert. 3 rooms, 150 m². 2–3 photo exhibitions/year. Artists: Josef Sudek, Václav Jirásek, František Drtikol, Jaroslav Rössler, Jaromír Funke, Eugen Wiškovský, Jindrich Marco, Václav Chochola, Karel Ludwig

Zellermayer Galerie, Ludwigkirchstr. 6/Ecke Uhlandstr. 46, D-10719 Berlin. Tel (030) 8834144, Fax (030) 8837316. Open: Tue–Fri 12–18, Sat 11–14. Director/curator: Carsta Zellermayer. Founded 1975. 2 rooms, 140 m². 1–2 photo exhibitions/year. Artists: Hans Pieler, Martin Zeller

Kunsthalle Bielefeld, Artur-Ladebeck-Str. 5, D-33602 Bielefeld. Tel (0521) 5124-79/80, Fax (0521) 513429. Open: Tue–Fri 11–18 (Wed –21), Sat 10–18. Director: Dr. Thomas Kellein. Curator: Dr. Jutta Hülsewig-Johnen. Founded 1968. 8 rooms, 600 m². 1–2 photo exhibitions/year. Artists: Jürgen Klauke, Jack Sal, Gottfried Jäger, A. T. Schaefer, Carl Strüwe

Lutz Teutloff Galerie, Weißenburger Str. 25, D-33607 Bielefeld. Tel (0521) 1360010, Fax (0521) 1360300. E-mail 100736.1255@compuserve.com. Website www.artud.com/teuloff. html. Open: Mon–Thu 9–13, 14–18, Fri 9–13, 14–17. Director/curator: Lutz Teutloff. Founded 1989. 2 rooms, 340 m². 3–4 photo exhibitions/ year. Artists: Lynn Hershmann, Vollrand Kutscher, Aziz + Cucher, Alex Flemming, Bettina Flitner, Jürgen Klauke, Frank Thiel, Gerd Bonfert, H. Döring-Spengler, Caroline Dlugos

m Fotografie Bochum, Schloßstr. 1a, Haus Weitmar D-44795 Bochum. Tel (0234) 431150, Fax (0234) 9432228. E-mail m.foto@m-bochum.de. Website www.m-bochum.de/fotogalerie. Open: Wed+Fri+Sat 17–19 and by appointment. Director: Susanne Breidenbach. Founded 1992. 4 rooms, 350 m². 4 photo exhibitions/year. Artists: Ger Dekkers, Nan Goldin, Florence Henri, André Kertész, Dirk Reinartz, Boris Savelev, Emmanuel Sougez, Ryszard Wasko, Lucinda Devlin, Thomas Florschuetz

Bonner Kunstverein, August-Macke-Platz/Hochstadenring 22, D-53119 Bonn. Tel (0228) 693936, Fax (0228) 695589. E-mail bonner.kunstverein@ gmx.de. Website www.kultur. nettrade.de/bkv. Open: Tue–Sun 11–17, Thu 11–19. Director: Dr. Annelie Pohlen. Curator: Harald Uhr. Founded 1963. 3 rooms, 600 m²

IfA-Galerie, Institut für Auslandsbe-ziehungen, Kaiserplatz 17, D-53113

Synopse:

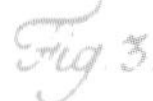

Was machen wir?

Struktur und Konzeption von Kulturmessen

Kunst, Buch, Architektur und Mode

Übernahme kuratorischer Aufgaben für Museen und Institutionen

Beschaffung von Kunstwerken als Leihgaben und für Ankäufe

Aufbau und Betreuung von Sammlungen für private Personen und Institutionen

Verkauf von Sammlungen und Umstrukturierung von Sammlungen

Beratung

Art & Concept in Progress · Thomas-Dehler-Str. 3 · D-10787 Berlin · Tel & Fax 030/262 48 12
e-mail synopse@synopse-online.de · Website http://www.synopse-online.de

Bonn. Tel (0228) 224450, Fax (0228) 212251. Website www.ifa.de. Open: Tue–Fri 12–18, Sat 11–14. Director: Beate Eckstein. Founded 1981. 4 rooms, 75 m². 2 photo exhibitions/year. Artists: Miguel Rio Branco, Anna Mariani, Enrique Bastelmann, Jerzy Lapinski, Igor Kuduz, Peter Magubane

Kunst- und Ausstellungshalle der Bundesrepublik Deutschland, Friedrich-Ebert-Allee 4, D-53113 Bonn. Tel (0228) 9171200, Fax (0228) 9171211. Website www.kah-bonn.de. Open: Tue–Wed 10–21, Thu+Sat–Sun 10–19, Fri 9–19. Founded 1992. 7 rooms, 5,400 m². 1–2 photo exhibitions/year

Kunstmuseum Bonn, Friedrich-Ebert-Allee 2, D-53103 Bonn. Tel (0228) 776262, Fax (0228) 776260. E-mail kunstmuseum@bonn.de. Website www.bonn.de/kunstmuseum. Open: Tue–Sun 10–18 (Wed –21). Director: Prof. Dr. Dieter Ronte. Curator: Dr. Stefan Gronert. Founded 1884. 28 rooms, 4,700 m². 1 photo exhibition/year

Rheinisches Landesmuseum Bonn, Fotografische Sammlung, Colmantstr. 14–16, D-53115 Bonn. Tel (0228) 98810, Fax (0228) 9881299. Open: Tue–Thu 9–17 (Wed –20), Fri 9–16, Sat–Sun 11–17. Director: Prof. Dr. Frank Zehnder. Founded 1874. 1 room, 200 m². 1 photo exhibition/year. Artists: Hugo Erfurth, Albert Renger-Patzsch, Alfred Eisenstaedt, Werner Mantz, Gabriele & Helmut Nothhelfer, F. C. Gundlach, Robert Lebeck, Jupp H. Darchinger

Museum für Photographie e. V., Helmstedter Str. 1, D-38102 Braunschweig. Tel (0531) 75000, Fax (0531)

75036. E-mail info@photomuseum.de. Website www.photomuseum.de. Open: Tue–Fri 14–18, Sat–Sun 15–18. Director: Ulrike Lahmann. Founded 1984. 5 rooms, 120 m². 6 photo exhibitions/year

Kunsthalle Bremen, Am Wall 207, D-28195 Bremen. Tel (0421) 329080, Fax (0421) 3290847. E-mail office@ kunsthalle-bremen.de. Website www.kunsthalle-bremen.de/Open: Tue 10–21, Wed–Sun 10–17. Director: Dr. Wulf Herzogenrath

Haus der Fotografie, Dr. Robert-Gerlich-Museum, Burg 1, D-84489 Burghausen. Tel (08677) 4734, Fax (08677) 911127. E-mail florian.fickert@ burghausen.de. Website www. burghausen.de. Open: Wed–Sun 10–18 (Apr–Oct). Director/curator: Hildegard Fickert. Founded 1983. 2 rooms, 100 m². 4 photo exhibitions/ year

Brandenburgische Kunstsammlungen Cottbus, Sammlung Fotografie, Spremberger Str. 1, D-03046 Cottbus. Tel (0355) 22042, Fax (0355) 22043. Open: Tue–Sun 10–18. Director: Dr. Perdita von Kraft. Curator: Carmen Schliebe. Founded 1979. 2 rooms, 355 m². 2–4 photo exhibitions/year. Artists: Claus Bach, Tina Bara, Micha Brendel, Kurt Buchwald, Gundula Schulze, Jens Rötzsch, Erasmus Schröter, Christian Borchert, Evelyn Richter, Manfred Paul

Bauhaus Dessau, Gropiusallee 38, D-06846 Dessau. Tel (0340) 65080, Fax (0340) 6508226. E-mail besuch@ bauhaus-dessau.de. Website www. bauhaus-dessau.de. Open: daily 10–18. Director: Omar Akbar. Curator: Wolfgang Thöner. Founded 1976. 4 rooms, 750 m². 1–2 photo exhibitions/year. Artists: Walter Peterhans, Werner D. Feist, Lucia Moholy, Hajo Rose, Marianne Brandt, Edmund Collein, Xanti Schawinsky, Irena Blühová, Albert Hennig, Erich Consemüller

Künstlerhaus Dortmund, Sunderweg 1, D-44147 Dortmund. Tel (0231) 820304, Fax (0231) 826847. Website www.kuenstlerhaus-dortmund.de. Open: Thu–Sun 16–19. Founded 1983. 4 rooms, 800 m². 1 photo exhibition/ year

Museum am Ostwall, Ostwall 7, D-44135 Dortmund. Tel (0231) 50232–47/48, Fax (0231) 5025244. Open: Tue–Sun 10–18. Director: Dr. Ingo Bartsch. Curator: Dr. Rosemarie Pahlke. Founded 1947. 12 rooms, 850 m². 1 photo exhibition/year. Artists: Simone Demandt, Astrid Klein, Rudolf Bonvie, Claudia Tersrappen, Pan Walther, Gerald Domenig, Andreas Müller-Pohle, Axel Schneider, Herbert Schwöbel

Westfälisches Industriemuseum, Zentrale Zeche Zollern II/IV, Grubenweg 5, D-44388 Dortmund. Tel (0231) 69610, Fax (0231) 6961114

Galerie Mitte, Fetscherplatz 7, D-01307 Dresden. Tel (0351) 4590052, Fax (0351) 4590052. E-mail dresden @galerie-mitte.de. Website www. galerie-mitte.de. Open: Wed–Fri 14–18, Sat 10–14. Director: Karin Weber. Founded 1979. 5 rooms, 160 m². 2 photo exhibitions/year. Artists: Gudrun Trendafilov, Leonore Adler, Andreas Dress, Günther Hein, Maik Perlich, Reinhard Springer, Wieland Richter, Thorsten Waak, Kerstin Quandt

Kunsthaus Dresden, Staatliche Galerie für Gegenwartkunst, Rähnitzgasse 8, D-01097 Dresden. Tel (0351) 8041456, Fax (0351) 8041582. Open: Tue–Fri 11–18, Sat–Sun 13–18. Director/cura-

tor: Harald Kunde. Founded 1984.
7 rooms, 400 m². 1 photo exhibition/
year

Staatliche Kunstsammlungen Dresden, Kupferstich-Kabinett, Güntzstr.
34, D-01307 Dresden. Tel (0351)
4914211, Fax (0351) 4914222. Open:
Mon–Fri 9–16 (Tue+Thu –18). Director: Dr. Wolfgang Holler. Curator:
Dr. Hans-Ulrich Lehmann. Founded
1899. 3 rooms, 220 m². 1 photo exhibition/year. Artists: Hugo Erfurth,
Franz Fiedler, Edmund Kesting,
Ulrich Lindner

Stadtmuseum Dresden, Wilsdruffer
Str. 2, D-01067 Dresden. Tel (0351)
498660, Fax (0351) 4951288. Open:
Sat–Thu 10–18. Director: Matthias
Griebel. Founded 1891. 10 rooms,
3,000 m². 1–2 photo exhibitions/year.
Artists: Hermann Krone, August
Kotzsch, Hugo Erfurth, Edmund
Kesting, Kurt Schaarschuch, Richard
Peter sen., Willy Pritsche, Erich Pohl,
Erich Höhne, Bernhard Braun

**Leopold-Hoesch-Museum der Stadt
Düren,** Hoeschplatz 1, D-52349 Düren. Tel (02421) 252561, Fax (02421)
252560. Open: Tue–Sun 10–13, 14–17
(Tue –21)

Galerie Bugdahn und Kaimer, Mühlengasse 3, D-40213 Düsseldorf. Tel
(0211) 329140, Fax (0211) 329147.
E-mail bugdahn.kaimer@t-online.de.
Website www.artnet.com/
bugdahnundkaimer.html. Open:
Tue–Fri 10–13, 14–18, Sat 11–14.
Director/curator: Udo Bugdahn.
Founded 1985. 2 rooms, 220 m².
4–5 photo exhibitions/year. Artists:
Robert Barry, Thomas Joshua Cooper,
Marianne Eigenheer, Jürgen Klauke,
Peter Hutchinson, Ingolf Timpner,
Marie-Jo Lafontaine, Abigail O'Brien,
Beverly Semmes, William Wegman

Galerie Conrads, Poststr. 3, D-40213
Düsseldorf. Tel (0211) 3230720, Fax
(0211) 3230722. E-mail galconrads@
aol.com. Open: Tue–Sat 11–13, Tue–
Fri 15–18. Director: Helga Weckop-
Conrads. Founded 1992. 1 room,
80 m². 3 photo exhibitions/year.
Artists: Hermann de Vries, Monika
Brandmeier, Marcia Hafif, Beat
Streuli, Boris Becker, Jörg Eberhard,
Sandra Voets, Gunda Foerster, Walter Niedermayr, Olav Christopher
Jenssen

Galerie Cora Hölzl, Citadellstr. 11, D-
40213 Düsseldorf. Tel (0211) 326412/
490958, Fax (0211) 131235. E-mail
cora.hoelzzl@t-online.de. Open: Tue–
Fri 11–18.30, Sat 12–16. Director: Cora
Hölzl. Founded 1984. 2 rooms, 80 m².
2–3 photo exhibitions/year. Artists:
Pidder Auberger, Cécile Bauer, Martin Eiter, Jochen Gerz, Inés Lombardi,
Brigitte Kowanz, Eva Schlegel

Galerie Zimmer, Oberbilker Allee 27,
D-40215 Düsseldorf. Tel (0211)
332919, Fax (0211) 332080. Open:
Tue–Fri 14.30–18.30, Sat 10–13 and by
appointment. Artists: Robert Lebeck,
Rolf Gillhausen, Barbara Klemm,
Arno Fischer

Konrad Fischer, Platanenstr. 7, D-
40233 Düsseldorf. Tel (0211) 685908,
Fax (0211) 689780. Open: Tue–Fri
11–18, Sat 11–13. Director: Dorothee
Fischer. Founded 1967. 6 rooms.
Artists: Bernd & Hilla Becher, Jan
Dibbets, Mischa Kuball, Simone
Nieweg, Petra Wunderlich, Daniela
Steinfeld, Lothar Baumgarten,
Richhard Long, Georg Schneider

**Kunstverein für die Rheinlande und
Westfalen,** Grabbeplatz 4, D-40213
Düsseldorf. Tel (0211) 327023, Fax
(0211) 329070. E-mail kunstverein.
duesseldorf@rp-online.de. Website
www.rp-online.de/duesseldorf/

kunstverein. Open: Tue–Sun 11–18.
Director: Dr. Raimund Stecker.
Founded 1829. 1 room, 350 m².
8–10 photo exhibitions/year

Wilhelm Lehmbruck Museum Duisburg, Europäisches Zentrum moderner Skulptur, Friedrich-Wilhelm-Str. 40, D-47049 Duisburg. Tel (0203) 2832630, Fax (0203) 2833892. Open: Tue–Sat 11–17, Sun 10–18. Director: Dr. Christoph Brockhaus. Curator: Dr. Renate Heidt Heller. Founded 1934. 3 rooms, 5,000 m². 1 photo exhibition/year. Artists: Stephan Balkenhol, Bernd & Hilla Becher, Tibor Henty, Ernst Ludwig Kirchner, Wilhelm Loth, Ernst Scheidegger, HA Schult, Stefan Moses, Franz Erhard Walther, Timm Rautert

Fotogalerie im Hause Bohl, Karlstr. 32, D-47051 Eisenach. Tel (03691) 742078. Open: Mon–Fri 9–18, Sat 9–12. Contact: Ulrich Kneise. Founded 1990. 1 room, 50 m²

Städtische Galerie Erlangen, Palais Stutterheim, Marktplatz 1, D-91054 Erlangen. Tel (09131) 862735, Fax (09131) 862117. Open: Tue–Fri 10–18. Sat–Sun 10–17. Director: Karl Manfred Fischer. Curator: Lisa Puyplat. Founded 1974. 11 rooms, 240 m²

Museum Folkwang, Fotografische Sammlung, Goethestr. 41, D-45128 Essen. Tel (0201) 8845100, Fax (0201) 8845130. Open: Tue–Sun 10–18 (Thu –21); Tue 10–13, 14–16 (collection). Director: Dr. Georg W. Költzsch. Curator: Ute Eskildsen. Founded 1979. 2 rooms, 310 running meters. 4–6 photo exhibitions/year. Artists: David Octavius Hill, Edouard Baldus, Heinrich Kühn, Aenne Biermann, Hugo Erfurth, Lotte Jacobi, Albert Renger-Patzsch, August Sander, Otto Steinert, Helmar Lerski, László Moholy-Nagy

Galerie der Stadt Esslingen, Villa Merkel, Pulverwiesen 25, D-73726 Esslingen. Tel (0711) 35122461, Fax (0711) 35122903. E-mail rwiehager@ esslingen.de. Open: Tue 11–20, Wed–Sun 11–18. Director/curator: Dr. Renate Wiehager. Founded 1974. 12 rooms, 500 m²

Deutsches Filmmuseum, Schaumainkai 41, D-60596 Frankfurt/Main. Tel (069) 21233369, Fax (069) 21237881. Open: Tue–Sun 10–17 (Wed –20). Director: Prof. Walter Schobert. Curator: Beate Dannhorn. Founded 1976. 2 rooms, 1,200 m². 4 photo exhibitions/year

Fotografie Forum International, Leinwandhaus, Weckmarkt 17, D-60311 Frankfurt/Main. Tel (069) 291726, Fax (069) 28639. Open: Tue–Fri 11–18 (Wed –20), Sat–Sun 11–17. Director/curator: Celina Lunsford. Founded 1984. 2 rooms, 150 m². 8–10 photo exhibitions/year. Artists: René Burri, Imogen Cunningham, Herman Försterling, Barbara Klemm, Miguel Rio Branco, Marco Breuer, Sarah Moon, Will McBride, Larry Fink, Elinor Carucci

Frankfurter Kunstverein e. V., Steinernes Haus am Römerberg, Markt 44, D-60311 Frankfurt/Main. Tel (069) 28533-0/9, Fax (069) 281253. Open: Tue–Fri 12–19 (Wed –20), Sat 11–19, Sun 11–18. Founded 1827. 4 rooms, 1,200 m². 8–10 photo exhibitions/ year. Artist: Ann Mandelbaum

Galerie Anita Beckers, Frankenallee 74, D-60327 Frankfurt/Main. Tel (069) 73900967, Fax (069) 73900968. E-mail galerie.beckers@t-online.de. Director: Anita Beckers. Founded 1995. 265 m². 2–3 photo exhibitions/year. Artists: Miron Schmückel, Horst Hamann, Ann Mandelbaum, Anton Corbijn, Mads Gamdrup

Galerie Monika Reitz, Domstr. 2,
D-60311 Frankfurt/Main. Tel (069)
20208, Fax (069) 20253. E-mail
reitz.galerie@t-online.de. Open: Tue–
Fri 13–18, Sat 11–14. Director: Monika
Reitz. Founded 1995. 2 rooms, 80 m².
2–3 photo exhibitions/year. Artists:
Richard Billingham, Gisela Bullacher,
Tamara Grcic, Christopher Muller

Galerie Wilma Tolksdorf, Hanauer
Landstr. 136, D-60313 Frankfurt/
Main. Tel (069) 43059427, Fax (069)
43059428. Open: Tue–Fri 14–18, Sat
11–15. Director: Meike Behm

Künstlerhaus Mousonturm, Wald-
schmidtstr. 4, D-60316 Frankfurt/
Main. Tel (069) 4058950, Fax (069)
40589540. Open: Tue–Sun 15–19.
Director: Dieter Buroch. Curator:
Dorothe Gebhart. Founded 1988. 2
rooms, 160 m². 2 photo exhibitions/
year. Artists: Andy Warhol, Alexander Paul Englert, Chris Nash

L. A. Galerie, Domstr. 6, D-60311
Frankfurt/Main. Tel (069) 288687,
Fax (069) 280912. Website www.
artnet.com. Open: Tue–Fri 12–18.30,
Sat 11–16. Directors: Agustin Lopez,
Lothar Albrecht. Founded 1990.
2 rooms, 90 m². 7 photo exhibitions/
year. Artists: Lukas Einsele, Joan
Fontcuberta, Mabel Palacín, Irene
Peschick, Arthur Tress, Javier Vall-
honrat, John Hilliard, Tracey Mof-
fatt, Robert F. Hammerstiel, Edgar
Lissel

Museum für Moderne Kunst, Domstr.
10, D-60311 Frankfurt/Main. Tel (069)
21230447, Fax (069) 21237882. E-mail
mmk@stadt-frankfurt.de. Website
www.frankfurt-business.de/mmk.
Open: Tue–Sun 10–17 (Wed –20).
Director: Prof. Dr. Jean-Christophe
Ammann. Founded 1981. 40 rooms,
4,150 m². 2 photo exhibitions/year.
Artists: Anna & Bernhard Blume,

Bernd & Hilla Becher, Jeff Wall,
Thomas Ruff, Bettina Rheims, Paul
Almasy, Abisag Tüllmann, Ryuji
Miyamoto, Nobuyoshi Araki

Portikus, Schöne Aussicht 2, D-60311
Frankfurt/Main. Tel (069) 21998760,
Fax (069) 21998761. E-mail portikus
@pop.stadt-frankfurt.de. Website
www.portikus.de. Open: Tue–Sun
11–18, Wed 11–20. Director: Prof.
Kasper König. Curator: Angelika
Nollert. Founded 1987. 1 room,
113 m². 1–3 photo exhibitions/year.
Artists: Anna & Bernhard Blume,
Thomas Struth, Gerald Domenig,
Thomas Ruff, Candida Höfer, Steven
Pippin, Andreas Gursky, Wolfgang
Tillmans, Boris Mikhailov, Esko
Männikkö

Schirn Kunsthalle, Römerberg,
D-60311 Frankfurt/Main. Tel (069)
2998820, Fax (069) 29988240. E-mail
schirn@schirn.de. Website www.
schirn.de. Open: Tue+Sun 11–19,
Wed–Sat 11–22. Director: Hellmut
Seemann. Founded 1986. 2,000 m².
4 photo exhibitions/year

Galerie Ruta Correa, Goethestr. 3,
D-79100 Freiburg. Tel (0761) 74163,
Fax (0761) 702624. E-mail galerie-
correa@t-online.de. Website www.
galerie-ruta-correa.de. Open: Tue–Fri
13–19 and by appointment. Director:
Ruta Correa. Founded 1980. 3 rooms,
80 m². 1 photo exhibition/year. Artists: Marta Maria Pérez, Ava Vargas,
Marie Orensanz, Liliana Porter

Kunstverein Freiburg im Marienbad,
Dreisamstr. 21, D-79098 Freiburg.
Tel (0761) 34944, Fax (0761) 24914.
Website www.ruf.uni-freiburg.de/
bildkunst/kunstver/kunstver.htm.
Open: Tue–Sun 10–17. Director: Dr.
Stephan Berg. Founded 1827. 1 room,
250 m². 1–2 photo exhibitions/year

Galerie O. Ahlers, Düstere Str. 20, 1. Etage, D-37073 Göttingen. Tel (0551) 57056, Fax (0551) 56187. E-mail galahlers@aol.com. Website www.galerieahlers.de. Open: Tue–Fri 9–13, 15–18, Sat 9–13. Director/curator: Oliver Ahlers. Founded 1982. 3 rooms, 190 m². 2 photo exhibitions/year

Staatliche Galerie Moritzburg Halle, Landeskunstmuseum Sachsen-Anhalt, Friedemann-Bach-Platz 5, D-06108 Halle/Saale. Tel (0345) 2125942, Fax (0345) 2029990. E-mail moritzburg@t-online.de. Website www.moritzburg.halle.de. Open: Tue 11–20.30, Wed–Fri 10–17.30, Sat–Sun 10–18. Director: Dr. Katja Schneider. Curator: T. O. Immisch. Founded 1885/1987. 4 rooms, 340 m². 5 photo exhibitions/year. Artists: Walter Danz, Karl Blossfeldt, Hans Finsler, Gerda Leo, Matthias Leupold, Evelyn Richter, Alexander Rodtschenko, Annelies Štrba, Helga Wallmüller, Ulrich Wüst

Deichtorhallen Hamburg, Deichtorstr. 2, D-20095 Hamburg. Tel (040) 32103240, Fax (040) 32103230. Open: Tue–Sun 11–18. Director: Dr. Zdenek Felix. Founded 1989. 2 rooms, 6,000 m². 3 photo exhibitions/year. Artists: Cindy Sherman, Anton Corbijn, Nan Goldin

Elke Dröscher, Kunstraum Falkenstein, Grotiusweg 79, D-22587 Hamburg. Tel (040) 810581, Fax (040) 818166. Open: Tue–Fri 11–17, Sat 11–14. Director/curator: Elke Dröscher. Founded 1968. 1 room, 80 m². 1–2 photo exhibitions/year. Artists: Armando, Abraham D. Christian, Claus Goedicke, Gotthard Graubner, Katsuhito Nishikawa, Norbert Radermacher, Ingo Ronkkolz, Jo Schöpfer, Ingolf Timpner, Dorothee von Windheim

Fabrik-Fotoforum, (exhibition space at Norddeutsches Landesmuseum in Hamburg) Barnerstr. 36, D-22765 Hamburg. Tel (040) 39107130, Fax (040) 3906362. Open: Tue–Sun 10–18. Director/curator: Denis Brudna. Founded 1979. 1 room, 120 m². 4–5 photo exhibitions/year. Artists: Volker Hinz, Bettina Clasen, Stephan Erfurt, Jürgen Königs, Jo Röttger, Ute Klophaus, Martin Pudenz, Clemens Kalischer, Pavel Odvody

Galerie Vera Munro, Heilwigstr. 64, D-20249 Hamburg. Tel (040) 484552, Fax (040) 472550. Open: Tue–Fri 10–13, 14–18, Sat 11–13. Director: Vera Munro. Founded 1977. 8 rooms, 350 m². Artists: Ian Anüll, John M. Armleder, Jean-Marc Bustamante, Walter Dahn, Michael Dörner, Günther Förg, Asta Gröting, Markus Hansen, Imi Knoebel, Mario Merz

Hamburger Kunsthalle, Glockengießerwall, D-20095 Hamburg. Tel (040) 24862612, Fax (040) 24862482. Open: Tue–Sun 10–18 (Thu –21). Founded 1869. Artists: Meister Bertram, Claude Lorrain, Philipp Otto Runge, Caspar David Friedrich, Wilhelm Leibl, Max Liebermann, Edvard Munch, Max Beckmann, Andy Warhol, Joseph Beuys

Kunstverein in Hamburg, Klosterwall 23, D-20095 Hamburg. Tel (040) 322157, Fax (040) 322159. Open: Tue–Sun 11–18 (Thu –21). Director: Corinna Koch. Founded 1816. 2 rooms, 1,200 m². 1 photo exhibition/year

Museum der Arbeit, Maurienstr. 19–21, D-22305 Hamburg. Tel (040) 428322364, Fax (040) 428323179. E-mail info@museum-der-arbeit.de. Open: Mon 13–21, Tue–Sun 10–17. Director: Prof. Gernot Krankenhagen. Curator: Dr. Lisa Kosok. Founded

1991. 2 rooms, 3,800 m². 1 photo exhibition/year

Museum für Kunst und Gewerbe, Forum Photographie, Steintorplatz 1, D-20099 Hamburg. Tel (040) 428542829, Fax (040) 428542087. E-mail photo@mkg-hamburg.de. Website www.mkg-hamburg.de. Open: Tue–Sun 10–18 (Thu –21). Director: Dr. Claudia Gabriele Philipp. Founded 1900. 5 photo exhibitions/year. Artists: Dörte Eißfeldt, Alfred Steffen, Edgar Lissel, Gerhard Vormwald, Michael Najjar, André Lützen, Jack Sal, Peter Dammann, Marco Breuer, Annegret Soltau

PPS.Galerie, Hochhaus 1, Feldstr. 66, D-20357 Hamburg. Tel (040) 43178373, Fax (040) 43178269. Open: Mon–Fri 10–13, 15–18. Director: Walter Remy. Founded 1975. 2 rooms, 120 m². 7 photo exhibitions/year. Artists: Peter Keetman, Wim Wenders, Olaf Martens

Produzentengalerie, Admiralitätstr. 71, D-20459 Hamburg. Tel (040) 378232, Fax (040) 363304. E-mail prodgal@aol.com. Open: Mon–Fri 11–13, 15–19, Sat 11–14. Director: Jürgen Vorrath. Founded 1973. 2 rooms, 250 m². Artists: Astrid Klein, Hermann Pitz, Anne & Bernhard Blume, Gisela Bullacher, Bernhard Prinz

Haus der Fotografie Hannover e. V., Klewergarten 4, D-30449 Hannover. Tel (0511) 714344, Fax (0511) 714347. E-mail hausfoto@bbs.bybyte.de. Website www.nananet.de/hausfoto. Open: Tue–Fri 17–20, Sat–Sun 14–18

Kestner-Gesellschaft, Goseriede 11, D-30159 Hannover. Tel (0511) 701200, Fax (0511) 7012020. E-mail kestner@real-net.de. Open: Tue–Sun 11–19 (Thu –21). Directors/curators: Dr.

Carl Haenlein, Carsten Ahrens. Founded 1916. 5 rooms, 1,400 m²

Sprengel Museum, Fotografische Sammlung, Kurt-Schwitters-Platz, D-30169 Hannover. Tel (0511) 16843875, Fax (0511) 16845093. E-mail sprengel-museum@hannover-stadt.de. Open: Tue 10–20, Wed–Sun 10–18. Director: Prof. Dr. Ulrich Krempel. Curator: Thomas Weski. Founded 1979. 2 rooms, 1,275 m². 6–7 photo exhibition/year. Artists: Karl Blossfeldt, August Sander, Albert Renger-Patzsch, Michael Schmidt, Robert Adams, Sigmar Polke, Thomas Struth, Rineke Dijkstra, Nicholas Nixon, Boris Mikhailov

Heidelberger Kunstverein e. V., Hauptstr. 97, D-69117 Heidelberg. Tel (06221) 18408-6/7, Fax (06221) 164162. E-mail hdkv@artgentur.de. Website www.artgentur.de/hdkv. Open: Tue–Sun 10–17 (Wed –21). Director: Hans Gercke. Founded 1869. 3 rooms, 555 m². 3–4 photo exhibitions/year. Robert Lebeck, Loris Cecchini, Irinel Stegaru

Badischer Kunstverein, Waldstr. 3, D-76133 Karlsruhe. Tel (0721) 28226, Fax (0721) 29773. E-mail badischer-kunstverein@karlsruhe.de. Website www.badischer-kunstverein. karlsruhe.de. Open: Tue–Fri 11–19, Sat–Sun 11–17. Director: Angelika Stepken. Founded 1818. 8 rooms, 900 m². 5 photo exhibitions/year

ZKM-Zentrum für Kunst und Medientechnologie Karlsruhe, Museum für Gegenwartskunst, P. O. Box 6909, D-76049 Karlsruhe. Tel (0721) 9340145, Fax (0721) 934019. E-mail ufro@zkm.de. Website www.zkm.de. Director: Peter Weibel. Curator: Dr. Ursula Frohne. Founded 1989. 3,000 m². Artists: Thomas Struth, Anna & Bernhard Blume, Peter Campus,

Günther Förg, Thomas Florschuetz, Frank Thiel, Thomas Ruff, Bernhard Prinz

Museum Fridericianum, Friedrichsplatz 18, D-34117 Kassel. Tel (0561) 7072720, Fax (0561) 774578. E-mail tb@documenta.de. Website www.documenta.de. Open: Tue–Sun 10–17. Director: René Block. Founded 1987. 18 rooms, 3,000 m². 1–2 photo exhibitions/year

Kunsthaus Kaufbeuren, Spitaltor 2, D-87600 Kaufbeuren. Tel (08341) 8644, Fax (08341) 8655. Open: Tue–Sun 10–18 (Thu –20). Director: Hilke Gesine Möller. Founded 1996. 2 rooms, 350 m². 1 photo exhibition/year

Agfa Foto-Historama, Bischofsgartenstr. 1, D-50667 Köln. Tel (0221) 2212411, Fax (0221) 2214114. Open: Tue–Fri 10–18, Sat–Sun 11–18. Director: Dr. Bodo von Dewitz. Curator: Ulrich Tillmann. Founded 1985. 3 rooms, 220 m². 2 photo exhibitions/year

Aurel Scheibler, Maria-Hilf-Str. 17, D-50667 Köln. Tel (0221) 311011, Fax (0221) 3319615. E-mail galerie.scheibler@netcologne.de. Open: Tue–Fri 11–13, 15–18.30, Sat 11–14. Director: Aurel Scheibler. Founded 1991. 4 rooms, 200 m². 1 photo exhibition/year. Artists: Dan Asher, Barclay Hughes, Chargesheimer, Jack Pierson, Weegee, Mark Morrisroe

Büro für Fotos, Nadia & Franz van der Grinten, Ewaldistr. 5, D-50670 Köln. Tel (0221) 7392936, Fax (0221) 7392936. E-mail burofurfotos@netcologne.de. Website www.burofurfotos.de. Open: Mon–Tue + Thu–Sat 15–19. Directors/curators: Nadia van der Grinten, Franz van der Grinten. Founded 1997. 1 room, 25 m². 7 photo exhibitions/year.

Artists: Bernd Arnold, Hella Berent, Mark Curran, Walde Huth, Miron Zownir, Izima Kaoru, Dirk Königsfeld, Rebecca Lewis, Christine Sommerfeldt

Galerie Alex Lachmann, St.-Apern-Str. 17–21, D-50667 Köln. Tel (0221) 2574953, Fax (0221) 2574951. Open: Tue–Fri 10–13, 14–18.30, Sat 10–14. Director: B. Remmen. Founded 1989. 3 rooms. 4 photo exhibitions/year. Artists: Alexander Rodtschenko, Georgy Petrusov, Boris Ignatovich, Georgy Zelma, Georgy Zimin, Arkady Shaykhet, Moysey Nappelbaum, Francisco Infante

Galerie Benninger, Moltkestr. 99, D-50674 Köln. Tel (0221) 9522198, Fax (0221) 514721. Open: Tue–Thu 16.30–19.30 and by appointment. Director: Horst Benninger. Founded 1998. 3 rooms, 40 m². 2–3 photo exhibitions/year. Artists: Peter H. Fürst, Katrin Nalop, Andrej Barov, Lena Bosch

Galerie Carla Stützer, Kamekestr. 21, D-50672 Köln. Tel (0221) 518214, Fax (0221) 511192. Open: Tue–Fri 10–13, 14.30–18, Sat 10–14. Director: Carla Stützer. Founded 1975. 1 room, 150 m². Artists: Victoria Bell, Carl Buchheister, Cordula Güdemann, Gisela Kleinlein, Wasa Marjanov, Hans van Meeuwen, Anton Räderscheidt, Patrick Raynaud, Andrei Roiter, Peter Nagel

Galerie Daniel Buchholz, Neven-DuMont-Str. 17, D-50667 Köln. Tel (0221) 2574946, Fax (0221) 253351. E-mail galeriebuchholz@t-online.de. Open: Tue–Fri 11–18.30, Sat 11–16. Director: Daniel Buchholz. Founded 1986. 2 rooms, 80 m². 1–5 photo exhibitions/year. Artists: Wolfgang Tillmans, Beat Streuli, Ken Lum

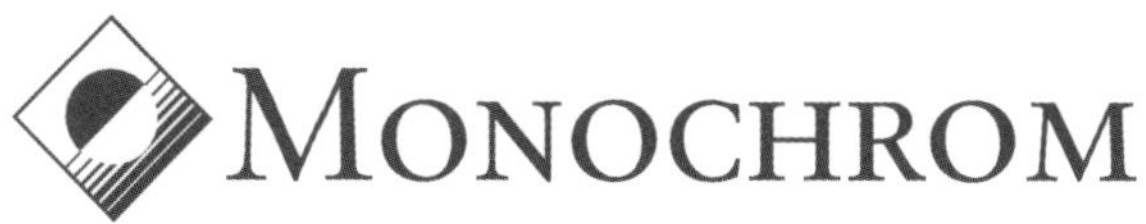

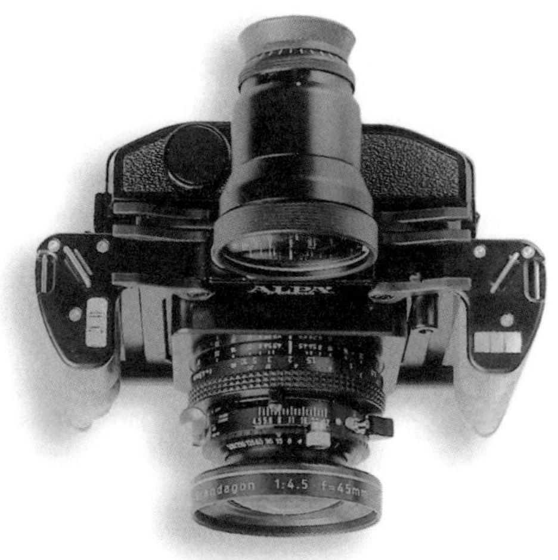

ALPA 125S/WA
(shift und scharf!)

Photographie
Präsentation
Archivierung

Fordern Sie Ihren Monochrom Katalog an

Für European Photography Guide-Leser kostenlos (bitte angeben: EPG/2000)

Complete illustrated catalogue on request

(in German only, unfortunately)

www.monochrom.com

Monochrom Archivierungs- und Photoprodukte Kunoldstr. 10–14 D-34131 Kassel

Fon 0561-935190 Fax 0561-9351919 email@monochrom.com

Galerie Fiedler, Lindenstr. 19, D-50674 Köln. Tel (0221) 9230800, Fax (0221) 249601. E-mail galerie-fiedler@netcologne.de. Open: Tue–Fri 11–13, 14–18, Sat 11–14. Director: Ulrich Fiedler. Founded 1986. 2 rooms, 130 m². 3–4 photo exhibitions/year. Artists: Albert Renger-Patzsch, Hans Finsler, Karl Blossfeldt, László Moholy-Nagy, Alexander Rodtschenko, Hiroshi Sugimoto, Boris Becker, Claus Goedicke, Heidi Specker

Galerie Gisela Capitain, Aachener Str. 5, 50674 Köln. Tel (0221) 256676, Fax (0221) 256593. Open: Tue–Fri 10–13, 14–18, Sat 11–16. E-mail info@galerie-capitain.de. Artists: Christopher Williams, Rachel Khedoori, Martin Kippenberger, Albert Dehlen, Anna Gaskell, Günther Förg, Laura Owens, Georg Herold

Galerie Johnen & Schöttle, Maria-Hilf-Str. 17, D-50677 Köln. Tel (0221) 310270, Fax (0221) 3102727. E-mail johnen.schoettle@gmx.de. Open: Tue–Fri 10–13, 14–18, Sat 10–16. Director/curator: Jörg Johnen. Founded 1985. 2 photo exhibitions/year. Artists: Candida Höfer, Thomas Ruff, Jeff Wall, Wiebke Siem, Inez van Lamsweerde, Yoshitomo Nara, Jim Shaw

Galerie Karsten Greve, Wallrafplatz 3, D-50667 Köln. Tel (0221) 2578737, Fax (0221) 2580479. Open: Mon–Fri 10–18.30, Sat 10–16. Director: Karsten Greve. Founded 1973. 2 rooms, 120 m². 1 photo exhibition/year. Artists: Josef Albers, John Chamberlain, Yves Charbonnier, Adam Fuss, Loïc Le Groumellec, Detleff Orlopp

Galerie Lichtblick, Steinbergstr. 21, D-50733 Köln. Tel (0221) 729149, Fax (0221) 729149. Website www.ora.de/quirl/. Open: Wed+Fri 19–21, Sat–Sun 11–15. Directors/curators: Tina Schellhorn, Stefan Worming, Wolf-gang Zurborn. Founded 1986. 3 rooms, 50 m². 6 photo exhibitions/year

Galerie Thomas Zander, Brühler Platz 1, D-50968 Köln. Tel (0221) 9348856. Open: Tue–Fri 14–18, Sat 11–14. Artist: Tom Wood

Heidi Reckermann Photographie, Albertusstr. 16, D-50667 Köln. Tel (0221) 2574868, Fax (0221) 2574867. E-mail heidi.reckermann@pironet.de. Website www.germangalleries.de. Open: Tue–Fri 11–18, Sat 11–16. Director: Heidi Reckermann. Founded 1990. 3 rooms, 180 m². 6 photo exhibitions/year. Artists: Constantin Brancusi, Adolf Lazi, Georges Rousse, Claudia Terstappen, Ulrich Tillmann, Bernhard Prinz, Angela Grauerholz, Katharina Bosse, Patrick Tosani, Albrecht Fuchs

in focus, Galerie am Dom, Marzellenstr. 9, D-50667 Köln. Tel (0221) 1300341, Fax (0221) 1300341. E-mail galeriefoc@aol.com. Website www.artist-info.com/gallery/in-focus-galerie-am-dom.html. Open: Tue–Fri 15–19, Sun 15–18. Director: Burkhard Arnold. Founded 1990. 2 rooms, 100 m². 8 photo exhibitions/year. Artists: Günter Blum, Bruce Davidson, Alvin Booth, Lucien Clergue, Heinrich Heidersberger, Frank Horvat, Gottfried Jäger, Floris M. Neusüss, Jan Saudek, Jeanloup Sieff

Josef-Haubrich-Kunsthalle, Josef-Haubrich-Hof 1, D-50676 Köln. Tel (0221) 2212335, Fax (0221) 2214552. Open: 11–20. Curator: Ralf Hofenbitzer. Founded 1967. 2 rooms, 2,000 m². Artists: Richard Avedon, Marc Riboud, Hans-Jürgen Burkard, Arwed Meemer

Kölnischer Kunstverein, Cäcilienstr. 33, D-50667 Köln. Tel (0221) 217021,

Fax (0221) 210651. Open: Tue–Sun 11–17. Director/curator: Udo Kittelmann. Founded 1839. 1 room, 500 m². 1–2 photo exhibitions/year. Artists: Joseph Albers, Bernd & Hilla Becher, Boris Becker, Jörg Sasse, Wolfgang Tillmans, Walter Dahn, Stan Douglas, Ann Mandelbaum, Ulrich Tillmann, Christa Näher

Kölnisches Stadtmuseum, Graphische Sammlung, Zeughausstr. 1, D-50667 Köln. Tel (0221) 2212352, Fax (0221) 2214154. Open: Tue–Thu 10–12, 13–15. Director: Dr. Dieckhoff. Founded 1888. 292 m². 1–2 photo exhibitions/year. Artists: Peter Frist, Henry Maitek, Annette Frick, Hans Meisenberg, August Sander, Carl-Heinz Chargesheimer, J. F. Michiels

Museum Ludwig, Photo- und Video-sammlung, Bischofsgartenstr. 1, D-50667 Köln. Tel (0221) 2213619, Fax (0221) 2214114. Open: Tue–Fri 10–18, Sat–Sun 11–18. Director: Dr. Jochen Poetter. Curator: Dr. Reinhold Mißelbeck. Founded 1977. 5 rooms, 500 m². 6 photo exhibitions/year

SK Stiftung Kultur, Die Photographische Sammlung, Im MediaPark 7, D-50670 Köln. Tel (0221) 2265900, Fax (0221) 2265901. E-mail asask1@aol.com. Website www.sk-kultur.de. Open: daily 12–17 (Tue –20), Wed closed. Director: Dr. Susanne Lange. Artist: August Sander

Galerie Arbeiterfotografie, Merheimer Str. 107, D-50733 Köln-Nippes. Tel (0221) 727999, Fax (0221) 7325588. E-mail mail@galerie-arbeiterfotografie.de. Website www.galerie-arbeiterfotografie.de. Open: Tue–Fri 9–13, Sat 10–14 and by appointment. Director/curator: Anneliese Fikentscher. Founded 1990. 3 rooms, 100 m². 6 photo exhibitions/year. Artists: Charly Cupic, Ibrahim

Demirel, Girogio von Arb, Eugen und Walter Heilig, Sabine Sauer, Anne E. Stärk, Werner Kohn, Herbert Döring-Spengler

Siebenhaar, Art Consulting, Schweizer Haus im Kurpark, D-61462 Königstein/Ts. Tel (06174) 1389, Fax (06174) 1380. Open: Mon–Fri 10–17 and by appointment. Director: Renate Siebenhaar-Zeller. Founded 1990. 3 rooms, 120 m². Artists: Luigi Ghirri, Gabriele Basilico, Franco Fontana, Pietro Donzelli, Mimmo Jodice, Guido Guidi, Olivo Barbieri, Arno Fischer, Frederico Patellani, Barbara Klemm

Caritas-Fotogalerie, St.-Stephans-Platz 39a, D-78462 Konstanz. Tel (07531) 120999, Fax (07531) 120930. Open: Mon–Thu 9–17, Fri 9–12. Director: Joachim Trautner. Founded 1990. 3 rooms, 100 m². 5–6 photo exhibitions/year

Ursula-Blickle-Stiftung, Mühlweg 18, D-76703 Kraichtal. Tel (07251) 60919, Fax (07251) 68687. Open: Tue 14–17, Sun 14–18 and by appointment. Director: Ursula Blickle. Curator: Gérard A. Goodrow. Founded 1990. 3 rooms, 200 m². 1 photo exhibition/year. Artists: Patrick Raynaud, Mercedes Barros, Lidy Jacobs, Sylvie Fleury, Piotr Dluzniewski, Manuel Pardo, Jack Pierson, Peter Wütherich, Bettina Gruber, Lukas Lasareishvili

Dogenhaus Galerie, Beethoven-str. 1, D-04107 Leipzig. Tel (0341) 9600054, Fax (0341) 9600036. E-mail dogenhaus@aol.com. Open: Tue–Fri 12–17, Sat 11–14. Director: Jochen Hempel. Founded 1991. 1 room, 90 m². 2–3 photo exhibitions/year. Artists: Matthias Hoch, Albrecht Tübke, Beat Streuli, Esko Männikkö

Galerie

D-50733 Köln, Merheimer Str. 107, fax 0049-221-7325588, fon 0049-221-727999, arbeiterfotografie@t-online.de

w w w . g a l e r i e - a r b e i t e r f o t o g r a f i e . d e

manfred förster charley cupic anna e stärk
raphael bolius giorgio van arb walter martin
anton tripp eugen heilig walter heilig
sabine sauer senne glanschneider ulrich
dahlinger ibrahim demirel sabattin sen werner
kohn herbert döring-spengler jörg boström
rahim fathi-baran anita schiffer-fuchs members
of german union arbeiterfotografie

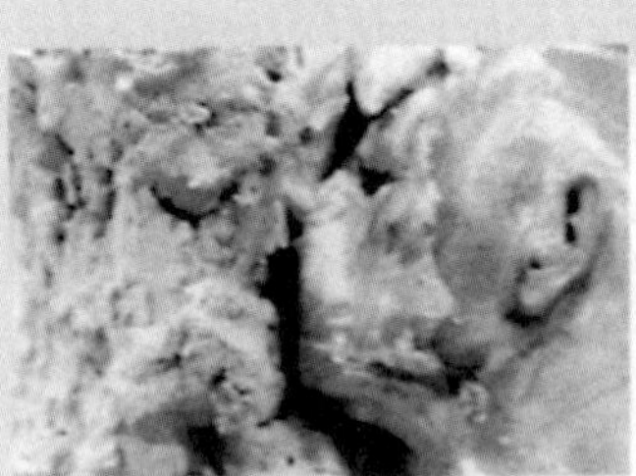

Manfred Förster: Lebensgröße, Heinz Breloh

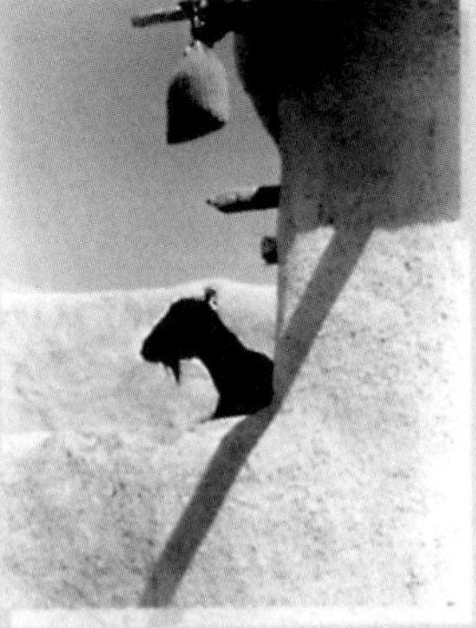

Ibrahim Demirel: Der Ort Kilis, 1970

Die
Welt
mit
anderen
Augen
sehn

Verband
Sitz: Bremen, Kontakt: Eugen Schanz, Luhering 27c, D-21147 Hamburg
Zeitschrift
2 Ausgaben/Jahr: Druckwerk, Mühlhofer Hauptstr. 5, D-90453 Nürnberg, fon: 0049 - 911 - 63 50 21

Galerie & Edition m, Grassisstr. 20, D-04107 Leipzig. Tel (0341) 4774553, Fax (0341) 4774553. Open: Tue–Fri 15–18, Sat 11–14. Director: Matthias Kleindienst. Founded 1994. 1 room, 100 m². 2–3 photo exhibitions/year. Artists: Erasmus Schröter, Michael Scheffer, Bernd Borchardt, Will McBride, Matthias Knoch, Uwe Walter

Galerie Eigen+Art, Ferdinand-Rhode-Str. 14, D-04107 Leipzig. Tel (0341) 9607886, Fax (0341) 9607886. Open: Tue–Fri 12–16, Sat 11–14. Director: Gerd Harry Lybke

Galerie für zeitgenössische Kunst, Karl-Tauchnitz-Str. 11, D-04107 Leipzig. Tel (0341) 140810, Fax (0341) 1408111. Open: Tue–Fri 13–17 (Thu –20), Sat+Sun 11–18

Galerie Kleindienst, Grassistr. 20, D-04107 Leipzig. Tel (0341) 4774553, Fax (0341) 4774553. Open: Tue–Fri 15–18, Sat 11–14 and by appointment. Director: Matthias Kleindienst

Hochschule für Grafik und Buchkunst, Wächterstr. 11, D-04107 Leipzig. Tel (0341) 2135133, Fax (0341) 2135166. Open: Tue–Fri 12–18, Sat 10–14. Artist: Tina Barney

Museum der bildenden Künste, Grimmaische Str. 1–7, D-04109 Leipzig. Tel (0431) 216990, Fax (0431) 9609925. Open: Tue, Thu–Sun 10–18, Wed 13–21.30. Director: Dr. Hans-Werner Schmidt

Kunstverein Lingen, Kunsthalle, Kaiserstr., D-49809 Lingen. Tel (0591) 59995, Fax (0591) 59905. E-mail kvlingen@t-online.de. Website www.kunstverein.de. Open: Tue–Fri 10–17 (Thu –20), Sat–Sun 11–17. Director: Heiner Schepers. Founded 1983. 8 rooms, 720 m². 1 photo exhibition/year. Artists: Heiner Blum, Joachim Brohm, Reinhard Matz, Andreas Horlitz, Volker Heinze, Gabriele Rothemann, Dörte Eißfeldt, Maix Mayer, Daniel Poensgen, Annelies Štrba

Kunstverein Ludwigsburg, Villa Franck, Franckstr. 4, D-71636 Ludwigsburg. Tel (07141) 929196, Fax (07141) 922873. Open: Tue–Fri 15–18, Sat–Sun 11–17. Directors: Ingrid Mössinger, Mrs. Jahnke. Founded 1973. 6 rooms, 180 m². 2–4 photo exhibitions/year. Artists: Jim Dine, Christiane Möbus, Nicola de Maria, Ilya Kabakov, Dimitri Prigov, Martin Pudenz, Norbert Badermacher, Lauren Ewing

Galerie Bausmann, Rochusstr. 22, D-55116 Mainz. Tel (06131) 236831, Fax (06131) 230289. Open: Wed–Fri 11–18, Sat 11–14. Director: Erik Bausmann. Founded 1990. 2 rooms, 120 m². 2 photo exhibitions/year. Artists: Werner Pawlok, Helmut Newton, Ernestine Ruben

Galerie Angelo Falzone, Bürohaus Luisenpark, Theodor-Heuss-Anlage 12, D-68165 Mannheim. Tel (0621) 416780, Fax (0621) 416782. Open: Tue–Fri 14.30–18.30, Sat 11–15. Director: Angelo Falzone. Founded 1990. 2 rooms, 1,050 m². 6 photo exhibitions/year. Artists: Klaus Wefringhaus, M & M Fasoli, Alba d'Urbano, Andreas Müller-Pohle, Francesco Illy, Günther Selichar, Gerhard Vormwald, Michael Najjar

Marburger Kunstverein, Gerhard-Jahn-Platz 5, D-35037 Marburg. Tel (06421) 25882, Fax (06421) 25882. Open: Tue–Sat 10–13, 14–17, Sun 11–13. Director: Dr. Wolfgang Tichy. Curator: Gisela Wengler. Founded 1953. 5 rooms, 170 m². 1–2 photo exhibitions/year

Kamera- und Fotomuseum Leipzig, Gottschalkstr. 9, D-04457 Mölkau. Tel (0431) 6515711, Fax (0341) 6513924. Open: Wed, Sat, Sun 13–17. Director: Kerstin Langner. Curator: Andreas J. Mueller. Founded 1989. 10 rooms, 150 m². 6 photo exhibitions/year. Artists: Horst P. Horst, Claude Fauville, Klaus-Dieter Weber, Olaf Martens, Jeanloup Sieff

Aktionsforum Praterinsel, Praterinsel 3–4, D-80538 München. Tel (089) 29160875, Fax (089) 29160876. Open: Tue+Sun 10–18, Wed–Sat 14–20

Ausstellungsfoyer, Vereinte Versicherungen, Fritz-Schäffer-Str. 9, D-81737 München. Tel (089) 67854671

Barbara Gross Galerie, Thierschstr. 51, D-80538 München. Tel (089) 296272, Fax (089) 295510. Director: Barbara Gross. Founded 1988. 4 rooms, 100 m². 2–4 photo exhibitions/year. Artists: Richard Billingham, Sophie Calle, John Davies, Valie Export, Boris Mikhailov, Ana Mendieta, Katharina Sieverding, Kiki Smith, Gabriel Orozco, James Welling

Edition Schellmann, Römer Str. 14, D-80801 München. Tel (089) 331717, Fax (089) 332800. Open: Mon–Fri 10–18. Director: Jörg Schellmann. Founded 1969. 2 rooms, 200 m². 1 photo exhibition/year. Artists: Bernd & Hilla Becher, Gilbert & George, Robert Mapplethorpe, Thomas Ruff, Cindy Sherman

Galerie Albrecht, Worzerstr. 16, D-80539 München. Tel (089) 268689, Fax (089) 2605292. Open: Tue–Fri 14–18, Sat 11–14. Artist: Pentii Sammallahti

Galerie Christa Burger, Fürstenstr. 8, D-80333 München. Tel (089) 28996550, Fax (089) 28996551. Open: Tue–Fri 14–18.30, Sat 11–14 and by appointment. Artists: Tina Bara, Andrew Phelps

Galerie der Moderne Stefan Vogdt, Kurfürstenstr. 5, D-80799 München. Tel (089) 987045/2716857/0172-8228850, Fax (089) 99750505. Director: Margot Utzschmid

Galerie Objekte, Kurfürstenstr. 17, D-80799 München. Tel (089) 2711345, Fax (089) 2711345. E-mail womamue @t-online.de. Open: Mon–Fri 14–18.30. Director: Wolfgang F. Maurer. 4 rooms, 100 m². 4 photo exhibitions/year. Artists: Jan Saudek, Franco Fontana, Claudia Böhm, Annemarie Schudel, Katharina Krauss-Vonow, Carlo Mollino, Martin Chambi, Ettore Sottsass, Vivienne Maricevic, Occhio Magico

Galerie Philomene Magers, Schellingstr. 48, D-80799 München. Tel (089) 28808685, Fax (089) 28808679. E-mail pm@philomenemagers.com. Open: Tue–Fri 11–14, 15–18, Sat 11–14 and by appointment. Director: Philomene Magers. Artists: John Baldessari, Anna & Bernhard Blume, Sylvie Fleury, Dan Flavin, Ed Ruscha

Galerie Wittenbrink, Jahnstr. 18, D-80469 München. Tel (089) 2605580, Fax (089) 2605868. Open: Tue–Fri 14–18, Sat 11–14. Directors: Bernhard Wittenbrink, Hanna Wittenbrink. Founded 1978. 3 rooms, 150 m². 3 photo exhibitions/year. Artists: Alexander Timtschenko, Katharina Bosse, Katrin Thomas, Ulrich Schmitt, Astrid Klein, Helmut Newton, Florian Thomas

Haus der Kunst, Prinzregentenstr. 1, D-80538 München. Tel (089) 211270, Fax (089) 21127157. Open: Tue–Fri 10–22, Sat–Mon 10–18. Director: Christoph Vitali. Curator: Prof. Dr. Hubertus Gaßner. Founded 1938.

Galerie Angelo Falzone

109 Germany

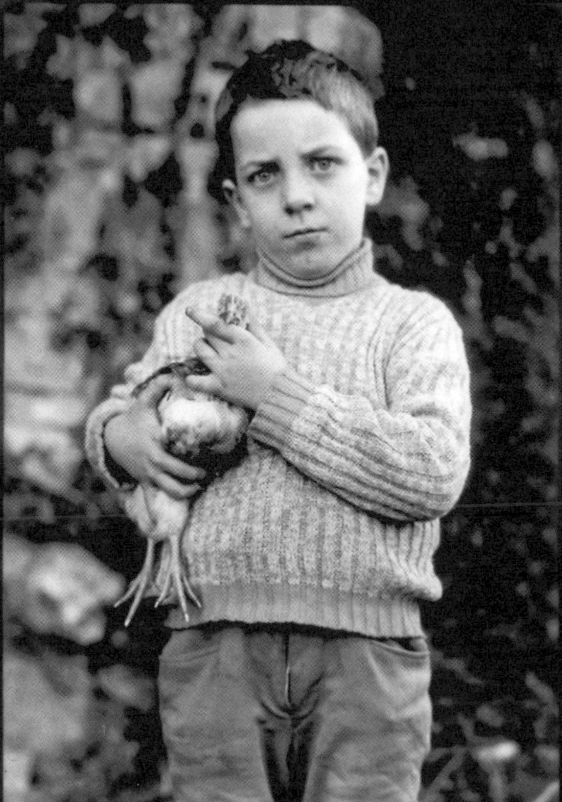

Pino Bertelli "Campiglia Marittima" 80er / Bromsilberabzug, Barytpapier

PHOTOGRAPHERS AND MEDIA ARTISTS OF THE GALLERY:

Pino Bertelli, Lewis Baltz, M&M Fasoli, Olivier Richon, Sinje Dillenkofer, Peter Schlör
Olivo Barbieri, Michael Najjar, Francesco Illy, Alba D'Urbano, Margret Eicher, Klaus
Wefringhaus, Andreas Müller-Pohle, Günther Selichar, Gerhard Vormwald

Galerie Angelo Falzone / Theodor-Heuss-Anlage 12
D - 68165 Mannheim / Phon (0049) 6 21 . 41 67 80
Fax (0049) 6 21 . 41 67 82

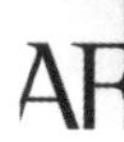

15 rooms, 2,000 m². 1–2 photo exhibitions/year

Münchner Stadtmuseum, Fotomuseum, St.-Jakobs-Platz 1, D-80331 München. Tel (089) 23322948, Fax (089) 23327967. E-mail stadtmuseum@compuserve.com. Open: Tue–Sun 10–18. Director: Dr. Ulrich Pohlmann. Founded 1961. 2 rooms, 350 m². 6–8 photo exhibitions/year. Artists: Frank Eugene, Franz Hanfstaengl, Theodor Hilsdorf, Hubs Flöter, Alois Löcherer, Philip Kester, Barbara Lüdecke, Stefan Moses, Regina Relang, Erich Retzlaff

Schneider-Henn, Galeriestr. 2b, D-80539 München. Tel (089) 297199, Fax (089) 2904515. Open: Mon–Fri 9–13, 14–18. 1 room. Artist: Hannes Kilian

Villa Stuck, Prinzregentenstr. 60, D-81675 München. Tel (089) 4555510, Fax (089) 45555124. E-mail villastuck@compuserve.com. Website www.muechen.de/villastuck. Open: Tue–Sun 10–18. Director: Jo-Anne Birnie Danzker. Founded 1968. 11 rooms, 1,500 m². 1–2 photo exhibitions/year

Walter Storms Galerie, Ismaninger Str. 51, D-81675 München. Tel (089) 41902828, Fax (089) 41902829. Artists: Ellen Auerbach, Michael Wesely, Arnold Newman

Westfälischer Kunstverein, Domplatz 10, D-48143 Münster. Tel (0251) 46157, Fax (0251) 45479. Open: Tue–Sun 10–18. Director: Dr. Susanne Gaensheimer. Founded 1831. 2 rooms, 300 m². 1 photo exhibition/year

Rheinisches Industriemuseum, Hansastr. 18, D-46049 Oberhausen. Tel (0208) 85790, Fax (0208) 8579101. E-mail r.wirtz@mail.lvr.de. Website www/lvr/dez9/amt91/rim. Open: daily 10–17 (Thu –20). Director: Prof.

Dr. Rainer Wirtz. Curator: Dr. Daniel Stemmrich. Founded 1987. 5 rooms, 850 m². 4 photo exhibitions/year

Galerie Hammer/Regensburger Fotogalerie, Untere Bachgasse 6, D-93047 Regensburg. Tel (0941) 563171. Open: Tue–Fri 11–18, Sat 10–13

Kunsthalle Rostock, Hamburger Str. 40, D-18069 Rostock. Tel (0381) 82336, Fax (0381) 8016288. Open: Wed–Sun 10–18. Director: Dr. Ulrich Ptak. Founded 1969. 3 rooms, 1,500 m². 1 photo exhibition/year. Artists: Per Kirkeby, Hermann Glöckner, Otto Niemeyer-Holstein, Willy Wolff, Felix Droese, Bernhard Kretzschmar, Theodor Rosenhauer, Robert Sterl

GAFF, Galerie für Fotografie, Distelweg 6, D-27356 Rotenburg/Wümme. Tel (04261) 83756, Fax (04261) 83756. E-mail gs.gaff@t-online.de. Open: Wed 17–20, Sun 11–13. Director: Gerd Schnakenwinkel. Founded 1988. 1 room, 58 m². 5–6 photo exhibitions/year. Artists: Sibylle Bergemann, Rudi Torunskí, Klaus Benhof, Alfred Ehrhardt, Arno Fischer, Andreas Rost, Klaus-Dieter Weber, Tristan Vankann, Christel Kremser

Staatliches Museum Schwerin, Kunstsammlungen Schlösser und Gärten, Alter Garten 3, D-19055 Schwerin. Tel (0385) 59580, Fax (0385) 563090. E-mail otto@museum-schwerin.de. Website www.museum-schwerin.de/. Open: Tue 10–20, Wed–Sun 10–18. Director: Dr. Kornelia von Berswordt-Wallrabe. Curator: Dr. Gerhard Graulich. Founded 1994. 3 rooms, 600 m². 1 photo exhibition/year. Artists: Valie Export, Tim Ulrichs, Dieter Kiessling

Stadtmuseum Siegburg, Markt 46, D-53721 Siegburg. Tel (02241) 9698511, Fax (02241) 9698525. E-mail stadtmuseum@siegburg.de. Website www.siegburg.de. Open: Tue–Sat 10–17 (Thu –20), Sun 10–18. Director: Dr. Gert Fischer. Founded 1990. 2 rooms, 250 m². 1 photo exhibition/year. Artists: Knut Wolfgang Maron, Hartmut Zander, Susanne Greven, Wojciech Prazmowski, Salvatore Puglia, Kapa, Angelika Bliese, Andreas Kuhlmann, Rainer Griese, Herbert Döring-Spengler

Leica Galerie, Oskar-Barnack-Str. 11, D-35606 Solms. Tel (06442) 208404, Fax (06442) 208410. E-mail cpr@leica-camera.com. Website www.leica-camera.com. Open: 7–18. Director: H. G. von Zydowitz. Founded 1976. 1 room, 20 m². 12 photo exhibitions/year. Artists: Eric Valli, Fred Hazel-hoff, Ann-Marie Grobet, Fee Schlapper, Takeshi Mizukoshi, Andrej Reiser, Hans W. Silvester

Galerie Kaess-Weiss, Grüneisenstr. 19, D-70184 Stuttgart. Tel (0711) 232627, Fax (0711) 248165. Open: Tue–Fri 14–18.30, Sat 10–14. Directors: Gudrun Weiss, Carl Kaess. Founded 1986. 3 rooms, 70 m². 1 photo exhibition/year. Artists: Helmut Newton, Alan David-Tu, Tjarda Sixma, Henk Tas

Staatsgalerie Stuttgart, Konrad-Adenauer-Str. 32, D-70038 Stuttgart. Tel (0711) 2124101, Fax (0711) 2124111. Open: Tue+Thu 10–20, Wed+Fri–Sun 10–17

Württembergischer Kunstverein Stuttgart, Schloßplatz 2, D-70173 Stuttgart. Tel (0711) 223370, Fax (0711) 293617. E-mail info@wkv-stuttgart.de. Website www.stuttgart.de. Open: Tue–Fri 11–18 (Wed –20), Sat–Sun and bank holidays 11–18. Director: Dr. Martin Hentschel. Founded 1827. 5 rooms, 2,500 m². 1–2 photo exhibitions/year

Pixel.Art Gallery, Niedernhart 1, D-94113 Tiefenbach. Tel (08546) 919110, Fax (08546) 919306. E-mail dkuehmeier@pixelnet.de. Website www.pixelnet.de. Open: Mon–Fri 13–17 and by appointment. Curators: Brigitte Blüml, Kurt Kaindl, Walter Landshuter, Doris Kühmeier

Klaus Hinrichs KunstRaum, Sichelstr. 4, D-54290 Trier. Tel (0651) 49092, Fax (0651) 43266. Open: Tue–Fri 14–18, Sat 10–14 and by appointment. Director: Klaus Hinrichs. Founded 1991. 4 rooms, 130 m². 4–5 photo exhibitions/year. Artists: Yehuda Altmann, Rudolf Bonvie, Rut Blees Luxemburg, Joachim Brohm, Sinje Dillenkofer, Robert Häusser, Astrid Klein, Laura Padgett, Ursula Wevers, Byrd Williams

Maisenbacher Art Gallery, Engels-trasse 12, D-54292 Trier. Tel (0651) 25900, Fax (0651) 21013. E-mail gallery@maisenbacher-art.de. Website www.maisenbacher-art.de. Open: Tue–Sat 15–19. Director/curator: Christoph Maisenbacher. Founded 1998. 2 rooms, 55 m². 3 photo exhibitions/year. Artists: Thomas Baumgärtel, Sebastiaan Spit, Christian Frosch, Sven Hoffmann, Helge Hommes, Claudia Pilsl, Ren Rong, Peter Schlör, Richard Tipping, Lisette Verkerk

Stadthaus Ulm, Münsterplatz 38, D-89073 Ulm. Tel (0731) 1617700, Fax (0731) 1617701. E-mail stadthaus@ulm.de. Website www.stadthaus.ulm.de

ACC Galerie, Burgplatz 1, D-99423 Weimar. Tel (03643) 62970, Fax (03643) 502280. Open: Mon–Sun 12–18

Kunstmuseum Wolfsburg, Porsche-str. 53, D-38440 Wolfsburg. Tel (05361)

26690, Fax (05361) 266911.
E-mail info@kunstmuseum-
wolfsburg.de. Website www.
kunstmuseum-wolfsburg.de. Open:
Tue 11–20, Wed–Sun 11–18. Director:
Dr. Gijs van Tuyl. Curators: Veit
Görner, Annelie Lütgens, Holger
Broeker. Founded 1993. 4 rooms,
3,411 m². 3–4 photo exhibitions/year.
Artists: Cindy Sherman, Wolfgang
Tillmans, Richard Billingham, Jeff
Wall, Andreas Gursky, Gilbert &
George

Lichtbild-Galerie, Neu-Bergedorfer
Damm 44a, D-27726 Worpswede. Tel
(04792) 4442, Fax (04792) 4442. Open:
Sat–Sun 14–17. Director: Wolfgang
Kleine. Founded 1987. 2 rooms, 90 m².
4 photo exhibitions/year. Artists:
Christer Strömholm, Fritz Henle,
Otmar Thormann, Vilém Reichmann,
Walter Ballhause, William Carter,
Jean-Paul Rohner, Willy Zielke
Estate, Heinrich Heidersberger,
Peter Keetman

Räume für neue Kunst, Rolf Henges-
bach, Vogelsangstr. 18, D-42109
Wuppertal. Tel (0202) 753532, Fax
(0202) 753634. Open: Wed–Fri 14–
19.30, Sat 10–14. Director: Rolf Hen-
gesbach. Founded 1991. 3 rooms,
200 m². 1–2 photo exhibitions/year.
Artists: Richard Caldicott, Clegg &
Guttmann, William Eggleston,
Graham Gussin, Christopher Muller,
Bridget Smith, Michael Seeling,
Dieter Kiessling

Von der Heydt-Museum, Turmhof 8,
D-42103 Wuppertal. Tel (0202)
5636231, Fax (0202) 5638091. Website
www.wuppertal.de/von-der-heydt-
museum. Open: Tue–Sun 11–18 (Thu
–20). Director: Dr. Sabine Fehlemann.
Founded 1902. 27 rooms, 7,000 m².
1 photo exhibition/year

Festivals & Fairs

Art Cologne, Internationaler Kunstmarkt, Messe- und Ausstellungs-
Ges.mbH, P. O. Box 210760, D-50532
Köln. Tel (0221) 8213215, Fax (0221)
8213437. E-mail artcologne@
koelnmesse.de. Website www.
artcologne.de

Art Frankfurt, International Fair for
Contemporary Art, Ludwig-Erhard-
Anlage 1, D-60327 Frankfurt/Main.
Tel (069) 75756664, Fax (069)
75756674. E-mail artfrankfurt@
messefrankfurt.com. Website
www.artfrankfurt.de

documenta, Museum Fridericianum,
Friedrichsplatz 18, D-34117 Kassel.
Tel (0561) 707270, Fax (0561) 774276.
E-mail 100433.1542@compuserve.
com

European Art Forum Berlin, Messe
Berlin GmbH, Erika Plies, Messe-
damm 22, D-14055 Berlin. Tel (030)
30382061, Fax (030) 30382070

Internationale Fototage, c/o Galerie
Lichtblick, Tina Schellhorn, Steinbergstr. 21, D-50733 Köln. Tel (0221)
729149, Fax (0221) 729149

Internationale Fototage Herten,
BildForum, Resser Weg 1, D-45699
Herten. Tel (02366) 303232, Fax
(02366) 104176. E-mail bildforum@
aol.com. Website www.agfaphoto.
com/herten

photokina, Messe- und Ausstellungs-
Ges.mbH, P. O. Box 210760, D-50532
Köln. Tel (0221) 8212380, Fax (0221)
8213415

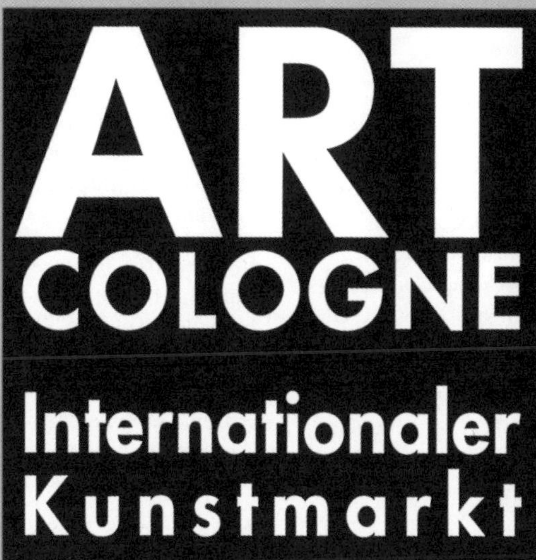

34th International Fair for Modern Art
ART COLOGNE
Internationaler Kunstmarkt
Cologne, Nov. 5–12, 2000
Information: KölnMesse GmbH,
P.O. Box 210760
D-50532 Cologne, Germany
Phone +49 221/821-0
Fax +49 221/821-3734
Internet: www.artcologne.de

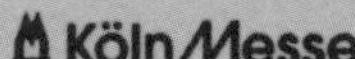

KölnMesse

Magazines

Arbeiterfotografie, Forum für Engagierte Fotografie, Merheimer Str. 107, D-50733 Köln. Tel (0221) 725298, Fax (0221) 7325588. E-mail arbeiterfotografie@t-online. Website www.arbeiterfotografie.de. Editor: Anneliese Fikentscher. German. Founded 1973. Copy price: DM 14.00. Annual subscription: DM 25.00, 2 issues/year

Art, Das Kunstmagazin, Am Baumwall 11, P. O. Box 110011, D-20459 Hamburg. Tel (040) 37030, Fax (040) 37035618. E-mail art.kunstmagazine @guj.de. Website www.art-magazine.de. Editor: Axel Hecht. German. Founded 1979. Copy price: DM 15.30. Annual subscription: DM 156.00, 12 issues/year

Artist, Außer der Schleifmühle 51, D-28203 Bremen. Tel (0421) 3398491, Fax (0421) 3398492. E-mail info@ artist-kunstmagazin.de

Belser Kunst Quartal, Vorschau auf Kunstausstellungen des In- und Auslandes, Senefelderstr. 12, D-73760 Ostfildern. Tel (0711) 4405226, Fax (0711) 4405228. E-mail rpalmer@ hatjecantz.de. Editor: Renate Palmer. German. Founded 1965. Copy price: DM 14.00. Annual subscription: DM 48.00, 4 issues/year

Color Foto, Heinrich-Vogl-Str. 22, D-81479 München. Tel (089) 791910, Fax (089) 7919111. Editor: Michael Tafelmaier. German. Founded 1970. Copy price: DM 9.00. Annual subscription: DM 96.00, 12 issues/year

Design Report, Blue C. Verlag GmbH, Große Elbstr. 68, D-22767 Hamburg. Tel (040) 30621400, Fax (040) 30621409. E-mail designreport@ macup.com. Website www.design-report.de. Editor: Klaus Thomas Edelmann. German (English summaries). Founded 1972. Copy price: DM 14.00. Annual subscription: DM132.00, 10 issues/year

European Photography, The international art magazine for contemporary photography and new media, P. O. Box 3043, D-37020 Göttingen. Tel (0551) 24820, Fax (0551) 25224. E-mail europhoto@equivalence.com. Website www.equivalence.com. Editor: Andreas Müller-Pohle. German/English. Founded 1980. Copy price: EUR 16.00, US$20.00. Two-year subscription: EUR 64.00 (Europe), US$80.00 (outside Europe), 2 issues/year

FotoMagazin, top special Verlag GmbH, Chiemgaustr. 109, D-81549 München. Tel (089) 68001121, Fax (089) 68001122. E-mail fotomag@ aol.com. Website www.evita.de. Editor: Klaus-Peter Bredschneider. German. Founded 1949, 12 issues/ year

Kultur-Chronik, Kennedyallee 91–103, D-53175 Bonn. Tel (0228) 880343, Fax (0228) 880384. Editor: Michael Hierholzer

Kunstforum International, P. O. Box 1147, D-53809 Ruppichteroth. Tel (02295) 5023, Fax (02295) 5021. Editor: Dieter Bechtloff. German. Copy price: DM 34.80. Annual subscription: DM 139.20, 4 issues/year

Kunsttermine.de, P. O. Box 150151, D-70075 Stuttgart. Tel (0711) 6143470, Fax (0711) 6143472. E-mail kontakt@ kunsttermine.de. Website www. kunsttermine.de. Editor: Reiner Brouwer. German. Copy price: DM 15.00. Annual subscription: DM 50.00, 4 issues/year

Kunstzeitung, Lindinger + Schmid, Margaretenstr. 8, D-93047 Regens-

EUROPEAN PHOTOGRAPHY

ART MAGAZINE · NUMBER 67

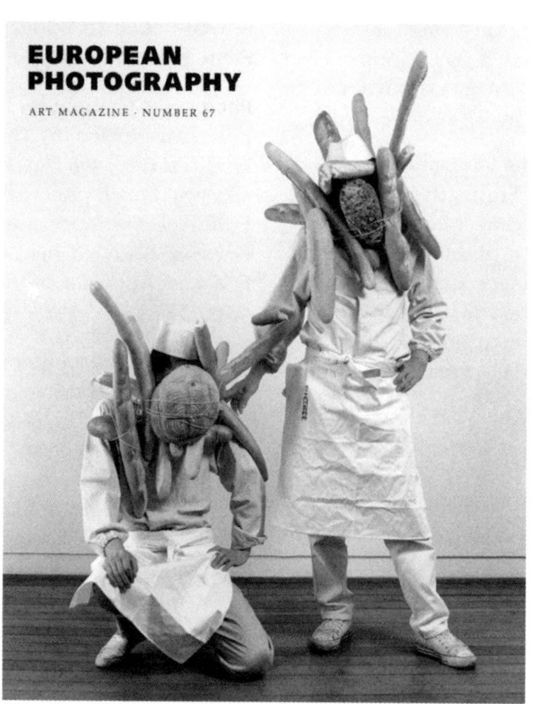

European Photography appears twice a year in English and German. 84 pages, duotone and full-color printing, sewn-binding. Copy price EUR 16.00 or US$20.00. Two-year subscription EUR 64.00 (Europe) or $80.00 (outside Europe), including postage. Order address: European Photography Subscriptions, P.O. Box 3043, 37020 Göttingen, Germany Visa, Eurocard, MasterCard welcome

European Photography is the international art magazine for contemporary photography and new media – a vital forum for images and ideas. Recent issues include works by Olivo Barbieri, Vik Muniz, Beth Yarnelle Edwards, Izima Kaoru, Philip-Lorca diCorcia, Tatsumi Orimoto, Adam Fuss, and Lucinda Devlin. *Looks excellent and contains impressive work by both artists and critics...* (Mark Haworth-Booth, Victoria & Albert Museum, London)

www.equivalence.com

115 Germany

burg. Tel (0941) 22177, Fax (0941) 270377. Editor: Karlheinz Schmid. German. Founded 1996. Annual subscription: DM 72.00 (only for handling and mail), 12 issues/year

Leica Fotografie International, Umschau Verlag, Stuttgarter Str. 18–24, D-60329 Frankfurt/Main. Tel (069) 26000, Fax (069) 2600609. Editor: Heiner Henninges. German/English/French. Founded 1949. Copy price: DM 10.40. Annual subscription: DM 78.80, 8 issues/year

Leica World, Abt. Marketing Communications, Oskar-Barnack-Str. 11, D-35606 Solms. Tel (06442) 208401, Fax (06442) 208455. Website www.leica-camera.com. Editor: Michael Koetzle

Photo-Presse, Nachrichtenmagazin für die Fotobranche, Klie Verlagsgesellschaft mbH, Sichelsteiner Weg 2, D-34346 Hann. Münden. Tel (05541) 98490, Fax (05541) 9849-98/99. E-mail zentrale@photopresse.de. Website www.photopresse.de. Editor: Hagen Klie. German. Founded 1945. Annual subscription: DM 161.20, 52 issues/year

Photo Technik International, The leading professional magazine, top special Verlag GmbH, Chiemgaustr. 109, D-81549 München. Tel (089) 68001115, Fax (089) 68001112. Editor: Hans-Eberhard Hess. German. Founded 1954. Copy price: DM 14.50. Annual subscription: DM 87.00, 6 issues/year

Photographie, VVA, Höherweg 278, D-40231 Düsseldorf. Tel (0211) 98494930, Fax (0211) 98494925. E-mail photographie@vva.de. Website www.photographie.de. Editor: Gerald Blauermel

Photography Now, Kantstr. 17, D-10623 Berlin. Tel (030) 31515180, Fax (030) 31515185. E-mail photography.now@t-online.de. Editor: Claudia Stein. Founded 1998

Photonews, Zeitung für Photographie, Chemnitzstr. 67, D-22767 Hamburg. Tel (040) 3895891, Fax (040) 3800779. E-mail phnewshh@aol.com. Editors: Denis Brudna, Anna Gripp. German. Founded 1989. Copy price: DM 5.00. Annual subscription: DM 50.00, 10 issues/year

ProfiFoto, Magazin für professionelle Fotografie + Electronic Imaging, Volmerswerther Str. 20, D-40221 Düsseldorf. Tel (0211) 390090, Fax (0211) 3981619. E-mail mail@profifoto.de. Website www.profifoto.de. Editor: Thomas Gerwers. German. Founded 1969. Copy price: DM 14.80. Annual subscription: DM 81.00, 6 issues/year

Rundbrief Fotografie, Sammeln, Bewahren, Erschließen, Vermitteln, P. O. Box 210256, D-01263 Dresden. Tel (0351) 3160990, Fax (0351) 3160992. E-mail rundbrief@dresden.nacamar.de. Website www.foto.unibas.ch/~rundbrief. Editor: Wolfgang Hesse. German. Founded 1993. Copy price: DM 23.00. Annual subscription: DM 75.00, 4 issues/year

Schwarzweiss, Das Magazine für Fotografie, Umschau Zeitschriftenverlag, Stuttgarter Str. 18–24, D-60329 Frankfurt/Main. Tel (069) 2600625, Fax (069) 2600609. E-mail n.jiptner@broenner-umschau.de. Website www.uzv.de. Editor: Norbert Jiptner. German. Founded 1991. Copy price: DM 26.50. Annual subscription: DM 91.20, 4 issues/year

Texte zur Kunst, Norbertstr. 2–4, D-50670 Köln. Tel (0221) 1390445, Fax (0221) 138229. E-mail tzk@

netcologne.de. Editor: Isabelle Graw. German. Founded 1990. Copy price: DM 25.00 + mailing. Annual subscription: DM 90.00, DM 100.00 (Europe), DM 130.00 (overseas)

Visuell International, PIAG-Verlag, Stephanienstr. 25, D-76530 Baden-Baden. Tel (07221) 3017560, Fax (07221) 3017570. E-mail piag. visuell@t-online.de. Website www. fotomarktplatz.de. Editor: Dieter Brinzer. English. Founded 1973. Copy price: DM 9.00. Annual subscription: DM 66.00, 6 issues/year

Book Publishers

Benedikt Taschen Verlag, Hohenzollernring 53, D-50672 Köln. Tel (0221) 201800, Fax (0221) 2018097/254919. E-mail info@taschen.de

Die Gestalten Verlag GmbH, Zehdenickerstr. 21, D-10119 Berlin. Tel (030) 4491272/44340773, Fax (030) 30871068. E-mail verlag@die-gestalten.de. Website www.die-gestalten.de

DuMont Buchverlag, Mittelstr. 12–14, D-50672 Köln. Tel (0221) 20530, Fax (0221) 2053-281/294. Website www.dumont.de

Edition Braus im Wachter Verlag GmbH, Hebelstr. 10, D-69115 Heidelberg. Tel (06221) 5029660, Fax (06221) 5029666. Website www.editionbraus.de

Elefanten Press, Am Treptower Park 28–30, D-12435 Berlin. Tel (030) 68834151, Fax (030) 68834159

European Photography, P. O. Box 3043, D-37020 Göttingen. Tel (0551) 24820,

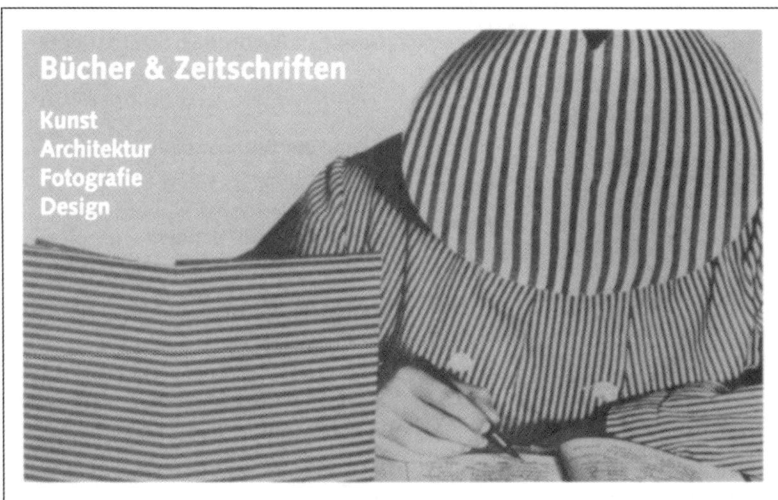

Fax (0551) 25224. E-mail europhoto@equivalence.com. Website www.equivalence.com

Ex posé Verlag, Yorckstr. 89a, D-10965 Berlin. Tel (030) 7858169, Fax (030) 7858169

Fotokunst-Verlag Groh, Hauptstr. 15, D-82237 Wörthsee. Tel (08153) 8830

Gina Kehayoff Verlag, Herzogstr. 60, D-80803 München. Tel (089) 390185, Fax (089) 338053

H. B. Wilson DMK CO sro, P. O. Box 22, D-91448 Emskirchen. Tel (09104) 86223, Fax (09104) 86225. E-mail hwilson@aol.com

Hatje Cantz Verlag, Senefelder Str. 12, D-73760 Ostfildern/Ruit. Tel (0711) 44050, Fax (0711) 4405220. E-mail sales@hatjecantz.de. Website www.hatjecantz.de

Jonas Verlag für Kunst und Literatur GmbH, Weidenhäuser Str. 88, D-35037 Marburg. Tel (06421) 25132, Fax (06421) 210572. E-mail jonas-verlag@soultek.de

Kruse Verlag GmbH, Meike Lottmann, Kampstr. 11, D-20357 Hamburg. Tel (040) 43282460, Fax (040) 432824612. E-mail lottmann@krusepublishers.com

Lindinger + Schmid GbR, Verlag und Kunstprojekte, Margaretenstr. 8, D-93047 Regensburg. Tel (0941) 22177, Fax (0941) 270377

Nazraeli Press, Waldemarstr. 81, D-10997 Berlin. Tel (030) 61609237, Fax (030) 61609238, E-mail nazraeli@aol.com

Nicolaische Verlagsbuchhandlung, Neuenburger Str. 17, D-10969 Berlin. Tel (030) 2537380, Fax (030) 25373840. E-mail info@nicolai-verlag.de

Nieswand-Verlag, Werftbahnstr. 8, D-24143 Kiel. Tel (0431) 735962, Fax (0431) 739031

Prestel Verlag, Mandlstr. 26, D-80802 München. Tel (089) 3817090, Fax (089) 38170935

Richter Verlag, Corneliusstr. 48, D-40215 Düsseldorf. Tel (0211) 370202, Fax (0211) 377099

Schaden Verlag, Burgmauer 10, D-50679 Köln. Tel (0221) 9252668, Fax (0221) 9252669. E-mail verlag@schaden.com. Website www.schaden.com

Schirmer/Mosel Verlag, Widenmayerstr. 16, D-80538 München. Tel (089) 2126700, Fax (089) 338695. Website www.schirmer-mosel.de

Steidl Verlag, Düstere Strasse 4, D-37073 Göttingen. Tel (0551) 496060, Fax (0551) 4960649. E-mail mail@steidl.de. Website www.steidl.de

Umschau Buchverlag, Stuttgarter Str. 18–24, D-60329 Frankfurt/Main. Tel (069) 26001, Fax (069) 2600223

Verlag der Buchhandlung Walther König, Ehrenstr. 4, D-50672 Köln. Tel (0221) 2059-53/54, Fax (0221) 2059660. E-mail verlag@buchhandlung-walther-koenig.de

Verlag der Kunst, G+B Fine Arts Verlag GmbH, Rosa-Menzer-Str. 12, D-01309 Dresden. Tel (0351) 3100052, Fax (0351) 3105245. E-mail verlag-der-kunst@t-online.de

Bookshops

Artificium, Hackische Höfe, Rosenthaler Str. 40–41, D-10178 Berlin

Buchhandlung L. Werner, Residenzstr. 18, D-80333 München

NAZRAELI PRESS *Art & Photography Books*

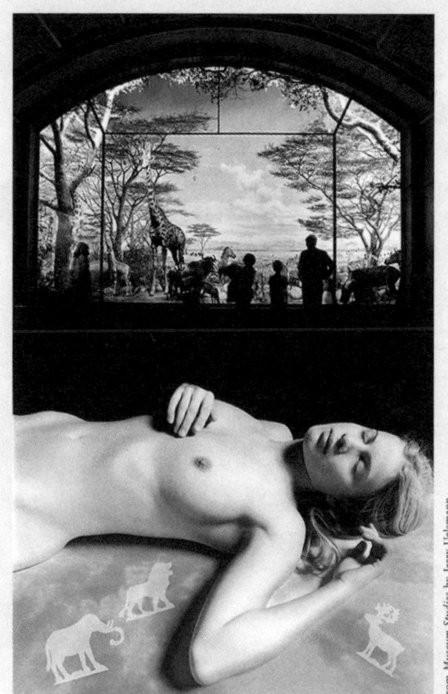

From *Museum Studies* by Jerry Uelsmann

Printed Catalogue on request: nazraeli@aol.com

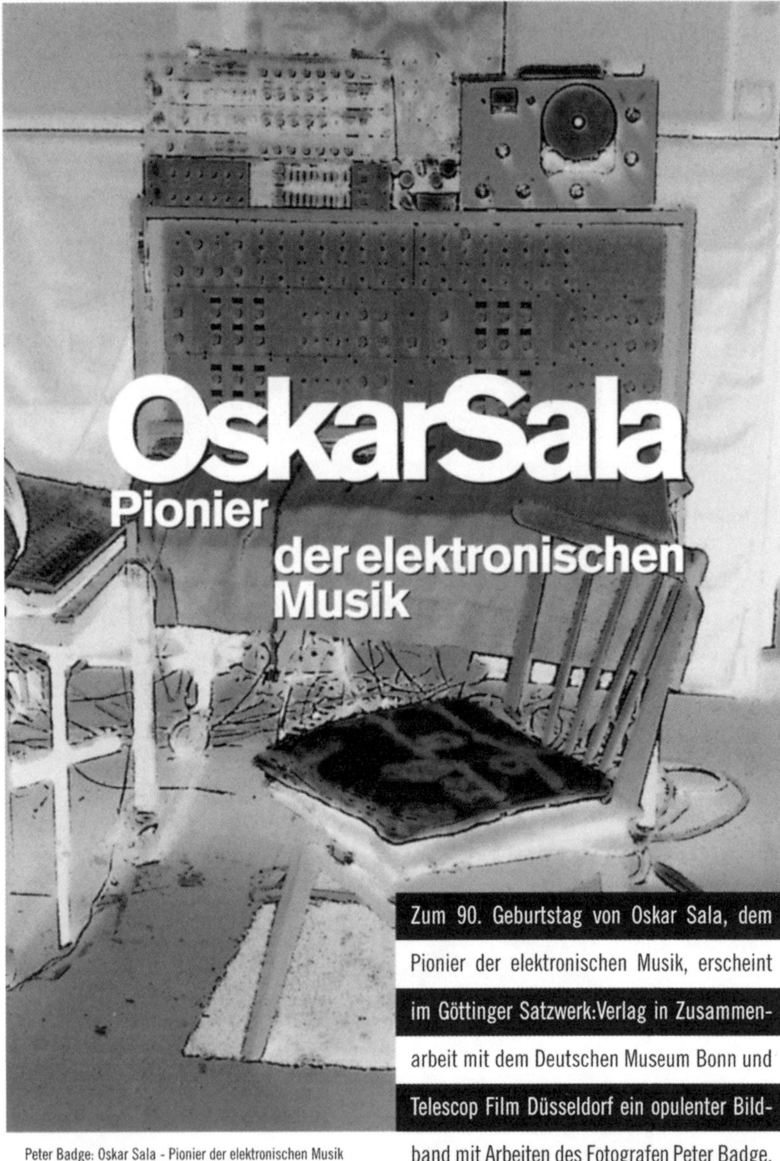

120 Germany

Peter Badge: Oskar Sala - Pionier der elektronischen Musik
Herausgegeben von Dr. Peter Frieß, Deutsches Museum Bonn
Erscheint im Satzwerk:Verlag, Göttingen
in Zusammenarbeit mit Telescop Film, Düsseldorf

Bildband in Duotone, ca. 120 Seiten + CD-ROM
DM 120,-- Euro 61,36
ISBN 3-930333-34-1

Peter Badge
wird vertreten durch Galerie Francoise Knabe, Frankfurt/Berlin
E-Mail: galerie.knabe@t-online.de
Tel.:   06181/25 14 18
Fax: 06181/25 14 86

Zum 90. Geburtstag von Oskar Sala, dem Pionier der elektronischen Musik, erscheint im Göttinger Satzwerk:Verlag in Zusammenarbeit mit dem Deutschen Museum Bonn und Telescop Film Düsseldorf ein opulenter Bildband mit Arbeiten des Fotografen Peter Badge, der Sala über einige Monate auf der Bühne, im Studio und auch privat begleitet hat. Dem Buch beigefügt ist eine CD-ROM mit Musik, Filmausschnitten, einem interaktivem Trautonium, etc.

Buchhandlung Walther König, Ehrenstr. 4, D-50672 Köln

Buchhandlung Walther König im Martin-Gropius-Bau, Niederkirchner Str. 7, D-10963 Berlin

Bücherbogen am Savignyplatz, Stadtbahnbogen 593, D-10345 Berlin. Tel (030) 31869511, Fax (030) 3137237

Galerie 2000, Knesebeckstr. 56/58, D-10719 Berlin. Tel (030) 8838467, Fax (030) 8824432

Goltz – Buchhandlung für Bildende Kunst und Photographie, Türkenstr. 54, D- 80799 München

Kunst-Buch, Schirn Kunsthalle, Römerberg, D-60311 Frankfurt/Main

Lindemanns, Nadler Str. 10, D-70173 Stuttgart. Tel (0711) 24899977, Fax (0711) 2369672

PPS-Fachbuchhandlung für Photographie, Hochhaus, Feldstr. 1, D-20357 Hamburg. Tel (040) 43178155, Fax (040) 43178140. E-mail bookshop @pps-online.de. Website www.pps-online.de

Schaden.com, Buchhandlung GmbH, Burgmauer 10, D-50667 Köln. Tel (0221) 9252667, Fax (0221) 9252669. E-mail books@schaden.com. Website www.schaden.com

Auctions

Lempertz, Neumarkt 3, D-50667 Köln. Tel (0221) 9257290, Fax (0221) 9257296

Schneider-Henn, Galeriestr. 2b, D-80539 München. Tel (089) 297199, Fax (089) 2904515

Villa Grisebach, Fasanenstr. 25, D-10719 Berlin. Tel (030) 8859150, Fax (030) 8854095

Critics & Journalists

Prof. Dr. Hubertus von Amelunxen, An den Eichen 1, D-24242 Felde. Tel (04340) 402701, Fax (04340) 402703. E-mail amelunxen@muthesius.de. *Fotogeschichte,* Wien; *European Photography,* Göttingen; Muthesius Hochschule, Kiel

Peter Badge, P. O. Box 360315, D-10973 Berlin. Tel (030) 5139080, Fax (030) 5139080. E-mail typos1 @aol.com. *Photo Presse,* Hann. Münden; *Berliner Zeitung,* Berlin

Dr. Angelika Beckmann, Südstr. 61, D-53340 Meckenheim. Tel (02225) 706286, Fax (02225) 706286. *Fotogeschichte, Eikon,* Wien

Susanne Boecker, Redaktionsbüro Dank, Gladbacher Str. 18–20, D-50672 Köln. Tel (0221) 9520464/734907, Fax (0221) 9520463. E-mail boecker@ artcontent.de. *Kölner Stadtanzeiger, WDR,* Köln; *Kunstforum,* Ruppichteroth; www.artthing.de

Prof. Jörg Boström, Steinweg 1, D-32049 Herford. Tel (05221) 840639. *Fotogeschichte,* Wien; *Arbeiterfotografie,* Köln; Fachhochschule Bielefeld

Denis Brudna, Photonews, Chemnitzstr. 67, D-22767 Hamburg. Tel (040) 3895891, Fax (040) 3895891. Editor of *Photonews,* Hamburg

W. P. Fahrenberg, Am Eikborn 15a, D-37079 Göttingen. Tel (0551) 43390, Fax (0551) 59175. E-mail ausstellungsbuero@ozet.de

Dr. Zdenek Felix, Deichtorhallen Hamburg, Deichtorstr. 2, D-20095 Hamburg. Tel (040) 32103240, Fax (040) 32103230

Dr. Gerhard Glüher, Alter Kirchhainer Weg 59, D-35039 Marburg. Tel

(06421) 15973. Kunstverein Marburg; *European Photography*, Göttingen

Gérard A. Goodrow, Forststr. 84, D-50767 Köln. Tel (0221) 9790190, Fax (0221) 7124932

Anna Gripp, Photonews, Chemnitzstr. 67, D-22767 Hamburg. Tel (040) 3895891, Fax (040) 3895891. Editor of *Photonews*, Hamburg

Prof. L. Fritz Gruber, Paulistr. 10, D-50933 Köln. Tel (0221) 494249

Dr. Wulf Herzogenrath, Kunsthalle Bremen, Am Wall 207, D-28195 Bremen. Tel (0421) 3290821, Fax (0421) 3290847

Hans-Eberhard Hess, Kazmairstr. 34, D-80339 München. Tel (089) 68001115, Fax (089) 68001122. Editor of *Photo Technik International*, München; *Süddeutsche Zeitung*, München

Prof. Klaus Honnef, Baumschulallee 3, D-53115 Bonn. Tel (0228) 655681, Fax (0228) 637660. E-mail art.honnef@ t-online.de. *Die Welt*, Berlin; *Art*, Hamburg; *Eikon*, Wien; *European Photography*, Göttingen; *Camera Austria*, Graz

Georg Imdahl, Frankfurter Allgemeine Zeitung, Hellerhofstr. 2–4, D-60327 Frankfurt/Main. *Frankfurter Allgemeine Zeitung*, Frankfurt/Main

Prof. Dr. Gottfried Jäger, August-Bebel-Str. 67, D-33602 Bielefeld. Tel (0521) 63542, Fax (0521) 138617. E-mail gjaeger@fhzinfo.fh-bielefeld.de. Website www.gottfried-jaeger.de. Fachhochschule Bielefeld; *European Photography*, Göttingen; Kerber Verlag, Bielefeld

Dr. Enno Kaufhold, Pohlstr. 69, D-10785 Berlin. Tel (030) 2618247, Fax (030) 2618247. *Photonews*, Hamburg, *European Photography*, Göttingen

Michael Köhler, Zieblandstr. 10, D-80799 München. Tel (089) 2723852, Fax (089) 2725836. E-mail s.press@az-online.net. Website www.spress.de/ foto. *Artis*, Bern; *Kunstforum International*, Ruppichteroth

Michael Koetzle, Kazmairstr. 81, D-80339 München. Tel (089) 50009890, Fax (089) 50029565. *Photo Technik International*, München; *European Photography*, Göttingen; *Leica World*, Solms; *Max*, Hamburg

Dr. Andreas Krase, Marienburger Str. 30a, D-10405 Berlin. Tel (030) 4424191, Fax (030) 4424191. E-mail krase@ iapp.de. *Berliner Zeitung*, Berlin; *Photonews*, Hamburg; *Fotogeschichte*, Wien; *Bauwelt*, Berlin

Dr. Dr. Rolf H. Krauss, Heusteigstr. 37, D-70180 Stuttgart. Tel (0711) 6492166, Fax (0711) 609616. E-mail rhkrauss@t-online.de

Freddy Langer, Wilhelmsbader Weg 9, D-60386 Frankfurt/Main. Tel (069) 426266, Fax (069) 424993. E-mail f.langer@faz.de. *Frankfurter Allgemeine Zeitung*, Frankfurt/Main

Claus Heinrich Meyer, Süddeutsche Zeitung, Sendlinger Str. 8, D-80331 München. Tel (089) 2183404, Fax (089) 2183787. *Süddeutsche Zeitung*, München

Dr. Reinhold Mißelbeck, Museum Ludwig, Photo- und Videosammlung, Bischofsgartenstr. 1, D-50667 Köln. Tel (0221) 2213619, Fax (0221) 2214114

Dr. Herbert Molderings, Leostr. 26, D-50823 Köln. Tel (0221) 519171

Andreas Müller-Pohle, P. O. Box 3043, D-37020 Göttingen. Tel (0551) 24820, Fax (0551) 25224. E-mail amp@ equivalence.com. Website www.

artificial
image

/ Digitale Kunstproduktion
Artists in new residence

Sorgfältige Digitalisierung
im medienneutralen Farbraum

Digitale Nachbearbeitung
an farbkalibrierten Arbeitsstationen

Iris-Giclée-Kunstdrucke
auf hochwertigen Materialien

Organisation und Farbmanagement
auch für grossflächige Kunstprojekte

123 Germany

Artificial Image

Köpenicker Straße 154a/157
10997 Berlin (Kreuzberg
Telefon 49 30) 25 79 99 15
Fax 49 30) 25 79 99 16
look@artificiality.com
www.artificiality.com

equivalence.com. Editor of *European Photography*, Göttingen

Dr. Claudia Gabriele Philipp, Museum für Kunst und Gewerbe, Steintorplatz 1, D-20099 Hamburg. Tel (040) 24862829, Fax (040) 24862834

Dr. Ulrich Pohlmann, Fotomuseum im Münchner Stadtmuseum, St.-Jakobs-Platz 1, D-80331 München. Tel (089) 23322948, Fax (089) 2337967. *Fotogeschichte*, Wien

Prof. Dr. Lothar Romain, Fichtestr. 2, D-10967 Berlin. Tel (030) 69041424, Fax (030) 69041425

Florian Rötzer, Kreittmayrstr. 26, D-80335 München. Tel (089) 182276. Editor of *Telepolis*, www.heise.de/tp; *European Photography*, Göttingen; *Kunstforum International*, Ruppichteroth

Dr. Peter Sager, Hummelsbütteler Kirchenweg 10, D-22335 Hamburg. Tel (040) 3280355. *Die Zeit*, Hamburg

Prof. Manfred Schmalriede, Schloßstr. 39, D-75245 Neulingen

Ulla Schmitz, P. O. Box 940105, D-60459 Frankfurt/Main. Tel (069) 788947, Fax (069) 788947. E-mail fotoinfo@fotoinfo.de. Website www.fotoinfo.de. AJPI – Photopädagogisches Büro, Frankfurt/Main

Thomas Seelig, Christinastr. 11, D-50733 Köln. Tel (0221) 7202021, Fax (0221) 7202023. E-mail thomasseelig@aol.com. *Eikon*, Wien; *Photonews*, Hamburg; *European Photography*, Göttingen

Ruprecht Skasa-Weiss, Roßhaustr. 6, D-70597 Stuttgart. Tel (0711) 766630

Christoph Tannert, Künstlerhaus Bethanien, Mariannenplatz 2, D-10997 Berlin. Tel (030) 61690314, Fax (030) 61690330. *European Photography*, Göttingen

Prof. Dr. Herta Wolf, Universität GH Essen/FB 4, D-45117 Essen. Tel (0201) 1834220, Fax (0201) 1833014. E-mail herta.wolf@uni-essen.de

Manfred Zollner, c/o FotoMagazin, top special Verlag GmbH, Chiemgaustr. 109, D-81549 München. Tel (089) 68001121, Fax (089) 68001122

Schools & Workshops

Akademie der Bildenden Künste München, Akademiestr. 2, D-80799 München. Tel (089) 38520

Akademie der Bildenden Künste Nürnberg, Bingstr. 60, D-90480 Nürnberg. Tel (0911) 94040

Akademie für Photographie Hamburg e. V., Langenfelder Str. 93, D-22769 Hamburg. Tel (040) 8504643, Fax (040) 8514378

Art & Rat, Klaus Küster, Ewaldstraße 25, D-42859 Remscheid. Tel (02191) 35229, Fax (02191) 35229

Bergische Universität Gesamthochschule Wuppertal, Fachbereich Design, Haspeler Str. 27, D-42285 Wuppertal

Burg Giebichenstein, Hochschule für Kunst und Design Halle, Neuwerk 7, D-06108 Halle/Saale. Tel (0345) 38661, Fax (0345) 25726

Europäische Akademie für Bildende Kunst Trier, Kunstzentrum Martiner Hof, Aachener Str. 63, D-54294 Trier

Fachhochschule Aachen, Fachbereich Design, Boxgraben 100, D-52064 Aachen. Tel (0241) 60090, Fax (0241) 64841

Fachhochschule Anhalt, Fachbereich Design, Gropiusallee 38, D-06846 Dessau

Fachhochschule Augsburg, Fachbereich Gestaltung, Henesiusstr. 1, D-86152 Augsburg. Tel (0821) 55860, Fax (0821) 741671

Fachhochschule Bielefeld, Fachbereich Gestaltung, Lampingstr. 3, D-33615 Bielefeld. Tel (0521) 1062485, Fax (0521) 1062444. E-mail dekan@ dmail.fh-bielefeld.de. Website www. gestaltung.fh-bielefeld.de

Fachhochschule Darmstadt, Fachbereich Gestaltung, Olbrichweg 10, D-64287 Darmstadt. Tel (06151) 168331, Fax (06151) 168940

Fachhochschule des Saarlandes, Fachbereich Design, Saaruferstr. 66, D-66117 Saarbrücken. Tel (0681) 33301, Fax (0681) 30775

Fachhochschule Dortmund, Fachbereich Design, Rheinlanddamm 203, D-44139 Dortmund. Tel (0231) 9112-426/447, Fax (0231) 9112415. Website www.fh-dortmund.de

Fachhochschule Düsseldorf, Fachbereich Design, Georg-Glock-Str. 15, D-40474 Düsseldorf. Tel (0211) 8100

Fachhochschule für Gestaltung Pforzheim, Holzgartenstr. 36, D-75175 Pforzheim. Tel (07231) 62861, Fax (07231) 69278

Fachhochschule für Gestaltung Schwäbisch Gmünd, Fachbereich Grafik-Design, Rektor-Klaus-Str. 100, D-73525 Schwäbisch Gmünd. Tel (07171) 602600

Fachhochschule Hamburg, Fachbereich Gestaltung, Armgartstr. 24, D-22087 Hamburg. Tel (040) 29188382-4/5/6, Fax (040) 291883374

Fachhochschule Hannover, Fachbereich Kunst und Design, Herrenhäuser Str. 8, D-30419 Hannover. Tel (0511) 755139, Fax (0511) 2798242

Fachhochschule Hildesheim/Holzminden, Fachbereich Kommunikationsgestaltung, Kaiserstr. 43–45, D-31134 Hildesheim. Tel (05121) 8810, Fax (05121) 881125

Fachhochschule Kiel, Fachbereich Gestaltung, Lorentzendamm 6–8, D-24103 Kiel. Tel (0431) 20000, Fax (0431) 570919

Fachhochschule Köln, Fachbereich Photoingenieurwesen, Betzdorfer Str. 2, D-50679 Köln. Tel (0221) 82752512, Fax (0221) 82752513. E-mail jponcar @gauss.fo.fh-koeln.de. Website www.gabor.fo.fh-koeln.de:80

Fachhochschule München, Fachbereich Gestaltung, Erzgießereistr. 14, D-80335 München. Tel (089) 12392240

Fachhochschule Münster, Fachbereich Design, Sentmaringer Weg 53, D-48151 Münster. Tel (0251) 834271

Fachhochschule Niederrhein, Fachbereich Design, Petersstr. 123, D-47798 Krefeld. Tel (02151) 8220, Fax (02151) 822153

Fachhochschule Potsdam, Fachbereich Design, Friedrich-Ebert-Str. 4, D-14167 Potsdam. Tel (0331) 2884554, Fax (0331) 2884555. Website www. design.fh-potsdam.de

Fachhochschule Rheinland-Pfalz, Fachbereich Design, Holzstr. 36, D-55116 Mainz. Tel (06131) 23920, Fax (06131) 239212

Fachhochschule Rheinland-Pfalz, Fachbereich Design, Paulusplatz, D-54290 Trier. Tel (0651) 81031, Fax (0651) 8103333

Fachhochschule Wiesbaden, Fachbereich 05 Gestaltung, Kurt-Schumacher-Ring 18, D-65195 Wiesbaden. Tel (0611) 9495-251/252, Fax (0611) 48862

Fachhochschule Würzburg/Schweinfurt, FB Gestaltung, Pavillion 1, Münzstraße 19, D-97070 Würzburg. Tel (0931) 3511206, Fax (0931) 3511329. E-mail design@mail.fh-wuerzburg.de. Website w3.fh-wuerzburg.de/gestaltung/

Fotografie Forum International, Leinwandhaus, Weckmarkt 17, D-60311 Frankfurt/Main. Tel (069) 291726, Fax (069) 28639

Fotowerk, Zollernstr. 31, D-86154 Augsburg. Tel (0821) 417854, Fax (0821) 417854

Freie Akademie der Künste zu Leipzig, Karl-Tauchnitz-Str. 2, D-04107 Leipzig. Tel (0341) 1499889, Fax (0341) 1499889

Georg-Simon-Ohm-Fachhochschule Nürnberg, Fachbereich Design für Elektronische Medien – Fotografie/Sekretariat, Wassertorstr. 10, D-90489 Nürnberg. Tel (0911) 5880690, Fax (0911) 5880696

Gesamthochschule Kassel, Universität, Fachbereich Visuelle Kommunikation, Menzelstr. 13–15, D-34121 Kassel. Tel (0561) 8042497

Hochschule der Bildenden Künste Saar, Keplerstr. 3–5, D-66117 Saarbrücken. Tel (0681) 926520, Fax (0681) 5847287

Hochschule der Künste Berlin, Fachbereich Visuelle Kommunikation, Ernst-Reuter-Platz 10, D-10587 Berlin. Tel (030) 31850, Fax (030) 31852659

Hochschule für Architektur und Bauwesen Weimar, Fakultät Gestaltung, Geschwister-Scholl-Str. 7, D-99421 Weimar. Tel (03643) 580

Hochschule für Bildende Künste Braunschweig, Fachbereich Freie Kunst, Johannes-Selenka-Platz 1, D-38118 Braunschweig. Tel (0531) 3919122

Hochschule für Bildende Künste Hamburg, Fachbereich Visuelle Kommunikation, Lerchenfeld 2, D-22081 Hamburg. Tel (040) 29840

Hochschule für Gestaltung Offenbach, Fachbereich Visuelle Kommunikation, Schloßstr. 31, D-63065 Offenbach/Main. Tel (069) 800590. E-mail fotohfg@bigfoot.de. Website www.fotohfg.de

Hochschule für Grafik und Buchkunst, Wächterstr. 11, D-04107 Leipzig. Tel (0341) 21350

Hochschule für Künste Bremen, Fachbereich Bildende Kunst, Am Wandrahm 23, D-28195 Bremen. Tel (0421) 30190

Hochschule Wismar, Fachbereich Design, Kühlungsborner Str. 16, D-18209 Heiligendamm. Tel (038203) 727, Fax (038203) 727

Institut für Kommunikations-Design an der FH Konstanz, Seestr. 33, Villa Prym, D-78464 Konstanz. Tel (0753) 50103

Johannes Gutenberg-Universität Mainz, Fachbereich Bildende Kunst, Am Taubertsberg 6, D-55099 Mainz. Tel (0631) 392309

Kunstakademie Düsseldorf, Fachbereich Freie Kunst, Eiskellerstr. 1, D-40213 Düsseldorf. Tel (0211) 13960

Kunstakademie Münster, Hochschule für Bildende Künste, Scheibenstr. 109, D-48153 Münster. Tel (0251) 972170

Kunsthochschule Berlin-Weißensee, Hochschule für Gestaltung, Bühringstr. 20, D-13086 Berlin. Tel (030) 477050

Kunsthochschule für Medien Köln, Peter-Welter-Platz 2, D-50676 Köln. Tel (0221) 201890, Fax (0221) 2018917. E-mail maas@khm.de. Website www.khm.de

Lehrinstitut für Design, Lippstädter Str. 133, D-33378 Rheda-Wiedenbrück. Tel (05242) 35938, Fax (05242) 37412. E-mail lehrdesign@aol.com. Website www.lehrdesign.de

Lette-Verein, Berufsfachschule für Fotografie, Grafik, Mode, Viktoria-Luise-Platz 6, D-10777 Berlin. Tel (030) 219940

Merz Akademie, Hochschule für Gestaltung Stuttgart, Kulturpark Berg, Teckstr. 58, D-70190 Stuttgart. Tel (0711) 268660, Fax (0711) 2686621. E-mail 100566.3420@compuserve.com

Muthesius-Hochschule, Forum, Lorentzendamm 6–8, D-24103 Kiel. Tel (0431) 5198-195/192, Fax (0431) 5199504. E-mail forum@muthesius.de. Website www.muthesius.de/~forum

Privatschule für Foto-Design, Christoph Eberbach GmbH, Stolzestr. 3–5, D-75175 Pforzheim. Tel (07231) 64949, Fax (07231) 650463

Ruhr-Universität Bochum, Musisches Zentrum, Arbeitsbereich Foto und Film, Universitätsstr. 150, D-44801 Bochum. Tel (0234) 7001

Staatliche Akadamie der Bildenden Künste Karlsruhe, Reinhold-Frank-Str. 67, D-76133 Karlsruhe. Tel (0721) 850180

Staatliche Akademie der Bildenden Künste Stuttgart, Am Weißenhof 1, D-70191 Stuttgart. Tel (0711) 25750

Staatliche Fachakademie für Fotodesign München, Clemensstr. 33, D-80803 München. Tel (089) 347673

Staatliche Fachschule für Optik und Fototechnik Berlin, Einsteinufer 43–53, D-10587 Berlin. Tel (030) 3479630

Staatliche Hochschule für Bildende Künste – Städelschule, Dürerstr. 10, D-60596 Frankfurt/Main. Tel (069) 6050080, Fax (069) 60500866

Staatliche Hochschule für Gestaltung Karlsruhe, Durmersheimer Str. 55, D-76185 Karlsruhe. Tel (0721) 95410

Städtische Fachhochschule für Gestaltung, Fachbereich Grafik-Design, E 3, Haus Nr. 16, D-68159 Mannheim. Tel (0621) 2920

Universität Gesamthochschule Essen, Fachbereich 4 Gestaltung, Universitätsstr. 12, D-45141 Essen. Tel (0201) 1831, Fax (0201) 1832151

Universität Hildesheim, Fachbereich II, Kulturwissenschaften und Ästhetische Kommunikation, Marienburger Platz 22, D-31141 Hildesheim. Tel (05121) 59484, Fax (05121) 511653. E-mail dierssen@rz.uni-hildesheim

Associations

Arbeitskreis Photographie Hamburg e. V., c/o FOCUS, Stresemannstr. 29, D-22769 Hamburg. Tel (040) 45037373, Fax (040) 45037373

Bund Freischaffender Foto-Designer e. V., Tuttlinger Str. 95, D-70619 Stuttgart. Tel (0711) 473422, Fax (0711) 475280. E-mail bff_de@compuserve.com

Bundesverband Arbeiterfotografie, Oslebshauser Dorfstr. 4, D-28239 Bremen

Bundesverband Bildender Künstlerinnen und Künstler, Bundesgeschäftsstelle, Weberstr. 61, D-53113 Bonn. Tel (0228) 216-107/108, Fax (0228) 216105

Bundesverband Deutscher Galerien e. V. (BVDG), St.-Apern-Str. 17–21, D-50667 Köln. Tel (0221) 2574939

Centralverband Deutscher Berufsphotographen (CV), Frankenwerft 35, D-50667 Köln. Tel (0221) 2070466, Fax (0221) 2070442

Deutsche Gesellschaft für Photographie (DGPh), Rheingasse 8–12, D-50676 Köln. Tel (0221) 9232069, Fax (0221) 9232070. E-mail dgph@dgph.photographie.com

Deutscher Künstlerbund e. V., Köthener Str. 44, D-10963 Berlin. Tel (030) 26552281

Deutscher Kunststudenten-Verband, Am Schloßgarten 3, D-50935 Köln

Deutscher Werkbund e. V., Nikolaiplatz 1b, D-80802 München. Tel (089) 346580, Fax (089) 397640. Website www.dsk.de/rds/19842.htm

Fachgruppe Bildende Kunst in der IG Medien, Friedrichstr. 15, D-70174 Stuttgart. Tel (0711) 20180

Fördergemeinschaft Fotografische Ausbildung e. V. Bielefeld, c/o Schindler, Herforder Str. 155a, D-33609 Bielefeld. Tel (0521) 34167, Fax (0521) 35359

FreeLens, Verein der Fotojournalistinnen und Fotojournalisten e. V., Markusstr. 9, D-20355 Hamburg. Tel (040) 340022, Fax (040) 344022. E-mail freelens@aol.com

FWU Institut für Film und Bild in Wissenschaft und Unterricht, Bavaria-Film-Platz 3, D-82031 Grünwald. Tel (089) 64971, Fax (089) 6497300. E-mail info-fwu@t-online.de. Website www.fwu.de

Gedok, Gemeinschaft der Künstlerinnen und Kunstfreunde e. V., Odeonstr. 2, D-30159 Hannover. Tel (0511) 131404 , Fax (0511) 131404. E-mail gedok-hannover@t-online.de

Gesellschaft für elektronische Kunst e. V., Gemarkenweg 1, D-51467 Bergisch Gladbach

Internationale Gesellschaft der Bildenden Künste e. V., Weberstr. 61, D-53113 Bonn. Tel (0228) 216141, Fax (0228) 216105

Internationaler Kunstkritiker-Verband e. V., Sektion der Bundesrepublik Deutschland, Maternusstr. 29, D-50678 Köln. Fax (0221) 315337

Lomographische Botschaft Berlin, Utrechterstr. 41, D-13347 Berlin. Tel (030) 4561687, Fax (030) 4561260. E-mail lomo@lomo.com. Website www.lomo.com

Verband der Amateurfotografen e. V., P. O. Box 25, D-14478 Potsdam

Verband der Deutschen Photographischen Industrie, Karlstr. 19–21, D-60329 Frankfurt/Main. Tel (069) 25561410

Verwertungsgesellschaft Bild-Kunst, Poppelsdorfer Allee 43, D-53115 Bonn. Tel (0228) 915340

Westdeutscher Künstlerbund, Hochstr. 73, D-58095 Hagen

Grants & Awards

Aenne-Biermann-Preis für deutsche Gegenwartsfotografie, to support contemporary German photography in the tradition of Aenne Biermann, total amount DM 19,000, every two years. Contact: Museum für Angewandte Kunst Gera, Greizer Str. 37–39, D-07545 Gera. Tel (0365) 28750, Fax (0365) 28750

Agfa-Nachwuchs-Wettbewerb, for students of photography, no application, photo equipment and supplies (value DM 17,000), publication, every year. Contact: Agfa-Gevaert AG, Werbeabteilung, Gebäude D 162/3, P. O. Box 100160, D-51301 Leverkusen. Tel (0214) 301

Albert-Renger-Patzsch-Preis, to support European photography book projects, nomination, DM 50,000, every three years. Contact: Museum Folkwang, Fotografische Sammlung, Goethestr. 41, D-45128 Essen. Tel (0201) 8845100, Fax (0201) 8845130

Bayerischer Fotopreis der Danner-Stiftung, to support young German photographers, below the age of 36, with five years residence in Bavaria, total amount DM 20,000, every three years. Contact: Danner'sche Kunstgewerbestiftung, Thomas-Wimmer-Ring 9, D-80539 München. Tel (089) 229267, Fax (089) 297482. E-mail danner-stiftung@t-online.de

Berliner Preis für Junge Kunst, below the age of 40. Contact: Staatliche Museen zu Berlin, Hamburger Bahnhof, Invalidenstr. 50–51, D-10557 Berlin. Tel (030) 2662647. E-mail aussenamt@smb.spk-berlin.de. Website www.smb.spk-berlin.de/d/

BFF-Förderpreis "Die besten Diplomarbeiten im Bereich Fotografie", to recognize thesis projects by graduating design students, no application, total amount DM 20,000, every two years. Contact: Bund Freischaffender Foto-Designer e. V., Tuttlinger Str. 95, D-70619 Stuttgart. Tel (0711) 473422, Fax (0711) 475280. E-mail bff_de@compuserve.com

Chargesheimer Stipendium der Stadt Köln, residence in Cologne, DM 18.000, every year. Contact: Kulturamt der Stadt Köln, Richartzstr. 2–4, D-50667 Köln. Tel (0221) 2213481

DAAD Stipendienprogramme, residencies abroad, every year. Contact: Deutscher Akademischer Austauschdienst, Kennedyallee 50, D-53175 Bonn. Tel (0228) 8820

David-Octavius-Hill-Medaille, to recognize a lifetime achievement, no application, DM 10,000, diploma, medal, every two years. Contact: Deutsche Fotografische Akademie e. V., Prof. Manfred Schmalriede, Schloßstr. 39, D-75245 Neulingen-Bauschlott. Tel (07237) 9408, Fax (07237) 5478

Deutscher Jugendfotopreis, photographers below the age of 22, total amount DM 18,000, every two years. Contact: Kinder- und Jugendfilmzentrum in Deutschland, Küppelstein 34, D-42857 Remscheid. Tel (02191) 794238, Fax (02191) 794230. E-mail kjfmedia@aol.com. Website www.kjf.de

Deutscher Photopreis der Landesgirokasse, encouraging artistic photography, for German residents, total amount DM 40,000, every two years. Contact: Landesgirokasse, Deutscher Photopreis – Kunst und Kultur 1120, Königstr. 3–5, D-70144 Stuttgart. Tel (0711) 1243935, Fax (0711) 1243699. E-mail kontakt@lgbank.de

DG BANK Stipendien für Fotografie, to support young talent, project-oriented work, DM 24,000, every year. Contact: DG BANK Deutsche Genossenschaftsbank, Abteilung Kommunikation/Presse, Am Platz der Republik, D-60325 Frankfurt/Main. Tel (069) 74472380, Fax (069) 74472959

DG BANK-Förderpreis Fotografie, to support young talent, appointed by the "Spectrum" prizewinner, solo exhibition with catalog at Sprengel Museum, Hannover, every two years. Contact: DG BANK Deutsche Genossenschaftsbank, Abteilung Kommunikation/Presse, Am Platz der Republik, D-60325 Frankfurt/Main. Tel (069) 74472380, Fax (069) 74472959. Website www.dgbank.de

Dr. Erich Salomon-Preis, for outstanding contributions in photo journalism, no application, every year. Contact: Deutsche Gesellschaft für Photographie e. V., Rheingasse 8–12, D-50676 Köln. Tel (0221) 2402037, Fax (0221) 2402035

Emma-und-Agfa-Preis für Fotojournalistinnen, only for women, total amount DM 16,000, every two years. Contact: Redaktion Emma, Alteburger Str. 2, D-50678 Köln. Tel (0221) 316071, Fax (0221) 316075

Erich-Stenger-Preis, history and theory of photography, DM 6,000, every two years, last one 1992. Contact: Deutsche Gesellschaft für Photographie e. V., Rheingasse 8–12, D-50676 Köln. Tel (0221) 2402037, Fax (0221) 2402035

Europäischer Kulturpreis für das Land Oldenburg, DM 5,000, every year. Contact: Dr. Schröder, Kardinal-von-Gahlen-Haus, D-49661 Stapelfeld/Cloppenburg

European Publishers Award, for European Photographers, to recognize a work which is suitable for a book project, US$5,000, book publication in six countries, every year. Contact: Edition Braus GmbH, Hebelstr. 10, D-69115 Heidelberg. Tel (06221) 14080, Fax (06221) 14086

Focus Award for Students, promotion of young photography and design, only for students of photography and design, total amount DM 10,000, exhibition, catalogue, every two years. Contact: Fachhochschule Dortmund, Fachbereich Design, Focus Büro, Rheinlanddamm 203, D-44139 Dortmund. Tel (0231) 9112436, Fax (0231) 9112415. E-mail post@focus2tausend.de. Website focus2tausend.de

Förderpreis für Dokumentarfotografie, to support the "exploration of real worlds" and to contribute to a "redefinition of documentary photography", DM 10,000. Contact: Wüstenrot-Stiftung, Deutscher Eigenheimverein, Hohenzollernstr. 45, D-71630 Ludwigsburg. Tel (07141) 164777, Fax (07141) 163900

Förderpreis für Fotografie der Landeshauptstadt München, promotion of young artists, Munich residence, DM 12.000, every year. Contact: Kulturreferat der Landeshauptstadt München, Rindermarkt 3/4, D-80331 München. Tel (089) 233-5153, Fax (089) 233-8622. E-mail 100773.1137@compuserve.com. Website www.muenchen.de

Fotografie als Kunst – Preis der Sparkasse Pforzheim, to support art-based photography, for artists below the age of 36, DM 25,000, every three years, last one 1994. Contact: Sparkasse Pforzheim, Poststr. 3, D-75172 Pforzheim. Tel (07231) 993303, Fax

(07231) 993398. E-mail mwm@ sparkasse-pforzheim.de. Website www.sparkasse-pforzheim.de

Fujifilm Shooting Stars, for young photo apprentices, attendence at a workshop in a foreign country, every year. Contact: Fuji Photo Film (Europe) GmbH, Abt. Professionals, Heesenstr. 31, D-40549 Düsseldorf. Tel (0211) 50890, Fax (0211) 5089344

Herbert-Schober-Förderpreis, for medicine and science photography, DM 2,000 or visit to Biomedical Photography Workshop in Rochester, every two years, last one 1992. Contact: Deutsche Gesellschaft für Photographie e. V., Rheingasse 8–12, D-50676 Köln. Tel (0221) 2402037, Fax (0221) 2402035

Hermann-Claasen-Preis, to recognize work relating to the Rheinland, Rheinland residence, DM 10,000, exhibition, every two years, last one 1993. Contact: Kreissparkasse Köln, Referat Öffentlichkeitsarbeit, Neumarkt 18-24, D-50667 Köln. Tel (0221) 227-2703/2279

Internationaler Polaroid Mikrofotografie Wettbewerb, to recognize scientific work in the field of microphotography, works done with Polaroid equipment, DM 15,000, every year. Contact: Polaroid GmbH, Sprendlinger Landstr. 109, D-63069 Offenbach/Main. Tel (069) 8404415

Kodak Fotobuchpreis. Contact: Kodak AG, GB Professional Imaging, D-70323 Stuttgart. Tel (0711) 4060, Fax (0711) 4062524

Kodak Nachwuchs Förderpreis, support of young photographers by offering opportunity a) to realize a photographic concept with Kodak professional consumables and b) to publish the results in professional photo magazines, for photography students/apprentices under 30, Kodak professional consumables up to DM 2,500 for each of the five winners, twice a year (spring and autumn). Contact: Kodak AG, GB Professional Imaging, D-70323 Stuttgart. Tel (0711) 4065473, Fax (0711) 4062524. E-mail 917766N@ knotes.kodak.com

Kulturpreis, to recognize a lifetime achievement, no application, every year. Contact: Deutsche Gesellschaft für Photographie e. V., Rheingasse 8–12, D-50676 Köln. Tel (0221) 2402037, Fax (0221) 2402035

Kunstfonds e. V., various art grants, for german visual artists only, total amount DM 800,000, every year. Contact: Kunstfonds e. V., Weberstr. 61, D-53115 Bonn. Tel (0228) 9153411, Fax (0228) 9153441. Website www. kunstfonds.de

Künstlerhäuser Worpswede, the artists must be present in Worpswede, 3–12 month free residence and DM 1,800/month, every year, application deadline 15th April. Contact: Dr. Anette Hulek, Bergstr. 1, D-27726 Worpswede. Tel (04792) 1380, Fax (04791) 2112

Kunstpreis der Stadtsparkasse Hannover, acknowledging the complete work of the award-winner, for participants of the autumn exhibition of artists from Niedersachsen, DM 15,000, catalogue, every two years. Contact: Kunstverein Hannover, Sophienstr. 2, D-30159 Hannover. Tel (0511) 324594, Fax (0511) 3632247

Kunstpreis der Ursula-Blickle-Stiftung, support of work by young artists, previous exhibition in the foundation, DM 10,000, every year. Contact: Ursula-Blickle-Stiftung, Mühlweg 18,

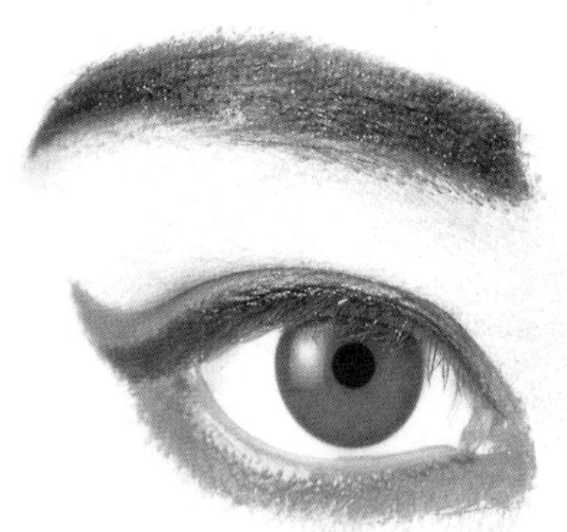

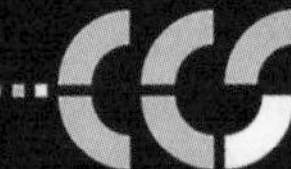

**Digitale Prints
für Präsentationen,
Werbung,
Ausstellungen**

**bis XXL
für innen und außen**

Fachlabor für
Farbfotografie und
Digitale Medien

CCS GmbH
Lützowstraße 100
10785 Berlin

Fon 030. 23 0811-0
Fax 030. 23 0811-15

photolab@ccsberlin.de
www.ccsberlin.de

Lambda Imaging
Ilfochrome Classic
C-Prints
Diasec
Leuchtkästen
Inkjets

132 Germany

D-76703 Kraichtal. Tel (07251) 60919, Fax (07251) 68687. E-mail ursula-blickle-stiftung@t-online.de

Kurt-Schwitters-Preis, to support contemporary art, especially concerning Kurt Schwitters, no application, DM 15,000, exhibition, every two years. Contact: Sprengel Museum, Kurt-Schwitters-Platz 1, D-30169 Hannover. Tel (0511) 1683875, Fax (0511) 1685093

Leica Medal of Excellence, award for fine-art photography, taken on 35mm film; completed in the last year, US$10,000, every year. Contact: Leica Camera GmbH, Oskar-Barnack-Str. 11, D-35606 Solms. Tel (06442) 208404, Fax (06442) 208410. E-mail cpr@leica-camera.com. Website www.leica-camera.com/lme

Leica Oskar-Barnack-Preis, to support committed photo journalism, applicants must submit a single photograph or a photo essay of up to 12 pictures, photographed in the year before, DM 10,000, every year. Contact: Leica Camera GmbH, Oskar-Barnack-Str. 11, D-35606 Solms. Tel (06442) 208404, Fax (06442) 208410. E-mail cpr@leica-camera.com. Website www.leica-camera.com/oskar-barnack

Medienpreis "Sozialfotografie", to draw attention to social problems in Germany, works published during the last year for the first time, DM 7,500, every year. Contact: Bundesarbeitsgemeinschaft der Freien Wohlfahrtspflege e. V., Pressestelle, Franz-Lohe-Str. 17, D-53129 Bonn. Tel (0228) 226286, Fax (0228) 226266

Otto-Steinert-Preis, German residence, DM 10,000, every two years, last one 1993. Contact: Deutsche Gesellschaft für Photographie e. V.,

Rheingasse 8–12, D-50676 Köln. Tel (0221) 2402037, Fax (0221) 2402035

Paper Art – Internationale Biennale der Papierkunst, every two years. Contact: Leopold-Hoesch-Museum, Dr. Dorothea Elmert, Hoeschplatz 1, D-52349 Düren. Tel (02421) 2525-58/61, Fax (02421) 252560

Polaroid Fotoschulwettbewerb, only for students who are working with Polaroid equipment, DM 10,000 in supplies and equipment, every two years. Contact: Polaroid GmbH, Sprendlinger Landstr. 109, D-63069 Offenbach/Main. Tel (069) 840450-2/3, Fax (069) 8404530

Preis für jungen Bildjournalismus von Agfa und Bilderberg, to support young photo-journalists, artists below the age of 31, total amount DM 30,000, every two years, last one 1993. Contact: Agfa-Gevaert AG, Werbeabteilung, Gebäude D 162/3, P. O. Box 100160, D-51301 Leverkusen. Tel (0214) 301

Reinhart-Wolf-Preis, to support young photographers, photo artists below the age of 32, total amount DM 10,000, every year. Contact: Reinhart Wolf Photographische Stiftung, P. O. Box 221140, D-80501 München. Tel (089) 336987, Fax (089) 336987. E-mail rwolfstiftung@ctv.es. Website www.ctv.es/users/rwolfstiftung/

Robert-Luther-Preis, to recognize scientific works in the field of photography, academic works, DM 3,000, every two years. Contact: Deutsche Gesellschaft für Photographie e. V., Rheingasse 8–12, D-50676 Köln. Tel (0221) 2402037, Fax (0221) 2402035

Schöneberger Fotopreis, contemporary photography, professional photographer living or working in Berlin, DM 8.000, every year. Contact:

Kunstamt Schöneberg, Haus am Kleistpark, Grunewaldstr. 6–7, D-10823 Berlin. Tel (030) 7833032

Siemens-Medienkunstpreis, to recognize artistic and scientific-theoretical involvement with new media, no application, total amount DM 115.000, every two years. Contact: ZKM-Zentrum für Kunst und Medientechnologie Karlsruhe, Sibylle Peine, P. O. Box 6909, D-76049 Karlsruhe. Tel (0721) 93400, Fax (0721) 934019. Website www.zkm.de

Spectrum – Internationaler Preis für Fotografie, to acknowledge work by an outstanding contemporary artist. Solo exhibition with catalogue at the Sprengel Museum, Hannover, and nomination of the recipient of "DG BANK-Förderpreis für Fotografie", every two years. Contact: Stiftung Niedersachsen, Ferdinandstr. 4, D-30175 Hannover. Tel (0511) 315081, Fax (0511) 314499. E-mail stiftung. nds@t-online.de. Website www. stiftungniedersachsen.hannover.de

Staatspreis für das Kunsthandwerk im Lande Nordrhein-Westfalen, over the age of 25, residence in Nordrhein-Westfalen, DM 10,000, every two years. Contact: Arbeitsgemeinschaft des Kunsthandwerks Nordrhein-Westfalen, Georg-Schulhoff-Platz 1, D-40221 Düsseldorf. Tel (0211) 8795390, Fax (0211) 8795110

Stipendium der Alfried Krupp von Bohlen und Halbach-Stiftung für zeitgenössische Fotografie, to support long-term projects in contemporary photography, for photographers of German nationality or residence of at least three years, DM 20,000, every two years. Contact: Museum Folkwang, Fotografische Sammlung, Goethestr. 41, D-45128 Essen. Tel (0201) 8845100, Fax (0201) 8845130

New Media

Digitale, Kunsthochschule für Medien Köln, Peter-Welter-Platz 2, D-50676 Köln. Tel (0221) 20189226, Fax (0221) 20189230. E-mail digitale@ kmh.de. Website www.digitale. khm.de

Duisburger Filmwoche, Am König-Heinrich-Platz, D-47049 Duisburg. Tel (0203) 2834171, Fax (0203) 2834130. E-mail filmwoche.vhs@ duisburg.de. Website www. duisburg.de/filmwoche

European Media Art Festival, Lohstr. 45a, D-49074 Osnabrück. Tel (0541) 21658, Fax (0541) 28327. E-mail info@ emaf.de. Website www.emaf.de

Femme Totale/Frauen-Filmfestival, c/o Kulturbüro Dortmund, Kleppingstr. 21–23, D-44122 Dortmund. Tel (0231) 5025162, Fax (0231) 5025734. E-mail femmetotale@ compuserve.com. Website www. femmetotale.de

Freiburger Film Forum, Ethnographic Film Festival, Urachstr. 40, D-79102 Freiburg. Tel (0761) 709594, Fax (0761) 706921. E-mail fifo@freiburger-medienforum.de. Website www. freiburger-medienforum.de

Internationale Kurzfilmtage Oberhausen, Grillostr. 34, D-46042 Oberhausen. Tel (0208) 8252652, Fax (0208) 8255413. E-mail info@ kurzfilmtage.de. Website www. kurzfilmtage.de

Internationaler Medienkunstpreis, ZKM – Zentrum für Kunst und Medientechnologie Karlsruhe, Lorenzstr. 19, D-76135 Karlsruhe. Tel (0721)

81001150, Fax (0721) 81001139. E-mail medienkunstpreis@zkm.de. Website www.medienkunstpreis.de. Television-based award established by ZKM and Südwestfunk in cooperation with SF DRS, deadline for entries normally in March, prize money totalling EUR 30,000

Kasseler Dokumentarfilm und Videofest, Filmladen Kassel e. V., Goethestr. 31, D-34119 Kassel. Tel (0561) 7076421, Fax (0561) 7076441. E-mail wissner@filmladen.de. Website www.filmladen.de/dokfest

Marler Video-Kunst-Preis/Marler Video-Installations-Preis, Skulpturenmuseum Glaskasten, Rathaus, Creiler Platz, D-45768 Marl. Tel (02365) 992257, Fax (02365) 7992603. Website www.marl.de

Medienhaus für Kunst und Kultur, Schwarzer Bär 6, D-30449 Hannover. Tel (0511) 441440, Fax (0511) 453572. E-mail service@medienhaus-hannover. Website www.medienhaus-hannover.de/index.html

Multimediale, ZKM – Zentrum für Kunst und Medientechnologie Karlsruhe, Kaiserstr. 64, D-76133 Karlsruhe. Tel (0721) 93400, Fax (0721) 934019. Website www.zkm.de

Ökomedia Filmtage, Festival for films and videos on environmental issues, Ökomedia Institut e. V., Habsburgerstr. 9a, D-79104 Freiburg. Tel (0761) 52024, Fax (0761) 555724. E-mail oekomedia@t-online.de. Website www.oekomedia-institut.de

Ostranenie, The International Electronic Media Forum, Studio Electronic Media Interpretation, Bauhaus Dessau Foundation, Gropiusallee 38, D-06846 Dessau. Tel (0340) 65080313, Fax (0340) 65080326. E-mail emi@stiftung_bauhaus.de. Website www.ostranenie.org/

Videoforum des Neuen Berliner Kunstvereins, Chausseestr. 128/129, D-10115 Berlin. Tel (030) 2807020, Fax (030) 2807019. E-mail nbk@nbk.org. Website www.nbk.org

Great Britain

Population: 59 million
Capital: London, 7.1 million
Currency: Pound (£)
International code: ++44
Tourist information: British
Tourist Authority, Thames
Tower, Black's Road, Hammer-
smith, GB-London W6 9EL

Galleries & Museums

Aberystwyth Arts Centre, University College of Wales, Penglais Hill, GB-Aberystwyth, Ceredigion SY23 3DE, Wales. Tel (01970) 622887, Fax (01970) 622883. E-mail lla@aber.ac.uk. Website www.aber.ac.uk/~arcwww/index.htm. Open: Mon–Sat 10–17. Director: Alan Hewson. Curator: Stephen West. Founded 1972. 5 rooms. 8 photo exhibitions/year. Artists: David Gepp, Yuri Ivanov, Jean Welstead, Cathy De Witt, Alexander Rodchenko

School of Art Gallery and Museum, University of Wales, Buarth Mawr, GB-Aberystwyth, Ceredigion SY23 1NE, Wales. Tel (01970) 622460/7, Fax (01970) 622461. E-mail neh@aber.ac.uk. Open: Mon–Fri 10–17.30. Director: Robert Meyrick. Curator: Neil Holland. Founded 1974. 3 rooms, 120 m². 1–3 photo exhibitions/year. Artists: Mario Giacomelli, Elio Ciol, Carlo Bevilacqua, Erich Lessing, Ron Davies, Angus Mc Bean, Ferrucio Leiss, Keith Vaughan, Guiseppe Cavalli, Paolo Monti

f.Stop Gallery, Green Park Station, Midland Bridge Road, GB-Bath BA1 1JB, Avon. Tel (01225) 316922, Fax (01225) 465135. E-mail f.stop@online.rednet.co.uk. Open: Tue–Sat 10–18, (Tue+Thu –21). Director: Dan Hopkins. Founded 1985. 1 room, 40 m². 6 photo exhibitions/year

The Royal Photographic Society, The Octagon, Milsom Street, GB-Bath BA1 1DN, Avon. Tel (01225) 462841, Fax (01225) 448688. E-mail rps@rps.org. Website www.rps.org. Open: 9.30–17.30. Director: Barry Lane. Curator: Pamela Roberts. Founded 1853. 2 rooms, 4,000 m². 4 photo exhibitions/year. Artists: Martin Parr, John Blakemore, Elliott Erwitt, Nick Waplington, Mary Ellen Mark, Calum Colvin, George Rodger, John Hinde, Duane Michals, Don McCullin

Bedford Community Arts, The Gatehouse, Foster Hill Road, GB-Bedford MK41 7TD. Tel (01234) 355870, Fax (01234) 359742. E-mail bcart@kbnet.co.uk. Website www.communityarts.org

Old Museum Arts Centre, 7 College Square North, GB-Belfast, Northern Ireland. Tel (01232) 235053, Fax (01232) 322912. E-mail info@oldmuseumartscentre.freeserve.co.uk. Open: Mon–Sat 9.30–17.30. Director: Ann McReynolds. Founded 1991. 2 rooms, 40 m². 8–10 photo exhibitions/year

Ikon Gallery, 1 Oozells Square, Brindleyplace, GB-Birmingham B1 2HS. Tel (0121) 2480708, Fax (0121) 2480709. E-mail art@ikon-gallery.co.uk. Website www.ikon-gallery.co.uk. Open: Tue–Sat 11–18 (Thu –20). Director: Jonathan Watkins. Founded 1964. 2 rooms, 440 m². 3 photo exhibitions/year

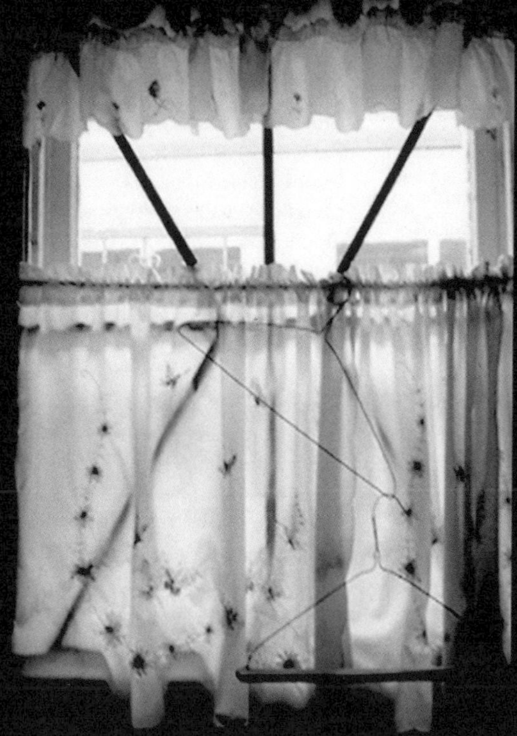

seeing the light

**events • folio reviews
publications • consultancy**

seeing the light works with image makers at
all stages of their development through
networking across the world with gallery
directors, publishers, agencies and picture
editors - physically and virtually •
events include international folio days,
presentations on the future of the sector,
managing the image and strategies for
enlightened vision •
consultants to groups and organisations with
an interest in the business of the image •

director : rhonda wilson
rx@seeingthelight.co.uk

212 the custard factory • gibb street • birmingham b9 4aa • united kingdom
tel +44 (0)121 773 7889 • fax +44 (0)121 773 7888 • www.seeingthelight.co.uk

the development agency for the contemporary image maker

MAC, Canon Hill, Edgbaston, GB-Birmingham B12 9QH. Tel (0121) 4404221, Fax (0121) 4464372. E-mail judy.dames@mac-birmingham.org.uk. Open: daily 9–23 (Space Galleries); Tue–Sun 12–20 (Cotton and Foyle Galleries). Director: Dorothy Wilson. Curator: Judy Dames. Founded 1960. 5 rooms, 340 m². 10 photo exhibitions/year

National Museum of Photography, Film & Television, Pictureville, GB-Bradford BD1 1NQ. Tel (01274) 202030, Fax (01274) 723155. E-mail talk.nmpft@nmsi.ac.uk. Website www.nmpft.org.uk. Open: Tue–Sun 10.30–18. Director: Amanda Nevill. Curator: Russel Roberts. Founded 1983. 8 rooms, 4,000 m². Artists: David Bailey, Michael Wilson

First Light Gallery, Nile Street, GB-Brighton BN1 1HW. Tel (01273) 327344. E-mail firstlightclick@hotmail.com. Website www.pavilion.co.uk/firstlight/. Open: Mon–Fri 9.30–17, Sat 10.30–16.30. Director: Mark Nelson. Founded 1981. 2 rooms, 35 m². 10 photo exhibitions/year. Artists: Thurston Hopkins, Nicholas Sinclair, Mark Nelson, Grace Robertson, Steve Parry, John Lynch

Arnolfini Gallery, 16 Narrow Quay, GB-Bristol BS1 4QA. Tel (0117) 9299191, Fax (0117) 9253876. E-mail arnolfini@arnolfini.demon.co.uk. Website www.arnolfini.demon.co.uk. Open: Mon–Sat 10–19.30, Sun 12–19. Director: Caroline Collier. 3 rooms

The Cambridge Darkroom, Dales Brewery, Gwydir Street, GB-Cambridge CB1 2LJ. Tel (01223) 566725, Fax (01223) 312188. E-mail darkroom@dircon.co.uk. Open: Tue–Sun 12–17. Director: Ronnie Simpson. Founded 1984. 1 room, 144 m². 8 photo exhibitions/year

Kettle's Yard, Northampton Street, GB-Cambridge CB3 0AQ. Tel (01223) 352124, Fax (01223) 324377. E-mail kettles-yard-gen@lists.cam.ac.uk. Website www.kettlesyard.co.uk

Museum & Gallery of Wales, Cathays Park, GB-Cardiff, S. Glam CF1 3NP, Wales. Tel (02920) 397951, Fax (02920) 226938. Website www.nmgw.ac.uk. Open: Tue–Sun 10–17. Director: Anna Sonthall. Founded 1907. 3 rooms, 628 m². 1 photo exhibition/year

The Ffotogallery, 31 Charles Street, GB-Cardiff CF1 4EA, Wales. Tel (029) 20341677, Fax (029) 20341672. E-mail info@ffotogallery.freeserve.co.uk. Open: Tue–Sat 10–17. Director: Sue Cunningham. Founded 1978. 3 rooms, 1,000 m². 10 photo exhibitions/year. Artists: John Davies, Sebastião Salgado, Raymond Moore, Susan Trangmar, Peter Greenaway, David Bailey, Ian Breakwell, Oliver Whitehead, Willie Doherty

Firstsite, The Minories, 74 High Street, GB-Colchester, Essex CO1 1UE. Tel (01206) 577067, Fax (01206) 577161. E-mail info@1stsite.keme.co.uk. Director: Katherine Wood

Q-Arts, Gallery, 35–36 Queen Street, GB-Derby DE1 3DS. Tel (01332) 295858, Fax (01332) 295859. E-mail create@q-arts.co.uk. Open: Wed–Fri 12–16, Sat 10–16. Director: Madeline Holmes. Curator: Richard Tomlinson. Founded 1999. 1 room, 102 m². 8–10 photo exhibitions/year. Artists: Olivier Richon, Michal Rovner, Boaz Tal, Oded Shimshon, Roshini Kempadoo, Clement Cooper, Paul Hill

Museum & Art Gallery, Chequer Road, GB-Doncaster, South Yorkshire DN1 2AE. Tel (01302) 734293, Fax

(01302) 735409. E-mail museum@ daicaster.gov.uk. Open: Mon–Sat 10–17, Sun 14–17. Director: Geoff Preece. Founded 1964. 5 rooms, 430 m². 2–3 photo exhibitions/year

DLI Museum & Durham Art Gallery, Aykley Heads, GB-Durham, Co. Durham DH1 5TU. Tel (0191) 3842214, Fax (0191) 3861770. E-mail dli@durham.gov.uk. Website www. durham.gov.uk. Open: Tue–Sat 10–17, Sun 14–17. Director: Dennis Hardingham. Founded 1968. 3 rooms, 340 m². 2–6 photo exhibitions/year

Beyond Words, 42–44 Cockburn Street, GB-Edinburgh EH1 1NY, Scotland. Tel (0131) 2266636. E-mail info@beyondwords.co.uk. Director: Neil McIlwraith. Founded 1998. 1 room. 4 photo exhibitions/year

Fruitmarket Gallery, 29 Market Street, GB-Edinburgh EH1 1DF, Scotland. Tel (0131) 2252383, Fax (0131) 2203130. E-mail bookshopdirector@ fruitmarket.co.uk. Open: Tue–Sat 10.30–17.30. Director: Graeme Murray. Founded 1974. 2 rooms. 1 photo exhibition/year

National Gallery of Scotland, The Mound, Belford Road, GB-Edinburgh EH2 2EL, Scotland. Tel (0131) 5568921, Fax (0131) 3324939. E-mail enquiries@natgalscot.ac.uk. Website www.natgalscot.ac.uk. Open: Mon–Sat 10–17, Sun 14–17. Director: Timothy Cliffard. Curator: James Holloway. Founded 1889. 5 rooms, 5,230 m². 3 photo exhibitions/year

Portfolio Gallery, 43 Candlemaker Row, GB-Edinburgh EH1 2QB, Scotland. Tel (0131) 2201911, Fax (0131) 2264287. E-mail portfolio@ ednet.co.uk. Website www.ednet. co.uk-portfolio. Open: Tue–Sat 12–17.30. Director/curator: Gloria

Chalmers. Founded 1988. 2 rooms, 120 m². 3 photo exhibitions/year. Artists: Calum Colvin, Maud Sulter, Helen Chadwick, Karen Knorr, Yve Lomax, Jim Harold, Paul Graham, John Stezaker

Scottish National Portrait Gallery, Queen Street, GB-Edinburgh EH1, Scotland. Tel (0131) 6246314, Fax (0131) 5583691. E-mail enquiries@ natgalscot.ac.uk. Website www. natgalscot.ac.uk. Director: Sarah Stevenson

Stills Gallery, 23 Cockburn Street, GB-Edinburgh EH1 1BP, Scotland. Tel (0131) 6226200, Fax (0131) 6226201. E-mail info@stills.demon.co.uk. Open: Tue–Sat 10–17. Director/ curator: Kate Tregaskis. Founded 1977. 2 rooms, 150 m². 8 photo exhibitions/year

Centre for Contemporary Arts, 350 Sauchiehall Street, GB-Glasgow G2 3JD, Scotland. Tel (0141) 3327521, Fax (0141) 3323226. E-mail jem@ cca-glasgow.com. Website www. cca-glasgow.com. Open: Mon–Sun 11–18. Contact: Graham McKenzie. Founded 1992. 2 rooms, 350 m². 4 photo exhibitions/year

Collins Gallery, University of Strathclyde, 22 Richmond Street, GB-Glasgow G1 1XQ, Scotland. Tel (0141) 5484145, Fax (0141) 5524053. E-mail collinsgallery@strath.as.uk. Open: Mon–Fri 10–17, Sat 12–16. Director: Laura Hamilton. Founded 1973. 1 room, 260 m². 3–10 photo exhibitions/year. Artists: Colin Cavers, Rita Hensen, Todd Garner, Ian McCulloch, Margaret Hunter, Jim Hardie, Ruth Stirling, Tom McKendrick

Street Level, 26 King Street, GB-Glasgow G1 5QP, Scotland. Tel (0141) 5522151, Fax (0141) 5522323. E-mail info@street.level.ndirect.co.uk. Open: Tue–Sat 10–17.30. Director: Malcolm Dickson. Curator: Janie Nicoll. Founded 1989. 2 rooms, 70 m². 12 photo exhibitions/year. Artists: Peter Finnemore, David Hatfield, Annette Heyer, Harry Kerr, Amanda McKittrick

Guildford House Gallery, 155 High Street, GB-Guildford GU1 3AJ. Tel (01483) 444740, Fax (01483) 444742. E-mail guildfordhouse@remote. guildford.gov.uk. Website www. guildfordborough.co.uk. Open: Tue–Sat 10–16.45. Director: Matthew Alexander. Curator: Tracey Mardless. Founded 1959. 5 rooms, 50 m². 1 photo exhibitions/year

Dean Clough Gallery, Dean Clough Industrial Park, GB-Halifax HX3 5AX. Tel (01422) 250250. E-mail dean.clough.ltd@deanclough.com. Curator: Doug Binder

Hereford City Museum & Art Gallery, Broad Street, GB-Hereford, Herefordshire HR4 9AU. Tel (01432) 260692, Fax (01432) 342492. E-mail p/young@herefordshire.gov.uk. Open: Tue–Sat 10–18 (Thu+Sat –17). Contact: Peter Young. Founded 1874. 2 rooms. 2 photo exhibitions/year

Huddersfield Gallery, Princess Alexander Walk, GB-Huddersfield, West Yorks HD1 2SU. Tel (01484) 221964/2, Fax (01484) 221952. E-mail robert-hall@kirkleesmc.gov.uk. Open: Mon–Fri 10–17, Sat 10–16. Contact: Robert Hall. 6 rooms, 850 m²

Ferens Gallery, Queen Victoria Square, GB-Hull, North Humberside HU1 3RA. Tel (01482) 613902, Fax (01482) 613710. Website www. hullcc.gov.uk/museum. Open: Mon–Sat 10–17, Sun 13.30–16.30. Director: Ann Bukantas. Curator: David Scruton. Founded 1927. 3 rooms, 896 m². 2–3 photo exhibitions/year. Artists: Helen Chadwick, Calum Colvin, Craigie Horsfield, Boyd Webb, Mark Wallinger, Gavin Turk

Brewery Arts Centre, Highgate, GB-Kendal LA9 4HE. Tel (01539) 725133. E-mail brewery@lakesnet.co.uk. Director: Anne Pierson. Founded 1972. 1 room, 72 m². 8 photo exhibitions/year

East Kilbridge Arts Centre, 51–53 Old Coach Bridge, GB-Kilbridge G74 4DU, Scotland. Tel (0135) 5261000. Contact: Paul Games

Folly Gallery, 26 Castle Park, GB-Lancaster LA1 1YQ. Tel (01524) 388550, Fax (01524) 338513. E-mail info@folly.co.uk. Director: Dave Clarke

Harewood House, Harewood, GB-Leeds LS17 9LQ. Tel (01132) 886331. E-mail business@harewood.org. Website www.harewood.org. Director: Terry Suthers. 100 m² approx.

The Pavilion, 235 Woodhouse Lane, GB-Leeds, West Yorks LS2 3AP. Tel (0113) 2332777, Fax (0113) 2335561. E-mail info@pavilion.org.uk. Website www.pavilion.org.uk. Open: Mon–Thu 10–16. Director: Julie Courtney. Founded 1983. 1 room, 380 m². 3–4 photo exhibitions/year

City Gallery, 90 Granby Street, GB-Leicester LE1 6FB. Tel (01162) 540595, Fax (01162) 540593. Director: Slyvia Wright

Picture House Centre for Photography Ltd., Belvoir House, 79 Voughan Way, GB-Leicester LE1 4SG. Tel (0116) 2531606. E-mail photo@ pichouse.demon.co.uk. Open: Mon–Fri 9–18 (Wed –21). Directors: Roger

Bradley, Anna Smalley. Founded 1993. 2 rooms, 300 m². 20 photo exhibitions/year

Bluecoat Gallery, School Lane, GB-Liverpool L1 3BX. Tel (0151) 7095689, Fax (0151) 7092777. E-mail bluecoat@ dircon.co.uk. Open: Tue–Sat 10.30–17. Director/curator: Catherine Gibson. Founded 1968. 4 rooms, 150 m²

Open Eye Gallery, 28–32 Wood Street, GB-Liverpool, L1 4AQ. Tel (0151) 7099460, Fax (0151) 7093059. E-mail info@openeye.u-net.com. Website www.openeye.org.uk. Open: Tue–Fri 10.30–17.30, Sat 10.30–17. Director/ curator: Paul Mellor. Founded 1977. 2 rooms. 8 photo exhibitions/year. Artists: Ed van der Elsken, Thecla Schiphorst, Gordon Bennett, Paula Latham, Stephanie Smith, Edward Stewart

Tate Gallery, The National Collections of British and Modern Art in London, Liverpool and St. Ives, Albert Dock, GB-Liverpool, Merseyside L3 4BB. Tel (0151) 7027400, Fax (0151) 7027401. E-mail liverpoolinfo @tate.org.uk. Website www.tate. org.uk. Open: Tue–Sun 10–17.50. Director: Lewis Biggs. Founded 1988. 4 rooms

Walker Art Gallery, William Brown Street, GB-Liverpool L3 8EL. Tel (0151) 4784199, Fax (0151) 4184190. Website www.connect.org.uk/ merseyworld/aande/museums. Open: Mon–Sat 10–17, Sun 12–17. Director: Sir Richard Foster. Curator: Dave Flower. Founded 1877. 3 rooms, 257 m². 1 photo exhibition/year

Anthony d'Offay, 9, 23, 24 Dering Street, GB-London W1R 9AA. Tel (020) 74994100, Fax (020) 74934443. E-mail infogallery@doffay.com. Website www.doffay.com. Director:

Mary Louise Laband. Artists: Andy Warhol, Georg Baselitz, Joseph Beuys, Gilbert & George, Jasper Johns, Jeff Koons, Richard Long, Bruce Nauman, Tatsuo Miyajima, Gabriel Orozco

Anthony Reynolds Gallery, 5 Dering Street, GB-London WIR 9AB. Tel (0171) 4910621, Fax (0171) 4952374. Open: Tue–Sat 10–18. Director: Anthony Reynolds. Founded 1985. 3 rooms, 100 m². Artists: Ian Breakwell, Alain Miller, Georgina Starr, Amikam Toren, Mark Wallinger, Richard Billingham, Steve McQueen, Keith Tyson, Ion Thompson, Paul Graham

Association Gallery, 81 Leonard Street, GB-London EC2A 4QS. Tel (020) 77393631, Fax (020) 77398707. E-mail aop@dircon.co.uk. Website www.aophoto.co.uk. Open: Mon–Fri 9.30–18, Sat 12–16.30. Director: Alex Steele-Mortimer. Founded 1986. 2 rooms, 100 m². 20 photo exhibitions/ year. Artists: Andreas Heumann, Barry Lategan, Claire Park, Martin Beckett, Marcus Lyon, Tony May, Bob Miller, Gilles Revell, Wendy Carrig, Duncan McNicol

Barbican Art Gallery, Barbican Centre, Level 8, Silk Street, GB-London EC2Y 8DS. Tel (020) 76384141, Fax (020) 79209648. E-mail barbican_press@ barbican.org.uk. Website www. barbican.org.uk. Open: Mon–Sat 10–18.45, Sun 12–17.45. Director: John Wholle. 1 photo exhibition/year

Bloomsbury Theatre Hall, 15 Gordon Street, GB-London WC1H 0AH. Tel (020) 76792777, Fax (020) 5042777. E-mail blooms.theatre@ucl.ac.uk. Website www.thebloomsbury.com. Open: 9.30–17.30. Director: Catriona Lenihan. Curator: Mark Feakins. Founded 1968. 1 room. 8 photo exhibitions/year. Artists: Gustava Espinosa, Kev Dutton, Suzanne Hutchinson, Louise Pim, Kim Jenkins, Tony Campbell

Camden Arts Centre, Arkwright Road, GB-London NW3 6DG. Tel (0171) 4352643/5224, Fax (0171) 7943371. E-mail info@camdenarts. org.uk. Open: Tue–Thu 11–19, Fri–Sun 11–17.30. Director: Jenni Lomax. Founded 1971. 3 rooms, 396 m². 1 photo exhibition/year. Artists: John Riddy, Lois Weinberger, Simon Starling, Li Yuan-Chia

Camerawork, 121 Roman Road, Bethnal Green, GB-London E2 0QN. Tel (0181) 9806256, Fax (0181) 9834714. E-mail info@camerawork. net. Website www.camerawork.net. Open: Tue–Sat 13–18. Director: Philip Sanderson. Curator: John Roberts. Founded 1975. 1 room, 100 m². 8 photo exhibitions/year

Curve Gallery, Barbican Centre, Level 5, Silk Street, GB-London EC2. Tel (0171) 6388891, Fax (0171) 2568586. E-mail artgalleries@barbican.org.uk. Website www.barbican.org.uk. Open: 10–17.30. Director: John Hoole. Founded 1982. 1 room, 190 running meters. 2–3 photo exhibitions/year

Hamiltons Gallery, 13 Carlos Place, GB-London W1Y 5AG. Tel (0171) 499949-3/4, Fax (0171) 6299919. E-mail photography@ hamiltonsgallery.com. Website www.hamiltonsgallery.com. Open: Tue–Sat 10–18. Director: Andrew Cowan. Curator: Nicole Stanner. Founded 1980. 3 rooms, 325 m². 10–12 photo exhibitions/year. Artists: David Bailey, Don McCullin, Norman Parkinson, Javier Vallhonrat, Tomio Seike, Irving Penn, Horst P. Horst, William Klein, Malcom Pasley, Robert Mapplethorpe

Hayward Gallery, South Bank Centre, Belvedere Road, GB-London SE1. Tel (0171) 9604242, Fax (0171) 4012664. E-mail visual_arts@hayward.org.uk. Website www.hayward-gallery.org. uk. Open: 10–18 (Tue+Wed –20). Director: Keith Hardy. Founded 1968. 5 rooms, 1,500 m². 1 photo exhibition/year

Institute of Contemporary Arts, 12 Carlton House Terrace, The Mall, GB-London SW1Y 5AH. Tel (0171) 9300493, Fax (0171) 8730051. E-mail info@ica.org.uk. Website www. illumin.co.uk/ica/. Open: 12–19.30 (Tue –21). Director: Philip Dadd. Founded 1947. 3 rooms, 395 m². 1–2 photo exhibitions/year

Islington Arts Factory, 2 Parkhurst Road, GB-London N7 0SF. Tel (0171) 6070561, Fax (0171) 7007229. E-mail artsfactory@netscape.online.co.uk. Website www.artec.org.uk/artec/ iafnet. Open: Mon–Fri 10–21.30, Sat 10–17.30, Sun 11–17.30. Director: Helen O'Hora. Curator: Phillippa Clayden. 1 room, 300 m². 9 photo exhibitions/year. Artists: Brendan Wilson, Dominic Chennell, Ian Welsby, Miriam Reik, Paul Smith, Jim Nelson

Jay Jopling/White Cube, 44 Duke Street, GB-London SW1Y 6DD. Tel (0171) 9305373, Fax (0171) 9309973. Website www.whitecube.com. Artists: Nobuyoshi Araki, Angus Fairhurst, Antony Gormley, Mona Hatoum, Damien Hirst, Clay Ketter, Sarah Lucas, Marc Quinn, Doris Salcedo, Sam Taylor-Wood

Laure Genillard, Gallery, 38a Foley Street, GB-London W1P 7LB. Tel (0171) 74908853, Fax (0171) 74908854. Open: Tue–Fri 11–18, Sat 11–15. Director: Laure Genillard. Founded 1988. 1 room, 25 m². 1 photo exhibition/year. Artists: Jürgen Albrecht, Tania Kovats, Vincent Shine, Gladstone Thompson, Padraig Timoney, Craig Wood, Catherine Yass, Günter Umberg, Sylvie Fleury, Dan Hays

Michael Hoppen Gallery, 3 Jubilee Place, GB-London SW3. Tel (0271) 3523649, Fax (0271) 3523669. E-mail michael.hoppen@getty-images.com. Website www.michaelhoppen-photo.com. Open: Mon–Fri 10–18, Sat by appointment. Director: Michael Hoppen. Curators: Michael Hoppen, Hilary Slater. Founded 1994. 6–8 photo exhibitions/year. Artists: André Kertész, Willy Ronis, Robert Frank, Nadar Kander, Lillian Bassman, David Parker

Museum of London, 150 London Wall, GB-London EC2Y 5HN. Tel (0171) 6003699, Fax (0171) 6001058. E-mail info@museumoflondon.org. uk. Website www.museumoflondon. org.uk. Open: Mon–Sat 10–17.50, Sun 12–17.50

National Portrait Gallery, St. Martin's Place, GB-London WC2H 0HE. Tel (0171) 3060055, Fax (0171) 3060056. E-mail csaumarezsmith@npg.org.uk. Website www.npg.org.uk. Open: Mon–Sat 10–18, Sun 12–18. Director: Dr. Charles Saumarez-Smith. Curator: Terence Pepper. Founded 1856. 3 rooms. 4 photo exhibitions/year

Photofusion, 17a Electric Lane, Brixton, GB-London SW9 8LA. Tel (020) 77385774, Fax (020) 77385509. E-mail gallery@photofusion.org.uk. Website www.photofusion.org. Open: Tue–Fri 10–18 (Wed –20), Sat 11–17, closed on Bank holidays. Director: Lynne Wealleans. Founded 1991. 2 rooms, 85 m². 9–12 photo exhibitions/year

Photology, 24 Litchfield Street, GB-London WC2 H9NJ. Tel (0171) 8368600, Fax (0171) 8367049. E-mail photology@mailbox.iunet.it. Website www.photology.com. Director: David Faccioli

Rebecca Hossack Gallery, 35 Windmill Street, GB-London W1P 1HH. Tel (0171) 4364899, Fax (0171) 3233182. E-mail rebecca@r-h-g.co.uk. Website www.r-h-g.co.uk. Open: Mon–Sat 10–18. Director: Rebecca Hossack. Founded 1987. 3 rooms. 4–5 photo exhibitions/year. Artists: Bernard Faucon, John Miles, Tim Allen, Shaun Brosnan, Chris Drury, Luke Elwes, Laura Godfrey-Isaacs, Colin Johnstone, Helen Flockhart, Simone Douglas

Royal Academy of Arts, Burlington House, Piccadilly, GB-London W1V 0DS. Tel (0171) 3005915, Fax (0171) 3005765. E-mail adam@ royalacademy.org.uk. Website www.royalacademy.org.uk

Tate Gallery, The National Collections of British and Modern Art in London, Liverpool and St. Ives, Millbank, GB-London SW1P 4RG. Tel (020) 78878000, Fax (020) 78878007. Website www.tate.org.uk. Director: Nicholas Seroto

The Canon Photography Gallery, c/o Victoria and Albert Museum, Cromwell Road, GB-London SW7 2RL. Tel (0171) 9388500, Fax (0171) 9388341. Website www.vam.ac.uk. Open: daily 10–17.50. Director: Dr. Alan Berg. Curator: Mark Haworth-Booth. Founded 1998. 1 room, 400 m². 3 photo exhibitions/year

The Photographers' Gallery, 5 & 8 Great Newport Street, GB-London WC2H 7HY. Tel (0171) 8311772, Fax (0171) 8369704. E-mail info@ photonet.org.uk. Website www. photonet.org.uk. Open: Mon–Sat 11–

18, Sun 12–18. Director: Paul Wombell. Curator: Kate Bush. Founded 1971. 3 rooms, 314 m². 6–8 photo exhibitions/year. Artists: Bert Hardy, Jacques-Henri Lartigue, Sebastião Salgado, Elinor Carucci, Dolores Marat, Andrew Douglas, Manuel Alvarez Bravo, Michael Kruger, Nigel Shafran, Iain Stewart

The Serpentine Gallery, Kensington Gardens, GB-London W2 3XA. Tel (020) 74026075, Fax (020) 74024103. E-mail rosed@serpentinegallery.org. Website www.serpentinegallery.org. Open: 10–18. Director: Julia Peyton-Jones. Founded 1970. 4 rooms, 500 m². 2 photo exhibitions/year

The Special Photographers Company, 21 Kensington Park Road, GB-London W11 2EU. Tel (020) 72213489, Fax (020) 77929112. E-mail info@ specialphoto.co.uk. Open: Mon–Fri 10–16, Sat 11–17. Directors: Catherine Turner, Chris Kewbank. Founded 1986. 2 rooms, 1,300 m². 10 photo exhibitions/year. Artists: Herman Leonard, Joyce Tenneson, Eddie Dayan, Lois Greenfield, Clare Park, Bruce Gilden, Simon Larbalestier, Gered Mankowitz, Edward S. Curtis, Ouka Lele

Tom Blau Gallery, 21 Queen Elizabeth Street, Butlers Wharf, GB-London SE1 2PD. Tel (0171) 3781300, Fax (0171) 2785126. E-mail tbg@dircon.co.uk. Open: Mon–Fri 09–18. Director: Keith Cavanagh. Founded 1993. 1 room, 62 m². 12 photo exhibitions/year. Artists: Simon Norfolk, Phil Knott, Rankin, Dennis Morris, Yousuf Karsh, Grace Lau

Whitechapel Art Gallery, 80–82 Whitechapel High Street, GB-London E1 7QX. Tel (020) 75227888, Fax (020) 73771685. E-mail info@whitechapel. org. Website www.whitechapel.org. Open: Tue–Sun 11–17 (Wed –20). Director: Catherine Lampert. Founded 1901. 3 rooms, 576 m²

Wigmore Fine Arts Ltd., 104 Wigmore Street, GB-London W1H 9DR. Tel (020) 72241962, Fax (020) 72241965. Website www.wigmore-fine-art. co.uk. Open: Tue–Fri 10–18, Sat 10–15. Director: Mary Los. Founded 1996. 2 rooms, 150 m². 3 photo exhibitions/year

Zelda Cheatle Gallery, 99 Mount St., GB-London W1. Tel (020) 74084448, Fax (020) 74081444. E-mail photo@ zcgall.demon.co.uk. Open: Mon–Sat 10–18. Director: Gareth Abbott. Founded 1989. 2 rooms, 92 m². 10 photo exhibitions/year. Artists: Keith Arnatt, Helen Chadwick, David Hiscock, Calum Colvin, Mari Mahr, Helen Sear, John Blakemore, Roger Mayne

Luton Museum & Art Gallery, Wardown Park, GB-Luton, Bedfordshire LU1 2NG. Tel (01582) 546722, Fax (01582) 546763. E-mail grabhamc@ luton.gov.uk. Website www.luton. gov.uk. Director: Chris Grabham. Founded 1928. 1 room, 90 m². 1 photo exhibition/year

Cornerhouse, 70 Oxford Street, GB-Manchester M1 5NH. Tel (0161) 2287621, Fax (0161) 2367323. E-mail Paul.Bayley@cornerhouse.org. Website www.cornerhouse.org. Open: Tue–Sat 11–18, Sun 14–18. Director: Paul Bayley. Founded 1985. 3 rooms, 429 m². 7 photo exhibitions/year

Documentary Photography Archive, Room GO II, Tylecote Building, Cavendish Street, GB-Manchester M15 6BG. Tel (01204) 840439. E-mail archives@gmcro.u-net.com. Website www.gmcro.co.uk. Open: by appointment only. Director: Audrey Lingman. Founded 1985. Artists: Martin Parr, Tom Wood, Shirley Baker, Clement Cooper, Paul Reas, Brian Lomas

Eastthorpe Visual Arts, St. Paul's Printworkshop, Huddersfield Road, GB-Mirfield WF14 8AT, West Yorkshire. Tel (01924) 497646, Fax (01924) 497646. E-mail eva@pop.3.poptel. org.uk. Open: Mon 17.30–21, Tue, Thu, Fri 12–16, Sat 10–17. Director: Don Myers. Curator: Jeff Jones. Founded 1984. 2 rooms. 2 photo exhibitions/year. Artists: Amanda Dodd, Jeff Jones

Pendle Arts Gallery, Town Hall, GB-Nelson, Pendle BB9 7LG. Tel (01282) 700492. Director: Roy Shoesmith. Founded 1993. 1 room, 6 m². 4 photo exhibitions/year. Artists: Roy Shoesmith, Melvyn Newman, Ross Ditchburn, John Malcolm, Alan Roberts, John Blakemore, Donald Holden, David Smith, Sharon Scaturo

Side Photographic Gallery, 5/9 Side, GB-Newcastle upon Tyne NE1 3JE. Tel (0191) 2322208, Fax (0191) 2303217. E-mail sidegallery@ hotmail.com. Website www.amber-online.com. Open: Mon–Sat 10–17, Sun 11–15. Director: Richard Grassick. Founded 1977. 2 rooms, 100 m². 8 photo exhibitions/year. Artists: Rich Grassick, Sirkka-Liisa Konttinen, Pete Roberts, Ellin Hare, Murray Martin, Pat McCarthy

University Gallery, University of Northumbria – Library Building, Sandyford Road, GB-Newcastle upon Tyne NE1 8ST. Tel (0191) 2274424, Fax (0191) 2274718. E-mail mara-helen.wood@unn.uc.uk. Open: Mon–Thu 10–17, Fri–Sat 10–16. Director: Mara-Helen Wood. Founded 1977. 2 rooms, 232 m². 3 photo exhibitions/year. Artist: Nick Danziger

Onsight Gallery, The Roadmender, 1 Lady's Lane, GB-Northhampton NN1 3AH. Tel (01604) 604603, Fax (01604) 603166. E-mail max@roadmender.org. Website www.roadmender.org. Director: Max Justice-Mills

Norwich Arts Centre, Reeves Yard, St. Benedicts Street, GB-Norwich, Norfolk NR2 4PG. Tel (01603) 660352. E-mail ian@norwichartscentre.co.uk. Director: Pam Reekie. Founded 1976. 30 running meters. 8 photo exhibitions/year

Norwich Gallery, School of Art & Design, St. George Street, GB-Norwich NR3 1BB. Tel (01603) 610561, Fax (01603) 615728. E-mail nor.gal@ nsad.ac.uk. Director: Lynda Morris

Sainsbury Centre for Visual Arts, University of East Anglla, GB-Norwich, Norfolk NR4 7TJ. Tel (01603) 456161, Fax (01603) 259401. E-mail scva@uea.ac.uk. Website www. uea.ac.uk. Open: Tue–Sun 11–17. Director: Nicola Johnson. Curator: Kay Poludniowski. Founded 1978. 4 rooms. 1 photo exhibition/year

Angel Row Gallery, 3 Angel Row, GB-Nottingham NG1 6HP. Tel (01159) 152869, Fax (01159) 152860. Curator: Deborah Dean

Broadway Media Centre, 14 Broad Street, GB-Nottingham NG1 3AL. Tel (01159) 526600, Fax (01159) 526662. E-mail enquiries@broadway.org.uk. Director: Loraine Porter

Djanogly Gallery, University of Nottingham, Arts Centre, University Park, GB-Nottingham NG7 2RD. Tel (0115) 9513192, Fax (0115) 9513194. Website www.nottingham.ac.uk/ artscentre. Open: Mon–Fri 10–18, Sat 11–18, Sun 14–17. Director: Johanne Wright

Museum of Modern Art, 30 Pembroke Street, GB-Oxford OX1 1BP. Tel (01865) 722733, Fax (01865) 722573. E-mail moma@demon.co.uk. Open: Tue–Sun 11–18 (Thu –21). Director: Karry Brougher. Founded 1965. 5 rooms, 512 m². 4 photo exhibitions/year

Ladylodge Arts Centre, Goldhay Way, Orton Goldhay, GB-Peterborough PE3 5JQ. Tel (01733) 237073, Fax (01733) 235462. E-mail postmaster@p-arts.demon.co.uk. Website www.peterborough.gov.uk. Director: Clifton Stewart

Plymouth Arts Centre, 38 Looe Street, GB-Plymouth PL4 0EB. Tel (01752) 206114, Fax (01752) 206118. E-mail stephen@eclipse.co.uk. Website www.eclipse.co.uk/pac. Open: Mon 10–17, Tue–Sat 10–20, Sun 17.30–19.30. Director/curator: Stephen Hobson. Founded 1947. 3 rooms, 158 m². 3–4 photo exhibitions/year

Aspex Gallery, 27 Brougham Road, Southsea, GB-Portsmouth, Hampshire PO5 4PA. Tel (01705) 812121, Fax (01705) 874523. E-mail 101661.3412@compuserve.com. Open: Wed–Sat 12–18, Sun 14–17. Director: Les Buckingham. Founded 1981. 1 room, 207 m²

Harris Museum & Art Gallery, Market Square, GB-Preston PR1 2PP. Tel (01772) 905408, Fax (01772) 886764. E-mail harris@pbch.demon.co.uk. Website www.preston.gov.uk. Director: Alexander Walker. Founded 1893. 9 rooms, 300 m². 3 photo exhibitions/year. Artists: Helen Chadwick, Nick Waplington, Maud Sulter, Cornelia Parker, Andy Goldsworthy, Keith Arnatt, Boyd Webb, Calum Colvin, Ron O'Donnell

Viewpoint Photography Gallery, Old Fire Station, The Crescent, GB-Salford M5 4NZ. Tel (0161) 7371040, Fax (0161) 7372044. E-mail info@vwpnt.demon.co.uk

Site Gallery, Media, Art, Photography, 1 Brown Street, GB-Sheffield S1 2BS. Tel (0114) 2812077, Fax (0114) 2812078. E-mail gallery@site-map.u-net.com. Website www.site-map.u-net.com. Open: Tue–Sat 11–18, Sun 13–17. Director: Carol Maund. Curators: Carol Maund, Jeanine Griffin. Founded 1977. 3 rooms. 7–8 photo exhibitions/year

John Hansard Gallery, The University, Highfield, GB-Southampton, Hants SO17 1BJ. Tel (02380) 592158, Fax (02380) 594192. E-mail hansard@soton.ac.uk. Open: Tue–Fri 11–17, Sat 11–16. Director: Stephen Foster. Founded 1979. 1 room, 300 m². 2 photo exhibitions/year

Focal Point Gallery, Central Library, Victoria Street, GB-Southend-On-Sea, Essex. Tel (01702) 612621. E-mail focal@mail.globalnet.co.uk. Contact: Lesley Farrell. Founded 1991. 1 room, 200 m². 7 photo exhibitions/year

Crawford Arts Centre, 93 North Street, GB-St. Andrews KYIG 9AL, Scot-land. Tel (01334) 474610, Fax (01334) 479880. E-mail crawfordarts@crawfordarts.free-online.co.uk. Website www.crawfordarts.free-online.co.uk. Open: Mon–Sat 10–17, Sun 14–17. Director: Diana Sykes. Founded 1977/78. 4 rooms, 180 m². 1–2 photo exhibitions/year

Jersey Photographic Museum, St. Saviour's Road, GB-St. Helier, Jersey, Channed Islands. Tel (01534) 614700, Fax (01534) 35354. E-mail ianparker@cinergy.co.uk. Website www.style2000.com. Open: Mon–Fri 9–

17.30, Sat 9–12. Director: Ian Parker. Founded 1983. 4 rooms, 350 m². 6 photo exhibitions/year. Artists: Cecil Beaton, Cornel Lucas, Terry O'Neil, Margaret Cameron, Lord Snowdon, Patrick Lichfield, Ian Parker

Wakefield Museum, Wood Street, GB-Wakefield, West York WF1 2EW. Tel (01924) 305351, Fax (01924) 305353. Website www.wakefield.gov.uk. Open: Mon–Sat 10.30–16.30, Sun 14.30–16.30. Director: Gordon Watson. Curator: Christine Johnstone. Founded 1920. 4 rooms, 400 m². 1–2 photo exhibitions/year

The New Art Gallery Walsall, Gallery Square, GB-Walsall WS2 8LG. Tel (01922) 654400, Fax (01922) 654401. E-mail info@artatwalsall.org.uk. Website www.artatwalsall.org.uk. Director: Peter Jenkinson. Open: Tue–Sat 10–17, Sun 12–17

The Sutcliffe Gallery, 1 Flowergate, GB-Whitby, North Yorkshire YO21 3BA. Tel (01947) 602239, Fax (01947) 820287. E-mail photographs@ sutcliffe-galleryfsnet.co.uk. Website www.sutcliffe-gallery.co.uk. Open: Mon–Sat 9–17. Directors: Bill Shaw, Michael Shaw. Founded 1965. 2 rooms, 950 m². 1 photo exhibition/ year. Artist: Frank Meadow Sutcliffe

Wrexham Library Arts Centre, Rhosddu Road, GB-Wrexham, Clwyd LL11 1AU. Tel (01978) 292090, Fax (01978) 292093. Open: 9.30–18.45. Director: Hazel Hawarden. Founded 1910. 2 rooms, 129 m². 2 photo exhibitions/year. Artists: Fred Langford Edwards, Maud Sulter, David Woodfall, Alvin Langdon Coburn, Kate Mellor

Impressions Gallery, 17 Colliergate, GB-York YO1 2BN. Tel (01904) 654724, Fax (01904) 651509. E-mail info@mpressions-gallery.com. Website www.impressions-gallery.com. Open: Mon–Sat 10.30–17.30. Founded 1972. 3 rooms, 700 m². 8 photo exhibitions/year

Festivals & Fairs

Herefordshire Photography Festival, Courtyard Arts Centre, P. O. Box 276, Edgar Street, GB-Hereford, Herefordshire HR41 9WW. Tel (01432) 351964, Fax (01432) 279899. E-mail enquiries@ photofest.org. Website www. photofest.org

K.O'C. Ltd., London Photographic Awards, 23 Roehamton Lane, GB-London SW15 5LS. Tel (0181) 3928557, Fax (0181) 8764625. E-mail koc@mailbox.co.uk. Website www. lpa-awards.com

Magazines

AN Magazine, 7–15 Pink Lane, 1st Floor, Turner Building, GB-Newcastle upon Tyne NE1 5DW. Tel (0191) 2418000, Fax (0191) 2418001. E-mail an@anpubs.demon.co.uk. Website www.anweb.co.uk. Contact: Louise Coysh. English. Founded 1980. Copy price: £3.00. Annual subscription: £26.00, 12 issues/year

Arts Review, Britain's only Fortnightly Art Magazine, 20 Prescott Place, GB-London SW4 6BT. Tel (0171) 9781000, Fax (0171) 9781102. Editor: Catriona Warron. English. Founded 1949. Copy price: £3.50. Annual subscription: £29.50, £57.00 (Europe), 10 issues/year

Audio Visual, Communications for Business, Maclaren House, Scarbrook Road, P. O. Box 109, GB-Croydon,

Surrey CR9 1QH. Tel (0208) 5654223, Fax (0208) 5654282. E-mail peterl@ gpp.co.uk. Editor: Peter Lloyd. English. Founded 1972. Copy price: £3.90. Annual subscription: £45.00, 10 issues/year

British Journal of Photography, Timothy Benn Publishing Ltd, 39 Earlham Street, Covent Garden, GB-London WC2H 9LD. Tel (0207) 3067000, Fax (0207) 3067017. E-mail bjp@bjphoto.co.uk. Website www. bjphoto.co.uk. Editor: Chris Dickie. English. Founded 1854. Copy price: £1.50. Annual subscription: £65.00, £85.00 (Europe/airmail), 50 issues/ year

Creative Review, St. Giles House, 50 Poland Street, GB-London W1V 4AX. Tel (0171) 9706277, Fax (0171) 9706712. E-mail patrickb@centaur. co.uk. Website www.creativereview. co.uk. Editor: Patrick Burgoyne. English. Founded 1980. Copy price: £4.25. Annual subscription: £49.95, 12 issues/year

Dpict, incorporating Creative Camera, 55–57 Tabernacle Street, GB-London EC2A 4AF. Tel (020) 74902068, Fax (020) 74902087. E-mail info@ ccamera.demon.co.uk. Website www. ccamera.demon.co.uk. Editor: David Brittain. English. Founded 1968

Eos Magazine, The Old Barn, Ball Lane, Tackley, Kidlington, GB-Oxfordshire OX5 3AG. Tel (01869) 331741, Fax (01869) 331641. E-mail rsa@macline.co.uk. Website www. eos-magazine.com. Editor: Robert Scott. English. Founded 1992. Annual subscription: £14.95, £19.95 (Europe), 4 issues/year

Frieze, Contemporary Art and Culture, 21 Denmark Street, GB-London WC2H 8NA. Tel (020) 73791533, Fax (020) 73791521. E-mail editors@ frieze.co.uk. Website www.frieze. co.uk. Contact: Helen Slater. English. Founded 1990. Copy price: £3.75. Annual subscription: £22.50 (UK), £30.00 (overseas), 6 issues/year

History of Photography, Taylor & Francis Ltd., 11 New Fetter Lane, GB-London EC4P 4EE. Tel (020) 78422313, Fax (020) 75839859. E-mail info@tandf.co.uk. Editors: Dr. Mike Weaver, Anne Hammond. English. Founded 1977. Annual subscription: US$89.00 (individuals), US$151.00 (institutions), 4 issues/year

Portfolio Magazine, The Catalogue of Contemporary Photography in Britain, 43 Candlemaker Row, GB-Edinburgh EH1 2QB, Scotland. Tel (0131) 2201911, Fax (0131) 2264287. E-mail portfolio@ednet.co.uk. Website www.ednet.co.uk/-portfolio. Editor: Gloria Chalmers. English. Founded 1988. Copy price: £8.95. Annual subscription: £17.00 (UK), £25.00 (Europe), 2 issues/year

Professional Photographer, The Mill, Berwalden Business Park, Wendens Ambo, GB-Essex CB11 45X. Tel (01799) 544246, Fax (01799) 544 205. E-mail eileen.martin@ marketlink.co.uk. Website www. professionalphotographer.co.uk. Editor: Eileen Martin. English. Founded 1960. Copy price: £2.95, 12 issues/year

Source, 3 Botanic Avenue, GB-Belfast BT7 1JG. Tel (01232) 329691, Fax (01232) 329691. E-mail editors@ sourcemagazine.demon.co.uk. Website www.sourcemagazine. demon.co.uk. Editors: John Duncan, Richard West

Stare, electronic Internet publication, David Glenn Rinehart, 16 Prospect

Court/Prospect Place, GB-New-castle-upon-Tyne NE4 6NS. E-mail dgr@stare.com. Website www. stare.com

The Art Newspaper, 70 South Lambeth Road, GB-London SW8 1RL. Tel (0207) 7353331, Fax (0207) 7353332. E-mail contact@ theartnewspaper.com. Website www.theartnewspaper.com. Editor: Anna Somers Cocks. English. Copy price: £4.5, 11 issues/year

The Art World Directory, Art Books International, 1 Stewarts Court, 220 Stewarts Road, GB-London SW8 4UD. Tel (0171) 9781222, Fax (0171) 7203158. E-mail sales@art-bks.com. Editor: Kate Sayner. English

The Photographic Journal, Official Journal of The Royal Photographic Society, Acorn House, 74–94 Cherry Orchard Road, GB-Croydon, Surrey CR9 6DA. Tel (0181) 6818339, Fax (0181) 6811880. E-mail roy@rps-pj.demon.co.uk. Editor: Roy Green. English. Founded 1839. Copy price: £3.00. Annual subscription: £55.00, £60.00 (overseas), 10 issues/year

Zoo, 245 Old Marylebone Road, GB-London NW1 5QT. Tel (020) 72586900, Fax (020) 72586901. E-mail info@zooworld.net. English. Copy price: £125.00. Annual subscription: £475.00, 4 issues/year

Book Publishers

A. H. Jolly (Editorial) Ltd., Yelvertoft Manor, GB-Yelvertoft, Northhampton NN6 7LF. Tel (01788) 823868, Fax (01788) 823915

AN Publications, P. O. Box 23, GB-Sunderland SR4 6DG. Tel (0191) 2418000. E-mail an@anpubs.demon. co.uk. Website www.anweb.co.uk

Art Data, Action Business Centre, School Road, GB-London NW10 6TD. Tel (0181) 9613643, Fax (0181) 9653092

ARTbibliographies, 35a Great Clarendon Street, GB-Oxford OX2 6AT. Tel (01865) 311350, Fax (01865) 311358. E-mail abm@abc-clio.la.uk. Website www.abc-clio.com

Arts Council of Great Britain, 14 Great Peter Street, GB-London SW1P 3NQ. Tel (0171) 3330100. E-mail enquiries@ artscouncil.org.uk. Website www. artscouncil.org.uk

Bloomsbury Publishing Ltd., 2 Soho Square, GB-London W1V 5DE. Tel (0171) 4942111, Fax (0171) 4340151. E-mail webmaster@Bloomsbury.com. Website www.bloomsbury.com

Butterworth Heinemann Ltd., Linacre House, Jordan Hill, GB-Oxford OX2 8DP. Tel (01865) 310366, Fax (01865) 310898. E-mail margaret.riley@ bhein.rel.co.uk. Website www. heinemann.co.uk

Calmann and King Ltd., 71 Great Russell Street, GB-London WC1B 3BN. Tel (0171) 8316351, Fax (0171) 8318356. E-mail enquiries@calman-king.co.uk. Website www.laurence-king.com

Cornerhouse Publications, 70 Oxford Street, GB-Manchester M1 5NH. Tel (0161) 2379662, Fax (0161) 2379664. E-mail chse-publ-dist@mcr1.poptel. org.uk. Website www. poptel.org.uk/chse-publ/home-html

David & Charles, Brunel House, Forde Road, GB-Newton Abbot TQ12 4PU. Tel (01626) 323200, Fax (01626) 364463. E-mail anna.watson@ davidcharles.co.uk. Website www. davidcharles.co.uk

150 Great Britain

Dewi Lewis Publishing, 8 Broomfield Road, Heaton Moor, GB-Stockport SK4 4ND. Tel (0161) 4429450, Fax (0161) 4429450. E-mail mail@ dewilewispublishing.com. Website www.dewilewispublishing.com

Ebury Press, Random House, 20 Vauxhall Bridge Road, GB-London SW1V 2SA. Tel (0171) 8408400, Fax (0171) 2337398. E-mail flaurent@ randomhouse.co.uk. Website www. randomhouse.co.uk

Focal Press, Linacre House, Jordan Hill, GB-Oxford OX2 8DP. Tel (01865) 314554, Fax (01865) 314572. E-mail marie.milmore@repp.co.uk. Website www.focalpress.com

Fountain Press, 2 Gladstone Road, GB-Kingston Upon Thames KT1 3HD. Tel (0181) 5414050, Fax (0181) 5473022. E-mail fountprs@ dircon.co.uk

Harper Collins, General Reference Div., 77–85 Fulham Palace Road, Hammersmith, GB-London W6 8JB. Tel (0181) 7417070, Fax (0181) 3074440. E-mail cathy.gosling@ harpercollins.co.uk. Website www. fireandwater.com

I. B. Tauris, Victoria House, 45 Bloomsbury Square, GB-London WC1B 4D2. Tel (0171) 8319060, Fax (0171) 8319061. E-mail mail@ ibtauris.com

Internos Books, 12 Percy Street, GB-London W1P 9FB. Tel (0171) 6374255, Fax (0171) 6374251. E-mail info@ booth-clibborn.com. Website www. booth-clibborn-editions.com

IPC Magazines – Book Division, King's Reach Tower, Stamford Street, GB-London SE1 9LS. Tel (0171) 2615000. Website www.ipc.co.uk

Mainstream Publishing, 7 Albany Street, GB-Edinburgh EH1 3 UG, Scotland. Tel (0131) 5572959, Fax (0131) 5568720. E-mail office. mainstream@btinternet.com. Website www.mainstreampublishing.com

Martin Secker & Warburg, 20 Vauxhall Bridge Road, GB-London SW1Z 2SA. Tel (020) 78408400, Fax (0171) 2336125

Mitchell Beazley, Michelin House, 81 Fulham Road, GB-London SW3 6RB. Tel (0171) 5819393, Fax (0171) 5810878

Nicholas Enterprises Limited, 28 Percy Street, GB-London W1P 0LD. Tel (0171) 3233319, Fax (0171) 3234829

Octopus, 2 Heron Keys, GB-London E14 4JP. Tel (020) 75318400, Fax (020) 75318650. Website www. octopuspublishing.co.uk

Phaidon Press Ltd., Regent's Wharf, All Saints Road, GB-London N1 9PA. Tel (020) 78431000, Fax (020) 78431010. Website www.phaidon. com

Photo-Historical Publications, 34 Bury Walk, GB-London SW3 6QB. Fax (0171) 8239058

Plexus Publishing, 55a Clapham Common 5th Side, GB-London SW4 9BX. Tel (0171) 6222440, Fax (0171) 62222441. E-mail plexus@plexusuk. demon.co.uk. Website www. plexusbooks.co.uk

Quartet Books Limited, 27 Goodge Street, GB-London W1P 2LD. Tel (0171) 6363992, Fax (0171) 6371866

Quarto Publishing plc, 6 Blundell Street, GB-London N7 9BH. Tel (0171) 7006700, Fax (0171) 7004191. Website www.quarto.com

Rivers Orum Press, 144 Hemmingford Road, GB-London N1 1De. Tel (020) 76070823

Robert Harding Picture Library, 58–59 Great Marlborough Street, GB-London W1V 1DD. Tel (0171) 2875414, Fax (0171) 6311070. E-mail info@robertharding.com. Website www.robertharding.com

Scottish Publishers Association, Scottish Book Centre, 137 Dundee Street, GB-Edinburgh EH 11 1BG, Scotland. Tel (0131) 2286866, Fax (0131) 2283220. E-mail enquiries@ scottishbooks.org. Website www. scottishbooks.org

Swan Hill Press, 101 Longden Road, GB-Shrewsbury SY3 9EB. Tel (01743) 235651, Fax (01743) 232944. E-mail airlise@airlisebooks.com

Thames & Hudson, 181A High Holborn, GB-London WC1V 7QX. Tel (020) 78455000, Fax (020) 78455050. E-mail mail@thameshudson.co.uk. Website www.thamesandhudson. com

The British Council, Bridgewater House, 58 Whiteworth St., GB-Manchester M1 6BB. Tel (0161) 9577000, Fax (0161) 9577168. E-mail gen.enquiries@britcoun.org

Victoria and Albert Museum Publications, 38–40 Clareville Street, GB-London SW7 5AJ. Tel (020) 79422966, Fax (020) 79422977. E-mail n.evans@ vam.ac.uk. Website www.vam.ac.uk

Bookshops

Daniella Dangoor, XIX Century Photographs, Museum Street 40a, GB-London WC1A 1LT. Tel (0171) 4043919, Fax (0171) 4043919

Dillons Art Bookstore, 8 Long Acre, GB-London WC2E 9HL. Tel (0171) 8361359

Ian Shipley Books, 70 Charring Cross Road, GB-London WC2. Tel (020) 78364872, Fax (020) 73794358. E-mail artbook@compuserve.com. Website www.artbook.co.uk

Photographers' Gallery Bookshop, 5/ 8 Great Newport Street, GB-London WC2H 7HY. Tel (0171) 8311772, Fax (0171) 2400591. E-mail bookshop@ photonet.org.uk. Website www. photonet.org.uk

Zwemmer Ltd., 80 Charring Cross Road, GB-London WC2H 0BE. E-mail enquiries@zwemmer.co.uk. Website www.zwemmer.co.uk

Auctions

Christie's South Kensington, 85 Old Brompton Road, GB-London SW7 3LD. Tel (020) 75817611, Fax (020) 73213321. E-mail mpritchard@ christies.com. Website www. christies.com

Sotheby's, 34–35 New Bond Street, GB-London W1A 2AA. Fax (0171) 2935000. Website www.sotheby's. com

Critics & Journalists

Claire Armistead, Guardian, 119 Farrlngdon Road, GB-London EC1R 3ER. Tel (020) 2182332. E-mail claire.armistead@guardian.co.uk. Website www.guardian.co.uk

Mo Bakaya, BBC Radio, Portland Place, GB-London W1A 1AA. Website www.bbc.co.uk/radio

Marina Benjamin, 10 Thene Villas, Holloway, GB-London N7 7PA

David Brittain, Dpict, 55–57 Tabernacle Street, GB-London EC2A 4AF. Tel (020) 74902068, Fax (020) 74902087. E-mail info@ccamera. demon.co.uk. Website www. ccamera.demon.co.uk. Editor of *Dpict*, London

Susan Butler, 7 Blewitt Street, GB-Newport NP20 4DB, Wales. Fax (0633) 211537

Emmanuel Cooper, 38 Chalcol Road, GB-London NW1

Thomas Joshua Cooper, Glasgow School of Art, 167 Renfrew Street, GB-Glasgow G3 6RQ, Scotland. Tel (0141) 3534500. Website www. gsa.ac.uk

Garry Coward-Williams, Amateur Photographer, King's Reach Tower, Stamford Street, GB-London SE1 8LS. Tel (0171) 2615100, Fax (0171) 2615404. E-mail amateurphotographer@ipa.co.uk. *Amateur Photographer*, London

Sascha Craddock, 89 Great Russell Street, GB-London W1X 1HD

Sue Davies, 53 Britwell Road, GB-Burnham, Bucks SL1 8DH. Tel (01628) 662677, Fax (01628) 662677

Wayne Ford, Observer Magazine, 75 Farringdon Road, GB-London EC1R 3ER. Tel (0171) 2782332. E-mail wayne.ford@observer.co.uk. *Observer Magazine*, London

Anna Fox, 5 Hoxton Square, GB-London N1 6NU. Tel (0171) 7394014, Fax (0171) 7297568

Richard Gott, 88 Lodbury Road, GB-London W8. Tel (0171) 7273967

Hilary Gresty, 2 George's Terrace, Halifax Road, GB-Cambridge CB4 3PY

Mark Haworth-Booth, Victoria and Albert Museum, Exhibition Road, South Kensington, GB-London SW7 2RL. Tel (020) 79422552, Fax (020) 79422561. E-mail m.haworth-booth@vam.ac.uk. Website www. vam.ac.uk

Francis Hodgson, 9 St. Mark's Place, GB-London W11 1MS

Amanda Hopkinson, 13 Conought Road, GB-London N4 4NT. Tel (0171) 2634034

Ian Jeffrey, Vine Cottage, Rodmell, GB-Lewes, Sussex BN7 3HF. *European Photography*, Göttingen

Sarah Kent, Time Out, 251 Tottenham Court Road, GB-London W1P 0AB. Tel (0171) 8133000. E-mail sarah@ timeart.com

Chris Miller, 16 Argyle Street, GB-Oxford OX4 1SS. Tel (01865) 724896, Fax (01865) 724896. *European Photography*, Göttingen

Charlotte Mullins, Independent on Sunday, The Garden Flat, 12a Tanza Road, GB-London NW3. Tel (0171) 2932000. E-mail charlotte.mullins@ independent.co.uk

Richard Pinsent, The Art Newspaper, 70 South Lambeth Road, GB-London SW8 1RL. Tel (0207) 7353331, Fax (0207) 7353332. E-mail contact@ theartnewspaper.com

David Glenn Rinehart, 16 Prospect Court/Prospect Place, GB-Newcastle-upon-Tyne NE4 6NS. E-mail dgr@stare.com. Website www. stare.com

John Russell-Taylor, Times, 11 Phoenix Lodge Mansions, GB-London W6. Tel (0171) 7825000, Fax (0171) 7825748. *Times*, London

John Stathatos, 212 Stapleton Hall Road, GB-London N4 4QR. Tel (020) 83405650, Fax (020) 83417610. E-mail stathatos@zeno.globalnet.co.uk. *European Photography*, Göttingen; *Portfolio*, Edinburgh

Sue Steward, Daily Telegraph, 1 Canada Square, GB-London E14 5DT. Tel (0171) 5385000. E-mail www. telegraph.co.uk

Sue Ward, Art Book, Laughton, GB-Nr. Lewis East Sussex BN8 6DD. Tel (01323) 811759. E-mail sward@ mistral.co.uk

Dr. Mike Weaver, History of Photography/Taylor & Francis Ltd., 11 New Fetter Lane, GB-London EC4P 4EE. Tel (020) 75839855, Fax (020) 78422373. E-mail info@tandf.co.uk. Editor of *History of Photography*, London

Liz Wells, 145b Ashley Gardens, Thirleby Road, GB-London SW1P 1HN. Tel (0374) 623108

Rhonda Wilson, Seeing the Light, 212 The Custard Factory, Gibb Street, GB-Birmingham B9 4AA. Tel (0121) 7737889. E-mail rx@seeingthelight. co.uk. Website www.seeingthelight. co.uk. *European Photography*, Göttingen

Paul Wombell, The Photographers' Gallery, 5 Great Newport Street, GB-London WC2H 7HY. Tel (0171) 8311772, Fax (0171) 8369704. E-mail info@photonet.org.uk. Website www.photonet.org.uk. Director of The Photographers' Gallery, London

Schools & Workshops

Edinburgh College of Art, Photography Courses, Lauriston Place, GB-Edinburgh EH3 9DF, Scotland. Tel (0131) 2216000, Fax (0131) 2216001. E-mail viscom@eca.ac.uk. Website www.eca.ac.uk

Exeter College of Art and Design, Earl Richard's Road North, GB-Exeter, Devon EX2 6AS. Tel (01392) 205301, Fax (01392) 205301

Glasgow School of Art, Fine Art Photography Department, 167 Renfrew Street, GB-Glasgow G3 6RQ, Scotland. Tel (0141) 3534575, Fax (0141) 3534575. E-mail v.judge@ gsa.ac.uk. Website www.gsa.ac.uk

Kent Institute of Art & Design, Oakwood Park, Oakwood Road, GB-Maidstone, Kent, ME16 8AG. Tel (01622) 757286, Fax (01622) 621100. E-mail kiadmarketing@kiad.ac.uk. Website www.kiad.ac.uk

London School of Photojournalism, 52–54 Kenway Road, Earls Court, GB-London SW5 0RA. Tel (0171) 2219977, Fax (0171) 2431730. E-mail lsp@easynet.co.uk

Manchester University, Dept. of Communication Arts and Design, Grosvenor Building, All Saints, GB-Manchester M15 6BR. Tel (0161) 2471285, Fax (0161) 2476805. E-mail j.magee@mmv.ac.uk. Website www. mmv.ac.uk

Napier University, Dept. of Photography, Film and Television, 61 Marchmont Road, GB-Edinburgh EH9 1HU, Scotland. Tel (0131) 4555203, Fax (0131) 4555224. Website www.napier.ac.uk

Photography at the Metropole, The Arts Centre, New Metropole, The

Leas, GB-Folkstone, Kent. Tel (01303) 244706

Picture House Centre for Photography Ltd., Belvoir House, 79 Voughan Way, GB-Leicester LE1 4SG. Tel (0116) 2531606. E-mail photo@ pichouse.demon.co.uk

Royal College of Art, Dept. of Photography, Kensington Gore, GB-London SW7 2EU. Tel (020) 75904444, Fax (020) 75904500. E-mail public-relations@rca.ac.uk. Website www. rca.ac.uk

School of Art, University of Wales, Old College, King Street, GB-Aberystwyth, Dyfed SY23 2AX, Wales. Tel (01970) 622021, Fax (01970) 627410. E-mail viawww@aber.ac.uk. Website www.aber.ac.uk

Sheffield Hallam University, School of Cultural Studies/Fine Art, Psalter Lane, GB-Sheffield, South Yorkshire S11 8UZ. Tel (0114) 2252646, Fax (0114) 2252603. Website www. shu.ac.uk

The University Wolverhampton, Dept. of Art and Design, Molineux Street, GB-Wolverhampton, West Midlands WV1 1SB. Tel (01902) 321945, Fax (01902) 321944

University of Brighton, Faculty of Art, Design and Humanities, Grand Parade, GB-Brighton BN2 2JY. Tel (01273) 600900, Fax (01273) 642825. Website www.brighton.ac.uk

University of Derby, Art and Design School/Britannia Mill, Mackworth Road, GB-Derby DE22 3BL. Tel (01332) 622222, Fax (01332) 622760. E-mail info@derby.ac.uk. Website www.derby.co.uk

University of Wales College, Newport Wales, GB-Newport, Gwent NP6 1YH. Tel (01633) 432432, Fax (01633) 432850. E-mail uic@newport.ac.uk. Website www.newport.ac.uk

University of Westminster, School of Communication Arts, Watford Rd., GB-Harrow, Middlesex HA1 3TP. Tel (020) 79115000, Fax (020) 79115955. E-mail g.h.jack@wmin.ac.uk. Website www.wmin.ac.uk

Wimbledon School of Art, Merton Road, GB-London SW19 3QA. Tel (0181) 4085000, Fax (0181) 4085050. Website www.wimbledon.ac.uk

Winchester School of Art, Park Avenue, GB-Winchester, Hampshire SO23 8DL. Tel (023) 80596900, Fax (023) 01703-596901. Website www. soton.ac.uk/~wsart

Associations

Birmingham Art Trust, Unit 4, Old Union Mill, 17–23 Grosvenor St. West, GB-Birmingham B16 8HW. Tel (0121) 6436040, Fax (0121) 6436040

British Institute of Professional Photography, Fox Talbot House, Amwell End, GB-Ware, Hertfordshire SG12 9HN. Tel (01920) 464011, Fax (01920) 487056. E-mail bipp@compuserve. com. Website www.bipp.com

Master Photographers' Association, 1 West Ruislip Station, GB-Ruislip, Middlesex HA4 7DW

Photographic Collectors Club of Great Britain, 38 Sutton Road, GB-Watford, Herts WD1 2QF. Tel (01923) 468356, Fax (01923) 468509. E-mail pccgb@ lightwave.demon.co.uk. Website www.lightwave.demon.co.uk/ pccgb/pccgb.htm

Royal Academy of Arts, Burlington House, Piccadilly, GB-London W1V 0DS. Tel (0171) 3005915, Fax (0171) 3005765. E-mail adam@royalacademy. org.uk. Website www.royalacademy. org.uk

Royal Birmingham Society of Artists, 69a New Street, GB-Birmingham B2 4DU. Tel (0121) 2364353. E-mail forbes@rbsa.org.uk. Website www. rbsa.org.uk

Royal Photographic Society, RPS National Centre of Photography, The Octagon, Milsom Street, GB-Bath BA1 1DN. Tel (01225) 462841. E-mail rps@rps.org.uk. Website www.rps. org.uk

Royal Society of Arts, John Adam Street, Adelphi, GB-London WC2N 6EZ. Tel (0171) 9305115

Seeing the Light, The International Development Agency for the Contemporary Image Maker, 212 The Custard Factory, Gibb Street, GB-Birmingham B9 4AA. Tel (0212) 7737889, Fax (0212) 7737888. E-mail info@seeingthelight.co.uk. Website www.seeingthelight.co.uk

The Association of Photographers, 81 Leonard Street, GB-London EC2A 4QS. Tel (020) 773936669, Fax (020) 77398707. E-mail aop@dircon.co.uk. Website www.aophoto.co.uk

Grants & Awards

BG Wildlife Photographer of the Year, to emphasize the beauty, wonder and importance of the natural world, £15,000, every year. Contact: Louise Grove-White, Wildlife Photographer of the Year, The Natural History Museum, GB-London SW7 5BD. Tel (020) 79425015, Fax (020) 79425084

European Publishers Award for Photography, to publish the best photography book project, to send IRC for entry form, royalty on minimum 5,500 print run, every year. Contact: Dewi Lewis Publishing, 8 Broomfield Road, Heaton Moor, GB-Stockport SK4 4ND. Tel (0161) 4429450, Fax (0161) 4429450. E-mail mail@ dewilewispublishing.com. Website www.dewilewispublishing.com

Ian Parry Memorial Scholarship, for photographers under 24 or students, £1,500 to fund a foreign project for the newspaper and £1,500 worth of Nikon products. Contact: The Sunday Times Magazine, 1 Pennington Street, GB-London E1 9XW. Tel (0171) 7827850

John Kobal Photographic Portrait Award, to promote contemporary portrait photography, over 18 years old, £5,000, exhibition at the National Portrait Gallery and UK tour, every year. Contact: The John Kobal Foundation, The Administrator, P. O. Box 3838, GB-London. Tel (020) 72788482, Fax (020) 72788482. E-mail swcrockeve@tconnect.com

Kraszna-Krausz Book Awards, to encourage outstanding achievements in the publishing and writing of books on photography and the moving image, books from publishers worldwide are accepted, in categories, £20,000, every year, alternating between photography and moving image. Contact: Kraszna-Krausz Foundation, Andrea Livingstone, 122 Fawnbrake Avenue, GB-London SE24 0BZ. Tel (020) 77386701, Fax (020) 77386701. E-mail k-k@dial.pipex.com. Website www.editor.net/k-k

North West Photography Open, the prize is open to all photographers in north-west England, every two years.

Contact: North West Photography Open, Open Eye Gallery, 28–32 Wood Street, GB-Liverpool L1 4AQ. Tel (0151) 7099460. E-mail info@openeye.unet.com. Website www.openeye.unet.com

Richard Hough Bursary, to provide a mid-career of a Scotland-based photographer with the opportunity to produce new work, £14,500, every year. Contact: Stills Gallery, 23 Cockburn Street, GB-Edinburgh EH1 1BP, Scotland. Tel (0131) 6226200, Fax (0131) 6226201. E-mail info@stills.denon.co.uk

Sarah Noble Memorial Fund, grants in the areas of women issues, health, peace, Third World, every year. Contact: Sarah Noble Memorial Fund, 29 Albany Street, GB-Edinburgh EH1 3QN, Scotland. Tel (0131) 5575242

The Citibank Private Bank Photography Prize, to identify and reward the individual who has made the most significant contribution to the medium of photography in the UK in the past year, candidates must have exhibited or published a body of work in the United Kingdom in the past 12 months, £10,000 plus specially commissioned trophy, every year. Contact: The Citibank Private Bank Photography Prize, Drum Venture Communications, 40 Berkeley Square, GB-London W1X 6AD. Tel (0171) 3042481, Fax (0171) 3042486. E-mail 106125.642@compuserve.com

The Observer Hodge Award, to reward and encourage both student and professional photographers under 30, first prize £3,000 and a photographic assignment on behalf of the Observer, second prize £1,000, third prize £500.00, best student photographer £1,000, every year. Contact: The Observer Hodge Award, P. O. Box 30518, GB-London SW16 2GS. Tel (0181) 6647353. Website www.newsunlimited.co.uk/observer/hodgeaward

New Media

Digital Dreams, P. O. Box 344, GB-Newcastle upon Tyne NE99 1FZ. E-mail 2cultures@dd-4.demon.co.uk. Website www.visartuk.org.uk/dd4/

ICA – Institute of Contemporary Arts, The Mall, GB-London SW1. Tel (071) 9303647. Website www.illum.co.uk/ica/home/html

New Visions International Festivals, New Visions Film Video Media, P. O. Box 1269, GB-Glasgow G3 6oA. Tel (0141) 5523436, Fax (0141) 5532660. E-mail newvisions@screenbase.com

North by Northwest Independent Film & Video Festival, NXN/The Workhouse, 13 Wolstenholme Street, GB-Liverpool L1 4JJ. Tel (0151) 7093979. Website www.merseyworld.com/nxnw/press.html

The Film and Video Institute's International Film and Video Festival, IAC – The Film and Video Institute, 24c West Street, Epsom, GB-Surrey KT18 7RJ. Tel (0372) 739672. E-mail mayfield@bcmweb.iclnet.co.uk

Video Positive Festival, Foundations for Arts & Creative Technology, Bluecoat Champers, School Lane, GB-Liverpool L1 3BX. Tel (0151) 7092663, Fax (0151) 7072150. E-mail fact@fact.co.uk. Website www.fact.co.uk

Volcano Film/Video Festival, Exploding Cinema, 4 Rodwell Road, GB-London SE22 9LF. Tel (0956) 823712. E-mail volcano@backspace.org. Website www.backspace/org/volcano/

Greece

Population: 10.5 million
Capital: Athens, 3.1 million
Currency: Drachma (Dr)
International code: ++30
Tourist information:
EOT – Ellinikos Organismos
Tourismou, Amerikis 2,
GR-10564 Athens
Tel (01) 322 31 11,
Fax (01) 322 41 48

Galleries & Museums

Agahthi, Mithymnis 12 & Eptanis-
sou, Amerikis sq., GR-11257 Athens.
Tel (01) 8640250/8655630, Fax (01)
8657909. Open: Mon–Fri 10.30–13.30,
18–21.30, Sat 10.30–13.30. Contact:
Yiorgos Kartalos. Artists: Alexandra
Maschori, Yiannis Scoulas, Errieta
Attali

Alpha-Delta Gallery, Pallados 3, Psirl,
GR-10554 Athens. Tel (01) 3602948,
Fax (01) 3602949. Open: Tue–Fri 11–
14, 18–21, Sat 11–14. Contact: Pantelis
Arapinis. Artists: Despina Mcimazo
glou, Yiannis Theodoropoulos, Nikos
Kessanlis

Benaki Museum, Koumbari 1, GR-
10674 Athens. Tel (01) 3671000, Fax
(01) 3622547. E-mail benaki@
benaki.gr. Website www.benaki.gr

Epikentro, Armodiou 10, GR-10552
Athens. Tel (01) 3312187, Fax (01)
3312377. Open: Tue–Fri 12–21, Sat 11–
16. Contact: Angeliki Antonopoulou.
Artist: Yiorgos Yerolymbos

Gallery Eleni Koronaiou, 5–7 Mitseon
St., GR-11742 Athens. Tel (01)
9244271, Fax (01) 9244271. Director:
Eleni Koronaiou. Artists: Michael
Smith, Christina Dimetriades, Maria
Papadimitriou, Axel Hütte, Larry
Clark

Ileana Tounta, Contemporary Art
Center, Armatolon & Klefton Street
48, GR-11471 Athens. Tel (01)
6439466, Fax (01) 6442852. E-mail
ileanatounta@art.tounta.gr. Website
www.art-tounta.gr. Open: Tue–Fri
10–14, 18–21, Sat 11–15 (Aug closed).
Director/curator: Ileana Tounta.
Founded 1988. 3 rooms, 350 m². 5
photo exhibitions/year. Artists: Hilde
Aagard, Per Barclay, Lila Cambanis,
Helen Glinou, Susy Gomez, James
Lane, Fryni Mouzakitou, Lia Nalban-
tidou, Aliki Palaska, Manthos San-
torinaios

Nees Morfes, Valaoritou 9, GR-10671
Athens. Tel (01) 3616165, Fax (01)
3637233. E-mail nmorfes@artgallery.
gr. Open: tue–Fri 10–14, 18–21, Sat
10–15. Contact: Julia Dimakopoulou.
Artists: Takis Zerderas, Ioanna Ralli

Photography Centre of Athens,
Sina 52, GR-10672 Athens. Tel (01)
3608825/3610495, Fax (01) 3543323.
E-mail pca@athens.otenet.gr. Website
www.pca.gr. Open: Tue–Fri 18–21
(Jun–Aug closed). Director: Kostis
Antoniades. Founded 1978. 1 room,
60 m². 6–10 photo exhibitions/year.
Artists: Periklis Alkides, Kostis
Antoniades, Lizzie Calligas, Yiorgos
Depollas, Stelios Efstathopoulos,
Sokrates Mavromatis, Nikos
Panayiotopoulos, John Stathatos

Rebekka M. Camchi, Sofokleous 23,
GR-10552 Athens. Tel (01) 3210448,
Fax (01) 3210448. E-mail
camchigallery@hotmail.com. Open:
Wed–Fri 12–20, Sat 12–15. Contact:

Rebekka M. Camchi. Artists: Nan Goldin, Nobuyoshi Araki

Photography Center of Thessaloniki, Menelaou 18, GR-54631 Thessaloniki. Tel (031) 256296, Fax (031) 920988/214708. Open: 18.30–22.00. Curator: Karkatselis Vassilis. Founded 1995. 3 rooms, 180 m². 14 photo exhibitions/year. Artists: Kostis Delakis, Loukas Konias, Stavros Dagtzidis, Thanasis Raptis, Euthimios Mouratidis, Chrysa Tzelepi, Theodorus Pitouras, Shakis Otampasidis, Photis Paleologos

Thessaloniki Museum of Photography, Aristotelous 18, GR-54622 Thessaloniki. Tel (031) 257052, Fax 257053. E-mail thmphoto@magnet.gr. Director: Aris Georgiou

Festivals & Fairs

Art Athina, Hellenic Art Galleries Association, 9 Valaoritoy St., GR-10671 Athens. Tel (01) 3616165, Fax (01) 3637233

Month of Photography in Athens, Hellenic Centre for Photography, P. O. Box 30564, GR-10033 Athens. Tel (01) 3234257, Fax (01) 3232082. E-mail hcp@photography.gr. Website www.monthof.photography.gr

Photography Festival of Skopelos, Town Hall, GR-37003 Skopelos. Tel (0424) 24121, Fax (0424) 24131. Website www.pcskopelos.gr

Photosynkyria, Thessaloniki Museum of Photography, Aristotelous 18, GR-54622 Thessaloniki. Tel (031) 257052, Fax (031) 257053. E-mail thmphoto@magnet.gr. Website www.magnet.gr/photosynkyria

Magazines

Fotografia, Iperidou 19, Plaka, P. O. Box 30564, GR-10033 Athens. Tel (01) 3234217, Fax (01) 3232082. E-mail fotomag@photography.gr. Editor: Stavros Moressopoulos. Greek. Founded 1977. Copy price: Dr 1,200. Annual subscription: Dr 4,800, 4 issues/year

Photographos Magazine, Troupaki 1 & Kourtidou St., GR-10445 Athens. Tel (01) 8541400, Fax (01) 8541485. E-mail photomag@photo.gr. Website www.photo.gr. Editor: Dimitris Tzimas. Greek. Founded 1989. Copy price: Dr 1,500. Annual subscription: US$80.00, 10 issues/year

Book Publishers

Agra Publications, 7 Fokianou St., GR-11635 Athens. Tel (01) 7011461, Fax (01) 7018649. Website www.agra.gr

Editions Moressopoulos/Fotografia, Iperidou 19, Plaka, P. O. Box 30564, GR-10033 Athens. Tel (01) 3234217, Fax (01) 3232082. E-mail fotomag@photography.gr. Website cultureontheroad.org

Gnosis Publishers, Ippokratous 31 & Solonos St., GR-10680 Athens. Tel (01) 362-0941/1194, Fax (01) 3605910

Kastaniotis, Zalogou 11, GR-10678 Athens. Tel (01) 3301208, Fax (01) 3822530

Press Photo Publications, Troupaki 1 Kourtidou St., GR-10445 Athens. Tel (01) 8541400, Fax (01) 8541485. E-mail photomag@photo.gr. Website www.photo.gr

University Studio Press, Armeno-poulou 32, GR-54636 Thessaloniki. Tel (031) 208731, Fax (031) 216647

Bookshops

Papasotiriou Bookstores, Stournari 35, GR-10682 Athens. Tel (01) 3841826, Fax (01) 3848254. Website www. papasotiriou.gr

Critics & Journalists

Kostis Antoniadis, Efpalinou 20, GR-11253 Athens. Tel (01) 8618401, Fax (01) 3543323. E-mail pcathens@ otenet.gr. *Fotografia,* Athens

John Demos, Apeiron Photos, Paleo-logou St. 7 A, Aghia Paraskevi, GR-15342 Athens. Tel (01) 6007925, Fax (01) 6007924. E-mail apeiron@ otenet.gr

Aris Georgiou, Mitrapoleos 23, GR-54624 Thessaloniki. Tel (031) 286847, Fax (031) 286847. *Entefktirio,* Thessa-loniki; Camera Obscura, Thessaloniki

Yorgos Katsaggelos, Thermopilon 36, GR-55535 Thessaloniki. Tel (031) 343842

Natassa Markidou, Efpalinou 20, GR-11253 Athens. Tel (01) 8618401, Fax (01) 3643323. *Fotografia,* Athens

Stavros Moressopoulos, Iperidou 19, Plaka, P. O. Box 30564, GR-10033 Athens. Tel (01) 3234217, Fax (01) 3232082. E-mail hcp@photography.gr. Editor of *Fotografia,* Athens

Alexandra Moschovi, Litons 16, GR-11853 Athens. Tel (01) 345352, Fax (01) 3232082. *Fotografia,* Athens

Nikos Panaiotopoulos, Dafnomili St. 23–25, GR-11471 Athens. Tel (01) 3644247, Fax (01) 3644247. E-mail nikopan@teiath.gr

Dimitris Tzimas, Troupaki 1 & Kour-tidou St., GR-10445 Athens. Tel (01) 8541400, Fax (01) 8541485. E-mail photomag@photo.gr. Website www. photo.gr. Editor of *Photographos Magazine,* Athens

Alkis Xanthakis, P. O. Box 4198, GR-102 Athens. Tel (01) 8051196/ 5227417-450, Fax (01) 8051196. E-mail alkisxanthakis@hotmail.com. *Photog-rapher,* Athens; Head of A.K.T.O. School of Photography, Athens

Schools & Workshops

A.K.T.O., Har. Trikoupi 21 & Solo-nos, GR-10681 Athens. Tel (01) 3613700, Fax (01) 3620215

EMEF, Patission 4, GR-10677 Athens. Tel (01) 3613319

E.S.P. Artikon, Iperidou 19, Plaka, P. O. Box 30564, GR-10033 Athens. Tel (01) 3243753, Fax (01) 3232082. E-mail esp@photography.gr

European School of Photography, Narmahian Ellis 3–5, GR-54625 Thessaloniki. Tel (031) 541148, Fax (031) 541709. E-mail esp@ photography.gr

Focus, Photographic Institute, Leofo-ros Papagou 112, Zografou, GR-15779 Athens. Tel (01) 7750675, Fax (01) 7716194. E-mail focus@otenet.gr

Leica Academy, Imitou 243, GR-11632 Athens. Tel (01) 7560485. E-mail info@leica-academy.gr

School of Fine & Applied Arts, Dept. of Photography, Pavlou Mela 40, GR-54622 Thessaloniki

School of Graphic and Fine Arts,
Technological Institute, Dept. of Photography, Ag. Spiridonos, Egaleo,
GR-12243 Athens. Tel (01) 59090024,
Fax (01) 5987719

Associations

Camera Obscura, Creative Photographers of Thessaloniki, Mitropoleos
23, GR-54624 Thessaloniki. Tel (031)
280743/286847, Fax (031) 286847

Friends of Creative Photography,
Photography Centre of Athens,
Sina 52, GR-10672 Athens. Tel (01)
3608825/3610495, Fax (01) 3543323.
E-mail pcathens@otenet.gr. Website
www.pca.gr

**Greek Union of Applied and Creative
Photography,** Artemonos 68, GR-
11631 Athens

Hellenic Centre of Photography,
Iperidou 19, Plaka, P. O. Box 30564,
GR-10033 Athens. Tel (01) 3234217,
Fax (01) 3232082. E-mail desk@
cultureontheroad.org. Website
cultureontheroad.org

Hellenic Photographiki Etairia,
Tinou 14a, GR-11257 Athens.
Tel (01) 8228131

Grants & Awards

Sanni Festival/Shell Award, for the
best exhibition and for the best young
photographer, shown at Photosynkyria. Contact: Aris Georgiou, Mitropoleos 23, GR-54624 Thessaloniki

Voula Papaioannou Award. Contact:
Voula Papaioannou, Hellenic Center
of Photography, Iperidou 19, P. O.
Box 30564, GR-10033 Athens. Tel (01)
3244548, Fax (01) 3232082

New Media

Media@Terra Festival, Mediterranean
& Balkan Art & Technology Festival,
Fournos Cultural Centre, Mavromihali 169, GR-11472 Athens. Tel (01)
6460749, Fax (01) 6420451. E-mail
festival@fournos-culture.gr. Website www.otenet.gr/fournos,
www.ournos-culture.gr/

Hungary

Population: 10.2 million
Capital: Budapest, 1.9 million
Currency: Forint (Ft)
International code: ++36
Tourist information: Hungarian
Tourist Office, Margit Körút
85, H-1024 Budapest
Tel (01) 355 11 33,
Fax (01) 375 38 19

Galleries & Museums

Bolt Fotógáleria, Podmaniczky utca.
69, H-1064 Budapest. Tel (01)
3022043, Fax (01) 3022043. E-mail
bolt@c3.hu. Website www.c3.hu/
bolt. Open: by appointment only.
Contact: Judit Hanggyál, Jenö Detvay

**Fövárosi Szabó Ervin Könyvtár Buda-
pest Gyüjteménye,** Photo Archives,
Szabó Ervin tér 1, H-1088 Budapest.
Tel (01) 1384933. E-mail santib@
fszek.hu. Open: 9–17. Contact: Tibor
Sándor. Founded 1957. 1 room 2
photo exhibitions/year

Hadtörténeti Múzeum Fotóarchívuma,
Photo Archives of the Museum of
War History, Tóth Árpad sétány 40,
H-1014 Budapest. Tel (01) 1569370,
Fax (01) 1561575. Open: Tue–Sat 9–17
(Nov–Feb 10–16), Sun 10–18. Contact:
Györgi Bánfyy-Kalavszky. Founded
1918. 3 rooms. Artists: József Kassák,
Ede Ellinger, Aladár Székely

Kassák Múzeum, Fö tér 1, H-1033
Budapest. Tel (01) 1687021. Open:
Tue–Sun 10–18. Contact: Dr. Ferenc
Csaplár. Founded 1976. 6 rooms, 200
m². 1 photo exhibition/year. Artists:
Lajos Kassák and his contemporaries

Magyar Fotográfusok Háza, House
of Hungarian Photographers in the
building of Mai Manó, Nagymezö
utca 20, H-1065 Budapest. Tel (01)
3024496, Fax (01) 3025847. E-mail
maimano@matavnet.hu. Open: Mon–
Fri 14–18. Director: András Török.
Founded 1995. 5 rooms. 36 photo
exhibitions/year

**Magyar Nemzeti Múzeum – Történeti
Fényképtára,** Hungarian National
Museum – Historical Photo Collec-
tion, Múzeum krt. 14–16, H-1088
Budapest. Tel (01) 3277784/3277779.
Open: Tue–Sun 10–18. Contact: Ilona
Balog. Founded 1802. 5 rooms,
1,500 m². 1 photo exhibition/year

Mücsarnok, Palace of Arts, Dózsa
György útca 37, H-1146 Budapest.
Tel. (01) 3437401, Fax (01) 3435205.
E-mail info@mucsarnok.hu. Website
www.mucsarnok.hu. Open: Tue–Sun
10–18. Director: Prof. Dr. László Beke.
Founded 1902. 2,000 m². 2–4 photo
exhibitions/year. Artists: Péter
Korniss, Josef Sudek, Cecil Beaton

Néprajzi Múzeum, Ethnographical
Museum, Kossuth Lájos tér. 12, H-
1055 Budapest. Tel (01) 1326340, Fax
(01) 2692419. Open: Tue–Sun 10–18.
Contact: János Tári, Klára Fogarasi.
Founded 1873, 40 rooms, 2,500 m².
2 photo exhibitions/year

Országos Müszaki Múzeum, Kapos-
vár utca 13–15, H-1117 Budapest

Privat Foto Galeria Lajos Györi, Mo-
ros u. 11, H-1122 Budapest. Tel (01)
1566332. Open: by appointment.
Founded 1990. Artists: Károly Deme-
ter, Ferenc Haár, Erwin Kankowszky,
István Kerny, Imre Kinszki, László
Osolna, Ernö Vadas

162 Hungary

Vintage Galéria, Vintage Gallery, Magyar utca 26, H-1053 Budapest. Tel (01) 3370584, Fax (01) 3370584. E-mail vintage@c3.hu. Website www.c3.hu/vintage. Director: Attila Pöcze. Founded 1996. 1 room. 37 m². 10 photo exhibitions/year. Artists: Imre Kinszki, Károly Escher, Márta Aczél, Lajos Csontó, Gábor Gerhes, Dezsö Szabó

Magyar Fotográfiai Múzeum, Hungarian Museum of Photography, Katona József tér 12, H-6000 Kecskemét. Tel (076) 483221, Fax (076) 483221. E-mail fotomuz@visio.c3.hu. Website www.c3.hu/fotomuz. Open: Tue–Sun 10–18. Director: Károly Kincses. Founded 1991. 1 room, 130 m². 10 photo exhibitions/year. Artists: André Kertész, László Moholy-Nagy, George Kepes, Brassaï, Imre Kinszki, Károly Escher, Tibor Honty, Jindrich Štreit

Fridrich-fényirda, Kossuth Lajos utca 6, H-6600 Szentes

Magazines

Balkon, Hollán Ernö u. 30, H-1136 Budapest. Tel (01) 3405187

Fotómüvészet, P. O. Box 72, H-1676 Budapest. Tel (01) 2913621. E-mail timfoto@elender.hu. Website www.ns.elender.hu/fotomuveszet. Editor: Péter Timár. Hungarian (English summaries). Founded 1966. 4 issues/year

Fotó Piac, Szent László tér 20, H-1102 Budapest. Tel (01) 2623674, Fax (01) 2623674. Email fotopiac@fotopiac.hu. Website www.fotopiac.hu. Editor: Takács Szabolcs. Hungarian

Fotóriporter, Andrássy útca 101, H-1062 Budapest. Editor: András Bánkuti. Hungarian, 4 issues/year

FotoVideo, Bécsi útca 141–143, H-1034 Budapest. Tel (01) 3688688, Fax (01) 3688688. Editor: József Rák. Hungarian

Szellemkép, Dob. útca 20, H-1072 Budapest. Tel (01) 1213637. Editors: Lehel Fuchs, Gabriella Medgyesi. Hungarian, 4 issues/year

Book Publishers

Balassi Kiadó, Margit u. 1, H-1023 Budapest. Tel (01) 1162885

Intera Könyvkiadó, Ürömi útca 24–28, H-1023 Budapest

Magyar Fotográfiai Múzeum, Hungarian Museum of Photography, Katona József tér 12, H-6000 Kecskemét. Tel (076) 483221, Fax (076) 483221. E-mail fotomuz@visio.c3.hu. Website www.c3.hu/fotomuz

Müszaki Könyvkiadó, Hess András tér 4, H-1014 Budapest. Tel (01) 1557122

Park Kiadó, Keleti Károly u. 29, H-1024 Budapest. Tel (01) 2125534

Critics & Journalists

Dr. Béla Albertini, P. O. Box 1, H-2043 Budaörs 3. Tel (01) 1537704. *Fotómüvészet,* Budapest

Tibor Bakáts, Bartók béla út 156, H-1115 Budapest. Tel (01) 2030871

András Bán, Márvány u. 29, H-1126 Budapest. Tel (01) 1750411. E-mail megaban@matavnet.hu. University of Miskolc, Department of Anthropology

Prof. Dr. László Beke, Pozsonyi u. 4, H-1137 Budapest. Tel (01) 1328802. E-mail beke@mucsarnok.hu. Director of the Mücsarnok Art Hall, Budapest;

Fotómüvészet, Budapest; *Imago*, Bratislava

Csilla E. Csorba, Igaz u. 7, H-1181 Budapest

Bálinth Flesch, V. Károlyi Mihály u. 14/c, H-1053 Budapest. Tel (01) 1179908, Fax (01) 1371557

Mihály Gera, Nyúl u. 4, H-1026 Budapest

Péter György, ELTE Média Tanszék, Múzeum krt. 6–8, H-1088 Budapest. Tel (01) 2664658

Lajos Györi, Maros u. 11, H-1122 Budapest. Tel (01) 3566332. Editor of *Hungarian Photography Yearbook*, president of the National Association of Hungarian Photographic Creative Groups, Budapest

Éva Hajdú, Tárnok u. 5, H-1014 Budapest. Tel (01) 1568362, Fax (01) 1568362. *Magyar Nemzet*, Budapest; School of Journalism of the Hungarian Journalist Section

István Hajdú, Fény u. 2, H-1024 Budapest. Tel (01) 1353294

Dr. Katalin Jalszovsky, Börzsöny u. 9, H-1098 Budapest. Tel (01) 1778975

Károly Kincses, Kossuth u. 92, H-2192 Hévizgyörk. Tel (076) 483221, Fax (076) 48322. E-mail fotomuzeum @matavnet.hu. Director of the Hungarian Museum of Photography, Kecskemét; *Fotómüvészet*, Budapest; *Imago*, Bratislava

Árpád Kiss-Kuntler, Királyok u. 40, H-1039 Budapest. Tel (01) 3555411, Fax (01) 3555693. E-mail a.kiss@hvg.hu

László Lugosi-Lugo, Haller u. 15, H-1096 Budapest. Tel (01) 2161172. E-mail lugo@matavnet.hu

Miklós Peternák, Dózsa Gy. u. 140, H-1134 Budapest. E-mail peternak@ c3.hu. Director of Center for Culture and Communication, Budapest; Hungarian Academy of Fine Arts, Budapest

Ilona Stemlerné Balog, Faludi u. 6/b, H-1131 Budapest. Tel (01) 1297019. Collection of Historical Photographs, Hungarian National Museum, Budapest

Dr. Margit Szakács, Üllöi út 708, H-1185 Budapest. Tel (01) 2924354

Klára Szarka, Kerepesi út 29/b, H-1087 Budapest. Tel (01) 2103741

Gábor Szilágyi, Vörösvári u. 1, H-1035 Budapest. Tel (01) 1885674

András Török, Nagymezö utca 20, H-1065 Budapest. Tel (01) 3024496, Fax (01) 3025847. E-mail maimano@ matavnet.hu. Director of the House of Hungarian Photography, Budapest

Klára Töry, Kalapács u. 9/a, H-1148 Budapest. Tel (01) 1843015. Secondary School of Fine and Applied Arts, Budapest

Prof. Dr. Lajos Végvári, Derkovits u. 10, H-3529 Miskolc. Tel (046) 363946

Schools & Workshops

27. sz. Ipari Szakmunkásképzö Intézet, Technical School No. 27, Práter u. 31, H-1082 Budapest

Bálint György Újságíró Iskola, György Bálint's School of Journalists, Andrássy ut 101, H-1062 Budapest

Képzö és Iparmüvészeti Szakközép-iskola, Secondary School for Fine and Applied Arts, Török Pál u. 1, H-1093 Budapest

Magyar Iparmüvészeti Föiskola, Hungarian Academy of Applied Arts,

Dept. of Visual Communication, Zugligeti u. 11–21, H-1121 Budapest

Magyar Müvelödési Intézet Kortárs Müvészetek Osztálya, Corvina tér 8, H-1011 Budapest

Sebesvíz Nemzetközi Fotómüvészeti Alkotótábor, International Creative Photography Workshop Sebesvíz, Széchenyi u. 30, H-3530 Miskolc

Associations

Fiatalok Fotomüvészeti Stúdiója, Association of Young Photographers, Negymezö utca 20, H-1065 Budapest. Tel (01) 3112626. E-mail pxl@ matavnet.hu

Magyar Fényképész Ipartestület, Kútvölgyi u. 19, H-1125 Budapest. Tel (01) 2141621, Fax (01) 2141621

Magyar Fotómüveszeti Alkotócsoportok Országos Szövetsége (MAFOSZ), National Association of Hungarian Photographic Creative Groups, Corvin tér 8, H-1011 Budapest. Tel (01) 2015692, Fax (01) 2015692. E-mail mfsz-bp@freemail.c3.hu. Website www.webdesign.hu/mfsz

Magyar Fotómüvészek Szövetsége, Association of Hungarian Art Photographers, Nagymezö u. 20, H-1065 Budapest. Tel (01) 3112626

Magyar Fotóriporterek Kamarája, Chamber of Hungarian Press Photographers, Andrássy út 101, H-1062 Budapest

Magyar Újságírók Országos Szövetsége, Association of Hungarian Journalists, Andrássy út 101, H-1062 Budapest

Grants & Awards

André Kertész Grant, for talented young photographers for a 3 month-stay in Paris and contact with French photographers in institutions, every year. Contact: Nemzeti Kulturális Alap, National Cultural Fund, Bajza u. 32, H-1062 Budapest

József Pécsi Award, for a lifetime achievement in applied photography, every year. Contact: Hungarian Advertising Association, Dob u. 45, H-1074 Budapest. Tel (01) 1220640

József Pécsi Grant, to recognize talented young photographers below the age of 35, four winners receive Ft 60,000 per month for three years, every year. Contact: Ministry of Cultural and Education, Szalay u. 10–14, H-1055 Budapest. Tel (01) 1530600

Rudolf Balogh Award, for outstanding achievements in photographic art and theory, a medal, a diploma and Ft 60,000 each for two winners, every year. Contact: Ministry of Cultural and Education, Szalay u. 10–14, H-1055 Budapest. Tel (01) 1530600

New Media

Center for Culture and Communication, P. O. Box 419, H-1537 Budapest. Tel (01) 2146856, Fax (01) 2146872. E-mail info@c3.hu. Website www.c3.hu

Ireland

Population: 3.66 million
Capital: Dublin, 1 million
Currency: Pound (£)
International code: ++353
Tourist information: Bord
Failte – Irish Tourist Board,
Baggot Street Bridge,
IRL-Dublin 2
Tel (01) 602 40 00,
Fax (01) 602 41 00

Galleries & Museums

Gallery of Photography, Meeting
House Square, Temple Bar, IRL-
Dublin 2. Tel (01) 6714654/6709293,
Fax (01) 6709293. E-mail gallery@
irish-photography.com. Website
www.irish-photography.com. Open:
11–18. Director: Tanya Kiang. Founded 1978. 3 rooms, 120 m². 12 photo
exhibitions/year

The Irish Museum of Modern Art,
Royal Hospital Kilmainhan, IRL-
Dublin 8. Tel (01) 6129900, Fax (01)
6129999. E-mail info@modernart.ie.
Website www.modernart.ie. Open:
Tue–Sat 10–17.30, Sun and bank
holidays 12–17.30. Director: Declan
Mc Gonagle. Founded 1991. 6 rooms.
2–6 photo exhibitions/year. Artists:
Lee Jaffe, Craigie Horsfield, Gilbert &
George, Hannah Collins, Grenville
Davey, Willie Doherty, Bernd & Hilla
Becher, Elaire Reichek, Dorothy Cross

Magazines

Circa, Arthouse, Curved Street,
Temple Bar, IRL-Dublin 2. Tel (01)
6797388, Fax (01) 6797388. E-mail
info@recirca.co. Website www.
recirca.com. Editor: Peter FitzGerald

Associations

Dublin Photographic Centre, 10
Lower Camden Street, IRL-Dublin 2.
Tel (01) 6624464. E-mail dcl@iol.ie

Photographic Society of Ireland, 11
Hume Street, IRL-Dublin 2

Grants & Awards

Glen Dimplex Artists Award, to mark
achievement or new development in
the practice of contemporary artists
who are either Irish or have exhibited
there recently, £15,000, every year.
Contact: The Irish Museum of Modern Art, Royal Hospital Kilmainhan,
IRL-Dublin 8. Tel (01) 6129900, Fax
(01) 6129999. E-mail info@
modernart.ie

Italy

Population: 57.6 million
Capital: Rome, 2.7 million
Currency: Lira (Lit)
International code: ++39
Tourist information:
Ente Nazionale Italiano per il
Turismo ENIT, Via Marghera
2/6, I-00185 Roma
Tel (06) 49711
Fax (06) 446-3379/9907

Galleries & Museums

Centro Culturale Pier Paolo Pasolini,
Via Atenea 123, I-92100 Agrigento.
Tel (0922) 20522, Fax (0922) 20522.
Open: 9–13, 16–19. Director: Maurizio
Masone. Curator: Angelo Pitrone.
Founded 1981. 1 room, 80 m². 7 photo
exhibitions/year. Artists: Tano Sira-
cusa, Lillo Rizzo, Angelo Pitrone

Free Gallery, Viale Leonardo Sciascia
29, I-92100 Agrigento. Tel (0922)
606527, Fax (0922) 25386. E-mail
mlab@mediatel.it. Open: 8.30–13, 16–
19. Director: Sabbia Gaetano. Curator: Pitrone Angelo. Founded 1996.
1 room, 15 m². 10–12 photo exhibi-
tions/year. Artists: Pitrone Angelo,
Tano Siracusa, Silvio Gouirnali,
Ludouico Bick, Saluiwa Falsone,
Carmelo Nicosia, Pilippo Serra
Bruno d'Andrea

Museo Nuova Era, Spazio Immagine,
Via Vallisa 11/12, I-70100 Bari. Tel
(080) 5531030, Fax (080) 5061158

Ex Teatro Sociale, Via Colleoni,
I-24100 Bergamo. Tel (035) 399230.
Website www.cite.bg.it. Open: Mon–
Fri 16–19.30, Sat+Sun 10–19.30

Ar/Ge Kunst, Galleria Museo, Via
Museo 29, I-39100 Bolzano. Tel (0471)
971601, Fax (0471) 979945. E-mail
argebz@dnet.it. Open: Tue–Fri 10–13,
15–19, Sat 10–13. Director: Dr. Marion
Piffer-Damiani. Curator: Christina
Busin. Founded 1985. 2 rooms,
150 m². 2–3 photo exhibition/year.
Artists: Walter Niedermayr, Marina
Ballo Charmet, Guido Guidi

Galleria Comunale d'Arte Moderna,
Piazza Costituzione 3, I-40100
Bologna. Tel (051) 502859, Fax
(051) 371032. E-mail infogam@
comune.bologna.it. Website www.
galleriadartemoderna.bo.it. Open:
Tue–Sun 10–18

Galerie Fotoforum, Via Weggenstein
2, I-39100 Bolzano. Tel (0471) 982159,
Fax (0471) 982159. Open: Tue–Fri 16–
19.30, Sat 10–12.30. Director/curator:
Dr. Gunther Waibl. Founded 1993.
2 rooms, 60 m². 8 photo exhibitions/
year. Artists: Paolo Biadene, Flavio
Faganello, Eduardo Gil, Leopold von
Glasersfeld, Rupert Larl, Bernard
Plossu, Brigitte Niedermair, Adalbert
Defner, Martin Pardatscher, Erika
Hubatschek

Museo Ken Damy, Fotografia Con-
temporanea, Corsetto S. Agata 22 –
Loggia delle Mercanzie, I-25122
Brescia. Tel (030) 3750295, Fax (030)
45259. E-mail kendamy@tin.it.
Website www.polimedia.it/
kendamy. Open: Tue–Sun 15.30–
19.30. Director/curator: Ken Damy.
Founded 1974. 9 rooms, 540 m². 8
photo exhibitions/year. Artists: Jeff
Dunas, Lucien Clergue, Franco
Fontana, Joyce Tenneson, Rafael
Navarro, Mario Giacomelli, Jan

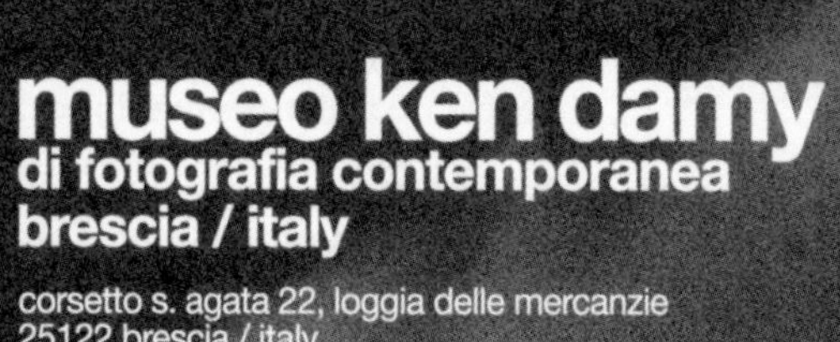

museo ken damy
di fotografia contemporanea
brescia / italy

corsetto s. agata 22, loggia delle mercanzie
25122 brescia / italy
tel. 030.3750295 fax 030.45259

e-mail: kendamy@tin.it
http://www.polimedia.it/kendamy

permanent
collections

temporary
exhibitions

library

bookshop

courses and
workshops

edizioni del museo
publishing house
books and
original prints portfolios

Saudek, Jean Janssis, William Ropp, Occhiomagico

Museo Nazionale della Fotografia, Cinefotoclub, Corso Matteotti 16b–18a, I-25100 Brescia. Tel (030) 49137, Fax (030) 49137. E-mail museo@ virgilio.it. Website www.freeyellow. com/members6/navigatore/. Open: Mon–Fri 9–11, 15–16, Sat–Sun 16–19. Director/curator: Alberto Sorlini Efiap. Founded 1953. 50 m²

Il Ponte, Via di Mezzo 42 B, I-50121 Firenze. Tel (055) 240617, Fax (055) 240617. Open: 10–13, 15–19. Director: Andrea Alibrandi. Founded 1965. 2 rooms, 170 m². 1 photo exhibition/ year

Museo di Storia della Fotografia Fratelli Alinari, Palazzo Rucellai, Via della Vigna Nuova 16, I-50123 Firenze. Tel (055) 2395206, Fax (055) 2382857. Giacomo Brogi, Domenico Anderson, Carlo Mollino, Carlo Wulz, Alberto Lattuada, Luigi Veronesi, Carlo Baravalle, Guido Rey, Bill Brandt, Giuseppe Primoli

Studio Marangoni, Via San Zanobi 32 R, I-50129 Firenze. Tel (055) 280368, Fax (055) 215052. E-mail info@ studiomarangoni.it. Website www. studiomarangoni.it. Open: Mon–Fri 10–13, 15.30–18.30, Sat 10–13 and by appointment. Director: Martino Marangoni. Curator: Alessandra Capodacqua. Founded 1988. 2 rooms, 100 m². 8 photo exhibitions/year. Artists: Olivo Barbieri, Gabriele Basilico, Ernesto Bazan, Vincenzo Castella, Mimmo Jodice, Alex Webb, Leonard Freed, John Davies, Bernard Plossu, Ferdinando Scianna

Martini e Ronchetti, Via Roma 9, I-16121 Genova. Tel (010) 586962, Fax (010) 583375. E-mail info@martini-ronchetti.com. Website www. ronchetti.com. Website www. martini-ronchetti.com. Open: Tue–Sun 10.30–12.30, 16–19.30. Director: Alberto Ronchetti. Founded 1969. 3 rooms, 100 m². 2 photo exhibitions/ year. Artists: Florence Henri, Cesar Domela, Wilhelm Maywald, Luigi Veronesi, Giorgio Sommer, Alfred Noack, Georges Hugnet

Care Of, Via Zucchi 39/G, I-20095 Cusano Milanino (Milano). Tel (02) 6197359, Fax (02) 6197359. E-mail careof@tin.it. Open: Tue–Sat 15–19. Contact: Mario Gorni, Zefferina Castoldi. Founded 1987. 2 rooms, 115 m². 1–2 photo exhibitions/ year

Claudia Gian Ferrari Arte Contemporanea, Via Brera 30, I-20121 Milano. Tel (02) 86461690, Fax (02) 801019. E-mail gferrari@tin.it. Director: Claudia Gian Ferrari. Founded 1990. Artists: Enrica Borghi, Giovanna Di Costa, Marco Papa, Alberta Pellacani, Sabrina Sabato, Bianca Sforni, Mario Sironi

Fabbrica Eos, Piazza Baiamonti 2, I-20154 Milano. Tel (02) 6596532. Website www.inforel.it/fabbricaeos. Open: Tue–Sun 10–13, 16–19.

Foto F.45, Viale Gorizia 12, I-20144 Milano. Tel (02) 58101682, Fax (02) 48100279

Fondazione Antonio Mazzotta, Foro Buonaparte 50, I-20121 Milano. Tel (02) 878197, Fax (02) 8693046. E-mail mazzotta@iol.it. Website www. milanoweb.com/mazzotta/. Open: 10–19.30 (Tue+Thu –22.30)

Fondazione Mudima, Via Tadino 26, I-20124 Milano. Tel (02) 29409633, Fax (02) 29401455. E-mail mudima@ mudima.com. Website www. mudima.com. Open: Mon–Fri 10–12.30, 16–19.30

Franca Speranza, Via Melzo 10, I-20129 Milano. Tel (02) 29402599, Fax (02) 29406440. E-mail francasperanza @francasperanza.it. Website www. francasperanza.it

Galleria Carla Sozzani, Corso Como 10, I-20154 Milano. Tel (02) 653531, Fax (02) 6592015. E-mail info@ galleriacarlasozzani.it. Website www.galleriacarlasozzani.it/com. Open: Mon 15.30–19.30, Tue–Sun 10.30–19.30 (Wed+Thu –21.00). Director: Carla Sozzani. Founded 1991. 3 rooms, 400 m². Artists: Ralph Gibson, Paolo Roversi, Mark Seliger, Shoji Ueda, Franco Grignani, Leni Riefenstahl, Manuel Alvarez Bravo, Lillian Bassman

Galleria del Credito Valtellinese, Refettorio delle Stelline, Corso Magenta 59, I-20123 Milano. Tel (02) 48008015, Fax (02) 48058249. E-mail creval@creval.it. Website www. creval.it. Open: Mon–Fri 10–12.30, 15.30–19, Sat 10–12

Galleria Emi Fontana, Viale Bligny 42, I-20136 Milano. Tel (02) 58322237, Fax (02) 58306855. Director: Emi Fontana

Galleria Karsten Greve, Via Santo Spirito 13, I-20121 Milano. Tel (02) 783840, Fax (02) 783866. Open: Tue–Sat 11–13.30, 14–19.30. Director: Karsten Greve. Founded 1969. 1 room. Artists: Josef Albers, John Chamberlain, Yves Charbonnier, Adam Fuss, Loic Le Groumellec, Detleff Orlopp

Galleria Laura Pecci, Via F. Bocconi 9, I-20136 Milano. Tel (02) 58430047, Fax (02) 58434287. E-mail galpecci@ electraline.com. Website www. gallerialaurapecci.com. Open: Tue–Sat 15–19 and by appointment. Director Laura Pecci. Curator: Manuela Klerkx. Founded 1999. 2 rooms,

200 m². 1 photo exhibition/year: Artists: Sislej Xhafa, Bettina von Zwehl, Hellen Van Meene, Jasper Joffe, Navin Ravanchaikul, Biarne Melgaard, Cees Krijnen, Tsuyoshi Ozawa, Job Koelewijn, Mark Wallinger

Galleria Milano, Via Manin 13/Via Turati 14, I-20121 Milano. Tel (02) 29000352, Fax (02) 29003283. Website www.iann.it/art1/milano.htm

Galleria Monica de Cardenas, Via Viganó 4, I-20124 Milano. Tel (02) 29010068, Fax (02) 29005784. E-mail decardemas@didonet.it. Open: 15–19. Director: Monica de Cardenas. Founded 1991. 4 rooms, 100 m². 2 photo exhibitions/year. Artists: Maurizio Arcangeli, Martino Coppes, Chiara Dynys, Jean-Frédéric Schnyder, Thomas Struth

Galleria Photology, Via delle Moscova 25, I-20100 Milano. Tel (02) 6595285, Fax (02) 624284. E-mail photology@ photology.com. Website www. photology.com. Open: Tue–Sat 10–13, 15–19. Director: Davide Faccioli. Founded 1991. 3 rooms, 150 m². 8 photo exhibitions/year. Artists: Mario Giacomelli, Jacques-Henri Lartigue, Robert Mapplethorpe, Helmut Newton, Irving Penn, Herb Ritts, Bettina Rheims, Bruce Weber, Edward Weston, André Kertész

Galleria Raffaella Cortese, Via Farneti 10, I-20129 Milano. Tel (02) 2043555, Fax (02) 2043555. E-mail rcortgal@ tin.it. Open: 15–19. Director/curator: Raffaella Cortese. Founded 1995. 3 rooms, 100 m². 4 photo exhibitions/ year. Artists: Angelo Candiano, Paola de Pietri, Jan Groover, Franco Uimercati, Barbara Bloom, Monica Carocci, Umberto Cavenago, Perino & Vele, Ugo Simeone, Roni Horn

Giò Marconi, Via Tadino 15, I-20124 Milano. Tel (02) 29404373, Fax (02) 29405573. E-mail giomarconi@ mclink.it. Website www.vol.it/arte/ marconi. Director: Giò Marconi. Founded 1965. Artists: John Bock, Michel, Majerus, Grazia Toderi, Francesco Vezzoli

Il Diaframma, Via dell'Annunciata 31, I-20121 Milano. Tel (02) 29000071, Fax (02) 6592631. Website www. archivio.it/lattuada.studio

Isu Bocconi, Via Sarfatti 25, I-20136 Milano. Tel (02) 58362147, Fax (02) 58362148. Website www.unibocconi.it

Le Case d'Arte, Via Gorani 8, I-20123 Milano. Tel (02) 8054071, Fax (02) 8054071. Director: Pasquale Leccese. Founded 1986. Artists: Vincenzo Castella, Peter Fischli and David Weiss, Marlene Dumas, Sara Rossi, Cindy Sherman, Rosemarie Trockel

Luciano Inga Pin, Via Pontaccio 12/A, I-20121 Milano. Tel (02) 875237, Fax (02) 875237. Open: Tue–Sun 15.30– 19.30. Artists: Alessandro Bellucco, Cosma Calzone, Renzo Chiesa, Paola Di Bello, Nicola Di Caprio, Giovanna Di Costa, Tarin Gartner, Giovanna Ricotta, Alberto Rizzi, Manuela Sonzogno

Marino alla Scala Art Center, Piazza della Scala 5, I-20121 Milano. Tel (02) 8068821. Website www.trussardi.it. Artists: David Byrne, Dennis Hopper, Rudolf Nurevev

Padiglione d'Arte Contemporanea, Via Palestro 14, I-20121 Milano. Tel (02) 62086537, Fax (02) 783330. E-mail segreteria@pac-milano.org. Website www.pac-milano.org. Open: Tue–Sun 9.30–18.30

Spazio Foto San Fedele, Via Hoepli 3/ A, I-20122 Milano. Tel (02) 86352233, Fax (02) 86352233. Open: Tue–Sat 10– 12.30, 16–19

Spazio Oberdan, Viale Vittorio Veneto 2, I-20124 Milano. Tel (02) 77406354, Fax (02) 77406356. Website www.provincia.milano.it. Artists: Gabriele Basilico, Guido Guidi, Luigi Ghirri, Mimmo Jodice, Olivo Barbieri, Vittore Fossati, Fulvio Ventura, Paolo Gioli, John Davies, Paul Graham

Studio Guenzani, Via Eustachi 10, I-20129 Milano. Tel (02) 29409251, Fax (02) 29408080. Open: Tue–Sat 15.30– 19.30 and by appointment. Director/ curator: Claudio Guenzani. Founded 1986. 4 rooms, 200 m². 4 photo exhibitions/year. Artists: Cindy Sherman, Louise Lawler, Robert Mapplethorpe, Armin Linke, Hiroshi Sugimoto, Gabriele Basilico, Nobuyoshi Araki, Dayanita Singh

Triennale Palazzo dell'Arte, Viale Alemagna 6, I-20121 Milano. Tel (02) 8052263, Fax (02) 89010693. E-mail triennale@com2000.it. Website www. triennale.it. Open: Tue–Sun 10–20

Viafarini, Via Farini 35, I-20154 Milano. Tel (02) 66804473, Fax (02) 66804473. E-mail viafarini@planet.it. Website www.undo.net/viafarini. Open: Tue–Sat 15–19. Director: Patrizia Brusarosso. Founded 1991. 1 room, 200 m²

Galleria Civica, Corso Canalgrande 103, I-41100 Modena. Tel (059) 206911, Fax (059) 206932. E-mail galcivmo@comune.modena.it. Website www.comune.modena.it/ galleria. Open: 10–13, 16–19. Director: Walter Guadagnini. Curator: Filippo Maggia. Founded 1959. 2 buildings, 725 m². 5–10 photo exhibitions/year. Artists: Francesca Woodman, Philip Lorca DiCorcia, Thomas Ruff, Ralph Eugene Meatyard, Joan Fontcuberta,

Franco Fontana, Man Ray, Henri Cartier-Bresson, Nan Goldin, Walker Evans

Studio Trisorio, Riviera di Chiaia 255, I-80121 Napoli. Tel (081) 414306/ 426987, Fax (081) 412969. E-mail trisorio@studiotrisorio.com. Open: 11–13, 17–20. Director: Lucia Trisorio. Founded 1974. 2 rooms, 50 m². 1 photo exhibition/year. Artists: Gabriele Basilico, Luigi Ghirri, Raffaela Mariniello, Ferdinando Scianna, Paul Thorel

Theoretical Events, Piazza del Gesù Nuovo 33, I-80134 80100 Napoli. Tel (081) 5800238, Fax (081) 5800237. Director: Guido Costa. Founded 1994. Artists: John Baldessari, Paolo Berardinelli, Eugenio Giliberti, Nan Goldin

Galleria del Centro Culturale Francese, Via Enrico Parisi 5, I-90100 Palermo. Tel (091) 586272/323041, Fax (091) 329492. Open: 9.30–13, 16–19.30. Director: Jean Fracchiolla. Founded 1952. 3 rooms, 50 m². 8–12 photo exhibitions/year. Artists: Ferrante Ferranti, Franco Donaggio, S. Bacciardi, Raoul Vecchiola, Carlo Fabre, C. Bellaiche, Giuseppe Leone, Mario Rizzi

Centro Studi e Archivio della Comunicazione, Padiglione Nervi, Via Palermo 6, I-43100 Parma. Tel (0521) 270847. Artists: Luigi Ghirri, Gabriele Basilico, Francesco Radino, Ugo Mulas, Paolo Gioli, Cuchi White, Nino Migliori, Olivo Barbieri, Vincenzo CasTella, Luigi Veronesi

Archivio Fotografico Toscano, Viale della Repubblica 235, I-59100 Prato. Tel (0574) 592228/592147, Fax (0574) 592269. E-mail aft@mbox.comune. prato.it. Website www.comune. prato.it/aft/home.htm. Open: Mon+ Thu 8.30–17.30, Tue+Wed+Fri 8.30–

13.30. Director: Sauro Lusini. Founded 1979. 2 rooms. 10 photo exhibitions/year

Centro per l'Arte Contemporanea, Luigi Pecci, Viale della Repubblica 277, I-59100 Prato. Tel (0574) 570620, Fax (0574) 572604. E-mail pecci@ mbox.comune.prato.it. Website www.comune.prato.it/pecci. Open: Wed–Mon10–19. Director: Ida Panicelli. Founded 1987. 10 rooms. Artists: Georges Rousse, Craigie Horsfield

Dryphoto, Via Pugliese 23, I-59100 Prato. Tel (0574) 604939, Fax (0574) 604939. Open: 17–20. Director: Ciolini Vittoria. Founded 1979. 2 rooms, 70 m². 5 photo exhibitions/year. Artists: Olivo Barbieri, Andrea Abati, Herman Bertiau, Eduard Olivella, Dennis Marsico, Marrie Bot, Alessandra Spranzi

Fototeca della Biblioteca Panizzi, Via Farini 3, I-42100 Reggio Emilia. Tel (0522) 456089, Fax (0522) 456081. E-mail panizzi@comune.re.it. Website www.panizzi.comune.re.it. Open: Mon–Sat 9–19. Curator: Laura Gasparini. Founded 1980. 2 rooms, 200 m². 1–2 photo exhibitions/year. Artists: Luigi Ghirri, Paola De Pietri, Fabio Boni, Miro Zagnoli, Olivo Barbieri, Stanislao Farri, Vasco Ascolini, Luigi Menozzi

Palazzo Magnani, Corso Garibaldi 29, I-42100 Reggio Emilia. Tel (0522) 454437/459391, Fax (0522) 452349. E-mail palazzomagnani@mbox. provinciare.it. Website www.rcs.re.it /provincia/palazzomagnani

Galleria dell'Immagine, Via Gambalunga 27, I-47900 Rimini. Tel (0541) 55082, Fax (0541) 28692. E-mail musei@comune.rimini.it. Website www.comune.rimini.it/musei/ esposizioni.htm. Open: Mon–Fri 9.30–

12.30, 16–19, Sat 10–12, 17–19. Director: Renzo Semprini. Curator: Piero Delucca. Founded 1979. 2 rooms, 60 m². 4–5 photo exhibitions/year

Collezione di Autori, de Pellegrin, Viale Vannetti 8, I-38066 Riva del Garda. Tel (0349) 8423025, Fax (071) 7390277. E-mail depellegrin@hotmail.com. Website www.hfnet.it/portfolio/orlandoni. Open: by appointment only. Curator: Fulvio de Pellegrin. Founded 1992. 50 m². 3–4 photo exhibitions/year. Artists: Judita Csaderova, Heidi Lichtenberger, Adriano Eccel, Igor Savchenko, Roberto Kusterie, Franco Sortini, Massimiliano Orlandoni, Enrico Prada, Jose Ramon Bas, Fulvio de Pellegrin

Museo Civico, Piazza Battisti 3, I-38066 Riva del Garda (Trento). Tel (0464) 573869, Fax (0464) 521680. E-mail museo@anthesi.com. Website www.garda.com/museocivico. Open: Tue–Sun 9.30–12.30, 14–18 (Jul–Aug 16–22)

Castello di Rivoli, Museo d'Arte Contemporanea, Piazza Mafalda di Savoia, I-10098 Rivoli (Torino). Tel (011) 9565222, Fax (011) 9561141. E-mail info@castellodirivoli.torino.it. Website www.castellodirivoli.torino.it. Director: Ida Gianelli. Curator: Giorgio Verzotti. Founded 1984. 36 rooms, 6,000 m². 2 photo exhibitions/year. Artists: Jan Dibbets, Günther Förg, Mimmo Jodice, Gilbert & George, Katharina Sieverding, Mario Giacomelli

Galleria Minima Peliti Associati, Largo della Fontanella di Borghese 19, I-00100 Roma. Tel (06) 6868622.

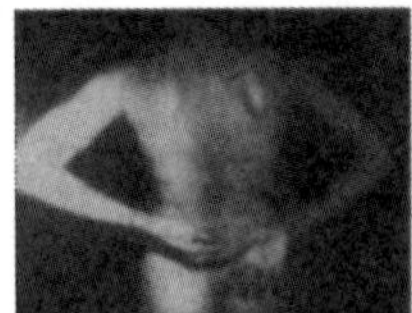
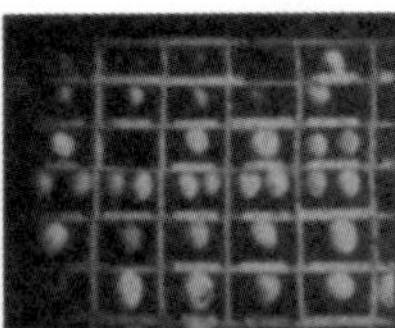

De Pellegrin

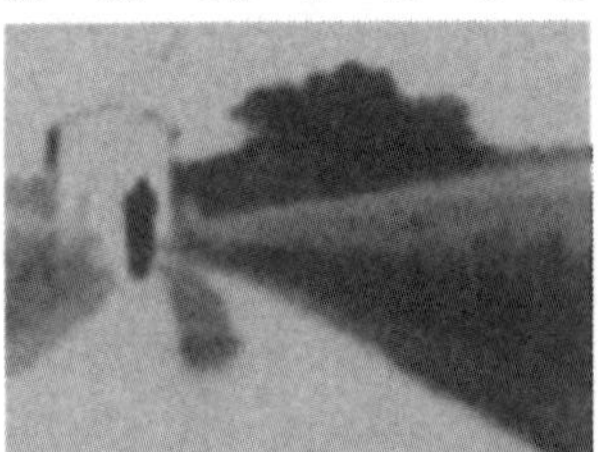

Orlandoni

Collezione di Autori

Judita Csaderova, Heidi Lichtenberger, Adriano Eccel,
Igor Savchenko, Roberto Kusterle, Franco Sortini,
Massimiliano Orlandoni, Enrico Prada,
José Ramon Bas, Fulvio De Pellegrin

Address: De Pellegrin - Viale Vannetti, 8 - I - 38066 Riva del Garda (TN) Italy
Tel.:++39.0349.8423025 Fax: ++39.071.7390277
Web: www.hfnet.it/portfolio/orlandoni
E-mail: depellegrin@hotmail.com

Open: Mon–Fri 17–20, Sat 10.30–13, 15.30–20

Instituto Nazionale per la Grafica, Calcografia, Via della Stamperia 6, I-00187 Roma. Tel (06) 69980218, Fax (06) 69921454. Artists: Giorgio Sommer, Carlo Naya, Francesco Agosti, Gianni Berengo Gardin, Mimmo Jodice, Roberto Salbitani, Studio Vasari

La Mente e l'Immagine, Via Caio Mario 8, I-00192 Roma. Tel (06) 3223392, Fax (06) 3223392. Open: Tue–Sat 11–13, 16–19.30 and by appointment. Director: Emanuele Cosentino. Curator: Giovanna Catania. Founded 1993. 2 rooms, 80 m². 6 photo exhibitions/year. Artists: Luigi Veronesi, Alain Fleischer, Giovanna Catania, Maria Miesenberger, Roberto Marzano, Cosimo Savina, Alessandro Formiconi, Giovanni Caccamo, Andrea Nocchia, Alessandro Vescovo

Palazzo delle Esposizioni, Via Nazionale 194, I-00100 Roma. Tel (06) 4828757, Fax (06) 4870776. E-mail palaexopo@tiscalinet.it. Website www.palaexpo.com. Artists: Sabina Cuneo, Jacques-Henri Lartigue, Francesca Woodman, Alan Volut

Linea di Confine per la Fotografia Contemporanea, L'Ospitale, Via Fontana 2, I-42048 Rubiera (Reggio Emilia). Tel (0522) 629403, Fax (0522) 628978. E-mail linconfine@comune. rubiera.re.it. Open: Mon–Sat 10–13. Director: William Guerrieri. Founded 1990. 3 rooms, 410 m². 4 photo exhibitions/year. Artists: Lewis Baltz, Walter Niedermayr, Stephen Shore, Guido Guidi, Olivo Barbieri, Paola De Pietri, Franco Vaccari, Luigi Ghirri, Gilbert Fastenaekens, Axel Hütte

Alberto Peola Arte Contemporanea, Via della Rocca 29, I-10123 Torino. Tel (011) 8124460, Fax (011) 8124460. E-mail a.peola@iol.it. Open: Tue–Sat 15.30–19.30, holiday closed. Director: Alberto Peola. Founded 1989. 3 rooms, 90 m². 3 photo exhibitions/year. Artists: Botto & Bruno, Monica Carocci, Seamus Nicolson, Paola De Pietri, Daniela Rossell

Fondazione Italiana per la Fotografia, Museo della Fotografia Storica e Contemporanea, Via Avogadro 4, I-10121 Torino. Tel (011) 546595, Fax (011) 5189799. E-mail fondfoto@ alpcom.it. Open: Tue–Fri 15–19, Sat–Sun 10–19. Director: Luisella d'Alessandro. Curator: Dennis Curti. Founded 1992. 3 rooms, 280 m². 6 photo exhibitions/year. Artists: Margaret Bourke-White, Eugene Omar Goldbeck

Galleria Civica d'Arte Moderna e Contemporanea, Via Magenta 31, I-10123 Torino. Tel (011) 5629911, Fax (011) 5628637. E-mail gam@comune. torino.it. Open: Tue–Sun 9–19

Photo & Co., Via Dei Mille 36, I-10123 Torino. Tel (011) 889884, Fax (011) 8178693. Open: Tue and Sat 15.30–19.30. Directors: Valerio Tazzetti, Marco Voena. Curator: Valerio Tazzetti. Founded 1996. 3 rooms, 120 m². 5–6 photo exhibitions/year. Artists: Arno Rafael Minkkinen, Hiroshi Sugimoto, Luis Gonzales Palma, Karen Knorr, Sandy Skoglund, Georges Rousse, Vik Muniz, Jürgen Klauke, Mimmo Jodice, Gabriele Basilico

Museo d'Arte Moderna e Contemporanea, Villa Mirabello, Piazza della Motta 4, I-21100 Varese. Tel (0332) 281590, Fax (0332) 281590. E-mail cultura@working.it

Sala Veratti, Via Veratti 20, I-21100 Varese. Tel (0332) 220256, Fax (0332) 822959. E-mail cultura@working.it, cultura@comune.varese.it

Galleria Imagina, Santa Margherita al Ponte dei Pugni, Dorsoduro 3126, I-30100 Venezia. Tel (041) 2410625, Fax (041) 2410625. E-mail paocasan@aol.com. Open: Tue–Sat 11-19. Directors/curators: Carmen Attisani, Paola Casanova. Founded 1999. 2 rooms, 80 m². 6–7 photo exhibitions/year. Artists: Luca Campigotto, Bruce Cratsley, Mark Feldstein, Flor Garduño, Mimmo Jodice, Alex Majoli, Marco Zanta, Alessandra Chemollo

Ikona Photo Gallery, Dorsoduro 48, I-30123 Venezia. Tel (041) 5205854, 5200428, Fax (041) 5205854. E-mail mail@ikonavenezia.com. Website www.ikonavenezia.com. Director: Ziva Kraus. Founded 1979. Artists: Berenice Abbott, Gisèle Freund, Lisette Model, Carlo Naya, Franco Fontana, William Klein, Robert Doisneau, Helmut Newton, Helen Levitt, Barbara Morgan

Imagina di Attisani & C., Dorsoduro 3126, I-30123 Venezia. Tel (041) 2410625, Fax (041) 2410625. E-mail photove@aol.com. Artists: Luca Campigotto, Flor Garduño, Mimmo Jodice, Ferdinando Scianna, Franco Vaccari, Marco Zanta

Palazzo Fortuny, Campo San Beneto, San Marco 3780, I-30100 Venezia. Tel (041) 2748881, Fax (041) 5200945. Open: Tue–Sun 9–19

Centro Internazionale di Fotografia, Cortile del Tribunale Piazza dei Signori, I-37121 Verona. Tel (045) 8007490/8077533, Fax (045) 8077239. E-mail maria-grazia_galdiolo@comune.verona.it

Castello di Vigevano, Piazza Ducale, I-Vigevano (Pavia). Tel (0381) 691965. E-mail cultura@comune.vigevano.pv.it. Open: Tue–Fri 11–13, 15–19, Sat+Sun 10–13, 14–22

Festivals & Fairs

Alberobello Fotografia, Associazione Culturale Nicéphore Niépce, Via Pola 16, I-70011 Alberobello (Bari). Tel (080) 4323291, Fax (080) 4323291. E-mail niepce@mailbox.media.it. Website www.lgs.it.niepce

Biennale Europea Fotografia d'Autore, Viale Volta 51, I-50131 Firenze. Tel (055) 582686, Fax (055) 583707

Biennale Internazionale di Fotografia, Fondazione Italiana per la Fotografia, Via Avogadro 4, I-10121 Torino. Tel (011) 546594, Fax (011) 544132. E-mail fondofoto@alpcom.it

Big Torino 2000, Biennial of Emerging Artists, Palazzo Cesare Alfieri di Sostegno, Via Maria Vittoria 18, I-10123 Torino. Tel (011) 4430010, Fax (011) 4430021. E-mail bigtorino@comune.torino.it. Website www.bigtorino.net

International Photographic Competition, Contrada Omagnano 20, I-47890 Repubblica di San Marino. Tel (0549) 8824-11/12, Fax (0549) 882575. E-mail statoturismo@omniway.sm. Website www.omniway.sm

International Photomeeting della Repubblica di San Marino, Contrada Omagnano 20, I-47031 San Marino. Tel (0549) 882410, Fax (0549) 882575. E-mail statoturismo@omniway.sm. Website www.omniway.sm/photomeeting

La Biennale di Venezia, S. Marco, Ca' Giustinian, I-30124 Venezia. Tel (041) 5218711, Fax (041) 5240817

Modena per la fotografia, Corso Canalgrande 103, I-41100 Modena. Tel (059) 206911, Fax (059) 206932. E-mail duretti@comune.modena.it. Website www.comune.modena.it/galleria

Photo Show, Centro Direzionale Milanofiori Strada 1, Palazzo F/1, I-20090 Assago (Milano). Tel (02) 8243390, Fax (02) 8258930. E-mail assoexpo@assoexpo.com. Website www.assoexpo.com

Spilimbergo Fotografia, Villa Ciani 2, I-33090 Lestans (Pordenone). Tel (0427) 91453, Fax (0427) 91453. E-mail craf@agemont.it. Website www.agemont/craf

Toscana Fotofestival, A.MA.TUR., Via Norma Parenti 22, I-58024 Massa Marittima (Grosseto). Tel (0566) 902756, Fax (0566) 940095. E-mail tff@cometanet.it. Website www.cometanet.it/tff

Venezia Immagine, Salone della Fotografia Storica, Moderna e Contemporanea, San Polo 2120, I-30125 Venezia. Tel (041) 714066, Fax (041) 713151. E-mail veimmagine@veneziafiere.it. Website www.veneziafiere.it

Magazines

Arte, Mensile di Arte, Cultura, Informazione, Giorgio Mondadori e Associati, Via Andrea Ponti 10, I-20143 Milano. Tel (02) 891661, Fax (02) 89125960. Editor: Nuccio Francesco Màdera. Italian. Copy price: Lit 9,000. Annual subscription: Lit 75,000, Lit 120,000 (outside Italy), 12 issues/year

Classic Camera, Viale Piceno 14, I-20129 Milano. Tel (02) 70002222, Fax (02) 713030. Editor: Paolo Namias. Italian. Founded 1992. Copy price: Lit 15,000. Annual subscription: Lit 50,000, 4 issues/year

D'Ars, Giardino Aristide Calderini 3 già Via S. Agnese, I-20123 Milano. Tel (02) 860290. E-mail darse@digibank.it. Website www.dars.it

F & D Foto e dintorni, Via Lanza 108, I-00184 Roma. Fax (06) 7009566. E-mail mifav@roma2.infn.it

Flash Art International, The Leading European Art Magazine, Via Carlo Farini 68, I-20159 Milano. Tel (02) 668-6150/73413, Fax (02) 6884784. Editors: Helena Kontova, Giancarlo Politi. English. Founded 1980. Copy price: US$7.00. Annual subscription: US$50.00 (8 issues), 6 issues/year

FotoComputer, Via Rucellai 7, I-20126 Milano. Tel (02) 27006844, Fax (02) 27006851. E-mail fotocomputer@ecitalia.com

Fotografare, Via Lipari 8, I-00141 Roma. Tel (06) 87183441, Fax (06) 87183995. Editor: Francesco Ciapanna. Italian. Founded 1967. Copy price: Lit 5,000. Annual subscription: Lit 50,000, 12 issues/year

Fotographia, Via Zuretti 2 a, I-20125 Milano. Tel (02) 66713604, Fax (02) 66981643. E-mail graphia@tin.it. Editor: Maurizio Rebuzzini. Italian. Founded 1994. Copy price: Lit 9,000. Annual subscription: Lit 90,000, 10 issues/year

Fotologia, Largo Fratelli Alinari 15, I-50123 Firenze. Tel (055) 288228, Fax (055) 2382857. E-mail infomore@alinari.it. Website www.alinari.it

Fotopratica Immagini, Lucano 3, I-20135 Milano. Tel (02) 5516109, Fax (02) 59902431. E-mail infodde@ designdiffusion.it. Website www. designdiffusion.it. Editor: Gianni Baumberger. Italian. Founded 1974. Copy price: Lit 15,000. Annual subscription: Lit 70,000

Fotostorica, Archivio Fotografico Storico, Via San Liberale 8, I-31100 Treviso. Tel (0422) 656139, Fax (0422) 410749. E-mail fotostorica@tin.it

Gente di Fotografia, Trimestrale di Cultura Fotografica e Immagini, Via Telesino 31, I-90135 Palermo. Tel (091) 406359, Fax (091) 406359. E-mail gente.di.fotografia@etabeta.it. Website www.etabeta.it/gente.di. fotografia. Editors: Francesca Ingoglia, Vincenzo Mirisola. Italian. Founded 1994. Copy price: Lit 10.000. Annual subscription: Lit 50.000, 4 issues/year

Il Giornale dell'Arte, Via Mancini 8, I-10131 Torino. Tel (011) 8193133, Fax (011) 8193090. Editor: Gianna Marini. Italian. Copy price: Lit 8,000. Annual subscription: Lit 80,000, Lit 100,000 (Europe), 11 issues/year

Immagine Cultura, Via Gradisca 3, I-33100 Udine. Tel (0432) 547525

Juliet, Art Magazine, Via Belpoggio 13, I-34123 Trieste. Tel (040) 313425/ 224648, Fax (040) 272119. E-mail juliet@arsmedia.net. Website www. arsmedia.net/news/juliet.htm. Editor: Roberto Vidali. Italian. Founded 1980. Copy price: Lit 15,000. Annual subscription: Lit 90,000 (Europe), 5+2 extra issues/year

Jump, Via Vanvitelli 10, I-20129 Milano. Tel (02) 700003588, Fax (02) 700003588. E-mail jump@ micronet.it

Photo, Via Cretese 12, I-20156 Milano. Tel (02) 38002901, Fax (02) 38010437. E-mail editor@photoitalia.com. Editor: Paoua Bergna. Italian. Founded 1996. Copy price: Lit 8,000. Annual subscription: Lit 56,000, Lit 76,000 (outside Italy), 10 issues/year

Private, Via Melloni 36, I-40124 Bologna. Tel (051) 433349, Fax (051) 433349. E-mail private@private.it

Progresso Fotografico, Professional Magazine, Viale Piceno 14, I-20129 Milano. Tel (02) 70002222, Fax (02) 713030. Editor: Paolo Namias. Italian. Founded 1894. Copy price: Lit 8,000. Annual subscription: Lit 92,000, 10 issues/year

Prospettive d'Arte, Via Carlo Torre 29, I-20143 Milano. Tel (02) 89408327, Fax (02) 89408329. Editor: Mimmo Dabbrescia. Italian. Founded 1975

Reflex Fotografia, Via di Villa Severini 54, I-00191 Roma. Tel (06) 36308595, Fax (06) 3295648. E-mail reflex@mclink.it. Website www. reflex.it

Risk Arte Oggi, Via Mecenate 76, I-20138 Milano. Tel (02) 58014112, 58010548, Fax (02) 58010860

Tema Celeste, Via Augusta 17, I-96100 Siracusa. Tel (0931) 757219/ 491597, Fax (0931) 491491. Editor: Demetrio Paparoni. Italian/English

Tutti Fotografi, Viale Piceno 14, I-20129 Milano. Tel (02) 70002222, Fax (02) 713030. Editor: Paolo Namias. Italian. Founded 1969. Copy price: Lit 7,000. Annual subscription: Lit 89,000, 11 issues/year

Zoom, International edition, Viale Piceno 14, I-20129 Milano. Tel (02) 70002222, Fax (02) 713030. Website www.zoom-net.com. Editor: Paolo

Namias. English. Founded 1980.
Copy price: US$10.00. Annual sub-
scription: US$49.90, 6 issues/year

Book Publishers

Baldini e Castoldi, Via Crocefisso 21,
I-20122 Milano. Tel (02) 584501/
58309445

Boringhieri Bollati, Corso Vittorio
Emanuele 86, I-10121 Torino. Tel
(011) 5612637

Bruno Mondadori, Via Archimede 23,
I-20129 Milano. Tel (02) 76009881

Casa Editrice Roberto Napoleone, Via
Antonio Chinotto 16, I-00195 Roma.
Tel (06) 3729103-9096, Fax (06)
3729103

Charta, Via della Moscova 27, I-20121
Milano. Tel (02) 6598098, Fax (02)
6598577. E-mail edcharta@tin.it.
Website www.artecontemporanea.
com/charta

Contrastodue, Via Calabria 32,
I-00187 Roma. Tel (06) 42086551,
Fax (06) 42821481

Edition Raetia, Via Grappoli 23,
I-39100 Bolzano. Tel (0471) 976904,
Fax (0471) 976908. E-mail info@
raetia.com

Editoriale Jaca Book, Via Saffi 19,
I-20123 Milano. Tel (02) 4390946

Edizioni Bolis, Via Zanica 58, I-24100
Bergamo. Tel (035) 317333, Fax (035)
316938

Edizioni Futuro s. r. l., Viale G. D.
Annunzio 3, I-37126 Verona. Tel (045)
8345955, Fax (045) 8300261

Edizioni Gruppo Abele, Via Carlo
Alberto 18, I-10123 Torino. Tel (011)
8142715, Fax (011) 545241. E-mail

egamedia@tin.it. Website www.
netbook.it/ega

Enzo Sellerio Editore, Via Siracusa 50
int. 2, I-90141 Palermo. Tel (091)
6254110/6259475, Fax (091) 6258802

Federico Motta Editore s. p. a., Via
Branda Castiglioni 7, I-20156 Milano.
Tel (02) 33400491, Fax (02) 38003625.
E-mail editor@mottaeditore.it.
Website www.mottaeditore.it

Franco Sciardelli, Via Giannone 6,
I-20154 Milano. Tel (02) 33105772

Fratelli Alinari, Largo Fratelli Alinari
15, I-50123 Firenze. Tel (055) 288228,
Fax (055) 2382857. E-mail info.
alinari@alinari.it. Website www.
alinari.it

Gabriele Mazzotta Editore, Foro
Bonaparte 52, I-20121 Milano. Tel
(02) 8055803/8690050, Fax (02)
8693046. E-mail mazzotta@iol.it.
Website www.milanoweb.com/
mazzotta/

Giulio Einaudi, Via Biancamano 2,
I-10121 Torino. Tel (011) 56561, Fax
(011) 542403

Grafis Edizioni, Via 2. Giugno 4,
I-40033 Casalecchio di Reno
(Bologna)

Gremese Editore s. r. l., Via Virginia
Agnelli 88, I-00151 Roma. Tel (06)
65740507, Fax (06) 65740509. E-mail
gremese@gremese.com. Website
www.gremese.com

Laterza, Via Dante 26, I-70121 Bari.
Tel (080) 213413

Leonardo Arte, Via Trentacoste 7,
I-20134 Milano. Tel (02) 215631,
Fax (02) 21563401

Magnus Edizioni s.p.a., Via Spilimbergo 180, I-33034 Fagagna Udine. Tel
(0432) 800081, Fax (0432) 810071

Novecento Editrice, Via Siracusa 16, I-90141 Palermo. Tel (091) 323513, Fax (091) 585702

Nuova Arnica Editrice, Via dei Rieti 19/A, I-00185 Roma. Tel (06) 4441611, Fax (06) 4441611. E-mail n.arnica@ flashnet.it

Peliti Associati, Viale Beata Vergine del Carmelo 12, I-00144 Roma. Tel (06) 5291340, Fax (06) 5292351. E-mail peliti@peliti.it. Website www.peliti.it

Photology, Via della Moscova 25, I-20121 Milano. Tel (02) 6595285

Priuli & Verlucca, Stradale Torino 11, P. O. Box 245, I-10018 Ivrea (Torino). Tel (0125) 239929, Fax (0125) 230085

Rossella Bigi Editore, Via Vigevano 10, I-20144 Milano. Tel (02) 58101870, Fax (02) 58100951. E-mail rbigiedi@ tin.it

Scala Istituto Fotografico, Editoriale s.p.a., Via Chiantigiana 62, I-50011 Antella (Firenze). Tel (055) 641541, Fax (055) 641124

Silvana Editoriale d'Arte, Via Margherita de Vizzi 86, I-20092 Cinisello Balsamo (Milano). Tel (02) 618361. Website www.silvanaeditoriale.it

Skira, Palazzo Casati Stampa, Via Torino 61, I-20123 Milano. Tel (02) 72444210, Fax 72444219

Tau Visual, Via Manara 7, I-20122 Milano. Tel (02) 55187195, Fax (02) 5465563

Umberto Allemandi & C. s.r.l., Via Mancini 8, I-10131 Torino. Tel (011) 8199111, Fax (011) 8193090. E-mail allemandi@artel.it

White Fotolibri, Via C. Sassone 22, I-13100 Vercelli. Tel (0161) 294203, Fax (0161) 393993

Zanichelli Editore s.p.a., Via Irnerio 34, I-40126 Bologna. Tel (051) 293111, Fax (051) 249782

Bookshops

A & M Bookstore, Via Tadino 30, I-20124 Milano. Tel (02) 29527729, Fax (02) 29526115. E-mail ambooks@ planet.it. Website www.undo.net/ ambookstore

Al Ferro di Cavallo Librogalleria, Via di Ripetta 67, I-00100 Roma. Tel (06) 3227303

Bourlot, Piazza San Carlo 183, I-10123 Torino. Tel (011) 537405

HF Distribuzione, Casella postale 56, I-13100 Vercelli. Tel (0161) 210727, Fax (0161) 214133. E-mail hf.distribuzione@hfnet.it. Website www.hfnet.it

IF Libri, Giovanna Chiti, Via Paganini 9, I-20131 Milano. Tel (02) 29405715, Fax (02) 29405715. E-mail iflibri@ tiscalinet.it. Website www.iflibri.it

Libreria di Brera, Via delle Erbe 2, I-20121 Milano. Tel (02) 72002206, Fax (02) 865885

Libreria Internazionale Ulrico Hoepli, Via Hoepli 5, I-20121 Milano. Tel (02) 864871, Fax (02) 864322

Milano Libri, Via Verdi 2, I-20121 Milano. Tel (02) 976871

Auctions

Associazione Pavia Fotografia, Via Toscana 4, I-27100 Pavia. Tel (0347) 2504089

Christie's, Via Manin 3, I-20121 Milano. Tel (02) 29001374, Fax (02) 29001156

Critics & Journalists

Augusto Baracchini Caputi, Corso Mazzini 167, I-57100 Livorno

Carlo Bertelli, Via Soresina 12, I-20144 Milano. Tel (02) 463638

Kitti Bolognesi, Largo Treves 2, I-20121 Milano. Tel (02) 6572580

Silvia Bordini, Via Labicana 58, I-00184 Roma. Tel (06) 70492897

Giovanna Calvenzi, Via Pergolesi 19, I-20124 Milano. Tel (02) 6701498, Fax (02) 6701498

Giacomo Carioti, Piazzale Ardeatino 6, I-00154 Roma. Tel (06) 5781357, Fax (06) 5781357. E-mail photogram@ katamail.com. Website www. machina.org. Editor of *Machina; Galleria Colonna* and Distampa, Roma

Dr. Cecilia Casorati, Via Nemorense 25, I-00199 Roma. Tel (06) 8553122, Fax (06) 8553122. *Carte*, Messina; *Avvenire*, Milano; i Libri Dizerynthia, Roma

Gualtiero Castagnola, Via Rossetti 6, I-20145 Milano

Pierangelo Cavanna, Via G. Bellezia 15, I-10122 Torino. Tel (011) 4364539/ 0161-921432

Giovanna Chiti, Via Paganini 9, I-20131 Milano. Tel (02) 29405715, Fax (02) 29405715. E-mail iflibri@ tiscalinet.it. Website www.iflibri.it

Dr. Frederick Clarke, Via Canneto il Lungo 6/5, I-16100 Genova. Tel (010) 2461550, Fax (010) 2461550. Accademia Ligustica di Belle Arti, Genova

Attilio Colombo, Via Dante 44, I-22060 Cabiate-Como

Cesare Colombo, Ripa Porta Ticinese 27, I-20143 Milano. Tel (02) 89402668, Fax (02) 89402668. *Abitare; Domus,* Milano

Mauro Corradini, Via Dobbeni 54, I-25060 Brescia

Dennis Curti, c/o Fondazione Italiana per la Fotografia, Museo della Fotografia Storica e Contemporanea, Via Avogadro 4, I-10121 Torino. Tel (011) 546595, Fax (011) 5189799. E-mail fondfoto@alpcom.it

Prof. Ken Damy, Corsetto S. Agata 22, I-25122 Brescia. Tel (030) 3750295, Fax (030) 45259. E-mail kendamy@tin.it. Website www.polimedia.it/ kendamy. *Zoom, Progresso Fotografico,* Milano. Director of Museo Ken Damy, Brescia and Milano; Professor of Fine Art, Accademia Brera, Milano

Anna D'Elia, Via Fanelli 206/23, I-70125 Bari. Tel (080) 5020526

Fulvio de Pellegrin, Viale Vannetti 8, I-38066 Riva del Garda. Tel (0464) 551700. E-mail depellegrin@ hotmail.com. Website www.hfnet.it/ portfolio/depellegrin. *Gente di Fotografia*, Palermo; *La Fotografia*, Barcelona

Luigi Erba, Via Polverara 41, I-22053 Lecco

Prof. Francesco Faeta, Universitá di Messina, Piazza Ugo Da Como 2, I-00139 Roma. Tel (06) 88328868

Vittorio Fagone, Via Vigoni 5, I-20122 Milano. Tel (02) 58313147

Gigliola Foschi, Via Urbano III 3, I-20123 Milano. Tel (02) 8321532

Luca Frigerio, Via Santa Tecla 5, I-20122 Milano. Tel (02) 860015/46, Fax (02) 860060

Laura Gasparini, Fototeca della Biblioteca Panizzi, Via Farini 3, 42100 Reggio Emilia. Tel (0522) 456089, Fax

(0522) 456081. E-mail panizzi@
comune.re.it

Sandra Giannatasio, Via Cosseria 1,
I-00192 Roma

Ando Gilardi, Via degli Imbriani 31,
I-20100 Milano. Tel (02) 39320380,
Fax (02) 39320380

Giovanna Ginex, Via Camperio 16,
I-20123 Milano. Tel (02) 876065

Antonio Giusa, Centro Regionale
di Catalogazione e Restauro dei
Beni Culturali, I-33030 Villa Manin
di Passariano (Udine). Tel (0432)
908527

Viviana Gravano, Piazza Sonnino 37,
I-00153 Roma. Tel (06) 5885801

Walter Guadagnini, Galleria Civica,
Corso Canalgrande 103, I-41100
Modena. Tel (059) 206883, Fax (059)
206932. E-mail galcivmo@comune-
modena.it. Website www.comune.
modena.it/galleria

Flaminio Gualdoni, Via Barbavara 9,
I-20144 Milano. Tel (02) 8361776

Dr. Thilo Koenig, Via Pateras 27,
I-00153 Roma. Tel (06) 5885341, Fax
(06) 5885341

Dr. Laura Leonelli, Via Palma il
Vecchio 24, I-24100 Bergamo. Tel
(035) 400177, Fax (035) 400177.
Fotopratica immagini, Milano

Angela Madesani, Via Pecchio 13,
I-20131 Milano. Tel (02) 29530040,
Fax (02) 29530040

Filippo Maggia, Via M. Broggi 4,
I-21019 Somma Lombardo (Varese).
Tel (0331) 255586

Prof. Claudio Marra, Via Savenella 10,
I-40124 Bologna. Tel (051) 580686,
Fax (051) 332850

Lorenzo Merlo, 11020 St. Christophe,
I-11100 Aosta. Tel (0165) 541875, Fax
(0165) 541875

Enzo Minervini, Archivio della
Comunicazione e dell'Immagine
per l'Etnografia e la Storia Sociale,
Regione Lombardia, Piazza IV
Novembre 5, I-20100 Milano. Tel
(02) 67652599. E-mail minervini@
regione.lombardia.it

Dr. Marina Miraglia, Viale dei
Quattro Venti 152, I-00152 Roma.
Tel (06) 5802273, Fax (06) 5886068

Dr. Vincenzo Mirisola, Via Telesino
31, I-90135 Palermo. Tel (091)
406359, Fax (091) 406359. E-mail
vmirisola@iol.it. Website www.
etabeta.it/gente.di.fotografia.
Director of Fotogalleria Libreria
Dante, Palermo; *Gente di Fotografia,*
Palermo; *Print Flash,* Messina

Diego Mormorio, C. F. 27, Roma
Centro C. P., I-00187 Roma. Tel (06)
70453288, Fax (06) 77205861

Massimo Mussini, Via Nazario Sauro
4, I-42100 Reggio Emilia. Tel (0522)
305785

Prof. Roberto Mutti, Corso Buenos
Aires 77 A, I-20124 Milano. Tel (02)
6704325. *La Repubblica, Fotographia,*
Milano

Luca Pagni, Via F. Tovaglieri 382 E,
I-00155 Roma. Tel (06) 39729972, Fax
(06) 39729973

Prof. Daniela Palazzoli, Via Mozart
2, I-20122 Milano. Tel (02) 76008872,
Fax (02) 76008872. *Il Giornale,* Mi-
lano; Accademia Brera/Dept. of
Theory and Method of Mass Media,
Milano

Roberto Pinto, Via Farini 36, I-20159
Milano. Tel (02) 66804195

Valeria Prina, Via M. Melloni 17,
I-20129 Milano. Tel (02) 718341,
Fax (02) 714067

Prof. Carlo Arturo Quintavalle, Viale
Duca Alessandro 48 bis, I-43100
Parma. Tel (0521) 494300

Dr. Antonio Ria, Corso Garibaldi 71,
I-20121 Milano. Tel (02) 864261, Fax
(02) 864261. *Corriere Del Ticino,*
Lugano; Radio Svizzera Italiana,
Lugano; *Il Mattino,* Napoli

Antonella Russo, Corso Duca degli
Abruzzi 74, I-10129 Torino. Tel (011)
502773

Prof. Angelo Schwarz, Via San Ber-
nardino 3, I-12037 Saluzzo (CN). Tel
(0175) 46894, Fax (0175) 45572. E-mail
angelo.schwarz@saluzzo.alpcom.it.
*Rivista di storia e critica della fotografia
& delle immagini tecnologiche,* Saluzzo;
Fotopratica, Milano

Prof. Giuliana Scimé, Via Farini 8,
I-20154 Milano. Tel (02) 6571006, Fax
(02) 29010329. E-mail g.scime@
libero.it. *Corriere della Sera, Immagini
Fotopratica,* Milano

Wladimiro Settimelli, Colle Lungo,
I-00039 Zagarolo, Roma

Valerio Soffientini, Viale Famagosta
44, I-20142 Milano. Tel (02) 8139322.
Albatross Press Agency, Milano

Ennery Taramelli, Via Cesare Massini
69, I-00155 Roma. Tel (06) 77205646

Silvana Turzio, Via Melzo 17, I-20129
Milano. Tel (02) 29407850

Prof. Roberta Valtorta, Via Tiraboschi
6, I-20135 Milano. Tel (02) 55192956,
Fax (02) 55192956. E-mail valtorta@
tiscalinet.it. *European Photography,*
Göttingen

Alessandro Zanazzo, Via Andrea
Doria 16/c, I-00192 Roma. Tel (06)
39744741. E-mail a.zanazzo@flashnet.
it. *RomArte,* Roma

Schools & Workshops

Accademia di Belle Arti, Piazza
Carrara 82, I-24100 Bergamo. Tel
(035) 399526

Accademia di Belle Arti, Via Belle Arti
54, I-40126 Bologna. Tel (051) 244252

Accademia di Belle Arti, Via San
Giuliano 257, I-Catania. Tel (095)
317350

Accademia di Belle Arti, Via Ricasoli
66, I-50122 Firenze. Tel (055) 215449

Accademia di Belle Arti, Palazzo di
Brera, Via Brera 28, I-20121 Milano.
Tel (02) 86460639

Accademia di Belle Arti, Via Con-
stantinopoli 107, I-80100 Napoli.
Tel (081) 5640557

Accademia di Belle Arti, Via Ripetta
222, I-00100 Roma. Tel (06) 3227025

Accademia di Belle Arti, Via Accademia Albertina 6, I-10100 Torino.
Tel (011) 889020

Accademia di Belle Arti, Via dei
Maceri 2, I-Urbino. Tel (0722) 320287

Accademia di Belle Arti, Campo della
Carità 1050, I-30100 Venezia. Tel (041)
5225396

**Accademia di Fotografia del Museo
Ken Damy,** Corsetto S. Agata 22,
I-25122 Brescia. Tel (030) 3750295,
Fax (030) 45259. E-mail kendamy@
tin.it. Website www.polimedia.it/
kendamy

Accademia di Moda e Arte "Altieri",
Via San Nicola da Tolentino 50,
I-00187 Roma. Tel (06) 4870207/
4820902

Art E – Scuola Internazionale di Design & Fotografia, Via Borgo Allegri 51 R, I-50122 Firenze. Tel (055) 2478510

Associazione Imago, Via Costantino 12, I-90147 Cardillo (Palermo). Tel (091) 243714

C.R.A.F., Villa Ciani, I-33090 Lestans (Pordenone). Tel (0427) 91453, Fax (0427) 91453. E-mail craf@agemont.it. Website www.agemont.it/craf

Casalgrande Fotografia, Assessorato alla Cultura del Comune, I-Casalgrande (Reggio Emilia). Tel (0522) 849397. E-mail biblio.casalgrande@gea.geanet.it

Centro di Formazione Professionale, Via Boccaccio 1, I-20052 Monza

Centro di Formazione Professionale Don Orione, Via della Camilluccia 112, I-00100 Roma

Centro di Formazione Professionale Riccardo Bauer, Via Pace 10, I-20122 Milano. Tel (02) 5455013. E-mail bauer@cfpbauer.com

Centro per il restauro e la conservazione della fotografia Berselli, Via Correggio 55, I-20149 Milano. Tel (02) 466031, Fax (02) 466031. E-mail berselli@meloria.iol.it

D.A.M.S., Università degli Studi di Bologna, Via Zamboni 33, I-40100 Bologna. Tel (051) 259750

Dryphoto, Via Pugliesi 23, I-59100 Prato. Tel (0574) 604939, Fax (0574) 604939

Fabrica, Villa Minelli, I-31050 Ponzano (Treviso). Tel (0422) 4491, Fax (0422) 969501

IF, Viale dei Mille 35, I-20129 Milano. Tel (02) 29405715, Fax (02) 29405715. E-mail iflibri@tiscalinet.it. Website www.iflibri.it

Incontri di Fotografia e Critica, Via E. Majorana 3, I-58024 Massa Marittima (Grosseto). Tel (0566) 901003, Fax (0566) 901003

Istituto Europeo di Design, Viale Trento 39, I-09123 Cagliari

Istituto Europeo di Design, Via Sciesa 4, I-20135 Milano. Tel (02) 5796951, Fax (02) 5469410. Website www.ied.it

Istituto Europeo di Design, Via Salaria 222, I-00198 Roma. Tel (06) 8842186, Fax (06) 8412640. E-mail ist.europeo.design@agora.stm.it

Istituto Europeo di Design, Via Pomba 17, I-10123 Torino. Tel (011) 8125668, Fax (011) 835720

Istituto Italiano di Fotografia, Via Forcella 13, I-20144 Milano. Tel (02) 58105598, Fax (02) 58103108. E-mail istituto@istit.it. Website www.istitfoto.it

Istituto Professionale di Stato Caterina da Siena, Via A. Costa 24, I-20100 Milano

Istituto Professionale Statale Cesare Correnti, Via Alcuino 4, I-20100 Milano

Istituto Professionale Statale per la fotografia Paravia, Via del Carmine 14, I-10100 Torino

Istituto Statale d'Arte, Via de Porta Romana 9, I-50100 Firenze

Istituto Statale d'Arte Adolfo Venturi, Via Belle Arti 16, I-41100 Modena

Istituto Superiore di Fotografia & Arti Visive, Via Tiziano Minio 19, I-35134 Padova. Tel (049) 8643984

Linea di Confine per la Fotografia Contemporanea, L'Ospitale, Via

Fontana 2, I-42048 Rubiera (Reggio Emilia). Tel (0522) 629403, Fax (0522) 628978. E-mail linconfine@comune. rubiera.re.it

Mifav, Università di Roma Tor Vergata, Dipartimento di Fisica, Via della Ricerca Scientifica 1, I-00133 Roma. Tel (06) 2023507, Fax (06) 2023507. E-mail mifav@roma2.infn.it. Website www.roma.infn.it

Nuova Accademia di Belle Arti, Via Bassi 3, I-20148 Milano. Tel (02) 6686867, Fax (02) 6684413

Scuola di Fotografia di Firenze, Via di Canacci 9, I-50100 Firenze. Tel (055) 289505

Scuola di Fotografia Istituto Superiore, Via degli Ausoni 1, I-00185 Roma. Tel (06) 4469269. Website www. netart.it/sfis

Scuola di Fotografia nella Natura di Roberto Salbitani, c/o Pierluigi Gentilini, Via Perisauli 4, I-47019 Tredozio (Forlì). Tel (06) 6534931

Scuola Permanente di Fotografia "Graffiti", Via Lavini 20, I-00183 Roma. Tel (06) 7005263

Scuola Professionale di Fotografia Click Up, Via San Francesco di Paola 15, I-50124 Firenze. Tel (055) 2298548, Fax (055) 2298430. E-mail clickup@ ats.it. Website www.clickup.net

Studio Marangoni Workshops, Via San Zanobi 32 R, I-50129 Firenze. Tel (055) 280368, Fax (055) 215052. E-mail info@studiomarangoni.it. Website www.studiomarangoni.it

Toscana Photographic Workshops, P. O. Box 931, Bologna Centrale, I-40100 Bologna. Tel (051) 6360519, Fax (051) 399626. E-mail info@tpw.it. Website www.tpw.it

Università di Parma, Centro Studi e Archivio della Comunicazione, P.le della Pace 5, I-43100 Parma

Associations

Associazione Culturale Al.b.um, Via Pace 10, I-20122 Milano. E-mail album.ass@tiscalinet.it. Website www.album.ass.it

Associazione Culturale Fotografica Antonino Paraggi, Via Santa Maria del Sile 13, I-31100 Treviso. Tel (0422) 321673, Fax (0422) 321673. E-mail paraggi@ptsc.net

Associazione Culturale Nicéphore Niépce, Via Pola 15, I-70011 Alberobello (Bari). Tel (080) 9323291, Fax (080) 9323291. E-mail niepce@ mailbox.media.it

Associazione Fotografi Italiani Professionisti, Via Perosi 5, I-20146 Milano. Tel (02) 48954001, Fax (02) 48954174

Associazione Fotografia & Informazione, Via Watt 4, I-20143 Milano. Tel (02) 89124802, Fax (02) 89124802. E-mail fotoinfo@transmat.it. Website www.fotoinfo.net

Associazione Italiana Reporter Fotografi AIRF, Via Sallustiana 15, I-00187 Roma

Associazione per la Fotografia Storica, Via Po 12, I-10123 Torino. Tel (011) 8395382, Fax (011) 835814

Associazione Studio Patellani, Piazza Tricolore 2, I-20129 Milano. Tel (02) 781986

FIAF, Corso S. Martino 8, I-10122 Torino. Tel (011) 5629479, Fax (011) 5175291. E-mail fiaf@arpnet.it. Website www.arpnet.it/fiaf

Fondazione Italiana per la Fotografia,
Via Avogadro 4, I-10121 Torino. Tel
(011) 546594, Fax (011) 5189799.
E-mail fifto@tin.it

Fondazione Primoli, Via Zanardelli 1,
I-00186 Roma. Tel (06) 68801136

**Fondazione Sandretto Re Rebauden-
go,** Corso Stasti Uniti 39, I-10129
Torino. Tel (011) 5625536, Fax (011)
549225

Fondazione Sella, Via Corradino Sella
10, I-13051 Biella. Tel (015) 2522445,
Fax (015) 2522455

Fondazione Studio Nocera, c/o
Laudie Nocera, Via Cola Monta-
no 40, I-20159 Milano. Tel (02)
66805977

GADEF, Via Manara 7, I-20122
Milano. Tel (02) 5501381, Fax (02)
5501381

Istituto di Fotografia Paolo Monti,
Via Vegezio 17, I-20140 Milano.
Tel (02) 70103445

L'occhio e l'idea, Via Santa Croce o/
E, I-10123 Torino. Tel (011) 835973,
Fax (011) 835973. E-mail occhio@
arpnet.it. Website www.arpnet.it/
occhio

Pavia Fotografia, Via Toscana 4,
I-27100 Pavia. Tel (0347) 2504089

SIAF/CNA, Via Guattani 13, I-00161
Roma. Tel (06) 441881, Fax (06)
44249515. E-mail siaf@uni.net.
Website www.net/CNA_SIAF

TAU Visual Associati, Via Manara 7,
I-20122 Milano. Tel (02) 55187195,
Fax (02) 5465563. E-mail tauvisual@
tauvisual.it. Website www.
tauvisual.it

Ultreya, Via San Gerolamo Emiliani,
I-20135 Milano. Tel (02) 5453636, Fax
(02) 5453638

Grants & Awards

**Biennale dei Giovani Artisti dell'
Europa Mediterranea,** Assessorato alla
Cultura, Comune di Bologna, Via
Oberdan 24, I-40126 Bologna. Tel
(051) 336686

**Canon Italia Premio Giovani Foto-
grafi,** Palazzo L, Strada 6, I-20089
Rozzano Milanofiori (Milano). Tel
(02) 82841, Fax (02) 82484600

Concorso Agfa-Gevaert, Via Grosioo
10/4, I-20151 Milano. Tel (02)
3074377, Fax (02) 38000229

**European Publishers Award for
Photography,** for European photographers, to recognize a work which is
suitable for a book project, book
publication in five countries, every
year. Contact: Peliti Associati, Viale
Beata Vergine del Carmelo 12, I-00144
Roma. Tel (06) 5295548, Fax (06)
5292351. E-mail peliti.f@peliti.it.
Website www.peliti.it

Fotoesordio, Mifav, Università di
Roma Tor Vergata, Dipartimento di
Fisica, Via della Ricerca Scientifica 1,
I-00133 Roma. Tel (06) 72594895, Fax
(06) 2023507. E-mail mifav@roma2.
infn.it

**I luoghi della vita, European Award
for Women Photographers,** Dryphoto, Via Pugliesi 23, I-59100 Prato.
Tel (0574) 604939, Fax (0574) 444508.
E-mail m.verdi@dada.it

Portfolio – Immagini in movimento,
Comune di Modena, Via Galaverna 8,
I-41100 Modena. Tel (059) 206404, Fax
(059) 206877. E-mail eferrari@
comune.modena.it. Website www.
comune.modena.it/gioarte/

Premio Federchimica, per un progetto
fotografico, awarded annually to
finance an unpublished project, Lit

5,000,000, every year. Contact: Studio
Marangoni Foundation, Via San
Zanobi 32 R, I-50129 Firenze. Tel
(055) 280368, Fax (055) 215052. E-mail
info@studiomarangoni.it. Website
www.studiomarangoni.it

Premio Oscar Goldoni, Galleria
Civica, Corso Canalgrande 103,
I-41100 Modena. Tel (059) 206890,
Fax (059) 206932

Premio Riccardo Pezza, Associazione
Culturale Al.b.um/CFP Bauer, Via
Pace 10, I-20122 Milano. Tel (02)
5455013. E-mail album.ass@
tiscalinet.it. Website www.album.
ass.it

Premio Yann Geoffrey, Agenzia
Grazia Neri, Via Maroncelli 14,
I-20154 Milano. Tel (02) 625271,
Fax (02) 6597839

Latvia

Population: 2.7 million
Capital: Riga, 900,000
Currency: Lat
International code: ++371
Tourist information: Latvian
Tourist Board, 4 Pils Square,
LV-1050 Riga
Tel 722 99 45,
Fax 722 99 45

Galleries & Museums

Saukas pagasta muzejs – M. Buclera fotografijas kabinets, Sauka Parish Museum – Photocabinet of M. Bucler, Saukas lauksaimniecibas škola, LV-5232 Jekabpils raj. Contact: Gunars Spidainis. Founded 1997. 1 room, 80 m². Artists: Vilnis Auzinš, Leons Balodis, Angela Klidzeja, Aivars Liepinš, Boris Mangolds, Dace Marga, Raitis Purinš

Gallery Mozums, Škunu iela 19/19, LV-1050 Riga. Tel 7062292/9548719. E-mail mozums@elva.org.lv. Open: Mon–Sat. Contact: Inga Štemaine. Founded 1997. 1 room, 50 m². Artists: Gunars Binde, Gvido Kajons, Janis Knakis, Raimo Lielbriedis, Vilhelms Mohailovskis, Imants Purinš

Gallery Riga, Blaumana iela 21/2, LV-1011 Riga. Tel 7282356. Open: Mon–Fri 10–18. Contact: Imansts Purinš. Founded 1994. Artists: Aivars Akis, Eizenija Freimane, Janis Gleizds, Imants Purinš, Guntis Ziemanis

Latvian Artist Union Gallery, 11 novembra krastmala 35, LV-1050 Riga. Tel 7228997. Open: Thu– Sat 11–18. Contact: Inese Baranovska. Artists: Vilnis Auzinš, Aldis Dubjans, Inta Ruka, Andrejs Grants, Arno Antums Jansons, Gvido Kajons, Ina Sture, Dainis Karkluvalks

Latvijas fotográfijas muzejs, Latvian Museum of Photography, Marstalu iela 8, LV-1050 Riga. Tel 7222713/7227231, Fax 7222713. E-mail lvfoto@lanet.lv. Open: Wed–Thu 12–19, Fri–Sun 10–17. Director: Vilnis Auzinš. Founded 1993. 5 rooms, 180 m², contemporary photography gallery 2 rooms, 80 m². 12–13 photo exhibitions/year. Artists: Gunars Binde, Shai Ginot, Gvido Kajons, Timo Kelaranta, Raimo Lielbriedis, Marie Nilsson, Antanas Sutkus, Karen Willeto, Steve Yates

Reitern's House, Union of Journalists, Marstalu iela 2, LV-1050 Riga. Tel 7224004. Contact: Ieva Neikena. Founded 1990. 6 rooms, 200 m². Artists: Stanislavs Graholskis, Arno Antumns Jansons, Rose Marosco, Vilhelm Mihailovskis, Imants Predelis, Augusts Upitis

Salon – Library "Vecriga", Pils iela 18, LV-1050 Riga. Tel 7210677. Contact: Arnis Zile. Founded 1996. 1 room, 40 m². Artists: Leonards Pastors, Leons Balodis, Christina Elsinger, Andris Ozois

Valts makslas muzejs, Museum of Fine Arts, K. Valdemara iela 10a, LV-1010 Riga. Tel 7325021. E-mail vmm@latnet.lv. Contact: Mara Lace. 1 room, 40 m². Artists: Roberts Auzinš, Gustav Klucis, Andris Zegners

Talsi novada muzejs, Talsi Regional Museum, K. Milenbaha iela 19, LV-3201 Talsi. Tel (032) 24541. Contact:

Guna Millersone. Artists: Vilnis Auzinš, Uldis Balga, Aldis M. Dublans, Andrejs Grants, Gvido Kajons, Valts Kleins, Modris Rubenis, Andris Zegners

Pedvales brivdabas makslas muzejs, Pedvale Open Air Art Museum, Pedvale, Abavas pag., LV-3294 Talsu raj. Tel (032) 52249. Contact: Ojars Feldbergs. 1 room, 60 m². Artists: Vilnis Auzinš, H. H. Capor, Karen Willeto, Christina Elsinger, Dainis Karkluvalks, Astrida Meirane, Marie Nilsson

Ventspils novada vestures un makslas muzejs, Ventspils Museum of Art and Regional Studies, Akmenu iela 3, LV-3601 Ventspils. Tel (036) 22031. 3 rooms, 120 m². Contact: Silvia Leruma. Artists: Vilnis Auzinš, Hideo Haga, Angela Klidzeja, Dace Marga, Okuda Minoru, Augusts Upitis

Festivals & Fairs

Baltars, International Art Exhibition, RTU – BT1, Šmerija iela 3-338, LV-1006 Riga. Tel 7529918/7542585, Fax 7821493/7545020. E-mail info@btl.lv

Fotosavara, BO SIA "ACD Fotoforma", Getrudes 5A, LV-1000 Riga. Tel 274429, Fax 7312871. E-mail acd@parks.lv

Photography – a Phenomenon of Visual Culture, Latvian Museum of Photography, Marstalu iela 8, LV-1050 Riga. Tel 7222713/7227231, Fax 7222713. E-mail lvfoto@lanet.lv

PhotoParade, Latvian Museum of Photography, Marstalu iela 8, LV-1050 Riga. Tel 7222713/7227231, Fax 7222713. E-mail lvfoto@lanet.lv – or BO SIA "ACD Fotoforma", Getrudes

5A, LV-1000 Riga. Tel 274429, Fax 7312871. E-mail acd@parks.lv

Magazines

Grafika un Poligrafija, Raina bulv. 29, LV-1459 Riga. Tel 7224689, Fax 7242397. E-mail grafika@ dtmediadia.lv. Editor: Janis Borgs. Latvian. Founded 1998, 4 issues/ year

Maksla plus, Akademijas laukums 1, LV-1027 Riga. Tel 7220722, Fax 7820608. E-mail makslaplus@ hotmail.com. Editor: Ligita Berzina. Founded 1997, 6 issues/year

Rigas Laiks, Laèpleša iela 25, LV-1011 Riga. Tel 7287922/7286416, Fax 7830542. E-mail pasts@rigaslaiks.lv. Editor: Inese Zandere. Latvian. Founded 1994, 12 issues/year

Studija, 11 novembra krastmala 35-103, LV-1050 Riga. Tel 7222647, Fax 7226066. E-mail studija@re-lab.net. Editor: Laima Slava. Latvian. Founded 1997, 6 issues/year

Book Publishers

Avots, Aspazijas bulv. 24, LV-1050 Riga. Tel 7225824

Jana Seta, Elizabetes iela 83/85, korp. 2, LV-1011 Riga. Tel 7217371/7092270

Jumava, Dzimavu iela 73/1, LV-1011 Riga. Tel 7280314

Nordik, Daugavgrivas iela 36/9, LV-1007 Riga. Tel 7602672, Fax 7602818

Critics & Journalists

Vilnis Auzinš, Lacpleša iela 2-6, LV-1050 Riga. Tel 290140, Fax 222713. E-mail acd@parks.lv. Director of Latvian Museum of Photography, Riga; *Diena, Rigas Laiks, Grafika un Poligrafija, Maksla Plus*, Riga; *Imago*, Bratislava

Sergejs Daugovišs, Staiceles iela 11-7, LV-1035 Riga. Tel 2586068. *Deina*, Riga

Helena Demakova, 11 novembra krastmala 35-103, LV-1050 Riga. Tel 2285568, Fax 7226066. E-mail studija@re-lab.net. *Studija, Diena*, Riga

Daiga Kalnina, Jana iela 5, LV-5200 Jekabpils. Tel (052) 21393. *Neatkariga Rita Avize*, Riga

Ieva Kalnina, E-mail ik@re-lab.net. *Studija, Diena*, Riga

Odrija Kalve, Arsenala iela 3, LV-1050 Riga. Tel 7223891, Fax 7322261. E-mail marcis@mail.bke.lv

Péteris Korsaks, Kveles iela 15/5-42, LV-1024 Riga. Tel 7525162, Fax 7222713. E-mail lvfoto@lanet.lv. *Dziesmusvetki, Literatura, Makskla*, Riga

Ieva Lejasmeijere, 11 novembra krastmala 35-103, LV-1050 Riga. Fax 7226066. E-mail studija@re-lab.net. *Studija, Literatura, Maksla, Mes*, Riga

Gatis Rozenfelds, Getrudes 5A, LV-1010 Riga. Tel 9657330, Fax 7312871. E-mail acd@parks.lv

Schools & Workshops

Jana Rozentala Rigas makslas koledza, Janis Rozentals Riga Art College, Hamana iela 2A, LV-1007 Riga. Tel 7601783. E-mail raimo@apollo.lv

Latvijas Kulturas Akademija, Latvian Academy of Culture, Ludzas iela 24, LV-1003 Riga. Tel 7140175, Fax 7141012. E-mail lka@ acad-latnet.lv

Latvijas Maksklas Akademija, Latvian Art Academy, Kalpaka bulv. 13, LV-1050 Riga. Tel 7332202, Fax 7228963. E-mail kampars@latnet.lv

Associations

ACD Fotoforma, Getrudes iela 5A, LV-1010 Riga. Tel 2274429, Fax 7312871. E-mail acd@parks.lv

Latvian Association of Professional Photographers, Marstalu iela 8, LV-1050 Riga. Tel 72222713, Fax 7222713. E-mail lvfoto@lanet.lv

Latvian Designers Society, Getrudes iela 5A, LV-1010 Riga. Tel 7222859, Fax 7313316

Latvian Photo Artists Union, Marstalu iela 6, LV-1098 Riga. Tel 7210327

Photo Club "Ezerzeme", Rigas iela 8, LV-5407 Daugavpils. Tel (054) 21201

Photo Club "Ogre", Ogre Culture House, Brivibas iela 15, LV-5001 Ogre. E-mail raimo@apollo.lv

Photo Club "Riga", Blaumana 21/2, LV-1011 Riga. Tel 7282356

Photo Club "Talsi", Milenbaha iela 19, LV-3201 Talsi

Youth Creative Center, Annas iela 2, LV-1001 Riga. Tel 7374093, Fax 7374093. E-mail tjn@www.tjn.lv

Lithuania

*Population: 3.7 million
Capital: Vilnius, 580,000
Currency: Lit (LT)
International code: ++370
Tourist information: Tourist
Board, Vilniaus 4/35,
LT-2600 Vilnius
Tel (02) 62 26 10,
Fax (02) 22 68 19*

Galleries & Museums

Fuji Film Fotografijos galerija, Fuji Film Gallery of Photography, Rotušes a. 1, LT-3000 Kaunas. Tel (07) 321145/321789, Fax (07) 207760. Open: Mon–Sun 12–18. Contact: Aleksandras Macijauskas. Founded 1979. 2 rooms, 400 m². Artists: Aleksandras Macijauskas, Evaldas Butkevicius, Romualdas Pozerskis, Romualdas Rakauskas, Snieguole Michelkeviciute

Klaipedos fotografijos galerija, Klaipeda Gallery of Photography, Tomo 7, LT-5800 Klaipeda. Tel (06) 410402. Open: Tue–Sat 10–17. Founded 1989. 1 room, 100 m². Artists: Algis Jankunas, Vaclovas Straukas, Aleksandras Dapkevicius, Mecislovas Šilinskas, Jonas Strazdauskas

Panevezio fotografijos galerija, Panevezys Gallery of Photography Vasario 16-osios 11, LT-5300 Panevezys. Tel (054) 67551. Open: Wed–Sat 11–19, Sun 11–18. Founded 1992. 3 rooms, 60 m². Artists: Algimantas Aleksandravicius, Marija Cicirkiene, Petras Kaupelis, Aurimas Strumila, Marius Abromavicius, Edis Jurcys, Ruta Kripaityte

Fotografijos muziejus, Photography Museum, Vilniaus 140, LT-5400 Šiauliai. Tel (01) 524396. E-mail sjurga@takas.lt. Open: Thu–Fri 10–18, Sat 11–16. Contact: Regina Sulskyte. Founded 1973. 1 room of permanent collection, 2 rooms, 194 m². Artists: Antanas Sutkus, Romualdas Pozerskis

Prospekto galerija, Gallery of Prospectus, Gedimino 43, LT-2000 Vilnius. Tel (02) 611665, Fax (02) 611665. Founded 2000

Vilniaus fotografijos galerija, Vilnius Gallery of Photography, Stikliu 4, LT-2001 Vilnius. Tel (02) 611665. Open: Wed–Sun 12–18. Contact: Stanislovas Zvirgzdas. Founded 1973. 2 rooms, 135 m². Artists: Algimantas Aleksandravicius, Antanas Sutkus, Algimantas Kuncius, Alvydas Lukys, Vytautas Karaciejus, Georgy, Borosz

Vilniaus šiuolaikinio meno centras, The Contemporary Art Center of Vilnius, Vokieciu 2, LT-2024 Vilnius. Tel (02) 629891, Fax (02) 623954. Open: Thu–Sun 11–19. Director: Kestutis Kuizinas. Founded 1968. 4 rooms, 2,000 m². Artists: Elke Krystufek, John Batho, Luisa Lambri

Magazines

Lietuvos fotografija vakar ir siandien, Lithuanian Photography Yesterday and Today, Almanac Universiteto 4, LT-2600 Vilnius. Tel (02) 611665, Fax (02) 611665. E-mail info@ photography.lt. 1 issue/year

"Nemunas", Gedimino 45, LT-3000 Kaunas. Tel (07) 220229. Lithuanian, 12 issues/year

Book Publishers

Baltos lankos, Mesiniu 4, LT-2001 Vilnius. Tel (02) 220126/220152. E-mail baltos.lankos@post.omnitel. net

R. Paknio leidykla, Isganytojo 4-10, LT-2001 Vilnius. Tel (02) 629950, Fax (02) 223156. E-mail pako@pako.vno. osf.lt

Vaga, Gedimino 50, LT-2600 Vilnius. Tel (02) 613159, Fax (02) 616902. E-mail vaga@post.omnitel.net

Critics & Journalists

Alfonsas Andriuskevicius, Braskiu 35, LT-2021 Vilnius. Tel (02) 701009

Algirdas Gaizutis, Saltiniu 9-16, LT-2001 Vilnius. Tel (02) 262035

Dainius Junevicius, Pasilaiciu 6-59, LT-2022 Vilnius. Tel (02) 479975

Virgilijus Juodakis, Architektu 182-36, LT-2029 Vilnius. Tel (02) 457309

Raminta Jurenaite, Pavasario 17-2, LT-2055 Vilnius. Tel (02) 612310

Agne Narusyte, Geliu 9-17a, LT-2000 Vilnius. Tel (02) 608411

Laima Skeiviene, Musninku 2-34, LT-2010 Vilnius. Tel (02) 411492

Skirmantas Valiulis, Jurginu 4-1, LT-2048 Vilnius. Tel (02) 677550

Schools & Workshops

Vilniaus aukstesnioji technologijos mokykla, Vilnius Technological College, Pamenkalnio 15/6, LT-2001 Vilnius. Tel (02) 618114/619961, Fax (02) 618114/619961. E-mail vatm@ pub.osf.lt

Vilniaus dailes akademija, Vilnius Academy of Arts, Fotografijos ir videomeno katedra, Department of Photography and Video Art, Maironio 6, LT-2600 Vilnius. Tel (02) 610539. E-mail alvydas.lukys@vda.lt

Vilniaus lengvosios pramones ir buitiniu paslaugu mokykla, Vilnius School of the Light Industry and Domestic Services, Didlaukio 84, LT-2057 Vilnius. Tel (02) 779357/ 763763, Fax (02) 779357/763763. E-mail root@mokykla.lpki.lt

Associations

Lietuvos fotografu sajunga, Association of Lithuanian Photographers, Universiteto 4, LT-2600 Vilnius. Tel (02) 611665, Fax (02) 611665. E-mail info@photography.lt. Website www. photography.lt

Luxembourg

Population: 422,000
Capital: Luxembourg, 80,000
Currency: Franc (F)
International code: ++352
Tourist information: National
Tourist Office, P. O. Box 1001,
L-1010 Luxembourg
Tel 42 82 82 10,
Fax 42 82 82 38

Galleries & Museums

Centre National de l'Audiovisuel,
5 route de Zoufftgen, L-3598 Dudelange. Tel 5224241, Fax 520655. E-mail
info@cna.etat.lu. Open: 8–12, 14–18.
Director: Jean Back. Founded 1988.
3–4 photo exhibitions/year

Casino Luxembourg, Forum d'art
Contemporain, 41 rue Notre-Dame,
L-2240 Luxembourg. Tel 225045, Fax
229595. E-mail casino-luxembourg@
ci.culture.lu. Website www.men.lu/
casino/casino.html. Open: Mon +
Wed–Sun 11–18 (Thu –20). Director:
Jo Kox. Curator: Enrico Lunghi.
Founded 1996. 13 rooms, 650 m².
2 photo exhibitions/year

Magazines

Café-Crème Art Magazine, Café
Crème Photo-Art-Image, 2 rue Al-
phonse-Munchen, P. O. Box 2655,
L-2172 Luxembourg. Tel 454619,
Fax 458674. E-mail pierre.stiwer@
ci.edua.lu. Website www.restena.lu/
index.html. Editors: Pierre Stiwer,
Paul di Felice. English/French.
Founded 1984. Copy price: F 500.00.
Annual subscription: F 1,000,
2 issues/year

Grants & Awards

Mosaïque Programme, to help the
creation, research and promotion of
photographic works on the theme of
Europe, EUR 37,184, every year.
Contact: Centre National de l'Audio-
visuel, 5 route de Zoufftgen, L-3598
Dudelange. Tel 5224241, Fax 520655.
E-mail info@cna.etat.lu

New Media

Casino Luxembourg, Video/media
activities, Fondation Casino Luxembourg – Forum d'art contemporain,
41 rue Notre Dame, P. O. Box 345,
L-2013 Luxembourg. Tel 225045,
Fax 229595. E-mail casino-
luxembourg@ci.culture.lu. Website
www2.men.lu/casino

Netherlands

*Population: 15.6 million
Capital: Amsterdam, 715,000
Currency: Florin (Fl)
International code: ++31
Tourist information: Neder-
lands Bureau voor Toerisme,
P. O. Box 458, NL-2260 MG
Leidschendam*

Galleries & Museums

**Amsterdams Centrum voor Fotogra-
fie,** Bethaniënstraat 9, NL-1012 BZ
Amsterdam. Tel (020) 6224899, Fax
(020) 6391481. Open: Wed–Sat 13–19.
Director: Bob van den Berg. Founded
1994. 3 rooms, 250 m². 20 photo
exhibitions/year

Aschenbach Galerie, Bilderdijkstraat
165c, NL-1053 KP Amsterdam. Tel
(020) 6853580, Fax (020) 6890009.
E-mail euronet@lippold. Open: Wed–
Sun 13–18. Director: G. L. Lippold.
Founded 1982. 3 rooms, 200 m².
3 photo exhibitions/year. Artists:
Thomas Florschuetz, Günter Förg,
Paul Graham, Conny Schleime,
Désirée Dolron

Fotogalerie 2,5 x 4,5, Prinsengracht
356, NL-1016 JA Amsterdam. Tel
(020) 6260757, Fax (020) 6279635.
Director/curator: Han Schoonhoven.
Founded 1983. 40 m². 16 photo exhi-
bitions/year. Artists: Paul Kooiker,
Koos Breukel, Leo Divendal, Catha-
rine Poncin

Galerie Akinici, Lijnbaansgracht 317,
NL-1017 WZ Amsterdam. Tel (020)
6380480, Fax (020) 6386485. E-mail
info@akinici.nl. Website www.
akinici.nl

**Galerie Ferdinand van Dieten –
d'Eendt,** Spuistraat 270, NL-1012
VW Amsterdam. Tel (020) 6265777,
Fax (020) 6243064. E-mail dieten@
worldonline.nl

Galerie Paul Andriesse, Prinsengracht
116, NL-1015 EA Amsterdam. Tel
(020) 6236237, Fax (020) 6390038.
E-mail andriesse@euronet.nl. Website
www.artnet.com. Open: Tue–Fri 11–
18.00, Sat–Sun 14–18 (first Sunday of
the month). Director: Paul Andriesse.
Founded 1984. 2 rooms. 2 photo
exhibitions/year. Artists: Jan Koster,
John Riddy, Thomas Struth, James
Welling, Hellen van Meene, Jean-
Marc Bustanabte, Vincenzo Castella,
Lidwien van de Ven

Galerie Rob Jurka, Singel 28, NL-1015
AA Amsterdam. Tel (020) 6276343,
Fax (020) 6278091. E-mail robjurka@
cable.a2000.nl. Open: Thu–Sat 13–16.
Director: Rob Jurka. Founded 1970.
1 room, 60 m². 4 photo exhibitions/
year. Artists: Robert Mapplethorpe,
Matthias Herrmann, Jean-Marc
Spaans, Marcel van der Vlugt,
Wouter van Riessen, Ken Probst

Huis Marseille, Stichting voor
Fotografie, Keizersgracht 401, NL-
1016 EK Amsterdam. Tel (020)
5318989, Fax (020) 5318988. E-mail
info@huismarseille.nl. Website
www.huismarseille.nl. Open: Tue–
Sun 11–17

Jewish Historical Museum, Jonas
Daniel Meyerplein 2–4, NL-1011 RH
Amsterdam. Tel (020) 6269945, Fax
(020) 6241721. E-mail info@jhm.nl.
Website www.jhm.nl. Open: 11–17.
Founded 1932. 3 rooms. 1–2 photo
exhibitions/year

Melkweg Galerie, Lijnbaansgracht 234a, NL-1017 PH Amsterdam. Tel (020) 5318181, Fax (020) 5318181. E-mail galerie-theater@melkweg.nl. Website www.melkweg.nl. Open: Wed–Sun 14–20 (free entry), 20–24 box-office. Director: Suzanne Dechert. Founded 1984. 2 rooms, 100 m². 11 photo exhibitions/year. Artists: Diana Blok, Erwin Olaf, Eugene Bavcar, Johan Vigeveno, Michel Szulc-Krzyzanowski, Laura Samsom, Gon Buurman, Cindy Marler, Martijn de Jonge, Christien Jaspars

Rijksmuseum, Dutch History, Stadhouderskade 42, NL-1070 DN Amsterdam. Tel (020) 47000, Fax (020) 47001. E-mail j.baruch@ rijksmuseum.nl. Website www. rijksmuseum.nl. Open: Mon–Sat 10–17, Sun 13–17. Director: P. J. Sigmond. Curator: J. Baruch. Founded 1885. 1 room, 300 m². 1 photo exhibition/year

Rijksmuseum, Print Room, Jan Luyckenstraat 1a, P. O. Box 74888, NL-1070 DN Amsterdam. Tel (020) 6747000, Fax (020) 6747001. E-mail m.boom@rijksmuseum.nl. Website www.rijksmuseum.nl. Open: Tue–Sat 10–17. Director: Dr. Peter Schatborn. Curators: Dr. Mattie Boom, Dr. Hans Rooseboom. Founded 1885. 1 room. 1 photo exhibition/year

SBK, Amsterdam Fine Arts Centre, Art Loan, Nieuwe Zydsvoorburgwal 325, NL-1012 RM Amsterdam. Tel (020) 6224018, Fax (020) 6224961. Open: Tue 11–21, Wed–Fri 11–17, Sat 9–17, first Sun/month 12–17. Director: P. Groot. Founded 1955. 3 rooms, 1,100 m². 1 photo exhibition/year

Stedelijk Museum Amsterdam, Paulus Potterstraat 13, NL-1070 AB Amsterdam. Tel (020) 5732911, Fax (020) 5752716. Website www.stedelijk.nl. Open: 11–17 (Oct–Mar), 11–19 (Apr–Sep). Director: Rudi H. Fuchs. Curator: Hripsimé Visser. Founded 1895. 47 rooms. 6–8 photo exhibitions/year

Stichting Fotoarchief Kees Scherer, Valeriusstraat 93, NL-1075 EP Amsterdam. Tel (020) 6793684. E-mail annick.visser@planet.nl

Torch Gallery, Lauriergracht 94, NL-1016 RN Amsterdam. Tel (020) 6260284, Fax (020) 6238892. Open: Thu+Fri+Sat 14–18 and by appointment. Director/curator: Adriaan van der Have. Founded 1984. 1 room, 140 m². 7 photo exhibitions/year. Artists: Henk Tas, Gerald van der Kaap, Teun Hocks, Anton Corbijn, Cor Dera, Wink van Kempen, Henk Elenga, Yuk Lin Tang, Inez van Lamsweerde, Alan David-Tu

Galerie Pennings, Geldropseweg 63, NL-5611 SE Eindhoven. Tel (040) 2120640, Fax (040) 2120640. E-mail galpen@iaehv.nl. Website www. iaehv.nl/users/galpen. Open: Wed– Sat 11–17. Director: Harry Pennings. Founded 1979. 1 room, 125 m². 6 photo exhibitions/year. Artists: Lili Almog, Ton Huybers, Hans Biezen, Betsy Green, José Ferrero Vilares, Phoebe Maas, Viviane Sassen, Lucia Radochonska, Patrick-Bailly-Maître Grand, Bernard Faucon, Hermann Försterling

Fotogalerie Objektief, Walstraat 33, NL-7511 GE Enschede. Tel (053) 4322507. Website www.go.to/ objektief. Open: Wed–Sat 13–17.30. Directors: Donny Scholten, Anna Pisula. Founded 1988. 1 room, 35 m². 10 photo exhibitions/year

Fotogalerie Lichtzone, Oude Kijk in 't Jatstraat 36, NL-9712 EK Groningen.

Tel (050) 5770139. Website www. lichtzone.nl. Open: Wed–Fri 13–18, Sat 12–17, Sun 13–17. Contact: Marco Tjassing. Artists: Ben Abma, Rudy Halm, Cecco, Heike Meyers, Menno Visser, Henny Stern, Stefan Strobl, Johan Rienska, Rein Paalman, Jan Bouwman

Groninger Museum, Museumeiland 1, NL-9711 ME Groningen. Tel (050) 3666555, Fax (050) 3120815. E-mail gronmus@inn.nl. Website www. groninger-museum.nl. Open: Tue–Sat 10–17, Sun 10–17. Director: Rein van der Lugt. Curator: Mark Wilson. Founded 1894. 20 rooms, 3,500 m². 2 photo exhibitions/year. Artists: Paul Blanca, Walter Dahn, Alan David-Tu, Barend van Herpe, Teun Hocks, Louis Jammes, Gerald van der Kaap, Anton Corbijn, Henk Tas, Peter Fischli & David Weiss

USVA Noorderlicht Fotogalerie, Munnekeholm 10, NL-9711 JA Groningen. Tel (050) 3182227, Fax (050) 3182204. E-mail photogallery@ noorderlicht.com. Website www. noorderlicht.com. Open: Mon–Fri 10– 21. Director: Ton Broekhuis. Curator: Wim Melis. Founded 1980. 1 room, 65 m². 7 photo exhibitions/year

Van, Hagestraat 18, NL-2011 CV Haarlem. Tel (023) 5334361. Open: by appointment only. Director: Piet van Leeuwen. Founded 1990. 1 room, 26 m². 3 photo exhibitions/year

Stadsgalery Heerlen, Museum of Con- temporary Art, Raadhuisplein 19, NL-6411 HK Heerlen. Tel (045) 5604449, Fax (045) 5717475. E-mail stadsgalery@heerlen.nl. Open: Tue– Fri 11–17, Sat–Sun 14–17. Director: Anke van der Laan. Founded 1986. 3 rooms, 80 running meters. 1 photo exhibition/year

Stelling Gallery, Kruisstraat 1b, NL- 2312 BH Leiden. Tel (071) 5127568, Fax (071) 5127568. Open: Thu–Sun 14–17 and by appointment. Director: Joyce de Gruiter. Curator: Peter Willemse. Founded 1982. 2 rooms, 200 m². 2 photo exhibitions/year. Artists: Nan Goldin, Weegee, David Byrne

Galerie Fotomania, Hoornbrekers- straat 22, NL-3011 CL Rotterdam. Tel (010) 4135055, Fax (010) 4132733. Open: Wed–Sun 12–17. Director: Robbert van Venetië. Curator: René van der Giessen. Founded 1985. 2 rooms, 150 m². 8 photo exhibitions/ year. Artists: Paul C. Bogaers, Wout Berger, Marjoleine Boonstra, Hans Aarsman, Fons Brasser, Mels van Zutphen, Wyn Geleynse, Ulay, Loodwicks Press Images, Aglaia Konrad

Galerie Kralingen, Gashouderstraat 9, NL-3061 EH Rotterdam. Tel (010) 4135454/2201818, Fax (010) 2200116. Open: Thu–Sat 14–19 and by appoint- ment. Directors: Georges Knap, Mi- cheline Nysten. Founded 1994. 3 rooms, 270 m². 2 photo exhibitions/ year. Artists: Hans Kok, Roswitha Freitag, Henny Maliangkay, Barbara Obst, Peter Badge, Inge Prokot, Annette Stranders, Marianne Klap- wijk, Dirk de Herder, Alain Garo

Kunsthal Rotterdam, Westzeedijk 341, NL-3015 AA Rotterdam. Tel (010) 4400345, Fax (010) 4367152. E-mail vansinderen@kunsthal.nl. Website www.Kunsthal.nl. Open: Tue–Sat 10–17, Sun 11–17. Director: Wim van Krimpen. Curator: Wim van Sinde- ren. Founded 1992. 7 rooms, 125 m² photogallery), 550 m² (printing cabi- net). 6–10 photo exhibitions/year. Artists: Germaine Krull, Alfred Stieg- litz, Dana Lixenberg, Tina Modotti, Leon Levenstein, Cas Oorthuys, Peter

Martens, Lord Snowdon, Martin Parr, Spencer Tunick

Museum Boijmans Van Beuningen, Museumpark 18–20, NL-3015 CX Rotterdam. Tel (010) 4419400, Fax (010) 4360500. E-mail info@boijmans.rotterdam.nl. Website www.boijmans.rotterdam.nl. Open: Tue–Sat 10–17, Sun 11–17. Director: C. Dercon. Curator: P. de Jonge. Founded 1847. 53 rooms, 6,750 m². 3 photo exhibitions/year. Artists: Dan Graham, Jeff Wall, Martin Kippenberger, Sharon Lockhart, Cindy Sherman, Louise Lawler, Rineke Dijkstra, Daan van Golden, Joep van Lieshout

Natural History Museum Rotterdam, Westzeedyk 345, NL-3015 AA Rotterdam. Tel (010) 4364222, Fax (010) 4364399. E-mail natuurmuseum@nmr.nl. Website www.nmr.nl. Open: Tue–Sat 10–17, Sun 11–17. Director: Dr. J. W. F. Reumer. Founded 1927. 6 rooms, 1,000 m². 1 photo exhibition/year

Nederlands Foto Instituut, The National Institute for Photography in the Netherlands, Witte de Withstraat 63, NL-3012 BN Rotterdam. Tel (010) 2132011, Fax (010) 4143465. E-mail info@nfi.nl. Website www.nfi.v2.nl. Open: Tue–Sun 11–17. Director: Loek C. B. van der Molen. Founded 1992. 3 rooms, 600 m². 10–15 photo exhibitions/year

Wereldmuseum Rotterdam, Willemskade 25, NL-3016 DM Rotterdam. Tel (010) 2707172, Fax (010) 2707182. Open: Tue–Fri 10–17, Sat–Sun 11–17. Director: H. Reedijk. Curator: Anneke Groeneveld. Founded 1885. 6 rooms, 4,000 m². 2 photo exhibitions/year

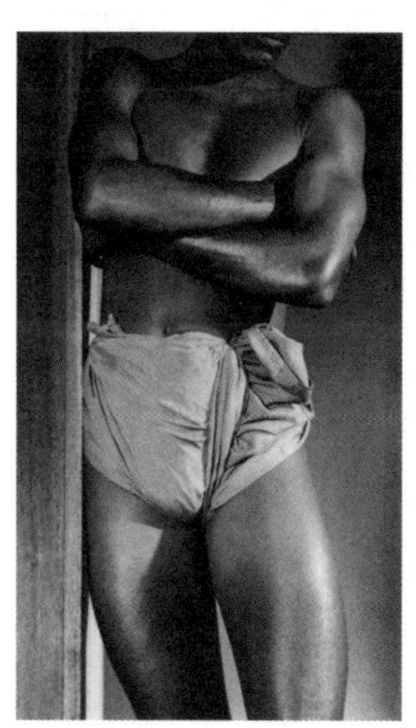

lionel wendt
ceylon 1900–1944
portrait c. 1937
brom-etching vintage print

artists in stock: alinari, anderson, arnoux, atget, baldus, barker, beato, bechard, bellmer, berssenbrugge, bisson frères, bonfils, bougault, bourne, braun, brogi, cameron, carjat, coburn, collard, curtis, d'ora, demanchy, disderi, drtikol, frith, giacomelli, green, hammerschmidt, hine, jackson, kertész, lehnert and landrock, lenormand, macpherson, mapplethorpe, misonne, molinier, muybridge, naya, negre, ninci, oorthuys, platt-lynes, sebah, sherman, sommer, taber, villers, von gloeden, watkins, wendt, woodbury and page

TON PEEK PHOTOGRAPHY

19th–20th century photographs
oudegracht 295 – 3511 pa utrecht

Witte de With, Center for Contemporary Art, Witte de Withstraat 50, NL-3012 BR Rotterdam. Tel (010) 4110144, Fax (010) 4117924. E-mail info@wdw.nl. Website www.wdw.nl. Open: Tue–Sun 11–18. Director: Barbera van Kooij. Founded 1990. 4 rooms, 1,250 m². 1–2 photo exhibitions/year

Stedelijk Museum, Het Domein, Kapittelstraat 6, NL-6130 AA Sittard. Tel (046) 4513460, Fax (046) 4529111. E-mail het.domein@wxs.nl. Website www.hetdomein.nl. Open: Tue–Sun 11–17. Director: Stijn Huijts. Founded 1993. 5 rooms, 800 m². 3 photo exhibitions/year

Ton Peek Photography, Oudegracht 295, NL-3511 PA Utrecht. Tel (030) 2312001, Fax (030) 2367898. E-mail tonpeek@xs4all.nl. Website www.xs4all.nl/~tonpeek. Open: Fri–Sat 12–17 and by appointment. Director: Ton Peek. Founded 1981. 1 room, 35 m². 3–4 photo exhibitions/year. Artists: Pierre Molinier, George Platt-Lynes, Adrien Bonfils, Eadweard Muybridge, Giuseppe Ninci, Carlo Brogi, Felice A. Beato, Lionel Wendt, André Kertész, Adolphe Braun

Herder-Museum, Fotohistorie en Moderne Kunst, Zijderveldselaan 58, NL-4122 GR Zijderveld. Tel (0345) 642601, Fax (070) 3838467. Open: Sat 11–16 (15 May – 15 Oct). Director: Dirk de Herder. Curator: L. v. d. Brink. Founded 1996. 1 room, 80 m². 2 photo exhibitions/year. Artists: Dirk de Herder, Harold Verhagen, Eric de Vries

Festivals & Fairs

Breda Fotografica, De Beyerd, Boschstraat 22, NL-4811 GH Breda. Tel (076) 5225025, Fax (076) 5223842

Fotobiënnale Enschede, P. O. Box 1355, NL-7500 BJ Enschede

Fotofestival Naarden, Utrechtsestraat 54b, NL-1017 VP Amsterdam. Tel (0299) 631634, Fax (0299) 631632. E-mail office@fotofestival.com. Website www.fotofestival.com

Fotografie Biënnale Rotterdam, Nederlands Foto Instituut, Witte de Withstraat 63, NL-3012 BN Rotterdam. Tel (010) 2132011, Fax (010) 4143465. E-mail nfi@nfi.v2.nl. Website www.nfi.v2.nl

KunstRAI, Europaplein, NL-1078 GZ Amsterdam. Tel (020) 5491212, Fax (020) 6464469

Noorderlicht Photofestival, Munnekeholm 10, NL-9711 JA Groningen. Tel (050) 3182227, Fax (050) 3182204. E-mail photofestival@ noorderlicht.com. Website www.noorderlicht.com

Magazines

Foto, Onafhankelijk maandblad voor beeld en techniek, Olmenlaan 6-E, P. O. Box 3, NL-3833 AV Leusden. Tel (033) 4947200, Fax (033) 4952251. E-mail foto.vof@tip.nl. Editor: Wim Broekman. Dutch. Founded 1946. Copy price: Fl 10.50. Annual subscription: Fl 98.00, 10 issues/year

Hollands Licht, W. G. Plein 753, NL-1054 Amsterdam. Tel (020) 6124627, Fax (020) 6125758. Dutch. Founded 1996. Copy price: Fl 10. Annual subscription: Fl 40, 4 issues/year

n o o r d e r l i c h t

ON THE EDGE OF PHOTOGRAPHY

Photography: that which tells stories about people and the world, about things and ideas, about art and its artists.

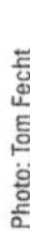

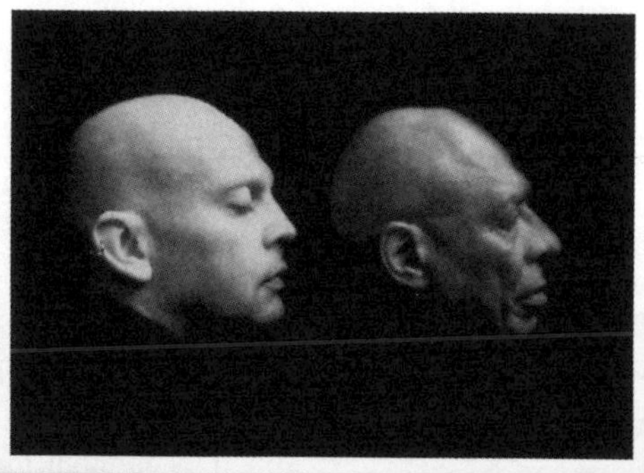

Running three organisations from one office, Noorderlicht ('Northern Lights') is the main center for photography in the Northern region of the Netherlands, and has been promoting the medium from 1980.

Our leading event is the annual Noorderlicht Photofestival which alternates between the Dutch cities Groningen and Leeuwarden, and includes an international main exhibition plus dozens of photography shows in galleries and museums.

Secondly, the USVA Noorderlicht Photogallery which features seven exhibitions each year, with artists ranging from local to international.

Lastly, Publisher Aurora Borealis which offers a portfolio of skillfully made photobooks and cd-roms.

http://www.noorderlicht.com

Visit Noorderlicht on the web and find thousands of webpages including images by hundreds of photographers. The website is updated continually with new information and keeps an archive of past events. To receive our monthly newsletter via email, please send a message to news@noorderlicht.com.

Munnekeholm 10 • 9711 JA Groningen • The Netherlands
tel +31 50 318 2227 • fax +31 50 318 2204 • email info@noorderlicht.com

Mediamatic, Willem Velthoven, P. O. Box 17490, NL-1001 JL Amsterdam. Tel (020) 6266262, Fax (020) 6263793. E-mail desk@mediamatic.nl. Website www.mediamatic.nl/. Editor: Jans Possel. Dutch/English

Metropolis M, Tijdschrift over Hedendaagse Kunst, P. O. Box 19263, NL-3501 DG Utrecht. Tel (030) 2342125, Fax (030) 2369161. E-mail metropol@euronet.nl. Editor: Let Geerling. Dutch. Founded 1979. Copy price: Fl 17.95. Annual subscription: Fl 92.50 (NL), Fl 122.50 (Europe), 6 issues/year

NFI news, Nederlands Foto Instituut, Witte de Withstraat 63, NL-3012 BN Rotterdam. Tel (010) 2132011, Fax (010) 4143465. E-mail info@nfi.nl. Website www.nfi.v2.nl. Editor: Loek van der Molen. Dutch/English

Nieuwsbrief Nederlands Fotogenootschap, 2e Schuystraat 135, NL-2517 Den Haag. Tel (070) 3647972, Fax (070) 3455969. E-mail josephine@joha.demon.nl. Editor: Josephine van Bennekom. Dutch. Founded 1992. Copy price: Fl 17.50. Annual subscription: Fl 60.00, 4 issues/year

P/F, Vakblad voor fotografie en imaging, P/F-Kunstbeeld v. o. f., P. O. Box 318, NL-2280 AH Ryswyk. Tel (070) 3941007, Fax (070) 3938382. E-mail info@profoto.nl. Website www.profoto.nl. Editor: Jan van der Schans. Dutch. Founded 1986. Copy price: Fl 16.50. Annual subscription: Fl 123.35, 9 issues/year

Book Publishers

Aurora Borealis, Munnekeholm 10, NL-9711 JA Groningen. Tel (050) 3182227, Fax (050) 3182204. E-mail aurora@noorderlicht.com. Website www.noorderlicht.com

BIS Publishers, Nieuwe Spiegelstraat 36, NL-1017 DG Amsterdam. Tel (020) 6205171, Fax (020) 6279251. E-mail bis@bispublishers.nl

Coen Sligting Bookimport, Van Oldenbarneveldstraat 77, NL-1052 JW Amsterdam. Tel (020) 6732280, Fax (020) 6640047. E-mail sligting@xs4all.nl

De Verbeelding, Sumatrakade 1425, NL-1019 RP Amsterdam. Tel (020) 4199143, Fax (020) 4195936. E-mail fred.verbeelding@planet.nl

Duo Duo, Mathenesserlaan 304, NL-3021 HW Rotterdam. Tel (010) 4778529

Focus Publishing BV, M. J. Kosterstraat 4, NL-1017 VX Amsterdam. Tel (020) 6264353, Fax (020) 6236049. E-mail focus@focusmagazine.nl. Website www.focusmedia.nl

Meulenhoff International, Herengracht 507, P. O. Box 100, NL-1000 AC Amsterdam. Tel (020) 5533500, Fax (020) 6258511

Paradox, P. O. Box 113, NL-1135 ZK Edam. Tel (0299) 315083, Fax (0299) 315082. E-mail server@paradox.nl. Website www.paradox.nl

Samenwerkende Uitgeverijen Prometheus en Bert Bakker, Herengracht 406, NL-1017 BX Amsterdam. Tel (020) 6241934, Fax (020) 6225461

SDU, P. O. Box 30446, NL-2500 EA Den Haag. Tel (070) 3429700, Fax (070) 3634903

Uitgeverij 010 Publishers, Watertorenweg 180, NL-3063 HA Rotterdam. Tel (010) 4333509, Fax (010) 4529825. E-mail office@

010publishers.nl. Website www.
010publishers.nl

Uitgeverij Voetnoot, Entrepotdok
60A, NL-1018 AD Amsterdam. Tel
(020) 6246129, Fax (020) 6206935.
E-mail voetnoot@knoware.nl

Bookshops

Antiquariat L. van Paddenburgh,
Diefsteeg 18, NL-2311 TS Leiden.
Tel (071) 5149805, Fax (071) 5149805.
E-mail padburgh@xs4all.nl. Website
www.antiqbook.nl/paddenburgh

Atheneum Boekhandel B. V., Spui
14–16, NL-1012 XA Amsterdam

Nijhof and Lee, Staalstraat 13a,
NL-1011 JK Amsterdam. Tel (020)
6203980, Fax (020) 6393294. E-mail
info@nijhoflee.nl. Website www.
nijhoflee.nl

Critics & Journalists

Dr. Josephine van Bennekom, 2e
Schuystraat 135, NL-2517 TL Den
Haag. Tel (070) 3647972, Fax (070)
3455969. E-mail josephine@joha.
demon.nl. *Nieuwsbrief Vereniging
Nederlands Fotogenootschap*, Rotterdam; *Foto*, Leusden

Flip Bool, 2e Schuytstraat 78, NL-2517
XH Den Haag. Tel (070) 3462420, Fax
(010) 2140375. E-mail bool@nfa.nl.
Website www.nfa.nl

Jan Coppens, Turfveldenstraat 30,
NL-5632 XJ Eindhoven. Tel (040)
2421252, Fax (040) 2927896. *Foto*,
Leusden

Rianne van Dijck, Noorder Ijdijk 91,
NL-1023 NT Amsterdam. Tel (020)
4904266, Fax (020) 4904266. E-mail
rianne@xs4all.nl. *AD-Magazine*,

Intermediair, Amsterdam; *Foto*,
Leusden

Leo Divendal, Hoofdweg 57-HS,
NL-1058 AX Amsterdam. Tel (020)
6120315, Fax (020) 6120315. E-mail
leo@divendal.demon.nl

Michael Gibbs, Overtoom 444, NL-
1054 JW Amsterdam. Tel (020)
6836665, Fax (020) 6181802

Dr. Frits Gierstberg, Abraham Kuy-
perlaan 82b, NL-3038 PN Rotterdam.
Tel (010) 4673440. Nederlands Foto
Instituut, Fotografie Biënnale,
Rotterdam

Jan Mattheus de Grauw, Oostzee-
dijk 6A, NL-3063 BB Rotterdam. Tel
(010) 4522625, Fax (010) 4522625.
Palet, Alkmaar; *Kunststof-Magazine
LOKV*, Utrecht; *Culture & Camp*,
Amsterdam

Jacqueline Hagman, Loenermark 157,
NL-1025 SN Amsterdam. Tel (020)
6322984/5732911, Fax (020) 5732789.
Website www.art.cwi.nl/stedelijk

Dr. Mariëtte Haveman, Achter de
Dom 14c, NL-3512 JP Utrecht

Herman Hoeneveld, Valeriusstraat 48,
NL-1071 MK Amsterdam. Tel (020)
6791230, Fax (020) 6756352. E-mail
hermanh@worldonline.nl. *Kunstbeeld,
P/F Professionele Fotografie, De Journalist*, Amsterdam

Eddie Marsman, Lage der A12–36,
NL-9718 BJ Groningen. Tel (050)
3186547, Fax (050) 3118650. E-mail
edmarsman@cs.com. *Foto*, Leusden;
NRC Handelsblad, Rotterdam

Pim Milo, Beethovenstraat 72/1, NL-
1077 Amsterdam. Tel (020) 6704444,
Fax (020) 6704447. E-mail pimmilo@
euronet.nl. *Credits*, Amsterdam; Foto-
Festival, Naarden

Philippe Moroux, Rijklof van Goens-straat 71, NL-2593 EG Hague. Tel (070) 3816014. E-mail philippe@ knoware.nl. Website www.come.to/ invitation

Dr. Linda Roodenburg, Claes de Vrieselaan 32b, NL-3021 JP Rotterdam. Tel (010) 4783324, Fax (010) 4783325. E-mail l.roodenburg@ planet.nl

Dr. Rik Suermondt, Jansveld 11a, NL-3512 BD Utrecht. Tel (030) 2334815, Fax (030) 2334815. E-mail suermond@ worldonline.nl. Website www.home-1.worldonline.nl/~suermond. *Vitrine,* Den Haag; *De Fotograaf,* Amsterdam; *Camera Austria,* Graz

Dr. M. G. Thijsen, International Photography Research (IPhoR), Ertskade 39, NL-1019 BB Amsterdam. Tel (020) 4194545, Fax (020) 4194546. E-mail mthijsen@xs4all.nl. *Foto,* Leusden; *Het Financieele Dagblad,* Amsterdam

Dr. Hripsimé Visser, Stedelijk Museum, P. O. Box 75082, NL-1070 AB Amsterdam. Tel (020) 5732911, Fax (020) 752716

Willem van Zoetendaal, Lijnbaansgracht 109, NL-1016 KT Amsterdam. Tel (020) 6249802, Fax (020) 4232197. E-mail basalt@knoware.nl

Hans Zonnevijlle, Steve Bikostraat 294, NL-3573 BH Utrecht. Tel (030) 2735904. E-mail hanzonnev@ knoware.nl. Nederlands Foto Instituut, Rotterdam

Schools & Workshops

A.K.I., Campus Universiteit Twente, Hallenweg 5, P. O. Box 1440, NL-7500 BK Enschede. Tel (053) 4824400/ 4824472, Fax (053) 4824463. E-mail post@aki.nl. Website www.aki.nl

Academie Minerva, Gedempte Zuiddiep 158, NL-9701 HN Groningen. Tel (050) 3666700, Fax (050) 3186083. E-mail academieminerva@ org.hanze.nl

Academie St. Joost, Beukenlaan 1, NL-4800 RA Breda. Tel (076) 5250302, Fax (076) 5250305. E-mail philippe@ knoware.nl. Website www.stjoost.nl

Academie voor Fotografie, Stoofsteeg 6zw, NL-2011 TE Haarlem. Tel (023) 315692, Fax (023) 5317194

Fotovakschool, Brinklaan 136, NL-7311 JE Apeldoorn. Tel (055) 5216722, Fax (055) 5225812

Gerrit Rietveld Academie, Fred. Roeskenstraat 96, NL-1076 ED Amsterdam. Tel (020) 6731869

Hogeschool voor de Kunsten, Onderlangs 9, NL-6812 CE Arnhem. Tel (026) 3535635, Fax (026) 3535677

Hogeschool voor de Kunsten, Ina Boudier-Bakkerlaan 50, NL-3582 VA Utrecht

Kon. Academie van B. K., Prinsessegracht 4, NL-2514 AN Den Haag. Tel (070) 3154777, Fax (070) 3154778. E-mail post@kabk.nl. Website www. kabk.nl

Kon. Academie voor Kunst en Vormgeving, Sportlaan 56, NL-5223 AZ Den Bosch

MTS voor Fotografie en Fotonica, Tarwekamp 3, NL-1592 XG Den Haag

Opleiding Restauratoren, Gabriel Metsustraat 8, NL-9071 AC Amsterdam. Tel (020) 6767933, Fax (020) 6755191

Rijksuniversiteit Leiden, Studie en Documentatiecentrum voor Fotografie, Rapenburg 65, NL-2311 GJ Leiden. Tel (071) 5272795, Fax (071) 5272615. E-mail fotohist@leiden. univ.nl

SKVR Foto- en Videoschool, Endrachstraat 12a, NL-3012 XL Rotterdam. Tel (010) 4334051, Fax (010) 4143281. E-mail tcoolsma@knoware.nl. Website www.skvr.nl

Willem de Kooning Academie, Blaak 10, NL-3011 TA Rotterdam. Tel (010) 2414750, Fax (010) 2414751. E-mail a.g.lagendaal@hro.nl. Website www. wdka.hro.nl

Associations

Chicago Albumen Works Nederland, Witte de Withstraat 63, NL-3012 BN Rotterdam. Tel (010) 2331696, Fax (010) 2331965

GKf, W. G. Plein 753, NL-1054 SK Amsterdam. Tel (020) 6124627, Fax (020) 6125758

Hollandse Hoogte, P. O. Box 14658, NL-1001 LD Amsterdam. Tel (020) 5306070, Fax (020) 6203729. E-mail info@hollandse-hoogte.nl. Website www.hollandse-hoogte.nl

International Photography Research (IPhoR), Ertskade 39, NL-1019 BB Amsterdam

Milton Guran Fundation, 2nd Schuytstraat 135, NL-2517 TL Den Haag. Tel (070) 3450675, Fax (070) 3455969

Nederlands Foto Instituut, The National Institute for Photography in the Netherlands, Witte de Withstraat 63, NL-3012 BN Rotterdam. Tel (010) 2132011, Fax (010) 4143465. E-mail info@nfi.nl. Website www. nfi.nl

Stichting Fotoconservering, Hans de Herder, 2nd Schuytstraat 135, NL-2517 TL Den Haag. Tel (070) 3450675, Fax (070) 3455969

Stichting NF&GC/Spaarnestad Foto-archief, P. O. Box 3118, NL-2001 DC Haarlem. Tel (023) 5323181/5329034, Fax (023) 5323311

V2 Centre for Art and Media Technology, Eendrachtsstraat 10, NL-3012 XL Rotterdam. Tel (010) 2067272, Fax (010) 2067271. E-mail alex@v2.nl. Website www.v2.nl

Vereniging Nederlands Fotogenootschap, W. de Koning Gans p/a Haags Gemcertearchief, Spui 70, NL-2511 BT Den Haag. Tel (070) 3537025, Fax (070) 3537010

World Press Photo, Van Baerlestraat 144, NL-1071 ZD Amsterdam. Tel (020) 6766096, Fax (020) 6764471. E-mail office@worldpressphoto.nl. Website www.worldpressphoto.nl

Grants & Awards

Apexchanges. Contact: Apex Changes, Apex Coordinator, Jan van Goyenkade 5, NL-1075 HN Amsterdam. Tel (020) 6760222, Fax (020) 6752231. E-mail apexchanges@eurocult.org. Website www.eurocult.org

Capi-Lux Alblas Prijs, to recognize a Dutch photographer or image-maker who uses the "still" as a characteristic tool, no application, video portrait of the artist, every year. Contact: Capi-Lux Alblas Stichting, Capi-Lux Vak, P. O. Box 8189, NL-1005 AD Amsterdam. Tel (020) 5858585, Fax (020) 5858390

Dunhill Distinction, to recognize a person/institution who/which has furthered good service to Dutch photography, no application, a monetary prize and an art work, every year. Contact: Stichting Dutch Photography, Weesperzijde 86, NL-1091 EK Amsterdam. Tel (020) 6630331, Fax (020) 6630646

Fotojaarprijs "Het ABC van het Bedrijfsleven", a contest for professional Dutch photographers who send in work on a different subjects every year. The themes refer to Dutch business. Professional Dutch photographers who reside in Holland can participate, Fl 10,000, every year. Contact: Fotojaarprijs/Het ABC van het Bedrijfsleven, P. O. Box 190, NL-2000 AD Haarlem. Tel (023) 5533533. E-mail abcgids@pi.net. Website www.abc_d.nl

Foto Kees Scherer Prijs, for the best Dutch photo book, open to Dutch photographers and their publishers, Fl 10,000, exhibition, every two years. Contact: Stichting Fotoarchief Kees Scherer, Valeriusstraat 93, NL-1075 EP Amsterdam. Tel (020) 6793684. E-mail annick.visser@planet.nl

Incentive Prize for Photographers, for a young photographer or for an established photographer who is taking a new direction in his/her work, photographers living and working in the Netherlands, Fl 5,000, every two years. Contact: Stichting Amsterdams Fonds voor de Kunst, Stadhuis, kamer 1296, Amstel 1, NL-1011 PN Amsterdam. Tel (020) 5522416

Maria Austria Prijs, to recognize outstanding recent photography, photographers living and working in the Netherlands, Fl 10,000, press release, every two years. Contact: Stichting Amsterdams Fonds voor de Kunst, Stadhuis, kamer 1296, Amstel 1, NL-1011 PN Amsterdam. Tel (020) 5522416

Oeuvreprijs (Prize for a body of work), to recognize established visual artists, designers and architects, Dutch nationals, Fl 50,000, exhibition, every two years. Contact: Fonds voor Beeldende Kunsten, Vormgeving en Bouwkunst, P. O. Box 773, NL-1000 AT Amsterdam. Tel (020) 5231523, Fax (020) 5231541. E-mail post@ fondsbkvb.nl. Website www. fondsbkvb.nl

Prix de Rome, for visual artists, artists below the age of 36, living for two years in Holland, 1st prize Fl 40,000, 2nd prize Fl 20,000, base prize Fl 10,000, every year. Contact: Prix de Rome, Rijksakademie van Beeldende Kunsten, Sarphatistraat 112, NL-1018 GW Amsterdam. Tel (020) 5270300, Fax (020) 5270301. E-mail prix@ rijksakademie.nl. Website www. rijksakademie.nl

World Press Photo of the Year and Golden Eye Awards, to recognize the best press photos of the year, no application, Fl 15,000 for World Press Photo of the Year, Fl 2,500 for Golden Eye Awards, group exhibition and catalog for every winner, every year. Contact: World Press Photo Foundation, Jacob Obrechtstraat 26, NL-1071 KM Amsterdam. Tel (020) 6766096, Fax (020) 6764471. E-mail office@worldpressphoto.nl

New Media

International Audio Visual Experimental Festival AVEcom.nl, GBK, Beekstraat 7, NL-6811 DV Arnhem. Tel (020) 6237101, Fax (026) 6244423. E-mail gbkunstenaars@compuserve. com. Website www.avecom.nl

Montevideo, Media Art Institute,
MonteVideo/TBA, Keizersgracht 264,
NL-1016 EV Amsterdam. Tel (020)
6237101, Fax (020) 6244423. E-mail
info@montevideo.nl. Website www.
montevideo.nl

Open Electronic Annual Festival,
Cyberlag Foundation, Munnekeholm
10, NL-9711 JA Groningen. Tel (050)
3637513, Fax (050) 3632209. E-mail
usva-th1@bureau.rug.nl, pianodeun@
hotmail.com. Website www.
cyberslag.com

The one minutes, Videos no longer
than one minute, Sandberg Instituut,
Generaal Vetterstraat 76, NL-1059
BW Amsterdam. Tel (020) 5882400,
Fax (020) 5882401. E-mail 1minute@
sandberg.nl. Website www.sandberg.
nl/1minute

World Wide Video Festival, Marnix-
straat 411, NL-1017 PJ Amsterdam.
Tel (020) 4707729, Fax (020) 4213828.
E-mail wwvf@wwvf.demon.nl.
Website www.wwvf.nl

Norway

Population: 4.4 million
Capital: Oslo, 500,000
Currency: Krone (Kr)
International code: ++47
Tourist information:
Nortra, P. O. Box 2893 Solli,
Drammensveien 40,
N-0230 Oslo

Galleries & Museums

Henie-Onstad Art Center, Sonja
Henies V. 31, N-1311 Hövikodden.
Tel 67543050, Fax 67543270. Website
www.hok.no. Open: Tue–Thu 10–21,
Fri–Mon 11–18. Director: Gavin
Jantjes. Founded 1968. 6 rooms,
2,000 m². 2–3 photo exhibitions/
year

Norsk Museum for Fotografi, Preus
Fotomuseum, Nedre vei 8, N-3192
Horten. Tel 33031630, Fax 33031640.
E-mail post@foto.museum.no. Direc-
tor: Oivind Storm Bjerke. Founded
1995

Fotogalleriet, Kongensg. 9, N-0153
Oslo 1. Tel 47424924, Fax 47424209.
E-mail fg@fotogallenet.no. Open:
Tue–Fri 12–17, Sat 11–15, Sun 12–16.
Director/curator: Ole John Aandal.
Founded 1977. 2 rooms, 120 m².
8 photo exhibitions/year. Artists:
artists of the Norwegian Association
of Fine Art Photographers

Magazines

Norsk Fotografiske Tidsskrift, Bettum
Gaard, N-3178 Vaale. Tel 33060916,
Fax 33060707. E-mail knut.evensen@
inter-view.no. Editor: Knut Evensen.
Norwegian. Founded 1914. Copy
price: Kr 59.00. Annual subscription:
Kr 350.00, Nok 375.00 (outside Nor-
way)

Critics & Journalists

Kristin Aasbø, P. O. Box 278, N-8601
Mo. Tel 75121202, Fax 75155460.
E-mail kristin.aasbo@nbr.no. Website
www.nbr.no/galnor/. National
Library, Rana; Sound and Image
Archive, Mo

Eva Klerck Gange, Kyrresv. 26, N-1320
Stabekk. Tel 67121671, Fax 67121671

Prof. Robert Meyer, The Robert
Meyer Collection, Wesselsg. 3b,
N-5006 Bergen. Tel 55310793, Fax
55310793

Prof. Jamie Parslow, Strømg. 1,
N-5015 Bergen. Tel 55312214, Fax
55326756. Website www.samson.
shkd.no

Lotte Sandberg, Neubergg. 4b,
N-0367 Oslo. Tel 22558120

Schools & Workshops

Fredrikstad Videregående Skole,
N-1601 Fredrikstad

Kunsthøgskolen i Bergen, Strømg. 1,
N-5015 Bergen. Tel 55587300, Fax
55587310. E-mail khib@khib.no.
Website www.khib.no

Sogn Videregående Skole, Fotolinjen,
Sognsv. 80, N-0855 Oslo 8

Statens Kunstakademie, St. Olavsg.
32, N-0166 Oslo 1

Strømmen Videregående Skole,
N-2011 Strømmen

Trondheim Videregående Skole,
N-7000 Trondheim

Associations

Forbundet Frie Fotografer, Kongensg.
9, N-0102 Oslo. Tel 22335981, Fax
22424209. E-mail fff@fotogalleriet.no.
Website www.fotogalleriet.no

Norges Fotografforbund, Kirsten
Stokmo, P. O. Box 250, N-9000
Tromsø

Norges Kunstnerråd, P. O. Box 643 –
Sentrum, N-0106 Oslo. Tel 22478040,
Fax 22424040. E-mail kunstner@
raadet.filmenshus.no. Website
www.filmenshus.no/kunstner/

New Media

Per Plexis, Alternative Bergen Short
Film/Video Festival, Mediaverkste-
det i Bergen, Georgernes Verft 2B,
N-5011 Bergen. Tel 55901097, Fax
55901097

Poland

Population: 38.6 million
Capital: Warsaw, 1.6 million
Currency: Zloty (Zl or PLN)
International code: ++48
Tourist information:
Urzad Kultury Fizycznej i
Turystyki, ul. Swietokrzyska
12, PL-00-916 Warszawa

Galleries & Museums

Galeria Fotografii B&B, Gallery of
Photography B & B, ul. Mickiewicza
24, PL-43-300 Bielsko-Biala. Tel (033)
8123488, Fax (033) 8140955. Open:
Tue–Sun 9–17 (winter), 10–17
(summer). Contact: Inez & Andrzej
Baturo, Boguslawa Kubieniec. Founded 1992. 1 room, 50 m². 12 photo
exhibitions/year. Artists: Tomasz
Sikora, Danuta Rago, Tadeusz Rolke,
Rafal Szopa, Tomas Sikora, Polish
Press Photography, Krzysztof Gieraltowski

**Gdanska Galeria Fotografii – Mu-
zeum Narodowe Gdansk,** Gdansk
Gallery of Photography – National
Muzeum, Gdansk, ul. Grobla I 3/5 ,
PL-80-834 Gdansk. Tel (058) 3017147,
Fax (058) 3011125. E-mail ller@box43.
gnet.pl. Website www.muzeum.
narodowe.gda.pl/html/galeria.html.
Open: Tue–Fri 11–13.30,14–17, Sat–
Sun 11–16. Contact: Stefan Figlaro-
wicz. Founded 1977. 1 room. 50 m².
10–11 photo exhibitions/year. Artists:
Wojciech Buyko, Kestutis Stoszkus,
Jerzy Lewczynski, Tomasz Zerek,
Zygmunt Wrzesniowski, Janusz
Uklejewski, Stefan Figlarowicz

Mala Galeria, Small Gallery, ul.
Chrobrego 4, PL-66-400 Gorzów
Wielkopolski. Tel (095) 72228532.
Open: Tue–Sun 10–18. Contact:
Marian Lazarski. Founded 1972.
1 room, 40 m². 3–4 photo exhibi-
tions/year. Artists: Marian Lazarski,
Grzegorz Przyborek, Leszek Weso-
lowski

Biuro Wystaw Artystycznych, Office
of Art Exhibitions, ul. Dluga 1, PL-
58-500 Jelenia Gora. Tel (075) 7526669,
Fax (075) 76751 32. Open: Tue–Fri
11–18, Sat–Sun 11–15. Contact: Janina
Hobgarska. Founded 1976. 2 rooms,
150m². 3–7 photo exhibitions/year.
Artists: Waldemar Wydmuch, Izabella Gustowska, Natalia LL, Krzysztof Cichosz, Wojciech Prazmowski,
Grzegorz Przyborek, Jozef Robakowski, Krzysztof Wojciechowski, Ewa
Andrzejewska, Andrzej Lech, Bogdan
Konopka

Galeria Korytarz RCK, Corridor Gallery RCK, ul. Bankowa 28/30, PL-
58-500 Jelenia Gora. Tel (075) 7526918,
Fax (075) 7526918. Open: Mon–Fri
11–18. Contact: Ewa Andrzejewska,
Wojciech Zawadzki. Founded 1990.
1 room, 50 m². 10–12 photo exhibi-
tions/year. Artists: Janusz Nowacki,
Slawomir Tobis, Piotr Komorowski,
Ewa Andrzejewska, Marek Szyryk,
Marek Likszet

Galeria Pusta, Pusta Gallery, Gornos-
laskie Centrum Kultury, pl. Sejmu
Slaskiego 2, PL-40-032 Katowice.
Tel (032) 2553806, Fax (032) 2517925.
E-mail pusta@gck.org.pl. Open: Tue–
Sun 11–18. Contact: Jakub Byrczek.
Founded 1984. 1 room, 140 m². 10–16
photo exhibitions/year. Artists: Zofia
Rydet, Aleksander Balicki, Malwina
Wieczorek, Jan Reich, Jaroslav Benes,

Natalia LL, Andrzej Lech, Grzegorz Przyborek, Krzysztof Cichosz

Galeria Sztuki KOK, Art Gallery KOK, Klodzki Osrodek Kultury, pl. Jagielly 1, PL-57-300 Klodzko. Tel (074) 8673501, Fax (074) 8673364. E-mail kok@netgate.com.pl. Website www.netgate.com.pl/kok. Contact: Boguslaw Michnik. Founded 1975. 2 rooms, 110 m². 9–10 photo exhibitions/year. Artists: Jerzy Olek, Naoya Yoshikawa, Akira Komoto, Magdalena Poprawska

Miedzynarodowe Centrum Kultury, International Center of Culture, Rynek Glowny 25, PL-31-008 Kraków. Tel (012) 4218601, Fax (012) 4218571. Open: Tue–Sun 11–17. Contact: Bogna Dziechciaruk. 3 rooms, 200 m². Founded 1991. 1–2 photo exhibitions/year

Muzeum Historii Fotografii, Museum of the History of Photography, Józefitów 16, PL-30-045 Kraków. Tel (012) 6345932, Fax (012) 6330637. E-mail foto@mhf.krakow.pl. Website www.mhf.krakow.pl. Open: Tue 12–17.30, Wed–Sun 10–15.30. Contact: Marek Lomnicki. Founded 1987. 8 rooms, 200 m². 10 photo exhibitions/year. Artists: Edward Hartwig, Jerzy Lewczynski, Erich Lessing, Terence Wright, August Sander, Zbigniew Lagocki, Waldemar Jama, Cecil Beaton

Galeria FF – Forum Fotografii, Gallery FF – Forum of Photography, Lodzki Dom Kultury, ul. Traugutta 18, PL-90-113 Lodz. Tel (042) 6337115/ 6339800/6337115, Fax (042) 6337096. E-mail galeriaff@infocentrum.com. Website www.galeriaff.infocentrum. com. Open: Tue–Sat 14–18. Contact: Krzysztof Cichosz. Founded 1983. 1 room, 70 m². 10–12 photo exhibitions/year. Artists: Zbigniew

Tomaszczuk, Witold Wegrzyn, Jerzy Wronski, Józef Robakowski, Jirí Šigut, Antoni Mikolajczyk, Dan Biferie, Jaroslaw Bartolowicz, Grzegorz Przyborek

Galeria Wymiany, Exchange Gallery, al. J. Pilsudskiego 7/29, PL-90-307 Lodz. Tel (042) 6363092, Fax (042) 6363092. E-mail konopka@mailcity. com. Open: by appointment only. Contact: Jozef Robakowski, Barbara Konopka. Founded 1978. 1 room, 40 m². Artists: Zbigniew Pronaszko, Henryk Stazewski, Stefan Themerson, Witkacy, Ryszard Winiarski, Stefan Wegner, Sharits, Jadwiga Sawicka

Muzeum Sztuki, Museum of Fine Art, ul. Wieckowskiego 36, PL-90-734 Lodz. Tel (042) 6339790, Fax (042) 6329941. E-mail museumct@krysia. uni.lodz.pl. Open: Tue 10–17, Thu 12–19, Wed+Fri 11–17, Sat–Sun 10–16. Curator: Dr. Krzysztof Jurecki. Founded 1930. 30 rooms. 2–4 photo exhibitions/year. Artists: Stanislaw Ignacy Witkiewicz, Turid Olsen, Aleksander Krzywoblocki, Stefan Themerson, Stefan Wojnecki, Zygmunt Rytka, Slawomir Kubala, Agnieszka Barkowska, Malene Pedersen

Galeria Biala, White Gallery, Centrum Kultury, ul. Peowiakow 12, PL-20-007 Lublin. Tel (081) 5325340, Fax (081) 5328700. E-mail ck@ck.lublin.pl. Contact: Irena Nawrot. 2 rooms, 70 m². 2–4 photo exhibitions/year. Artists: Hanna Luczak, Irena Nawrot, Katarzyna Korzeniecka, Boaz Tal

Galeria "Prezentacje" – Foto-Medium-Art Zamek Wojnowice, Gallery "Presentation" – Foto-Medium-Art, Wojnowice Castle, PL-55-334 Mrozow. Tel (071) 3170726, Fax (071) 3170726. Open: Mon–Sun 10–19. Contact: Franciszek Oborski, Jerzy Olek.

Founded 1991. 3–4 photo exhibitions/year. Artists: Janusz Oleksa, Yaning Hedel, Zbigniew Dlubak, Jacek Lalak

Centum Kultury "Zamek", Cultural Center "Castle", ul. Sw. Marcin 80/82, PL-61-809 Poznan. Tel (061) 8536081 ext. 130, Fax (061) 8520503. Open: Mon–Sat 12–20. Contact: Janusz Nowacki. 2–3 rooms, 480 m². 2–4 photo exhibitions/year. Artists: Ryszard Horowitz, László Moholy-Nagy, Jan Saudek, Andrzej Florkowski, Leszek Szurkowski, Students of Silesian University in Opava, World Press Photo, National Geographic

Galeria Fotografii "pf", Gallery of Photography "pf", ul. Sw. Marcin 80/82 , PL-61-809 Poznan. Tel (061) 8536081 ext. 130, Fax (061) 8520503. E-mail sekretariat@zamek.poznan.pl. Open: Mon–Sat 11–18. Contact: Janusz Nowacki. Founded 1994. 1 room, 75 m². 12 photo exhibitions/year. Artists: Irene Torebiarte, Bogdan Konopka, Erich Salomon, August Sander, Ewa Rubinstein, Edward Hartwig

Galeria Miejska "Arsenal", Municipal Gallery "Arsenal", ul. Stary Rynek, PL-61-772 Poznan. Tel (061) 8529501-2, Fax (061) 8529501. E-mail office@arsenal.info.poznan.pl. Website www.arsenal.info.poznan.pl. Open: Tue–Sun 11–18. Contact: Wojciech Makowiecki. Founded 1949. 2 rooms, 200 m². 3–4 photo exhibitions/year. Artists: Izabella Gustowska, Stefan Wojnecki, Grzegorz Sztabinski, Natalia LL, Jan Berdyszak, Zofia Kulik, Fortunata Obrapalska, Rafal Drozdowski

Muzeum Narodowe, Poznan, National Museum, Poznan, Al. Marcinkowskiego 9, PL-61-745 Poznan. Tel (061) 8568134/8568000, Fax (061) 8512898/8515898. E-mail mnoffice@man.poznan.pl. Open: Tue 10–18, Wed+Fri 9–17, Thu+Sat 10–16, Sun 11–15. Contact: Wlodzimierz Nowaczyk. Several rooms. Founded 1903. 3–4 photo exhibitions/year. Artists: Izabella Gustowska, Stefan Wojnecki, Zofia Kulik, Jaroslaw Kozlowski, Poznan Photography ZPAF

Panstwowa Galeria Sztuki, State Gallery of Fine Art, Powstancow Warszawy 2-6, PL-81-718 Sopot. Tel (058) 5513261. E-mail sopotpgs@polbox.com. Open: Tue–Sun 11–18. Contact: Zbigniew Buski. Founded 1954. 3 rooms, 1,080 m². 2–3 photo exhibitions/year. Artists: Wojciech Prazmowski, Jerzy Hejber, Hanns Karlewski

Galeria Fotografii "PA-Camera", Regionalny Osrodek Kultury i Sztuki, ul. Noniewicza 71, PL-16-400 Suwalki. Tel (087) 5664211/5664934

Klub 13 Muz, Club of 13 Muses, pl. Zolnierza Polskiego 2, PL-70-551 Szczecin. Tel (091) 4347173, Fax (091) 4347173. Contact: Krystyna Lyczywek. 3 rooms, 120 m². 5 photo exhibitions/year. Artists: Ozawa Toshiki, Krystyna Lyczywek, Anna Pisula-Mandziej, Czeslaw Czaplinski

Mala Galeria Fotografiki ZPAF, Small Gallery of Photography ZPAF, ul. Podmurna 5, PL-87-100 Torun. Tel (056) 6225094, Fax (056) 6226298. Open: Wed–Sun 10–18 (summer), 10–17 (winter). Contact: Jerzy Wadak. Founded 1980. 1 room, 45 m². 10–12 photo exhibitions/year. Artists: Zbigniew Lagocki, Edward Hartwig, Pawel Pierscinski

Biblioteka Narodowa, National Library, Dzial Ikonografii, pl. Krasinskich 5, PL-00-973 Warszawa. Tel (022) 5313241-5, Fax (022) 6354498.

Open: Tue–Sun 11–18. Contact: Alicja Zendara. Founded 1928. 2 rooms, 300 m². 3 photo exhibitions/year

Centrum Sztuki Wspolczesnej "Zamek Ujazdowski", Center for Contemporary Art "Ujazdowski Castle", Al. Ujazdowskie 6, PL-00-461 Warszawa. Tel (022) 6281271-3, Fax (022) 6289550. E-mail csw@art.pl. Website www.csw.art.pl. Open: Tue–Sun 11–17. Contact: Marek Grygiel. Founded 1990. 20 rooms, 3,000 m². 6–10 photo exhibitions/year. Artists: Annie Leibovitz, Tomek Sikora, Jirí David, Wojciech Prazmowski, Hannah Collins, Andres Serrano, Zbigniew Dlubak

Galeria Abakus, Abakus Gallery, Stoleczne Centrum Edukacji Kulturalnej, ul. Jezuicka 4, PL-00-277 Warszawa. Tel (022) 5313762, Fax (022) 5313335. Founded 1990. 3 rooms, 100 m²

Galeria Goethe Institut, Goethe Institut Gallery, Plac Defilad 1, PL-00-901 Warszawa. Tel (022) 6566044/6566050. Contact: Dorota Swinarska. 3 photo exhibitions/year

Galeria/Studio Gieraltowskiego, Gallery/Studio of Krzysztof Gieraltowski, ul. Dzielna 1 m. 15a, PL-00-162 Warszawa. Tel (022) 8397123/6186314, Fax (022) 6358181. E-mail galeria-studio@gieraltowski-foto.com.pl. Website www.gieraltowski-foto.com.pl. Open: Fri–Mon 13–19 and by appointment. Founded 1996. 2 rooms, 66 m². Artists: Krzysztof Gieraltowski, Wiktor Wolkow, Stanislaw J. Woš, Zbigniew Furman, Stanislav Woš, Bogdan Krezel

Mala Galeria ZPAF – CSW, Mala Gallery of the Union of Polish Art Photographers and the Center for Conterporary Art, Plac Zamkowy 8, PL-00-277 Warszawa. Tel (022) 8312339, Fax (022) 8310386. E-mail marekg@csw.art.pl. Website www.fototapeta.art.pl. Open: Tue–Sun 12–18. Contact: Marek Grygiel. Founded 1977. 1 room, 42 m². 13–16 photo exhibitions/year. Artists: Edward Hartwig, Janusz Szczucki, Slawomir Kubala, Zbigniew Dlubak, Zygmunt Rytka, Jozef Robakowski, Pawel Kwiek, Josef Moucha, Allan Ginsberg

Panstwowa Galeria Sztuki "Zacheta", State Gallery of Fine Art "Zacheta", Plac Malachowskiego 3, PL-00-916 Warszawa. Tel (022) 8275854, Fax (022) 8277886. E-mail office@zacheta_gallery.waw.pl. Website www.zacheta_gallery.waw.pl. 2–3 photo exhibitions/year. Artists: Ryszard Horowitz, Edward Hartwig, Zofia Kulik, Roman Cieslewicz

Stara Galeria ZPAF, Old Gallery of the Union of Polish Art Photographers, Plac Zamkowy 8, PL-00-277 Warszawa. Tel (022) 8310386/8312339/6354783, Fax (022) 8310386. Open: Mon–Sun 10–18. Contact: Danuta Rago. Founded 1970. 3 rooms, 200 m². 20 photo exhibitions/year. Artists: Elliott Erwitt, Edward Hartwig, Chris Niedenthal, Janusz Kobylinski, Danuta Rago, Zbyszko Siemaszko, Tomasz Tomaszewski, Vladimír Birgus, Adam Bujak, Bill Brandt

Biuro Wystaw Artystycznych, Office of Art Exhibitions, ul. Wita Stwosza 32, PL-50-149 Wroclaw. Tel (071) 3441056, Fax (071) 3441056. Open: Tue–Sun 10–18. Contact: Wojciech Stefanik. Founded 1957. 9 rooms, 500 m². 4–5 photo exhibitions/year. Artists: Marek Pozniak, Tina Bara, Jiri Šigut, Natalia LL, Peter Mackerich

Dolnoslaskie Centrum Fotografii, Silesian Center of Photography, Plac Biskupa Nankiera 8, PL-50-140 Wroclaw. Tel (071) 3447840, Fax (071)

3447840. Open: Tue–Sun 10–18. Contact: Jan Bortkiewicz. Founded 1970. 3 rooms, 200 m². 6–8 photo exhibitions/year. Artists: Jeanloup Sieff, Edward Hartwig, Josef Beuys, Günter Grass

Galeria Entropia, Entropia Gallery, Rzeznicza 4, PL-50-129 Wroclaw. Tel (071) 3444634, Fax (071) 3444634. E-mail entropia@entropia. wroclaw.art.pl. Website www. entropia.wroclaw.art.pl/. Open: Mon–Fri 13–18. Contact: Mariusz Jodko. 1 room, 40 m². 3–4 photo exhibitions/year. Artists: László Moholy-Nagy, Tadeusz Parcej, Piotr Komorowski

Galeria Fotografii WTF, Photography Gallery WTF, ul. Wlodkowicza 31, PL-50-950 Wrolaw. Tel (071) 3445792. Open: Tue+Thu 16–18, Sat–Sun 10–16. Contact: Zbigniew Stoklosa. Founded 1986. 1 room, 40 m². 12 photo exhibitions/year

Galeria "W Podziemiu" – Foto-Medium-Art, Gallery "In Underground" – Foto-Medium-Art, Dom Aukcyjny ul. Mikolaja, PL-50-125 Wroclaw. Tel (071) 3429677. Contact: Grazyna Horszowska. 2–3 photo exhibitions/year. Artists: Zbigniew Dlubak, Gottfried Jäger, Zdzislaw Jurkiewicz, Witold Wegrzyn, Witold Liszkowski

Muzeum Narodowe Wroclaw, National Museum Wroclaw, Plac Powstancow Warszawy 5, PL-50-153 Wroclaw. Tel (071) 3438830, Fax (071) 3435643. E-mail muzeumnarodowe@ wr.onet.pl. Website www.rej.com.pl/ m_narodowe. Open: Tue–Sun 10–16, Thu 9–16. Curator: Adam Sobota. Founded 1963. 7 rooms, 300 m². 2–3 photo exhibitions/year. Artists: Hermann Krone, Zofia Rydet, Franciszek Groer, Natalia LL, Stefan Arczynski, Zbigniew Staniewski, Wojciech Zawadzki

Festivals & Fairs

Biennale Fotografii Górskiej, Biennial of Mountain Photography, Regionalne Centrum Kultury, ul. Bankowa 28/30, PL-58-500 Jelenia Góra

Biennale Fotografii Polskiej, Biennial of Polish Photography, Galeria Miejska Arsenal, Stary Rynek, PL-61-772 Poznan. Tel (061) 8529501-2, Fax (061) 8529501. E-mail office@ arsenal.info.poznan.pl

Konfrontacje Fotograficzne Gorzów, Photographic Confrontation Festival Gorzów, Gorzowskie Towarzystwo Fotograficzne & Zwiazek Polskich Artystow Fotografikow, ul. Chrobrego 4, PL-66-400 Gorzow. Tel (095) 7228532, Fax (095) 7228532

Konkurs Polskiej Fotografii Prasowej, Warszawa, Competition of Polish Press Photography, Warszawa, Andrzej Zygmuntowicz. Tel (022) 8390613, Fax (022) 8390613

Miedzynarodowe Spotkania Fotograficzne "Profile" Skoki, International Photographic Meeting "Profiles" Skoki, Academy of Fine Art, Al. Marcinkowskiego 29, PL-60-967 Poznan. Tel (061) 8552521, Fax (061) 8522309. E-mail fotografia@asp. poznan.pl

Magazines

Dagerotyp, Stowarzyszenie Historii Fotografii, ul. Dluga 26, PL-00-950 Warszawa. Tel (022) 8313149/ 8313271, Fax (022) 8318056. Editor: Dr. Wanda Mossakowska. Polish. Founded 1993

Exit, Nowa Sztuka w Polsce, New Art in Poland, Rynek Starego Miasta 2, PL-00-272 Warszawa. Tel (022)

8319931. Editor: Jacek Werbanowski. Polish/English. Founded 1990, 4 issues/year

Format, Art Journal, Plac Polski 3/4, PL-50-156 Wroclaw. Tel (071) 3438031 ext. 209, Fax (071) 3460327. Editor: Dr. Andrzej Saj. Polish/English. Founded 1990, 3–4 issues/year

Foto, Magazyn Fotograficzny, ul. Slomiana 25, P. O. Box 53, PL-01-353 Warszawa. Tel (022) 6661085, Fax (022) 6661073. E-mail foto@foto.com.pl. Website www.foto.com.pl. Polish, 12 issues/year

Fotografia, ul. Fabryczna 11, PL-62-300 Wrzesnia. Tel (061) 4367285, Fax (061) 6400726. Editor: Zbigniew Tomaszczuk. Polish (English summaries). Founded 2000. 4 issues/year

Foto-Kurier, ul. Kleszczowa 13, PL-02-485 Warszawa. Tel (022) 831303/8634702/8634703, Fax (022) 8634702/8634703. E-mail f-kurier@pol.pl. Website www.fraktal.com.pl/f_kurier/. Editor: Krzysztof Patrycy. Polish, 12 issues/year

Fototapeta, Mala Galeria, Pl. Zamkowy 8, PL-00-277 Warszawa. Tel (022) 8312339, Fax (022) 8310386. E-mail marekg@csw.art.pl. Website www.fototapeta.art.pl. Editor: Marek Grygiel. Polish

Foto-Zeszyty, Stowarzyszenie-Klub Fotograficzny, ul. Gorna Wilda 68/7, PL-61-564 Poznan. Tel (061) 8332855, Fax (061) 8332855. Editor: Zbigniew Grzegorski. Founded 1992. Polish, 4 issues/year

Gazeta Malarzy i Poetow, Galeria Miejska Arsenal, Stary Rynek 3, PL-61-772 Poznan. Tel (061) 8529501-2, Fax (061) 8529501. E-mail office@asenal.info.poznan.pl. Editors: Wojciech Makowiecki, Ryszard

K. Przybylski, Eugeniusz Sterna-Wachowiak. Polish

Konteksty, Antropologia, kultura, etnografia, sztuka, Instytut Sztuki PAN, ul. Dluga 28, PL-00-950 Warszawa. Tel (022) 8313271, Fax (022) 8313149. Editor: Zbigniew Benedyktowicz. Polish (English summaries). Founded 1947. 4 issues/year

Magazyn Sztuki, ul. Zakopianska 32b/4, PL-80-142 Gdansk. Tel (058) 321001, Fax (058) 321001. Editor: Ryszard Ziarkiewicz. Polish/English, 4 issues/year

Pozytyw, ul. Piotrkowska 143, PL-90-434 Lodz. Tel (042) 6372398 ext. 351/6372315, Fax (042) 6372315. E-mail pozytyw@kki.net.pl. Editor: Cezary Janicki. Polish. Founded 1999, 12 issues/year

Wiadomosci Fotograficzne, ul. Grójecka 75, PL-02-094 Warszawa. Tel (022) 8223917. Editor: Mieczyslaw Cybulski. Polish, 12 issues/year

Book Publishers

Festina, ul. Sobolewska 18a, PL-02-908 Warszawa. Tel (022) 425453, Fax (022) 425453

Multic O. W., ul. Lektykarska 4a, PL-01-687 Warszawa. Tel (022) 8322355, Fax (022) 8322358

Muza S. A., ul. Marszalkowska 8, PL-00-590 Warszawa. Tel (022) 6211775-6, Fax (022) 6292349. E-mail muza@com.pl. Website www.muza.com.pl

Ossolineum, Plac Solny 14a, PL-50-062 Wroclaw. Tel (071) 3444471/3438625, Fax (071) 3448103. E-mail osso-bn@pw.wroc.pl. Website www.ossolineum.wroc.pl

Panstwowy Instytut Wydawniczy, ul. Foksal 17, PL-00-372 Warszawa. Tel (022) 8260201, Fax (022) 8261536. E-mail piw@piw.pl. Website www. piw.pl

Proszynski i S-ka S. A., ul. Garazowa 7, PL-02-651 Warszawa

Split Trading, Wydawnictwo Fundacji Buchnera, Aleja Róz 2, PL-00-556 Warszawa. Tel (022) 6225457, Fax (022) 6281796

Videograf II, ul. Korfantego 191, PL-40-153 Katowice. Tel (032) 2036559/7302512, Fax (032) 2036559/ 7302512. E-mail videograf@ videograf.dnd.com.pl. Website www.videograf.dnd.pl

Wydawnictwo Adam Marszalek, ul. Przy Kaszowniku 37, PL-87-100 Torun. Tel (056) 6232238, Fax (056) 6608160. E-mail info@marszalek. com.pl. Website www.marszalek. com.pl

Wydawnictwo Arkady, ul. Dobra 28, PL-00-344 Warszawa. Tel (022) 6358344, Fax (022) 8274194. E-mail arkady@arkady.com.pl. Website www.arkady.com.pl

Wydawnictwo Artystyczne i Filmowe, ul. Pulawska 61, PL-00-595 Warszawa. Tel (022) 8454041 ext. 125, Fax (022) 8455301

Wydawnictwo Baturo, ul. Powstañców Slaskich 6, PL-43-300 Bielsko-Biala. Tel (033) 8140455, Fax (033) 8125086

Wydawnictwo Buffi, ul. J. Poniatowskiego 6, PL-43-300 Bielsko-Biala. Tel (033) 8149535, Fax (033) 8149535

Wydawnictwo Kropka, J. W. Sliwczynski, Fabryczna 11, PL-62-300 Wrzesnia. Tel (061) 4367285

Wydawnictwo Literackie, ul. Dluga 1, PL-37-147 Kraków. Tel (012) 4228950, Fax (012) 4225423

Wydawnictwo Lukrum, ul. Cyniarska 10, PL-43-300 Bielsko-Biala. Tel (033) 8110421, Fax (033) 8110421

Wydawnictwo Podsiedlik, Reniowski i Spolka, ul. Zmigrodzka 41/49, PL-60-171 Poznan. Tel (061) 8679546, Fax (061) 8676850. E-mail office@ priska.com.pl. Website www. priska.com.pl

Wydawnictwo UMCS, pl. Marie Curie-Sklodowskiej 5, PL-20-031 Lublin. Tel (081) 5375303

Wydawnictwo Znak, ul. Kosciuszki 37, PL-30-105 Kraków. Tel (012) 4291469, Fax (012) 4219860

Auctions

Stara Galeria ZPAF, Old Gallery of the Union of Polish Art Photographers, Plac Zamkowy 8, PL-00-277 Warszawa. Tel (022) 8310386/8312339/ 6354783, Fax (022) 8310386

Critics & Journalists

Dr. Andrzej Florkowski, ul. Brandstaettera 6, PL-61-659 Poznan. Tel (061) 8230737. E-mail aflorkow@soho-online.com. Academy of Fine Art, Poznan

Marek Grygiel, ul. Lokajskiego 20/8, PL-02-793 Warszawa. Tel (022) 6487706/8312339, mobil 0603670160, Fax (022) 8310386/6289550. E-mail marekg@csw.art.pl. Editor of *Fototapeta,* Warszawa; *Edit, Gazeta Wyborcza,* Warszawa; *Imago,* Bratislava; Direktor of Mala Galeria ZPAF,

Curator of Center of Conterporary Art "Ujadowski Castle", Warszawa

Ewa Hornowska, ul. Wojska Polskiego 102k, PL-62-030 Lubon. Tel (061) 8625645. E-mail hornaku@amu.edu.pl

Dr. Krzysztof Jurecki, ul. Szczanieckiej 3/9, Pl-93-342 Lodz. Tel (042) 6339790, Fax (042) 6329941. E-mail kjurecki@friko.sos.com.pl. Curator of the Museum of Art, Lodz; *Exit, Fototapeta,* Warszawa; *Format,* Wroclaw

Prof. Alicja Kepinska, ul. Jezycka 31/2, PL-60-864 Poznan. Tel (061) 8433885

Barbara Kosinska-Filocha, ul. Zwierzyniecka 1 m. 76, PL-00-719 Warszawa. Tel (022) 403001

Jan Kurowicki, ul. Prosta 53a m. 29, PL-65-783 Zielona Gora. Tel (068) 3232630

Lech Lechowicz, al. Pilsudskiego 25/11, PL-90-308 Lodz. Tel (042) 6747945. E-mail llechowi@asp.lodz.pl. State School of Cinema, Television and Theatre, Lodz

Dr. Marta Lesniakowska, ul. Askenazego 7/37, PL-03-580 Warszawa. Tel (022) 6793546, Fax (022) 8313149. *Dagerotyp,* Warszawa

Jerzy Lewczynski, P. O. Box 71, PL-44-100 Gliwice. Tel (032) 2383625

Elzbieta Lubowicz, ul. Obornicka 12 m. 13, PL-51-113 Wroclaw. Tel (071) 3441056. BWA, Wroclaw; *Fotografia,* Wrzesnia

Krystyna Lyczywek, ul. Curie-Sklodowskiej 19, PL-71-332 Szczecin. Tel (091) 4870621, Fax (091) 4870621. *Format,* Wroclaw; *Foto, Przekroj,* Warszawa; *Foto Zeszyty,* Poznan; *Glos Szczecinski,* Szczecin

Marianna Michalowska, os. Przyjazni 5/143, PL-61-000 Poznan. Tel mobil 0606251908. E-mail marianna@arsenal.info.poznan.pl. *Magazyn Sztuki,* Warszawa; *Gazeta Malarzy i Poetow,* Poznan; *Kultura Wspolczesna,* Opcje

Dr. Wanda Mossakowska, ul. Gamerskiego 3/9, PL-00-089 Warszawa. Tel (022) 8313271, Fax (022) 8313149. *Dagerotyp,* Warszawa

Janusz Nowacki, Centrum Kultury „Zamek", ul. Sw. Marcin 80/82, PL-61-809 Poznan. Tel (061) 8536081 ext 130, Fax (061) 8520503. Curator of the Cultural Censter "Castle" and the Gallery of Photography pf

Jerzy Olek, P. O. Box 197, PL-50-950 Wroclaw 2. *Wiadomosci Kulturalne,* Wroclaw; *Imago,* Bratislava; Academy of Fine Art, Poznan, Wiadomosci Kulturalne

Prof. Ryszard K. Przybylski, ul. Jackowskiego 30a/32, PL-60-509 Poznan. Tel (061) 8434399. *Gazeta Malarzy i Poetow,* Poznan; *Teksty,* Warszawa

Dr. Jerzy Saj, ul. Sepa Sarynskiego 70/2, PL-50-334 Wroclaw. Tel (071) 3438031 ext. 209/239, Fax (071) 3460327. E-mail asa@cybis.asp.wroc.pl. Editor of *Format,* Wroclaw

Slawomir Sikora, ul. Ogrodowa 39/41 m. 39, PL-00-873 Warszawa. *Konteksty,* Warszawa

Adam Sobota, ul. Wejherowska 67/3, PL-54-239 Wroclaw. Tel (071) 3508749, Fax (071) 3435643. Curator of the National Museum, Wroclaw; *Format, Odra,* Wroclaw; *Foto, Exit,* Warszawa

Zbigniew Tomasczuk, ul. Wilenska 18 m. 195, PL-03-416 Warszawa. Tel (022) 8184511. E-mail turgul@

priv3.onet.pl. Editor of *Fotografia,*
Wrzesnia

Prof. Stefan Wojnecki, ul. Sw. Marcin
29/34, PL-61-806 Poznan. Tel (061)
8525043. E-mail stewoj@polbox.com.
Academy of Fine Art, Poznan, Union
of Polish Art Photogaphers, Warszawa

Dr. Piotr Wolynski, ul. Wiosenna 21a,
PL-60-592 Poznan. Tel (061) 8430205.
Academy of Fine Art, Poznan

Dr. Zbigniew E. Zegan, ul. Majora
1/19, PL-31-422 Krakow. Tel (042)
4111792, Fax (042) 4226566. Academy
of Fine Art, Kraków

Schools & Workshops

Akademia Sztuk Pieknych, Gdansk,
Academy of Fine Arts, Gdansk,
ul. Targ Weglowy 6, PL-80-836
Gdansk. Tel (058) 3012801, Fax (058)
3012200. E-mail office@asp.gda.pl.
Website www.asp.gda.pl

Akademia Sztuk Pieknych, Krakow,
Academy of Fine Arts, Kraków,
ul. Pilsudskiego 38, PL-30-000
Krakow. Tel (012) 4226422, Fax
(012) 4226566. E-mail zerektor@
kinga.cys_kr.edu.pl

Akademia Sztuk Pieknych, Lodz,
Academy of Fine Arts, Lodz, ul.
Wojska Polskiego 121, PL-91-726
Lodz. Tel (042) 6561056, Fax (042)
6562192

Academy of Fine Art in Poznań

Department of Multimedia Communication
Art Photography Studio
Extramurial Photography Studio

leads art photography study

full-time M.A. study / 5 years
part-time B.A. study / 3 years
post-degree part-time M.A. study / 2.5 years

PL-60-967 Poznań, Al. Marcinkowskiego 29
tel +48 61 855 25 21, fax +48 61 852 23 09, e-mail fotografia@asp.poznan.pl

Akademia Sztuk Pieknych, Poznan,
Academy of Fine Art, Poznan, Wydzial Komunikacji Multimedialnej, Katedra Fotografii/full time students/Zaoczne Studium Fotografii/ part time students, al. Marcinkowskiego 29, PL-60-967 Poznan. Tel (061) 8552521, Fax (061)8522309. E-mail fotografia@asp.poznan.pl. Website www.asp.poznan.pl/asp/ uczelnia.html

Akademia Sztuk Pieknych, Warszawa,
Academy of Fine Arts, Warszawa, Wydzial Grafiki, ul. Krakowskie Przedmiescie 5, PL-00-068 Warszawa. Tel (022) 8266251, Fax (022) 8262114

Panstwowa Wyzsza Szkola Filmowa, Telewizyjna i Teatralna, Lodz, State School of Film, Television and Theatre, Studia Zaoczne Fotografii, ul. Targowa 61/63, PL-90-323 Lodz. Tel (042) 6743943, Fax (042) 6748139

Regionalne Centrum Kultury, Jelenia Gora, Regional Center of Culture, Jelenia Gora, Studium Fotografii, ul. Grabowskiego 7, PL-58-500 Jelenia Gora. Tel (075) 7523542/7524254, Fax (075) 7526569

Szkola Reportazu Collegium Civitas, School of Reportage Collegium Civitas, ul. Marii Kazimiery 31, PL-01-641 Warszawa. Tel (022) 8338539, Fax (022) 8338539

Uniwersytet Mikolaja Kopernika, Torun, Kopernik University, Torun, Wydzial Sztuk Pieknych, ul. Sienkiewicza 30/32, PL-87-100 Torun. Tel (056) 6227051

Wyzsza Szkola Pedagogiczna, Zielona Gora, Instytut Sztuki i Kultury Plastycznej, ul. Wisniowa 10, PL-61-517 Zielona Gora. Tel (068) 3263520, Fax (068) 3265449. E-mail rektorat@ asia.aw.wsp.zgora.pl. Website www.wsp.zgora.pl

Associations

Naukowe Towarzystwo Fotografii, Science Society of Photography, al. Marcinkowskiego 29, PL-60-967 Poznan. Tel (061) 8525043. E-mail fotografia@asp.poznan.pl, stewoj@ polbox.com

Stowarzyszenie Historykow Fotografii, Society of Photography Historians, ul. Dluga 26, PL-00-950 Warszawa. Tel (022) 8313271, Fax (022) 8313149

Stowarzyszenie Polska Korporacja Fotografii, Izabella Wojciechowska, Warszawa. Tel (022) 8270217, Fax (022) 8270217

Zwiazek Polskich Artystow Fotografikow, Union of Polish Art Photographers, Plac Zamkowy 8, PL-00-277 Warszawa. Tel (022) 8310386

Grants & Awards

Fundusz Promocji Tworczosci, Ministerstwo Kultury i Dziedzictwa Narodowego, ul. Krakowskie Przedmiescie 15/17, PL-00-071 Warszawa. Tel (022) 6200231, Fax (022) 8261470

New Media

WRO International Media Art Biennale, Media Art Biennale, Open Studio/WRO Foundation, P. O. Box 1385, PL-54-137 Wroclaw 16. Tel (071) 3422691, Fax (071) 3422691. E-mail wro@info.wcss.wroc.pl. Website www.asp.wroc.pl/~ppo/ wro/, www.wro.art.pl

Portugal

Population: 9.94 million
Capital: Lisbon, 2.1 million
Currency: Escudo (Esc)
International code: ++351
Tourist information: ICEP –
Investimentos, Comércio e Tu-
rismo de Portugal, Av. Conte
de Valbom 30-5°, P-1050 Lisboa

Galleries & Museums

Centro de Estudos de Fotografia,
Rua Padre António Vieira 1, P-3000
Coimbra. Tel (0239) 27452/23072,
Fax (0239) 20154. Open: 10–13, 15–19.
Director: Albano da Silva Pereira.
Founded 1974. 3 rooms, 40 m². 15–20
photo exhibitions/year. Artists:
Albano Pereira, Leitao Marques,
Macas de Carvalho, José Afonso
Furtado, José Manuel Rodrigues

Museu – Photographia "Vicentes",
Rua da Carreira 43, P-9000 Funchal.
Tel (0291) 225050, Fax (0291) 232714.
Open: Mon–Fri 9–12.30, 14–17.30.
Director: Maria Helena Araujo.
Founded 1982. 2 rooms, 111 m².
Artists: Vicente Gomes da Silva,
Alexander Lamont Henderson,
Visconde Valparaiso, João Anacleto
Rodrigues, Alvaro Nascimento,
Joaquim Augusto de Sousa, Russel
Manners Gordon, Gino Romoli,
Photo Figueiras, Perestrellos Photo-
graphos

Centro Cultural de Belém, Centro de
Exposiçoes, Praca do Imério, P-1400
Lisboa. Tel (021) 3622772, Fax (021)

3622685. Open: 11–20. Director:
Margarite Waiga. Founded 1993.
4 rooms, 6,000 m². 3–4 photo exhi-
bitions/year

Centro de Arte Moderna, Fundaçao
Calouste Gulbenkian, Rua Dr. Nico-
lau Bettencourt, P-1000 Lisboa. Tel
(021) 7935131, Fax (021) 7939294.
Open: Tue–Sun 10–17, summer:
Wed+Sat 14–19.30. Director: Jorge
Molder. Founded 1983. 4 rooms,
4,000 m². 2–3 photo exhibitions/year.
Artists: Thomas Joshua Cooper,
Fernando Lemos, Cindy Sherman,
John Baldessari

Galeria Diferenca, Rua S. Filipe Néri
42, P-1250 Lisboa. Tel (021) 3832193,
Fax (021) 3853664. Open: Tue–Sat 15–
20. Director: Monteiro Gil. Curator:
Agostinho Gonçalves. Founded 1979.
3 rooms, 120 m². 6 photo exhibitions/
year. Artists: Afonso Furtado, Agostinho Gonçalves, André Gomes,
Curado Matos, Francisco Azevedo,
Monteiro Gil, Paulo Ferro, Alberto
Picco, Valente Alves

Galeria Graça Fonseca, Rua da
Emenda 26 CV, P-1200 Lisboa. Tel
(021) 3477037, Fax (021) 3427314.
Artists: Paul den Hollander, Joao
Tabarra, Luis Palma

Galeria Palmira Suso, Rua des
Flores 109, P-1200 Lisboa. Tel (021)
3427242, Fax (021) 3427242. E-mail
palmirasuso@mail.telepac.pt. Web-
site www.galeriapalmirasuso.pt.
Open: Tue–Sat 15–20. Director:
António Bacalhau. Founded 1991.
1 room, 120 m². 1–2 photo exhibi-
tions/year. Artists: Domingos Rego,
Philip-Lorca diCorcia, Jaime Lebre,
Ana Marchand, Carlos Medeiros,
Jorge Pinheiro, Gonçalo Ruivo,
Inez Teixeira, Martin Parr, Maria
Beatriz

Casa das Artes, Secretaria de Estado da Cultura, Rua António Cardoso 175, P-4100 Porto. Tel (022) 6006153, Fax (022) 6006152. Open: 14–24. Director: Manuel Matos Fernandes. Founded 1991. 2 rooms, 395 m². 4–5 photo exhibitions/year

Centro Portugues de Fotografia, Rua António Cardoso 175, P-4150-081 Porto. Tel (022) 6061170, Fax (022) 6002375. E-mail cpfot@mail. telepac.pt. Open: Tue–Fri 15–18, Sat–Sun 15–19. Director: Tereza Siza. Founded 1997. 6 rooms, 978 m²

Fundaçao de Serralves, Rua de Serralves 977, P-4100 Porto. Tel (022) 6180057, Fax (022) 6173862. Open: Tue–Fri 14–20, Sat–Sun 10–20 (summer), 14–18, Sat–Sun 10–18 (winter). Director: Prof. Fernando Pernes. Curator: Odete Patricio.

Founded 1989. 9 rooms, 600 m². 1 photo exhibition/year

Imago Lucis, Photogallery, Rua de S. Francisco 22, P-4000 Porto. Tel (022) 2004347. Open: Mon–Fri 14.30–19 (Fri 21.30–24), Sat 15–19. Director: Manuel Magalhaes. Curator: Anibal Lemos. Founded 1989. 1 room, 30 m². 11 photo exhibitions/year. Artists: Anibal Lemos, Manuel Magalhaes, Eurico Cabral

Festivals & Fairs

Encontros da Imagem, Associação de Fotografia e Cinema de Braga, Rua de S. Marcos 41, P-4700 Braga. Tel (0253) 616108, Fax (0253) 277725. E-mail eimagem@mail.bragatel.pt. Website www.bragatel.pt/eimagem

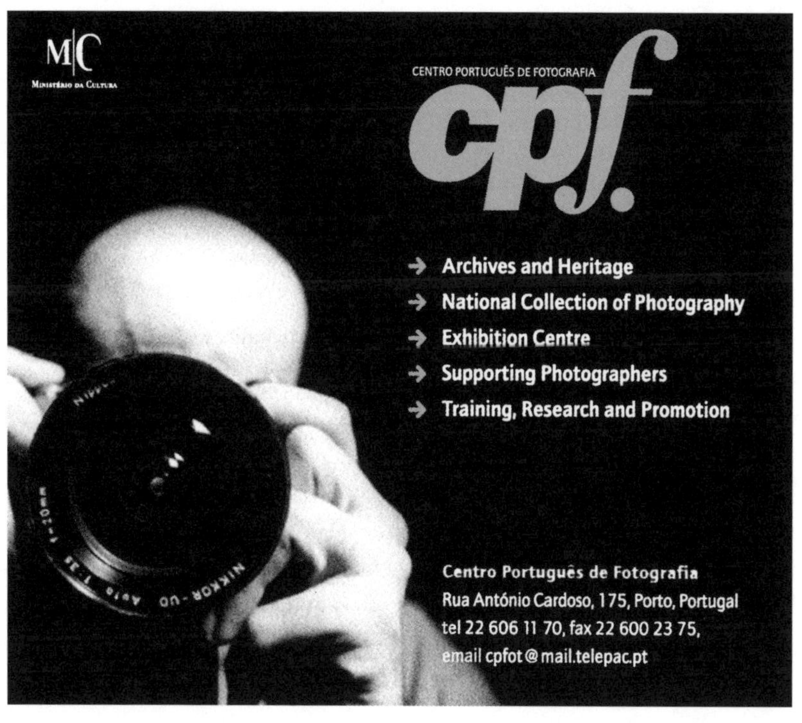

218 Portugal

Encontros de Fotografia, Rua Padre António Vieira, Edf° AAC, P-3000 Coimbra. Tel (0239) 20154/26178, Fax (0239) 20154. E-mail encontrosphoto@mail.interacesso.pt

Magazines

Colóquio/Artes, Fundaçao Calouste Gulbenkian, Av. de Berna 45a, P-1093 Lisboa Codex. Tel (021) 7937542, Fax (021) 7935139. Editor: José Augusto Franca. Portuguese/French/English/Spanish/Italian. Founded 1959. Copy price: US$8.00. Annual subscription: US$60.00 (Europe), US$80.00 (outside Europe), 4 issues/year

Book Publishers

Assírio & Alvim, Rua Passos Manuel 67b, P-1100 Lisboa. Fax (021) 3555580 Difusao Cultural, Rua Luis de Freitas Branco 3 A/B, P-1600 Lisboa. Tel (021) 7599364, Fax (021) 7594418

Ediçoes 70 Lda., Rua Luciano Cordeiro 123-2, Esq., P-1069-157 Lisboa. Tel (021) 3190240, Fax (021) 3190249. E-mail edi.70@mail.telepac.p

Ediçoes Afrontamento, Rua de Costa Cabral 852, P-4200 Porto

Ediçoes ASA, Rua dos Mártires da Liberdade 77, P. O. Box 4263, P-4004 Porto Codex. Tel (022) 222-79/70, Fax (022) 9716610

Editorial Caminho, Al Santo António dos Capuchos 6-B, P-1169-051 Lisboa. Tel (021) 3152683, Fax (021) 3534346. E-mail webmaster@editorial-caminho.pt. Website www.editorial-caminho.pt

Imprensa Nacional Casa da Moeda E. P., Rua D. Francisco Manuel de Melo 5, P-1092 Lisboa Codex. Fax (021) 7978632

Publicaçoes Don Quixote Lda., Rua Luciano Cordeiro 116, P-1098 Lisboa Codex. Tel (021) 3158079-82, Fax (021) 574595

Vega, Rua Joao Saraiva 36-3°, P-1700 Lisboa

Critics & Journalists

Jorge Calado, Rua Fernao Gomes 19, P-1400 Lisboa

António Cerveira Pinto, Palácio dos Corucheus, Rua Alberto Oliveira, Estúdio 27, P-1700 Lisboa. Tel (021) 7939161, Fax (021) 7939161. *O Independente,* Lisboa

Joao Miguel Fernandes Jorge, Avenida Rainha D. Leonor 21-6° F, P-1600 Lisboa

Joao Lopes, Expresso, Rua Duque de Palmela 37-3°, P-1296 Lisboa Codex

Margarida Medeiros, Público, Rua Amílcar Cabral, Lote 1, P-1700 Lisboa. Tel (021) 7501036, Fax (021) 758-7373/7138. *Público,* Lisboa

Alexandre Melo, Rua Serpa Pinto 3-3° Esq., P-1200 Lisboa

Joao Pinharanda, Rua D. Estefânia 9-1°, P-1100 Lisboa. Tel (021) 7584002, Fax (021) 7587373. *Público,* Lisboa

Alexandre Pomar, Rua do Vale 6-1° D, P-1200 Lisboa. Tel (021) 3965078, Fax (021) 3965078. E-mail pomar@mail.telepac.pt. *Expresso,* Lisboa

António Sena, Cancela da Areia, Santa Cruz-Ribeiras, P-9930 Lajes do Pico. Tel (0292) 678169, Fax (0292) 678169

Teresa Siza, Rua Brito Capelo 827,
P-4450 Matosinhos. Tel (022) 9380252,
Fax (022) 9380252

Carlos Vidal, Praça 5 de Outubro 20,
P-2870 Montijo

Schools & Workshops

**AR.CO Centro de Arte e Comunicaçao
Visual,** Rua de Santiago 18, P-1100
Lisboa. Tel (021) 8882749, Fax (021)
8870261

**Arvore – Cooperativa de Actividades
Artísticas (CRL),** Rua Azevedo de
Albuquerque 1, P-4000 Porto. Fax
(022) 200684

Aula do Risco, Rua Nova da Trindade
15a, P-1200 Lisboa. Tel (021) 3431179,
Fax (021) 3431180

**ETIC – Escola Técnica de Imagem e
Communicaçao,** Rua Tomás Ribeiro
8-1° Dt°, P-1000 Lisboa. Tel (021)
3527064

**MAUMAUS – Escola de Fotografia
e Artes Visuais,** Campo dos Mártires
da Pátria 100-1° Esq., P-1150-227
Lisboa. Tel (021) 3547383, Fax (021)
3956860. E-mail maumaus@
esoterica.pt

Associations

Clube Português de Artes e Ideias,
Rua do Sol ao Rato, 73-1.°, P-1250
Lisboa

Grants & Awards

Centro Nacional de Cultura, Dr. Helena Vaz da Silva, Rua António Maria
Cardoso 68, P-1200 Lisboa. Tel (021)
3466722, Fax (021) 3428250

Fundaçao Calouste Gulbenkian, Ser-
viço de Belas-Artes, Av. Berna 45-A,
P-1093 Lisboa Codex. Tel (021)
7937542, Fax (021) 7935139

**Fundaçao Lusi-Americana para o
Desenvolvimento,** Eng° Luis dos
Santos Ferro, Director dos Serviços
Culturais, Rua do Sacramento à Lapa
21, P-1200 Lisboa. Tel (021) 3960297,
Fax (021) 3963358

Secretaria de Estado da Cultura,
Departamento das Artes, D.G.E.A.,
Rua Castilho 71-4° D., P-1200 Lisboa.
Tel (021) 3884530, Fax (021) 3863206

New Media

VideoLisboa, International Festival,
Club Português de Artes e Ideias,
Rua do Sol ao Rato, 73-1.°, P-1250-262
Lisboa. Tel (021) 387812-1/2, Fax
(021) 3876667. E-mail videolisboa@
videolisboa.com. Website www.
videolisboa.com

Romania

Population: 22.6 million
Capital: Bucharest, 2 million
Currency: Lei (ROL)
International code: ++40
Tourist information: Ministry
for Tourism, Apolodor 17,
RO-7000 Bucuresti

Galleries & Museums

Fotogaleria GAD, National Office for
Art Exhibitions, Bd. N. Balcescu 2,
RO-7000 Bucuresti. Tel (01) 3139115,
Fax (01) 3121502. Open: Tue–Sun 10–
18 (closed for renovation till autumn
2000). Contact: Mihai Oroveanu,
Ruxandra Balaci. 80 m². 8–10 photo
exhibtions/year. Artists: Vlad Iacob,
Andrei Dirlau, Nicoletta Montalbetti,
Filip Habart

**Muzeul National de Arta al Roma-
niei,** National Romanian Museum of
Art, Department of Contemporary
Art, Photography and Video, Calea
Victoriei 49–53, RO-7000 Bucuresti.
Tel (01) 3133030, Fax (01) 3124327.
Website www.art.museum.ro. Open:
Wed–Sun 10–18. Contact: Ruxandra
Balaci. Founded 1948, department
1994. Several rooms from 100 m² to
500 m². 2 photo exhibitions/year

**Oficiul National pentru Docementare
si Expozitii de Arta si Fundatia
ARTEXPO,** National Office for Fine
Art Exhibitions and ARTEXPO
Foundation, Bd. N. Balcescu 2, RO-
7000 Bucuresti. Tel (01) 3139115, Fax
(01) 3121502. Open: Tue–Sun 10–18.
Contact: Mihai Oroveanu, Ruxandra
Balaci. Founded: National Office
1968, ARTEXPO Foundation 1992.
Several rooms from 100 m² to 500 m².
2 photo exhibitions/year. Artists:
William Henry Fox Talbot, Heinrich
Zille, Martin Parr

Magazines

**Artelier – contemporary art magazine
for new media,** CIAC, Spatarului 52,
RO-7000 Bucuresti. Tel (01) 2107777,
Fax (01) 2107777. E-mail icca@icca.ro.
Editors: Ruxandra Balaci, Magda
Carneci. Romanian/English. Found-
ed 1997, 2 issues/year

Balkon, IDEA Print, Calea Paris
5–7, RO-3400 Cluj. Tel (064) 194634,
Fax (064) 431661. E-mail balkon@
idea.dntcj.ro. Editor: Timotei Na-
dasan. Romanian. Founded 1999,
2 issues/year

Book Publishers

ARTEXPO Foundation, Bd. N. Balcescu 2, RO-7000 Bucuresti. Tel (01)
3139115, Fax (01) 3121502. E-mail
artexpop@tag.vsat.ro

Critics & Journalists

Emanuel Badescu, Library of the
Romanian Academy, Calea Victoriei
125, RO-7000 Bucuresti. Tel (01)
3503043

Ruxandra Balaci, National Romanian
Museum of Art, Calea Victoriei 49–
53, RO-7000 Bucuresti. Tel (01)
3133030, Fax (01) 3124327. E-mail
balaci@art.museum.ro. Editor of *Artelier* Magazine, Bucuresti; Fotogaleria GAD, Bucuresti; *Imago,* Bratislava

Mihail Oroveanu, ARTEXPO Foundation, Bd. N. Balcescu 2, RO-7000 Bucuresti. Tel (01) 3139115, Fax (01) 3121502. E-mail artexpop@tag.vset.ro

Gheorghe Rasovszky, Intr. Popa Nan 5, RO-7000 Bucuresti. Tel (0040) 092652918. *Artelier*, Bucuresti

Schools & Workshops

Institutul de Arta Ion Andreescu, Institute of Fine Arts Ion Andreescu, Department of Photography and Video, Romania Str., RO-3400 Cluj-Napoca. Tel (064) 111577, Fax (064) 192890

Universitatea de Arta, University of Arts, Department of Photography and Video, Str. G-ral Budisteanu 19, RO-7000 Bucuresti. Tel (01) 3103977, Fax (01) 3103977

Russia

Population: 147.3 million
Capital: Moscow, 12.4 million
Currency: Ruble (R)
International code: ++7
Tourist information:
Russian National Tourist
Office, Kitaigorodski Proesd 7,
RUS-103693 Moskva

Galleries & Museums

Galereja Sojuza fotokhudozhnikov Rossii v Cheboksarakh, Gallery of the Union of Photo Artists of Russia in Cheboksary, P. O. Box 16, RUS-428000 Cheboksary. Tel (8352) 576456/560761, Fax (8352) 214252. E-mail master@gorod.chuvashia.ru. Curator: Andrey Dobrynkin

Gosudarstvenny obiedinenny istorich-no-arkhitekturny i literatyrny muzei Kirova, State Unite Historical, Architectural and Literature Museum of Kirov City, Drelevskogo ulitsa 6, RUS-610000 Kirov. Tel (8332) 623738. Director: Sergey Elshin. Artists: Sergey Lobovikov, Anatoly Skyrikhin, Arkady Shishkin

Kirovsky Oblastnoy Khudozhestvenny Muzei imeni V. i A.Vasnetsovykh, Kirov Region Art Museum n. a. V. & A.Vasnetsovs, Karl Marx ulitsa 70, RUS-610000 Kirov. Tel (8332) 622646, Fax (8332) 627903. Director: Alla Noskova. Artist: Sergey Lobovikov

Aidan-Gallery, 1-st Tverskaya-Yamskaya street, 22/1, 3d floor, RUS-125047 Moskva. Tel (095) 2513734, Fax (095) 2513734. Contact: Aidan Salakhova.12–15 photo exhibitions/year. Artists: Aidan Salakhova, Olga Chernyshova, Sergey Shutov, Mikhail Rosanov, Tatiaru Panova, Timur Novikov

Art-media centre TV-Gallery, Bolshaya Yakimanka ulitsa 6, RUS-123459 Moskva. Fax (095) 2389666. Director: Nina Zaretskaya. 3–5 photo exhibitions/year. Artists: Sergey Shutov, Olga Chernyshova, Gor Chakhal, Gia Rigvava

Dom, kultyrny tsentr, Cultural Centre Dom (House), Bolshoy Ovchinnikovsky pereulok 24/4, RUS-113134 Moskva. Tel (095) 9537236, Fax (095) 9537242. E-mail dommsk@ postman.ru. Open: Wed–Sun 14–20. Contact: Dr. Vitaly Patsyukov. 120 m². Artists: Aleksander Slyusarev, Aleksander Lapin, Boris Smelov, Lulia Kouznetsova, Evgeny Gladkov, Gennady Bodrov, Sergey Gitman, Pavel Krivtsov

Feniks, Phoenix, Exhibition Hall, Kutuzovsky prospect 3, RUS-121248 Moskva. Tel (095) 2434958, Fax (095) 2430462. Open: Tue–Sun 13–18. Contact: Ludmila Zelayaskova. 5–7 photo exhibitions/year. Artists: Valery & Natascha Cherkashins, Sergey Kasianov, Aleksander Maslenitsyn, Pavel Kiselev, Valeri Stigneev, Leonid Shokin

Fotocentr, Photocentre, Gogolevsky bulvar 8/2, RUS-121019 Moskva. Tel (095) 2906996. Open: Wed–Sun 12–19. Director: Valery Nikiforov. Founded 1985. 2 rooms, 590 m². 12–15 photo exhibitions/year. Artists: Karl Bulla, Yuri Polygalov

Gelman Gallery, Malaya Polyanka 7/7, str. 5, RUS-109180 Moskva. Tel (095) 2316654, Fax (095) 2388492. E-mail guilman@russ.ru. Curator: Marat Gelman. 10–12 photo exhibitions/year. Artists: Sergey and Svetlana Osmachkin, Igor Mukhin, Dima Gutov, Evgeny Semenov

Gosudarstvenny Istorichesky muzei, State Historic Museum, Krasnaya ploshchad 1/2, RUS-103012 Moskva. Tel (095) 2923731/9244529. Open: Mon, Wed–Sun 11–19. Director: Dr. Aleksandr Shkurko. 2–5 photo exhibitions/year

Gosudarstvenny istorichno-arkhitekturny, khudozhestvenny i landshaftny muzei-zapovednik "Tsaritsyno", State Historical, Architectural, Art and Landscape Museum "Tsaritsyno", Dolskaya ulitsa 1, RUS-115569 Moskva. Tel (095) 3216366/2875992/4521777. Director: Vsevolod Anikovich. Curator: Dr. Andrey Erofeev

Gosudarstvenny muzei Lva Tolstogo, State Museum of Lev Tolstoy, Prechistenka ulitsa 11, RUS-109034 Moskva. Tel (095) 2022190/2013811

Gosudarstvenny muzei V.V. Mayakovskogo, State Museum of Vladimir Mayakovsky, Lubyansky proezd 3/6, RUS-101000 Moskva. Tel (095) 9219387, Fax (095) 9286092. Open: Mon, Tue, Fri–Sun 10–18, Thu 13–19. Director: Svetlana Strizhenova. Artists: Alexander Rodchenko, Boris Ignatovich, Arkady Shaykhet

Gosudarstvenny nauchno-issledovatelsky muzei arkhitektury imeni A.V. Shchuseva, State Scientific Museum of Architecture A. V. Shchusev, Vozdvizhenka ulitsa 5, RUS-121019 Moskva. Tel (095) 2911978, Fax (095) 291209. Director: Vladimir Rezvin.

Artists: Yury Yeremin, Mikhail Dashevsky

Gosudarstvenny Politekhnichesky muzei, State Polytechnical Museum, Novaya Ploshad 3/4, RUS-101000 Moskva. Tel (095) 9230756, Fax (095) 9251290. Open: Tue, Wed, Fri–Sun 10–17. Director: Dr. Gurgen Grigorian. 2–3 photo exhibitions/year

Gosudarstvenny tsentr sovremennogo iskusstva, State Centre for Contemporary Art, Vorotnikovsky pereulok 11/3, RUS-103006 Moskva. Tel (095) 2998142, Fax (095) 2998142. Curator: Leonid Bazhanov. Artists: Vladimir Kupreyanov, Sergey Faibisovich, Gia Rigvava

Gosydarstvennaya Tretyakovskaya galeria, State Tretyakov Gallery, Lavryshinski pereylok 10, RUS-109017 Moskva. Tel (095) 2311362/2307788. Open: Tue–Sun 10–20. Director: Valentin Rodionov. 2–4 photo exhibitions/year

Institut sovremennogo iskusstva, Institute for Contemporary Art, Sretensky bulvar 6/1, RUS-101878 Moskva. Tel (095) 4334022. Contact: Josef Bakshtein. 2–3 photo exhibitions/year

Junion Galereja, Union Gallery, Smolenskaya ulitsa 6, RUS-121099 Moskva. Tel (095) 2410131, Fax (095) 2417136/2416982. Open: Mon–Sat 12–18. Contact: A. Kotlyar. 3–5 photo exhibitions/year. Artists: Wols, Valery Stigneev

Manezh, Exhibition Hall, Manezhnaya ploshchad 2, RUS-101000 Moskva. Tel (095) 2028976, Fax (095) 2025242. Several rooms. 2–3 photo exhibitions/year. Artists: Henri Cartier-Bresson, Annie Leibovitz

Moskovsky dom fotografii, Moscow House of Photography, Ostozhenka 16/1, RUS-119034 Moskva. Tel (095) 2020610/2027612, Fax (095) 2024346. E-mail mdf@cityline.ru, fotofest@cityline.ru. Website www.mdf.cityline.ru. Director: Olga Sviblova. Artists: Boris Ignatovich, Dmitry Baltermants, Georgi Zelma, Max Penson, Igor Mukhin, Valery Stigneev, Valery Tschekoldin, Vladimir Syomin

Moskovsky gosudarstvenny vystavochny zal Novy Manezh, Moscow State Exhibition Hall New Manezh, Georgievsky pereulok 3/3, RUS-103009 Moskva. Tel (095) 2921577/2924459, Fax (095) 2921577. Contact: Sergey Balan, Tatyana Ameshina. 3–5 photo exhibitions/year

Muzei fotograficheskikh kolektsiy, Museum of Photographic Collections, RUS-Moskva. Tel (095) 2083151. Open: by appointment only. Contact: Yury Rybchinsky. 1–2 photo exhibitions/year. Artists: Aleksander Slyusarev, Boh Mikhailov, Aleksander Lapin, Lulia Kouznetsova, Boris Smelov, Gennady Bodrov, Sergey Gitman, Pavel Krivtsov, Evgeny Gladkov

Muzei istorii goroda Moskvy, Museum of the History of Moscow, Novaya Ploshchad 12, RUS-103012 Moskva. Tel (095) 9248490/9243145, Fax (095) 9244142. Open: Tue, Thu–Sun 12–18, Wed 12–20. Contact: Galina Vedernikova. Several rooms. 2–3 photo exhibitions/year

Muzei izobrazitelnykh iskusstv imeni A. S. Pushkina, Pushkin Museum of Fine Arts, Volkhonka 12, RUS-121019 Moskva. Tel (095) 2039578/2037998. Open: Tue–Sun 10–19. Director: Dr. Irina Antonova. Founded 1912. 1–2 photo exhibitions/year. Artists: Boris Ignatovich, Moisey Nappelbaum, Arkady Shaykhet, Josef Sudek, Franco Fontana, August Sander

Muzei izobrazitelnykh iskusstv imeni A. S. Pushkina – Muzei chastnykh kollekciy, Pushkin Museum of Fine Arts – Museum for Private Collections, Volkhonka 14, RUS-121019 Moskva. Tel (095) 2039578/2037998. Open: Wed–Sun 10–17. Contact: Aleksey Savinov. Founded 1994. 2–3 photo exhibitions/year. Artists: Alexander Rodchenko, Henri Cartier-Bresson, William Klein

Muzei M. Gorkogo, Museum of Maksim Gorky, Malaya Nikitskaya ulitsa 6/2. RUS-121069 Moskva. Tel (095) 2900535. Open: Wed, Fri 12–17, Thu, Sat, Sun 10–17. Artists: Moysey Nappelbaum, Maxim Dmitriev

Novaya Tretyakovskaya galeria, New Tretyakov Gallery, Krymsky Val 10, RUS-117049 Moskva. Tel (095) 2307788. Open: Tue–Sun 10–20. 2–4 photo exhibitions/year. Artists: Boris Smelov, Francisco Infante

Obscuri Viri Gallery, Bolshaya Polyanka 1/3, kv. 71, RUS-109180 Moskva. Tel (095) 2386227/9281445. Director: Aleksander Malyutin. Artists: Anten Olshvang, Lena & Vera Samorodovy, Igor Makarevich

Regina Gallery, 1st Tverskaya-Yamskaya ulitsa, 22/1, 2d floor, RUS-125047 Moskva. Tel (095) 9211653, Fax (095) 2081653. E-mail regina.art@relcom.ru. Website www.regina.ru. Director: Regina Ovcharenko. 3–5 photo exhibitions/year. Artists: Oleg Kulik, Olga Tobreluts, Vlad Efimov

ROSIZO – Gosudarstvenny muzeino-vystavochny tsentr Ministerstva Kultury Rossiyskoy Federatsii, ROSIZO State Centre for Museums and Exhibitions of the Ministry of

Culture of Russian Federation, Petrovka 28/2, RUS-103051 Moskva. Tel (095) 9217997, Fax (095) 9219291. E-mail berezner@mtu-net.ru. Contact: Oleg Shandybin, Evgeny Berezner. 1 room, 100 m². Artists: Sergey Lobovikov, Vladimir Guchshin, Alexey Goga, Aleksander Zabrin, Grigory Maiofis, Igor Terekhov, Andrey Chezhin, Nikolay Bakharev, Vlad Efimov, Valery Stigneev

Spider & Mouse Gallery, Leningradsky prospekt 58, RUS-Moskva. Tel (095) 2128347, 4129765. E-mail spider@ica.msk.ru. Director: Marina Perchikhina. Curator: Nikolay Polizhechenko. 3–5 photo exhibitions/year. Artists: Igor Ioganson, Malina Perchikhina, Timur Novikov, Andrey Barov

Tondo, Photographic and Art Gallery, Myasnitskaya street 21/8, str. 8–9, RUS-101878 Moskva. Tel (095) 1811012, Fax (095) 1811977. Contact: Aleksandr Seleznev. 2–3 photo exhibitions/year

Tsentralny dom khudozhnikov, Central House of Artists, Krymsky Val 10/14, RUS-117049 Moskva. Tel (095) 2389843. Open: Tue–Sun 11–20. Several rooms. 5–7 photo exhibitions/year

Tsentralny muzei Velikoi otechestvennoi voiny 1941–1945, Central Museum of the Great Patriotic War 1941–1945, Bratiev Fonchenko ulitsa 11, RUS-121293 Moskva. Tel (095) 4498044, Fax (095) 1455558. Director: Leonid Kotlyar

Tsentr sovremennogo iskusstva, Centre for Contemporary Art, Bolshaya Yakimanka ulitsa, 6, RUS-109180 Moskva. Tel (095) 2384422, Fax (095) 2389666. Curator: Dr. Victor Miziano. 3–5 photo exhibitions/year

Tsentr sovremennogo iskusstva Sorosa, Soros Centre for Contemporary Art, Chernyakhovsky ulitsa 4a, RUS-125319 Moskva. Tel (095) 1518706, Fax (095) 1518816. E-mail sccamsk@transts.ru. Open: Mon–Fri 12–18. Contact: Irina Alpatova. 3–5 photo exhibitions/year. Artists: Valery Stigneev, FENSO group, Yury Avvakumov, V. Glazychev

XL-Gallery, Bolshaya Sadovaya 6, RUS-103111 Moskva. Tel (095) 2993724. Open: Tue–Fri 16–20. Curator: Elena Selina. 1 room, 27 m². 10–12 photo exhibitions/year. Artists: Igor Moukhin, Tatyana Liberman, AES group, FENSO group, Oleg Kulik

Nizhegorodsky istorichno-arkhitekturny muzei-zapovednik, History and Architecture Museum of Nizhny Novgorod, Verkhne-Volzhskaya naberezhnaya, RUS-603005 Nizhny Novgorod. Tel (8312) 367661. Director: Zinaida Khalimylina. Artists: Maxim Dmitriev, Andrey Karelin

Nizhegorodsky literaturno-memorialny muzei A. M. Gorkogo, Literature Museum of A. M. Gorky, Milin ulitsa 26, RUS-603155 Nizhny Novgorod. Tel (8312) 363606. Director: Tamara Ryzhova. Artists: Maxim Dmitriev, Andrey Karelin

Art Collegia Gallery, Ligovsky prospect 64, RUS-191000 Sankt Peterburg. Tel (812) 1649564. 5–7 photo exhibitions/year. Artists: Andrey Chezhin, Alexey Titarenko

Borey Art Center, Liteiny prospekt 58, RUS-191104 Sankt Peterburg. Tel (812) 2733693, Fax (812) 2728098. E-mail borey@ragtim.ru. Open: Tue–Sat 12–20. Contact: Tatyana Ponomarenko. 5 rooms, 200 m². 5–6 photo exhibitions/year

Delta Gallery, Nevsky prospekt 51 (courtyard), P. O. Box 525, Glavpostamt, RUS-190000 Sankt Peterburg. Tel (812) 2196241. Open: Tue–Sat 12–19. Contact: Irina Bolotova. 2 rooms, 80 m². 4 photo exhibitions/year. Artists: Leonid Bogdanov, Boris Smelov, Andrey Chezhin, Olga Korsunova, Alexey Titarenko

Gosudarstvenny Ermitage, State Hermitage, Dvortsovaya naberezhnaya 34, RUS-191186 Sankt Peterburg. Tel (812) 1109601. Open: Tue–Sun 10.30–17. Director: Prof. Dr. Mikhail Piotrovsky

Gosudarstvenny Muzei istorii religii, State Museum of History of Religion, Kazanskaya square 2, RUS-191186 Sankt Peterburg. Tel (812) 3123586, Fax (812) 3119483. Open: Mon, Tue, Thu, Fri 12.30–17, Sat 11–17, Sun 12–17. Artists: Maxim Dmitriev, Karl Bulla

Gosudarstvenny Muzei istorii Sankt Peterburga, State Museum of the History of St. Petersburg, Petropavlovskaya krepost, RUS-197046 Sankt Peterburg. Tel (812) 2384728, Fax (812) 2384243. Open: Mon 10–17, Tue, Thu–Sun 11–16. Contact: Vassily Pankratov, Ludmila Myasnikova. Artists: Karl Bulla, Boris Kudoyarov

Gosudarstvenny Russky muzei, State Russian Museum, Inzhenernaya ulitsa 4, RUS-191011 Sankt Peterburg. Tel (812) 2191680, Fax (812) 3144153. Open: Mon 10–18, Wed–Sun 10–17. Director: Vladimir Gusev. Curator: Dr. Alexander Borovsky. Founded 1898. 1–3 photo exhibitions/year

Khudozhestvenny Tsentr Borey, Borey Art Centre, Liteyny prospekt 58, RUS-191104 Sankt Peterburg. Tel (812) 2733693. 5–7 photo exhibitions/year. Artist: Aleksander Kitaev

Muzey Novoy akademii iskusstv, Museum of the New Academy of Fine Arts, Tsentr sovremennogo iskusstva, Pushkinskaya 10–14, RUS-191040 Sankt Peterburg. Tel (812) 2728222. Open: Sat 16–19. Contact: Timur Novikov. 6–7 photo exhibitions/year. Artists: Olga Tobreluts, Yulia Strausova, Timur Novikov, Andrey Barov

National Center for Contemporary Art, St. Petersburg branch, Nevsky prospekt 60, RUS-191011 Sankt Peterburg. Tel (812) 3258975, Fax (812) 2196133. E-mail office@spbgcsi.spb.su. Open: Mon–Sat 11–18. Contact: Zakhar Kolovsky. 1 room, 40 m²

Photo Image Gallery, Tsentr sovremennogo iskusstva, Pushkinskaya 10, RUS-191040 Sankt Peterburg. E-mail chegin@mail.ru. Open: Sat 16–19. Contact: Andrey Chezhin, Dmitry Pilikin. 1 room, 20 m². Artists: Vita Bujvid, Andrey Chezhin, Alexander Kitaev, Igor Lebedev, Igor Vasiljev, Evgeniy Mohorev, Boris Smelov, Alexey Titarenko, Willy Usov, Dmitry Vilensky

Rossiysky etnografichesky muzei, Russian Museum of Ethnography, Inzhenernaya ulitsa 4a/1, RUS-191011 Sankt Peterburg. Tel (812) 3118622, Fax (812) 3158502. Open: Tue 11–16, Wed–Sun 11–18. Founded 1934. Several rooms

Sankt Peterburgsky gosudarstvenny universitet, St. Petersburg State University, Faculty of Journalism, Vassilevsky ostrov, 1-aya liniya 26, RUS-199034 Sankt Peterburg. Tel (812) 3285996, Fax (812) 3285937. Open: Tue–Sun 11–19. Contact: Dr. Vladimir Nikitin, Yuri Matveev, Pavel Ivanov. 6–8 photo exhibitions/year

Sankt Peterburgsky tvorchesky sojuz khudozhnikov (IFA), St. Petersburg Union of Artists, Nevsky prospekt 60, RUS-191011 Sankt Peterburg. Tel (812) 2981473. Open: Tue–Sat 15–19. Contact: Natalya Dokka. 2 rooms, 200 m². 2–3 photo exhibitions/year

Tsentr sovremennogo iskusstva Pushkinskaya 10, Center for Contemporary Art Pushkinskaya 10, Pushkinskaya 10 (entrance from Ligovsky prospekt 53), RUS-191040 Sankt Peterburg. Tel (812) 1645371, Fax (812) 1645207. E-mail p10@ neva.spb.ru. Contact: Liudmila Vorontsova. Several galleries with different opening times

Tsentralnyj vystavochny sal Manezh, Central Exhibition Hall Manezh, Isaakievskaya ploshad 1, RUS-190000 Sankt Peterburg. Tel (812) 3148248, Fax (812) 3148254. E-mail srgey.bilyk @pop3.rcom.ru. Open: Fri–Wed 11– 18. Contact: Larisa Skob-kina. 1st floor 1,900 m², 2nd floor 1,600 m², hall 800 m². 2–4 photo exhibitions/year

Festivals & Fairs

InterFoto – Annual Moscow International Festival of Professional Photography, Commitee of InterFoto in Russia. Tel (095) 2403149, Fax (095) 2403149. E-mail interfoto@glas.apc. org. Website www. interfoto.ru

Osenny Maraphon, Autumn Maraphon, St. Petersburg Annual Month of Photography, Art Collegia Gallery, Ligovsky prospect 64, RUS-191000 Sankt Peterburg. Tel (812) 1649564, 2794273

Photobiennale – Month of Photography in Moscow, Moskovsky dom fotographii, Moscow House of Photography, Ostozhenka 16/1, RUS-

109034 Moskva. Tel (095) 2020610/ 2027612, Fax (095) 2024346. E-mail mdf@cityline.ru, fotofest@cityline.ru. Website www.mdf.cityline.ru

Rossiysky festival reklamy, Annual Russian Festival of Advertising, The Guild of Advertising Photographers. Contact: Yuri Zheludev, Leningradskee shosse 8, exit 12, RUS-125871 Moskva. Tel (095) 1506965, Fax (095) 1506965

Magazines

29, Bolshaya Andronikovskaya ulitsa 17, RUS-121019 Moskva. Tel (095) 2413545, Fax (095) 2413545. E-mail spdvsl@mail.ru. Editor: Evgeny Nesterov. Russian. Founded 1997, 4 issues/year

Foto magazin, Fizkulturny proezd 8, RUS-121309 Moskva. Tel (095) 7378868, Fax (095) 7378867. E-mail photomag@cityline.ru. Editor: Aleksandr Blaganadezhin. Russian. Founded 1996, 12 issues/year

Foto – Sibirsky Uspekh, Dobrolyubova 16, P. O. Box 62, RUS-630009 Novosibirsk. Tel (383-2) 660839, Fax (383-2) 660839. E-mail sibphoto@uspekh.nsk.ru. Editor: Oleg Romanyuk. Russian. Founded 1997, 4 issues/year

Foto & Video, Ordgenikidze ulitsa 11, RUS-117908 Moskva/P. O. Box 903, RUS-103009 Moskva. Tel (095) 9551584/2344797/9551742, Fax (095) 2344770. Website www.photo-video.ru. Editor: Andrey Andreev. Russian. Founded 1997, 12 issues/ year

Khudozhestvenny zhurnal, Art Magazine, Tverskaya 48/80, RUS-125047 Moskva. Contact: Dr.Victor Miziano. Tel (095) 2384422. E-mail

martmag@glasnet.ru. Russian.
Founded 1993, 4 issues/year

Na Nevskom, Peterburg, P. O. Box 63,
RUS-191025 Sankt Peterburg. Tel
(812) 3157753, Fax (812) 3154186.
E-mail express@infopro.spb.su.
Editor: Mikhail Borisov. Russian.
Founded 1999

PhotographerRu, Free Internet Maga-
zine on Russian Photography, Zabe-
lina 9/2, ap. 23, RUS-101001 Moskva.
Tel (095) 9246870, Fax (095) 9246870.
E-mail andrey@photographer.ru.
Website www.photographer.ru.
Editor: Andrey Bezukladnikov.
Russian/English. Founded 1998

Ptyuch, P. O. Box 725, RUS-117296
Moskva. Tel (095) 9382990, Fax (095)
9303154. Editor: Igor Shulinsky.
Russian. Founded 1995, 6 issues/year

Retikulatsia, Photoherald of Russian
Union of Photographers, P. O. Box 16,
RUS-428000 Cheboksary. Tel (8352)
576456/560761, Fax (8352) 214252.
E-mail master@gorod.chuvashia.ru.
Editor: Andrey Dobrynkin. Russian.
Founded 1990, 6 issues/year

Book Publishers

Galart, Chernyukhovsky ulitsa 4a,
RUS-101000 Moskva. Tel (095)
1513761

IMA-Press, Derbenevskaya ulitsa 10/
1, str. 3, RUS-101000 Moskva. Tel
(095) 2352937/2357904, Fax (095)
2353522

Iskusstvo, Sobinovsky pereulok 3,
RUS-103009 Moskva. Tel (095)
2035872, Fax (095) 2918882

Izobrazitelnoe iskusstvo, Sushchevsky
val 64, RUS-101000 Moskva. Tel (095)
2816548/2813320, Fax (095) 2814111

Bookshops

Dom knigi, House of Book, Nevsky
prospekt 28, RUS-191001 Sankt
Peterburg

Moskovsky Dom knigi, Moscow
House of Book, Novy Arbat 8, RUS-
110001 Moskva

Critics & Journalists

Ekaterina Andreeva, Gosudarstvenny
Russky muzei, State Russian Museum, Inzhenernaya ulitsa 4, RUS-
191011 Sankt Peterburg. Tel (812)
2191680/3522624, Fax (812) 3144153

Faina Balakhovskaya, Bolshaya
Nikitskaya 52, kv. 4, RUS-121069
Moskva. Tel (095) 2906723

Josef Bakshtein, 26 Bakinsky komissa-
rov ulitsa 3/1, kv. 202, RUS-117571
Moskva. Tel (095) 4334022. Institute
for Contemporary Art, Moskva

Dr. Elena Barhkatova, Russian
National Library, Nevsky prospect
76, RUS-190000 Sankt Peterburg. Tel
(812) 3123459. Chief of graphic-art
department

Andrey Baskakov, Semenovskaya
naberezhnaya 3/1-1, RUS-103094
Moskva. Tel (095) 3665501/3605501,
Fax (095) 3605501. President of the
Union of Russian Photo Artists,
Moskva

Leonid Bazhanov, Vorotnikovsky
pereulok 11/3, RUS-103006 Moskva.
Fax (095) 2998142. E-mail ncca@
aha.ru. Curator of State Centre for
Contemporary Art

Evgeny Berezner, Petrovka 28/2, RUS-
103051 Moskva. Tel (095) 9217997,
Fax (095) 9219291. E-mail berezner@
mtu-net.ru. Deputy-director of

ROSIZO State Centre for Museums and Exhibitions of the Ministry of Culture of Russian Federation, Vice-Chairman of Commission on Photo, Ministry of Culture of Russian Federation, Moskva; *Imago*, Bratislava

Andrey Bezukladnikov, Zubelina 9/2, ap. 23, RUS-101001 Moskva. Tel (095) 9246870, Fax (095) 9246870. Editor of *PhotographerRu*, Moskva

Mikhail Bode, Sirenevy bulvar 72, kv. 89, RUS-105484 Moskva. Tel (095) 2411653

Dr. Aleksander Borovsky, Zhakha-revskaya 7, kv. 24, RUS-190000 Sankt Peterburg. Tel (812) 2725420/2191680 (of). Chief of contemporary art de-partment of State Russian Museum, Ludwig Museum, Sankt Peterburg

Andrey Chezhin, Leninsky prospect, 178/2, kv. 50, RUS-196066 Sankt Peterburg. Tel (812) 108 3761

Grigory Chudakov, Lomonosovsky prospect 18, kv. 497, RUS-117296 Moskva. Tel (095) 9301042. *Imago*, Bratislava; Thames and Hudson, London

Julia Demidenko, Lenina ulitsa 12, kv. 44, RUS-191000 Sankt Peterburg. Tel (812) 2322201. Gosudarstvenny Russky Muzei, State Russian Muse-um, Sankt Peterburg

Andrey Dobrynkin, Leninskogo Komsomola 36-48, RUS-428000 Cheboksary. Tel (8352) 576456/ 223308, Fax (8352) 214252. E-mail master@gorod.chuvashia.ru. Editor of *Retikulatsia*, Cheboksary; curator of Gallery of Union of Photo Artists of Russia, Cheboksary

Dr. Andrey Erofeev, Prospect Mira 116/b, kv. 53, RUS-129620 Moskva. Tel (095) 2875992/4521777. E-mail art@art.hist.msu.su. Curator of

contemporary art department of State Art Museum Tsaritsyno, Moskva

Marat Gelman, Prospekt Mira 124/2, kv. 223, RUS-101001 Moskva. Tel (095) 2316654/(office) 1819634, Fax (095) 238 8492. Curator of Gelman Gallery, Moskva

Prof. Dr. Aleksander Jakimovich, Salvador Aliende ulitsa 7, kv. 59, RUS-125252 Moskva. Tel (095) 1980319. Department of Art History of Moscow State University

Lilya Jashchenko, Foto magazin, Fizkulturny proezd 8, RUS-121309 Moskva. Tel (095) 7378868, Fax (095) 7378867. E-mail photomag@ cityline.ru.

Olga Kabanova, Tverskaya ulitsa 18/ 1, RUS-103791 Moskva. Tel (095) 2095394/2302303, Fax (095) 2093620. *Izvestiya*, Moskva

Andrey Khlobystin, Nevsky prospekt 27 kv. 50, RUS-191011 Sankt Peter-burg. Tel (812) 3101798, Fax (812) 2728222. E-mail p10@neva.spb.ru

Pavel Khoroshilov, Ministry of Cul-ture of Russian Federation, Kitai-porodsky proezd 7, RUS-103693 Moskva. Tel (095) 9241786. Chief of the Commission of Photographic Art and Heritage

Dmitry Kyian, Foto & Video, Ordgenikidze ulitsa 11, RUS-117908 Moskva/P. O. Box 903, RUS-103009 Moskva. Tel (095) 9551584/2344797/ 9551742, Fax (095) 2344770. E-mail dmiki@foto-video.ru. Website www. photo-video.ru

Prof. Dr. Aleksander Lavrentyev, Myasnitskaya 21-18, RUS-101878 Moskva. Tel (095) 9281565. Design Academy (Stroganovskoe Uchilish-che); Photo Poche, Paris; Thames and

Hudson, London; Könemann, Köln; MOMA, New York

Vladimir Levashov, Krutitskaya naberezhnaya 13, kv. 81, RUS-109044 Moskva. Tel (095) 2743823/1813373. Soros Center of Contemporary Art, *iskusstvo kino magazin*, Moskva

Nina Martynova, Karl Marx ulitsa 70, RUS-610000 Kirov (Vyatka). Tel (8332) 38 1111. Kirov Region Art Museum n. a. V.&A. Vasnetsovs chief of storage

Dr. Victor Miziano, Tverskaya 48/80, RUS-125047 Moskva. Tel (095) 2384422 (office)/2512086. E-mail martmag@glasnet.ru. Editor of *Khudozhesvenny zhurnal*, Moskva; curator of Contemporary Art Centre

Dr. Vladimir Nikitin, Vasilyevsky ostrov, 14aya linia, 1a, kv.3. RUS-199034 Sankt Peterburg. Tel (812) 2185986/3285986. E-mail VN1902@ spb.edu. Faculty of Journalism of the St. Petersburg State University

Dr. Vitaly Patsyukov, Bolshoy Ovchinnikovsky pereulok 24/4, RUS-113134 Moskva. Tel (095) 9537236, Fax (095) 9537242. Curator of Cultural Centre Dom (House), Moskva

Dmitry Pilikin, Prospekt Prosvesheniya 53, korp. 1, kv. 178, RUS-195274 Sankt Peterburg. Tel (812) 5944341, Fax (812) 5944341. E-mail pilikin@dp5422.spb.edu

Tatiana Saburova, Lavochkina 48, kor. 3, kv. 5, RUS-125502 Moskva. Tel (095) 4554623. State Historic Museum of Russia, Moskva

Tatiana Salzirn, Prospect Mira 184-2-196, RUS-129301 Moskva. Tel (901) 7742710, Fax (095) 2926511. E-mail salzirn@glasnet.ru, interfoto@ glasnet.ru. InterFoto, Moskva

Prof. Dr. Ph. Valery Savchuk, P. O. Box 40, RUS-191011 Sankt Peterburg. Tel (812) 5285288. E-mail savchuk@ VS1334.spb.edu. Philosophy department of St. Petersburg State University

Elena Selina, 3 Sokolnicheskaya ulitsa 4, kv.15, RUS-107011 Moskva. Tel (095) 2695126. Curator of XL Gallery, Moskva

Irina Semakova, Bolshaya Filevskaya ulitsa 57, kv. 36, RUS-121467 Moskva. State Historic Museum of Russia, Moskva

Oleg Shishkin, Medelina 10/24, kv. 55, RUS-121354 Moskva. Tel (095) 4474236

Mikhail Sidlin, Sovietskoj Armii ulitsa 17/52, kv. 333, RUS-127018 Moskva. Tel (095) 2895540. *Nezavisimaya gazeta*, Moskva

Dr. Valery Stigneev, Bolshaya Spasskaya 6, kv. 128, RUS-129010 Moskva. Tel (095) 2801045. Institute of History and Theory of Art, Moskva; *Imago*, Bratislava; St. Martin Press, New York

Dr. Anatoly Strigalev, Ac. Pilyugina 14, kv. 10, RUS-120000 Moskva. Tel (095) 1323314. Institute of History and Theory of Art, Moskva

Olga Sviblova, Klimentovsky pereulok 6, kv. 23, RUS-113184 Moskva. Tel (095) 2020610/2027612, Fax (095) 2024346. E-mail mdf@ cityline.ru, fotofest@cityline.ru. Director of the Photobiennal, Moscow House of Photography, Moskva; Galerie Carré Noir, Paris

Irina Tchmyreva (Rena Gvozdeva), Petrovka 28/2, RUS-103051 Moskva. Tel (095) 9217997, Fax (095) 9219291. E-mail ira@photographer.ru. Chief-editor of *PhotographerRu*, Moskva; *Imago*, Bratislava; *Foto &Video*, ROSIZO State Centre for Museums and Exhibitions of the Ministry of Culture of Russian Federation, Moskva

Valery Volran, Baskov pereulok 3, kv. 10, RUS-191104 Sankt Peterburg. Tel (812) 2794273

Dr. Anri Vartanov, Chernyakhovsky ulitsa 2, kv. 56, RUS-125319 Moskva. Tel (095) 1510368. Institute of History and Theory of Art, Moskva

Schools & Workshops

Moskovsky gosudarstvenny universitet, Moscow State University, Faculty of Journalism, Volkhonka 20, RUS-101000 Moskva

Moskovsky gosudarstvenny universitet kultury, Moscow State University of Culture, Bibliotechnaya 7, Khimky 6, RUS-141400 Moskva

Sankt Peterburgsky gosudarstvenny universitet, St. Petersburg State University, Faculty of Journalism, Vassilievsky ostrov, 1-aya linia 26, RUS-199034 Sankt Peterburg

Associations

Gildiya reklamnykh fotografov, Guild of Advertising Photographers, Leningradskoe shosse 8, exit 12, RUS-125871 Moskva. Tel (095) 1506965, Fax (095) 1506965

Gildiya reklamnykh fotografov, Guild of Advertising Photographers, Torzhkovskaya 4, kv. 308, RUS-197342 Sankt Peterburg. Tel (812) 2469651, Fax (812) 2469651. E-mail nasonov@usa.net

Komissya po fotograficheskomu iskusstvu i naslediu Ministerstva kultury Rossiskoy federatsii, Commission of Photographic Art and Heritage, Ministry of Culture of Russian Federation, Kitaigorogsky proezd 7, RUS-103693 Moskva. Tel (095) 9241786, Fax (095) 9289979

Sojuz fotokhudozhnikov Rossii, Union of Photo Artists of Russia, Semenovskaya naberezhnaya, 3/1-1, RUS-103094 Moskva. Tel (095) 3605501, Fax (095) 3605501

Tvorchesky soyuz Fotoiskusstvo, Creative Union Fotoiskusstvo, Moskva, P. O. Box 220, RUS-121019 Moskva. Tel (095) 5481508/9567553, Fax (095) 5481508/9567553

Slovakia

Population: 5.4 million
Capital: Bratislava, 450,000
Currency: Slovenská koruna (Sk)
International code: ++421
Tourist information: Slovak
Tourist Board, Namestie slobody
2, P. O. Box 497, SK-974 01
Banska Bystrica
Tel (088) 414 28-60/62,
Fax (088) 414 66 26

Galleries & Museums

Štátná galéria výtvarného umenia,
State Gallery of Fine Art, Dolná 8,
SK-975 90 Banská Bystrica. Tel (088)
4126080/4124167, Fax (088) 4126080.
E-mail sgbb@isternet.sk. Website
www.isternet.sk/sgbb. Open: Tue–
Fri 10–18, Sat–Sun 10–17. Contact:
Helena Hudcovicova. Founded 1956.
4 rooms, 250 m². 2–3 photo exhibi-
tions/year. Artists: Pavol Breier,
Vasil Stanko, Peter Rónai, Group
Bratrstvo, Robert Vano

Múzeum Karola Plicku, Karol Plicka
Museum, SK-038 15 Blatnica. Tel
(0849) 5522758, Fax (0842) 32457.
Open: Tue–Sat 9–13, Sun 9–17 (Dec–
Feb), Tue–Sun 9–17 (Mar–Nov).
Founded 1988. Permanent exposition
of photographs of Karel Plicka (1894–
1987)

Francúzsky inštitút – Fotogaléria,
French Institute – Photo Gallery,
Sedlárska 7, SK-812 83 Bratislava.
Tel (07) 59347777, Fax (07) 59347799.
E-mail institut@france.sk. Website
www.france.sk. Open: Mon–Fri 9–18.
Contact: Michel Gies. Founded 1993.
2 rooms, 100 m². 5–6 photo exhibi-
tions/year. Artists: Henri Cartier-
Bresson, Frank Horvat, Jacques-Henri
Lartigue, Marc Riboud, Josef Koudel-
ka, Jeanloup Sieff

Galéria Artotéka, Municipal Library,
Kapucínska 18, SK-811 01 Bratislava.
Tel (07) 54435718/54435148. Open:
Mon, Wed, Thu 12.30–18, Tue, Fri 10–
16. Founded 1991. 2 rooms, 120 m².
2 photo exhibitions/year. Artists:
Roger Ballen, Sergey Lobovikov,
Luc Choquer, Gábor Kerekes, Gábor
Enikö, Janez Vlachy, Herman Pivk,
Lado Jaksa

Galéria Focus, Comenius University,
Štúrova 9, SK-811 00 Bratislava. Tel
(07) 52926530/52964192, Fax (07)
52926530. E-mail kzur@phil.uniba.sk,
vatral@phil.uniba.sk. Website www.
sphil.uniba.sk. Open: Mon–Fri 9–17.
Contact: Dr. Ján Lofaj. Founded 1992.
1 room, 50 m². 10–11 photo exhibi-
tions/year. Artists: Jaro Sýkora, Ivan
Kozácek, Andrej Bán, Irena Blühová,
Andrea Rašlová, Michal Suchý, Alan
Hyza

Galéria fotografie Profil, Gallery of
Photography Profil, Prepoštská 4,
SK-811 01 Bratislava. Tel (07)
54430459, Fax (07) 54430459. E-mail
fotofo@seznam.cz. Website www.
fotofo.sk. Open: Mon–Sun 13–18.
Contact: Prof. Václav Macek, Richard
Friedemann. Founded 1992. 3 rooms,
120 m². 10–11 photo exhibitions/year.
Artists: Philippe Pache, Ján Krízik,
Costas Ordolis, Jindrich Štreit, Jozef
Sedlák, Jana Šebestová, Pavel Pecha,
Judita Csáderová, Patrice Bouvier,
Filip Vanco, Chris Girrip, Zdenek
Lhoták, Tomasz Michalowski, Karel
Kameník

Galéria Médium, Vysoká skola výtvarných umení – Academy of Fine Arts, Hviezdoslavovo nám. 18, SK-814 37 Bratislava. Tel (07) 544435334, Fax (07) 54432340. Open: Mon–Fri 10–17, Sat 10–16. Contact: Mária Hudecová. Founded 1991. 4 rooms, 170 m². 2–3 photo exhibitions/year. Artists: Lubo Stacho, Ján Krízik, Milota Havránková, Duane Michals, Maria Hahnenkamp

Galéria mesta Bratislavy, Bratislava Municipal Gallery, Pálffy Palace, Panská ul., SK-815 35 Bratislava. Tel (07) 5444344. E-mail gmb@netlab.sk. Open: Tue–Sun 10–18 (Jun–Sep), 10–17 (Oct–May). Contact: Alena Kianicková. Founded 1959. Several rooms for photo exhibitions in different buildings. 4 photo exhibitions/year. Artists: Alexander Rodchenko, Jan Saudek, Eikoh Hosoe, Pierre Molinier, Rudo Sikora, Werner Bischof

Slovenská národná galéria, Slovak National Gallery, Riecna 1, SK-815 13 Bratislava. Tel (07) 54432081/54430746/54431703, Fax (07) 54433971. E-mail xsnggic@savba.savba.sk. Websites www.culture.gov.sk, www.savba.sk/logos/vytvar/galerie/sng.sng.html. Open: Tue–Sun 10–18. Contact: Aurel Hrabušický. 1 room, 400 m². 1–2 photo exhibitions/year. Artists: Joel-Peter Witkin, Annie Leibovitz, Sebastião Salgado, William Klein, Karol Kállay, Martin Martincek

Oravská galéria, Gallery of Orava Region, Hviezdoslavovo nám. 43, SK-026 01 Dolný Kubín. Tel (0845) 5864395. E-mail ogaleria@nextra.sk. Contact: Dr. Eva Luptáková. 2–3 photo exhibitions/year

Galéria Vihorlatského osvetového centra, Gallery of the Vihorlat Cultural Centre, Sokolovská 11, SK-066 15 Humenné. Tel (0933) 7752262, Fax (0933) 7753286. Contact: Mária Mišková. Founded 1990. 1 room, 90 m². 4–5 photo exhibitions/year. Artists: Jozef Sedlák, Jozef Ondzik, Tomáš Leno, Robo Kocan, Jano Pavlík

Fotogaléria Nova, Photogallery Nova, Verejná kniznica Jána Bocatia, Hlavná 48, SK-042 61 Košice. Tel (095) 62223291/6223291, Fax (095) 6223292. E-mail vkjb@KE.telecom.sk. Open: Mon–Fri 8–20, Sat 8–13. Contact: Gabriel Balogh. Founded 1981. 1 room, 50 m². 10–11 photo exhibitions/year. Artists: Judita Csáderová, Juraj Lipták, Magdaléna Robinsonová, Alexander Jiroušek

Východoslovenská galéria, East Slovakia Gallery, Hlavná 27, SK-040 01 Košice. Tel (095) 6221187-8, Fax (095) 6220340. Open: Tue–Sat 10–18, Sun 10–14. Contact: Helena Nimcová. Founded 1951. 1 room, 150 m². 2–3 photo exhibitions/year. Artists: Don McCullin, Ken Reynolds, Jan Saudek, Peter Zupník, Martin Martincek, Magdaléna Robinsonová

Galéria P. M. Bohúna, P. M. Bohún Gallery, Tranovského 3, SK-031 01 Liptovský Mikuláš. Tel (0849) 5522758, Fax (0848) 5514032. E-mail gpmb@mail.viapvt.sk. Open: Tue–Sun 9–17. Contact: Dr. Zuzana Gazíková, Zita Ziaranová. Founded 1955. 3 rooms, 100 m². 2–3 photo exhibitions/year. Artists: Josef Sudek, Ján Krízik, Dezo Hoffman, Martin Martincek, René Burri, Michal Kern, Peter Zupník, Robo Kocan

Múzeum moderného umenia Andyho Warhola, Andy Warhol Museum of Modern Art, Andyho Warhola 749, SK-068 01 Medzilaborce. Tel (0939) 21059, Fax (0939) 21069. Open: Tue–Sun 10–18. Contact: Dr. Michal Bycko.

Founded 1991. 4 rooms, 340 m². 2–3
photo exhibitions/year. Artists: Andy
Warhol, Billy Name, Rudo Prekop,
Dana Kyndrová, Robert Vano

Dom fotografie, House of Photogra-
phy, Námestie Sv. Egídia 3633/33,
SK-058 01 Poprad. Tel (092) 7723818,
Fax (092) 7723818. E-mail domfoto@
domfoto.sk. Website www.domfoto.
sk. Open: Tue–Sun 10–18. Contact:
Lucia Benická. Founded 1996. 1 room,
120 m². 10–12 photo exhibitions/year.
Artists: Robo Kocan, Cecil Beaton,
Pavol Breier, Peter Zupnik, Lubo
Stacho, Andrej Bán, John Kippin,
Miro Zeman, Marie Zavadilová

Tatranská galérie – Elektráren, Tatra
Gallery – Power Station, Hviezdo-
slavova 12, SK-058 01 Poprad. Tel
(092) 65315/7721670, Fax (092)
7721670. E-mail galeria@isternet.sk.
Open: 10–18 (May–Sep). Contact:
Lucia Benická. Founded 1993. 4
rooms, 1,200 m². 2 photo exhibitions/
year. Artists: John Kippin, Nicky
West, Chris Wainwright, Ray Lee,
Ian Wiblin, Andrej Bán, Jindrich
Štreit, Pavel Pecha, Lubo Stacho,
Robo Kocan

Múzeum J. M. Petzvala, J. M. Petzval
Museum, Petzvalova 30, SK-059 01
Spišská Belá. Tel (0968) 4591307.
Open: Mon–Fri 8–14 (Oct–Mar),
8.30– 17 (Apr–Sep). Contact: Antónia
Ronckevicová. Founded 1968 as a
branch of Slovak Technical Museum.
Permanent exposition of J. M. Petzval
(1807–1891). 4–5 photo exhibitions/
year

Galéria umelcov Spiša, Gallery of
Artists of Spiš Region, Zimná 46, SK-
052 01 Spišská Nová Ves. Tel (0965)
24710, Fax (0965) 24259. Open: Tue–
Fri 8.30–17, Sat–Sun 8–12. Contact:
Jozef Joppa. Founded 1987. Several
rooms for exhibitions. 2–3 photo

exhibitions/year. Artists: Pavol
Breier, Margita Strohmeyer, Peter
Zupník, Andrej Barla, Andrej Bán,
Robo Kocan, Rudo Prekop

Povazská galéria umenia, The Art
Gallery of Povazie Region, Štefáni-
kova 2, SK-010 01 Zilina. Tel (089)
5622522/5622415, Fax (089) 5626931.
Open: Tue–Fri 9–17, Sat–Sun 10–17.
Contact: Milan Mazur. Founded 1960.
2–3 photo exhibitions/year. Several
rooms for exhibitions. Artists: Michal
Kern, Ján Krízik, Rudo Sikora, Lubo
Stacho, Jindrich Štreit

Festivals & Fairs

Mesiac fotografie Bratislava, Month
of Photography Bratislava, FOTOFO,
Prepoštská 4, P. O. Box 290, SK-
814 99 Bratislava. Tel (07) 63831529,
Fax (07) 54430459. E-mail mac@kfv.
ftf.vsmu.sk, fotofo@seznam.cz.
Website www.fotofo.sk

Magazines

Dart, Stredoeurópsky inštitút
súcasného umenia, Central European Institute of Contemporary Art,
Vajnorká 52, SK-831 04 Bratislava.
Tel (07) 44257702, Fax (07) 43331232.
E-mail dart@pobox.sk. Editor:
Richard Gregor. Slovak. Founded
1999. Copy price: Sk 49. Annual
subscription: Sk 490, 10 issues/year

Fototip, Garmond, Skuteckého 39,
SK-974 01 Banská Bystrica. Tel (088)
414-2061/6737/5631, Fax (088)
4145631. E-mail garmond@isternet.sk.
Website www.w2sk. Editor: Marta
Svítková. Slovak. Founded 1994.
Copy price: Sk 45. Annual subscrip-
tion: Sk 492, 12 issues/year

Imago, Photography in Middle and East Europe. FOTOFO, Prepoštská 4, P. O. Box 290, SK-814 99 Bratislava. Tel (07) 63831529, Fax (07) 54430459. E-mail mac@kfv.ftf.vsmu.sk, fotofo@ seznam.cz. Website www.fotofo.sk. Editor: Prof. Dr. Václav Macek. English. Founded 1995. Copy price: US$15.00, 2 issues/year

Revue vizuálnej komunikácie, Revue of visual communication, Štúdio V&V, Uršulínska 2, SK-040 01 Košice. Tel (095) 6220202, Fax (095) 6220202. Editors: Vladimír Vološín, Jana Zitová. Slovak. Founded 1996. Copy price: Sk 80. Annual subscription: Sk 320, 4 issues/year

Výtvarnické noviny, Fine Art Newspapers, Slovenská výtvarnícka únia, Partizánska 21, SK-813 51 Bratislava.

Tel (07) 54412425, Fax (07) 54433154. Editor: Viera Kleinová. Slovak. Founded 1996. Copy proce: Sk 50. Annual subscription: Sk 200, 4 issues/year

Book Publishers

FOTOFO, Prepoštská 4, P. O. Box 290, SK-814 99 Bratislava. Tel (07) 63831529, Fax (07) 54430459. E-mail mac@kfv.ftf.vsmu.sk, fotofo@ seznam.cz. Website www.fotofo.sk

Osveta, Osloboditeľov 21, SK-036 54 Martin. Tel (0842) 4134121

Slovart, Pekná cesta 6/B, P. O. Box 14, SK-830 04 Bratislava 34. Tel (07) 44871164, Fax (07) 44871210

I M A G O

A UNIQUE BI-ANUAL MAGAZINE ABOUT CONTEMPORARY PHOTOGRAPHY IN CENTRAL AND EASTERN EUROPE

The magazine informs about current issues and publishes critical essays. It is the only magazine focused on Central and Eastern European Photography and is published in English. Three portfolios by contemporary artists from Slovakia, The Czech Republic, Poland, Hungary, Russia, Ukraine, Croatia, Slovenia, Latvia, Lithuania, Estonia, Romania and other countries are included in each issue along with essays on current issues, interviews with critics and artists, reviews of books and events in Central and Eastern Europe. ▶ The magazine focuses on experimental contemporary work which pushes the bounderies of the medium ▶ The readership is mainly critics, curators and artists ▶ 80 pages, size 24 x 29 cm, duo-tone printing

SUBSCRIPTION INFORMATION:
Volume 5 (2000) ISSN 1335-1362 ▶ Copy price: USD 15
▶ Annual subscription: Europe USD 30

For further information or to receive your FREE sample copy please contact:
FOTOFO, Prepoštská 4, P.O. Box 290, 814 99 Bratislava, Slovakia
tel. / fax: 00 421-7-5443 0459, E-mail: lucia.lendelova@usa.net,
fotofo@seznam.cz, www.fotofo.sk

Bookshops

Dom fotografie, House of Photography, Námestie Sv. Egídia 3633/33, SK-058 01 Poprad. Tel (092) 7723818, Fax (092) 7723818. E-mail domfoto@domfoto.sk. Website www.domfoto.sk

Galéria fotografie Profil, Gallery of Photography Profil, Prepoštská 4, SK-811 01 Bratislava. Tel (07) 54430459, Fax (07) 54430459. E-mail fotofo@seznam.cz. Website www.fotofo.sk

Critics & Journalists

Lucia Benická, Banícka 22, SK-058 01 Poprad. Tel (092) 7764588, Fax (092) 64588. Director of Dom fotografie/House of Photography, Poprad; *Sme, Imago,* Bratislava; *Fototip,* Banská Bystrica; *Fotografie Magazín,* Praha; *Zoom,* Milano

Slávka Breierová, Jurigovo nám. 15, SK-841 05 Bratislava. Tel (07) 65429538. *Imago,* Bratislava

Richard Friedmann, SENP 163, SK-05916 Hranovnica. Tel (092) 7795179. Gallery Profil, Bratislava

Petra Hanáková, Gorkého 9, SK-81103 Bratislava. Tel (07) 54131217. *Domino,* Bratislava

Ludovít Hlavác, Poloreckého 2, SK-85103 Bratislava. Tel (07) 62246475

Aurel Hrabušický, Na Revíne 17, SK-831 01 Bratislava. Tel (07) 54776912. Curator of the Slovak National Gallery, Bratislava; *Imago, Galéria,* Bratislava

Lucia Lendelová, Korenicova 3, SK-811 03 Bratislava. Tel (07) 54411414. E-mail lucia.lendelova@usa.net. *Imago, Domino,* Bratislava

Dr. Ján Lofaj, Furdekova 10, SK-851 03 Bratislava. Tel (07) 62314453. *Fotografie Magazín,* Praha; *Otázky zurnalistiky, Národná osveta,* Bratislava

Prof. Dr. Václav Macek, Krásnohorská 7, SK-851 01 Bratislava. Tel (07) 63831529, Fax (07) 63831529. E-mail mac@kfv.ftf.vsmu.sk, fotofo@seznam.cz. Director of the Month of Photography in Bratislava; editor of *Imago,* Bratislava

Dr. Juliana Menclová, Hlavná 999/56, SK-900 31 Stupava

Dr. Marián Pauer, Znievska 28, SK-851 06 Bratislava. Tel (07) 63828064. *Národná obroda,* Bratislava; *Fototip,* Banská Bystrica; *Fotografie Magazín,* Praha

Jozef Ridilla, Juzná 4/506, SK-086 56 Pecovská Nová Ves. *Imago,* Bratislava

Lubo Stacho, Povraznícka 13, SK-811 05 Bratislava. Tel (07) 52493822. Associate Professor of the Academy of Fine Arts, Bratislava

Fero Tomík, Víglašská 54, SK-851 07 Bratislava. Tel (07) 63828372

Vladimír Vorobjov, Krízna 17, SK-811 07 Bratislava. Tel (07) 554211194. *Fototip,* Banská Bystrica; *Imago,* Bratislava

Schools & Workshops

Letná fotoškola Domu fotografie, Summer Photo School of the House of Photography, Námestie Sv. Egídia 3633/33 , SK-058 01 Poprad. Tel (092) 7723818, Fax (092) 7723818. E-mail domfoto@domfoto.sk. Website www.domfoto.sk

Národné osvetové centrum, National Enlightenment Center, Námestie SNP 12, SK-811 03 Bratislava. Tel (07) 52964383/52923736

Škola uzitkového výtvarníctva, Secondary School of Applied Arts, Jakobyho 15, SK-040 84 Košice. Tel (095) 6237251/6237481

Škola uzitkového výtvarníctva Josefa Vydru, Josef Vydra Secondary School of Applied Arts, Dúbravská cesta 9, SK-841 04 Bratislava. Tel (07) 54791361, Fax (07) 54793466

Vysoká škola výtvarných umení, Katedra vizuálnych umení, Academy of Fine Arts, Visual Arts Department, Hviezdoslavovo nám 18, SK-814 37 Bratislava. Tel (07) 532251, Fax (07) 5332340

Warholova ulica – letná fotoškola, Warhol Street – Summer Photoschool, Múzeum moderného umenia Andy Warhola, Andyho Warhola 749, SK-068 01 Medzilaborce. Tel (0939) 21059, Fax (0939) 21059

Associations

Národné osvetové centrum, National Enlightenment Center, Dr. Zuzana Skoludová, Námesetie SNP 12, SK-811 03 Bratislava. Tel (07) 52964383/52923736

Slovenský syndikát novinárov, The Union of Slovak Journalists, Foto-klub, Zupné nám. 7, SK-811 03 Bratislava. Tel (07) 5334534

Zdruzenie profesionálnych fotografov, The Union of Professional Photographers, Slovenská výtvarná únia, Partizánska 21, SK-811 01 Bratislava. Tel (07) 54412425

Zväz slovenských fotografov, The Union of Slovak Photographers, ul. Slobody 10, SK-034 01 Ruzomberok

Grants & Awards

Award for the best photographic book published in Central and East European Countries. Contact: FOTOFO, Prepoštská 4, P. O. Box 290, SK-81 499 Bratislava. Tel (07) 638831529, Fax (07) 5440459. E-mail fotofo@ seznam.cz

Slovenia

Population: 2 million
Capital: Ljubljana, 276,000
Currency: Tolar (SLT)
International code: ++386
Tourist information: Slovenian
Tourist Board WTC, Dunajska
156, SLO-1000 Ljubljana
Tel (061) 18 91 840
Fax (061) 18 91 841

Galleries & Museums

Galerija Loggia, Titov trg 2, SLO-6000 Koper. Tel (066) 742688, Fax (066) 742690. E-mail obalne.galerije@guest.arnes.si. Open: Tue–Sat 10–13, 16–19, Sun 10–12. Contact: Toni Biloslav. Founded 1972. 2 photo exhibitions/year. Artists: Robert Mapplethorpe, Man Ray, Joze Kološa

Arhitekturni muzej, Museum of Architecture, Grad Fuzine, Studenec 2a, SLO-1260 Ljubljana. Tel (061) 1409798, Fax (061) 1409457. E-mail aml@siol.si. Open: Mon–Fri 8–15. Contact: Dr. Primoz Lampic. Founded 1972. 2 rooms, 800 m². 2 photo exhibitions/year. Artists: Ivan Dvorzak, Christian Vogt, Branko Lenart, Heribert Burkert, Stojan Kerbler, Stane Jagodic

Cankarjev dom – Mala fotogalerija, Kulturni i kongresni center, Cultural and Congress Centre "Cankarjev dom" – Small Photogallery, Prešernova 10, SLO-1000 Ljubljana. Tel (061) 1258121/1767152, Fax (061) 224279. E-mail nina.pirnat@cd-cc.si. Website www.cd-cc.si. Open: Tue–Sat 10–19, Sun 10–14. Contact: Nina Pirnat Spahic. Founded 1981. 3 rooms, 400 m². 6 photo exhibitions/year. Artists: Josef Sudek, Tono Stano, Sylvia de Swaan, Mario Vidor, Marko Modic, Arne Hodalic, Herman Pivk

Galerija Kapelica, Kapelica Gallery, Kersnikova 4, SLO-1000 Ljubljana. Tel (061) 1317010, Fax (061) 319448. E-mail galerija@kapelica.org. Website www.kapelica.org. Open: Mon–Fri 8–18. Contact: Jurij Krpan. Artists: Rajko Bizjak, Talent Factory, Mathias Herman, Students of FAMU, Praha

Galerija KUD – France Prešeren, Karunova 14, SLO-1000 Ljubljana. Tel (061) 332288/332299, Fax (061) 331128. E-mail tadeja@kud-fp.si. Website www.kud-fp.si. Open: Mon–Sat 11–23. Contact: Alma Stjepic Popovska, Tadeja Kovac. Founded 1991. 2 rooms, 75 m². 6 photo exhibitions/year. Arists: Goran Bertok, Jure Breceljnik, Lado Jakša, Luciano Kleva

Jakopiceva Galerija, Jakopic Gallery, Slovenska 9, SLO-1000 Ljubljana. Tel (061) 1252393, Fax (061) 1400344. Open: Tue–Sat 10–18, Sun 10–13. Contact: Mica Planinc. 2 rooms, 80 m². Artists: Dusan Pirih-Hup, Mario Magajna, Karlo Kocjancic

Mestska Galerija, City Art Gallery, Mestni trg 5, SLO-1000 Ljubljana. Tel (061) 212896, Fax (061) 221125. Open: Tue–Sat 10–18, Sun 10–13. Contact: Aleksander Bassin. Founded 1963. 10 rooms, 371 m². 2–3 photo exhibitions/year. Artists: Jure Breceljnik, Joze Suhadolnik, Bozidar Dolenc

Moderna galerija, Modern Gallery, Tomsiceva 14, SLO-1000 Ljubljana. Tel (061) 214106, Fax (061) 214120. E-mail info@mg-lj.si. Open: Tue–Sat

10–18, Sun 10–13. Contact: Lara Štrumej. Founded 1991. 2 rooms, 340 m². 4 photo exhibitions/year. Artists: Jeanloup Sieff, Annie Leibovitz, Werner Bischof, Wim Wenders, Andres Serrano

Fotogalerija Stolp, Fotoklub Maribor, Zidovska ulica, P. O. Box 1512, SLO-2001 Maribor. Tel (062) 212490, Fax (062) 412500. E-mail fotogalerija.stolp@guest.ames.si. Website www.margarina.uni-mb/fotogalerija.stolp. Open: Tue–Fri 15–19, Sat 10–12. Contact: Bogomir Cerin, Branimir Ritonja. Founded 1989. 4 rooms, 85 m². 12 photo exhibitions/year. Artists: Bogo Cerin, Branko Konicek, Manfred M. Pichler, Janko Jelnikar, Manfred Kriegelstein, Branimir Ritonja, Arpad Szentivanyi, Matjaz Wenzel

Galerija KID-Kibla-Kibela, Kneza Koclja 9, SLO-2000 Maribor. Tel (062) 2294012, Fax (062) 2294020. E-mail aleksandra.kostic@kibla.org. Website www.kibla.org. Open: Mon–Fri 10–14, 16–22. Contact: Aleksandra Kostic. Founded 1996. 1 room, 135 m². Artists: Goran Bertok, Ziga Korotnik, Jure Breceljnik, Aleksandra Vajd, Damjan Švarc

Festivals & Fairs

International Photographers Ex-Tempore Idrija, Janko Prelovec, Lapajnetova 59, SLO-5280 Idrija. Tel (065) 72774, Fax (065) 71331

Mlada Svetovna Fotografija, World Young Photography, Jure Breceljnik, Kneza Koclja 13, SLO-1000 Ljubljana.

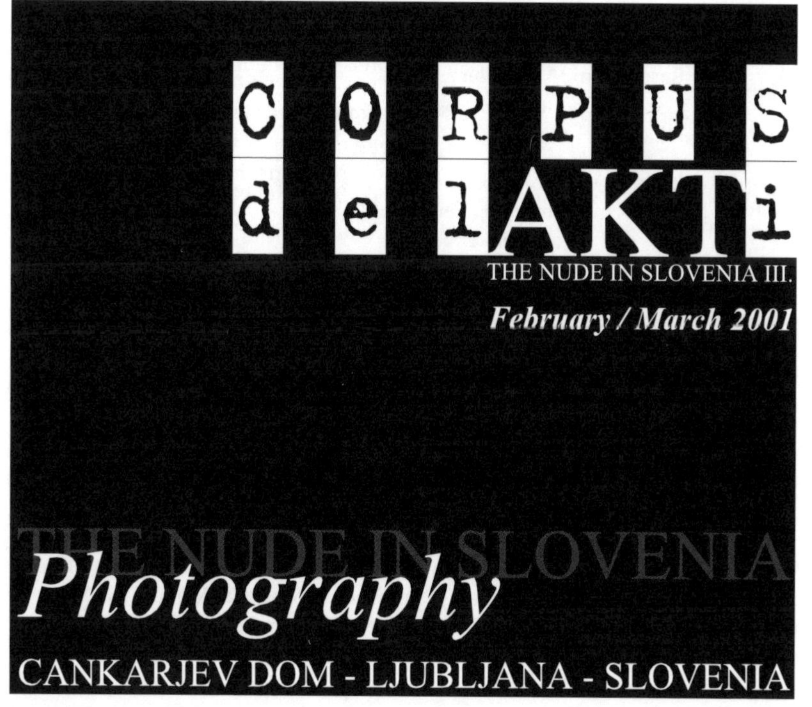

Tel (061)1553483, 942664. E-mail
jure.b@k2.net. Every year

Magazines

Emzin/Art Magazine, Metelkova 6/II,
SLO-1000 Ljubljana. Tel (061) 13035-
40/44, Fax (061) 1303540. E-mail
emzin@guest.arnes.si. Editors:
Dušan Dovc, Metka Dariš. Copy
price: US$8.00, 6 issues/year

Fotografija, Photography Magazine,
Cebelarska 20, SLO-1117 Ljubljana.
Tel (061) 1503570. E-mail studio.
graffit@siol.net. Editor: Meta Krese.
Copy price: US$5.00, 5 issues/year

M'ARS, Magazine of the Modern
Gallery, Tomsiceva 14, SLO-1000
Ljubljana. Tel (061) 214120, Fax (061)
214120. E-mail info&@mg-lj.si.
Website www.mg-lj.si

Critics & Journalists

Aleksander Bassin, City Art Gallery,
Mestni trg 5, SLO-1000 Ljubljana. Tel
(061) 212896, Fax (061) 221125

Rajko Bizljak, Vrtojba, Ulica 9. Sep-
tembra 113, SLO-5290 Šempeter. Tel
(041) 732562. E-mail rajko.bizjak@
k2.net

Marina Grzinic, Pohlinova 14, SLO-
1000 Ljubljana. Tel (061) 1403736,
Fax (061) 1403736. E-mail margrz@
nhs.zrc-sazu.si

Mirko Kambic, Gosposvetska 4/II,
SLO-1000 Ljubljana. Tel (061) 1332158

Stojan Kerbler, Potrceva cesta 46,
SLO-2250 Ptuj. Tel (062) 777429

Aleksandra Kostic, Kneza Kocjlja
9, SLO-2000 Maribor. Tel (062)
2294012, Fax (062) 2294020. E-mail

aleksandra.kostic@kibla.org. Galerija
KID, Maribor

Brane Kovic, Ilirska 6, SLO-1000
Ljubljana. Tel (061) 321648, Fax (061)
214120. E-mail info@mg-lj.si. Modern
Gallery, Ljubljana

Dr. Primoz Lampic, Dunajska 351,
SLO-1231 Lj-Crnuce. Tel (061)
375561/(041) 866420. E-mail
neda.lampic@sid.net

Andrej Medved, Krozna pot 6, SLO-
6000 Koper. Tel (066) 282048

Sarival Sesic, City Art Museum,
Mestni trg 5, SLO-1000 Ljubljana.
Tel (061) 212896, Fax (061) 221125

Jelka Sutej-Adamic, DELO d.o.o.,
Dunajska cesta 5, SLO-1000 Ljubljana.
Tel (061) 1737290, Fax (061) 1737290

Associations

Društvo fotografov Slovenije, Asso-
ciation of Slovenian Photographers,
Trzaška 2/a, SLO-1000 Ljubljana.
Tel (061) 1252307

FAIR, Koblarjeva 34, SLO-1000
Ljubljana. Tel (041) 732562. E-mail
rajko.bizjak@k2.net-projektfair

Fotografska zveza Slovenije, Photographic Union of Slovenia, P. O. Box
98, SLO-4220 Škofja Loka. E-mail
fotografska.zveza@fzs-zveza.si.
Website www.fzs-zveza.si

Grants & Awards

Photography of the Year, Exhibition
of the best Slovenian photographs of
the year. Contact: Emzin/Art Magazine, Metelkova 6/II, SLO-1000
Ljubljana. Tel (061) 13035-40/44, Fax

(061) 1303540. E-mail emzin@guest.
arnes.si

New Media

Festival of Computer Arts, Multime-
dia Center KiberSRCeLab – KIBLA,
Kneza Koclja 9, SLO-2000 Maribor.
Tel (062) 2294012/2294013, Fax (062)
225376. E-mail peco@kibla.org.
Website www.kibla.org

Spain

Population: 39.3 million
Capital: Madrid, 5 million
Currency: Peseta (Pta)
International code: ++34
Tourist information:
Turespana – Instituto de Pro-
motion del Turismo de España,
José Lazaro Goldiano 6,
E-28036 Madrid

Galleries & Museums

Centro Galego de Artes da Imaxe,
Durán Loriga 10, E-15003 A Coruña.
Tel (981) 203499, Fax (981) 204054.
E-mail dir@cgai.org. Website www.
cgai.org. Director/curator: Jose Luis
Cabo. Founded 1991. 1 room, 200 m².
4 photo exhibitions/year

Alter Ego, C/Doctor Dou 11, E-08001
Barcelona. Tel (93) 3023698, Fax (93)
3023698. E-mail doctordou@
hotmail.com

Centre d'Art Santa Mònica, Rambla
Santa Mònica 7, E-08002 Barcelona.
Tel (93) 4122279, Fax (93) 4122288.
Director: Josep Miquel Garcia.
Founded 1988

**Centre de Cultura Contemporània de
Barcelona,** Montalegre 5, E-08001
Barcelona. Tel (93) 3064100, Fax (93)
3064101. E-mail troig@cccb.org.
Website www.cccb.org

Espai Fotogràfic Can Basté, Passeig
Fabra i Puig 274–276, E-08031 Barcelona. Tel (93) 4206651, Fax (93)
4201797. E-mail globalid@

lix.intercom.es. Website www.
noubarris.net/cccanbaste

Fundació Antoni Tàpies, Aragó 255,
E-08007 Barcelona. Tel (93) 4870315,
Fax (93) 4870009. E-mail museu@
ftapies.com. Open: Tue–Sun 10–20.
Director: Miquel Tàpies. Curator:
Nuna Enquita. Founded 1990. 3
rooms, 1,135 m². 1–2 photo exhibi-
tions/year. Artists: Antoni Tàpies,
Mario Merz, Louise Bourgeois,
Brassaï, Gary Winogrand, Krszysztof
Wodiczko, Franz Kline, Craigie Hors-
field, Hans Haacke, Chris Marker

Galeria Estrany, de la Mota, Passatge
Mercader 18, E-08008 Barcelona. Tel
(93) 2157051, Fax (93) 4873552. E-mail
estranydelamota@teleline.es. Open:
Tue–Sat 10.30–13.30, 16.30–20.30.
Directors: Antoni Estrany, Angels de
la Mota. Founded 1990. 2 rooms,
400 m². 2–3 photo exhibitions/year.
Artists: Antoni Abad, Pep Agut,
Ignasi Aballí, Jean-Marc Bustamante,
Nuria Canal, Daniel Canogar, Alicia
Framis, Jorge Ribalta, Thomas Ruff,
Helena Almeida, Esko Mänikkö

Galería Joan Prats, Ramba de Cata-
lunya 54, E-08007 Barcelona. Tel (93)
2160284, Fax (93) 4871614. Open:
Tue–Sat 10.30–13.30, 17–20.30. Direc-
tor: Steve Afif. Founded 1976. 1 room,
120 m². 2 photo exhibitions/year.
Artists: Frederic Amat, Perejaume,
Alfons Borrall, Joan Buossa, Hannah
Collins, Ricardo Cotanda, Guinovart,
Hernandez Pijuan, Rafols Casamada,
Jose Noguero

Galeria Ras, Doctor Dou 10, E-08001
Barcelona. Tel (93) 4127199. E-mail
ras@oike.com

Kowasa, Gallery Arte Fotográfico,
Mallorca, 235, E-08008 Barcelona. Tel
(93) 4873588, Fax (93) 2158054. E-mail
kowasa@abaforum.es. Website www.

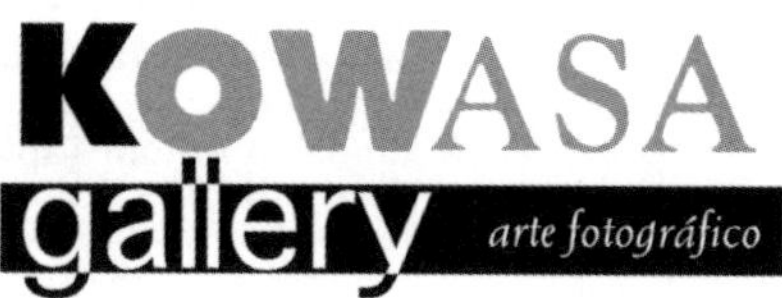

Photographers represented:

Agustí Centelles	Sonia Fort	Ramón Masats
Eduardo Cortils	Martí Llorens	Rafael Navarro
Ramón David		

Work available by spanish artists:

Ramón Batlles	Josep Esclusa	Anna Malagrida
Pere Catalá Pic	Joan Fontcuberta	Xavier Miserach
Francesc Catalá Roca	Emili Godes	Ouka Lele
Tony Catany	Joaquim Gomis	Aleydis Rispa
Marga Clark	Chema Madoz	Josep Sala

Work available by other artists:

Dimitri Baltermants	Annelise Hager	Vilém Reichmann
Herbert Bayer	Heinz Hajek-Halke	Alexander Rodtchenko
Férenc Berko	Arthur Harfaux	Jaroslav Rösseler
Edouard Boubat	Raoul Hausmann	Jan Saudek
Bill Brandt	Florenece Henri	Christian Schad
Théodore Brauner	Tibor Honty	Joost Schmidt
Robert Capa	M. Jacob Kjeldgaard	Arthur Siegel
Étienne Carjat	Lotte Jacobi	Aaron Sisking
Lynwood Chase	Václav Jírû	Bohumil Stastny
Arthur Cheesman	Tony Keeler	Alfreed Stieglitz
Vladimir Chlebnikov	Peter Keetman	Paul Strand
Václav Chochola	Willy Keesels	Carl Struwe
Lucien Clergue	William Klein	Josef Sudek
Charles Clifford	August Kreyenkamp	Jaime David Thischler
Erick Consemuller	Clarence J. Laughlin	Jerry Uelsmann
Pierre Cordier	J.Laurent	Paolo Verzone
Carlotta Corpron	Dora Maar	Brett Weston
Cesar Domela	Arnold Newman	Eugen Wiskowsky
Frantísek Drtikol	Mathieu Pernot	Gérard Vulliamy
Jaromir Funke	Gérard Petremand	Alexander Zhitomirsky
Jérôme Galland	Pablo Picasso/André Villers	
Flor Garduño	Bernard Plossu	Mariano Zuzunaga
Ralph Gibson	Gilles-Henri Polge	Piet Zwart
Grancel W. Fitz	Edward Quigley	

MALLORCA, 235 - 08008 BARCELONA - España
TEL. 93 487 35 88 - FAX 93 215 80 54

abaforum.es/kowasa. Open: Tue–Sat 16.30–20.30. Director: Hubert de Wangen. Curator: Juan Naranjo. Founded 1997. 2 rooms, 60 m². 6–7 photo exhibitions/year. Artists: Marti Llorens, Ramon David, Rafael Navarro, Eduardo Cortils

Libreria Tartessos, c. Canuda 35, E-08002 Barcelona. Tel (93) 3018181. Open: 10–14, 16.30–20. Director: Jos Framis. Founded 1981. 1 room, 100 m². 12 photo exhibitions/year. Artists: Flor Garduño, Toni Catany, Frederic Barthes, Eugenia Baicells

Metrònom, c. Fussina 9, E-08003 Barcelona. Tel (93) 2684298, Fax (93) 2684298. Open: Tue–Sat 10–14, 16.30–20.30. Director: Rafael Tous. Founded 1980. 4 rooms, 500 m². 6–8 photo exhibitions/year

Museu d'Art Contemporani MACBA, Plaça dels Àngels 1, E-08001 Barcelona. Tel (93) 4120810, Fax (93) 4124602. E-mail macba@macba.es. Website www.macba.es

Museu Nacional d'Art de Catalunya, Palau Nacional-Parc de Montjuïc, E-08038 Barcelona. Tel (93) 6220360, Fax (93) 6220374. E-mail mnac@correu.gencat.es. Website www.mnac.es. Open: Tue–Sat 10–17, Sun+holidays 10–14.30. Director: Eduard Carbonell. Curator: David Balsells. Founded 1996. 4 rooms, 1,200 m². 2–3 photo exhibitions/year. Artists: Joaquim Pla Janini, Josep Masana, Emili Godes, Josep Lladó, Otho Lloyd, Antoni Arissa, Oriol Maspons, Carles Fontsere

Posada del Potro, Plaza del Potro 10, E-14002 Córdoba. Tel (957) 472000207, Fax (957) 478050. Open: 9–14, 19–21. Director: Alicia Recuera. Founded 1972. 3 rooms, 200 m². 14 photo exhibitions/year. Artists:

Robert Hammerstiel, Miguel Oriola, Gabriel Cualladó, Franco Fontana, Isabel Muñoz, Lucien Clergue, Carlos Perez Siquier, Xurso Lobato, Juan Vacas, Jose Carlos Nievas

Museo Internacional de Electrografia, Ronda Julian Romero 20, E-16001 Cuenca. Tel (969) 179115, Fax (969) 179118. E-mail mide@mide-cu.uclm.es. Website www.uclm.es/mide/

Canal de Isabel II, Santa Engracia 125, E-28003 Madrid. Tel (91) 4451000, Fax (91) 4474763. Open: Tue–Sat 11–14, 17–20.30, Sun 11–14. Director: Teresa Zaragoza. Founded 1986. 1 room, 400 m². 5 photo exhibitions/year. Artists: Lisette Model, Inge Morat, Alex Webb, Elliot Erwitt, Johannes Muggenthaler, José Gomez, Martin Sampedro, Daniel Canogar, Jana Leo, Marcelo Exposito

Circulo de Bellas Artes, Calle Alcalá 42, E-28014 Madrid. Tel (91) 5317700, Fax (91) 5310552. Open: Tue–Sun 11–14, 17–21. Director: Alejandro Castellote. Founded 1981. 3 rooms, 2,000 m². 8 photo exhibitions/year

Elba Benítez Galería, San Lorenzo 11, E-28004 Madrid. Tel (91) 3080468, Fax (91) 3190169. Open: Tue–Sat 11–14, 17–21. Director: Elba Benitez. Founded 1990. 2 rooms, 140 m². Artists: Pep Agut, Juan Luis Moraza, Jürgen Partenheimer, Ana Prada, Elena Del Rivero, Francisco Ruitz De Infante, Reiner Ruthenbeck, Manuel Saiz, Francesc Torres, Dario Urzay

Galería Helga de Alvear, Doctor Fourquet, 12, E-28012 Madrid. Tel (91) 4680506, Fax (91) 4675134. E-mail dealvear@w3art.es. Website w3art.es/dealvear. Open: Tue–Sat 11–14, 17–21. Directors: Helga de Alvear, Carlos Urroz. Founded 1964.

PHOTO PROJECTS
Rosalind Williams

EXHIBITIONS
SEMINARS
in
SPAIN
and
ABROAD

Plaza Conde de Miranda, 4 ▪ 28005 MADRID
Tel. 34 91 542 96 58 ▪ Fax: 34 91 894 30 13
e-mail: rosphopro@grn.es

2 rooms, 150 m². 2–3 photo exhibitions/year. Artists: Pep Agut, Daniel Canogar, Christine Davis, Joan Fontcuberta, Kazuo Katase, José Maldonado, Mabel Palacín, Frank Thiel, Eulàlia Valldosera, Javier Vallhonrat

Museo Nacional, Centro de Arte Reina Sofía, Santa Isabel 52, E-28012 Madrid. Tel (91) 4675062/4683002, Fax (91) 4673163. E-mail catherine.coleman@cars.mcu.es. Website www.museoreinasofia.mcu.es. Open: Mon+Wed–Sat 10–21, Sun 10–14.30. Director: Jose Guirao Cabrera. Curator: Catherine Coleman. Founded 1990. 23 rooms. 4–5 photo exhibitions/year. Artists: Madrid photographers

Centro de Fotografía Isla de Tenerife, Pza. Isla de la Madera, s/n, E-38003 Santa Cruz de Tenerife. Tel (922) 290951, Fax (922) 240553. E-mail avela@museoscabtf.rcanaria.es. Open: 8–15. Director: Antonio Vela. Founded 1989. 3 rooms, 450 m². 5 photo exhibitions/year

Forvm Gallery, Carrer dels Cavallers 4-2°-3a, E-43003 Tarragona. Tel (977) 224098, Fax (977) 224098. E-mail forvm@sct.ictnet.es. Open: 18–20. Director: Chantal Grande. Founded 1981. 1 room, 45 m². 8 photo exhibitions/year. Artists: Humberto Rivas, Pere Formiguera, Gabriel Cualladó, Jorge Ribalta, Javier Vallhonrat, Valentin Vallhonrat, Bernard Plossu, Ralph Gibson, David Escudero, Xavier Rivas

Instituto Valenciano de Arte Moderno, Calle Guillem de Castro 118, E-46003 València. Tel (96) 3863000, Fax (96) 3921094. E-mail ivam@ivam.es. Website www.ivam.org. Open: Tue–Sun 10–19. Director: Juan Manuel Bonet. Curator: Josep Vicent Monzó. Founded 1989. 9 rooms, 10,800 m².

3–4 photo exhibitions/year. Artists: Julio González, Eugène Atget, André Kertész, Walker Evans, Robert Capa, Weegee, Robert Frank, Gabriel Cualladó, Cindy Sherman, Richard Prince, Bernard Plossu

Railowsky Foto-Galeria, Grabador Esteve 34, E-46004 València. Tel (96) 3517218, Fax (96) 3517218. E-mail railowsky@mundicom.com. Open: 10–14, 16.30–20.30. Director: José Font de Mora. Founded 1985. 1 room, 60 m². 7 photo exhibitions/year

Visor Centre Fotogràfic, Calle Corretgeria 26 bajo, E-46001 València. Tel (96) 3922399, Fax (96) 3922399. Open: Tue–Sat 17–21. Director: Pep Benlloch. Founded 1982. 2 rooms, 40 m². 8 photo exhibitions/year. Artists: Ana Teresa Ortega, Luis Gonzales Palma, Marketa Luskakowa, Iñigo Royo, Eulalia Valldosera, Maria Bleda & Jose MaRosa, Mira Bernabeu, Mayte Vieta, Gabriele Basilico, Mario Cravo Neto

Spectrum, Concepción Arenal 19–23, E-50005 Zaragoza. Tel (976) 359473, Fax (976) 568487. E-mail galeriaspectrum@teleline.es. Open: Mon–Sat 17–21. Director: Julio Alvarez. Founded 1977. 3 rooms, 80 m². 9 photo exhibitions/year. Artists: Rafael Navarro, Pablo Genoves, Anna Fox, Pedro Avellaned, Toto Frima, Lucien Clergue, Antonio Uriel, Jean Dieuzaide

Photomuseum, Villa Manuela, 3.a planta, P. O. Box 251, E-20800 Zarautz. Tel (943) 130906, Fax (943) 831823. Open: 10–13, 16–20. Director: Leopoldo Zugaza. Founded 1993. 1 room, 60 m². 12 photo exhibitions/year

Festivals & Fairs

Arco, International Contemporary Art Fair, Parque Ferial, Juan Carlos I., E-28067 Madrid. Tel (91) 7225017, Fax (91) 722-5798/5800. E-mail arco@ifema.es. Website www.arco.ifema.es

Fotobienal de Vigo, Centro de Estudios Fotográficos, Plaza do Rei, E-36201 Vigo-Pontevedra. Tel (986) 810170, Fax (986) 221666

Fotonoviembre, Centro de Fotografia "Isla de Tenerife", Plaza Isla de la Madera, s/n, E-38003 Santa Cruz de Tenerife. Tel (922) 290735, Fax (922) 240553. Website www.cabtf.es

Photo España, Alameda 9, E-28014 Madrid. Tel (91) 3601320, Fax (91) 3601322. Website www.photoes.com

Primavera Fotogràfica, Centre d'Art Santa Mònica, Rambla Santa Mònica 7, E-08002 Barcelona. Tel (93) 3162812, Fax (93) 3162817. E-mail primavef@correu.gencat.es. Website www.cultura-gencat.es/casm

Magazines

Agenda de la Imatge, Rambla de Catalunya 10, E-08007 Barcelona. Tel (93) 4121111, Fax (93) 3178386

Archivos de la Fotografia, San Ignacio 11, P. O. Box 251, E-20800 Zarautz. Tel (043) 130906, Fax (043) 831823. Editor: Leopoldo Zugaza. Spanish. Founded 1995. Copy price: Pts 1,750, US$20.00. Annual subscription: Pts 3,500, US$40.00, 2 issues/year

Arte Fotográfico, Santo Angel 76, E-28043 Madrid. Tel (91) 3886533, Fax (91) 7597584. Editor: Antonio Cabello. Spanish. Founded 1952. Copy price: Pta 550.00. Annual subscription: Pta 5,500, 12 issues/year

Diorama, Fotografía y Video International, Tembleque 96, bajo C y D, E-28024 Madrid. Tel (91) 7192413, Fax (91) 7192494. Spanish. Founded 1984

FV/Foto-Video Actualidad, Omnicon, S. A., Hierro 9-3a-7, E-28045 Madrid. Tel (91) 5278249, Fax (91) 5281348. E-mail omnicon@skios.es. Website www.omnicon.es. Editor: Juan M. Varela. Spanish. Founded 1988. Copy price: Pta 650.00. Annual subscription: Pta 6,300, 12 issues/year

La Fotografía, P. O. Box 1808, E-08080 Barcelona. Tel (93) 3198724, Fax (93) 3492692. Editor: F. Gori. Spanish/English. Founded 1989. Copy price: Pta 650.00. Annual subscription: Pta 6,500, Pta 8,500 (Europe), 10 issues/year

Lápiz, International Art Magazine, Gravina 10, 1°, E-28004 Madrid. Tel (91) 52229-71/72, Fax (91) 5224707. Editor: José Alberto López. Spanish/English. Founded 1982

Papel Alpha, Cuadernos de fotografía, Ediciones Universidad de Salamanca, Departamento de Suscripciones, P. O. Box 325, E-37080 Salamanca. Tel (923) 262579. Editor: Alberto Martín Expósito. Spain/English. Founded 1996. Copy price: Pta 1,000. Annual subscription: Pta 2,000, 2 issues/year

PhotoVision, Arte y Proyectos Editoriales, s. l., P. O. Box 164, E-41710 Utrera. Tel (95) 4862895, Fax (95) 4862895. E-mail photovision@photovision.es. Website www.photovision.es. Editor: Joan Fontcuberta. Spanish/English. Founded 1981. Copy price: US$12.00. Annual subscription: US$24.00, 2 issues/year

Revista Foto, Real 22, E-28230 Madrid Las Rozas. Tel (91) 6377948, Fax (91)

6361665. Editor: Manuel López. Spanish. Founded 1982. Copy price: Pta 600.00. Annual subscription: Pta 6,000, Pta 13,000 (Europe), 12 issues/year

Book Publishers

Actar, Roca i Batlle 2–4, E-08023 Barcelona. Tel (03) 4187759, Fax (03) 4186707. E-mail actar@arquired.es

Arteleku, Loiola, Kristobaldegui 14, E-20014 San Sebastian. Tel (943) 453662, Fax (943) 462256

Ediciones El Viso, Roncal 2, E-28002 Madrid

Editorial Gustavo Gili, c. Rosselló 87–89, E-08015 Barcelona

Focal Ediciones, P. O. Box 89054, E-08080 Barcelona. Tel (93) 670766699, Fax (93) 3217644

La Fabrica, Alameda 9, E-28014 Madrid. Tel (913) 601320, Fax (913) 601322

Lunwerg Editores, S. A., Beethoven 12, E-08021 Barcelona

Lunwerg Editores, S. A., Manuel Silva 12 bajo, E-28010 Madrid. Tel (91) 5930058, Fax (91) 5930070

Mestizo, Vinadel 6 bajos, E-30004 Murcia. Tel (968) 217651, Fax (968) 217651. E-mail mestizo@mestizo.org. Website www.mestizo.org

Omega/Medici/Iberia, Plató 26, E-08006 Barcelona. Tel (93) 2010599, Fax (93) 2097362

Bookshops

Libreria, Centre Culturel Fundacio "la Caixa", Passeig de Sant Joan 108, E-08037 Barcelona

Libreria, Museo Nacional Centro de Arte Reina Sofia, Santa Isabel 52, E-28012 Madrid

Libreria Kowasa, Mallorca 235, E-08008 Barcelona. Tel (93) 2158058, Fax (93) 2158054. E-mail kowasa@abaforum.es. Website www.abaforum.es/kowasa

Critics & Journalists

José Abad, Argentina 8 bajo, E-15011 A Coruña. Tel (981) 272729

Cecilia Andersson, Alameda de Mazarredo 21 4 B, E-48001 Bilbao. Tel (94) 4247759

José Ramón Cancer, Padre Ferris 20, Puerta 9, E-46009 Valencia. Tel (96) 3499558

Alejandro Castellote, Bravo Murillo 33, E-Madrid. Tel (91) 4473945

Manel Clot, Pl. Maluquer I Salvador 6, E-08400 Granollers. Tel (93) 8706740

Estrella de Diego, Potosi 8, E-28016 Madrid. Tel (91) 4588407

Ramón Esparza, Rampas de Uribitarte, 1-4º DD, E-48001 Bilbao. Tel (94) 4248375. E-mail cypeses@lg.ehu.es. *El Correo*, Bilbao

Horacio Fernandez, P. O. Box 477, E-03700 Alacant

Joan Fontcuberta, P. O. Box 114, E-08430 La Roca (Barcelona). Tel (93) 8420283, Fax (93) 8420038. E-mail fontcuberta_joan@caud.upf.es. Editor of *PhotoVision*, Utrera; *European Photography*, Göttingen

Manolo García, c. Poeta Bodria 10, E-46010 València

Lola Garrido, San Buenaventura 5, 2°, E-28005 Madrid. Tel (91) 3667765, Fax (91) 3667765

Marta Gili, Urgell 90, E-08011 Barcelona. Tel (93) 4530289, Fax (93) 4530289

Ignacio González, Plaza Trianilla 4, P. O. Box 91, E-41710 Utrera-Sevilla. Tel (95) 4862895, Fax (95) 4862895. E-mail ignacio@photovision.es. Editor of *PhotoVision*, Utrera-Sevilla

Prof. Dr. Manolo Laguillo, Pau Claris 188, E-08037 Barcelona. Tel (93) 4881255. University of Barcelona

Margarita Ledo, Rua Loureiros 29, 2°, E-15704 Santiago de Compostela. Tel (981) 575210

Manuel López, Calle Real 22, E-28230 Madrid Las Rozas. Tel (91) 6377948, Fax (91) 6361665. E-mail foto@ teleline.es

Antonio Molinero Cardenal, Puigcerdà 294, 13, 3c, E-08020 Barcelona. Tel (93) 3146340

Angel Mollà, Canaveral 16, E-38208 La Laguna (Tenerife). Tel (922) 262851/610342342. E-mail angelmolla @teleline.es

Joan Naranjo, Renart 46, E-08030 Barcelona. Tel (91) 2379407

Astrid Nordentoft, Avenida Republica Argentina 159, 4° 1a, E-08023 Barcelona. Tel (93) 2123107. *Katalog*, Odense

Salvador Obiols, Jaume Abril 2, E-08840 Viladecans (Barcelona). Tel (93) 6580200, Fax (93) 6590815

Rosa Olivares, Juan de Mena 25 2 IZQ, E-28004 Madrid. Tel (91) 5329189, Fax (91) 5329492. E-mail zurilla@retemoil.es

Enric Mira Pastor, Pintor S. Abril 14/ P8 Apt. 10, E-46005 Valencia

Gloria Picazo, Goya 16, E-08012 Barcelona. Tel (93) 2370299

Jesús Angel Prieto Villanueva, Av. Pere Planes 274, E-08190 Sant Cugat del Vallés. Tel (93) 6748597, Fax (93) 4417844. E-mail emassana@mail. ben.es. *La Vanguardia*, Barcelona; *Papers D'Art*, Girona

Jorge Ribalta, Aroles 16, 2°, E-08002 Barcelona. Tel (93) 4127513

Bernardo Riego, P. O. Box 342, E-39080 Santander. Tel (942) 227032

Josep Rigol, Calaf 29, E-08021 Barcelona. Tel (93) 2011716

Salvador Rodes, Tiradors 3, 4°-1a, E-08003 Barcelona. Tel (93) 3106666

Rafael Doctor Roncero, Las Fuentes 5, 2°C, E-28013 Madrid. Tel (91) 5483660

Manuel Santos, Urb. Parque Real 3-413, E-El Escorial. Tel (91) 3693552

Marie-Loup Sougez, c. Ibiza 32-7°B, E-28009 Madrid. Tel (91) 4094976

Jose Lebrero Stals, P. O. Box 32015, E-08015 Barcelona. Tel (93) 3253420

Dr. Carmelo Vega, Albéniz 5, 3°B, E-38007 Santa Cruz de Tenerife. Tel (922) 214089, Fax (922) 317723. E-mail cvega@ull.es

Anatxu Zabalbeascoa, Sors 27 Atico 1, E-08024 Barcelona. Tel (93) 2194630, Fax (93) 2194630

Cristina Zelich, Comuneros 105–109, E-37003 Salamanca. Tel (923) 120369. *PhotoVision*, Utrera; Fundació La

Caixa; Centre d'Art Santa Mònica; Primavera Fotogràfica, Barcelona

Santos Zunzunegui, Egana 21, E-48010 Bilbao. Tel (94) 4446833

Schools & Workshops

Arteleku, Loiola, Kristobaldegui 14, E-20014 San Sebastian. Tel (943) 453662, Fax (943) 462256

Aula de Fotografía UFCA, C/Millán Picazo 38, E-Algeciras. Tel (956) 667649/633428

Barcelona Centro de Imagen, C/Pons i Gallarza 25, E-08030 Barcelona. Tel (93) 3119273

Cámara oscura, Portales 43 (pje. Los Leones), E-26001 Logroño

Centre d'Estudis d'Art Contemporani, Fundació Joan Miró, Parc de Montjuïc, E-08038 Barcelona. Tel (93) 3291908, Fax (93) 3298609. E-mail fjmiro@bcn.fjmiro.es. Website www.bcn.fjmiro.es

Centro de la Imagen, Provenza 269-1°, E-08008 Barcelona

CEV, c. Regueros 3, E-28004 Madrid

Escola Municipal de Belles Arts, Cavallers 15, E-25002 Lleida. Tel (977) 270995, Fax (977) 260928

Escola Universitaria d'Optica de Terrassa, Universitat Politècnica de Barcelona, c. Violinista Vellsolà 37, E-08222 Barcelona. Tel (93) 7398300

Escuela de Artes y Oficios, Julián Claveria 12, E-33006 Oviedo-Asturias

Escuela de Fotografia, Aula de especializaci, C/San Joaquin 19, E-08012 Barcelona. Tel (93) 2372818

Escuela de Fotografia Centro de Imagen EFTI, C/Fuenterrabía 4–6, E-28014 Madrid. Tel (91) 55299999. E-mail efti@efti.es. Website www.efti.es

Escuela Superior de Fotografía e Imagen, C.E.U. "San Pablo", Edificio Seminario, E-46113 Moncada (Valencia). Tel (96) 1391616/1391666, Fax (96) 1395272

Escuela Superior de Fotografia Flash, Plaza Luca de Tena 13-1°, E-28045 Madrid. Tel (91) 5397468, Fax (91) 5396485

Fac. Bellas Artes, Departament de Fotografia, c. Pau Gargallo s/n., E-08028 Barcelona. Tel (93) 3345004

Fac. Bellas Artes de Cuenca, Benito Péres 42, E-16002 Cuenca

Fac. Bellas Artes Euzkadi, Universidad del País Vasco, E-48080 Bilbao

Fac. Bellas Artes Madrid, El Greco 2, Ciudad Universitaria, E-28040 Madrid

GrisArt, Corcega 415-2, E-08037 Barcelona. Tel (93) 4579733, Fax (93) 2077025. E-mail grisart@mx2.redestb.es. Website www.grisart.com

Institut d'Estudis Fotogràfics, Escola Industrial, c. Urgell 187, E-08029 Barcelona. Tel (93) 3212394

Institut d'Estudis Politècnics, Avgda. Diagonal 401, E-08008 Barcelona. Tel (93) 4161012

Masia Can Serrat, Can Serrat, E-08294 El Bruc (Barcelona). Tel (993) 7710037. E-mail galina@online.no, pete@fotem.demon.co.uk

Mecad Media Centre d'Art i Disseny, Avda. Marquej de Comillas 79, E-08202 Sabadell (Barcelona). Tel (93)

7457040, Fax (93) 7268183. E-mail
info@mecad.org. Website www.
mecad.org

Universidad de Cantabria, Aula de
Fotografia, Avda. de Los Castros s/n,
E-39005 Santander. Tel (942) 211276,
Fax (942) 201183

**Universitat de Autònoma de Barce-
lona,** Facultat de Ciències de la infor-
mació, Campus del Bellaterra s/n,
E-08193 Barcelona. Tel (93) 5811338

Universitat Pompeu Fabra, Facultat
de Comunicació Audiovisual, La
Rambla 30–32, E-08002 Barcelona.
Tel (93) 5422272

Visor Centre Fotogràfic, c. Corretgeria
26 bajos, E-46001 València. Tel (96)
3922399, Fax (96) 3922399

Associations

Agrupación Fotogràfica de Navarra, c.
Zapatería 42-2° D, E-31001 Pamplona.
Tel (948) 222358, Fax (948) 222358

Agrupación Fotogràfica de Reus,
Plaça Prim 1, E-Reus-Tarragona

Asoc. Fotog. Publicidad – Moda, Juan
Hurtado de Mendoza 9, 507, E-28036
Madrid

**Asoc. Nal. Informadores Gráficos
Prensa,** Espronceda 32-6°, E-28003
Madrid

Associació de Fotògrafs Professionals,
Ptge. Maluquer 8–10, E-08022 Barcelona. Tel (93) 4184525, Fax (93)
4184435. E-mail afppmc@ibernet.com.
Website www.afppmc.com

Colectivo Fotografico Ongarri, P. O.
Box 123, E-20870 Elgoibar-Guipúz-
coa. Tel (943) 742301/743431, Fax
(943) 740601

Confederación Española Fotografia,
P. O. Box 1614, E-20080 San Sebastián

Escuela Superior de Fotografia Flash,
Plaza Luca de Tena 13-1°, E-28045
Madrid. Tel (91) 5397468, Fax (91)
5396485

Real Sociedad Fotográfica, c. Príncipe
16, E-28029 Madrid

New Media

Art Futura, Media, computer animation, installations, performances,
Fernando el Santo 11, E-28010
Madrid. E-mail artfutura@artfutura.
org. Website www.artfutura.org/
index2.html

**Festival Internacional de Video y
Multimedia de Canarias,** Cabildo
Insular de Gran Canaria, c/Bravo
Murillo 23, E-35002 Las Palmas,
Canary Islands. Tel (928) 371011,
Fax (928) 364239. E-mail imagen.
cultura@cabgc.org. Website
www.cabgc.org/area-cultura

Sonar, International Festival of
Advanced Music and Multimedia
Arts, P. O. Box 38024, E-08080
Barcelona. Tel (93) 4422972, Fax (93)
4415338. E-mail sonar@sonar.es.
Website www.sonar.es

Sweden

Population: 8.9 million
Capital: Stockholm, 736,000
Currency: Krona (Skr)
International code: ++46
Tourist information: FörTur –
Föreningen Turism i Sverige,
P. O. Box 7542, S-103 93
Stockholm
Tel (08) 789 24 80,
Fax (08) 789 24 50

Galleries & Museums

Amidol, Gallery of Contemporary
Photography, Ejdergatan 11, S-416 68
Göteborg. Tel (031) 258884. Open:
Tue+Thu 15–19, Sat–Sun 12–15 and
by appointment. Director: John
Ljungkvist. Founded 1993. 2 rooms,
50 m². 10 photo exhibitions/year

Gallery Fotohuset, Parkgatan 2, S-
411 38 Göteborg. Tel (031) 7110908,
Fax (031) 7110908. Website www.
netg.se/fotohuset. Open: Tue-Wed
13–18, Thu–Sun 12–16. Director:
Thomas at Ekenstam. Curator: Hans
Yxell. Founded 1979. 3 rooms, 150 m².
15 photo exhibitions/year

Hasselblad Center, Ekmansgatan 8,
S-412 56 Göteborg. Tel (031) 203530,
Fax (031) 203480. E-mail info@
hasselbladcenter.o.se. Website www.
hasselbladcenter.o.se. Open: Tue–Fri
11–16 (Wed –21), Sat–Sun 11–17 (Sep–
Apr); Mon–Fri 11–16, Sat–Sun 11–17
(May–Aug). Director: Gunilla Knape.
Curator: Val Williams. Founded 1989.
2 rooms, 350 m². 6–8 photo exhibi-

tions/year. Artists: Lennart Nilsson,
Manuel Alvarez Bravo, Josef Kou-
delka, William Klein, Sebastião
Salgado, Sune Jonsson, Edouard
Boubat, Christer Strömholm, Miriam
Bäckstrom, Marjaana Kella

Naturhistoriska Museet, Museum of
Natural History, Slottsskogen, P. O.
Box 7283, S-402 35 Göteborg. Tel (031)
7752400, Fax (031) 129807. E-mail
info@gnm.se. Website www.gnm.se.
Open: Mon–Fri 9–16, Sat–Sun 10–17
(Sep–Dec Wed –21, Sep–Apr Mon
closed). Curator: Sture Myhrén.
Founded 1833. 7,000 m². 1–2 photo
exhibitions/year

Norrbottens museum, Storgatan 2,
S-971 08 Luleå. Tel (0920) 220355, Fax
(0920) 67966/87350. Open: Mon–Fri
10–16 (Wed –20), Sat–Sun 12–16
(winter time), Mon–Fri 10–18 (Wed
–20), Sat–Sun 12–18 (summer time).
Director: Börje Ekström. Founded
1886. 3 rooms, 235 m². 2–5 photo
exhibitions/year

Fotogalleriet, Svartbrödersgatan 3,
S-223 50 Lund. Tel (046) 184838.
Open: Tue–Fri 12–17, Sat–Sun 12–16
(Jun–Aug closed). Director: Hans-
Inge Bernstrup. Founded 1983. 3
rooms, 100 m². 9 photo exhibitions/
year. Artists: Tove Kurtzweil, Lars
Schwander, Jan Fridlund, Marco
Plüss, Tuija Lindström, Tove Falk-
Olsson, Lotta Schwarz, Torbjörn
Andersson, Erik Wipp, Åke Hed-
ström

Forum Galleriet, Stora Nygatan 1,
S-211 37 Malmö. Tel (040) 979210.
Open: Mon–Fri 12–18, Sat–Sun 12–16.
Director: Marit Lindberg. Founded
1992. 2 rooms, 100 m². 6 photo exhi-
bitions/year. Artists: Lena Mattson,
Bengt Olov Johansson, Marko Vouk-
hola, Lotta Antonsson, Annika
Karlsson-Rixon, Lars-Ola Bergquist,

Fredrik Sandblom, Jörgen Svensson,
Lisa Jevbratt

Malmö Konsthall, Sankt Johannes-
gatan 7, S-200 10 Malmö. Tel (040)
341293/86, Fax (040) 301507. Open:
11–17 (Wed –22). Director: Sune
Nordgren. Founded 1975. Rooms
of various size, 2,250 m²

Rooseum, Center for Contemporary
Art, Gasverksgatan 22, S-200 11
Malmö. Tel (040) 121716, Fax (040)
304561. E-mail office@rooseum.se.
Website www.rooseum.se. Open:
Tue–Sun 11–17 (Thu –20). Founded
1988. 3 rooms, 1,700 m². Artist:
Mariko Mori

Arbetets Museum, Museum of Work,
Laxholmen, S-602 21 Norrköping. Tel
(011) 189800, Fax (011) 182290. E-mail
info@arbetetsmuseum.e.se. Website
www.arbetetsmuseum.e.se. Open:
11–17. Director: Anders Lindh.
Founded 1991. 5 rooms, 3,000 m².
5–8 photo exhibitions/year. Artists:
Ulla Lemberg, Horst Tuuloskorpi,
Stig T. Karlsson, Jens Assur

Norrköpings Konstmuseum, Kristina-
platsen, S-602 34 Norrköping. Tel
(011) 152600, Fax (011) 135897. Open:
12–16, Mon+Thu 19–21. Curator:
Onita Wass. Founded 1946. 8 rooms.
1 photo exhibition/year

Galleri Andréhn-Schiptjenko, Sture-
parken 1, S-114 26 Stockholm. Tel
(08) 6760515, Fax (08) 6760516. E-mail
gas@algonet.se. Open: Tue–Fri 12–17,
Sat 12–16, Sun 13–16. Directors:
C. Andréhn, M. Schiptjenko. Founded 1991. 1 room, 85 m². Artists: Annika von Hausswolff, Peter Hagdahl,
Carin Carlsson, Peter Johansson

Galleri Charlotte Lund, Skeppargatan
70, S-114 59 Stockholm. Tel (08)
6630979, Fax (08) 6630978. Open:
Tue–Fri 12–18, Sat 12–17. Director:

Charlotte Lund. Founded 1993.
3 rooms, 140 m². 2–3 photo exhibi-
tions/year. Artists: Maria Friberg,
Charlotte Gyllenhammar, Mikael
Lundberg, Anders Widoff, Gregory
Crewdson, Adam Fuss, Andres
Serrano, Mats Gustafson, Liam
Gillick, Denise Grünstein

Galleri Roger Björkholmen, Karlavä-
gen 24 , S-114 31 Stockholm. Tel (08)
6112630, Fax (08) 6112630. E-mail
bjoerkholmen@artnope.se. Open: Fri–
Sun 12–16. Artists: Magnus Bártas,
Patrik Karlström, Jack Pierson, Can-
dice Breitz, Olof Glemme, Hans
Isaksson, Richhard Kern, Paul
Ramirez-Jonas

**Index – The Swedish Contemporary
Art Foundation,** St. Paulsgatan 3,
S-104 65 Stockholm. Tel (08) 6409492,
Fax (08) 6419608. E-mail karina@
algonet.se. Website www.aim.se/
galleri_index. Open: Tue–Sun 12–16.
Director: Karina Ericsson Wärn.
Founded 1974/1998. 2 rooms, 100 m².
8 photo exhibitions/year. Artists:
Annika von Hausswolff, Larry Clark,
Wolfgang Tillmans, Nobuyoshi Araki,
Joel-Peter Witkin, Eija-Liisa Antila,
Rineke Dijkstra, Stan Douglas,
Douglas Gordon

Moderna Museet, Skeppsholmen,
P. O. Box 16382, S-103 27 Stockholm.
Tel (08) 51955200, Fax (08) 51955242.
Website www.modernamuseet.se.
Open: Tue–Thu 11–20, Fri–Sun 11–18.
Director: David Elliott. Curator: Leif
Wigh. Founded 1958/1998. 5 rooms,
20,000 m². 10 photo exhibitions/year

Nordiska Museet, Djurgardsvägen
6–16, S-115 93 Stockholm. Tel (08)
6664600, Fax (08) 6653853. E-mail
nordiska@nordm.se. Open: Tue–Sun
11–17 (Thu –22). Director/curator:
Eva Dahlman. Founded 1873/1990.
1–2 photo exhibitions/year

254 Sweden

The City Museum of Stockholm, Peter Myndes Backe 6, S-116 46 Stockholm. Tel (08) 50831600, Fax (08) 50831699. E-mail stm-ch@nordm.se. Open: Tue–Sun 11–17 (Thu –19/winter –21). Director: Nanna Hermansson. Curator: Carl Heideken. Founded 1937. 5 rooms. 5 photo exhibitions/year. Artists: Mike Stott, Nick Waplington, Anna Gerden, Michael Tongue, Kent Klich, Berenice Abbott, Andreas Feininger, Joseph Rodriguez, Eugène Atget

Zinc Gallery, Skeppargatan 86, S-114 54 Stockholm. Tel (08) 6623009, Fax (08) 6623048. E-mail info@ zincgallery.com. Website www. zincgallery.com. Open: Tue–Fri 12–18, Sat 12–17. Director: Aldy Milliken. Curator: Ben Loveless. Founded 1997. 3 rooms, 70 m². 5 photo exhibitions/ year. Artists: Shimon Attie, Bill Jacobson, Gábor Kerekes, Helen Sear, Ola Kolehmainen, Elisabeth Ohlson, Jyrki Parantainen, Riitta Päiväläinen, Lars Siltberg, Jean-Marc Spaans

BildMuseet, Umeå University, S-901 87 Umeå. Tel (090) 7865227, Fax (090) 7867733. E-mail info@ bildmuseet.umu.se. Website www. umu.se/bildmuseet. Director: Jan-Erik Lundström

Uppsala Konstmuseum, slottet ingang E, S-752 37 Uppsala. Tel (018) 272482, Fax (018) 507690. E-mail konstinfo@ konstmuseum.uppsala.se. Website www.uppsala.se/konstmuseum. Open: Wed–Thu 11–16 (summer), Wed–Thu 11–19, Sat–Sun 11–17. Director/curator: Deborah Thompson. Founded 1982. 7 rooms, 300 m². Artists: Öyvid Fahlström, Helen Chadwick, Ana Mendieta, Ike Ude, Lyle Ashton Harris, Wim Delvoye, Rogelio Lopez-Cuenca, Carlos Capelán, Inez van Lamsweerde

Festivals & Fairs

Fotomässan, Mässansgata 14, P. O. Box 5222, S-402 24 Göteborg. Tel (031) 7088400, Fax (031) 209103. E-mail magdalena.ronstrom@bok-bibliothek.se

Xposeptember, Stockholm Fotofestival, P. O. Box 15146, S-10465 Stockholm. Tel (08) 50831646, Fax (08) 6460370. Website www. xposeptember.com

Magazines

90 – Tal, P. O. Box 19074, S-104 32 Stockholm. Tel (08) 6121049, Fax (08) 6121077

Aktuell Fotografi & Foto, Landskronavägen 25 A, S-251 85 Helsingborg. Tel (042) 173500, Fax (042) 173790. Editor: Jan Almlöf. Swedish. Founded 1992. Copy price: Skr 39.00. Annual subscription: Skr 410.00, 12 issues/year

Fotografi, P. O. Box 1079, S-251 10 Helsingborg. Tel (042) 147040, Fax (042) 146060. E-mail fotografi@ helsingborg.se. Website www. fotografi.ipro.se. Editor: Lars Kjellberg. Swedish. Founded 1992. Copy price: Skr 39.00. Annual subscription: Skr 325.00, 10 issues/year

Fotografisk Tidskrift, Grindsgatan 31, S-118 57 Stockholm. Tel (08) 6418472, Fax (08) 6406988. E-mail flemming@ journal-media.se. Website www. sfoto.se/f. Editor: Gösta Flemming. Swedish. Founded 1888. Copy price: Skr 45.00. Annual subscription: Skr 350.00, 6 issues/year

Fotografiska Föreningen i Malmö, P. O. Box 19091, S-200 73 Malmö. Tel (040) 977143, Fax (040) 977143. Editor: Anders Andersson. Swedish. Copy

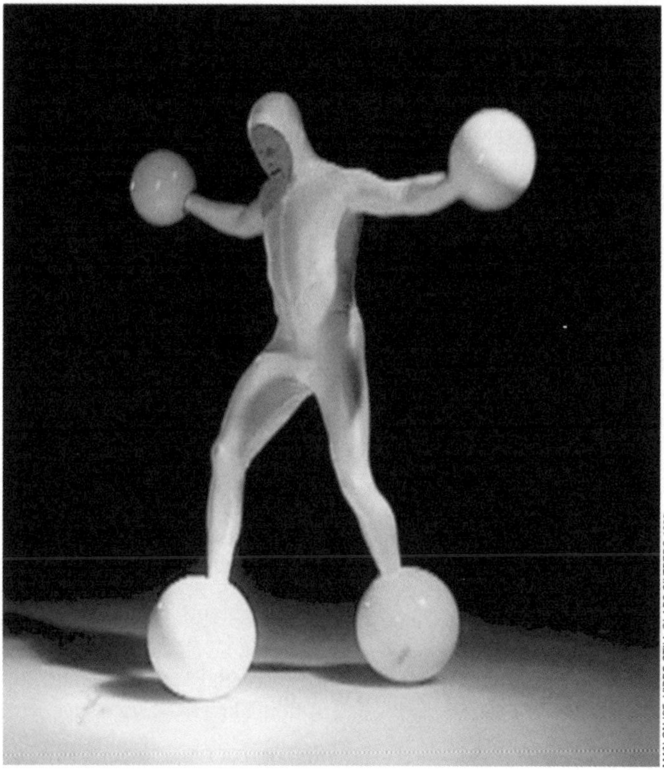

Artwork by:
Shimon Attie
Andras Bozsó
Bill Jacobson
Gábor Kerekes
Ola Kolehmainen
Monika Larsen Dennis

Elisabeth Ohlson
Jyrki Parantainen
Riitta Päiväläinen
Helen Sear
Lars Siltberg
Jean-Marc Spaans

photography and contemporary art

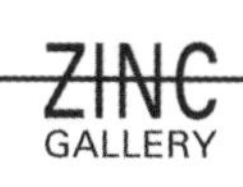

Skeppargatan 86, 114 59 Stockholm Sweden
t 46 8 662 3009 f 46 8 662 3048 www.zincgallery.com

255 Sweden

price: only postage. Annual subscription: only postage, 4 issues/year

Hasselblad Forum, Victor Hasselblad
AB, P. O. Box 220, S-401 23 Göteborg.
Tel (031) 102400, Fax (031) 135074.
E-mail forum@hasselblad.se. Website
www.hasselblad.se. Editor: Sören
Gunnarsson. English/French/Ger-
man/Spain. Copy price: Skr 42.50.
Annual subscription: Skr 170.00,
4 issues/year

Material, Tidskrift för Samtidskonst,
Skeppsholmen, S-111 49 Stockholm.
Tel (08) 6119613, Fax (08) 6118199.
Editor: Sven-Olov Wallenstein.
Swedish. Founded 1991. Copy price:
Skr 30.00. Annual subscription: Skr
150.00, 5 issues/year

Nu, Siksi Index – The Nordic Art
Review, Jacobsgatan 27 nb, S-111 52
Stockholm. Tel (08) 4023890, Fax (08)
4023899. E-mail nu@nordicartreview.
nu. Editors: Sara Arrhenius, John
Peter Nilsson. Copy price: Skr 95.00.
Annual subscription: Skr 550.00
(Europe), 6 issues/year

Paletten, Karl Gustavsgatan 10 C,
S-411 25 Göteborg. Tel (031) 117873/
118739, Fax (031) 117785. Editor:
Elizabeth Pethrus. Swedish. Founded
1940. Copy price: Skr 65.00. Annual
subscription: Skr 280.00, 4 issues/
year

Book Publishers

Alfabeta Bokförlag, P. O. Box 4284,
S-102 66 Stockholm. Tel (08) 71493-
53/36, Fax (08) 6432431

Bildibok, Gammelsträng, S-820 64
Näsviken. Tel 65035344, Fax 65033433

Edition Eriksson, Rörmansgatan 42,
S-216 11 Malmö

Journal, Grindsgatan 31, S-118 57
Stockholm. Tel (08) 6430094, Fax (08)
6406988. E-mail flemming@journal-
media.se

Kaleidoscope, P. O. Box 125, S-296 00
Åhus

Raster Förlag AB, Östgötagatan 27,
S-116 25 Stockholm. Tel (08) 6422016,
Fax (08) 6424123

Bookshops

Akademibokhandeln, Mäster
Samuelsgatan 32, S-10394 Stockholm

Arbetets Museum, Museum of Work,
Laxholmen, S-602 21 Norrköping. Tel
(011) 189800, Fax (011) 182290. E-mail
info@arbetetsmuseum.e.se. Website
www.arbetetsmuseum.e.se

Konst-IG, Sergels Torg 3, S-10326
Stockholm. Tel (08) 50831518, Fax
(08) 50831519. E-mail info@konstig.se.
Website www.konstig.se

Konst-IG, Konstmuseet, Götaplatgen,
S-41256 Göteborg. Tel (031) 189145,
Fax (031) 189154. E-mail info@
konstig.se. Website www.konstig.se

Auctions

Göteborgs Auktionsverk AB, Tredje
Länggatan 9, S-40235 Göteborg.
Tel (031) 124430, Fax (031) 127047.
E-mail myriam.lindberg@gbg-
auktionsverk.se. Website www.
gbg-auktionsverk.se

Critics & Journalists

Hans Alenius, Mossgränd 5, S-773 00
Fagersta. Tel (0223) 14907

Peder Alton, Svampvägen 156,
S-122 33 Enskede. Tel (08) 392502

Kari Andén-Papadopoulos, Blekin-
gegatan 61, S-116 62 Stockholm.
Tel (08) 6410660. *Dagens Nyheten,*
Stockholm

Sara Arrhenius, Aftonbladet, Arena-
vägen 63, S-105 18 Stockholm. Tel
(08) 328016, Fax (08) 6419608. E-mail
sara.arrhenius@aftonbladet.se.
Aftonbladet, Index, Stockholm

Ingamaj Beck, Aftonbladet, Arena-
vägen 63, S-105 18 Stockholm. Tel
(08) 7252443, Fax (08) 6000175.
Aftonbladet, Stockholm

Irene Berggren, Svartågatan 17:1,
S-128 45 Bagarmossen. Tel (08)
6488899, Fax (08) 6004090

Marta Edling, Aspstigen 9, S-171 34
Solna. Tel (0468) 270446. University
of Stockholm/Dept. of Art History,
Stockholm

Lars O. Eriksson, Dagens Nyheten,
S-105 15 Stockholm. Tel (08) 6448371,
Fax (08) 6419608. *Dagens Nyheten,*
Stockholm; *Artforum,* New York

Gösta Flemming, Grindsgatan 31,
S-118 57 Stockholm. Tel (08) 6430094,
Fax (08) 6406988. E-mail flemming@
journal-media.se

Sören Gunnarsson, Hasselblad Fo-
rum/Victor Hasselblad AB, P. O. Box
220, S-401 23 Göteborg. Tel (031)
102400, Fax (031) 135074. Editor of
Hasselblad Forum, Göteborg

Rune Hassner, Bastugatan 12 B,
S-11820 Stockholm. Tel (08) 6443030,
Fax (08) 6460370

Hans Hedberg, St. Paulsgatan 11,
S-118 46 Stockholm. Tel (08) 6435763,
Fax (08) 6673786. *Index,* Stockholm

Rune Jonsson, Hanna Paulis gata 31,
S-126 65 Hägersten

Maria Lind, Vindragarvägen 12, II,
S-117 50 Stockholm

Jan-Erik Lundström, Kungsgatan 17a,
S-90321 Umeå. Tel (090) 7865227,
Fax (090) 7867733. E-mail jan-erik.
lundstrom@bildmuseet.umu.se.
Website www.umu.se/bildmuseet.
European Photography, Göttingen;
Director of BildMuseet, Umeå

Patric Moreau, Tjärhovsgatan 41,
S-116 29 Stockholm. Tel (08) 6497240,
Fax (08) 6497240. E-mail chateu.
moreau@swipnet.se

John Peter Nilsson, Hagagatan 7,
S-113 48 Stockholm. Tel (08) 344918,
Fax (08) 344918. E-mail jpn@
algonet.se. *Aftonbladet,* Stockholm;
Siksi, Helsinki

Stefan Nilsson, Nerihes Allehanda,
P. O. Box 1603, S-701 16 Örebro. Tel
(019) 155057, Fax (019) 105290. Editor
of *Nu,* Stockholm

Ralph Nykvist, Karl X Gustafs gata 32,
S-252 39 Helsingborg

Annette Rosengren, Nordiska Museet,
P. O. Box 27820, S-115 93 Stockholm.
Tel (08) 51956000, Fax (08) 51954580.
E-mail ar@nordm.se. Website www.
nordm.se

John S. Webb, Thorsgatan 5, S-26321
Höganäs. Tel (042) 333715. E-mail
john.webb@foto.gu.se. Website
www.foto.gu.se. *Helsingborgs Dagblad,* Helsingborg

Peter Wiklund, Wrangels väg 4a,
S-178 33 Ekerö. Tel (08) 841415,
Fax (08) 841516. E-mail peter.
wiklund@mailbox.swipnet.se.
Fotografi, Helsingborg; *Pressens
Bild,* Stockholm

Val Williams, Hasselblad Center,
Ekmansgatan 8, S-412 56 Göteborg.
Tel (031) 203530, Fax (031) 203480.
E-mail info@hasselbladcenter.o.se.
Website www.hasselbladcenter.o.se

Schools & Workshops

Bergnässkolan, Västra Skolgatan,
S-972 53 Luleå

GFU, Folkuniversitetet, Estetavdel-
ningen, Brunnsgatan 3, S-103 98
Stockholm

Göteborgs Universitet, Fotohög-
skolan, Haraldsgatan 2 A, S-413 14
Göteborg

Konstfack, Fotoakademin, P. O. Box
24115, S-104 51 Stockholm

Kulturama, P. O. Box 732, S-10134
Stockholm. Tel (08) 4023406, Fax (08)
103430

Nordens Fotoskola, Biskops-Arnö,
S-198 00 Bålsta

Associations

Pressfotografernas Klubb, Vasagatan
50, S-111 20 Stockholm. Tel (08)
6137544

Svenska Fotografers Förbund, Ass. of
Swedish Professional Photographers,
Götgatan 48, S-118 26 Stockholm. Tel
(08) 7020345, Fax (08) 6412210. E-mail
sff@sfoto.se. Website www.sfoto.se

Sveriges Allmänna Konstförening,
P. O. Box 2151, S-103 14 Stockholm

Grants & Awards

Gullers Stipendiat, for a Swedish
photographer, every year. Contact:

Fotografiska Museet, P. O. Box 16382,
S-103 27 Stockholm. Tel (08) 6664250

Konstnärsnämnden, The Arts Grants
Commitee, for artists and photog-
raphers of Swedish nationality or
residency, every year. Contact:
Konstnärsnämnden, P. O. Box 1212,
S-112 82 Stockholm. Tel (08) 141490

Sveriges författarfond, The Swedish
Author's Fund, several awards and
grants for photographers of Swedish
residency who illustrate or edit
books. Contact: Sveriges författarfond, Schönfeldts gränd 1–3, 4tr.,
S-111 27 Stockholm. Tel (08) 7914780,
Fax (08) 206178

The Erna and Victor Hasselblad
Foundation, international grants for
scientific research and education in
natural sciences and photography,
total amount US$200,000, every year.
Contact: Hasselblad Stiftelse, Hasselblad Center, P. O. Box 53098, S-400 14
Göteborg. Tel (031) 7781990, Fax
(031) 7784640. E-mail info@
hasselbladfoundation.o.se. Website
www.hasselbladfoundation.o.se

The Hasselblad Award, US$40.000,
every year or every second year.
Contact: Hasselblad Stiftelse, Hasselblad Center, P. O. Box 53098, S-
400 14 Göteborg. Tel (031) 7781980,
Fax (031) 7784640. E-mail info@
hasselbladfoundation.o.se

The Swedish Environmental Protection
Agency's Prize (Nature and Environ-
ment Photographer of the Year), for a
Swedish photographer who has
reached the great public with his/her
photography on natural and environ-
ment, no application, Skr 25,000,
every year. Contact: Naturvardsver-
ket, Peter Hanneberg, S-10 648 Stockholm. Tel (08) 6981087, Fax (08)
6981485. E-mail pth@environ.se

Switzerland

*Population: 7.1 million
Capital: Bern, 124,400
Currency: Franc (SFr)
International code: ++41
Tourist information: Schweiz
Tourismus, Tödistr. 60, P.O.
Box, CH-8027 Zürich
Tel (01) 2881111,
Fax (01) 2881205*

Galleries & Museums

Fabian Walter Galerie, Wallstr. 13,
CH-4010 Basel. Tel (061) 2713877,
Fax (061) 2713887. E-mail
fabianwalter@swissart.ch. Website
www.swissart.ch/fabianwalter

Galerie Anita Neugebauer, St.-Al-
ban-Vorstadt 10, CH-4052 Basel.
Tel (061) 2722157. Open: Wed–Fri
15–18, Sat 11–13 and by appointment.
Artists: René Mächler, Rudolf Licht-
steiner

Galerie Gisèle Linder, Elisabethenstr.
54, CH-4051 Basel. Tel (061) 2728377,
Fax (061) 2722728. E-mail glinder@
datacom.ch. Website www.
artgalleries.ch/linder. Open: Tue–Fri
14–18.30 (Thu –20), Sat 10–16. Direc-
tor/curator: Gisèle Linder. Founded
1984. 2 rooms, 160 m². 1 photo exhi-
bition/year. Artists: Serge Hasenböhler, Anne Sauser-Hall, Ursula
Mumenthaler, Hans Jürg Kupper,
Christoph Klauke, Werner von
Mutzenbecher, Hélène Delprat,
Eric Emo

Kunsthalle Basel, Steinenberg 7,
CH-4051 Basel. Tel (061) 2069900,
Fax (061) 2069919. E-mail info@
kunsthallebasel.ch. Website www.
kunsthallebasel.ch

Pep + No Name, Unterer Heuberg 2,
CH-4051 Basel. Tel (061) 2615161,
Fax (061) 2615161. E-mail
pepnoname@balcab.ch. Website
www.pepnoname.ch. Open: Mon–Fri
12–19 (Thu –20), Sat 11–16. Director:
Tobias Toggweiler. Founded 1980.
1 room, 50 m². 10 photo exhibitions/
year. Artists: Monika Brogle, Gerald
Axelrod, Georg Freuler, Beat Frutiger,
Christopher Gmuender, Lukas Hand-
schin, Serge Hasenböhler, Michael
Marzik, Ursula Zihler, D'Ark Zitt

XS! Atelier & Gallery, N. Trächslin &
Co., Feldbergstr. 40, CH-4057 Basel.
Tel (061) 6920031, Fax (061) 6924507.
Open: Mon 21–24, Thu–Sun 16–20
(Sat –19)

Kunstmuseum Bern, Bernische
Stiftung für Fotografie, Film und
Video (FFV), Hodlerstr. 8–12, CH-
3000 Bern 7. Tel (031) 3110944/
3122960, Fax (031) 3117263. E-mail
thomas.pfister@kmb.unibe.ch.
Website www.kunstmuseumbern.ch.
Open: Tue 10–21, Wed–Sun 10–17.
Director: Thomas Pfister. Founded
1879. 1–2 photo exhibitions/year

Photoforum Pasquart, 71 faubourg du
Lac, CH-2502 Biel-Bienne. Tel (032)
3224482, Fax (032) 3224513. E-mail
fsiegfried@bielstar.ch. Website
www.pasquart.ch/photoforum/.
Open: Tue–Sat 14–18, Sun 11–17.
Director: Francis Siegfried. Founded
1984. 3 rooms, 80 m². 9 photo exhi-
bitions/year

Galleria Cons Arc, Via Soldini 15,
CH-6830 Chiasso. Tel (091) 6837949,
Fax (091) 6829043. E-mail consarc@

bluewin.ch. Website www.mypage.
bluewin.ch/consarc/. Open: Mon–
Fri 9–12, 14–18.30, Sat 9–12. Director/
curator: Guido Giudici. Founded
1990. 3 rooms, 50 m². 4 photo exhi-
bitions/year. Artists: Gabriele Basilico, Francesco Radino, Mimmo
Jodice, Alberto Flammer, Max Huber,
Leo Matiz, Massimo Vitali, Stefan
Kirchner, Cora Büttenbender, G. P.
Minelli

Art Photographique, rue des Bains 22,
CH-1205 Genève. Tel (022) 3291464.
Artists: Jacques Bélat, Xavier
Lecoultre, Denis Yutzeler

Centre de la Photographie, 16 rue du
Général Dufour, CH-1204 Genève.
Tel (022) 3292835. Open: Tue–Sat 15–
19. Directors: Mayte Garcia, Carole
Potier. Founded 1984. 2 rooms,
100 m². 12 photo exhibitions/year

Galerie Saint-Gervais photographie,
5 rue du Temple, CH-1201 Genève.
Tel (022) 9082060, Fax (022) 9082001.
E-mail jboesch/sgg@sgg.ch. Website
www.sgg.ch. Open: Tue–Sat 14–21.
Director: Jacques Boesch. Founded
1963. 3 rooms, 300 m². 10 photo
exhibitions/year

Galerie Christian Schneeberger,
Unionstr. 17, CH-9403 Goldbach.
Tel (079) 2213455, Fax (079) 8451355.
E-mail snowgallery@paus.ch. Web-
site www.hso.ch/snowgallery. Open:
Fri 17–19.30, Sat 14.17 and by
appointment

Nikon Image House, Seestr. 157, CH-
8700 Küsnacht. Tel (01) 9136333, Fax
(01) 9136300. E-mail imagehouse@
nikon.ch. Website www.nikon.ch.
Open: Tue–Fri 12–18 (Thu –21),
Sat 10–16. Director/curator: Marc
Strebel. Founded 1996. 4 rooms,
100 m². 6 photo exhibitions/year

Musée de l'Elysée, avenue de l'Elysée
18, CH-1014 Lausanne. Tel (021)
6174821, Fax (021) 6170783. E-mail
musee.elysee@serac.vd.ch. Website
www.elysee.ch. Open: Tue–Sat 10–18
(Thu –21). Director: William Ewig.
Curator: Daniel Girardin. Founded
1985. 8 rooms, 1,000 m². 20–30 photo
exhibitions/year

Galleria Gottardo, Una fondazione per
la cultura della Banca del Gottardo,
Viale Stefano Franscini 12, CH-6901
Lugano. Tel (091) 8081988, Fax (091)
8082447. E-mail galleria@gottardo.ch.
Website www.gottardo.ch. Open:
Tue–Fri 10–17. Director: Alberto
Bianda. Curator: Luca Patocchi.
Founded 1989. 3 rooms, 240 m².
2 photo exhibitions/year

Museo Cantonale d'Arte, Via Canova
10, CH-6900 Lugano. Tel (091)
9104780, Fax (091) 9104789. Open:
Tue 14–17, Wed–Sun 10–17. Director/
curator: Marco Franciolli. Founded
1987. 23 rooms, 1,600 m². 2 photo
exhibitions/year. Artists: J. M. William Turner, Edgard Degas, August
Renoir, Camille Pissarro, Paul Klee,
Florence Henri, Thomas Struth,
Joseph Beuys, Stephan Balkenhol,
Rineke Dijkstra

Galerie Meile, Rosenberghöhe 4a, CH-
6004 Luzern. Tel (041) 4203318, Fax
(041) 4202169. E-mail ursmeile@-
galerieursmeile.ch. Website www.
galerie-meile.ch. Open: Tue–Fri 14–19,
Sat 14–16. Director/curator: Urs
Meile. Founded 1992. 3 rooms, 150 m².
1–2 photo exhibitions/year. Artists:
Rémy Markowitsch, Annelies Štrba,
Anatolij Shuravlev, Christoph
Draeger, Lang & Baumann

Galerie Focale, 4 place du Château,
CH-1260 Nyon. Tel (022) 3610966,
Fax (022) 3610966. E-mail focale@
swissonline.ch. Open: Tue–Sun 14–18.

Founded 1982. 2 rooms, 30 m².
10 photo exhibitions/year. Artists:
Zalmaï Ahad, Luc Chessex, Bernard
Dubuis, Anne-Marie Grobet, Alain de
Kalbermatten, Simone Oppliger, Jean
Revillard, Charles Weber, Bertrand
Rey, Anna Halm Schudel

Kunstmuseum Solothurn, Werkhofstr.
30, CH-4500 Solothurn. Tel (032)
6222307, Fax (032) 6225001. Open:
Tue–Sat 10–12, 14–17 (Thu –21), Sun
10–17. Director: André Kamber.
Founded 1900. 2 rooms, 100 m².
1 photo exhibition/year. Artists:
Hansjörg Sahli, Leonardo Bezzola,
Hansruedi Riesen, Jakob Tuggener,
Oscar Wiggli, Roland Schneider,
Rosemarie Hausheer, Hugo Jäggi,
Jean Mohr

**Musée Suisse de l'appareil Photogra-
phique,** 6 ruelle des Anciens Fossés,
CH-1800 Vevey. Tel (021) 9252140,
Fax (021) 9216458. E-mail
cameramuseum@bluewin.ch. Website www.cameramuseum.ch. Open:
Tue–Sun 11–17.30 (Mar–Oct), 14–
17.30 (Nov–Feb). Directors: Pascale &
Jean-Marc Bonnard Yersin. Founded
1979. 5 rooms, 450 m². 3–4 photo
exhibitions/year

Raum F, Forum und Verlag für Fotografie und Performance, Einsiedler-
str. 34, CH-8820 Wädenswil. Tel (01)
7800751, Fax (01) 7800751. E-mail
ffvogel@mus.ch. Open: by appointment only. Director: Fritz Franz
Vogel. Founded 1987. 1 room, 200 m².
1–3 photo exhibitions/year. Artists:
Pierre Schauwecker, Thomas Karsten,
Theo Stalder, Klaus Elle, Fritz Franz
Vogel

Kunstmuseum des Kantons Thurgau,
Kartause Ittingen, CH-8532 Warth.
Tel (052) 7484120, Fax (052) 7400110.
E-mail kunstmuseum.thurgau@
bluewin.ch. Website www.

kunstmuseum.ch. Open: Mon–Fri
14–17, Sat–Sun 11–17. Director:
Markus Landert. 2 rooms, 300 m².
1–2 photo exhibitions/year

COALmine fotografie, Volkarthaus
Winterthur, Turnerstr. 1, CH-8401
Winterthur. Tel (052) 2686868.
Curator: Urs Stahel

Fotomuseum Winterthur, Grüzenstr.
44, CH-8400 Winterthur. Tel (052)
2336086, Fax (052) 2336097. E-mail
fotomuseum@fotomuseum.ch.
Website www.fotomuseum.ch. Open:
Tue–Fri 12–18 (Wed –19.30), Sat–Sun
11–17. Director/curator: Urs Stahel.
Founded 1993. 5 rooms, 550 m². 5–7
photo exhibitions/year. Artists: Gilles
Peress, Lewis Baltz, Peter Hujar,
Astrid Klein, Seiichi Furuya, Paul
Graham, Axel Hütte, Nan Goldin,
Daido Moriyama, Nicolas Faure

Birgit Filzmaier, 19th & 20th Century
Fine Art Photography, Oescherstr. 26,
CH-8702 Zollikon. Tel (01) 3919459,
Fax (01) 3919459. E-mail bfilzmaier@
access.ch. Open: by appointment
only. Director: Birgit Filzmaier.
Founded 1998

Galerie Arrigo, Hirschengraben 3,
CH-8001 Zürich. Tel (01) 2622544.
Open: Tue–Fri 12–18.30, Sat–Sun
11–16

Galerie Ars Futura, Bleicherweg 45,
CH-8002 Zürich. Tel (01) 2018810,
Fax (01) 2018811. E-mail arsfutura@
bluewin.ch. Website www.
arsfutura.ch. Open: Tue–Fri 13–18,
Sat 12–16. Director: Nicola von
Senger. Founded 1992. 1 room, 75 m².
3 photo exhibitions/year. Artists:
Henry Bond, Wolfgang Tillmans,
Stefan Banz, Markus Hansen, Inez
van Lamsweerde, Dominique
Gonzales-Foerster, Daniele Buetti

Galerie Bob van Orsouw, Limmatstr. 270, CH-8005 Zürich. Tel (01) 2731100, Fax (01) 2731102. E-mail mail@bobvanorsouw.ch. Open: Tue–Fri 12–18, Sat 11–16 and by appointment

Galerie Peter Kilchmann, Limmatstr. 270, CH-8005 Zürich. Tel (01) 4403931, Fax (01) 4403932. E-mail kilchmann@access.ch. Open: Tue–Fri 12–18, Sat 12–16. Director: Peter Kilchmann. Founded 1992. 2 rooms, 150 m². 4 photo exhibitions/year. Artists: John Coplans, Stefan Altenburger, Willie Doherty, Thomas Demand, Felix Stephan Huber, Steffen Koohn, Zitta Leutenegger

Galerie Schedler, Josefstr. 53, CH-8005 Zürich. Tel (01) 44606120, Fax (01) 4406121. E-mail zurich@ schedler.ch. Website www. schedler.ch. Director: Patrik Schedler. 1 room, 124 m². 4 photo exhibitions/ year. Artists: Stephen Barker, Allen Frame, Gabriela Domeisen, Roland Iselin, Marget Morgan, Richard Müller, Walter Pfeiffer, Mauro Restiffe, Eliane Rutishauser, Christoph Schneeberger

Galerie "Zur Stockeregg", Stockerstr. 33, CH-8022 Zürich. Tel (01) 2026925, Fax (01) 2028251. E-mail stockeregg@ bluewin.ch. Open: Mon–Fri 9–17, Sat–Sun by appointment. Director: Kaspar M. Fleischmann. Curators: Claudia Coellen, Joy Neri. Founded 1978. 1 room, 120 m². 4 photo exhibitions/ year. Artists: Henri Cartier-Bresson, André Kertész, Paul Strand, Bill Brandt, Brassaï, Paul Outerbridge, Roman Vishniac, Michael Kenna, Izu Kenro, Berenice Abbott

Kunsthalle Zürich, Limmatstr. 270, CH-8005 Zürich. Tel (01) 2721515, Fax (01) 2721888. E-mail kunsthallezh@ access.ch. Open: Tue–Fri 12–18, Sat–Sun 11–17. Director: Bettina Marbach. Founded 1985. 5 rooms, 650 m². 2 photo exhibitions/year

Kunsthaus Zürich, Heimplatz 1, CH-8001 Zürich. Tel (01) 2516765, Fax (01) 2512464. E-mail info@kunsthaus.ch. Website www.kunsthaus.ch

Mai 36 Galerie, Rämistr. 37, CH-8001 Zürich. Tel (01) 2616880, Fax (01) 2616881. E-mail mai36@artgalleries.ch. Website www.artgalleries.ch/mai36. Open: Tue–Fri 12–18.30, Sat 11–16. Directors: Victor Gisler, Luigi Kurmann. Founded 1987. 3 rooms, 120 m². 2 photo exhibitions/year. Artists: John Baldessari, Robert Mapplethorpe, Thomas Ruff, Vito Acconci, Stephan Balkenhol, Piotr Uklanski, Franz Ackermann, Rita McBride, Jörg Sasse, Andreas Gursky

Museum für Gestaltung Zürich, Ausstellungsstr. 60, CH-8031 Zürich. Tel (01) 4462211, Fax (01) 4462233. Website www.museum-gestaltung.ch. Open: Tue–Fri 10–18 (Wed –21), Sat–Sun 11–18. Director: Dr. Erika Keil. Founded 1875. 2 rooms, 1,500 m². 1–2 photo exhibitions/year

Scalo Galerie, Weinbergstr. 22a, CH-8001 Zürich. Tel (01) 2610928, Fax (01) 2619262. E-mail gallery@scalo.com. Website www.scalo.com. Open: Tue–Fri 12–18.30, Sat 10–16. 1 room, 250 m². 6 photo exhibitions/year

Schweizerische Stiftung für die Photographie, Kunsthaus, Heimplatz 1, CH-8024 Zürich. Tel (01) 2516765, Fax (01) 2512464. E-mail ssp.@ kunsthaus.ch. Website www. kunsthaus.ch.ssp.stiftung.html. Open: Tue–Thu 10–21, Fri–Sun 10–17. Director: Dr. Peter Pfrunder. Founded 1971. 3 rooms, 180 m². 2–3 photo exhibitions/year

Galerie Zur Stockeregg

Stockerstrasse 33, CH-8022 Zürich
P: +41-1-202 69 25 F: +41-1-202 82 51
stockeregg@bluewin.ch

Galerie Zur Stockeregg is specialized in vintage 19th and 20th century and contemporary photography and maintains a large collection of high quality vintage masterprints from 1900 to 1950.

Vintage photographs by:
Berenice Abbott
Ansel Adams
Eugène Atget
Herbert Bayer
Ilse Bing
Constantin Brancusi
Bill Brandt
Brassaï
Pierre Dubreuil
André Kertész
Heinrich Kühn
Arnold Newman
Man Ray
Paul Outerbridge
Albert Renger-Patzsch
Edward Steichen
Albert Steiner
Alfred Stieglitz
Paul Strand
Karl Struss
Josef Sudek
Roman Vishniac
Edward Weston
and others....

Contemporary photographs by:
Dick Arentz
Richard Avedon
René Burri
Michel Comte
Robert Frank
Kenro Izu
Michael Kenna
Richard Misrach
Irving Penn
Christian Vogt
and others....

Member of AIPAD

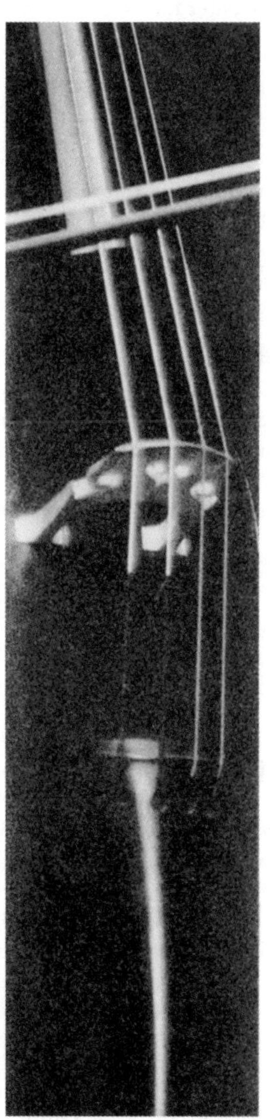

André Kertész
Cello Study, 1926
22,6cm x 4,8cm

263 Switzerland

Semina rerum – Irène Preiswerk, Cäcilienstr. 3, CH-8032 Zürich. Tel (01) 2512639, Fax (01) 2513419

Shedhalle Zürich, Seestr. 395, CH-8038 Zürich. Tel (01) 4815950, Fax (01) 4815951. Director: Tue–Fri 14–20, Sat–Sun 14–17

Zwischenraum der Schweizerischen Stiftung für die Photographie, Weinbergstr. 22a, CH-8001 Zürich. Tel (01) 2516765, Fax (01) 2512464. E-mail ssp.@kunsthaus.ch. Website www.kunsthaus.ch.ssp.stiftung.html. Open: Tue–Thu 10–21, Fri–Sun 10–17. Director: Dr. Peter Pfrunder

Festivals & Fairs

Art Basel, Messe Basel, P. O. Box , CH-4021 Basel. Tel (061) 6862020, Fax (061) 6862686. E-mail art@ messebasel.ch. Website www.art.ch

Images, Festival International de la Photographie et des Arts Visuels, 14 route de Châtel, CH-1807 Blonay. Tel (021) 9431900, Fax (021) 9432769. E-mail museum@vtx.ch

Magazines

Das Kunst-Bulletin, Zeughausstr. 55, CH-8026 Zürich. Tel (01) 2416300, Fax (01) 2416373. E-mail info@ kunstbulletin.ch. Website www.kunstbulletin.ch. Editor: Claudia Jolles. German/French. Founded 1968. Copy price: SFr 6.00. Annual subscription: SFr 48.50, 10 issues/year

Du, Die Zeitschrift der Kultur, Baslerstr. 30, CH-8048 Zürich. Tel (01) 4046030, Fax (01) 4046040. Editor: Marco Meier. German (English summaries). Founded 1941. Copy price: DM 20.00. Annual subscription: DM 162.00, 12 issues/year

Parkett Editionen und Verlag, Kunstzeitschrift/Art Magazine, Quellenstr. 27, CH-8005 Zürich. Tel (01) 2718140, Fax (01) 2724301. E-mail parkettmag @aol.com. Website www.parkettart. com. Editor: Bice Curiger. English/ German. Founded 1984. Copy price: DM 45.00. Annual subscription: DM 122.00, 3 issues/year

Passagen/Passages, A Swiss Cultural Magazine/Eine schweizerische Kulturzeitschrift, Pro Helvetia, P. O. Box, CH-8024 Zürich. Tel (01) 2677171, Fax (01) 2677106. E-mail mlarre@prohelvetia.ch. Editor: Michael Guggenheimer. German/French/English. Founded 1985. Annual subscription: free, 2 issues/year

Photo-Video-Expert, Le magazine suisse des passionnés de l'image, route de Bellebouche 13, CH-1246 Corsier. Tel (022) 7511653, Fax (022) 7511871. Editor: Jean Spinatsch. French. Copy price: FF 6.50–7.50. Annual subscription: FF 60.00, 9 issues/year

Visual, Mengis Druck und Verlag, P. O. Box 364, CH-3930 Visp. Tel (028) 462633, Fax (028) 462128. German. Annual subscription: SFr 92.00, 10 issues/year

Book Publishers

Benteli Verlags AG, Seftigenstr. 310, CH-3084 Bern. Tel (031) 9608484, Fax (031) 9617414. E-mail benteli-verlag@btm.ch. Website www.benteliverlag.ch

Diopter, Verlag für Kunst und Fotografie, Wesemlinrain 9, CH-6006 Luzern. Tel (041) 4108470, Fax (041)

4108417. E-mail info@diopter.ch.
Website www.diopter.com

Edition Stemmle AG, Alte Landstr. 55,
CH-8802 Kilchberg. Tel (01) 7154300,
Fax (01) 7154360

Editions Ides et Calendes, Evole 19,
CH-2001 Neuchâtel. Tel (032)
7253861, Fax (032) 7255880

Graphis Press Corp., Dufourstr. 107,
CH-8008 Zürich. Tel (01) 3838211,
Fax (01) 3831643

IMS/Studio 6, 60 avenue des Col-
lèges, CH-1009 Pully (Lausanne). Tel
(021) 7295562, Fax (021) 7295564

Memory/Cage Editions, Projekt-
verlag für zeitgenössische Kunst,
Fotografie und Literatur, Edenstr.
12 , CH-8045 Zürich. Tel (01) 2813565,
Fax (01) 2813566. E-mail mail@
memorycage.com. Website www.
memorycage.com

Punktum AG, Edition 91, Klusstr. 50,
CH-8032 Zürich. Tel (01) 4224540,
Fax (01) 4224813

Raum F, Forum und Verlag für Fotografie und Performance, Einsiedler-
str. 34, CH-8820 Wädenswil. Tel (01)
7800751, Fax (01) 7800751. E-mail
ffvogel@mus.ch

Reich-Verlag, terra magica, Musegg-
str. 12, CH-6000 Luzern 5. Tel (041)
4103721, Fax (041) 4103227

Scalo Verlag AG, Weinbergstr. 22a,
CH-8001 Zürich. Tel (01) 2610910,
Fax (01) 2619262. E-mail publisher@
scalo.com. Website www.scalo.com

Simonett Projects, P. O. Box 767,
CH-8038 Zürich. Tel (01) 4800351,
Fax (01) 4800354. E-mail projects@
simonett.com. Website www.
simonett.com

U. Bär Verlag, Mainaustr. 35, CH-
8008 Zürich. Tel (01) 3891666

Verlag Lars Müller, P. O. Box 912, CH-
5401 Baden. Tel (056) 2822700, Fax
(056) 2822701

Bookshops

Librairie du Musée de l'Elysée, avenue
de l'Elysée 18, CH-1014 Lausanne

Pep + No Name, Unterer Heuberg 2,
CH-4051 Basel. Tel (061) 2615161,
Fax (061) 2615161. E-mail
pepnoname@pepnoname.ch. Website www.photobuch.ch, www.
pepnoname.ch

Scalo Books & Looks, Weinbergstr.
22a, CH-8001 Zürich. Tel (01)
2610928, Fax (01) 2619262. E-mail
bookshop@scalo.com. Website
www.scalo.com

Critics & Journalists

Dr. Erika Billeter, 10 chemin Pelaz-
Beau, CH-1806 St. Légier. Tel (021)
9433261, Fax (021) 9434804. Benteli
Edition, Bern

Markus Britschgi, Wesemlinrain 9,
CH-6006 Luzern. Tel (041) 4108470,
Fax (041) 4108417. E-mail mbritschgi
@swissonline.ch. Diopter, Luzern

Birgit Filzmaier, Oescherstr. 26, CH-
8702 Zollikon. Tel (01) 3919459, Fax
(01) 3919459. E-mail bfilzmaier@
access.ch. *Rundbrief Fotografie,* Dresden; *Photonews,* Hamburg

Stefan Frey, Gesellschaftsstr. 31, CH-
3012 Bern. Tel (031) 3020138, Fax
(031) 3020138. Kunstmuseum Bern;
Bernische Stiftung für Fotografie,
Bern

Peter Killer, Kaeppel, CH-3367 Ochlenberg

Gerhard Johann Lischka, Gerberngasse 21, CH-3011 Bern

Allan Porter, Weinmarkt 18, CH-6004 Luzern. Tel (041) 4103205. E-mail aporter@access.ch. Philadelphia Verlag, Schindler, Luzern

Dr. Martin Schaub, Steinhaldenstr. 73, CH-8002 Zürich. Tel (01) 2022258, Fax (01) 2484607

Urs Stahel, Fotomuseum Winterthur, Grüzenstr. 44, CH-8400 Winterthur. Tel (052) 2336086, Fax (052) 2336097. Director of Fotomuseum Winterthur

Birgit Ulmer, Dufour Str. 61, CH-8008 Zürich. Tel (01) 3805015, Fax (01) 3805016. E-mail b.ulmer@ swissonline.ch

Schools & Workshops

Hochschule für Gestaltung und Kunst Zürich, Studienbereich Fotografie, Sihlquai 125, CH-8005 Zürich. Tel (01) 4462340, Fax (01) 2732254. E-mail fotografie@hgkz.ch. Website www. hgkz.ch/fotografie

Université de Bâle, Département de Photographie Scientifique, Klingelbergstr. 80, CH-4056 Basel. Tel (061) 2673836

Associations

Association Suisse des Institutions pour la Photographie, c/o Jacques Boesch, Saint-Gervais Genève – Images, 5 rue du Temple, CH-1201 Genève. Tel (022) 9802062, Fax (022) 9082001

Fondation Suisse pour la Restauration et la Conservation du Patrimoine Photographique, 14 faubourg de l'Hôpital, CH-2000 Neuchâtel

Images, Association pour les Arts visuels, 14 route de Châtel, CH-1807 Blonay. Tel (021) 9431900, Fax (021) 9432769. E-mail museum@vtx.ch

Schweizerischer Photographen-Verband, Spitalgasse 4, CH-3001 Bern

Schweizerischer Werkbund, Limmatstr. 118, CH-8031 Zürich. Tel (01) 2727176

Vereinigung fotografischer GestalterInnen, P. O. Box, CH-8033 Zürich. Website www.swissartwork.ch/vfg

Grants & Awards

Grand Prix de la Ville de Vevey, European Photography Competition, discovering new talent in European photography and giving them the opportunity to express themselves on a subject of their choice; no age limit, selection by a national committee, SFr 40,000, Special prizes SFr 5,000– 10,000, every two years. Contact: Images, Association pour les Arts visuels, Case postale, CH-1800 Vevey 1. Tel (021) 9218251, Fax (021) 9211884. E-mail mberney@cepv.ch. Website www.cepv.ch

Preis der Theater-Photographie, to support theatre photography as an artistic genre, every two years. Contact: Schweizerischer Bühnenverband, P. O. Box 46, CH-8126 Zumikon. Tel (01) 9181880, Fax (01) 9181880. Contact: The Selection vfg, P. O. Box , CH-8026 Zürich. Tel (01) 2402203, Fax (01) 2402202. E-mail theselectionvfg@swissartwork.ch. Website www.swissartwork.ch/vfg/selection

Prix Michel Jordi de Photographie,
first prize SFr 10,000. Contact: Prix
Michel Jordi de Photographie, St.
Gervais Photographie, 5 rue du
Temple, CH-1201 Genève. Tel (022)
7322060, Fax (022) 7384215

"The Selection vfg", The Selection vfg
(Vereinigung fotografischer Gestalterinnen), P. O. Box, CH-8026 Zürich.
Tel (01) 2402203, Fax (01) 2402202. E-
mail theselectionvfg@swissartwork.
ch. Website www.swissartwork.ch/
vfg/selection

New Media

Semaine Internationale de Vidéo,
Saint-Gervais Geneve, André Iten,
5 rue du Temple, CH-1201 Genève.
Tel (022) 9082060, Fax (022) 9082001.
E-mail sgg@sgg.ch. Website www.
sgg.ch

Solothurner Filmtage, Büro der
Solothurner Filmtage, I. Kummer,
P. O. Box 140, CH-4504 Solothurn.
Tel (032) 6258080, Fax (032) 6236410.
E-mail filmtage@cuenet.ch. Website
www.filmtage-solothurn.ch

Video Art Festival Locarno, P. O. Box
146, CH-6604 Locarno 4. Tel (091)
7512208, Fax (091) 7512207. E-mail
avart@tinet.ch. Website www.
tinet.ch/videoart

**Viper – Internationales Film-, Video-
und Multimedia Festival Luzern,** P. O.
Box 4929, CH-6002 Luzern. Tel (041)
3621717, Fax (041) 3621718. E-mail
info@viper.ch. Website www.
viper.ch

Ukraine

Population: 52 million
Capital: Kiev, 3 million
Currency: Grivna (UAH)
International code: ++380
Tourist information: State
Committee for Tourism, 36,
Yaroslaw Val, UA-253034 Kiev

Galleries & Museums

Dom khudozhnikov Kharkova, House
of Kharkov Artists, ul. Darvina 11,
UA-61057 Kharkov. Tel (0572) 439040.
Artists: Brad A. Smith, Evgeniy
Pavlov,Vladimir Shaposhnikov

Galereya Palitra, Palitra Gallery, 11
(4), Vorobyova, UA-61057 Kharkov.
Tel (0572) 235292, Fax (0572) 120015.
Director: Andrey Avdeenko. 1 room,
20 m². Artists: Sergey Bratkov, Sergey
Kochetov, Viktor Kochetov, Anatoli
Makienko, Evgeni Pavlov, Roman
Pyatkovka, Arsen Savadov, Edward
Stranadko

**Kharkovskiy Khudozhestvenny
Muzey,** Kharkov Art Museum,
11, Sovnarkomovskaya, UA-61057
Kharkov. Tel (0572) 433585, Fax
(0572) 433585. Director: Valentina
Mysgina. 5 rooms, 150 m². 2–3
photo exhibitions/year. Artists:
Oleg Malyovany, Boris Mikhailov,
Evgueni Pavlov, Alexander Suprun,
Sergey Solonsky, Yuri Voroshilov

**Kharkovskaya Municipalnaya Gale-
reya,** Kharkov City Art Gallery,
15, Chernyshevskogo, UA-61057
Kharkov. Tel (0572) 474034, Fax

(0572) 478100. Contact: Tatyana
Tumasyan. Founded 1996. 2 rooms,
185 m². 4–5 photo exhibitions/year.
Artists: Vladimir Bisov, Sergey Brat-
kov,Vladimir Ogloblin, Bill Davis,
Mikhle Johnson, Konny Salliven

Centr suchasnogo mystetsva, Center
for Contemporary Art, ul. Skovorody
2, UA-254070 Kiev. Tel (044) 2382446,
Fax (044) 2382448. E-mail art@
cca.kiev.ua. Website www.cca-
kiev.ua. Contact: Jerzy Onuch.
Founded 1994. 600 m². 2–3 photo
exhibitions/year. Artists: Sergey
Bratkov, Ilia Chichkan, Boris
Mikhailov, Arsen Savadov, Igor
Chursin, Alexander Kharchenko

**Centr suchasnogo mystetstva "Sovi-
art",** Center for Contemporary Art
"Soviart", 11, Kostyolna, UA-251001
Kiev. Tel (044) 2296157, Fax (044)
2296157. E-mail pro@iptelecom.
net.ua. Director: Viktor Khamatov.
Founded 1989. 80 m². Artists: Andrey
Avdeyenko, Sergey Bratkov, Anatoli
Makienko, Evgueni Pavlov, Igor
Karpenko, Alexander Suprun, Sergey
Chursin

Centralny Budynok Khudozhnikiv,
Central House of Artists, 1/5 Artema,
UA-254053 Kiev. Tel (044) 2120535.
Director: Evhen Solonin

Foto-centr "Eksar", Photo-center
"Eksar", 112, Velika Vasilkivska,
UA-251001Kiev. Tel (044) 2611868,
Fax (044) 2690514. Artists: Vladimir
Ogloblin, Evgeni Pavlov, Vladimir
Shaposhnikov, Eduard Stranadko

**Fotogalereya Spilky Fotokhudozhnikiv
Ukrainy,** Photogallery of the Union of
Ukrainian Photographers, 25e, Sahaidachnogo, UA-254070 Kiev. Tel (044)
4163374, Fax (044) 4163563

Galereya Atelier Karas, Studio Karas
Gallery, 22a, Andrievskiy uzviz, UA-

252025 Kiev. Tel (044) 4160247, 2386531, Fax (044) 2386531. E-mail karas@cca.kiev.ua. Website www.karas.cca.kiev.ua. Contact: Evhen Karas. Founded 1995. 100 m². Artists: Evgueni Pavlov, Vladimir Shaposhnikov

Ukrainski Dim, Ukrainian House, 2, Khreschatyk, UA-252001 Kiev. Tel (044) 2280006

Magazines

Art-Gallery, Magazine of Ukrainian Art Galleries Association, 11, Kostyolna, UA-253146 Kiev. Tel (044) 2296157, Fax (044) 2296157. E-mail pro@iptelecom.net.ua. Editor: Alexey Titarenko. Founded 1999, 2 issues/year

Foto-Novosti, 43, Moskovska, P. O. Box 384, UA-253146 Kiev. Tel (044) 2904162, Fax (044) 29041162. E-mail fotonews@nbi.com.ua. Editor: Olexander Lyapin. Founded 1998, 6 issues/year

Terra incognita, International magazine for contemporary art and culture, UA-252000 Kiev. Tel (044) 2243339. E-mail terraincognita@mail.ru. Editor: Hlib Vysheslavsky

Critics & Journalists

Olexandr Lyapin, 4g, Uzhviy, kv. 198, UA-254108 Kiev. Tel (044) 4607110. *Foto-Novosti*, Kiev

Tatiana Pavlova, Mira 76-6, UA-61106 Kharkov. Tel (0572) 990621. E-mail pavlovat@yahoo.com. *Imago*, Bratislava; *Parta, Art-Gallery*, Kiev

Nadia Prigodich, Centr suchasnogo mystetstva, ul. Skovorody 2, UA-254070 Kiev. Tel (044) 2421560. E-mail prigod@cca-kiev.ua. *Parta, Art-Gallery*, Kiev

Olexandr Soloviev, 10a, prosp. Vatutina, kv. 101, UA-251001 Kiev. Tel (044) 5338330. E-mail soloviov@cca.kiev.ua. *Parta, Terra Inkognita, Art-Gallery*, Kiev

Kateryna Stukalova, Centr suchasnogo mystetstva, ul. Skovorody 2, UA-254070 Kiev. Tel (044) 2421560, 2382446. E-mail katyast@cca.kiev.ua. *Terra Inkognita, Art-Gallery*, Kiev

Schools & Workshops

Kharkovsky Khodozhestvenno-promyshlenny Institut, Kharkov Institute of Applied Arts, Krasnoznamionnaya 8, UA-61000 Kharkov. Tel (0572) 400669, Fax (0572) 432873. E-mail root@design.kharkov.ua

Ukrainskaya Academya Iskusstva, Ukrainian Academy of Arts, 20, Smirnova-Lastochkina, UA-254053 Kiev

Associations

Soyuz Fotokhudoznikiv Kharkova, Union of Photographers Artists of Kharkov. Tel (0572) 931269

Soyuz Fotokhudoznikiv Kieva, Union of Photographers Artists of Kiev, O. Gonchara 55, kv. 31, UA-252034 Kiev. Tel (044) 2288141, Fax (044) 2288141. E-mail victor@cos.ambernet.kiev.ua

Spilka Fotokhudozhnikiv Ukrainy, Union of Photo Artists of Ukraine, 25e, Sahaidachnogo, UA-25254070 Kiev. Tel (044) 4163374, Fax (044) 4163563

Yugoslavia

Population: 10.6 million
Capital: Beograd, 1.2 million
Currency: Dinar (Din)
International code: ++381
Tourist information: Tourist
Association of Yugoslavia, Mose
Pijade 1, YU-11000 Beograd
Tel (011) 32 54 34

Galleries & Museums

Etnografski muzej, Ethnographical
Museum, Studentski trg 13, YU-11000
Beograd. Tel (011) 3281888. Open:
Tue–Sun 10–17. Contact: Vesna Bizic-
Omcikus. 600 m². 1–2 photo exhibi-
tions/year. Artists: Petar Z. Petrovic,
Stajone Bojovic, Zoran Milovanovic

Foto Galerija u Šumicama, Centar za
Kulturu i sport Šumice, Ustanicka
125/1, YU-11000 Beograd. Contact:
Milorad Djuric

Galerija SANU, Gallery of the Serbian
Academy of Science and Arts, Knez
Mihailova 35, YU-11000 Beograd. Tel
(011) 187144. E-mail imsuboti@
f.bg.ac.yu. Open: Mon–Sat 11–19.
Contact: Dr. Gojko Subotic. Founded
1955. 300 m². 1 photo exhibition/year.
Artist: Milan Jovanovic

Galerija Singidunum, Knez Mihajlova,
YU-11000 Beograd. Tel (011) 688721,
Fax (011) 685780. E-mail ulupuds@
beotel.yu. Open: Mon–Sat 9–20.
Contact: Djurdja Crevar

Kulturni centar Beograda, Cultural
Centre of Beograd, Knez Mihajlova 6,
YU-11000 Beograd. Tel (011) 621469.
Website: www.kcb.org.yu. Contact:
Vesna Danilovic, Svetlana Petrovic.
Founded 1959. 450 m². 2 photo
exhibitions/year. Artist: Tina Modotti

Muzej primenjene umetnosti, Museum of Applied Art, Vuka Karadzica
18, YU-11000 Beograd. Tel (011)
626841, Fax (011) 629121. Open: Tue–
Sun 10–17. Contact: Marijana Petro-
vic-Raic. Founded 1950. 600 m². 1–3
photo exhibitions/year. Artist: Nicola
Vucho

Nikon Galerija, Vuka Karadjica 7a,
YU-11000 Beograd. E-mail refotb@
eunet.yu. Contact: Slobodan Vuka-
dinovic

Salon fotografije, Salon of Photogra-
phy, Gospodar Jovanova 2, YU-32000
Cacak. Tel (032) 22729. Contact:
Zoran Milosevic

Narodni muzej Kragujevac, National
Museum Kragujevac, Vuka Karadzica
1, YU-34000 Kragujevac. Open:
Tue–Sun 10–17. Contact: Miroslav
Banovic, Milomir Minic. Founded
1960. 600 m². 1 photo exhibition/
year. Artists: Svetozar Nikolic Sosa,
Cedomil Pavlovic Bojadzic

Art Gallery Pecat, Strazilovska 4,
YU-21000 Novi Sad. Tel (021) 422659.
E-mail jovanovs@eunet.yu. Website
www.artmagazin.co.yu/galerije/
pecat/index.htm. Contact: Jasna
Jovanov. Founded 1995. 2 rooms,
45 m². 1–2 photo exhibitions/year.
Artist: Goranka Matic

Multimedia Arts, Pasiceva 28, YU-
21000 Novi Sad. Tel (021) 20780.
E-mail multivision@satto.co.yo.
Website www.multivision.co.yu.
Open: Mon–Sat 11–21. Contact:
Milorad Putnik. Founded 2000.
Artists: Young Photographers in
Vojvodina

Muzej savremene umetnosti, Museum of Contemporary Art, Usce Save bb, YU-11070 Novi Beograd. Tel (011) 3116965, Fax (011) 3112955. Open: Wed–Mon 10–17. Contact: Jasna Tijardovic Popovic. Founded 1965. 500 m². 1 photo exhibition/year. Artists: Vane Zavidovic-Bor, Mirko Lovric

Galerija Zlatno oko, Gallery Golden Eye, Trg mladenaca 10, YU-21000 Novi Sad. Tel (021) 29075. Open: Tue–Sun 10–13, 17–20. Contact: Sava Stepanov. Founded 1972. 1 room, 70 m². 2–3 photo exhibition/year

Festivals & Fairs

Dani jugoslovenske fotografije, Days of Yugoslav Photography, Foto savez Jugoslavije, Trg Republike 6, YU-11000 Beograd. Tel (011) 630363

Dan Nacionalnogo centra za fotografiju, Day of National Center of Photography, Obilicev venac 10, YU-11000 Beograd. Contact: Stevan Ristic, Salvadora Aljendea 1, YU-11000 Beograd. E-mail ristics@eunet.yu, fotogram@beotel.yu

Dogadjaj godine u srpskoj fotografiji, Event of the year in Serbian Photography, Obilicev venac 10, YU-11000 Beograd. Contact: Mirko Lovric and Stevan Ristic, Salvadora Aljendea 1, YU-11000 Beograd. E-mail ristics@eunet.yu, fotogram@beotel.yu

Magazines

Art Magazine On Line, On line casopis za savremenu likovnu umetnost, Online magazine for contemporary art, Hajduk Veljkova 11a, YU-21000 Novi Sad. Tel (021) 21061. E-mail office@artmagazin.co.yu. Website www.artmagazin.co.yu. Founded 1997. Editor: Luka Salapura

Beorama, Nehruova 109, YU-11070 Novi Beograd. Tel (011) 1778283, Fax (011) 1778283. E-mail beorama@bits.net. Website www.beograd.org.yu/beorama. Editor: Slavko Timotijevic

Kvadart, Nikole Tesle 2, YU-11070 Novi Beograd. Tel (011) 691644, Fax (011) 691644. E-mail kvadart@beotel.yu. Editor: Radomir Vukovic

Likovni ivot, Kej oslobodjenja 8, YU-11040 Beograd-Zemun. Editor: Bratislav Ljubišic

Book Publishers

Fotogram, Sarajevska 77, YU-11000 Beograd. Tel (011) 3548655. E-mail fotogram@beotel.yu. Website www.beotel.yu/~fotogram

Nacionalni centar za fotografiju NCF, Obilicev venac 10, YU-11000 Beograd. Tel (011) 631113

Critics & Journalists

Milan Aleksic, Academy of Arts Braca Karic, Department of Photography, Cara Dusana 98, YU-11080 Beograd- Zemun. Tel (011) 191794. E-mail aleksic@net.yu

Jasna Jovanov, Drage Spasic 13/VII, YU-21000 Novi Sad. Tel (021) 451084, E-mail jovanovs@eunet.yu. *Dnevnik, Projektart, Vreme,* Novi Sad

Mirko Lovric, Obilicev venac 10, YU-11000 Beograd. E-mail fotogram@beotel.yu. President of National Center of Photography, Beograd

Goran Malic, Nacionalni centar za fotografiju, Obilicev venac 10, YU-11000 Beograd. E-mail fotogram@beotel.yu. Website www.beotel.yu/~fotogram. Editor of *Fotogram*, Beograd; custodian of National Center of Photography, Beograd; president of Association of Serbian Applied Artists and Designers; *Politika*, Beograd

Milan Miletin, Branicevska 9, YU-11000 Beograd. Tel (011) 452582. Faculty of Performing Art, Department of Photography

Luka Salapura, Bulevar Cara Lazara 25, YU-21000 Novi Sad. Tel (021) 367136. E-mail luka@satto.co.yu. Website www.planet.satto.co.yu/luka. Chief-editor of *Art magazine On line*, Novi Sad

Andrej Tisma, Modene 1, YU-21000 Novi Sad. Tel (021) 28067. E-mail aart@eunet.yu. *Dnevnik*, Novi Sad

Milanka Todic, Vojvode Milenka 7, YU-11000 Beograd. E-mail btodic@f.bg.ac.yu. Faculty of Applied Arts and Design, Beograd

Schools & Workshops

Akademija lepih umetnosti u Novom Sadu, Academy of Fine Arts in Novi Sad, Djure Jakšica 7, YU-21000 Novi Sad

Akademija umetnosti Univerziteta Braca Karic, Academy of Art of Brother Karic, Department of Photography, Nemanjina 28, YU-11000 Beograd. Tel (011) 191794/3618715, Fax (011) 3618716. E-mail aleksic@net.yu

Fakultet dramskih umetnosti, Faculty of Performing Arts, Department of Film and TV Camera, Branicevska 9, YU-11000 Beograd

Fakultet primenjenih umetnosti i dizajna, Faculty of Applied Arts and Design, Department of Applied Graphic Arts (Atelier of Photography), Kralja Petra 4, YU-11000 Beograd. Tel (011) 638812, Fax (011) 182047

Graficka škola, Graphic School, Department of Photography, Otona Zupancica 19. YU-11070 Novi Beograd. Tel (011) 696931

Škola za dizajn, School of Design, Krupanjska 3, YU-11000 Beograd

Srednja Graficka Škola Milic Rakic, High Graphic School Milic Rakic, Otona Zupancica 19, YU-11000 Novi Beograd

Associations

Foto savez Jugoslavije, Yugoslav Union of Photographers, Trg Republike 6, YU-11000 Beograd. Tel (011) 636363

Nacionalni centar za fotografiju NCF, National Center of Photography NCF, Obilicev venac 10, YU-11000 Beograd. Tel (011) 631113. E-mail fotogram@beotel.yu. Website www.beotel.yu/~fotogram

Udruzenje likovnih umetnika primenjenih umetnosti i dizajnera Srbije, Association of Serbian Applied Artists and Designers, Art Photography Division, Terazije 26/3. YU-11000 Beograd. Tel (011) 688721, Fax (011) 685780. E-mail ulupuds@beotel.yu. Website www.beotel.yu/~ulupuds

Grants & Awards

Nagrada za zivotno delo u oblasti fotografije NCF Award, to recognize a lifetime achievement. Contact: National Center of Photography, Obilicev venac 10, YU-11000 Beograd. Tel (011) 631113. E-mail fotogram@ beotel.yu. Website www.beotel.yu/ ~fotogram

New Media

Video Medeja, International Video Summit, Jugoslovensko Udruzenja za Video Umetnost videomedeja, Jevrejska 4, YU-21000 Novi Sad. Tel (021) 621308, Fax (021) 621308. E-mail videomed@fodns.opennet.org. Website www.videomedeja.org.yu

Discover

SWANN S

AUCTIONS

*Man Ray,
Portrait of Lee Miller
(detail),
vintage silver print,
circa 1929,
sold on Oct 7, 1999
for $27,600.*

*Quarterly newsletter with
full auction schedule and
brochure, "Selling and
Buying at Swann
Auctions," on request.
For further information,
please contact Daile Kaplan,
dkaplan@swanngalleries.com*

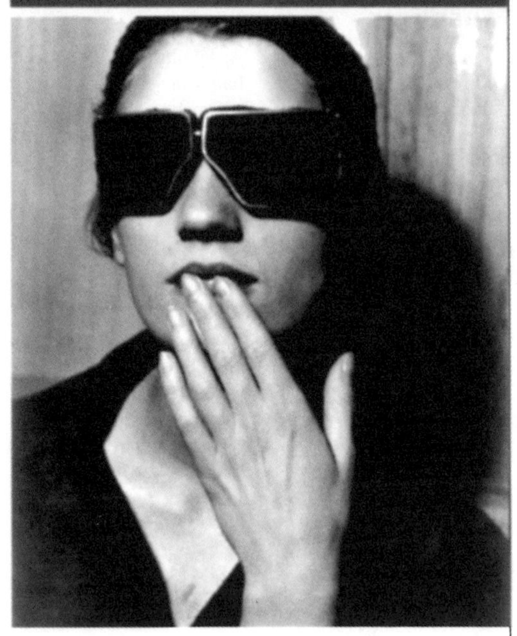

Five or more auctions per year of:

**Important 19th & 20th Century
Photographs**

Photographic Literature

Cameras and Viewing Devices

*Illustrated Catalogues available individually or by subscription.
Now accepting consignments for forthcoming auctions.*

AUTOGRAPHS
BOOKS/MANUSCRIPTS
MAPS/ATLASES
PHOTOGRAPHS
POSTERS
WORKS OF ART ON PAPER

Swann Galleries, Inc.
104 East 25th Street, New York, NY 10010
212 254 4710 Fax: 212 979 1017
www.swanngalleries.com

Index Section

Galleries & Museums

A l'Enseigne des Oudin 69
A l'Image du Grenier sur l'Eau 69
A.R.P.A. 65
Aberystwyth Arts Centre 136
ACC Galerie 111
Agahthi 157
Agfa Foto-Historama 102
Aidan-Gallery 222
Aineen Taidemuseo 61
Aktionsforum Praterinsel 108
Alberto Peola Arte Contemporanea 173
Alpha-Delta Gallery 157
Alter Ego 242
Amidol 252
Amsterdams Centrum voor Fotografie 192
Angel Row Gallery 145
Anthony d'Offay 141
Anthony Reynolds Gallery 141
Ar/Ge Kunst 166
Arbetets Museum 253
Archivio Fotografico Toscano 171
Argos 20
Arhitekturni muzej 238
Arhiv Tošo Dabac 36
Arken 53
Arnolfini Gallery 138
Arrêt sur Images 67
Arrêt sur l'Image Galerie 65
Art Center MONO 33
Art Collegia Gallery 225
Art Gallery Pecat 270
Art Kiosk – Art Gallery 20
Art Photographique 260

Art Rencontres Internationales 69
Art-centr imeni Marka Shagala 18
Art-media centre TV-Gallery 222
Artothèque 67
Aschenbach Galerie 192
Aspex Gallery 146
Association Gallery 141
ATA Galeria 33
Aurel Scheibler 102
Ausstellungsfoyer 108
Badischer Kunstverein 101
Barbara Gross Galerie 108
Barbican Art Gallery 141
Bauhaus Dessau 96
Bauhaus-Archiv 89
Bedford Community Arts 136
Belorussky gosudarstvenny muzei istorii Velikoi otechestvennoi voiny 17
Benaki Museum 157
Berlinische Galerie 89
Beyond Words 139
Biblioteka Narodowa 208
Bibliothèque Nationale de France 69
Bièvres – Foire à la Photographie 69
BildMuseet 254
Birgit Filzmaier 261
Biuro Wystaw Artystycznych 206, 209
Bloomsbury Theatre Hall 141
Bluecoat Gallery 141
Bolt Fotógáleria 161
Bonner Kunstverein 94
Borey Art Center 225
Brandenburgische Kunstsammlungen Cottbus 96
Brewery Arts Centre 140
Broadway Media Centre 145
Büro für Fotos 102
Busche Galerie 89
Cafe Aroma Photogalerie 90
Camden Arts Centre 142
Camera Obscura 69
Camerawork 142

Canal de Isabel II 244
Cankarjev dom – Mala fotogalerija 238
Care Of 168
Caritas-Fotogalerie 105
Casa das Artes 217
Casino Luxembourg 191
Castello di Rivoli 172
Castello di Vigevano 174
Centr sovremennogo iskusstva 18
Centr suchasnogo mystetsva 268
Centr suchasnogo mystetstva "Soviart" 268
Centralny Budynok Khudozhnikiv 268
Centre Atlantique de la Photographie 66
Centre Culturel du Triangle 77
Centre d'Art Contemporain 20
Centre d'Art d'Ivry 67
Centre d'Art Santa Mònica 242
Centre de Cultura Contemporània de Barcelona 242
Centre de la Photographie 260
Centre de la Vieille Charité 68
Centre for Contemporary Arts 139
Centre International d'Art Contemporain Château Beychevelle 69, 77
Centre Méditerranéen de la Photographie 65
Centre National de la Photographie 70
Centre National de l'Audiovisuel 191
Centre Photographique d'Île de France 77
Centre Photographique Nicéphore 68
Centre Régional de la Photographie 66
Centro Cultural de Belém 216
Centro Culturale Pier Paolo Pasolini 166

Centro de Arte
  Moderna 216
Centro de Estudos de
  Fotografia 216
Centro de Fotografía Isla
  de Tenerife 246
Centro Galego de Artes da
  Imaxe 242
Centro Internazionale di
  Fotografia 174
Centro per l'Arte Contem-
  poranea 171
Centro Portugues de
  Fotografia 217
Centro Studi e Archivio
  della Comunica-
  zione 171
Centrum Sztuki
  Wspolczesnej "Zamek
  Ujazdowski" 209
Centum Kultury
  "Zamek" 208
Ceské centrum
  fotografie 42
Circulo de Bellas
  Artes 244
City Gallery 140
Claudia Gian Ferrari Arte
  Contemporanea 168
COALmine fotografie 261
Collezione di Autori, de
  Pellegrin 172
Collins Gallery 139
Cornerhouse 144
Crawford Arts Centre 146
Cultureel Centrum 23
Cultureel Centrum
  Gildhof 23
Curve Gallery 142
Danmarks
  Fotomuseum 53
Das Verborgene
  Museum 90
De Warande 25
Dean Clough Gallery 140
Deichtorhallen
  Hamburg 100
Delta Gallery 226
Det Kongelige
  Bibliotek 53
Det Nationalhistoriske
  Museum paa
  Frederiksborg 53
Deutsches
  Filmmuseum 98

Divadlo hudby 40
Djanogly Gallery 145
DLI Museum & Durham
  Art Gallery 139
Dobra Galerie 42
Documentary Photography
  Archive 144
Dogenhaus Galerie 105
Dolnoslaskie Centrum
  Fotografii 209
Dom fotografie 234
Dom khudozhnikov
  Kharkova 268
Dom, kultyrny tsentr 222
Dorothée de Pauw
  Gallery 22
Dryphoto 171
Dum umení 41
Dum umení mesta
  Brna 38
East Kilbridge Arts
  Centre 140
Eastthorpe Visual
  Arts 145
Edition Schellmann 108
Elba Benítez Galería 244
Elke Dröscher, Kunstraum
  Falkenstein 100
Epikentro 157
Espace d'Art Yvonamor
  Palix 70
Espace Image 65
Espace Images 65
Espace Malraux 66
Espace Photographique
  Contretype 22
Espai Fotogràfic Can
  Basté 242
Etnografski muzej 270
Euregio Galerie 10
Ex Teatro Sociale 166
f.Stop Gallery 136
Fabbrica Eos 168
Fabian Walter Galerie 259
Fabrik-Fotoforum 100
Feniks 222
Ferens Gallery 140
First Light Gallery 138
Firstsite 138
FLUSS – Niederöster-
  reichische Fotoiniti-
  ative 11
Focal Point Gallery 146
Folly Gallery 140
Foma Bohemia 39

Fondation Cartier pour
  l'art contemporain 70
Fondazione Antonio
  Mazzotta 168
Fondazione Italiana per la
  Fotografia 173
Fondazione Mudima 168
Forum Galleriet 252
Forvm Gallery 246
Foto Art 40
Foto F.45 168
Foto Galerija u
  Šumicama 270
Foto-centr "Eksar" 268
Fotocentr 222
Fotocentrum Raseborg
  Valokuvakeskus 60
Fotoforum West 9
Fotogalereya Spilky
  Fotokhudozhnikiv
  Ukrainy 268
Fotogaleria GAD 220
Fotogaléria Nova 233
Fotogalerie 90
Fotogalerie 2,5 x 4,5 192
Fotogalerie Camera
  Austria 9
Fotogalerie im Hause
  Bohl 98
Fotogalerie Kralupy 40
Fotogalerie
  Lichtzone 193
Fotogalerie Objektief 193
Fotogalerie Wien 10
Fotogalerie Zelená
  sedma 40
Fotogalerij Cultureel
  Centrum Hasselt 23
Fotogalerija Spot 36
Fotogalerija Stolp 239
Fotogalleriet 204, 252
Fotografie Forum
  International 98
Fotografijos muziejus 189
Fotografisk Center 54
Fotomuseum
  Winterthur 261
Fotosammlung in der
  Albertina 10
Fototeca della Biblioteca
  Panizzi 171
Fövárosi Szabó Ervin
  Könyvtár Budapest
  Gyüjteménye 161
Franca Speranza 169

Francúzsky inštitút –
Fotogaléria 232
Frankfurter Kunstverein
e. V. 98
Free Gallery 166
Fridrich-fényirda 162
Fruitmarket Gallery 139
Fuji Film Fotografijos
galerija 189
Fundaçao de
Serralves 217
Fundació Antoni
Tàpies 242
GAFF 110
Galereja Sojuza foto-
khudozhnikov Rossii v
Cheboksarakh 222
Galereya Atelier
Karas 268
Galereya Evropeiskogo
gumanitarnogo
universiteta 17
Galereya Natsional'noj
biblioteki Belarusi 17
Galereya Nova 17
Galereya Palitra 268
Galereya Vilnius 17
Galeria Abakus 209
Galéria Artotéka 232
Galeria Biala 207
Galeria Diferenca 216
Galeria Entropia 210
Galeria Estrany, de la
Mota 242
Galeria FF – Forum
Fotografii 207
Galéria Focus 232
Galéria fotografie
Profil 232
Galeria Fotografii
B&B 206
Galeria Fotografii
"PA-Camera" 208
Galeria Fotografii
"pf" 208
Galeria Fotografii
WTF 210
Galeria Goethe
Institut 209
Galeria Graça Fonseca 216
Galería Helga de
Alvear 244
Galería Joan Prats 242
Galeria K.E.V.A. 33
Galeria Korytarz RCK 206

Galéria Médium 233
Galéria mesta
Bratislavy 233
Galeria Miejska
"Arsenal" 208
Galéria P. M. Bohúna 233
Galeria Palmira Suso 216
Galeria "Prezentacje" –
Foto-Medium-Art Zamek
Wojnowice 207
Galeria Pusta 206
Galeria Ras 242
Galeria Sredec 33
Galeria Sztuki KOK 207
Galéria umelcov
Spiša 234
Galéria Vihorlatského
osvetového centra 233
Galeria "W Podziemiu" –
Foto-Medium-Art 210
Galeria Wymiany 207
Galeria/Studio
Gieraltowskiego 209
Galerie & Edition m 107
Galerie 1900–2000 70
Galerie 213 71
Galerie 4 39
Galerie 5020 10
Galerie AB 38
Galerie Agathe
Gaillard 71
Galerie Akinici 192
Galerie Alain Gutharc 71
Galerie Albrecht 108
Galerie Alex
Lachmann 102
Galerie Ambrosiana 38
Galerie Angelo
Falzone 107
Galerie Anita Beckers 98
Galerie Anita
Neugebauer 259
Galerie Anne Barrault 71
Galerie
Arbeiterfotografie 105
Galerie Arena 65
Galerie Argus
Fotokunst 90
Galerie Arrigo 261
Galerie Ars Futura 261
Galerie Barbara
Thumm 90
Galerie Baudoin Lebon 71
Galerie Bausmann 107
Galerie Benninger 102

Galerie Berinson 90
Galerie Bob van
Orsouw 262
Galerie Bugdahn und
Kaimer 97
Galerie Caesar 40
Galerie Camera Work 90
Galerie Carla Stützer 102
Galerie Carré Noir 72
Galerie Christa
Burger 108
Galerie Christian
Schneeberger 260
Galerie Condé 72
Galerie Conrads 97
Galerie Cora Hölzl 97
Galerie Daniel
Buchholz 102
Galerie DB-S 20
Galerie der Moderne Stefan
Vogdt 108
Galerie der Stadt
Esslingen 98
Galerie des Archives 72
Galerie Dieter Tausch 9
Galerie du Forum 77
Galerie du Jour
Agnès B. 72
Galerie du Théâtre 67
Galerie du Théâtre de
l'Agora 66
Galerie Eigen+Art 90, 107
Galerie Esther
Woerdehoff 72
Galerie Eva Poll 90
Galerie Faber 10
Galerie Fairt et Cause 72
Galerie FAMU 42
Galerie Farideh Cadot 72
Galerie Ferdinand van
Dieten – d'Eendt 192
Galerie Fiducia 41
Galerie Fiedler 104
Galerie Focale 260
Galerie Foma 38
Galerie Fotoforum 166
Galerie Fotohof 10
Galerie Fotomania 194
Galerie Françoise et Alain
Paviot 72
Galerie Françoise
Knabe 91
Galerie Fronta 42
Galerie für zeitgenössische
Kunst 107

Galerie Gisela Capitain 104
Galerie Gisèle Linder 259
Galerie Hammer/Regensburger Fotogalerie 110
Galerie hlavního mesta Prahy 42
Galerie Institutu tvurcí fotografie 41
Galerie J & J Donguy 72
Galerie Jána Šmoka 39
Galerie Johnen & Schöttle 104
Galerie Josefa Sudka 42
Galerie Kaess-Weiss 111
Galerie Karsten Greve 74, 104
Galerie Kleindienst 107
Galerie Kralingen 194
Galerie Laage-Salomon 74
Galerie Laurent Herschtritt 74
Galerie Le Lieu 67
Galerie les Filles du Calvaire 74
Galerie Lichtbilder 91
Galerie Lichtblick 104
Galerie Lichtenštejnský palác 42
Galerie L'Œil Écoute 67
Galerie Lisi Hämmerle 9
Galerie Maecenas 41
Galerie Maeght 74
Galerie Marion Meyer 74
Galerie Meile 260
Galerie Mestské knihovny 47
Galerie Michèle Chomette 74
Galerie Mitte 96
Galerie Monika Reitz 99
Galerie Municipale du Château 68
Galerie Municipale du Château d'Eau 77
Galerie Nadar 78
Galerie Nationale du Jeu de Paume 74
Galerie O. Ahlers 100
Galerie Objekte 108
Galerie Opera 41
Galerie Paul Andriesse 192
Galerie Pecka 44
Galerie Pennings 193

Galerie Périscope 23
Galerie Peter Kilchmann 262
Galerie Philomene Magers 108
Galerie Pierre Brullé 74
Galerie Pod kamennou zábou 39
Galerie Polaris 74
Galerie Régine Lussan 74
Galerie Renn 74
Galerie Rob Jurka 192
Galerie Robert Doisneau 78
Galerie Rodolphe Janssen 22
Galerie Rudolf Kicken 91
Galerie Rudolfinum 44
Galerie Ruta Correa 99
Galerie Saint-Gervais photographie 260
Galerie Samia Saouma 75
Galerie Schedler 262
Galerie sel d'Argent 68
Galerie Škola 39
Galerie Stadtpark 9
Galerie Štepánská 35 44
Galerie Šternberk 47
Galerie Suzel Berna 75
Galerie Tammen & Busch 91
Galerie Thaddaeus Ropac 75
Galerie Thierry Marlat 75
Galerie Thomas Zander 104
Galerie U Bílého jednorozce 40
Galerie umelecké fotografie 40
Galerie Václava Špály 44
Galerie ve sklepe 42
Galerie Velryba 44
Galerie Vera Munro 100
Galerie Vu 75
Galerie výtvarného umení 39
Galerie Willy D'Huysser 22
Galerie Wilma Tolksdorf 99
Galerie Wittenbrink 108
Galerie Wohnmaschine 91
Galerie Xippas 75
Galerie Yvon Lambert 75

Galerie Zero 65
Galerie Zimmer 97
Galerie Zlutá ponorka 47
Galerie "Zur Stockeregg" 262
Galerie-Atelier de Photographie 77
Galerija fotografija 36
Galerija Kapelica 238
Galerija KID-Kibla-Kibela 239
Galerija KUD – France Prešeren 238
Galerija Loggia 238
Galerija SANU 270
Galerija Singidunum 270
Galerija Zlatno oko 271
Galleri Andréhn-Schiptjenko 253
Galleri Charlotte Lund 253
Galleri Image 53
Galleri Roger Björkholmen 253
Galleria Carla Sozzani 169
Galleria Civica 170
Galleria Civica d'Arte Moderna e Contemporanea 173
Galleria Comunale d'Arte Moderna 166
Galleria Cons Arc 259
Galleria del Centro Culturale Francese 171
Galleria del Credito Valtellinese 169
Galleria dell'Immagine 171
Galleria Diana 60
Galleria Emi Fontana 169
Galleria Fotokram 60
Galleria Gottardo 260
Galleria Imagina 174
Galleria Karsten Greve 169
Galleria Laura Pecci 169
Galleria Milano 169
Galleria Minima Peliti Associati 172
Galleria Monica de Cardenas 169
Galleria Photology 169
Galleria Raffaella Cortese 169

Gallery Eleni
  Koronaiou 157
Gallery Fotohuset 252
Gallery L'Aquarium 78
Gallery Mozums 186
Gallery of Estonian
  Academy of Art 58
Gallery of Fine Arts of the
  Association of Bulgarian
  Fine Artists 33
Gallery of
  Photography 165
Gallery Riga 186
Gdanska Galeria Fotografii
  – Muzeum Narodowe
  Gdansk 206
Gelman Gallery 223
Georg-Kolbe-Museum 91
Giedre Bartelt Galerie 91
Gilbert Brownstone
  et Cie 75
Giò Marconi 170
Goethe-Institut 75
Golem Photo Art 91
Gosudarstvenny
  Ermitage 226
Gosudarstvenny
  Istorichesky muzei 223
Gosudarstvenny
  istorichno-arkhitekturny,
  khudozhestvenny i land-
  shaftny muzei-zapoved-
  nik "Tsaritsyno" 223
Gosudarstvenny Muzei
  istorii religii 226
Gosudarstvenny Muzei
  istorii Sankt
  Peterburga 226
Gosudarstvenny muzei
  istorii teatral'noi i
  muzikal'noi kultury
  Belarusi 17
Gosudarstvenny muzei Lva
  Tolstogo 223
Gosudarstvenny muzei
  V. V. Mayakovs-
  kogo 223
Gosudarstvenny nauchno-
  issledovatelsky muzei
  arkhitektury imeni A.V.
  Shchuseva 223
Gosudarstvenny
  obiedinenny istorichno-
  arkhitekturny i literatyrny muzei Kirova 222

Gosudarstvenny Politekh-
  nichesky muzei 223
Gosudarstvenny Russky
  muzei 226
Gosudarstvenny tsentr
  sovremennogo
  iskusstva 223
Gosydarstvennaya
  Tretyakovskaya
  galeria 223
Groninger Museum 194
Guildford House
  Gallery 140
Hadtörténeti Múzeum
  Fotóarchívuma 161
Hamburger
  Kunsthalle 100
Hamiltons Gallery 142
Harewood House 140
Harris Museum & Art
  Gallery 146
Hasselblad Center 252
Haus am Waldsee 92
Haus der Fotografie 96
Haus der Fotografie
  Hannover e. V. 101
Haus der Kulturen der
  Welt 92
Haus der Kunst 108
Hayward Gallery 142
Heidelberger Kunstverein
  e. V. 101
Heidi Reckermann
  Photographie 104
Henie-Onstad Art
  Center 204
Herder-Museum 196
Hereford City Museum
  & Art Gallery 140
Hochschule für Grafik und
  Buchkunst 107
Huddersfield Gallery 140
Huis Marseille 192
IfA-Galerie 92, 94
Ikon Gallery 136
Ikona Photo Gallery 174
Il Diaframma 170
Il Ponte 168
Ileana Tounta 157
Illegaard 58
Imagina di
  Attisani & C. 174
Imago Lucis 217
Impressions Gallery 147
in focus 104

Index – The Swedish
  Contemporary Art
  Foundation 253
Institut de Radioélectri-
  cité et de Cinémato-
  graphie 23
Institut sovremennogo
  iskusstva 223
Institute of Contemporary
  Arts 142
Instituto Nazionale per la
  Grafica 173
Instituto Valenciano de
  Arte Moderno 246
Instituut voor Fotografie en
  Nieuwe Media –
  Vlaanderen 20
Islington Arts
  Factory 142
Isu Bocconi 170
Jakopiceva Galerija 238
Jay Jopling/White
  Cube 142
Jersey Photographic
  Museum 146
Jewish Historical
  Museum 192
John Hansard Gallery 146
Josef-Haubrich-
  Kunsthalle 104
Junion Galereja 223
Kamera- und Fotomuseum
  Leipzig 108
Kassák Múzeum 161
Kestner-Gesellschaft 101
Kettle's Yard 138
Kharkovskaya
  Municipalnaya
  Galereya 268
Kharkovskiy Khudozhest-
  venny Muzey 268
Khudozhestvennaya
  galereya Belart 17
Khudozhestvenny Tsentr
  Borey 226
Kiek in de Kök 58
Kirovsky Oblastnoy Khu-
  dozhestvenny Muzei
  imeni V. i A. Vasnet-
  sovykh 222
Klaipedos fotografijos
  galerija 189
Klaus Hinrichs
  KunstRaum 111
Klub 13 Muz 208

KMZA Kunst- und Medien-
    zentrum Adlershof 92
Kölnischer
    Kunstverein 104
Kölnisches
    Stadtmuseum 105
Komorní galerie Domu
    fotografie Josefa
    Sudka 44
Konrad Fischer 97
Konserttitalon
    valokuvagalleria 60
Koralm-Fotogalerie 9
Kowasa 242
Kulturni centar
    Beograda 270
Kunst- und Ausstellungs-
    halle der Bundesrepublik
    Deutschland 95
Kunstakademiets
    Bibliothek 54
Kunsthal Rotterdam 194
Kunsthalle Basel 259
Kunsthalle Bielefeld 94
Kunsthalle Bremen 96
Kunsthalle Exnergasse 11
Kunsthalle Krems 10
Kunsthalle Rostock 110
Kunsthalle Wien am
    Karlsplatz 11
Kunsthalle Wien im
    Museumsquartier 11
Kunsthalle Zürich 262
Kunsthaus Apolda
    Avantgarde 89
Kunsthaus Bregenz 9
Kunsthaus Dresden 96
Kunsthaus
    Kaufbeuren 102
Kunsthaus Zürich 262
Künstlerhaus
    Bethanien 92
Künstlerhaus
    Dortmund 96
Künstlerhaus
    Mousonturm 99
Kunstmuseum Bern 259
Kunstmuseum Bonn 95
Kunstmuseum des Kantons
    Thurgau 261
Kunstmuseum
    Solothurn 261
Kunstmuseum
    Wolfsburg 111
Kunstraum im BDI 92

Kunstverein Freiburg im
    Marienbad 99
Kunstverein für die Rhein-
    lande und Westfalen 97
Kunstverein in
    Hamburg 100
Kunstverein Lingen 107
Kunstverein
    Ludwigsburg 107
L. A. Galerie 99
La Filature – La Galerie 68
La Galerie Photo 68
La Laverie 75
La Mente e
    l'Immagine 173
L'Abattoir 66
Ladylodge Arts
    Centre 146
Lagerfeld Gallery 76
Laoutlieff Gallery 33
Laterna Magica 60
Latvian Artist Union
    Gallery 186
Latvijas fotográfijas
    muzejs 186
Laure Genillard 142
Le bar Floréal.
    photographie 76
Le Botanique 23
Le Case d'Arte 170
Le Réverbère 2 67
Leica Galerie 111
Leopold-Hoesch-Museum
    der Stadt Düren 97
Les Ateliers Nadar 68
L'Hippodrome 66
Libreria Tartessos 244
Lichtbild-Galerie 112
L'Imagerie 67
Linea di Confine per la
    Fotografia Contempora-
    nea 173
Linnagalerii 58
Louisiana Museum of
    Modern Art 53
Luciano Inga Pin 170
Ludwig Forum für
    internationale Kunst 89
Luton Museum & Art
    Gallery 144
Lutz Teutloff Galerie 94
m Fotografie Bochum 94
MAC 138
Magyar Fotográfiai
    Múzeum 162

Magyar Fotográfusok
    Háza 161
Magyar Nemzeti Múzeum
    – Történeti
    Fényképtára 161
Mai 36 Galerie 262
Maisenbacher Art
    Gallery 111
Maison de la Villette 76
Maison Européenne de la
    Photographie 76
Maison Robert
    Doisneau 67
Mala Galeria 206
Mala Galeria Fotografiki
    ZPAF 208
Mala Galeria ZPAF –
    CSW 209
Malá galerie Ceské
    sporitelny 39
Malá výstavní sín –
    Fotogalerie 40
Malmö Konsthall 253
Mánes 44
Mánes – fotografická
    galerie 44
Manezh 223
Marburger
    Kunstverein 107
Marino alla Scala Art
    Center 170
Martini e Ronchetti 168
Melkweg Galerie 193
Mestska Galerija 238
Metrònom 244
Michael Hoppen
    Gallery 143
Miedzynarodowe
    Centrum Kultury 207
Minigalerie
    Waldemar 41
MJC de Rosendaël 66
Moderna galerija 238
Moderna Museet 253
Moravská galerie v
    Brne 38
Moravské zemské muzeum
    – Etnografický ústav 38
Moskovsky dom
    fotografii 224
Moskovsky gosudarst-
    venny vystavochny zal
    Novy Manezh 224
Mücsarnok 161
Multimedia Arts 270

Münchner
    Stadtmuseum   110
Musée Albert Kahn   66
Musée Carnavalet   76
Musée d'Art
    Contemporain   68, 69
Musée d'Art Moderne
    de la Ville de Paris   76
Musée d'Art Moderne et
    d'Art Contemporain   68
Musée de la Mer   66
Musée de la
    Photographie   23
Musée de l'Elysée   260
Musée de
    l'Holographie   76
Musée des Beaux-Arts
    de Nantes   68
Musée Français de la
    Photographie   65
Musée National d'Art
    Moderne   76
Musée Nicéphore
    Niépce   66
Musée Réattu   65
Musée Suisse de l'appareil
    Photographique   261
Museet for Fotokunst   54
Museo Cantonale
    d'Arte   260
Museo Civico   172
Museo d'Arte Moderna e
    Contemporanea   173
Museo di Storia della
    Fotografia Fratelli
    Alinari   168
Museo Internacional de
    Electrografia   244
Museo Ken Damy   166
Museo Nacional   246
Museo Nazionale della
    Fotografia   168
Museo Nuova Era   166
Museu – Photographia
    "Vicentes"   216
Museu d'Art Contempo-
    rani MACBA   244
Museu Nacional d'Art de
    Catalunya   244
Museum & Art Gal-
    lery   138
Museum & Gallery of
    Wales   138
Museum
    am Ostwall   96

Museum Boijmans Van
    Beuningen   195
Museum der Arbeit   100
Museum der bildenden
    Künste   107
Museum Folkwang   98
Museum
    Fridericianum   102
Museum für Gestaltung
    Zürich   262
Museum für Kunst und
    Gewerbe   101
Museum für Moderne
    Kunst   99
Museum für Photographie
    e. V.   95
Museum Ludwig   105
Museum Moderner Kunst
    Stiftung Ludwig   11
Museum of Modern
    Art   146
Museum of London   143
Museum van Heden-
    daagse Kunst Ant-
    werpen   20
Museum voor
    Fotografie   20
Muzei Belorusskoi
    akademii iskusstv   17
Muzei fotograficheskikh
    kolektsiy   224
Muzei istorii goroda
    Moskvy   224
Muzei izobrazitelnykh
    iskusstv imeni A. S.
    Pushkina   224
Muzei izobrazitelnykh
    iskusstv imeni A. S.
    Pushkina – Muzei
    chastnykh kollekciy   224
Muzei M. Gorkogo   224
Muzei sovremennogo
    izobrazitelnogo
    iskusstva   17
Muzej grada Rijeke   36
Muzej primenjene
    umetnosti   270
Muzej savremene
    umetnosti   271
Muzej suvremene
    umjetnost Zagreb   36
Muzej za umjetnost
    i obrt   36
Muzeul National de
    Arta al Romaniei   220

Muzeum Historii
    Fotografii   207
Muzeum hlavního mesta
    Prahy   44
Múzeum J. M.
    Petzvala   234
Múzeum Karola
    Plicku   232
Múzeum moderného
    umenia Andyho
    Warhola   233
Muzeum Narodowe,
    Poznan   208
Muzeum Narodowe,
    Wroclaw   210
Muzeum Sztuki   207
Muzeum umení
    Olomouc   41
Muzeum východnich
    Cech   39
Muzeum výtvarného
    umení   38
Muzey Novoy akademii
    iskusstv   226
Národní galerie – Sbírka
    moderního a soucasného
    umení   44
Narodni muzej
    Kragujevac   270
Národní technické
    muzeum   45
National Center for
    Contemporary Art   226
National Gallery of
    Fine Art   33
National Gallery of
    Scotland   139
National Museum of
    Photography, Film &
    Television   138
National Palace of
    Culture   33
National Portrait
    Gallery   143
Natsional'ny khudozhes-
    venny muzei   18
Natsional'ny muzei istorii
    i kul'tury Belarusi   18
Natural History Museum
    Rotterdam   195
Naturhistoriska
    Museet   252
NCE   76
Nederlands Foto
    Instituut   195

Nees Morfes 157
Néprajzi Múzeum 161
Neue Galerie am Landes-
 museum Joanneum 9
Neue Galerie der Stadt
 Linz 10
Neue Gesellschaft für
 Bildende Kunst e. V. 92
Neue Nationalgalerie 92
Neuer Berliner
 Kunstverein 92
Nikon Galerija 270
Nikon Image House 260
Nizhegorodsky istorichno-
 arkhitekturny muzei-
 zapovednik 225
Nizhegorodsky literaturno-
 memorialny muzei A. M.
 Gorkogo 225
Nordiska Museet 253
Norrbottens museum 252
Norrköpings
 Konstmuseum 253
Norsk Museum for
 Fotografi 204
Norwich Arts Centre 145
Norwich Gallery 145
Novaya Tretyakovskaya
 galeria 224
Nykytaiteen Museo 60
Obecní dum 45
Obecní galerie Beseda 45
Obscuri Viri Gallery 224
Oficiul National pentru
 Docementare si Expozitii
 de Arta si Fundatia
 ARTEXPO 220
Old Museum Arts
 Centre 136
Onsight Gallery 145
Open Eye Gallery 141
Oravská galéria 233
Országos Müszaki
 Múzeum 161
Österreichische Fotogalerie
 im Rupertinum 10
Österreichisches Museum
 für Angewandte
 Kunst 11
Oulu Taidemuseo 61
Padiglione d'Arte Contem-
 poranea 170
Palais des Beaux-Arts 23
Palazzo delle
 Esposizioni 173

Palazzo Fortuny 174
Palazzo Magnani 171
Panevezio fotografijos
 galerija 189
Panstwowa Galeria
 Sztuki 208
Panstwowa Galeria Sztuki
 "Zacheta" 209
Passage de Retz 76
Patrimoine de la photo-
 graphique – Hotel
 Sully 76
Pedvales brivdabas
 makslas muzejs 187
Pendle Arts Gallery 145
Pep + No Name 259
Photocellar "LEE" 58
Photo & Co. 173
Photo Image Gallery 226
Photo-Galerie Altstadt 89
Photoforum Pasquart 259
Photofusion 143
Photography Center of
 Thessaloniki 158
Photography Centre of
 Athens 157
Photography Now 92
Photology 143
Photomuseum 58, 246
Picto Bastille 77
Picture House Centre for
 Photography Ltd. 140
Picture Perfect 93
Pixel.Art Gallery 111
Plymouth Arts Centre 146
Pohjoinen
 valokuvakeskus 61
Porin Taidemuseo 61
Portfolio Gallery 139
Portikus 99
Posada del Potro 244
Povazská galéria
 umenia 234
PPS.Galerie 101
Prazský dum
 fotografie 45
Prazský hrad 47
Privat Foto Galeria Lajos
 Györi 161
Produzentengalerie 101
Prospekto galerija 189
Provinciaal Museum
 Hasselt 23
Q-Arts, Gallery 138
Raab Galerie 93

Railowsky Foto-
 Galeria 246
Rantagalleria 61
Raum F 261
Räume für neue
 Kunst 112
Rebecca Hossack
 Gallery 143
Rebekka M. Camchi 157
Regina Gallery 224
Reitern's House 186
Rheinisches Industrie-
 museum 110
Rheinisches Landes-
 museum Bonn 95
Rijksmuseum 193
Rooseum 253
ROSIZO – Gosudarstvenny
 muzeino-vystavochny
 tsentr Ministerstva
 Kultury Rossiyskoy
 Federatsii 224
Rossen Kolarov
 Gallery 33
Rossiysky etnografichesky
 muzei 226
Rovaniemi Art
 Museum 61
Royal Academy of
 Arts 143
Ruimte Morguen 20
Sainsbury Centre for Visual
 Arts 145
Sala Veratti 174
Salon – Library
 "Vecriga" 186
Salon fotografije 270
Sankt Peterburgsky
 gosudarstvenny
 universitet 226
Sankt Peterburgsky
 tvorchesky sojuz
 khudozhnikov (IFA) 227
Saukas pagasta muzejs –
 M. Buclera fotografijas
 kabinets 186
SBK 193
Scalo Galerie 262
Schirn Kunsthalle 99
Schneider-Henn 110
School of Art Gallery and
 Museum 136
Schweizerische Stiftung für
 die Photographie 262
Schwules Museum 93

Scottish National Portrait Gallery   139
Semina rerum – Irène Preiswerk   264
Serge Aboukrat   77
Severoceské muzeum   40
Shedhalle Zürich   264
Side Photographic Gallery   145
Siebenhaar   105
Site Gallery   146
SK Stiftung Kultur   105
Slezské zemské muzeum   41
Slovenská národná galéria   233
Sofijska gradska galeria   33
Spazio Foto San Fedele   170
Spazio Oberdan   170
Spectrum   246
Spider & Mouse Gallery   225
Sprengel Museum   101
Staatliche Galerie Moritzburg Halle   100
Staatliche Kunsthalle Baden-Baden   89
Staatliche Kunstsammlungen Dresden   97
Staatliche Museen zu Berlin   93, 94
Staatliches Museum Schwerin   110
Staatsgalerie Stuttgart   111
Stadsgalery Heerlen   194
Stadthaus Ulm   111
Städtische Galerie Erlangen   98
Stadtmuseum Dresden   97
Stadtmuseum Siegburg   110
Stara Galeria ZPAF   209
State Fine Arts Gallery   33
Štátná galéria výtvarného umenia   232
Stedelijk Museum Amsterdam   193
Stedelijk Museum, Het Domein   196
Stelling Gallery   194
Stichting Fotoarchief Kees Scherer   193
Stills Gallery   139

Stop Gallery   42
Street Level   139
Studio Guenzani   170
Studio Marangoni   168
Studio Trisorio   171
Suermondt-Ludwig-Museum   89
Sylviane de Decker Heftler   77
Synopse   94
Talsi novada muzejs   186
Tate Gallery   141, 143
Tatranská galérie – Elektráren   234
The Cambridge Darkroom   138
The Canon Photography Gallery   143
The City Museum of Stockholm   254
The Ffotogallery   138
The Finnish Museum of Photography   60
The Irish Museum of Modern Art   165
The New Art Gallery Walsall   147
The Pavilion   140
The Photographers' Gallery   143
The Royal Photographic Society   136
The Serpentine Gallery   144
The Special Photographers Company   144
The Sutcliffe Gallery   147
Theatre de la Photographie et de l'Image   69
Theoretical Events   171
Thessaloniki Museum of Photography   158
Tom Blau Gallery   144
Ton Peek Photography   196
Tondo   225
Torch Gallery   193
Triennale Palazzo dell'Arte   170
Tschechisches Zentrum   94
Tsentr sovremennogo iskusstva   225
Tsentr sovremennogo iskusstva Pushkinskaya 10   227

Tsentr sovremennogo iskusstva Sorosa   225
Tsentralny dom khudozhnikov   225
Tsentralny muzei Velikoi otechestvennoi voiny 1941–1945   225
Tsentralnyj vystavochny sal Manezh   227
Ukrainski Dim   269
Umeleckoprumyslové muzeum   47
University Gallery   145
Uppsala Konstmuseum   254
Ursula-Blickle-Stiftung   105
USVA Noorderlicht Fotogalerie   194
Valokuvagalleria Hippolyte   60
Valokuvakeskus Nykyaika   61
Valokuvakeskus Peri   61
Valts makslas muzejs   186
Van   194
Velge & Noirhomme   23
Ventspils novada vestures un makslas muzejs   187
Viafarini   170
Victor Barsokevitsch Photographic Center   61
Viewpoint Photography Gallery   146
Villa Stuck   110
Vilniaus fotografijos galerija   189
Vilniaus šiuolaikinio meno centras   189
Vintage Galéria   162
Visor Centre Fotogràfic   246
Viviane Esders   77
Von der Heydt-Museum   112
Vrais Rêves   68
Východoslovenská galéria   233
Výtvarné centrum Chagall – Galerie Na schodišti   41
Wakefield Museum   147
Walker Art Gallery   141
Walter Storms Galerie   110

Wereldmuseum Rotter-
dam 195
Westfälischer
Kunstverein 110
Westfälisches
Industriemuseum 96
Whitechapel Art
Gallery 144
Wiener Secession 11
Wigmore Fine Arts
Ltd. 144
Wilhelm Lehmbruck
Museum Duisburg 98
Witte de With 196
Wrexham Library Arts
Centre 147
Württembergischer
Kunstverein Stutt-
gart 111
Xavier Hufkens
Gallery 23
XL-Gallery 225
XS! Atelier & Gallery 259
Zelda Cheatle Gallery 144
Zellermayer Galerie 94
Zinc Gallery 254
ZKM – Zentrum für Kunst
und Medientechnologie
Karlsruhe 101
Zwischenraum der
Schweizerischen Stiftung
für die Photographie 264

Festivals & Fairs

Alberobello
Fotografia 174
Arco 247
Ars Electronica 11
Art Athina 158
Art Basel 264
Art Cologne 112
Art Frankfurt 112
Baltars 187
Biarritz Terre d'Images 78
Biennale d'Art
Contemporain 78
Biennale Europea
Fotografia d'Autore 174
Biennale Fotografii
Górskiej 210
Biennale Fotografii
Polskiej 210
Biennale Internationale de
l'Image 78
Biennale Internazionale di
Fotografia 174
Biennale
Photographique 78
Bièvres-Foire à la
Photographie 78
Big Torino 2000 174
Breda Fotografica 196
Cholet-Quinzaine de la
Photographie 78
Dan Nacionalnogo centra
za fotografiju 271
Dani jugoslovenske
fotografije 271
Découvertes 78
documenta 112
Dogadjaj godine u srpskoj
fotografiji 271
Encontros da Imagem 217
Encontros de
Fotografia 218
European Art Forum
Berlin 112
Festival de l'Image 78
FIAC 78
Fotobienal de Vigo 247
Fotobiënnale
Enschede 196
Fotofestival Naarden 196
Fotografie Biënnale
Rotterdam 196
Fotografiecircuit -
Vlaanderen 25
Fotomässan 254
Fotonoviembre 247
Fotosavara 187
Funkeho Kolín 47
Herefordshire Photography
Festival 147
Image/Imatge 78
Images 264
Images et Pages 78
InterFoto 227
Interkamera 47
Internationaal Fotofestival
Knokke-Heist 25
Internationaal Fotofestival
Turnhout 25
International Meetings of
Photography 33
International Photo Salon
"Art – Document –
Photo" 33
International Photogra-
phers Ex-Tempore
Idrija 239
International Photographic
Competition 174
International Photomeeting
della Repubblica di San
Marino 174
Internationale
Fototage 112
Internationale Fototage
Herten 112
Journées de l'Image
Professionnelle 79
Journées Photographiques
à Grignan 79
K.O'C. Ltd. 147
Konfrontacje Fotograficzne
Gorzów 210
Konkurs Polskiej Fotografii
Prasowej, Warszawa 210
KunstRAI 196
La Biennale di
Venezia 175
Laboratorium 25
Le Printemps de la
Photo 79
L'Été Photographique de
Lectoure 79
Mai Photographies 79
Mesiac fotografie
Bratislava 234
Miedzynarodowe
Spotkania Fotograficzne
"Profile" Skoki 210
Mlada Svetovna
Fotografija 239
Modena per la
fotografia 175
Mois de la Photo à
Paris 79
Mois de la
Photographie 79
Month of Photography in
Athens 158
Montpellier
Photovisions 79
Noorderlicht
Photofestival 196
Normandie-Rencontres
Photographiques 79
Odense Foto Triennale 54
Osenny Maraphon 227
Österreichische Triennale
zur Fotografie 11

Photo España 247
Photo Show 175
Photobiennale – Month of Photography in Moscow 227
Photofestivals Narvas Spring & Narvas Automn 58
Photography – a Phenomenon of Visual Culture 187
Photography Festival of Skopelos 158
photokina 112
PhotoParade 187
Photosynkyria 158
Photovacation festival 34
Pohjoinen Valokuva 62
Primavera Fotogràfica 247
Rencontres Internationales de la Photographie 79
Rencontres Photogràphiques 79
Rencontres Photographiques en Bretagne 79
Rossiysky festival reklamy 227
Seneffe Arts & Culture 25
Septembre de la Photo 79
Spilimbergo Fotografia 175
Théâtre de la Photographie et de l'Image 79
Toscana Fotofestival 175
Valokuvataide-Arkitaide 62
Venezia Immagine 175
View-finder asbl 25
Visa pour l'Image 79
Xposeptember 254
Zomer van de Fotografie 25

Magazines

29 228
90 – Tal 254
Advanced – Foto Video 47
Agenda de la Imatge 247
Aktuell Fotografi & Foto 254
AN Magazine 147
Arbeiterfotografie 114
Archivos de la Fotografia 247
Art 114
Art Magazine On Line 271
Art Press 79
Art-Gallery 269
Arte 175
Arte Fotográfico 247
Artelier 220
Artist 114
Arts Review 147
Ateliér 47
Audio Visual 147
Balkon 162, 220
Beaux-Arts 79
Belser Kunst Quartal 114
Beorama 271
British Journal of Photography 148
Bulletin Moravské galerie v Brne 47
Café-Crème Art Magazine 191
Camera Austria 12
Circa 165
Classic Camera 175
Colóquio/Artes 218
Color Foto 114
Colors 79
Connaissance des arts 80
Contretype 25
Creative Review 148
Dagerotyp 210
Dansk Fotografisk Tidsskrift 54
D'Ars 175
Dart 234
Das Kunst-Bulletin 264
Der Photograph 12
Design Report 114
Diorama 247
Dpict 148
Du 264
Eikon 12
Emzin/Art Magazine 240
Eos Magazine 148
Estonian Art 58
Études photographiques 80
European Photography 114
Exit 210
F & D Foto e dintorni 175
Flash Art International 175
Form Function Finland 62
Format 211
Forum International 25
Foto 196, 211
Foto – Sibirsky Uspekh 227
Foto & Video 227
Foto magazin 227
Fotó Piac 162
Foto-Kurier 211
Foto-Novosti 269
Foto-Zeszyty 211
FotoComputer 175
Fotogeschichte 12
Fotografare 175
Fotografi 254
Fotografia 158, 211
Fotografie Magazín 48
Fotografija 240
Fotografisk Tidskrift 254
Fotografiska Föreningen i Malmö 254
Fotographia 175
Fotologia 175
FotoMagazin 114
Fotómüvészet 162
Fotooko 34
Fotopratica Immagini 176
Fotóriporter 162
Fotostorica 176
Fototapeta 211
Fototip 234
FotoVideo 162
Frame 12
Frieze 148
FV/Foto-Video Actualidad 247
Galeries Magazine 80
Gazeta Malarzy i Poetow 211
Gente di Fotografia 176
Geographic Camera 48
Grafika un Poligrafija 187
Hasselblad Forum 256
History of Photography 148
Hollands Licht 196
Il Giornale dell'Arte 176
Imago 235
Immagine Cultura 176
Journal des Arts 80
Juliet 176
Jump 176
Kameralehti 62
Katalog 54

Khudozhestvenny
  zhurnal 227
Konteksty 211
Kultur-Chronik 114
Kunst.ee. 58
Kunstforum Interna-
  tional 114
Kunsttermine.de 114
Kunstzeitung 114
Kvadart 271
La Fotografía 247
Labyrint 48
Lápiz 247
Le Journal 80
Le Photographe 80
Leica Fotografie
  International 116
Leica World 116
Lietuvos fotografija vakar
  ir siandien 189
Likovni ivot 271
L'Oeil 80
Listy o fotografii 48
Magazyn Sztuki 211
Maksla plus 187
M'ARS 240
Mastatstva 18
Material 256
Mediamatic 198
Metropolis M 198
Monolog 18
Musta Taide 62
Na Nevskom.
  Petersburg 227
"Nemunas" 189
NFI news 198
Nieuwsbrief Nederlands
  Fotogenootschap 198
Norsk Fotografisk
  Tidsskrift 204
NU 256
Obscuur 25
Øjeblikket 54
P/F 198
Paletten 256
Papel Alpha 247
Parkett Editionen und
  Verlag 264
Passagen/Passages 264
Phot'Argus 80
Photo 80, 176
Photo Life 48
Photo Technik
  International 116
Photo work 80

Photo-Presse 116
Photo-Video-Expert 264
PhotographerRu 228
Photographie 116
Photographie Ouverte 25
Photographos
  Magazine 158
Photography Now 116
Photonews 116
Photoscoop 25
PhotoVision 247
Plages 80
Portfolio Magazine 148
Pozytyw 211
Private 176
Profession
  Photographe 80
Professional
  Photographer 148
ProfiFoto 116
Progresso Fotografico 176
Prospettive d'Arte 176
Ptyuch 228
Reflex Fotografia 176
Retikulatsia 228
Revista Foto 247
Revolver Revue & Kritická
  príloha 48
Revue Noire 80
Revue vizuálnej
  komunikácie 235
Rigas Laiks 187
Risk Arte Oggi 176
Rundbrief Fotografie 116
Schwarzweiss 116
Source 148
Springerin 12
Stare 148
Studija 187
Szellemkép 162
Taide 62
Teater-Muusika-Kino 58
Tema Celeste 176
Terra incognita 269
Texte zur Kunst 116
The Art Newspaper 149
The Art World
  Directory 149
The Photographic
  Journal 149
Tutti Fotografi 176
Umelec 48
Valokuva 62
Vikerkaar 58
Visual 264

Visuell International 117
Výtvarnické noviny 235
Wiadomosci
  Fotograficzne 211
Zoo 149
Zoom 176

Book Publishers

A. H. Jolly (Editorial)
  Ltd. 149
A. van Ginneken 81
Actar 248
Actes Sud 81
Agra Publications 158
Alfabeta Bokförlag 256
AN Publications 149
Anatolia 81
Ariadne Verlag 12
ARP Editions 26
Art Data 149
ARTbibliographies 149
Arteleku 248
ARTEXPO
  Foundation 220
Arts Council of Great
  Britain 149
Assírio & Alvim 218
Aurora Borealis 198
Avots 187
Balassi Kiadó 162
Baldini e Castoldi 177
Baltos lankos 190
Belarus 18
Benedikt Taschen
  Verlag 117
Benteli Verlags AG 264
Bildibok 256
BIS Publishers 198
Bloomsbury Publishing
  Ltd. 149
Booking International 81
Borgens Forlag 54
Boringhieri Bollati 177
Bruno Mondadori 177
Butterworth Heinemann
  Ltd. 149
Calmann and King
  Ltd. 149
Casa Editrice Roberto
  Napoleone 177
Charta 177
Christian Brandstätter 12

Coen Sligting
   Bookimport   198
Contrastodue   177
Cornerhouse
   Publications   149
Créaphis   81
David & Charles   149
De Verbeelding   198
Dewi Lewis
   Publishing   150
Die Gestalten Verlag
   GmbH   117
Diopter   264
DuMont Buchverlag   117
Duo Duo   198
Ebury Press   150
Ediciones El Viso   248
Ediçoes 70 Lda.   218
Ediçoes
   Afrontamento   218
Ediçoes ASA   218
Edition Braus im Wachter
   Verlag GmbH   117
Edition Camera
   Austria   12
Edition Eriksson   256
Edition Raetia   177
Edition Stemmle AG   265
Éditions Alain Sebe
   Images   81
Éditions Assouline   81
Éditions de la
   Martiniere   81
Éditions Denoël   81
Éditions du
   Collectionneur   81
Éditions du Regard   81
Éditions du Seuil   81
Éditions Hazan   81
Editions Ides et
   Calendes   265
Editions Images en
   Manœuvres   81
Editions Moressopoulos/
   Fotografia   158
Éditions Nathan   81
Éditions Pierre Belfond   81
Éditions V. M.   81
Editorial Caminho   218
Editorial Gustavo Gili   248
Editoriale Jaca Book   177
Edizioni Bolis   177
Edizioni Futuro s.r.l.   177
Edizioni Gruppo
   Abele   177

Elefanten Press   117
Enzo Sellerio Editore   177
European
   Photography   117
Ex posé Verlag   118
Fanlac   81
Federico Motta
   Editore s.p.a.   177
Festina   211
Filigranes   81
Focal Ediciones   248
Focal Press   150
Focus Publishing BV   198
Forlaget Politisk Revy   54
Foto Mida   48
FOTOFO   235
FotoFolio   81
Fotografisk Center   54
Fotogram   271
Fotohof Edition   12
Fotokunst-Verlag
   Groh   118
Fountain Press   150
Franco Sciardelli   177
Fratelli Alinari   177
Gabriele Mazzotta
   Editore   177
Galart   228
Gina Kehayoff Verlag   118
Giulio Einaudi   177
Gnosis Publishers   158
Grada Publishing   48
Grafis Edizioni   177
Graphis Press Corp.   265
Gremese Editore s.r.l.   177
Gyldendal   54
H. B. Wilson DMK CO
   sro   118
Harper Collins   150
Hatje Cantz Verlag   118
I. B. Tauris   150
IMA-Press   228
Imprensa Nacional Casa da
   Moeda E. P.   218
IMS/Studio 6   265
Intera Könyvkiadó   162
Internos Books   150
IPC Magazines – Book
   Division   150
Iskusstvo   228
Izdatel'stvo
   Vinograd   18
Izobrazitelnoe
   iskusstvo   228
Jana Seta   187

Jonas Verlag für Kunst und
   Literatur GmbH   118
Journal   256
Jumava   187
Kaleidoscope   256
Kant   48
Kastaniotis   158
Kruse Verlag GmbH   118
Kuklik   48
La Fabrica   248
Laterza   177
Leonardo Arte   177
Librairie Artheme
   Fayard   81
Lindinger + Schmid
   GbR   118
Lionel Hoebeke   81
Löcker Verlag   12
Lunwerg Editores,
   S. A.   248
Maeght   81
Magnus Edizioni
   s.p.a.   177
Magyar Fotográfiai
   Múzeum   162
Mainstream
   Publishing   150
Martin Secker &
   Warburg   150
Marval   81
Memory/Cage
   Editions   265
Mestizo   248
Meulenhoff
   International   198
Mitchell Beazley   150
Multic O. W.   211
Museum of London
   Publishing   143
Musta Taide   62
Müszaki Könyvkiadó   162
Muza S. A.   211
Nacionalni centar za
   fotografiju NCF   271
Nazraeli Press   118
Nicholas Enterprises
   Limited   150
Nicolaische
   Verlagsbuchhandlung   118
Nieswand-Verlag   118
Nordik   187
Novecento Editrice   178
Nuova Arnica
   Editrice   178
Octopus   150

Omega/Medici/
  Iberia 248
Ossolineum 211
Osveta 235
Otto Müller Verlag 12
Panstwowy Instytut
  Wydawniczy 212
Paradox 198
Park Kiadó 162
Peliti Associati 178
Phaidon Press Ltd. 150
Philippe Sers 81
Photo-Historical
  Publications 150
Photology 178
Plexus Publishing 150
Plume 81
Press Photo
  Publications 158
Prestel Verlag 118
Priuli & Verlucca 178
Proszynski i S-ka S. A. 212
Publicaçoes Don Quixote
  Lda. 218
Punktum AG 265
Quartet Books Ltd. 150
Quarto Publishing plc 150
R. Paknio leidykla 190
Raster Förlag AB 256
Raum F 265
Reich-Verlag 265
Residenz Verlag
  GmbH 12
Rhodos Internationalt
  Forlag 54
Richter Verlag 118
Rivers Orum Press 151
Robert Harding Picture
  Library 151
Rossella Bigi Editore 178
Samenwerkende
  Uitgeverijen Prometheus
  en Bert Bakker 198
Scala Istituto
  Fotografico 178
Scalo Verlag AG 265
Schaden Verlag 118
Schirmer/Mosel
  Verlag 118
Schroll-Verlag 14
Scottish Publishers
  Association 151
SDU 198
Silvana Editoriale
  d'Arte 178

Simonett Projects 265
Skira 178
Slovart 235
Split Trading 212
Steidl Verlag 118
Studio JB 48
Swan Hill Press 151
Tau Visual 178
Thames & Hudson 151
The British Council 151
Torst 48
Triton Verlag 14
U. Bär Verlag 265
Uitgeverij 010
  Publishers 198
Uitgeverij Ludion 26
Uitgeverij Voetnoot 199
Umberto Allemandi
  & C. s.r.l. 178
Umschau Buchverlag 118
University Studio
  Press 159
Vaga 190
Vega 218
Verlag der Buchhandlung
  Walther König 118
Verlag der Kunst 118
Verlag Lars Müller 265
Verlag Niederösterrei-
  chisches Pressehaus 14
Verlag Turia & Kant 14
Victoria and Albert Muse-
  um Publications 151
Videograf II 212
White Fotolibri 178
Wydawnictwo Adam
  Marszalek 212
Wydawnictwo
  Arkady 212
Wydawnictwo Artystyczne
  i Filmowe 212
Wydawnictwo Baturo 212
Wydawnictwo Buffi 212
Wydawnictwo
  Kropka 212
Wydawnictwo
  Literackie 212
Wydawnictwo
  Lukrum 212
Wydawnictwo
  Podsiedlik 212
Wydawnictwo UMCS 212
Wydawnictwo Znak 212
Zanichelli Editore
  s.p.a. 178

Bookshops

A l'Enseigne des
  Oudin 83
A & M Bookstore 178
Akademibokhandeln 256
Al Ferro di Cavallo
  Librogalleria 178
Antiquariat L. van
  Paddenburgh 199
Arbetets Museum 256
Artificium 118
Atheneum Boekhandel
  B. V. 199
Blow Up Photography
  Bookshop 26
Bourlot 178
Bücherbogen am
  Savignyplatz 121
Buchhandlung L.
  Werner 118
Buchhandlung Lia
  Wolf 14
Buchhandlung Walther
  König 121
Buchhandlung Walther
  König im Martin-
  Gropius-Bau 121
Ceské centrum
  fotografie 48
Comptoir de l'Image 83
Copyright Art & Architec-
  ture Bookshop 26
Daniella Dangoor 151
Dillons Art Bookstore 151
Dom fotografie 236
Dom knigi 228
Dum knihy – Jan
  Kanzelsberger 48
Fnac Etoile 83
Fnac Montparnasse 83
Foto Art 26
Fotografisk Center 56
Galéria fotografie
  Profil 236
Galerie 2000 121
Gibert Joseph 83
Goltz 121
HF Distribuzione 178
Ian Shipley Books 151
IF Libri 178
Konst-IG 256
Kunst-Buch 121
La Chambre Claire 83
La Hune 83

Laterna Magica 62
Librairie Contacts 83
Librairie de la Maison
  Européenne de la
  Photographie 83
Librairie du Centre Georges
  Pompidou 83
Librairie du Musée de
  l'Elysée 265
Librairie Maupetit 83
Librairie Mollat 83
Librairie Objectifs 26
Libreria 248
Libreria di Brera 178
Libreria Internazionale
  Ulrico Hoepli 178
Libreria Kowasa 248
Lindemanns 121
Louisiana Museum of
  Modern Art 56
Milano Libri 178
Moskovsky Dom
  knigi 228
Nijhof and Lee 199
Papasotiriou
  Bookstores 159
Pep + No Name 265
Photo Librairie 83
Photographers' Gallery
  Bookshop 151
Posada Art Books 26
PPS-Fachbuchhandlung für
  Photographie 121
Prazský dum fotografie 48
Scalo Books & Looks 265
Schaden.com 121
Serge Plantureux – Livres
  anciens 83
Temps de Pose 83
Zwemmer Ltd. 151

Auctions

Associazione Pavia
  Fotografia 178
Aukcní agentura a
  Antikvariát Prošek 49
Ceské centrum
  fotografie 49
Christie's 178
Christie's South
  Kensington 151
Dorotheum 14
Dorotheum Praha 49
Etude Binoche 83
Etude Pescheteau-Badin,
  Godeau, Leroy 83
Etude Tajan 83
Galerie de Chartres 83
Göteborgs Auktionsverk
  AB 256
Lempertz 121
Michel Grommen 26
Millon et Associe's 83
Olivier Coutau-Bégarie 83
Schneider-Henn 121
Sotheby's 151
Stara Galeria ZPAF 212
Villa Grisebach 121
Viviane Esders/Esders
  Concept 83

Critics & Journalists

Aasbø, Kristin 204
Abad, José 248
Aigner, Carl 14
Albertini, Dr. Béla 162
Aleksic, Milan 271
Alenius, Hans 256
Alton, Peder 257
Amelunxen, Prof. Dr.
  Hubertus von 121
Andén-Papadopoulos,
  Kari 257
Andersson, Cecilia 248
Andreeva, Ekaterina 228
Andriuskevicius,
  Alfonsas 190
Antoniadis, Kostis 159
Armistead, Claire 151
Arrhenius, Sara 257
Arrouye, Jean 83
Auer, Anna 14
Auzinš, Vilnis 188
Badescu, Emanuel 220
Badge, Peter 121
Baetens, Pascal 26
Bakáts, Tibor 162
Bakaya, Mo 151
Bakshtein, Josef 228
Balaci, Ruxandra 220
Balakhovskaya, Faina 228
Bán, András 162
Bancheva, Adriana 34
Baracchini Caputi,
  Augusto 179
Baran, Prof. Dr. Ludvík 49
Barazna, Mikhail 18
Barhkatova, Dr. Elena 228
Baskakov, Andrey 228
Bassin, Aleksander 240
Bauret, Gabriel 83
Bazhanov, Leonid 228
Beck, Ingamaj 257
Beckmann, Dr.
  Angelika 121
Beke, Prof. Dr. László 162
Benická, Lucia 236
Benjamin, Marina 152
Bennekom, Dr. Josephine
  van 199
Berezner, Evgeny 228
Berggren, Irene 257
Bertelli, Carlo, 179
Bertelsen, Lars Kiel 56
Bezukladnikov,
  Andrey 229
Bigday, Irina 18
Billeter, Dr. Erika 265
Birgus, Prof. Dr.
  Vladimír 49
Bizljak, Rajko 240
Bode, Mikhail 229
Bodson, Jean-Marc 26
Boecker, Susanne 121
Bolognesi, Kitti 179
Bool, Flip 199
Bordini, Silvia 179
Borhan, Pierre 83
Borovsky, Dr.
  Aleksander 229
Boström, Prof. Jörg 121
Boubnova, Jara 34
Bouqueret, Christian 83
Brandt, Carsten 56
Braun, Reinhard 14
Breierová, Slávka 236
Brezovecki, Iva Bidjin 36
Britschgi, Markus 265
Brittain, David 152
Brudna, Denis 121
Butler, Susan 152
Calado, Jorge 218
Calvenzi, Giovanna 179
Cancer, José Ramón 248
Carioti, Giacomo 179
Casorati, Dr. Cecilia 179
Castagnola, Gualtiero 179
Castant, Alexandre 84

Castellote, Alejandro 248
Caujolle, Christian 84
Cavanna, Pierangelo 179
Cerveira Pinto,
  António 218
Chevrier, Jean-François 84
Chezhin, Andrey 229
Chiti, Giovanna 179
Chocholová, Blanka 49
Chuchma, Josef 49
Chudakov, Grigory 229
Clarke, Dr. Frederick 179
Clot, Manel 248
Colombo, Attilio 179
Colombo, Cesare 179
Cooper, Emmanuel 152
Cooper, Thomas
  Joshua 152
Coppens, Jan 199
Corradini, Mauro 179
Coward-Williams,
  Garry 152
Craddock, Sascha 152
Csorba, E. Csilla 163
Curti, Dennis 179
Damgaard, Mogens 56
Damy, Prof. Ken 179
Daugovišs, Sergejs 188
Davies, Sue 152
Davydchik, Alexander 18
De Pellegrin, Fulvio 179
De Vos, Johan 26
Dean, Philip 62
D'Elia, Anna 179
Delic-Gozze, Vesna 36
Demakova, Helena 188
Demidenko, Julia 229
Demos, John 159
D'Hooghe, Alain 26
Diego, Estrella de 248
Dijck, Rianne van 199
Dister, Alain 84
Divendal, Leo 199
Dobrynkin, Andrey 229
Dubrovic, Ervin 36
Dufek, Dr. Antonín 49
Durand, Régis 84
Dvorák, Tomáš 49
Edling, Marta 257
Eelbode, Erik 26
Erba, Luigi 179
Eriksson, Lars O. 257
Erofeev, Dr. Andrey 229
Esders, Viviane 84
Esparza, Ramón 248

Faeta, Prof. Francesco 179
Fagone, Vittorio 179
Fahrenberg, W. P. 121
Fárová, Dr. Anna 49
Fassati, Tomáš 49
Felix, Dr. Zdenek 121
Fenz, Dr. Werner 14
Fernandes Jorge, Joao
  Miguel 218
Fernandez, Horacio 248
Filzmaier, Birgit 265
Fischer Jonge, Ingrid 56
Fleig, Alain 84
Flemming, Gösta 257
Flesch, Bálinth 163
Florkowski, Dr.
  Andrzej 212
Fontcuberta, Joan 248
Ford, Wayne 152
Foschi, Gigliola 179
Fox, Anna 152
Frey, Stefan 265
Friedmann, Richard 236
Frigerio, Luca 179
Frisinghelli, Christine 14
Frizot, Michel 84
Gade, Rune 56
Gaizutis, Algirdas 190
García, Manolo 249
Garrido, Lola 249
Gasparini, Laura 179
Gattinoni, Christian 84
Gautrand, Jean-Claude 84
Gelman, Marat 229
Georgieff, Anthony 56
Georgiev, Prof.
  Roumen 34
Georgiou, Aris 159
Gera, Mihály 163
Giannatasio, Sandra 180
Gibbs, Michael 199
Gierstberg, Dr. Frits 199
Gilardi, Ando 180
Gili, Marta 249
Gilsoul, Guy 26
Ginex, Giovanna 180
Giusa, Antonio 180
Glüher, Dr. Gerhard 121
Goffaux, Pascal 26
González, Ignacio 249
Goodrow, Gérard A. 122
Gott, Richard 152
Grauw, Jan Mattheus
  de 199
Gravano, Viviana 180

Gresty, Hilary 152
Gripp, Anna 122
Gruber, Prof. L. Fritz 122
Grygiel, Marek 212
Grzinic, Marina 240
Guadagnini, Walter 180
Gualdoni, Flaminio 180
Gudac, Vladimir 37
Guerrin, Michel 84
Gunnarsson, Sören 257
György, Péter 163
Györi, Lajos 163
Gysegem, Marc van 26
Hagman, Jacqueline 199
Hajdú, Éva 163
Hajdú, István 163
Hanáková, Petra 236
Härm, Anders 59
Hassner, Rune 257
Havelková, Jolana 49
Haveman, Dr.
  Mariëtte 199
Haworth-Booth, Mark 152
Hedberg, Hans 257
Herzogenrath, Dr.
  Wulf 122
Hess, Hans-Eberhard 122
Hlavác, Ludovít 236
Hlevnjak, Branka 37
Hodgson, Francis 152
Hoeneveld, Herman 199
Hofleitner, Johanna 14
Honnef, Prof. Klaus 122
Hopkinson, Amanda 152
Hornowska, Ewa 213
Hrabušický, Aurel 236
Imdahl, Georg 122
Ivan, Dina 37
Ivancevic, Dr. Radovan 37
Jäger, Prof. Gottfried 122
Jakimovich, Prof. Dr.
  Aleksander 229
Jalszovsky, Dr.
  Katalin 163
Janata, Michal 49
Järvinen, Jukka 62
Jashchenko, Lilya 229
Jeffrey, Ian 152
Jonsson, Rune 257
Jovanov, Jasna 271
Junevicius, Dainius 190
Juodakis, Virgilijus 190
Jurecki, Dr. Krzysztof 213
Jurenaite, Raminta 190
Kabanova, Olga 229

Kaindl, Dr. Kurt 14
Kalnina, Daiga 188
Kalnina, Ieva 188
Kalter, Marion 84
Kalve, Odrija 188
Kambic, Mirko 240
Katsaggelos, Yorgos 159
Kaufhold, Dr. Enno 122
Kemppainen, Kari 62
Kent, Sarah 152
Kepinska, Prof. Alicja 213
Kerbler, Stojan 240
Khlobystin, Andrey 229
Khoroshilov, Pavel 229
Killer, Peter 266
Kincses, Károly 163
Kirschner, Prof. Dr.
   Zdenek 49
Kiss-Kuntler, Árpád 163
Kleivan, Birna
   Marianne 56
Klerck Gange, Eva 204
Koenig, Dr. Thilo 180
Koetzle, Michael 122
Köhler, Michael 122
Korol, Dmitry 18
Korotkina, Nadezhda 18
Korsaks, Péteris 188
Košcevic, Dr. Zelimir 37
Kosinska-Filocha,
   Barbara 213
Kostic, Aleksandra 240
Kovic, Brane 240
Krabbe Meyer, Mette
   Kia 56
Krase, Dr. Andreas 122
Krauss, Dr. Dr.
   Rolf H. 122
Kroutvor, Dr. Josef 49
Kuneš, Aleš 49
Kurowicki, Jan 213
Kyian, Dmitry 229
Laanemets, Mari 59
Laguillo, Prof. Dr.
   Manolo 249
Lamarche-Vadel,
   Bernard 84
Lampic, Dr. Primoz 240
Langer, Freddy 122
Laoutliev, Nikolay 34
Larsen, Lotte Tauber 56
Lavrentyev, Prof. Dr.
   Aleksander 229
Le Goff, Hervé 84
Lechowicz, Lech 213

Ledo, Margarita 249
Lejasmeijere, Ieva 188
Lemagny, Jean-Claude 84
Lendelová, Lucia 236
Leonelli, Dr. Laura 180
Lesniakowska,
   Dr. Marta 213
Levashov, Vladimir 230
Lewczynski, Jerzy 213
Lind, Maria 257
Linkov, Krassimir 34
Linnap, Peeter 59
Lintonen, Kati 63
Lintunen, Martti 63
Lischka, Gerhard
   Johann 266
Liska, Dr. Pavel 49
Lobko, Valery 18
Lofaj, Dr. Ján 236
Lopes, Joao 218
López, Manuel 249
Lovric, Mirko 271
Lozanov, Georgi 34
Lubowicz, Elzbieta 213
Lugosi-Lugo, László 163
Lundström, Jan-Erik 257
Lyapin, Olexandr 269
Lyczywek, Krystyna 213
Macek, Prof. Dr.
   Václav 236
Madesani, Angela 180
Maggia, Filippo 180
Malic, Goran 272
Mandéry, Guy 84
Marcelis, Bernard 26
Markidou, Natassa 159
Marra, Prof. Claudio 180
Marsman, Eddie 199
Martynova, Nina 230
Mateju, Dr. Vera 50
Mauracher, Michael 14
Medeiros, Margarida 218
Medved, Andrej 240
Melikian, Arsen 18
Melo, Alexandre 218
Menclová, Dr. Juliana 236
Merlo, Lorenzo 180
Metken, Dr. Günter 84
Meyer, Claus
   Heinrich 122
Meyer, Prof. Robert 204
Michalowska,
   Marianna 213
Miletin, Milan 272
Miller, Chris 152

Millet, Bernard 84
Milo, Pim 199
Minervini, Enzo 180
Miraglia, Dr. Marina 180
Mirisola, Dr. Vincenzo 180
Mißelbeck, Dr.
   Reinhold 122
Missirkov, Boris 34
Miziano, Dr. Victor 230
Mlcoch, Jan 50
Molderings, Dr.
   Herbert 122
Molinero Cardenal,
   Antonio 249
Mollà, Angel 249
Monterosso, Jean-Luc 84
Mora, Gilles 84
Moreau, Patric 257
Moressopoulos,
   Stavros 159
Mormorio, Diego 180
Moroux, Philippe 200
Moschovi, Alexandra 159
Mossakowska, Dr.
   Wanda 213
Moucha, Josef 50
Mrázková, Daniela 50
Müller-Pohle,
   Andreas 122
Mullins, Charlotte 152
Mussini, Massimo 180
Mutti, Prof. Roberto 180
Naranjo, Joan 249
Narusyte, Agne 190
Niegelhell, Franz 14
Nikitin, Dr. Vladimir 230
Nilsson, John Peter 257
Nilsson, Stefan 257
Nordentoft, Astrid 249
Nori, Claude 84
Nowacki, Janusz 213
Nuridsany, Michel 84
Nykvist, Ralph 257
Obiols, Salvador 249
Olek, Jerzy 213
Olivares, Rosa 249
Ollier, Brigitte 84
Oroveanu, Mihail 221
Oujezdský, Karel 50
Pachmannová, Martina 50
Pagni, Luca 180
Palazzoli, Prof.
   Daniela 180
Panaiotopoulos,
   Nikos 159

Papakochev, Georgi 34
Parfianok, Uladzimir 18
Parslow, Prof. Jamie 204
Pastor, Enric Mira 249
Pastor, Suzanne 50
Patsyukov, Dr. Vitaly 230
Pauer, Dr. Marián 236
Pavlova, Tatiana 269
Peikova, Ralica 34
Pekari, Mikko 63
Peternák, Miklós 163
Philipp, Dr. Claudia
  Gabriele 124
Picazo, Gloria 249
Pilikin, Dmitry 230
Pinharanda, Joao 218
Pinsent, Richard 152
Pinto, Roberto 180
Podestát, Václav 50
Pohlmann, Dr. Ulrich 124
Pomar, Alexandre 218
Porter, Allan 266
Pospech, Tomáš 50
Poulsen, Tage 56
Prieto Villanueva, Jesús
  Angel 249
Prigodich, Nadiya 269
Primus, Dr. Zdenek 50
Prina, Valeria 181
Przybylski, Prof.
  Ryszard K. 213
Pujade, Robert 84
Quintavalle, Prof. Carlo
  Arturo 181
Räni, Piret 59
Rasovszky, Gheorghe 221
Remeš, Vladimír 50
Remy, Patrick 84
Reut, Inna 19
Ria, Dr. Antonio 181
Ribalta, Jorge 249
Ridilla, Jozef 236
Riego, Bernardo 249
Rigol, Josep 249
Rinehart, David
  Glenn 152
Ripatti, Mika 63
Roche, Denis 84
Rodes, Salvador 249
Roegiers, Patrick 85
Roisselle, Josiane 26
Romain, Prof. Dr.
  Lothar 124
Roncero, Rafael
  Doctor 249

Roodenburg, Dr.
  Linda 200
Rosengren, Annette 257
Rossi, Leena-Maija 63
Rötzer, Florian 124
Rouillé, André 85
Rousseva, Iglena 34
Rozenfelds, Gatis 188
Russell-Taylor, John 153
Russo, Antonella 181
Saburova, Tatiana 230
Sager, Dr. Peter 124
Saj, Dr. Jerzy 213
Salapura, Luka 272
Salo, Merja 63
Salzirn, Tatiana 230
Sandberg, Lotte 204
Sandbye, Mette 56
Santos, Manuel 249
Saraste, Leena 63
Savchenko, Igor 19
Savchuk, Prof. Dr. Ph.
  Valery 230
Sayag, Alain 85
Schaub, Dr. Martin 266
Scheufler, Pavel 50
Schmalriede, Prof.
  Manfred 124
Schmitz, Ulla 124
Schwander, Lars 56
Schwarz, Prof. Angelo 181
Scimé, Prof. Giuliana 181
Seelig, Thomas 124
Selina, Elena 230
Semakova, Irina 230
Sena, António 218
Sesic, Sarival 240
Settimelli, Wladimiro 181
Shishkin, Oleg 230
Sidlin, Mikhail 230
Sikora, Slawomir 213
Silverio, Robert 50
Siza, Teresa 219
Skasa-Weiss,
  Ruprecht 124
Skeiviene, Laima 190
Slijepcevic, Branka 37
Sne, Martin 56
Sobota, Adam 213
Soffientini, Valerio 181
Soloviev, Olexandr 269
Sougez, Marie-Loup 249
Srp, Dr. Karel 50
Stacho, Lubo 236
Stahel, Urs 266

Stals, Jose Lebrero 249
Starl, Timm 14
Stathatos, John 153
Steffensen, Erik 56
Steiner, Barbara 14
Stemlerné Balog,
  Ilona 163
Steward, Sue 153
Stigneev, Dr. Valery 230
Strigalev, Dr. Anatoly 230
Stukalova, Kateryna 269
Suermondt, Dr. Rik 200
Sunila, Sakari 63
Sutej-Adamic, Jelka 240
Sviblova, Olga 230
Swinnen, Dr. Johan 26
Szakács, Dr. Margit 163
Szarka, Klára 163
Szilágyi, Gábor 163
Tannert, Christoph 124
Taramelli, Ennery 181
Tchmyreva, Irina (Rena
  Gvozdeva) 230
Thage, Tove 56
Thijsen, Dr. M. G. 200
Thrane, Finn 56
Tisma, Andrej 272
Todic, Milanka 272
Tomasczuk, Zbigniew 213
Tomík, Fero 236
Tonkovic, Marija 37
Török, András 163
Töry, Klára 163
Travirka, Antun 37
Treier, Heie 59
Turzio, Silvana 181
Tzimas, Dimitris 159
Uimonen, Anu 63
Ulmer, Birgit 266
Valiulis, Skirmantas 190
Valjakka, Timo 63
Valtorta, Prof. Roberta 181
Van Deuren, Karel
  R. L. 28
Van Tieghem, Jean-
  Pierre 28
Vanhanen, Hannu 63
Varblane, Reet 59
Vartanov, Dr. Anri 231
Vassileva, Maria 34
Vega, Dr. Carmelo 249
Végvári, Prof. Dr.
  Lajos 163
Vidal, Carlos 219
Visser, Dr. Hripsimé 200

Vitvar, Jan H.   50
Vojtechovský, Prof.
   Miroslav   50
Volran, Valery   231
Vorobjov, Vladimír   236
Vossi, Leo   63
Vránová, Dr. Jana   50
Ward, Sue   153
Weaver, Dr. Mike   153
Webb, John S.   257
Weiermair, Prof. Peter   14
Wells, Liz   153
Wettendorff,
   Henning S.   56
Wiklund, Peter   257
Williams, Val   258
Wilson, Rhonda   153
Wisniewski, Jana   15
Wojnecki, Prof. Stefan   214
Wolf, Prof. Dr. Herta   124
Wolynski, Dr. Piotr   214
Wombell, Paul   153
Wynants, Jean-Marie   28
Xanthakis, Alkis   159
Yordanov, Boyko   34
Zabalbeascoa, Anatxu   249
Zanazzo, Alessandro   181
Zegan, Dr.
   Zbigniew E.   214
Zelich, Cristina   249
Zoetendaal,
   Willem van   200
Zollner, Manfred   124
Zonnevijlle, Hans   200
Zuckriegl, Dr. Margit   15
Zunzunegui, Santos   250

Schools & Workshops

27. sz. Ipari Szakmunkás-
   képzö Intézet   163
A.K.I.   200
A.K.T.O.   159
Académie des Beaux-Arts
   Alphonse Darville   28
Academie Minerva   200
Académie Royale des
   Beaux-Arts de
   Bruxelles   28
Academie St. Joost   200
Academie voor
   Fotografie   200

Accademia di Belle
   Arti   181
Accademia di Fotografia
   del Museo Ken
   Damy   181
Accademia di Moda e Arte
   "Altieri"   181
Akademia Sztuk Pieknych,
   Gdansk   214
Akademia Sztuk Pieknych,
   Krakow   214
Akademia Sztuk Pieknych,
   Lodz   214
Akademia Sztuk Pieknych,
   Poznan   215
Akademia Sztuk Pieknych,
   Warszawa   215
Akademie der Bildenden
   Künste   15
Akademie der Bildenden
   Künste München   124
Akademie der Bildenden
   Künste Nürnberg   124
Akademie für Photogra-
   phie Hamburg e. V.   124
Akademija dramske
   umjetnosti   37
Akademija lepih umetnosti
   u Novom Sadu   272
Akademija umetnosti
   Univerziteta Braca
   Karic   272
AR.CO Centro de Arte e
   Comunicaçao Visual   219
Arrêt sur l'Image   28
Art & Rat   124
Art E – Scuola Internazio-
   nale di Design & Foto-
   grafia   182
Arteleku   250
Arvore – Cooperativa de
   Actividades Artísticas
   (CRL)   219
Associazione Imago   182
Atelier de
   Photographie   85
Aula de Fotografía
   UFCA   250
Aula do Risco   219
Bálint György Újságíró
   Iskola   163
Barcelona Centro de
   Imagen   250
Belarusskaya akademiya
   iskusstv   19

Belorussky gosudarstvenny
   universitet – fakul'tet
   zhurnalistiki   19
Bergische Universität
   Gesamthochschule
   Wuppertal   124
Bergnässkolan   258
Burg Giebichenstein   124
C.R.A.F.   182
Cámara oscura   250
Casalgrande
   Fotografia   182
Centre de Formation des
   Techniques de Communi-
   cations Visuelles   85
Centre de Formation
   Technologique de la
   Chambre de Commerce et
   d'Industrie de Paris "Les
   Gobelins"   85
Centre d'Estudis d'Art
   Contemporani – Fundació
   Joan Miró   250
Centre d'étude et de
   Recherche de l'Image et
   du Son   85
Centro de la Imagen   250
Centro di Formazione
   Professionale   182
Centro di Formazione
   Professionale Don
   Orione   182
Centro di Formazione
   Professionale Riccardo
   Bauer   182
Centro per il restauro e la
   conservazione della
   fotografia Berselli   182
Centrum voor Volwasse-
   nenonderwij Technicum
   Noord-Antwerpen   28
CEV   250
Coloma Instituut   28
Cours Professionels
   de la Chambre des
   Métiers   85
CVO Elishout avond-
   school COOVI   28
D.A.M.S.   182
Danmarks Designskole   57
Dryphoto   182
École de Photographie de
   la Ville de Bruxelles   28
École de Photographie de
   Paris   85

École des Arts de
Valenciennes 85
École Française d'Enseigne-
ment Technique 85
École Louis Lumière 85
École Municipale des
Beaux-Arts 85
École Municipale des
Beaux-Arts de Metz 85
École Municipale des
Beaux-Arts d'Orléans 85
École Nationale de la
Photographie 85
École Nationale des Arts
Décoratifs de Nice 85
École Nationale Supérieure
des Arts Décoratifs 85
École Nationale Supérieure
Estienne 85
École Nationale Supérieure
Louis Lumière 85
École Supérieure d'Arts
Graphiques 85
École Technique Privée de
la Photographie et de
l'Audiovisuel 85
Edinburgh College of
Art 153
EMEF 159
Escola Municipal de Belles
Arts 250
Escola Universitaria
d'Optica de Terrassa,
Universitat Politècnica
de Barcelona 250
Escuela de Artes y
Oficios 250
Escuela de Fotografia 250
Escuela de Fotografia Cen-
tro de Imagen EFTI 250
Escuela Superior de Foto-
grafía e Imagen, C.E.U.
"San Pablo" 250
Escuela Superior de
Fotografia Flash 250
E.S.P. Artikon 159
ETIC – Escola Técnica de
Imagem e Communi-
caçao 219
Europäische Akademie für
Bildende Kunst Trier 124
European School of
Photography 159
Exeter College of Art and
Design 153

Fabrica 182
Fac. Bellas Artes 250
Fac. Bellas Artes de
Cuenca 250
Fac. Bellas Artes
Euzkadi 250
Fac. Bellas Artes
Madrid 250
Fachhochschule
Aachen 124
Fachhochschule
Anhalt 125
Fachhochschule
Augsburg 125
Fachhochschule
Bielefeld 125
Fachhochschule
Darmstadt 125
Fachhochschule des
Saarlandes 125
Fachhochschule Dort-
mund 125
Fachhochschule
Düsseldorf 125
Fachhochschule für Gestal-
tung Pforzheim 125
Fachhochschule für
Gestaltung Schwäbisch
Gmünd 125
Fachhochschule Ham-
burg 125
Fachhochschule
Hannover 125
Fachhochschule Hildes-
heim/Holzminden 125
Fachhochschule Kiel 125
Fachhochschule Köln 125
Fachhochschule
München 125
Fachhochschule
Münster 125
Fachhochschule
Niederrhein 125
Fachhochschule
Potsdam 125
Fachhochschule Rheinland-
Pfalz 125
Fachhochschule
Wiesbaden 126
Fachhochschule Würz-
burg/Schweinfurt 126
Fakulta sociálních ved
Karlovy univerzity 50
Fakultet dramskih
umetnosti 272

Fakultet primenjenih
umetnosti i dizajna 272
FAMU – Filmová a tele-
vizní fakulta Akademie
múzick 51
Fatamorgana 57
FLUSS – Niederösterrei-
chische Fotoinitiative 15
Focus 159
Fotografie Forum
International 126
Fotovakschool 200
Fotowerk 126
Fredrikstad Videregående
Skole 204
Freie Akademie der Künste
zu Leipzig 126
Gemeentelijke Academie
voor Beeldende
Kunsten 28
Gemeentelijke
Tekenacademie 28
Georg-Simon-Ohm-
Fachhochschule
Nürnberg 126
Gerrit Rietveld
Academie 200
Gesamthochschule Kassel,
Universität 126
GFU, Folkuniver-
sitetet 258
Glasgow School of Art 153
Göteborgs Universitet 258
Graficka škola 272
GrisArt 250
Hochschule der Bildenden
Künste Saar 126
Hochschule der Künste
Berlin 126
Hochschule für
Angewandte Kunst 15
Hochschule für Architektur
und Bauwesen
Weimar 126
Hochschule für Bildende
Künste Braun-
schweig 126
Hochschule für Bildende
Künste Hamburg 126
Hochschule für Gestaltung
Offenbach 126
Hochschule für Gestaltung
und Kunst Zürich 266
Hochschule für Grafik und
Buchkunst 126

Hochschule für Künste
  Bremen 126
Hochschule Wismar 126
Hoger Instituut voor
  Schone Kunsten 28
Hoger Onderwijs Imelda
  Instituut 28
Hoger Onderwijs Imelda
  Instituut HONIM 28
Hogeschool Sint-Lucas
  Brussel 28
Hogeschool voor de
  Kunsten 200
Höhere Bundeslehr-
  anstalt für Kunst und
  Design 15
Höhere Graphische Bun-
  deslehr- und Versuchs-
  anstalt 15
Hradecká fotografická
  konzervator 51
IF 182
Image Ouverte 86
Incontri di Fotografia e
  Critica 182
Inraci 28
Institut d'Estudis
  Fotogràfics 250
Institut d'Estudis
  Politècnics 250
Institut für Kommunika-
  tions-Design an der FH
  Konstanz 126
Institut marketing a
  reklamní tvorby 51
Institut tvurcí fotografie
  Slezské univerzity 51
Institute of
  Photography 204
Institutul de Arta Ion
  Andreescu 221
Instituut Saint-Luc 28
Internationale Sommer-
  akademie für Bildende
  Kunst 15
Istituto Europeo di
  Design 182
Istituto Italiano di
  Fotografia 182
Istituto Professionale
  di Stato Caterina da
  Siena 182
Istituto Professionale
  Statale Cesare
  Correnti 182

Istituto Professionale
  Statale per la fotografia
  Paravia 182
Istituto Statale d'Arte 182
Istituto Statale d'Arte
  Adolfo Venturi 182
Istituto Superiore di
  Fotografia & Arti
  Visive 182
Jana Rozentala Rigas
  makslas koledza 188
Johannes Gutenberg-
  Universität Mainz 126
Katholieke Hogeschool
  Limburg 28
Kent Institute of Art &
  Design 153
Képzö és Iparmüvészeti
  Szakközép-iskola 163
Keski-Suomen käsi- ja
  taideteollisuusoppi-
  laitos 63
Kharkovsky Khodozhest-
  venno-promyshlenny
  Institut 269
Kon. Academie van
  B. K. 200
Kon. Academie voor Kunst
  en Vormgeving 200
Koninklijk Technisch
  Atheneum 2 31
Koninklijke Academie voor
  Audiovisuele en
  Beeldende Kunst 31
Konstfack 258
K.U.B.A. 57
Kulturama 258
Kunstakademie
  Düsseldorf 126
Kunstakademie
  Münster 126
Kunstakademiets
  Konservatorskole 57
Kunsthochschule Berlin-
  Weißensee 127
Kunsthochschule für
  Medien Köln 127
Kunsthøgskolen
  i Bergen 204
La Cambre Ensav 31
Lahden taide- ja
  käsiteollisuusoppi-
  laitos 63
Latvijas Kulturas
  Akademija 188

Latvijas Maksklas
  Akademija 188
Le "75" 31
Lehrinstitut für
  Design 127
Leica Academy 159
Letná fotoškola Domu
  fotografie 236
Lette-Verein 127
Lidová konzervator
  Ostrava 51
Linea di Confine per la
  Fotografia Contem-
  poranea 182
London School of
  Photojournalism 153
Magyar Iparmüvészeti
  Föiskola 163
Magyar Müvelödési
  Intézet Kortárs
  Müvészetek
  Osztálya 164
Manchester
  University 153
Masia Can Serrat 250
MAUMAUS – Escola de
  Fotografia e Artes
  Visuais 219
Mecad Media Centre
  d'Art i Disseny 250
Merz Akademie 127
Mifav, Università di Roma
  Tor Vergata 183
Moskovsky gosudarst-
  venny universitet 231
Moskovsky gosudarst-
  venny universitet
  kultury 231
MTS voor Fotografie en
  Fotonica 200
Muthesius
  Hochschule 127
Napier University 153
Národné osvetové
  centrum 237
National Academy of
  Theatre and Cinema
  Kr. Sarafov 34
New Bulgarian
  University 34
Nordens Fotoskola 258
Nuova Accademia
  di Belle Arti 183
Opleiding
  Restauratoren 200

Panstwowa Wyzsza Szkola Filmowa, Telewizyjna i Teatraina, Lodz 215
Périscope 31
Photography at the Metropole 153
Picture House Centre for Photography Ltd. 154
Prager Fotoschule 15
Prazská fotografická škola 51
Privatschule für Foto-Design 127
Regionalne Centrum Kultury, Jelenia Gora 215
Rijkscentrum Hoger Kunstonderwijs 31
Rijksuniversiteit Leiden 200
Roskilde University 57
Royal Academy of Fine Arts 57
Royal College of Art 154
Ruhr-Universität Bochum, Musisches Zentrum 127
Salzburg College 15
Samsø Folkehøjskole 57
Sankt Peterburgsky gosudarstvenny universitet 231
School of Art 154
School of Fine & Applied Arts 159
School of Graphic and Fine Arts 160
School of Polygraphy and Photography 34
Schule für Künstlerische Photographie 15
Scuola di Fotografia di Firenze 183
Scuola di Fotografia Istituto Superiore 183
Scuola di Fotografia nella Natura di Roberto Salbitani 183
Scuola Permanente di Fotografia "Graffiti" 183
Scuola Professionale di Fotografia Click Up 183
Sebesvíz Nemzetközi Fotómüvészeti Alkotótábor 164

Sheffield Hallam University 154
Škola primijenjenih umjetnosti i dizajna 37
Škola uzitkového výtvarníctva 237
Škola uzitkového výtvarníctva Josefa Vydru 237
Škola za dizajn 272
SKVR Foto- en Videoschool 201
Sofia University 34
Sogn Videregående Skole 204
Soukromá škola uzitého umení a podnikání 51
Soukromá strední umelecká škola grafická 51
Speos 86
Srednja Graficka Škola Milic Rakic 272
Staatliche Akadamie der Bildenden Künste Karlsruhe 127
Staatliche Akademie der Bildenden Künste Stuttgart 127
Staatliche Fachakademie für Fotodesign München 127
Staatliche Fachschule für Optik und Fototechnik Berlin 127
Staatliche Hochschule für Bildende Künste – Städelschule 127
Staatliche Hochschule für Gestaltung Karlsruhe 127
Städtische Fachhochschule für Gestaltung 127
Statens Kunstakademie 205
Stedelijk Instituut voor Sierkunsten en Ambachten 31
Stedelijke Academie voor Schone Kunsten 31
Strední odborné ucilište 51
Strední odborné ucilište sluzeb 51
Strední integrovaná škola obchodu, sluzeb a podnikaní 51

Strední škola umeleckých remesel 51
Strední umeleckoprumyslová škola 51
Strømmen Videregående Skole 205
Studio Marangoni Workshops 183
Svenska Konstskola 63
Szkola Reportazu Collegium Civitas 215
Taideteollinen Korkeakoulu 63
Tekhnikum tekhnologicheskij 19
The Danish School of Journalism 57
The University Wolverhampton 154
Toscana Photographic Workshops 183
Trondheim Videregående Skole 205
Turun taiteen ja viestinnän oppilaitos 63
Ukrainskaya Academya Iskusstva 269
Universidad de Cantabria 251
Università di Parma 183
Universitat de Autònoma de Barcelona 251
Universitat Pompeu Fabra 251
Universität für künstlerische und industrielle Gestaltung 15
Universität Gesamthochschule Essen 127
Universität Hildesheim 127
Universitatea de Arta 221
Université de Bâle 266
Université Paris VIII 86
University of Brighton 154
University of Derby 154
University of Wales College 154
University of Westminster 154
Univerzita J. E. Purkyne 51
Uniwersytet Mikolaja Kopernika, Torun 215

Vestbirk Højskole   57
Vilniaus aukstesnioji
   technologijos
   mokykla   190
Vilniaus dailes
   akademija   190
Vilniaus lengvosios
   pramones ir buitiniu
   paslaugu mokykla   190
Visor Centre
   Fotogràfic   251
Vrå Folkehøjskole   57
Vrij Instituut voor
   Kunstambachten   31
Vrij Instituut voor
   secundair Onderwijs   31
Vrije Universiteit
   Brussel   31
Vyšší odborná škola gra-
   fická a Strední prumys-
   lová škola grafická   51
Vysoká škola
   umeleckoprumyslová   51
Vysoká škola výtvarných
   umení   237
Warholova ulica – letná
   fotoškola   237
Willem de Kooning
   Academie   201
Wimbledon School of
   Art   154
Winchester School of
   Art   154
Wyzsza Szkola Pedago-
   giczna, Zielona Gora   215

Associations

A.R.P.A.   86
ACD Fotoforma   188
Agrupación Fotogràfica de
   Navarra   251
Agrupación Fotogràfica de
   Reus   251
Aktiv volné fotografie   52
Arbeitskreis Photographie
   Hamburg e. V.   127
Art & Recherche   86
Art Center MONO   34
Asoc. Fotog. Publicidad –
   Moda   251
Asoc. Nal. Informadores
   Gráficos Prensa   251
Asociace fotografu   52

Associació de Fotògrafs
   Professionals   251
Association of Advertising
   Photographers   34
Association Photo-
   graphique Contem-
   poraine en Bretagne   86
Association Regionale de
   Diffusion de l'Image   86
Association Suisse des
   Institutions pour la
   Photographie   266
Associazione Culturale
   Al.b.um   183
Associazione Culturale
   Fotografica Antonino
   Paraggi   183
Associazione Culturale
   Nicéphore Niépce   183
Associazione Fotografi
   Italiani Professio-
   nisti   183
Associazione Fotografia &
   Informazione   183
Associazione Italiana
   Reporter Fotografi
   AIRF   183
Associazione per la
   Fotografia Storica   183
Associazione Studio
   Patellani   183
Assotsiatsiya "Sovremen-
   noe iskusstvo"   19
Berufsvereinigung Bil-
   dender Künstler
   Österreichs   15
Birmingham Art Trust   154
BKF (Danish Artists'
   Association)   57
British Institute of Profes-
   sional Photography   154
Bulgarian Photo-Club   34
Bulgarian Photographic
   Association   34
Bund Freischaffender Foto-
   Designer e. V.   127
Bundesinnung der Photo-
   graphen Österreichs   15
Bundesverband
   Arbeiterfotografie   128
Bundesverband Bildender
   Künstlerinnen und
   Künstler   128
Bundesverband Deutscher
   Galerien e. V.   128

Camera Obscura   160
Center for Contemporary
   Photography   59
Centralverband Deutscher
   Berufsphotographen
   (CV)   128
Centre d'Action Culturelle
   Théâtre de la Ville   86
Centre Photographique
   d'Ile de France   86
Ceské foto – sdruzení na
   podporu fotografie   52
Chicago Albumen Works
   Nederland   201
Clube Português de Artes
   e Ideias   219
Colectivo Fotografico
   Ongarri   251
Confederación Española
   Fotografia   251
Czech Photo   52
Dansk Fotografisk
   Forening   57
Dansk Fotohistorisk
   Selskab   57
Deutsche Gesellschaft für
   Photographie
   (DGPh)   128
Deutscher Künstlerbund
   e. V.   128
Deutscher Kunststudenten-
   Verband   128
Deutscher Werkbund
   e. V.   128
Društvo fotografov
   Slovenije   240
Dublin Photographic
   Centre   165
EFÜ – Estonian Society
   for Photographic Art   59
Escuela Superior de
   Fotografia Flash   251
Europhot   31
Fachgruppe Bildende
   Kunst in der IG
   Medien   128
FAIR   240
FIAF   183
Fiatalok Fotomüvészeti
   Stúdiója   164
Finnfoto ry   63
Foire Internationale d'Art
   Contemporain   86
Fondation Cartier pour l'art
   contemporain   86

Fondation Suisse pour la Restauration et la Conservation du Patrimoine Photographique 266
Fondazione Italiana per la Fotografia 184
Fondazione Primoli 184
Fondazione Sandretto Re Rebaudengo 184
Fondazione Sella 184
Fondazione Studio Nocera 184
Forbundet Frie Fotografer 205
Fördergemeinschaft Fotografische Ausbildung e. V. Bielefeld 128
Forum de l'Image 86
Foto savez Jugoslavije 272
Fotografska zveza Slovenije 240
Fotoklub "Minsk" 19
Fotoklub "Raduga" 19
FreeLens 128
Friends of Creative Photography 160
FWU Institut für Film und Bild in Wissenschaft und Unterricht 128
GADEF 184
Gedok 128
Gens d'Images 86
Gesellschaft für elektronische Kunst e. V. 128
Gildiya reklamnykh fotografov 231
GKf 201
Greek Union of Applied and Creative Photography 160
Groupe d'Animation Photographique de Cholet 86
Hélio 86
Hellenic Centre of Photography 160
Hellenic Photographiki Etairia 160
Hollandse Hoogte 201
Hrvatski fotosavez 37
Image/Imatge 86
Images 266
International Photography Research (IPhoR) 201

Internationale Gesellschaft der Bildenden Künste e. V. 128
Internationaler Kunstkritiker-Verband e. V. 128
Istituto di Fotografia Paolo Monti 184
Komissya po fotograficheskomu iskusstvu i naslediu Ministerstva kultury Rossiskoy federatsii 231
Komora fotografu 52
Latvian Association of Professional Photographers 188
Latvian Designers Society 188
Latvian Photo Artists Union 188
Lietuvos fotografu sajunga 190
L'Oeil Écoute 86
L'Oeil Quimpérois 86
L'occhio e l'idea 184
Lomographische Botschaft Berlin 128
Lomographische Gesellschaft 15
Magyar Fényképész Ipartestület 164
Magyar Fotómüveszeti Alkotócsoportok Országos Szövetsége (MAFOSZ) 164
Magyar Fotómüvészek Szövetsége 164
Magyar Fotóriporterek Kamarája 164
Magyar Újságírók Országos Szövetsége 164
Master Photographers' Association 154
Metz pour la Photographie 86
Milton Guran Fundation 201
Montpellier Photovisions 86
Nacionalni centar za fotografiju NCF 272
Národné osvetové centrum 237
Naukowe Towarzystwo Fotografii 215

Nederlands Foto Instituut 201
Norges Fotografforbund 205
Norges Kunstnerråd 205
Österreichisches Institut für Photographie und Medienkunst 15
Patrimoine Photographique 86
Pavia Fotografia 184
Photo Club 30 x 40 87
Photo Club "Ezerzeme" 188
Photo Club "Ogre" 188
Photo Club "Riga" 188
Photo Club "Talsi" 188
Photo Information Center 35
Photographic Academy 35
Photographic Collectors Club of Great Britain 154
Photographic Society of Ireland 165
Photographies and Co 87
Pohjoinen valokuvakeskus 63
Pressfotografernas Klubb 258
Priorité Ouverture 87
Real Sociedad Fotográfica 251
Royal Academy of Arts 143, 155
Royal Birmingham Society of Artists 155
Royal Photographic Society 155
Royal Society of Arts 155
Schweizerischer Photographen-Verband 266
Schweizerischer Werkbund 266
Seeing the Light 155
Sellit 150 87
SIAF/CNA 184
SIRP 87
Slovenský syndikát novinárov 237
Société de la Propriété Artistique et des Dessins, et Modèles (SPADEM) 87

Société Française de
Photographie 87
Sojuz fotokhudoznikov
Rossii 231
Soyuz Fotokhudoznikiv
Kharkova 269
Soyuz Fotokhudoznikiv
Kieva 269
Spilka Fotokhudozhnikiv
Ukrainy 269
Spolecenost pratel
fotografie 52
Stichting
Fotoconservering 201
Stichting NF&GC /
Spaarnestad
Fotoarchief 201
Støttekredsen (Members'
Association) 57
Stowarzyszenie History-
kow Fotografii 215
Stowarzyszenie Polska
Korporacja Fotografii 215
Suomen Luonnon-
valokuvaajat ry 63
Suomen Mainosvalo-
kuvaajat ry 63
Suomen Valokuvaajain
Liitto ry 64
Svaz ceských fotografu 52
Svenska Fotografers
Förbund 258
Sveriges Allmänna
Konstförening 258
Syndikát novináru Ceské
republiky 52
TAU Visual Associati 184
The Association of
Photographers 155
Tvorchesky soyuz
Fotoiskusstvo 231
Udruzenje likovnih
umetnika primenjenih
umetnosti i dizajnera
Srbije 272
Ultreya 184
UMMAF 87
V2 Centre for Art and
Media Technology 201
Vakka-Suomen
Taideyhdistys ry 64
Valokuvataiteilijoiden
Liitto ry 64
Verband der Amateur-
fotografen e. V. 128

Verband der Deutschen
Photographischen
Industrie 128
Verband Österreichischer
Galerien moderner
Kunst 16
Vereinigung Bildender
Künstlerinnen
Österreichs 16
Vereinigung fotografischer
GestalterInnen 266
Vereniging Nederlands
Fotogenootschap 201
Verwertungsgesellschaft
Bild-Kunst 128
Verwertungsgesellschaft
Bildender Künstler 16
Vienne la Photographie 87
Volné sdruzení východoces-
kých fotografu 52
Westdeutscher
Künstlerbund 128
World Press Photo 201
Youth Creative Center 188
Zdruzenie profesionálnych
fotografov 237
Zväz slovenských
fotografov 237
Zwiazek Polskich Artystow
Fotografikow 215

Grants &
Awards

Académie de France à
Rome / Villa Médicis 87
Agfa-Nachwuchs-
Wettbewerb 129
Albert-Renger-Patzsch-
Preis 129
André Kertész Grant 164
Aenne-Biermann-Preis für
deutsche Gegenwarts-
fotografie 129
Apexchanges 201
Award for the best photo-
graphic book published
in Central and East
European Countries 237
Award of City
of Prague 52
Bayerischer Fotopreis der
Danner-Stiftung 129

Berliner Preis für Junge
Kunst 129
BFF-Förderpreis 129
BG Wildlife Photographer
of the Year 155
Biennale dei Giovani
Artisti dell' Europa
Mediterranea 184
Bulgarian Photographic
Association 34
Camera Austria Preis für
zeitgenössische Fotografie
der Stadt Graz 16
Canon Italia Premio
Giovani Fotografi 184
Capi-Lux Alblas Prijs 201
Centro Nacional de
Cultura 219
Chargesheimer Stipendium
der Stadt Köln 129
Concorso Agfa-
Gevaert 184
DAAD Stipendien-
programme 129
David-Octavius-Hill-
Medaille 129
Deutscher Jugendfoto-
preis 129
Deutscher Photopreis der
Landesgirokasse 129
DG BANK Stipendien für
Fotografie 130
DG BANK-Förderpreis
Fotografie 130
Dr. Erich Salomon-
Preis 130
Dunhill Distinction 201
Emma-und-Agfa-Preis
für Fotojournalistin-
nen 130
Erich-Stenger-Preis 130
Europäischer Kulturpreis
für das Land Olden-
burg 130
European Publishers
Award 130
European Publishers
Award for Photogra-
phy 155, 184
Focus Award for
Students 130
Fondation CCF pour la
Photographie 87
Förderpreis für
Dokumentarfotografie 130

Förderpreis für Fotografie der Landeshauptstadt München 130
Förderungspreis für Fotografie 16
Foto Kees Scherer Prijs 202
Fotoesordio 184
Fotofinlandia 64
Fotografie als Kunst – Preis der Sparkasse Pforzheim 130
Fotojaarprijs "Het ABC van het Bedrijfsleven" 202
Fujifilm Shooting Stars 131
Fundaçao Calouste Gulbenkian 219
Fundaçao Lusi-Americana para o Desenvolvimento 219
Fundusz Promocji Tworczosci 215
Glen Dimplex Artists Award 165
Grand Prix de la Ville de Vevey 266
Grand Prix Scam du Portfolio Photographique 87
Großer Österreichischer Staatspreis für Fotografie 16
Gullers Stipendiat 258
Herbert-Schober-Förderpreis 131
Hermann-Claasen-Preis 131
I luoghi della vita, European Award for Women Photographers 184
Ian Parry Memorial Scholarship 155
Incentive Prize for Photographers 202
Internationaler Polaroid Mikrofotografie Wettbewerb 131
John Kobal Photographic Portrait Award 155
József Pécsi Award 164
József Pécsi Grant 164
Kodak Fotobuchpreis 131
Kodak Nachwuchs Förderpreis 131

Kodak Prize of the Photographic Critique 87
Konstnärsnämnden 258
Kopiosto Grant 64
Kraszna-Krausz Book Awards 155
Kulturpreis 131
Kunstfonds e. V. 131
Künstlerhäuser Worpswede 131
Kunstpreis der Stadtsparkasse Hannover 131
Kunstpreis der Ursula-Blickle-Stiftung 131
Kurt-Schwitters-Preis 133
Landesförderungspreis für Fotografie in der Steiermark 16
Leica Medal of Excellence 133
Leica Oskar-Barnack-Preis 133
Maria Austria Prijs 202
Medienpreis "Sozialfotografie" 133
Mosaïque Programme 191
Nagrada za zivotno delo u oblasti fotografije NCF Award 273
North West Photography Open 155
Oeuvreprijs 202
Otto-Steinert-Preis 133
Paper Art – Internationale Biennale der Papierkunst 133
Photographic Book of the Year 52
Photography of the Year 240
Plovdiv Photographic Foundation 35
Polaroid Fotoschulwettbewerb 133
Portfolio – Immagini in movimento 184
Preis der Theater-Photographie 266
Preis für jungen Bildjournalismus von Agfa und Bilderberg 133
Premio Federchimica 184
Premio Oscar Goldoni 185
Premio Riccardo Pezza 185

Premio Yann Geoffrey 185
Prix de Rome 202
Prix Henri Vincenot de la Photographie 87
Prix Michel Jordi de Photographie 267
Prix Niépce 87
Prizes of Interkamera 52
Prizes of the Chamber of Photographers 52
Reinhart-Wolf-Preis 133
Richard Hough Bursary 156
Robert-Luther-Preis 133
Römerquelle-Fotopreis 16
Rudolf Balogh Award 164
Rupertinum-Fotopreis 16
Sanni Festival/Shell Award 160
Sarah Noble Memorial Fund 156
Schöneberger Fotopreis 133
Secretaria de Estado da Cultura 219
Siemens-Medienkunstpreis 134
Spectrum – Internationaler Preis für Fotografie 134
Staatspreis für das Kunsthandwerk im Lande Nordrhein-Westfalen 134
Stichting Reind M. de Vries Prijs 31
Stipendium der Alfried Krupp von Bohlen und Halbach-Stiftung für zeitgenössische Fotografie 134
Sveriges författarfond 258
The Citibank Private Bank Photography Prize 156
The Erna and Victor Hasselblad Foundation 258
The Hasselblad Award 258
The Observer Hodge Award 156
"The Selection vfg" 267
The Swedish Environmental Protection Agency's Prize 258
Villa Médicis Hors les Murs 87

Voula Papaioannou
  Award 160
World Press Photo of the
  Year and Golden Eye
  Awards 202
Würdigungspreis
  für Fotografie 16

New Media

A Bao A Qou 87
APA Art Video Danse 88
Arcanal 88
Argos 32
Ars Electronica 16
Art Futura 251
Casino Luxembourg 191
Center for Culture and
  Communications 164
Centre Audiovisuel Simone
  de Beauvoir 88
Centre de Recherche Pierre
  Schaeffer 88
Centre Georges Pompi-
  dou/Musée National
  d'Art Moderne 88
Computer Space 35
Copenhagen Film und
  Video Workshop
  Festival 57
Danish Film Institute
  Workshop 57
dig_in_time: International
  Offline@online Media Art
  Festival 59
Digital Dreams 156
Digitale 134
Duisburger
  Filmwoche 134
European Media Art
  Festival 134
Femme Totale/Frauen-
  Filmfestival 134
Festival Cinema/Video de
  Lyon 88
Festival Internacional de
  Video y Multimedia de
  Canarias 251
Festival International du
  Film Indépendant (Mon-
  dial de la Vidéo) 32
Festival of Computer
  Arts 241

Festival Video Liège
  International 32
Freiburger Film
  Forum 134
Heure Exquise! 88
ICA – Institute of
  Contemporary Arts 156
Institut National de
  l'Audiovisuel 88
International Audio Visual
  Experimental Festival
  AVEcom.nl 202
International Festival of
  Film, Video & New
  Media 37
International Internet
  FilmVideoFestival "King
  Nobel" 32
Internatioale Kurzfilmtage
  Oberhausen 134
Internationaler
  Medienkunstpreis 134
Interspace Media Arts
  Center 35
Interstanding 4 59
Kasseler Dokumentarfilm
  und Videofest 135
Kiasma Mediatheque &
  screenings 64
Les dérives
  magnétiques 88
Marler Video-Kunst-Preis/
  Marler Video-Installa-
  tions-Preis 135
Media@Terra
  Festival 160
Medienhaus für Kunst
  und Kultur 135
Medienwerkstatt Wien 16
Montevideo, Media Art
  Institute 203
Multimediale 135
MuuMedia Festival –
  Annual Nordic Media
  Arts Festival 64
New Visions International
  Festivals 156
North by Northwest
  Independent Film &
  Video Festival 156
Ökomedia Filmtage 135
Open Electronic Annual
  Festival 203
Ostranenie 135
Per Plexis 205

Rencontres Arts
  Electroniques 88
Rencontres Internationales
  Art Cinema/Art
  Video 88
Rencontres Vidéos Arts
  Plastiques 88
Semaine Internationale de
  Vidéo 267
Solothurner Filmtage 267
Sonar 251
The Danish Video Art Data
  Bank 57
The Film and Video Insti-
  tute's International Film
  and Video Festival 156
The one minutes 203
Video Art Festival
  Locarno 267
Vidéoformes 88
Videoforum des Neuen
  Berliner Kunst-
  vereins 135
VideoLisboa 219
Video Medeja 273
Video Positive
  Festival 156
Viper – Internationales
  Film-, Video- und
  Multimedia Festival
  Luzern 267
Volcano Film/Video
  Festival 156
World Wide Vídeo
  Festival 203
WRO International Media
  Art Biennale 215

Edition Flusser

BAND I: FLUSSER-QUELLEN
Herausgegeben von Klaus Sander in Zusammenarbeit mit dem Flusser-Archiv
Köln. Mit rund 1500 Einträgen bieten die Flusser-Quellen eine vollständige
Bibliografie sämtlicher dem Archiv bekannter Text-, Bild- und Tonveröffent-
lichungen Vilém Flussers von 1961 bis 2000 in allen Sprachen und Auflagen: eine
unverzichtbare Navigationshilfe für die Erforschung Flusserscher Tiefen. Neben
der Basis-Buchausgabe ist eine CD-ROM mit Texten und audiovisuellen Doku-
menten geplant. Erscheint Ende 2000.

BAND II: DIE GESCHICHTE DES TEUFELS
"Der Mensch hat Gott und den Teufel nach seinem Gleichnis erschaffen."
Flussers Erstlingswerk, in den Jahren 1957/58 in Brasilien geschrieben und dort
1965 unter dem Titel *A história do diabo* erschienen, liegt hier in seiner deutschen
Originalversion vor: die Geschichte des Teufels als Geschichte des Fortschritts
und Kritik der Wissenschaft, Technik, Ökonomie, Kunst, erzählt anhand der
sieben Todsünden. 200 Seiten, 2. Auflage 1996.

BAND III: FÜR EINE PHILOSOPHIE DER FOTOGRAFIE
Die Analyse der Fotografie in ihren ästhetischen, wissenschaftlichen und poli-
tischen Aspekten bildet den Schlüssel zur Untersuchung der gegenwärtigen
Kulturkrise und der sich in ihr herauskristallisierenden neuen Daseins- und Ge-
sellschaftsform. Dieser Klassiker philosophischer Fotokritik, 1983 erschienen
und 1989 überarbeitet, liegt mittlerweile in zwölf Übersetzungen vor, darunter
ins Japanische, Französische und Englische. 79 Seiten, 9. Auflage 2000.

BAND IV: INS UNIVERSUM DER TECHNISCHEN BILDER
Im Jahre 1984 als Erweiterung der "Fotophilosophie" auf das Gesamtgebiet der
technischen Bilder herausgekommen, erweist sich Flussers Modell der telema-
tischen Informationsgesellschaft inzwischen als brillante Philosophie des Internet: ein Buch von atemberaubender visionärer Brisanz. "Alle Autoren, Gründer,
Stifter, Mosesse, Founding Fathers und Marxe (inklusive dem Göttlichen Schöpfer) sind angesichts der kybernetischen Verknüpfung der Dialoge und angesichts der Copyshops redundant geworden." 192 Seiten, 6. Auflage 2000.

BAND V: DIE SCHRIFT – HAT SCHREIBEN ZUKUNFT?
Vilém Flusser stellt das Schreiben schriftlich in Frage. Er macht deutlich, wel-
che Rolle der lineare, alphanumerische Code in der westlichen Kultur einnimmt
und was wir zurücklassen, wenn wir zu schreiben aufhören. "Nie zuvor ist der
Fortschritt der Geschichte so atemlos gewesen wie seit der Erfindung der bilder-
machenden Apparate. Denn endlich hat die Geschichte ein konkretes Ziel, dem
entgegen sie läuft, das Ziel, ins Bild gesetzt zu werden." 160 Seiten, 4. Auflage
1992.

BAND VI: VAMPYROTEUTHIS INFERNALIS
Zusammen mit dem französischen Künstler Louis Bec, der zu diesem Band fünf-
zehn fulminante Zeichnungen beisteuerte, entwirft Flusser eine Philosophie des
Menschen aus der Sicht des Anti-Menschen, eines Unterwasserungeheuers na-
mens Vampyroteuthis infernalis. Die Exkursion mit Flusser und Bec wird zur
Höllenfahrt ins Paradies. 84 Seiten, 2. Auflage 1993.

BAND VII: ANGENOMMEN – EINE SZENENFOLGE
In dieser Sammlung überaus vergnüglich zu lesender Zukunftsszenarien bün-
delt sich Flussers Beitrag zu einer neuen experimentellen, fiktiven Philosophie,
die statt von Wahrheiten von Möglichkeiten und Wahrscheinlichkeiten zu er-
zählen weiß. Ein philosophisches Juwel, das seine Zukunft vor sich hat, zugleich
Flussers letzte Monografie: "Wahrscheinlichkeit ist eine Chimäre, ihr Kopf ist
wahr, ihr Schwanz ist scheinlich. Futurologen versuchen, den Kopf zum Fres-
sen des Schwanzes zu bewegen. Hier hingegen wird zu wedeln versucht."
108 Seiten, 1989.

BAND VIII: STANDPUNKTE. TEXTE ZUR FOTOGRAFIE
Herausgegeben von Andreas Müller-Pohle. Das Erscheinen des Essays *Für eine
Philosophie der Fotografie* im Jahre 1983 löste im deutschen Sprachraum eine leb-
hafte Debatte über das Kulturphänomen Fotografie aus, an der sich Vilém
Flusser auf mannigfache Weise beteiligte. In der Folge entstanden zahlreiche
Exposés, Skizzen, Werkanalysen, Essays und Vorträge, aus denen der vorliegende Band, in chronologischer Zusammenstellung, eine reiche Auswahl bietet. Ein
spannendes Fotolesebuch und glänzendes Pendant zur "Fotophilosophie".
256 Seiten, 1999.

BAND IX: ZWIEGESPRÄCHE. INTERVIEWS 1967–1991
Herausgegeben von Klaus Sander. Vilém Flusser war ein außergewöhnlicher
Redner und enthusiastischer Gesprächspartner. Eine Sammlung seiner Interviews bietet insofern eine treffliche Einführung in sein verzweigtes philosophisches Denken – ein Denken, das über den in den 80er Jahren vorherrschend ge-
wordenen Medien- und Kommunikationsansatz weit hinausreicht und Vilém
Flusser als universalen Kritiker unserer Kultur vorstellt. 256 Seiten, 1996.

BAND X: BRIEFE AN ALEX BLOCH
Herausgegeben von Edith Flusser und Klaus Sander. Alex Bloch teilte mit Vilém
Flusser das Schicksal eines nach Brasilien emigrierten Prager Juden. Er war für
Flusser der Kritiker par excellence und zugleich ein "Steppenwolf", der zahlreiche Persönlichkeiten und Rollen verkörperte, jedoch die eines Freundes vermis-
sen ließ. Eine ergreifende Korrespondenz, begonnen 1951 in Rio de Janeiro und
wiederaufgenommen 1972 nach Flussers Rückkehr nach Europa. Erscheint 2000.

equivalence

European Photography Guide online:
updates, changes of address, entry requests
at www.equivalence.com